# The 1975 Compton Yearbook

A summary and interpretation of the events of 1974 to supplement Compton's Encyclopedia

**F. E. Compton Company, a division of Encyclopædia Britannica, Inc.**

CHICAGO · LONDON · TORONTO · GENEVA · SYDNEY · TOKYO · MANILA · JOHANNESBURG · SEOUL

# The 1975 Compton Yearbook

| | |
|---|---|
| Editor | Richard Pope |
| Assistant Editor | Christine Timmons |
| Contributing Editors | Robert Beran, Patricia Dragisic, Dave Etter, Alan Kimmel, Robert McHenry, Robert Rauch, Linda Tomchuck, Edith Wasserman, Richard Weisenseel, Joseph Zullo |
| Editorial Production Manager | J. Thomas Beatty |
| Production Coordinator | Barbara Whitney Cleary |
| Assistant Coordinator | Anita K. Wolff |
| Production Staff | Sujata Banerjee, Charles Cegielski, Elizabeth Chastain, Jeanne Deitel, Emilie Fall, Barbara Gardetto, Susan Goodfellow, Marilyn Klein, Lawrence Kowalski, Thomas Radko, Susan Recknagel, Julian Ronning, Mark Schoene, Harry Sharp, Denise Tinberg, Cheryl M. Trobiani, Coleen Withgott, Melinda Ann Wright |
| Copy Control Supervisor | Mary C. Srodon |
| Copy Recorder | Mary K. Finley |
| Art Director | Cynthia Peterson |
| Picture Editors | Jeannine Deubel, Catherine Judge |
| Assistant Picture Editor | Julie A. Kunkler |
| Design Supervisor | Ron Villani |
| Layout Artist | John L. Draves |
| Art Coordinator | Richard Heinke |
| Art Staff | Richard Batchelor, Miguel Rodriguez |
| Index Supervisor | Frances Latham |
| Assistant Supervisor | Rosa Casas |
| Index Staff | Mary Neumann, Mary Reynolds |
| Librarian | Terry Miller |
| Manuscript Typist | Eunice L. Mitchell |
| Secretary | Marie Lawrence |

Managing Editor, Encyclopædia Britannica, Inc.
Margaret Sutton

ENCYCLOPÆDIA BRITANNICA, INC.

| | |
|---|---|
| Chairman of the Board | Robert P. Gwinn |
| President | Charles E. Swanson |
| Vice-President/Editorial | Charles Van Doren |

# Contents

# compton's pictured highlights and chronology of

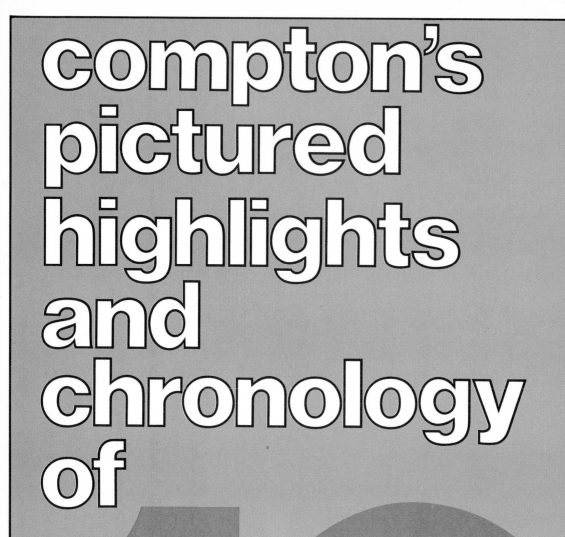

# JAN

**1** A coalition governing body, consisting of 15 Protestant and Roman Catholic members, takes office in Northern Ireland, ending 21 months of direct British rule.

**3** Carlos Arias Navarro, sworn in yesterday as the new premier of Spain, names his cabinet and promises some liberalization in the future.

**4** U.S. President Richard M. Nixon informs the Senate Watergate committee that he will not comply with committee subpoenas calling for the surrender of White House tapes and documents.

James D. St. Clair is retained by President Nixon as special counsel to the president in charge of Watergate matters; St. Clair replaces J. Fred Buzhardt, Jr., who assumes another White House post.

William B. Saxbe is sworn in as U.S. attorney general; he is the fourth person to hold that post in the Nixon Administration.

**7** The Bank of Japan suspends its artificial support of the yen on world money markets; a 6.7% de facto devaluation of the yen results, and the value of the dollar rises.

**9** Great Britain's House of Commons extends the national state of emergency for a third month, as the three-day workweek continues and coal miners stage a slowdown.

The Organization of Petroleum Exporting Countries (OPEC) concludes a three-day meeting in Geneva, Switzerland, with the announcement that there will be no change in the price of crude oil before April 1.

The White House announces that President Nixon has invited the foreign ministers of the major oil-consuming nations to meet in Washington, D.C., in February to discuss energy problems.

**15** A panel of experts reports to U.S. District Court Judge John J. Sirica that an 18½-minute gap on a crucial Watergate tape was caused by at least five separate erasures and rerecordings; accident is ruled out as a possible cause of the controversial gap.

**17** The U.S. Department of Commerce reports a slowdown in the growth of the gross national product (GNP) during the last quarter of 1973, along with the highest quarterly rise in inflation since 1951.

*The severe drought that afflicted Africa in 1973 continued unabated in January, hitting hardest the sub-Saharan region, where famine threatened to claim millions of lives.*

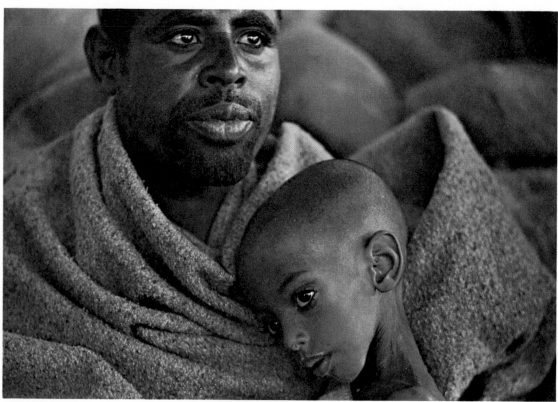

ABBAS—GAMMA

**18** Egypt and Israel sign an agreement to separate their forces along the Suez Canal, putting a formal end to the conflict that began on Oct. 6, 1973; the withdrawal accord, which does not include Syria, was negotiated by U.S. Secretary of State Henry Kissinger.

**19** The government of France announces that the franc will be allowed to float for six months—which, in practice, amounts to a devaluation.

**23** Addeke H. Boerma, director general of the United Nations (UN) Food and Agriculture Organization (FAO), reports that the severe drought in sub-Saharan Africa has worsened; the countries most affected are Chad, Mali, Mauritania, Niger, Senegal, and Upper Volta.

**25** Israel begins formal withdrawal of its troops along the Suez Canal; details of the disengagement were drawn up yesterday at a meeting of Israeli and Egyptian military authorities.

Rioting continues in the state of Gujarat, India, over severe food shortages and rising food prices;

a number of persons have been killed in the rioting, which began January 18.

**26** Turkey's President Fahri Koruturk formally approves the coalition cabinet formed by Bulent Ecevit, leader of the Republican People's party.

Nineteen bombing attacks against leftists are reported in various Argentine cities, one day after the national legislature passed a strong antiterrorism bill.

**27** Syria claims heavy Israeli casualties in sporadic fighting along the Golan Heights; the U.S. and Egypt continue to pressure Syria to enter into negotiations with Israel.

**30** President Nixon delivers his state of the union address, outlining major programs in health care, welfare reform, and mass transit; he urges an end to consideration of the Watergate scandal.

Fighting continues in Cambodia between government troops and Khmer Rouge insurgents; Cambodia's President Lon Nol declares a six-month state of emergency.

*The Nixon Administration's credibility gap widened on Jan. 15 when experts reported to Judge Sirica that the 18 ½-minute gap on a key Watergate tape was not an accidental erasure. (Right) Great Britain's energy crisis entered its third month, forcing English shopkeepers to devise their own sources of power for light and heat in order to stay open for business.*

DENNIS BRACK—BLACK STAR

JULIAN CALDER—WOODFIN CAMP

# FEB

**2** The People's Republic of China launches a campaign against the teachings of Confucius and the policies of the late Defense Minister Lin Piao—indicating that a new "cultural revolution" is under way.

**4** President Nixon submits his proposed budget for fiscal 1975, calling for $304.4 billion in expenditures; this is the first time a U.S. budget has surpassed $300 billion.

Patricia Hearst, 19, granddaughter of the late newspaper publishing magnate William Randolph Hearst, is kidnapped from her Berkeley, Calif., apartment by members of the Symbionese Liberation Army, a radical terrorist group.

U.S. Secretary of State Kissinger warns Arab countries that continuation of their oil embargo against the U.S. "must be construed as a form of blackmail."

**7** The Caribbean island of Grenada becomes independent, after 200 years of British rule; Prime Minister Eric M. Gairy urges an end to antigovernment demonstrations in the new country.

**8** Skylab 4, the last scheduled U.S. Skylab mission until a joint U.S.-Soviet mission planned for 1975, splashes down in the Pacific Ocean; the three astronauts aboard spent a record 84 days 1 hour 16 minutes in space.

*British troops prepared in February to leave the newly independent state of Grenada and 34th member of the Commonwealth of Nations.*

*Cambodia's capital city, Phnom Penh, was the center of heavy fighting in February as the country's four-year-old civil war raged on.*

**10** British coal miners, rejecting a 16.5% pay raise offered by the government, begin a strike for a pay raise of 30% to 40%.

**11** Nearly 200 civilians are reported killed at Phnom Penh, Cambodia, in one of the worst rebel shellings in the fighting between Khmer Rouge insurgents and government troops.

The government of South Vietnam announces that its troops have killed 118 Communists in clashes near the city of Pleiku.

**13** The Soviet Union deports dissident novelist Aleksandr I. Solzhenitsyn, a Nobel prize winner, and issues a decree stripping him of his Soviet citizenship.

At the end of a three-day meeting of 13 major oil-consuming countries, a communiqué is issued endorsing a U.S. proposal for cooperation in dealing with the energy crisis; the 13 nations are Belgium, Canada, Denmark, France, Great Britain, West Germany, Ireland, Italy, Japan, Luxembourg, the Netherlands, Norway, and the U.S.

**19** Randolph Hearst announces a plan to distribute $2 million worth of food to low-income persons; his plan is a compromise with the original ransom demand of the Symbionese Liberation Army, the group that kidnapped his daughter Patricia.

**23** A conference of Western Hemisphere foreign ministers adjourns in Mexico City, Mexico, and issues the Declaration of Tlatelolco, calling for future conferences on inter-American cooperation but containing few concrete proposals; ministers from 25 countries in the hemisphere attended.

**24** A three-day meeting of more than 30 Islamic government leaders at Lahore, Pakistan, ends with issuance of the Declaration of Lahore—which establishes a committee to study ways of helping less developed Muslim nations affected by high oil prices; the representatives also recognized the Palestine Liberation Organization (PLO) as sole representative of the Palestinians.

**27** A list of Israeli prisoners of war (POW's) held by Syria is delivered to Israel's Prime Minister Golda Meir by U.S. Secretary of State Kissinger; Israel later announces that receipt of the list fulfills its conditions for holding disengagement talks with Syria.

Jules Léger, newly appointed governor-general of Canada, opens the second session of the 29th Canadian Parliament in Ottawa with a speech calling for a record $22 billion in government spending.

**28** During a visit to Cairo, Egypt, by U.S. Secretary of State Kissinger, it is announced that the U.S. and Egypt are resuming full-scale diplomatic relations.

The Labour and Conservative parties both fail to gain a majority of seats in Parliament in the British elections; Labour wins 301 seats, Conservatives 296, Liberals 14, and others 24.

*On Feb. 4 the Symbionese Liberation Army abducted newspaper executive Randolph Hearst's daughter Patricia. On Feb. 13 the Soviets stripped author Aleksandr Solzhenitsyn of his citizenship.*

# MAR

**1** Seven former White House and Republican campaign officials are indicted on Watergate-related charges, including conspiracy, obstruction of justice, and making false statements to a grand jury; among the indicted are former Attorney General John N. Mitchell and White House aides John Ehrlichman and H. R. (Bob) Haldeman.

**2** In accordance with Burma's new constitution, adopted in January, Prime Minister Ne Win dissolves the ruling Revolutionary Council and turns its powers over to the new People's Assembly.

**4** The European Economic Community (EEC) offers to explore the possibilities of long-range economic cooperation with 20 Arab countries.

Harold Wilson, leader of Britain's Labour party, is appointed prime minister; Edward Heath, Conservative party leader, resigned as prime minister after failing to win Liberal party support for a coalition.

**5** Haile Selassie I, emperor of Ethiopia, agrees to call a constitutional convention; he moves in response to nationwide unrest that has included rioting in the capital, Addis Ababa, and an army mutiny in Asmara.

**10** Prime Minister Meir and her new 22-member coalition cabinet, including Moshe Dayan as defense minister, are sworn in as the government of Israel; Mrs. Meir announced formation of the coalition on March 6, ending a nine-week government crisis and a threat of resignation by Dayan.

**11** The British government ends the state of emergency that began in November 1973 because of acute fuel shortages; an agreement to end the miners' strike was made on March 6, and the national three-day workweek was canceled by the government on March 7.

**12** Carlos Andrés Pérez, in his inaugural address as president of Venezuela, promises to seek a rational consensus for nationalization of U.S. oil interests.

**14** Kurdish rebels, led by Gen. Mustafa al-Barzani, climax several days of fighting with Iraqi government troops by seizing a large area on Iraq's border with Turkey.

**15** Ernesto Geisel is sworn in as Brazil's first freely elected president in ten years; he is the fourth military officer to hold the office since the armed forces seized power in the country in 1964.

*In Great Britain's March elections, Labour leader Harold Wilson (top) was called upon to form a government after Edward Heath's attempted Conservative-Liberal coalition failed. On March 15 Gen. Ernesto Geisel (right), choice of Brazil's ruling military junta, was sworn in as president of Brazil for a five-year term.*

*When Iraq's Kurdish population rejected the government's March proclamation of limited Kurdish autonomy, the underground Kurdish army resumed its fight for a fully independent Kurdistan, including the oil-rich city of Kirkuk, over which the government wanted to retain control.*

**18** At a meeting of OPEC in Vienna, Austria, seven oil-producing countries agree to lift the embargo on oil shipments to the U.S.; Syria and Libya plan to continue the embargo against the U.S., and a general embargo is still in effect against Denmark and the Netherlands.

**19** Twenty-two persons are reported killed in several days of rioting over rising food prices and reported political corruption in Bihar State, India.

**21** The U.S. Court of Appeals upholds a ruling by U.S. District Court Judge Sirica that the grand jury report on Nixon's possible involvement in the Watergate cover-up should be turned over to the House of Representatives for its impeachment inquiry.

**28** U.S. Secretary of State Kissinger returns to Washington, D.C., after three days of talks with Soviet leaders in Moscow; a general communiqué issued by both countries indicates that little progress was made on disarmament or the other issues under discussion.

Turkey sends bombers on unauthorized sorties into Greece's airspace during a North Atlantic Treaty Organization (NATO) naval exercise; Greece withdraws from the exercise—relations between the two countries were already strained by tensions over Cyprus and oil rights in the Aegean.

Romania's Communist party leader Nicolae Ceausescu is elected to the newly created post of president of Romania; Ion Gheorge Maurer resigned as premier two days ago and was replaced by Deputy Premier Manea Manescu.

**29** Israeli proposals for troop disengagement are submitted by Defense Minister Dayan to U.S. Secretary of State Kissinger in Washington, D.C., in the first round of indirect negotiations between Israel and Syria.

In Zurich, Switzerland, exiled Soviet novelist Solzhenitsyn is reunited with his family; his wife and four sons had remained in the Soviet Union when he was expelled.

# APR

**1** At a meeting of EEC foreign ministers in Luxembourg, Britain's Foreign Secretary James Callaghan presents a strongly worded bid for renegotiation of the terms under which Britain joined the EEC in 1973; Callaghan represents the new Labour government, which campaigned on a promise to improve the country's economy by improving its position within the EEC.

**2** Georges Pompidou, Gen. Charles de Gaulle's successor to the presidency of France in 1969, dies in Paris; Alain Poher, president of the Senate, becomes interim president.

**3** President Nixon agrees to pay $432,787.13 plus interest in back taxes for his first term in office, after separate reports by the Internal Revenue Service and a Congressional committee indicate that he owes the money.

**5** In Laos a coalition government—the third since 1957—is formed by the neutralist, rightist, and Pathet Lao factions; Prince Souvanna Phouma continues as premier, and Pathet Lao leader Prince Souphanouvong comes out of exile to head an advisory body.

**8** Hank Aaron of the Atlanta Braves baseball team, in a game against the Los Angeles Dodgers, hits his 715th career home run, surpassing the late Babe Ruth's record total of 714.

**9** India, Pakistan, and Bangladesh sign an agreement in New Delhi, India, dealing with the aftermath of the 1971 Indo-Pakistani war—the first indication of an easing in relations between the three countries.

**10** Israel's Prime Minister Meir announces her decision to resign, only one month after the current coalition government was formed; her decision is prompted by Labor party dissension over a report on the nation's lack of military preparedness for the 1973 war.

**11** After rejecting a White House compromise offer, the House Judiciary Committee votes to issue a subpoena ordering President Nixon to turn over tapes and other materials relating to 42 White House conversations; deadline for compliance is set at April 25.

Three Palestinian guerrillas attack Qiryat Shemona, Israel, near the Lebanese border, killing 18 Israelis; on April 12 Israel retaliates by raiding six villages in Lebanon.

**13** Syria's chief of military intelligence submits his country's plan for troop disengagement with Israel to U.S. Secretary of State Kissinger in Washington, D.C.

**18** After 18 years of exclusive reliance on Soviet military material, the government of Egypt announces

*Portugal's "Junta of National Salvation" that took power in an almost bloodless coup on April 25 promised liberal reform of the government. (Right) The April 28 acquittal of Mitchell and Stans temporarily buoyed the Nixon Administration's hopes of surviving the Watergate scandal.*

HENRI BUREAU—SYGMA

J.-P. LAFFONT—SYGMA

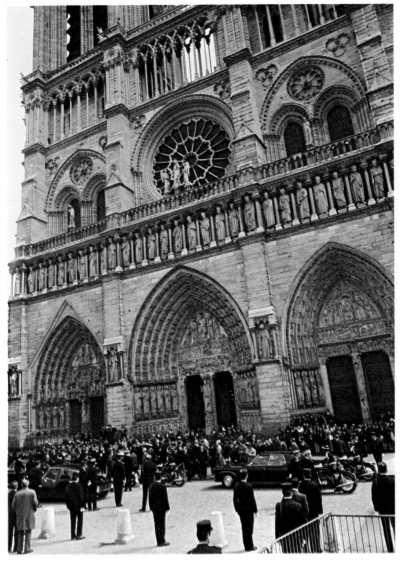

*French President Georges Pompidou, who died on April 2 after a lengthy illness, was honored with a state funeral followed by a simple, private burial service at Orvilliers.*

that it is seeking other sources of arms; the U.S.S.R. had been ignoring Egyptian requests for supplies for six months.

**19** Syria and Israel fight their first air battle over the Golan Heights since the October 1973 war, shortly after Kissinger received troop disengagement proposals from both countries.

**21** Alfonso López Michelsen, Liberal party candidate, is elected president of Colombia in the country's first free election for that office in more than two decades.

**22** The Central Committee of Israel's ruling Labor party elects Yitzhak Rabin to form a new cabinet.

**24** The Nationalist party of South Africa's Prime Minister B. J. Vorster increases its parliamentary majority by four seats in national elections, a virtual mandate for Vorster's apartheid policies.

**25** In Portugal a seven-man junta, led by Gen. António de Spínola, deposes the government of President Americo Tomas and Premier Marcello Caetano.

**28** A federal district court jury in New York City acquits former Attorney General Mitchell and former Secretary of Commerce Maurice Stans of all charges relating to a secret Nixon campaign contribution from financier Robert Vesco.

**29** President Nixon responds obliquely to the House Judiciary Committee subpoena of April 11; he announces that he will release pages of edited tape transcripts of Watergate-related conversations to the public—as opposed to releasing the actual tapes to the committee, as ordered.

**30** The Economic Stabilization Act of 1970, which gave the president authority to impose mandatory wage and price controls, expires; only petroleum product prices remain controlled, under the authority of the 1973 Emergency Petroleum Allocation Act.

# MAY

**1** U.S. newspapers begin publishing installments or excerpts of the White House-edited Watergate tape transcripts released yesterday by President Nixon; the House Judiciary Committee votes to notify Nixon that his release of the transcripts, rather than the actual tapes, does not constitute compliance with the committee's subpoena.

**6** Willy Brandt resigns as chancellor of West Germany, confessing "negligence" in employing an aide recently discovered to be an East German spy.

**8** Railway workers in India begin a nationwide strike, demanding higher wages and shorter working hours.

**9** The House Judiciary Committee opens formal hearings on whether to recommend that the full House impeach President Nixon; in the initial session, the events leading up to the Watergate burglary of June 1972 are summarized.

The minority Liberal government of Canada's Prime Minister Pierre Elliott Trudeau is dissolved after a vote of no confidence in the House of Commons yesterday; elections are set for July 8.

**13** In a two-day referendum, Italy's voters overwhelmingly support retention of the three-year-old law permitting divorce.

**15** General Spínola becomes provisional president of Portugal and announces formation of a cabinet, with Adelino da Palma Carlos as premier; Mário Soares, a socialist exiled under the old regime, becomes foreign minister.

Three Palestinian guerrillas enter the village of Ma'alot, Israel, and hold 90 schoolchildren hostage, demanding release of guerrillas already held by Israel; after a mixup in negotiations between the guerrillas and the authorities, Israeli troops storm the school and the ensuing battle kills 20 children and the 3 guerrillas.

**16** In the heaviest raids ever carried out by Israeli jets against Lebanon, more than 40 persons are reported killed and at least 170 injured in reprisal for the Ma'alot massacre.

Helmut Schmidt, finance minister under Willy Brandt, is sworn in as chancellor of West Germany; on May 15 the presidential electoral college elected Walter Scheel to replace retiring President Gustav Heinemann.

**17** Six members of the Symbionese Liberation Army are killed in a shoot-out with Los Angeles police; they had kidnapped and claim to have converted to their cause heiress Patricia Hearst; when it is determined that Patricia was not killed in the shoot-out, the FBI subsequently issues a warrant for her arrest.

**18** In an underground test in the Rajasthan Desert, India explodes its first nuclear device, thus becoming the world's sixth nuclear power—after the U.S., the U.S.S.R., Great Britain, France, and China.

Argentina's federal police begin mass arrests in Tucuman Province in a drive against the left-wing People's Revolutionary party.

*The May 15 raid by Lebanese-based Palestinian guerrillas on the Israeli village of Ma'alot left 20 school children dead and was followed by public outrage at the continuing terrorist attacks and by subsequent Israeli reprisal attacks on Lebanon.*

WILLIAM KAREL—GAMMA

# GISCARD D'ESTAING

*Finance Minister Valéry Giscard d'Estaing campaigned for the French presidency on a reform platform that gained him a narrow 400,000-vote margin in the May 19 runoff elections. Inaugurated on May 27, Giscard instituted symbolic innovations in the inaugural ceremonies and proceeded immediately to work for the political reforms promised in his campaign.*

**22** In a letter to the chairman of the House Judiciary Committee, President Nixon states that he will not comply with two subpoenas issued by the committee on May 15 for additional Watergate tapes and documents and, further, that he will not comply with any future subpoenas.

**27** Valéry Giscard d'Estaing is sworn in as president of France after narrowly defeating François Mitterrand in a runoff election May 19.

**28** Union officials end the 20-day rail strike in India after the government begins mass arrests of union leaders and workers.

Yitzhak Rabin, premier-designate of Israel, announces formation of a new cabinet; notably among those missing are ranking members of Mrs. Meir's government, including General Dayan and Abba Eban.

Northern Ireland's executive coalition of Protestants and Roman Catholics collapses, and the coalition's head, Brian Faulkner, resigns; this was brought about by a general strike that began May 15 and ends the day after the strike goal, the fall of the coalition, is achieved.

**29** Australia's Prime Minister Gough Whitlam formally claims victory for his Labor party in the May 18 elections; Labor won 66 seats.

**31** After a month of intensive negotiation by U.S. Secretary of State Kissinger, Israel and Syria formally sign an agreement to disengage their forces on the Golan Heights.

The U.S. Supreme Court grants a plea by Watergate prosecutor Leon Jaworski for prompt consideration of Nixon's refusal, on grounds of executive privilege, to turn over 64 White House tapes.

*On May 17, police raided a suspected Symbionese Liberation Army (SLA) hideout in Los Angeles, and in the subsequent shootout and fire six members of the organization were killed. The dead included Donald DeFreeze (Cinque), believed to be head of the SLA, but not, as was earlier feared, Patricia Hearst, kidnapped by the SLA on Feb. 4.*

# JUNE

**3** Charles W. Colson, one of President Nixon's former aides, pleads guilty to a charge that he obstructed justice in the Pentagon papers trial of Daniel Ellsberg in 1973; in return for that guilty plea, all other charges pending against him are dropped.

Premier-designate Rabin is approved by the Israeli Knesset with a vote of 61–51 and 5 abstentions.

**4** At a meeting of EEC foreign ministers in Luxembourg, British Foreign Secretary Callaghan again calls for renegotiation of the terms of Britain's membership in the EEC; on this occasion, however, he is considerably more conciliatory than he was on this topic in April.

The International Commission of Jurists, based in Geneva, after a three-year study accuses Uganda's President Idi Amin of creating a "reign of terror."

**11** In Salzburg, Austria, U.S. Secretary of State Kissinger holds an emotional news conference in which he threatens to resign unless his name is cleared of charges that he participated in illegal wiretaps undertaken by the White House in 1971.

**12** Argentina's President Juan Perón withdraws his threat to resign after at least 50,000 workers demonstrate in support of his policies; he had made the threat to quit in the wake of rising inflation and crippling strikes.

**13** The Committee of 20 of the International Monetary Fund (IMF) ends its sixth and final meeting with the adoption of interim rules for dealing with international monetary affairs; attempts at solving the world monetary crisis were abandoned in January, after soaring inflation and skyrocketing oil prices were added to existing problems.

Posters denouncing the Municipal Revolutionary Committee, Peking's equivalent of a city council, are put up outside committee offices by private citizens angry at some conservative officials; this move accords with a party directive issued May 18 authorizing the people to criticize local officials.

**14** Between 10,000 and 30,000 persons are reported dead in India, primarily in Bihar State, in one of the worst smallpox epidemics in recent history.

Talks between Portugal and the African Party for the Independence of Guinea and Cape Verde (PAIGC) collapse, presumably in response to a speech delivered June 11 by Portugal's President Spínola; in that speech he offered independence to the African territories of Angola, Portuguese Guinea (Guinea-Bissau), and Mozambique only after "a climate of freedom" and democratic institutions were established there.

**15** The U.S. Supreme Court agrees to broaden its consideration of the White House tapes matter to include the question of whether the Watergate grand jury had the right to name President Nixon as an unindicted co-conspirator in the Watergate cover-up.

*Nixon's June tour of the Mideast, designed to promote the May Golan Heights disengagement agreement and to better U.S.-Arab relations, included a visit with Egyptian President Sadat.*

**17** The Houses of Parliament in London are damaged by a bomb explosion that injures 11 persons; police blame the bombing on the Provisional wing of the Irish Republican Army (IRA).

**19** President Nixon returns to Washington, D.C., after a one-week triumphal tour of the Middle East that included stops in Egypt, Saudi Arabia, Syria, Israel, and Jordan; in Cairo he signed an agreement that the U.S. will provide Egypt with nuclear technology for peaceful purposes.

**20** A number of House Judiciary Committee staff memos are released, indicating that some of the edited tape transcripts made public by the White House differ significantly from the committee's version of the tapes.

Italy's Premier Mariano Rumor informs President Giovanni Leone that his cabinet is functioning again; Leone had refused to accept Rumor's resignation, offered June 10, and had ordered the coalition cabinet to settle its differences.

**23** Israeli troops complete their withdrawal from Syrian territory occupied during the 1973 war.

**25** Israel files a complaint with the UN Security Council that Lebanon should be held responsible for a June 24 guerrilla attack on Nahariya, Israel, because Lebanon permitted the guerrillas to operate freely from its territory.

**27** President Nixon arrives in Moscow for his third summit meeting with Soviet Communist Party General Secretary Leonid I. Brezhnev.

After the British government resumed direct control of Northern Ireland in May, the IRA increased its terrorist activities in Great Britain, including among its June targets the Houses of Parliament in London.

Warming up with a June victory in the French Open, Chris Evert moved on to the Wimbledon stakes, defeating Olga Morozova to capture the title on July 5; the next day Jimmy Connors' easy victory over Ken Rosewall completed the U.S. sweep of the Wimbledon singles titles.

# JULY

**1** Argentina's President Perón dies in Buenos Aires and is succeeded by his wife and vice-president, Isabel; Mrs. Perón, who took over the duties of the presidency on June 29 because of her husband's illness, thus becomes the first woman chief of state in the Americas.

**2** Satellite reports from Moscow by correspondents of three major U.S. television networks are cut off abruptly when the correspondents try to discuss Soviet dissidents; the correspondents were in Moscow for President Nixon's visit.

**7** West Germany defeats the Netherlands 2–1 in the World Cup soccer finale at Olympic Stadium in Munich.

**8** Presidential defense counsel St. Clair and Watergate prosecutor Leon Jaworski present oral arguments to the Supreme Court on the constitutionality of President Nixon's claim of executive privilege in withholding Watergate tapes and other materials.

Israeli naval commandos sink 30 fishing boats in three southern Lebanese ports in a retaliation

J.-P. LAFFONT—SYGMA

raid following the June 24 Palestinian attack on Nahariya, Israel.

The Liberal party of Canada's Prime Minister Trudeau wins an absolute majority in the House of Commons in national elections; Trudeau regains the majority he lost in the 1972 election.

**9** The House Judiciary Committee releases its own transcripts of eight Watergate-related taped conversations; the House transcripts differ in major respects from those released by the White House, chiefly in pointing toward greater involvement of President Nixon in the Watergate cover-up.

**13** Army Col. Vasco dos Santos Gonçalves, considered a leftist, is named premier of Portugal by President Spínola; Gonçalves replaces the centrist Da Palma Carlos, who resigned July 9.

After a 17-month investigation, the Senate Select Committee to Investigate the 1972 Presidential Campaign Activities releases its final report, which lists 35 recommendations for cleaning up campaign practices.

**15** Greek officers lead the Cypriot national guard in a coup that ousts Archbishop Makarios III as president of Cyprus; Greek Cypriot publisher and former guerrilla leader Nikos Sampson is sworn in to replace Makarios—who is at first reported killed but who actually escapes to London.

**16** Takeo Fukuda, finance minister of Japan, resigns his powerful post in the wake of demands for organizational reform in the ruling Liberal-Democratic party; the demands were brought on by the party's loss, in elections on July 7, of eight seats in the country's upper chamber of the national legislature.

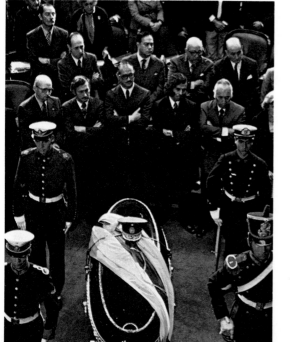

ALAIN NOGUES—SYGMA

The House Judiciary Committee (left) began televised hearings on July 24 on the possible impeachment of President Nixon. By month's end the committee had approved by a large bipartisan majority three articles recommending impeachment to the full House. Burial services (lower left) were conducted on July 4 for Argentinian President Juan Perón, who was succeeded by his wife and vice-president, Isabel. The July 15 military coup in Cyprus took on new dimensions when Turkish troops (below) invaded the island five days later.

**20** Turkey, claiming its right to protect Turkish Cypriots, invades Cyprus by sea and air at sunrise; in the next two days, Turkey gains control of a 16-mile corridor, fighting erupts in Nicosia, and Greece orders a general mobilization of forces.

**23** Greece's military junta, under the leadership of Brig. Gen. Demetrios Ioannides, resigns; Greece's President Phaidon Gizikis summons former Prime Minister Constantine Caramanlis from self-imposed exile to form a new civilian government.

In Cyprus President Sampson resigns and is succeeded by Glafkos Clerides, speaker of the Cypriot House of Representatives and a moderate.

**24** The Supreme Court rules 8–0 that claims of executive privilege cannot be used to withhold evidence in a criminal trial and that President Nixon must therefore provide the tapes and other Watergate materials subpoenaed by Jaworski.

**27** Portugal's President Spínola promises to start transferring power immediately to the three African territories of Angola, Mozambique, and Portuguese Guinea (Guinea-Bissau).

**30** The House Judiciary Committee recesses after approving three articles—the first on July 27, the second, July 29, the third, July 30—recommending that the full House impeach President Nixon and seek his removal from office through a Senate trial.

Turkey, Greece, and Great Britain sign an agreement in Geneva providing for a standstill cease-fire on Cyprus—the three countries are guarantors of Cyprus' sovereignty under a 1960 treaty; fighting had continued on Cyprus despite a UN-sponsored cease-fire of July 22.

AZZI—MAGNUM

# AUG

**1** Greece's Prime Minister Caramanlis reinstates the 1952 constitution, abolished in 1967 by the military junta; provisions of the constitution relating to the monarchy are temporarily suspended.

**3** Ethiopia's Emperor Haile Selassie approves a new provisional cabinet to be headed by Michael Imru; on July 22 Endalkachew Makonnen had been deposed as prime minister by the powerful military, and on August 1 it was announced that he had been arrested.

**5** President Nixon releases transcripts of three subpoenaed tapes recording conversations of June 23, 1972—six days after the Watergate burglary—revealing that on June 23 Nixon ordered that the FBI investigation of Watergate be suppressed; Nixon formerly had insisted that he did not know of the Watergate cover-up until 1973.

**6** The Senate Foreign Relations Committee issues a report clearing U.S. Secretary of State Kissinger of any responsibility for the wiretapping of 17 officials and newsmen between 1969 and 1971; in June Kissinger had threatened to resign unless cleared of all complicity in the illegal wiretaps.

**8** President Nixon announces that he is resigning his office effective tomorrow, because he has lost his "political base in the Congress"; following his statement of August 5 admitting involvement in the Watergate cover-up from the beginning, even Nixon's most conservative supporters expressed serious reservations about their continued support —impeachment in the House was considered a certainty, conviction in the Senate a strong probability.

Canada's Prime Minister Trudeau, who won a majority in the July 8 elections, announces a reorganization of his Cabinet.

As fighting continues on Cyprus, peace talks resume in Geneva, Switzerland, between Greece, Turkey, and Great Britain on the Cypriot situation; at the same time, representatives of the three nations and the UN are in Nicosia attempting to establish cease-fire lines in accord with the July 30 cease-fire declaration.

**9** Vice-President Gerald R. Ford is sworn in as 38th president of the United States by Chief Justice Warren Burger; Nixon's formal resignation is

J.-P. LAFFONT—SYGMA

*Following the Aug. 5 release of transcripts of recorded conversations that clearly implicated him in the Watergate cover-up, President Nixon announced in a televised address to the nation on Aug. 8 that he was resigning the next day.*

delivered to Secretary of State Kissinger, as required by law, while Nixon is en route from Washington, D.C., to San Clemente, Calif.

**14** The Geneva talks on Cyprus break down when Turkey refuses to allow time for Greek and Greek Cypriot consultations on a Turkish plan for a federal system on Cyprus; within hours Turkey's military forces unleash heavy air and ground attacks on Cyprus.

**15** Greece's Prime Minister Caramanlis announces that Greece will not go to war with Turkey over Cyprus, a decision evidently made in view of Turkey's military superiority and geographic advantages.

Yook Young Soo, wife of South Korean President Park Chung Hee, is killed during an attempt to assassinate her husband.

**16** By military means Turkey achieves its objective of partitioning Cyprus into autonomous Greek and Turkish areas; Turkey then declares a unilateral cease-fire.

A committee of the armed forces in Ethiopia abolishes the Crown Council and the Court of Appeal — further eroding the power of Haile Selassie.

**19** Rodger P. Davies, U.S. ambassador to Cyprus, is shot and killed in the U.S. embassy in Nicosia during an anti-American demonstration by Greek Cypriots who believe that the U.S. has sided with Turkey on Cyprus.

**20** President Ford announces that he has nominated Nelson Rockefeller, former governor of New York, to be the next vice-president of the U.S.

**24** Fakhruddin Ali Ahmed formally takes office as president of India; he was elected on August 17 to succeed V. V. Giri.

**26** Portugal signs an agreement, effective September 10, granting independence to Portuguese Guinea (Guinea-Bissau); the agreement ends 400 years of dominance over the African territory by Portugal.

**27** In the U.S. the stock market continues to lose ground, with the Dow Jones industrial average dropping to a four-year low of 671.54.

**29** The third UN Conference on the Law of the Sea adjourns in Caracas, Venezuela, without having reached specific agreement on international governing of the seas.

**31** West Germany agrees to lend $2 billion to Italy in order to ease the serious economic crisis in that country; on August 24 West Germany's Chancellor Schmidt had warned the Ford Administration that extreme measures taken to curb U.S. inflation could seriously disrupt the world economy.

*After submitting his formal letter of resignation and bidding his staff farewell, Nixon left immediately by helicopter for his California home. (Right) Vice-President Gerald R. Ford was sworn in as 38th president of the United States shortly after noon on Aug. 9.*

DON CARL STEFFEN—RAPHO GUILLUMETTE

J.-P. LAFFONT—SYGMA

# SEPT

*Motorcyclist Evel Knievel and his "Sky-Cycle" parachuted to safety after an abortive attempt to jump Idaho's Snake River Canyon in September.*

**2** President Ford signs into law a pension reform bill that will protect the retirement benefits of an estimated 23 million workers from the vagaries of their companies' finances.

**4** Meeting in Vienna, Austria, participants in the 24th Pugwash Conference approve a resolution calling for a world disarmament conference; it is said to be the first such unanimous appeal in the history of the Pugwash conferences—uniting scientists from East and West on the need for disarmament.

The U.S. establishes formal diplomatic relations with East Germany, thus becoming the last major Western country to do so since the Communist country emerged from isolation in 1971; embassies were to be opened in both countries by early 1975.

A Palestinian guerrilla detachment is intercepted by an Israeli patrol near Israeli Arab village of Fassuta, close to the border with Lebanon; observers believe that the guerrillas were planning an attempt to free Archbishop Hilarion Capucci, indicted on September 3 on three counts involving smuggling arms to the Arabs.

**5** President Ford presides over the first of several meetings scheduled as preliminaries for an economic summit to be held September 27 and 28; most of the 28 U.S. economists assembled for the meeting agree that the Federal Reserve Board should ease its tough monetary policy.

**8** Invoking the sweeping power to pardon granted in the U.S. Constitution, President Ford announces that he has given former President Nixon a full pardon for all federal crimes he "committed or may have committed or taken part in" while in office; it is also announced that Nixon was given title to his presidential papers and tapes but that they would be kept intact and available for use in judicial proceedings for three years.

U.S. stuntman Evel Knievel fails in his much publicized attempt to cross the Snake River Canyon in Idaho in a steam-propelled rocket; Knievel was rescued by helicopter after the vehicle parachuted safely to the bottom of the canyon.

**10** A poll taken by *The New York Times* indicates that public support for President Ford has dropped sharply as a result of his pardon of Nixon.

**12** Haile Selassie, emperor of Ethiopia since 1930, is peacefully deposed by the ruling military committee; Crown Prince Asfa Wossen is asked to return from Switzerland as a figurehead monarch, and parliament is dissolved and the constitution suspended.

Incidents of violence mark the opening of Boston, Mass., public schools; a number of schools, mainly in South Boston, are boycotted by white students to protest a court-ordered busing plan designed to promote racial integration.

*At a pro-busing rally in Boston (above), demonstrators carried signs urging whites not to boycott the city's newly integrated schools. A military coup in Ethiopia in September ended the 40-year reign of Emperor Haile Selassie (above right).*

*The* Courageous *was successful in its September defense of the America's Cup.*

**16** President Ford signs a proclamation offering conditional amnesty to thousands of Vietnam war deserters and draft resisters in return for an oath of allegiance and up to 24 months of alternative service; the proclamation is received coolly by most of the estimated 7,000 war resisters living in Canada.

**17** Abdelaziz Bouteflika, foreign minister of Algeria, is unanimously elected president of the 29th General Assembly of the UN at its opening session.

Jacques Senard, France's ambassador to the Netherlands, and eight other hostages are freed by the Japanese terrorists who had taken over the French embassy in The Hague on September 13; the captors had successfully demanded the release of a comrade from a prison in France.

**18** Britain's Prime Minister Harold Wilson calls for a general election on October 10, the second to be held in 1974.

After a six-month recess, the second round of the Strategic Arms Limitation Talks resumes in Geneva, Switzerland.

**19** Special Watergate prosecutor Leon Jaworski subpoenas former President Nixon to appear as a witness for the prosecution in the Watergate cover-up trial; Nixon had already received a subpoena ordering him to appear in the same trial as a witness for the defense of John Ehrlichman.

**20** Ron Nessen, a correspondent for the National Broadcasting Co., is named White House press secretary by President Ford; Jerald F. terHorst, Ford's first press secretary, had resigned on September 8 to protest the pardon of Nixon.

**30** Gen. António de Spínola resigns as provisional president of Portugal and is replaced by Gen. Francisco da Costa Gomes.

23

# OCT

*The nation's capital finally acquired its own modern art museum with the Oct. 1 opening of the Hirshhorn Museum (above); a work (below) by Jean Ipoustéguy graces the museum's Sculpture Garden.*

**1** Fireworks displays and dance performances in Peking's parks mark the 25th anniversary celebration of Communist rule in China; notably absent from the festivities is Communist Party Chairman Mao Tse-tung, believed to be too frail to appear.

The Watergate cover-up trial opens, with U.S. District Court Judge Sirica presiding; the five defendants are all former Nixon associates: John Ehrlichman, H. R. Haldeman, Robert C. Mardian, John N. Mitchell, and Kenneth Parkinson.

**3** The Dow Jones industrial average falls below the 600 mark for the first time in almost 12 years, closing at 587.61; the Dow Jones had peaked at 1,051.7 on Jan. 11, 1973.

After a five-day joint meeting with the World Bank in Washington, D.C., the International Monetary Fund announces that it is drawing up plans for a major lending operation; funds from the oil-producing nations will be used to aid countries that have encountered severe financial difficulties after paying the new high prices for imported oil.

**5** Under pressure from the Ford Administration, officials of two major U.S. grain-exporting firms agree to cancel orders from the U.S.S.R. for corn and wheat valued at $500 million.

**8** Edward Gierek, first secretary of Poland's Communist party, arrives in Washington, D.C., and begins two days of meetings with President Ford; in the course of the meetings, Ford and Gierek sign nine documents including declarations of "friendship" and of "good political relations."

**9** Left-wing guerrillas release a U.S. official and six other hostages held for almost two weeks in the Venezuelan consulate in Santo Domingo, Dominican Republic; in exchange, the guerrillas accept a government offer of safe-conduct to Panama.

**10** Prime Minister Wilson and his Labor party are returned to power in the second general elections of 1974 in Great Britain; Labor now has a slim majority of three seats in the House of Commons.

**14** The UN General Assembly votes 105–4 to recognize the Palestine Liberation Organization (PLO) as "the representative of the Palestinian people" and to invite the PLO to participate in the assembly's debate on Palestine in November.

Management and labor leaders in France agree on a plan that gives 20 million wage earners a guarantee of one year's unemployment pay if they are laid off because of poor economic conditions.

**15** Massachusetts Gov. Francis Sargent orders mobilization of 450 National Guardsmen as racial violence continues in Boston's public schools; Sargent had asked President Ford to send federal troops to Boston, but Ford refused on the grounds that local remedies must be exhausted first.

**17** President Ford appears before a House subcommittee to defend his pardon of former President Nixon and to assert that no "deal" was made about the pardon; this is believed to be the first formal appearance by a U.S. president before a Congressional committee.

**18** President Ford signs a federal spending resolution permitting U.S. military aid to Turkey until December 10, providing that Turkey does not send U.S. arms to Cyprus.

In an announcement at the White House, Senator Henry M. Jackson (D, Wash.) reveals an agreement —which he was instrumental in making—that the U.S. will provide trade benefits to the U.S.S.R. in exchange for more liberal emigration policies for Soviet Jews.

**20** South Koreans continue their protest demonstrations against the regime of President Park Chung Hee.

**23** Former military junta leader Georgios Papadopoulos and four other leaders of the 1967 military coup in Greece are arrested and placed in exile, in preparation for democratic elections to take place in November.

**25** After 11 days of negotiations, Amintore Fanfani abandons his attempt to form a coalition government in Italy; a caretaker government under Mariano Rumor continues in power.

**27** The Social Democratic party of West Germany's Chancellor Helmut Schmidt loses seats in local elections, reportedly because of voter unrest over steadily worsening economic conditions.

**28** At a meeting in Morocco, 20 Arab heads of state, including Jordan's King Hussein, unanimously issue a declaration calling for creation of an independent Palestinian state and recognizing the PLO as the "sole legitimate representative" of Palestinians.

*Twenty Arab leaders assembled in late October at Rabat, Morocco, for an Arab summit meeting on the Palestine problem.*

G. CHAUVEL–SYGMA

# NOV

**5** In off-year U.S. elections, the Democratic party scores major victories, raising its majority to nearly two thirds in both the Senate and the House of Representatives; the Democrats also win 27 governorships, and the Republicans 7.

**6** Argentina's President Isabel Perón places the nation under a state of siege following the assassination of the federal police chief; about 140 persons have died in political violence since the death of her husband on July 1.

**8** Eight former Ohio National Guardsmen are acquitted of violating the civil rights of students at a demonstration at Kent State University in 1970 in which four students were killed and nine wounded by the guardsmen.

**12** The UN General Assembly votes 91–22 to suspend South Africa's participation in the current session of the assembly.

Britain's Labour party government submits a budget to the House of Commons with the announcement that the tax on gasoline will be tripled in order to discourage waste of energy resources.

**13** The UN General Assembly opens debate on "the Palestine question," with Yasir Arafat, head of the PLO, informing the delegates that his organization's goal is the dissolution of the state of Israel and the establishment of a Palestinian state to include Muslims, Christians, and Jews.

**15** In the freest elections held in more than ten years, the Brazilian Democratic Movement—the only officially tolerated opposition group in Brazil—defeats the government's ARENA party in federal and state elections; the results were seen as a repudiation of the government's economic and social policies and a protest against rampant inflation.

**16** At the final session of its 11-day meeting in Rome, the World Food Conference approves the formation of a new UN agency (the World Food Council) to supervise programs that provide less developed nations with more and better food.

**17** Greece's Prime Minister Caramanlis wins an overwhelming victory in the first democratic election held in the country since 1964; Caramanlis' New Democratic party was expected to control almost 200 seats in the 300-member parliament.

U.S. President Ford departs for Japan, the first stop on an eight-day goodwill tour of East Asia.

**20** The U.S. Department of Justice files an antitrust suit in a federal court in Washington, D.C., against the American Telephone & Telegraph Co. (AT & T), the world's largest privately held corporation; the suit is an attempt to force AT & T to divest itself of Western Electric Co., an equipment subsidiary.

As the UN General Assembly debate on Palestine continues, Great Britain, France, and Italy urge a settlement that would enable Israel to live in peace within its pre-1967 borders.

**22** Canada, the largest single supplier of oil to the U.S., announces that exports of crude oil to the U.S. will be reduced by 100,000 barrels a day, effective Jan. 1, 1975; further reductions were expected, and Canada—which needs the oil for its own use—plans eventually to halt all oil exports.

The UN General Assembly grants observer status in the UN to the PLO.

Four Palestinian guerrillas hijack a British airliner with 47 persons aboard in the Persian Gulf sheikhdom of Dubai; they land the plane in Tunis and demand the release of 13 terrorists held in Cairo.

**23** Aldo Moro, a Christian Democrat, forms a minority government in Italy, ending the crisis that began October 3 with Rumor's resignation.

*Dressed in formal morning attire, U.S. President Ford and Japanese Emperor Hirohito reviewed an honor guard of Japanese troops on Nov. 19, the first day of Ford's historic visit to Japan.*

WIDE WORLD

*Speaking before the UN General Assembly on Nov. 13, PLO leader Yasir Arafat (left) presented the case for the creation of a secular state in Palestine and the abolition of the state of Israel. In Greece, where free elections were held in November for the first time since 1964, Constantine Caramanlis (above) won enough votes to become head of the country's new democratic government.*

**24** Sixty persons are executed by the military government in Ethiopia; most were associated with Emperor Haile Selassie, who was overthrown in September.

Police charge six men from Northern Ireland with the bombings of two crowded pubs in Birmingham, England, on November 21; 19 persons died in the bombings.

**26** Japan's Prime Minister Tanaka announces his resignation from office, amid political scandal.

**27** The PLO announces that it has arrested 16 persons for alleged involvement in the hijacking of a British airliner on November 22.

**29** In the wake of bombings and other terrorism, Britain's House of Commons outlaws the IRA and gives the police expanded powers to fight terrorism.

A court-appointed panel of three physicians informs Judge Sirica that former President Nixon's poor health will prevent his appearing at the Watergate cover-up trial until at least Feb. 16, 1975.

# DEC

**3** The U.S. space vehicle Pioneer 11 heads toward Saturn after surviving a pass within 26,600 miles of Jupiter; Pioneer 11 was able to gather substantial information on Jupiter's atmospheric conditions and internal properties.

**5** U.S. District Court Judge Sirica rules that former President Nixon need not testify in any way—either on the witness stand or by deposition—at the Watergate cover-up trial.

Leaders of the United Mine Workers sign a new three-year contract with the coal industry, ending a 24-day miners' strike.

**7** Thousands of enthusiastic Greek Cypriots greet President Makarios of Cyprus in Nicosia, the capital, from which he fled for his life during a coup in July; in a speech to the crowd, he promises not to accept any partition of the island nation between the Greeks and the Turks.

**9** One day after Greece's electorate voted to make the country a republic and eliminate the monarchy, 300 members of the new parliament are sworn in; the parliament had not been convened for seven years.

Takeo Miki of the Liberal Democratic party is formally elected prime minister of Japan by the parliament; he succeeds Tanaka, who announced in November that he would resign. The government of Britain announces a mandatory energy-saving program, including lower speed limits on many highways and a maximum temperature of 68° F. in most buildings, except homes and hospitals.

**10** Solzhenitsyn receives the Nobel prize for literature that he won in 1970; the Soviet government had

prevented him from accepting it at that time, but he is now in exile.

Reports that the major oil-exporting countries will refuse to accept the pound sterling in payment for oil touch off a new run on that currency, driving it down to a new low of $2.32.

Rep. Wilbur D. Mills (D, Ark.) resigns as chairman of the House Ways and Means Committee, a post he has held since 1958; earlier in December he was stripped of much of his power as chairman by his Democratic colleagues, following public disclosure of his association with an exotic dancer.

**11** Students begin rioting in Rangoon, Burma, after troops and policemen remove the body of former UN Secretary-General U Thant from a mausoleum on the university campus; the students and U Thant represent one political faction in Burma, the current government another.

Rhodesia's Prime Minister Smith announces a cease-fire after years of fighting between government troops and black nationalists on Rhodesia's northern border; he also announces a conference to discuss how the black majority can enter the government.

**19** Nelson A. Rockefeller is sworn in as vice-president of the U.S. by Chief Justice Burger; the occasion marks the first time in American history that both the presidency and the vice-presidency are filled by persons appointed and not elected to office.

**24** Christian pilgrims attending midnight mass in the Church of the Nativity in Bethlehem are searched by Israeli security forces because of recent terrorism in Jerusalem and Tel Aviv.

WIDE WORLD

*After four months of Congressional hearings that focused on his vast personal fortune and his controversial handling of the 1971 Attica prison riot while governor of New York, Nelson A. Rockefeller was confirmed and sworn in as the nation's 41st vice-president on Dec. 19.*

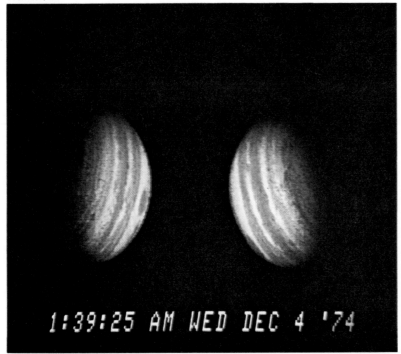

1:39:25 AM WED DEC 4 '74

*Swinging past Jupiter in early December, Pioneer 11 provided scientists with their first close-up view of the Jovian poles; at left are two photos taken from above Jupiter's north pole, showing the planet's striated equatorial cloud belts and the giant Red Spot.*

*Evidence of the changing focus of international power and wealth, Time magazine selected Saudi Arabia's oil-baron King Faisal as man of the year.*

**26** An airlift begins to evacuate victims of Cyclone Tracy that struck Darwin, Australia, on Christmas Eve; about 90% of the city was destroyed or damaged and relief operations were hampered by the city's remote location.

**29** A source in the administration of U.S. President Ford says that Ford has abandoned his proposal for an anti-inflationary income tax surcharge; economists were reportedly putting strong pressure on Ford to do the opposite and cut taxes as an antirecession move.

**30** Official reports indicate that at least 5,200 persons were killed and 16,000 injured in an earthquake that struck nine villages in northern Pakistan on December 28–29.

Soviet Communist Party General Secretary Brezhnev indefinitely postpones his visits to Egypt, Syria, and Iraq, planned for January 1975; the postponement is thought to reflect a decline of Soviet influence in the Arab world.

**31** President Ford receives an official report from the current CIA director, confirming recent allegations by *The New York Times* that the CIA has for years been involved in spying on U.S. citizens—an activity expressly forbidden the CIA under law.

The widely heralded "gold rush" in the U.S. fails to materialize, and only a small number of sales are made on the first day that private gold sales are again legal in the U.S.

# a new american art – by the people, for the people

## by Harold Haydon

'California Falling into the
Ocean' by Victor Henderson
and Terry Schoonhoven of
the Fine Arts Squad, Los
Angeles.

HANK LEBO / JEROBOAM – EB INC.

**Harold Haydon**

As teacher, critic, painter, sculptor, and mosaic muralist, Professor Haydon has distinguished himself in the cultural life of the U.S. He was awarded a prize for excellence in teaching at the University of Chicago and is the author of 'Great Art Treasures in America's Smaller Museums'.

'The Wall of Love', 'The Wall of Brotherhood', 'The Wall of Meditation', 'The Wall of Truth', 'The Peace and Salvation Wall of Understanding'—great classic themes of Western art in the service of religion echo in these street mural titles, but with a difference, for these paintings spring from the hearts, minds, and hands of artists self-appointed as spokesmen for the people. Often they are cries of despair mingled with hope.

In a remarkable expression of democracy and a simultaneous demonstration of the power of painting to communicate ideas and feelings to people with little formal experience with art, street murals have appeared almost overnight, primarily in major cities. They give permanence, measured in months and years, to causes, ideas, and images that are ephemeral in demonstrations and marches. They also are capable of tapping deep wellsprings of emotion through color and form. Like other artistic expressions of the human spirit, the murals seem sacrosanct, protected by the people for whom they speak and respected by the establishment they frequently attack.

Beginning in Chicago in 1967 with hope in the heart of the city's south-side black community expressed in 'The Wall of Respect', serious street art has proliferated across the country, involving all sorts of artists and institutions in all manner of styles and levels of aesthetic quality.

Not since Doctor Atl's challenge to create public art was taken up by Diego Rivera, José Clemente Orozco, David Alfaro Siqueiros, and a host of other artists in the Mexican mural renaissance of the 1920's have so many walls found tongues to articulate the social and spiritual concerns of the people. By 1974 there were more than 95 murals in Boston, Mass., 150 in Chicago, 60 in Philadelphia, Pa., 90 in Detroit, Mich., 50 in Portland, Ore., and considerable numbers in Cincinnati, Ohio, New Orleans, La., Los Angeles, San Francisco, Calif., Baltimore, Md., and other cities.

*Murals in progress: 'I Am the People' (above) by Caryl Yasko, Chicago, and (at left) an untitled work.*

*Portraits of Stokely Carmichael and Eldridge Cleaver on an adjunct by Eugene Eda to 'The Wall of Respect' by William Walker's group of artists, Chicago.*

*'Rip-Off', (opposite) a detail of the mural series 'Universal Alley', by Mitchell Caton, Chicago.*

## Anger and Abstraction

The subject matter of street art ranges widely, from self-assertive graffiti to pleas for understanding, from outbursts of anger to appeals for ethnic and national pride and solidarity, and from portraits to abstract decorations. Without denying the significance of the first and the last, graffiti and abstractions, it seems clear that the community-sponsored and community-approved mural expressions of social concerns constitute a new and distinctly American genre.

Who are the artists? Some are self-taught, and some are young people, including children, working under direction. Most are experienced painters, trained in art schools and universities but not for mural painting. Many belong to or represent the minorities whose fears and aspirations are subjects for murals: blacks; Latin Americans from Mexico, Puerto Rico, and Cuba; American Indians; and Japanese. More than a few are white professional artists who enjoy working on the grand scale of outdoor murals and justify it as a contribution to the visual environment. Some are impelled by the desire to make a social contribution by devoting time and talent to particular communities and causes.

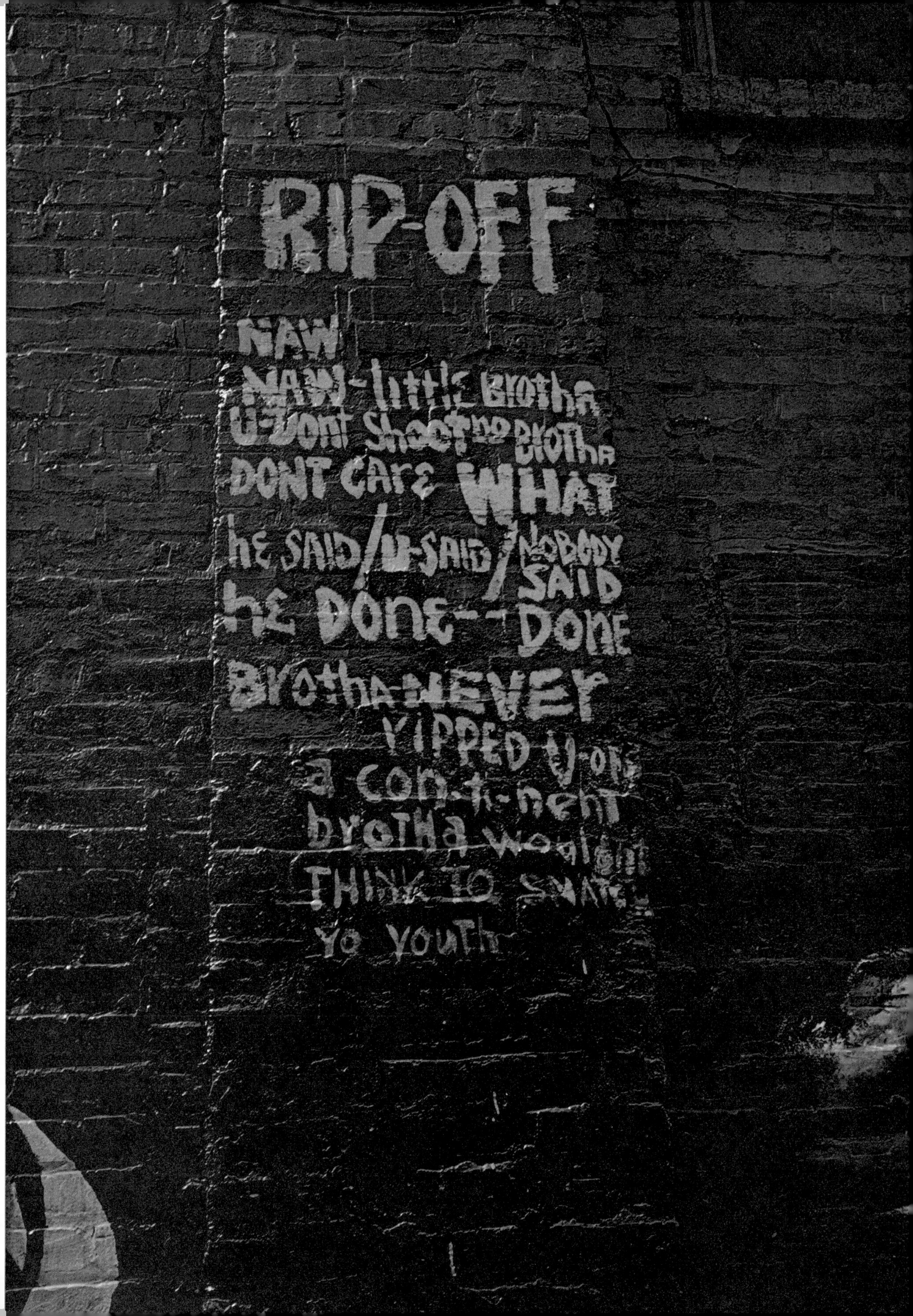

# RIP-OFF

NAW
NAW-little Brotha
U-Dont Shoot no Brotha
DONT CARE WHAT
he said/U-said/ NOBODY
                SAID
he DONE--DONE
Brotha-NEVER
        RIPPED U-off
a con-ti-nent
brotha wouldn't
THINK TO SNATCH
yo youth

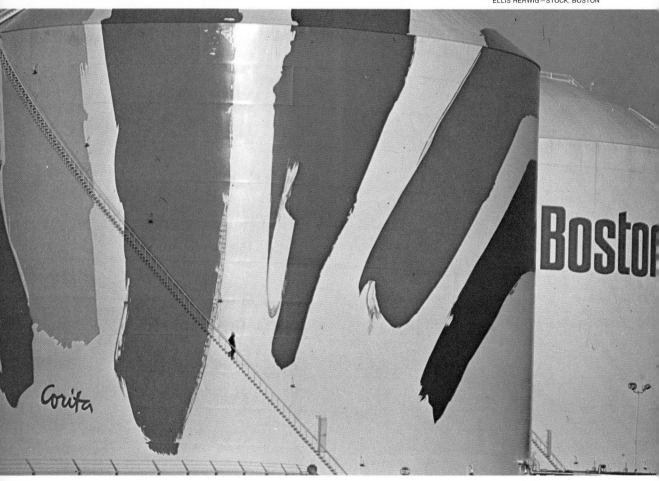

*Painted oil tank by Corita, Boston, Mass. 'The Wall of Love' (opposite), in progress, by William Walker, Chicago.*

There are artists who work as individuals wherever a wall is available, organizing their own support. Many others are sponsored by schools, churches, social agencies, business, and other community groups. There are major centers for mural painting in some cities, such as City Walls, directed by Doris Freedman, and City Arts Workshop, directed by Susan Green, in New York City; the Community Mural Project, directed by John Weber, and the Public Art Workshop, directed by Mark Rogovin, in Chicago; and in Boston the city-government-sponsored Summerthing and the Boston Redevelopment Authority. In the country as a whole, few artists are commissioned by governmental and private agencies to create permanent murals for buildings, although this is common in some parts of Europe and Latin America.

As might be expected, when government, museums, and big business get involved with public art, the fashionable abstract decorative styles are likely to be favored, as are big-name artists. Boston's Redevelopment Authority, with 1% of its funds for public art, turned to famous painters and sculptors, among them Robert Motherwell, Frank Stella, Larry Rivers, Herbert Ferber, Beverly Pepper, Constantino Nivola, Dmitri Hadzi, Alan D'Arcangelo, and Arnaldo Pomodoro.

This was not true of Chicago, however, when Museum of Contemporary Art President Joseph Randall Shapiro brought mural painting into the museum in 1971. He invited leading artists of the mural movement—William Walker, Mark Rogovin, Eugene Eda, John Weber, and Mitchell Caton—to paint murals, during a month-long demonstration, that later were placed in or on buildings.

City Walls in New York City has been criticized for being too involved with gallery artists, whose colorful abstract compositions, painted by professional sign painters on the sides of large buildings, enhance the purely visual experience of the city but contribute little to people-to-people dialogue. One abstract wall in the Borough of Queens is said to have drawn fire from local artists who wanted to participate and felt they had something to say through murals.

Boston's Summerthing festival of the arts began sponsoring outdoor murals in 1968 under the auspices of the Mayor's Office of Cultural Affairs, following proposals for murals by Boston painter Adele Seronde and Andrew Hyde, director of the Insitute of Contemporary Art (I.C.A.). With museum cooperation, 16 murals were completed in 1970, uniting government, business, and the arts in sponsorship. In 1971, Summerthing took over administration of the mural project, locating walls and supplying equipment. Effecting a notable union of people, art, and habitat, the goal was to transform the visual environment while making political and social statements. The most controversial murals, including Roy Cato's 'We All Belong Here', centered on the black experience in America. In an effort to revitalize the Boston mural activity, the I.C.A. sponsored a national conference on "Arts Renewal" in 1974.

JEAN-CLAUDE LE JEAUNE

Schoolchildren, aided by artists, also paint murals. Children in New York City painted the space-warping Henry Street Settlement House mural guided by Susan Green and James Jannuzzi of the City Arts Workshop. In Chicago, William Walker helped children paint murals on their own school buildings. In Portland, KGW Radio and the Arts and Crafts Society cosponsored murals, and children signed up to paint 35 walls in two years. In San Francisco, children made the richly detailed mosaic mural at the Alvarado School, aided by Ruth Asawa and Nancy Thompson. Guided by Kathy Judge, children composed their own Creation myth and modeled tons of clay to make 'The Beginning' for the First Unitarian Church in Chicago, while Nina Ward helped schoolchildren invent and paint a very childlike mural for an Illinois Central Gulf Railroad underpass. In each case, it is safe to say, the artist-director had much to do with the outcome.

### Distinctive Styles

Cities have their distinctive styles in mural painting. While Chicago murals have been deeply involved with social criticism, with few purely decorative walls, New York City has brightened its gray buildings mainly with the vivid hues of abstract art. A quizzical spirit in Cincinnati produced the illusionistic paintings of a giant bolt and wing nut apparently holding the building together; a whirling cartoon dog holding a paintbrush with its tail and painting itself into a circular maze of color; and the blind windows of a building painted with enormous eyes, staring and leering, as if giants were looking out. In Los Angeles, realist painting by the Fine Arts Squad—Victor Henderson, Terry Schoon-

JEAN-CLAUDE LE JEAUNE

HANK LEBO / JEROBOAM — EB INC.

*Detail of 'Protect the People's Homes' (opposite) by Mark Rogovin, Chicago.*

*Untitled mural (above) by Kent Twitchell, Los Angeles.*

*'At the Astor Bar' (left) by Robert Wiegand of City Walls, New York City.*

GEORG GERSTER — RAPHO GUILLUMETTE

'Past, Present, and Humanity'
by the City Arts Workshop,
guided by James Jannuzzi,
New York City.

hoven, and James Frazen—gave the city a portrait of one of its streets as if seen in a mirror, a fantasy of Venice, Calif., deep in snow, that now is completely hidden by a high-rise housing development. Henderson and Schoonhoven depicted on a four-story building the last chunk of California collapsing into the Pacific Ocean.

Even the ubiquitous graffiti artists, especially prominent in Philadelphia and New York City while nearly nonexistent in Chicago, have been recruited to mural painting as a way of channeling their creative energies constructively. Some of the graffiti masters who persistently mark up New York City transit cars with their names and street numbers, in what has been explained as a striving for identity in an impersonal metropolis, have been to some extent constrained by threats of fines and imprisonment but encouraged to paint graffiti murals and helped to exhibit them at New York's City College, Chicago's Museum of Science and Industry, and elsewhere. Graffiti bulletin boards have been tried as a way of restricting the spray-paint and lipstick artists, while Northwestern University artist William Stipe painted a graffiti

mural for an Evanston, Ill., transit station, leaving areas of the wall blank for writing. Several of Philadelphia's avid graffiti specialists have been diverted to legitimate murals that give them the same or greater satisfaction. In the summer of 1974 six murals by local artists were initiated by Philadelphia communities with help from the Philadelphia Museum of Art's Department of Urban Outreach.

A brief review of the rich and seminal mural activity in Chicago will suggest the range and variety of street art everywhere. Murals titled 'Wall of Black Saints', by Louis Boyd, 'Nation Time', by Mitchell Caton, 'Mural de la Raza', by Ray Patlan, and 'Nikkeijin No Rekishi—History of Japanese America', by Santi Isrowuthakul and Jim Yanagisawa, indicate some of the sources of the energy poured into street art. The struggle of minorities to be heard and for self-respect has been a major part of the Chicago mural movement since its beginning in 1967, when William Walker led a group of 21 black artists in creating 'The Wall of Respect' at 43d and Langley streets on a building now demolished.

With the temperament and sensitivity of a natural leader, Walker consciously sought to dedicate his art to black people. "In questioning myself as to how I could best give my art to black people," Walker says, "I came to the realization that art must belong to *all* people. That is when I began to think of public art."

### The Chicago Movement

With support from the Organization for Black American Culture and the 43d Street Community Organization, Walker's group painted 'The Wall of Respect' on the bricks and on panels covering windows and bays. This sectional mural praised black leaders in many fields of endeavor, and for a time Walker styled himself "keeper of the wall," touching up and repainting sections of the wall as he thought necessary. Soon the facing building across the street blossomed with 'The Wall of Truth' by Walker and other black artists. When urban renewal claimed the buildings, removable parts of the two murals were relocated outside Chicago's Malcolm X College, where one of the muralists, Eugene Eda, became for a time artist in residence, painting doors and walls with African themes. In 1968 and 1969, Walker and Eda joined black artists in Detroit to complete 'The Wall of Dignity', 'The Wall of Pride', and other murals.

Very soon white artists joined the mural movement, attracted by the revolutionary nature of the murals and also by the challenge of large-scale painting. Youthful Mark Rogovin, graduate of the Rhode Island School of Design and the School of the Art Institute of Chicago, arrived in Chicago after working as one of Siqueiros' assistants on the 'March of Humanity' murals for the Polyforum Cultural Siqueiros in Mexico City, Mexico. Rogovin established the Public Art Workshop as a mural-painting training and production center, began collecting information on murals worldwide as a resource center, and directed groups of young people in painting the murals 'Unity of the People', 'Protect the People's Homes', and 'Break the Grip of the Absentee Landlord'.

About the same time, another young painter, John Weber, graduate of Harvard University and the School of the Art Institute of Chicago, established the Community Mural Project as a center to sponsor murals. He, too, led groups of young people in painting walls, while coordinating the efforts of other artists. Weber created two of the more controversial murals—'The Wall of Choices' and 'Unidos Para Triunfar'—urging unity and tolerance where conflict still reigned, as well as the readily accepted 'Break the Chains', 'Defend the Bill of Rights', and 'People of Lakeview Together'.

While Walker stressed love and brotherhood to achieve racial harmony, other black artists lashed out at social evils—Turtle Onli, for example, with 'No More Drugs', and Don McIlvaine with 'Black Man's Dilemma'. The latter was also commissioned to paint and design murals for underpass walkways when the city discovered that murals stay virtually graffiti-free, eliminating the need to repaint marked walls several times a year, while also en-

Within the mural: FOR A NEW WORLD ... PARA UN NUEVO MUNDO

'For a New World' by John Weber and Oscar Martinez, Chicago.

hancing the walkways. The Puerto Rican Art Association and individual Chicano and Japanese artists meanwhile focused on ethnic and nationalist pride in the murals they painted.

In a lighter vein, Art Institute and University of Chicago graduate Ricardo Alonzo led teenagers in painting ecology murals on a block-long concrete embankment of the Chicago and North Western Railway. From these came a commission by Clipper Exxpress, a Chicago shipper, to paint on giant truck trailers traveling murals depicting the blue whale, bald eagle, ivory-billed woodpecker, and other endangered species. Pedestrian underpasses of the Illinois Central Gulf Railroad provided walls for socially oriented but less

*'Stop Whaling' from the series 'Endangered Species', commissioned by Clipper Exxpress and painted on a trailer truck by Ricardo Alonzo, Chicago.*

*'The Wave' (below) by Sachio Yamashita, Chicago.*

urgent murals in which imagination and even whimsy dominate. Fantasy bordering on the fantastic appears in former Art Institute student Don Pellett's 'Wall of Games' in tiny Wrightwood Park, where his 22-foot × 110-foot 'Wall of Thought and Ideas' was painted with help from about 100 neighborhood residents ranging in age from 5 to 60 years.

Like pure abstraction, self-expression for the artist as the main reason for mural painting is rare in Chicago, although prominent in other parts of the country. Bruce Brice in New Orleans, painting jazz events and neighborhood scenes, says "I paint to make myself happy and people around me happy. What I paint is just me."

Rare anywhere is Chicago's environmental artist Sachio Yamashita, who has painted rainbow stripes on walls and chimneys, splashed Ando Hiroshige's famous wave around two sides of a three-story building, set out to change Chicago's skyline by painting each of one thousand water towers a bright color, proposes color-keying neighborhoods by painting light poles different hues, and hopes to persuade the city to turn O'Hare airport into a colorful welcome mat by a massive seeding of flowers.

## A People's Art

Throughout this astonishing development of public art several things stand out: the initiative taken by the artists in the creation of murals; their desire to make the streets into art galleries for the people; the artist-to-people communication engendered by the murals and the dialogue that ensues with comment and participation by the public; the acceptance and appreciation of the people, their possessiveness and pride in the murals; and, on the negative side, the impermanence of the murals, painted on exposed surfaces of crumbling buildings destined in many cases for imminent destruction. The murals suffer remarkably little vandalism, and rarely is a mural simply painted over by the new owner of a wall, although this happened to Rogovin's 'Protect the People's Homes'.

The sudden appearance of a people's art in the last eight years adds a dimension to American art that can be measured only in time. Yet it seems to be growing and changing, involving more people and becoming more professional. Institutions are taking interest in the murals. Leslie F. Orear, for example, of the Amalgamated Meat Cutters and Butcher Workmen of North America, AFL/CIO, in Chicago, gets out a listing of murals, updated twice a year; the union's Civil Rights Committee published 'Cry for Justice', a pamphlet featuring color illustrations of a number of murals, and is commissioning murals on labor history in Illinois with William Walker given the first commission.

Many articles have been written about the murals, several books are in preparation, data is being collected, a national center for the study of murals has been proposed, and the government-sponsored Works Progress Administration and Department of the Treasury murals of the depression years are being rediscovered, cataloged, and preserved.

# Paul Dirac, antimatter, and you

by Robert A. Heinlein

V. HEINLEIN

## Robert A. Heinlein

Internationally acclaimed science writer and novelist Robert A. Heinlein, a retired U.S. naval officer, lives in California with his wife, Virginia, and his favorite collaborator, Taffrail Lord Plushbottom, who is equally at home in mathematics or in high-energy particles laboratories. "The dean of science fiction," Heinlein has won the prestigious Hugo Award an unprecedented four times.

### A Riddle

What have these in common?
1. 1926: A graduate student, Cambridge University
2. Billions of years ago: Quasars exploding
3. 1908: A Siberian forest devastated
4. 10 million years ago: A galaxy exploding
5. 1932: A cloud-chamber track, Pasadena, Calif.

Answer: All may, and 1 and 5 *do*, involve antimatter.
(*ANTI*matter?)

Yes—like ordinary matter with electrical properties of particles reversed. Each atom of matter is one or more nucleons surrounded by one or more electrons; charges add up to zero. A hydrogen atom has a proton with positive charge as nucleus, surrounded by an electron with negative charge. A proton is 1836.11 times as massive as an electron, but their charges are equal and opposite: $+1 -1 = 0$. Uranium-235 (or $_{92}U^{235}$, meaning "an isotope of element 92, uranium, nuclear weight 235") has 235 nucleons: 143 neutrons of zero charge and 92 protons of positive charges ($143 + 92 = 235$; hence its name); these 235 are surrounded by 92 electrons (negative), so total charge is zero: $0 +92 -92 = 0$. (Nuclear weight is never zero, being the mass of all the nucleons.)

Make electrons positive, protons negative: charges still balance; nuclear weight is unchanged—but it is *not* an atom of matter; it is an antiatom of antimatter.

*In galaxy M 82 (opposite), 10 million light-years from Earth, the extremely violent explosion of hot hydrogen from the galactic nucleus has been in progress for 1.5 million years with no end in sight. The force of the continuing explosion is so great that the neighboring (though many light-years away) galaxy M 81 is being shaken up. Is a thin cloud of antimatter slowly drifting through the M 82 galaxy, causing the violent explosion in the ensuing encounter of matter with antimatter? Scientists find this a plausible explanation but readily admit that they simply do not yet know.*

### " Touch Me Not!"

In an antimatter world, antimatter behaves like matter. Bread dough rises, weapons kill, kisses still taste sweet. You would be antimatter and not notice it.

*WARNING*! Since your body is matter (else you could not be reading this), *don't* kiss an antimatter girl. You both would explode with violence unbelievable.

But you'll never meet one, nor will your grandchildren. (I'm not sure about *their* grandchildren.)

### $E = mc^2$

Antimatter is no science-fiction nightmare; it's as real as Texas. That Cambridge graduate student was Paul A. M. Dirac inventing new mathematics to merge Albert Einstein's special theory of relativity with Max Planck's quantum theory. Both theories worked—but conflicted. Dirac sought to merge them without conflict.

He succeeded.

His equations were published in 1928, and from them, in 1930, he made an incredible prediction: each sort of particle had antiparticles of opposite charge: "antimatter."

Scientists have their human foibles; a scientist can grow as fond of his world concept as a cat of its "own" chair. By 1930 the cozy 19th-century "world" of physics had been repeatedly outraged. This ridiculous new assault insulted all common sense.

But in 1932 at the California Institute of Technology, Carl D. Anderson photographed proof of the electron's antiparticle (named "positron" for its positive charge but otherwise twin to the electron). Radical theory has seldom been confirmed so quickly or rewarded so promptly: Dirac received the Nobel prize in 1933, Anderson in 1936—each barely 31 years of age when awarded it.

Since 1932 so many sorts of antiparticles have been detected that no doubt remains: antimatter matches matter in every sort of particle. Matching is not always as simple as electron ($e^-$) and positron ($e^+$). Photons are their own antiparticles. Neutrons and neutrinos (zero charges) are matched by antineutrons and antineutrinos, also of zero charge—this sounds like meaningless redundancy because English is not appropriate language; abstract mathematics is the language required for precise statements in physical theory. (Try writing the score of a symphony solely in words *with no musical symbols whatever*.)

But a hint lies in noting that there are reaction series in which protons and electrons yield neutrons—one example: the *soi-disant* "Solar Phoenix" (solar power theory, Hans Bethe); if we ignore details, the Solar Phoenix can be summarized as changing four hydrogen atoms (four of $_1H^1$) into one helium atom ($_2He^4$). We start with four protons and four electrons; we end up six stages later with two neutrons, two protons, and two electrons—and that is neither precise nor adequate and is not an equation and ignores other isotopes involved, creation of positrons, release of energy

*A photograph (lower left), taken in 1932 by Carl D. Anderson (left) through the glass wall of a Wilson cloud chamber at the California Institute of Technology, provided the first proof of the existence of an antiparticle. Using a lead plate (viewed edge on as the vertical band in photo) to slow down the rapidly moving particle and thereby increase the curvature (caused by an applied magnetic field of known strength and polarity) of its track, Anderson first determined from the leftward movement that the particle was positively charged like a proton. Calculations based on the degree of the track's arc and magnetic field strength, however, revealed the particle's mass to be that of an electron. The particle tracked was therefore a positively charged electron—an antiparticle, or "positron" as Anderson dubbed it.*

through mutual annihilations of positrons and free electrons, and several other features, plus the fact that this transformation can occur by a variety of routes.

(But such are the booby traps of English or *any* verbal language where abstract mathematics is the *only* correct language.)

A wide variety of other transformations permits antiprotons and positrons to yield antineutrons. The twin types of varieties of transformations mentioned above are simply samples; there are many other types being both predicted mathematically and detected in the laboratories almost daily—and many or most transformation series involve antiparticles of antimatter.

**51**

Nevertheless, antimatter is scarce in our corner of the universe —lucky for us because, when matter encounters antimatter, *both* explode in total annihilation. $E = mc^2$ is known to everyone since its awful truth was demonstrated at Hiroshima, Japan. It states that energy is equivalent to mass, mass to energy, in this relation: energy equals mass times the square of the velocity of light in empty space.

That velocity is almost inconceivable. In blasting for the moon our astronauts reached nearly 7 miles/second; light travels almost 27,000 times that speed—186,282.4 ($\pm$0.1) miles or 299,792.5 ($\pm$0.15) kilometers each second. Round off that last figure as 300,000; then use the compatible units of science (grams, centimeters, ergs) and write in centimeters $3 \times 10^{10}$, then square it: $9 \times 10^{20}$, or 900,000,000,000,000,000,000. (!!!)

This fantastic figure shouts that a tiny mass can become a monstrous blast of energy—grim proof: Hiroshima.

But maximum possible efficiency of $U^{235}$ fission is about 1/10 of 1%; the Hiroshima bomb's actual efficiency was much lower, and H-bomb fusion has still lower maximum (H-bombs can be more powerful through having no limit on size; all fission bombs have sharp limits). But fission or fusion, almost all the reacting mass splits or combines into other elements; only a trifle becomes energy.

In matter-antimatter reaction, however, *all* of *both* become energy. An engineer might say "200% efficient" as antimatter undergoing annihilation converts into raw energy an equal mass of matter.

### Mathematical Physicists

An experimental physicist uses expensive giant accelerators to shoot particles at 99.9%+ of the speed of light, or sometimes gadgets built on his own time with scrounged materials. Large or small, cheap or costly, he works with *things*.

A mathematical physicist uses pencil, paper, and brain. Not my brain or yours—unless you are of the rare few with "mathematical intuition."

That's a tag for an unexplainable. It is a gift, not a skill, and cannot be learned or taught. Even advanced mathematics ("advanced" to laymen) such as higher calculus, Fourier analysis, *n*-dimensional and non-Euclidean geometries are skills requiring only patience and normal intelligence ... *after* they have been invented by persons having mathematical intuition.

The oft-heard plaint "I can't cope with math!" may mean subnormal intelligence (unlikely), laziness (more likely), or poor teaching (extremely likely). But that plaint usually refers to common arithmetic—a trivial skill in the eyes of a mathematician. (*Creating* it was not trivial. Zero, positional notation, decimal-or-base point all took genius; imagine doing a Form 1040 in Roman numerals.)

Of billions living and dead perhaps a few thousand have been gifted with mathematical intuition; a few hundred have lived in

*The mathematical or theoretical physicist provides the abstract thought and theory upon which all sciences are based; in the laboratory of the experimental physicist, these theories are confirmed or disproved.*

*'The Thinker' (opposite, above) by Auguste Rodin (1840–1917) and (below) an experimental physicist at work with a polarized-proton target system at the Argonne National Laboratory, Argonne, Ill.*

The world's great theoretical physicists have included (left to right, top to bottom) Nicolaus Copernicus (1473–1543); Johannes Kepler (1571–1630); Sir Isaac Newton (1643–1727) James Clerk Maxwell (1831–1879); Max Planck (1858–1947); Albert Einstein (1879–1955); and Paul A. M. Dirac (1902–    ).

LEFT TO RIGHT, TOP TO BOTTOM: COURTESY, YERKES OBSERVATORY AND THE UNIVERSITY OF CHICAGO PRESS; ARCHIV FÜR KUNST UND GESCHICHTE; COURTESY, NATIONAL PORTRAIT GALLERY, LONDON; COURTESY, NATIONAL PORTRAIT GALLERY, LONDON; EB INC.; COURTESY, GERMAN INFORMATION CENTER; COURTESY MARY COLLERAINE

circumstances permitting use of it; a smaller fraction have been mathematical physicists. Of these a few dozen have left permanent marks on physics.

But without these few we would not have science. Mathematical physics is basic to *all* sciences. No exceptions. *None.*

Mathematical physicists sometimes hint that experimentalists are frustrated pipefitters; experimentalists mutter that theoreticians are so lost in fog they need guardians. But they are indispensable to each other. Piling up facts is not science—science is facts-*and*-theories. Facts alone have limited use and lack meaning; a valid theory organizes them into far greater usefulness. To be valid a theory must be confirmed by *all* relevant facts. A "natural law" is theory repeatedly confirmed and drops back to "approximation" when *one* fact contradicts it. Then search resumes for better theory to embrace old facts plus this stubborn new one.

No "natural law" of 500 years ago is "law" today; all our present laws are probably approximations, useful but not perfect. Some scientists, notably Paul Dirac, suspect that perfection is unattainable.

A powerful theory not only embraces old facts and new but also discloses unsuspected facts. These are landmarks of science: Nicolaus Copernicus' heliocentric theory, Johannes Kepler's refining it into conic-sections ballistics, Isaac Newton's laws of motion and theory of universal gravitation, James C. Maxwell's equations linking electricity with magnetism, Planck's quantum theory, Einstein's relativity, Dirac's synthesis of quantum theory and special relativity—a few more, not many.

Mathematical physicists strive to create a mathematical structure interrelating all space-time events, past and future, from infinitesimally small to inconceivably huge and remote in space and time, a "unified field theory" embracing 10 or 20 billion years and light-years, more likely 80 billion or so—or possibly eternity in an infinity of multiple universes.

Some order!

They try. Newton made great strides. So did Einstein. Nearly 50 years ago Dirac brought it closer, has steadily added to it, is working on it today.

Paul Dirac may be and probably is the greatest living theoretical scientist. Dirac, Newton, and Einstein are equals.

### Paul A. M. Dirac

The experimentalists' slur about theoretical physicists holds a grain of truth. Newton apparently never noticed the lovely sex in all his years. Einstein ignored such trivialities as socks. One mathematical physicist who swayed World War II could not be trusted with a screwdriver.

Dirac is *not* that sort of man.

Other than genius, his only unusual trait is strong dislike for idle talk. (His Cambridge students coined a unit, the *dirac*—one word per light-year.) But he lectures and writes with admirable clarity. Taciturn, he is not unsocial; in 1937 he married a most charming Hungarian lady. They have two daughters and a son.

He can be trusted with tools; he sometimes builds instruments and performs his own experiments. He graduated in engineering before he became a mathematical physicist; this influenced his life. Engineers find working solutions from incomplete data; approximations are close enough if they do the job—too fussy wastes man-hours. But when a job needs it, a true engineer gives his utmost to achieve as near perfection as possible.

Dirac brought this attitude to theoretical physics; his successes justify his approach.

He was born in Bristol, England, Aug. 8, 1902, and named Paul Adrien Maurice Dirac. His precocity in mathematics showed early; his father supplied books and encouraged him to study on his own. Solitary walks and study were the boy's notion of fun— and are of the man today. Dirac works (and plays) hardest by doing and saying *nothing* . . . while his mind roams the universe.

When barely 16 years old, he entered the University of Bristol. At 18 he graduated, bachelor of science in electrical engineering. In 1923 a grant enabled him to return to school at the foremost institution for mathematics, Cambridge University. In three years of study for a doctorate Dirac published 12 papers in mathematical physics, 5 in *The Proceedings of the Royal Society*. A cub with only an engineering degree from a minor university has trouble getting published in *any* journal of science; to appear at the age of 22 in the most highly respected of them all is amazing.

Dirac received his doctorate in May 1926, his dissertation being "Quantum Mechanics"—the stickiest subject in physical science. He tackled it his first year at Cambridge and has continued to unravel its paradoxes throughout his career; out of 123 publications over the last 50 years the word *quantum* can be found 45 times in his titles.

Dirac remained at Cambridge—taught, thought, published. In 1932, the year before his Nobel prize, he received an honor rarer than that prize, one formerly held by Newton: Lucasian professor of mathematics. Dirac kept it 37 years, until he resigned from Cambridge. He accepted other posts during his Cantabrigian years: member of the Institute for Advanced Study at Princeton, N.J., professor of the Dublin Institute for Advanced Studies, visiting professorships here and there.

Intuitive mathematicians often burn out young. Not Dirac!—he is a Michelangelo who started very young, never stopped, is still going strong. Antimatter is not necessarily his contribution most esteemed by colleagues, but his other major ones are so abstruse as to defy putting them into common words:

A mathematical attribute of particles dubbed "spin"; coinvention of the Fermi-Dirac statistics; an abstract mathematical replacement for the "pellucid aether" of classical mechanics. For centuries, ether was used and its "physical reality" generally accepted either as "axiomatic" or "proved" through various negative proofs. Both "axiom" and "negative proof" are treacherous; the 1887 Michelson-Morley experiment showed no physical reality behind the concept of ether, and many variations of that experiment over many years gave the same null results.

So Einstein omitted ether from his treatments of relativity—while less brilliant men ignored the observed facts and clung to classical ether for at least 40 years.

Dirac's ether (circa 1950) is solely abstract mathematics, more useful thereby than classical ether as it avoids the paradoxes of the earlier concepts. Dirac has consistently warned against treating mathematical equations as if they were pictures of something that could be visualized in the way one may visualize the Taj Mahal or a loaf of bread; his equations are *rules* concerning space-time events—*not* pictures.

(This may be the key to his extraordinary successes.)

One more example must represent a long list: Dirac's work on Georges Lemaître's "primeval egg"—later popularized as the "big bang."

Honors also are too many to list in full: fellow of the Royal Society, its Royal Medal, its Copley Medal, honorary degrees (always refused), foreign associate of the American Academy of Sciences, Oppenheimer Memorial Prize, and (most valued by Dirac) Great Britain's Order of Merit.

Dirac "retired" by accepting a research professorship at Florida State University, where he is now working on gravitation theory. In 1937 he had theorized that Newton's "constant of gravitation" was in fact a decreasing variable . . . but the amount of decrease he predicted was so small that it could not be verified in 1937.

Today the decrease can be measured. In July 1974 Thomas C. Van Flandern of the U.S. Naval Observatory reported measurements showing a decrease in gravitation of about a ten-billionth each year (1 per $10^{10}$ per annum). This amount seems trivial, but it is *very* large in astronomical and geological time. If these findings are confirmed and if they continue to support Dirac's mathematical theory, he will have upset physical science even more than he did in 1928 and 1930.

Here is an incomplete list of the sciences that would undergo radical revision: physics from micro- through astro-, astronomy, geology, paleontology, meteorology, chemistry, cosmology, cosmogony, geogony, ballistics. It is too early to speculate about effects on the life sciences, but we exist inside this physical world and gravitation is the most pervasive feature of our world.

Theory of biological evolution would certainly be affected. It is possible that understanding gravitation could result in changes in engineering technology too sweeping easily to be imagined.

### Antimatter and You

Of cosmologies there is no end; astrophysicists enjoy "playing God." It's safe fun, too, as the questions are so sweeping, the data so confusing, that any cosmology is hard to prove or disprove. But since 1932 antimatter has been a necessary datum. Many cos-

mologists feel that the universe (universes?) has as much antimatter as matter—but they disagree over how to balance the two.

Some think that, on the average, every other star in our Milky Way galaxy is antimatter. Others find that setup dangerously crowded—make it every second galaxy. Still others prefer universe-and-antiuniverse with antimatter in ours only on rare occasions when energetic particles collide so violently that some of the energy forms antiparticles. And some like higher numbers of universes—even an unlimited number.

One advantage of light's finite speed is that we can see several eons of the universe in action, rather than just one frame of a *very* long moving picture. Today's instruments reach not only far out into space but also far back into time; this permits us to test in some degree a proposed cosmology. The LST (Large Space Telescope), to be placed in orbit by the Space Shuttle in 1981, will have 20 times the resolving power of the best ground-based and atmosphere-distorted conventional telescope—therefore 20 times the reach, or more than enough to see clear back to the "beginning" by one cosmology, the "big bang."

(Q: What happened *before* the beginning? A: *You* tell *me*.)

When we double that reach—someday we will—what will we see? Empty space? Or the backs of our necks?

(Q: What's this to *me*? A: Patience one moment. . . .)

The star nearest ours is a triplet system; one of the three resembles our sun and may have an Earthlike planet—an inviting target

*Among the exceedingly sophisticated instruments used to study our universe is the world's largest radio telescope (opposite, above) at Arecibo, Puerto Rico, recently made much more powerful when the wire-mesh surface of its 1,000-foot-diameter dish was replaced by aluminum reflector panels. The Nicholas U. Mayall 158-inch reflecting mirror telescope (opposite) at Arizona's Kitt Peak National Observatory has the widest field of view of all existing large reflecting telescopes, effectively reaching out to the edges of the universe. Currently in the design stage, the LST (Large Space Telescope, above) is to be orbited in 1981 and is expected to be 20 times more powerful than any current ground-based telescope.*

*In 1908 the Tunguska region of Siberia was struck by a blast equivalent to 30 million tons of TNT, the impact of which was felt by residents 400 miles from the site and which left in its wake a 20-mile radius of charred forests. Numerous theories attempting to explain the occurrence have been suggested over the years, but none has gained consensus in the scientific community. Among the more recent theories to explain the blast is the proposal that an antimeteor, composed of antimatter, plunged through Earth's atmosphere and, upon coming in contact with ordinary matter, exploded with devastating force.*

for our first attempt to cross interstellar space. Suppose that system is antimatter—*BANG!* Scratch one starship.

(Hooray for Zero Population Growth! To hell with space-travel boondoggles!)

Then consider this: June 30, 1908, a meteor struck Siberia, so blindingly bright in broad daylight that people 1,000 miles away saw it. Its roar was "deafening" at 500 miles. Its ground quake brought a train to emergency stop 400 miles from impact. North of Vanavara its air blast killed a herd of 1,500 reindeer.

Trouble and war and revolution—investigation waited 19 years. But still devastated were many hundreds of square miles. How giant trees lay pinpointed impact.

A meteor from inside our Galaxy can strike Earth at 50 miles/-second.

But could one hit us from *outside* our Galaxy?

*Yes!* The only unlikely (but not impossible) routes are those plowing edgewise or nearly so through the Milky Way; most of the sky is an open road—step outside tonight and *look*. An antimeteor from an antigalaxy could sneak in through hard vacuum —losing an antiatom whenever it encountered a random atom but nevertheless could strike us massing, say, one pound.

*One pound* of antimatter at any speed or none would raise as much hell as *28,000 tons* of matter striking at 50 miles/second.


Today no one knows how to amass even a gram of antimatter or how to handle and control it either for power or for weaponry. Experts assert that all three are impossible.

However . . .

Two relevant examples of "expert" predictions:

Robert A. Millikan, Nobel laureate in physics and distinguished second to none by a half-century of research into charges and properties of atomic particles, in quantum mechanics, and in several other areas, predicted that all the power that could ever be extracted from atoms would no more than blow the whistle on a peanut vendor's cart. (In fairness I must add that most of his colleagues agreed—and the same is true of the next example.)

Forest Ray Moulton, for many years top astronomer of the University of Chicago and foremost authority in ballistics, stated in print (1935) that there was "not the slightest possibility of such a journey" as the one the whole world watched 34 years later: Apollo 11 to the moon.


In 1938, when there was not a pinch of pure uranium-235 anywhere on Earth and no technology to amass or control it, Lise Meitner devised mathematics that pointed straight to atom bombs. Less than seven years after she did this, the first one blazed "like a thousand suns."

No *possible* way to amass antimatter?

Or *ever* to handle it?

Being smugly certain of *that* (but mistaken) could mean to *you* . . . and me and everyone . . .

the **End**

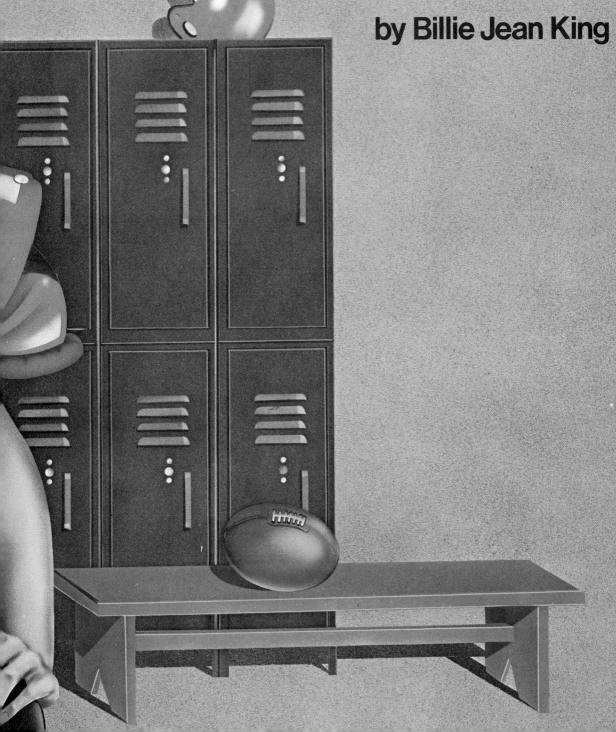

# the women's sports revolution

## by Billie Jean King

## Billie Jean King

Uncompromising on and off the tennis courts, Ms. King is a champion player and a champion of other sportswomen and, by extension, of all women. She led the fight for equal prize money for men and women tennis players and twice was named Sportswoman of the Year. She is co-publisher of the magazine *WomenSports*.

It's really given me a great deal of pleasure to see the current rise in interest in women's sports. I say that not only because I am a sportswoman, not only because I've been involved in sports all my life but because I feel so strongly that the benefits of sports for women are tremendous—physically, psychologically, and intellectually.

I guess I was born at the right time in history to see this interest in women's sports swell into what is now called a revolution. When I was 11 years old, and determined to become a baseball player, I was dismayed to learn that a woman couldn't earn a living in that sport.

My choices were the "ladylike" sports of swimming, golf, and tennis. Well, I hated swimming, was bored by golf, but, lucky for me, I fell in love with tennis. Otherwise, I might have spent the rest of my life as a frustrated baseball fan who would rather have run those bases than sat in the stands.

Well, there's no question about it now. The women's sports revolution is upon us.

Bred by the women's liberation movement, and fed by the torrents of social change in the 1960's, the women's athletic rebellion now touches all phases of American life.

Although the forces leading up to its creation gestated a long time, the women's sports revolution is surely the most talked about and misunderstood movement of the 1970's. But I see it as part of a larger trend.

In the 1960's, I remember that a lot of my contemporaries sat around contemplating their navels. I heard about drugs and alpha waves, pharmaceutically induced "highs." It seemed that everybody was looking inward to find answers to questions that had plagued civilization for centuries. Well, I'm not sure if all that interior speculation provided any real answers to the hard questions, but it seems to me that with the coming of the 1970's, people started opening up again, looking outward. They started experiencing the joys of good, hard physical exertion. They found

*Great Britain's Donna Murray (opposite) runs to victory in the 400-meter race at the British International Games on October 8.*

that a sports high was a real and an enjoyable thing. For example, the sport of backpacking—taking off into the woods for a hearty hike—became almost a national pastime. And the bicycle craze can be traced to the same desire to keep physically fit while enjoying the outdoors.

So, given the impetus from the women's movement, which argued that an independent body is a free body, the country's women were ready and waiting to take part in all sorts of sports, on all levels, from Sunday duffer to professional.

How do I know there's a revolution? Well, for one thing, participation and interest seem to be growing phenomenally. Let's take a look at a few facts:

1. There are 3 million women members of the Women's International Bowling Congress.

2. Seven million American women play tennis.

3. Five million women each month buy such "male" sports magazines as *Sports Illustrated* and *Sport*.

4. Women's participation in high school interscholastic athletics went up 175% between 1971 and 1973. (For boys, the figure is 3%.) Specifically, track and field participation increased from 62,000 to 186,000, or a 200% increase. Gymnastics figures doubled; softball figures rose from 9,800 to 81,000.

If changes in the law reflect social change, maybe we have another measure of whether or not we have a revolution on our hands. One recent piece of legislation has got to be historic in what it means for high school and college athletics: Title IX of the Education Amendments of 1972 requires equal opportunity for women to participate in athletics. We'll see just what that really means later, but a law with teeth goes a long way toward bringing about equality, and it naturally reflects the desires of the general population.

*Track star Barbara Ferrell (near right) signs an autograph for a fan, and billiards ace Jean Balukas, the 1973 top money winner in that sport, contemplates a shot during the U.S. Open Pocket Billiards Championship.*

ART SEITZ

WIDE WORLD

So, if we look just at participation figures and recent legislation, we'd say that things look as though they're on the upswing. If we had to measure the impact of this movement in dollars, we'd see some increases in prize monies at the professional level, but we'd have to conclude that the revolution has a long way to go before monies and facilities are equal to what men in comparable sports get. Let's take a look at top prize monies and the highest paying tournaments for five sports (below). If you'll look carefully, you can see an average ratio of 4 to 1 comparing the men's earnings with the women's.

I don't think you can attach a dollar value to people's attitudes, though, and that's perhaps the first thing that's changing. The money and the equal facilities, I am certain, will follow.

| SPORT | TOP MONEY WINNER—1973 | | HIGHEST PAYING TOURNAMENT FIRST PRIZE—1974 | |
| --- | --- | --- | --- | --- |
| | WOMEN | MEN | WOMEN | MEN |
| bowling | Judy Cook Soutar $11,200 | Don McCune $69,000 | Red Crown Classic $12,500 | Tournament of Champions $25,000 |
| golf | Kathy Whitworth $82,864 | Jack Nicklaus $308,362 | Winner's Circle $32,000 | World Open $60,000 |
| tennis | Margaret Court $191,495 | Ilie Nastase $225,290 | Virginia Slims Championships $35,000 | World Championship Tennis (WCT) Finals $50,000 |
| track | Wyomia Tyus $8,225 | Ben Jipcho $16,700 | International Track Association (ITA) 1–3 events per meet $500 | ITA 12 events per meet $500 |
| billiards | Jean Balukas $6,000 | Steve Mizerak $25,000 | U.S. Open $3,000 | U.S. Open $8,000 |

ART SEITZ

*Australia's Margaret Court returns a volley—and followed through to become the 1973 top tennis money winner. After giving birth to her second child in 1974, she returned to the courts with a December victory in the West Australian Open.*

*Although significant progress has been made—the fettering myths of lost feminity and sports-induced physical ills have fallen; recent antidiscriminatory laws have opened all sports to women; some sportswomen now capture six-digit incomes; franchises for women's professional teams are being planned; and women's collegiate athletic scholarships (nonexistent three years ago) have burgeoned—women athletes readily admit that total equality in sports is still a long way off.*

### Realities of the Revolution

Sometimes tactics such as the boycott have had to be employed to make the establishment promoters of sports events face up to the realities of the women's revolution. Take what happened with women's tennis as a case in point.

Tennis had gone from an amateur to a professional sport in 1968. That was great because it did away with all the hypocrisy and under-the-table expense monies that players were getting to retain their amateur status under the old requirements of the United States Lawn Tennis Association (USLTA). The women, however, were not being invited to participate in the same number of tournaments as in the past. The promoters thought men drew better crowds and sank all their money into setting up men's pro tours. When they did include women, it was for peanuts.

So at Forest Hills, N.Y., in 1970, Rosie Casals and I tried to organize a boycott of the upcoming Pacific Southwest Open in Los Angeles, at which top prize money was $12,500 for the men and *total* prize money for the women was $7,500. We contacted *World Tennis* publisher Gladys Heldman, who arranged a tournament for us in Houston the same week as the Pacific Southwest. So nine of us passed up the Pacific Southwest, effectively boycotting it.

Gladys announced that Philip Morris had decided to put up $7,500 for our outlaw match, and it was called the Virginia Slims Invitational. Naturally, the stodgy USLTA kicked all nine of us out. (They later reinstated us.) The point had been made, and the Virginia Slims circuit had been born. The first circuit tournament was held in San Francisco, Calif., in January 1971, with prize money of at least $10,000 per tournament. Well, as you all know, the 1974 Virginia Slims Championship playoff purse was the richest ever—$100,000. And that happened in just three years.

So in women's tennis, thanks to a little organizing and a lot of help from the commercial sponsors, a woman can make a living as a professional in her sport for the first time in history. Along with the bigger purses comes, almost automatically, greater media exposure—and along with that comes the creation of new sports heroines that women can identify with. In tennis there are Chris Evert, Rosie Casals, and Margaret Court, to name just a few of the most visible headline makers.

I tell that tennis story not only because it is the sport I know best but because I fully believe that it is the prototype for what will happen in other women's sports as this movement gains momentum. It's beginning to happen in women's golf, where the circuit went from the table-crumb figures of $520,000 in 1970 to $1.8 million in 1974.

And they've got angels, too—David Foster, president of the Colgate-Palmolive Co., sponsored the biggest golf event ever in April of 1974 at Palm Springs, Calif. It was called the Colgate-Dinah Shore Winner's Circle Classic, and boasted a purse of $200,000.

*Star golfer Sandy Palmer (left) and Olympic diving champion Micki King head for a break during the early rounds of the first women's Superstars competition at the Houston, Tex., Astrodome, in December.*

ART SEITZ

Golf personalities, like Carol Mann (who won $47,734 in 1973) and Kathy Whitworth, are emerging, along with media successes such as Sandra Haynie and Jane Blalock, not to mention popular Laura Baugh.

Colgate has lined up 33 of its women golfers to do television and print ads selling a vast array of Colgate's products. That means that not only are the women making money from these endorsements but the viewers and readers are getting exposure to real golf personalities for the first time. Who knows how many women have decided to take up the game as a result of all this exposure?

Two other measurable increases can be seen in professional track and bowling. Women's bowling had long been in the doldrums. In 1973 Judy Cook Soutar earned $11,200, while the top male won $69,000. But in January of 1974, Brunswick (which manufactures bowling equipment) put up $85,000 to fund the richest women's bowling event ever—the Red Crown Classic at Baltimore, Md. Personalities such as Paula Sperber and Loa Boxberger are emerging, who will attract more women to the sport.

Professional track, which didn't even exist until three years ago, has equal prize money for the men and the women—$500 per event—but there are no more than 3 events for women in any given meet, while there are 12 for the men. That's why Wyomia Tyus, who may be this country's best woman sprinter, made only $8,250 during 1973.

So a look at the record shows progress in some areas, growth in others, and agonizingly slow, snail-paced growth in too many areas of women's sports. We emerge on the scene of this newest social revolution not without a certain sense of déjà vu. Sure, in the 19th century the sports that were acceptable for women— archery, croquet, bowling, tennis, and golf—were almost entirely dictated by the Victorian mode of dress. When the bicycle craze hit in the 1880's, however, women all across the country started clamoring for Amelia Bloomer's curious pantaloons (which she had invented about 30 years earlier) and spun off into the country. There is a diary left by a Margaret Valentine Le Long, who rode her bicycle alone from Chicago to San Francisco in 1896. Truly, the bicycle has been well named as the first vehicle of women's liberation.

Physical fitness via sports became all the rage at the exclusive women's schools well before the turn of the century, and in 1896, Harriet Ballintine started track at Vassar College. In 1901, Smith, Radcliffe, Wellesley, Bryn Mawr, and Vassar colleges started field hockey clubs. At Vassar, about 500 young women turned out to sign up.

### The Golden Decade and the Decline

It seemed for a while that women at last would come into their own physically. Sports participation grew during the 1910's, and with the passage of the 19th Amendment in 1920, granting women the vote, many sportswomen thought they were home free. In

*Chris Evert prepares for a backhand, displaying the style that eventually won her the 1974 Italian, French, and Wimbledon titles—events in which she had been a runner-up the previous year.*

KEN REGAN—CAMERA 5

fact, the years 1925–35 have been called the Golden Decade in women's sports.

It was during these years that Hazel Hotchkiss Wightman made her mark in tennis, Glenna Collett in golf, and Babe Didrikson Zaharias in almost every sport imaginable. Sportswomen were heroines in those days. It was also the era that produced Amelia Earhart, whose daring exploits and liberating marriage contract inspired many women to become independent.

Many women participated in volleyball, softball, basketball, field hockey, lacrosse, polo, squash, you name it. And the sports had spread from the exclusive schools into the masses. Almost every factory had some kind of team.

But it wasn't to last. Perhaps the schools were the first to feel the pinch, just as they had been first to participate. The decline started in 1923, when Herbert Hoover's wife, who might not be remembered in history for anything else, banned boys' and girls' basketball double-headers on the grounds that the spectators came to watch the girls perform in gym clothes. For some reason, this shocked her Victorian sensibilities, and she felt that the girls were being exploited. Her ban was effective, and by 1930 the number of colleges sponsoring varsity competition dropped from 22% to 12%, and the emphasis went from "winning" to "play-days." To compete in earnest became unladylike. Women's competitive drive was thwarted, and women rapidly lost the ground they had gained in achieving their physical freedom.

The damage done to competitive women athletes was devastating. Suddenly, their "femininity" came into question. Nobody had thought to hurl that epithet lightly before. And the same kind of thinking gave rise to what I've labeled "shamateurism."

If sport were for fun only, then a woman shouldn't expect to be paid for what she was doing, according to this thinking. Certainly she shouldn't be given scholarships or financial assistance. This credo was given validity since the U.S. Olympic requirements stipulated that an athlete must be an "amateur" to participate. And so the greatest rip-off of all time was (and still is) perpetrated upon those who defied society's disapproval and developed their athletic abilities.

Outside the collegiate arena, women's sports were de-emphasized for other reasons. The depression of 1929 meant that fewer women were able to go to college, fewer women worked, fewer women could afford to live away from home and be independent. This tide away from women's participation was stemmed somewhat when the women returned to the work force during World War II. Again, women's teams sprang up in the factories. Nationally, there were 40,000 semi-professional women's softball teams during the War. In 1943, Phil Wrigley, owner of the Chicago Cubs, started the All-America Girls Professional Ball League, which expanded to include ten clubs in the Midwest. They played 126 games per season, and star players made up to $125 per week. Changing mores caught up to them, too, and the league folded in 1954.

### Toward Lasting Liberation

My but the 1950's and early 1960's were lazy years! Betty Friedan in her 1963 book, 'The Feminine Mystique', traced the socialization of women away from independent action by listing story titles from women's popular magazines through the years. In the 1920's the titles encouraged women to learn to fly planes, become pilots, be independent. After World War II, they emphasized dependency, domesticity, and child care.

Socialization of pubertal girls away from sport by calling such interest "unladylike" was perpetrated against almost every female child born in this country between 1940 and 1972.

But now, in the 1970's, many more women are part of the work force—most often because they are heads of households and *need* to work. (By the first of the decade nearly 50% of all American women between the ages of 18 and 64 were in the labor force, as compared with nearly 20% in 1900.) So the new feminism is partially a reflection of the economic necessity of a woman who has to bring home enough bacon to feed not only herself but her 2 to 12 children. And just as financial independence inspires women to seek their fair chare of the paycheck, so does physical independence encourage women to seek their fair share of the physical goodies that sport has to offer them. So we're now in the throes of an upsurge in sports participation that makes the Golden Decade seem like the dark ages.

It seems peculiar, in retrospect, that the women's liberation movement, which naturally spawned the women's sports revolu-

*With the invention of bloomers in about 1850, the women's sports revolution was off and running—or cycling, as was the Victorian craze (opposite, bottom). Women's athletic vistas were later broadened by such pioneers as Amelia Earhart (top), whose 1932 solo transatlantic flight ushered women pilots into the cockpit, and multitalented Babe Didrikson Zaharis (center, shown with Babe Ruth), whose outstanding performances in basketball, track and field, and golf provided an encouraging example to other early women athletes.*

*Among the 23 competitors in the December qualifying rounds of the women's Superstars competition at Texas' Houston Astrodome were (left to right) Olympic gymnast Cathy Rigby, ace bowler Paula Sperber, and world women's softball champion Joan Joyce. U.S. golfer Judy Rankin (far right) took the $52,140 winner's purse at the August Colgate European Women's Open in Sunningdale, England.*

tion, did not immediately appreciate the values of an independent body made strong through sports. In fact, it was not until 1973 that the National Organization for Women held a symposium on the place of women in sport.

Early feminists like Gloria Steinem turned down sports stories in *Ms.* magazine (until July of 1973) because she felt that sports embodied all the negative male values that women were trying to get away from—competitiveness, the killer instinct, the will to win, and other such attributes. It is refreshing to note that she has since rethought her stand and has come to appreciate that making women strong through sports can't possibly hurt them.

In fact, Agnes Kurtz, who now heads up the women's athletic department at Dartmouth College, related that while in a previous position she was approached by the school psychiatrist, who demanded to know why none of the women actively involved in sports seemed to have emotional problems.

Thomas Boslooper, a New Jersey clergyman who had counseled women for many years, found that physically active women had fewer emotional problems, and that the most disturbed seemed to be the aggressive women who had no outlets for their drives.

It's a competitive world out there, and the more weapons a woman has in her psychic arsenal of self-defense, the better prepared she is to meet the battle and win. Yes, I've always felt that winning counts a lot. Surely, the benefits of sport that men derive must be good for women, too. I mean teamwork, discipline, learning how to lose, how to win, and how to weigh an opponent's strengths and weaknesses. It's not for nothing that the British are fond of saying that the Battle of Waterloo was won upon the playing fields of Eton.

## Participation and the Law

Many of the battles in the women's sports revolution have been won not on the playing fields but in the courts of law. Certainly, Little League's stand against allowing girls on their teams was highly illegal. The teams used municipal fields and facilities, and by denying the girls the right to play they were clearly in violation of the girls' civil rights. A suit on behalf of Maria Pepe of Hoboken, N.J., was instituted in 1972, but Maria passed the maximum age for Little Leaguers while the case was pending, so she never won. It became a class action suit, however, and after two years in the courts, the New Jersey State Superior Court ruled in March 1974 that National Little League should comply with the New Jersey court order that the Little League permit girls to play on local teams throughout the state. The national organization decided in June 1974 to rescind its ban on girls by rewording its charter to delete the references excluding girls. I'm not convinced that girls wouldn't be better off having their own teams to begin with, because that way all of them would get a chance to play. As it is now, only the best girls can make the team. But I naturally support the right of the girls to play on the Little League teams if they wish.

In Nebraska, Debbie Reed wanted to play high school golf but was rejected despite her powerful swing. Debbie sued—and won in 1972. In Philadelphia, Pa., Heidi Beth Kaplan won the right in 1974 for girls to swim on that city's high school teams—not because she actually sued but because her sister was a feminist and a lawyer and made the right threatening noises.

UPI COMPIX

The battle to end the discriminatory barring of girls from Little League play was initiated by a 1972 suit filed on behalf of Maria Pepe (left) of Hoboken, N.J., that was eventually won in March 1974 in the New Jersey State Superior Court. In light of that ruling and 22 similar suits filed across the country in 1974, the Little League organization petitioned the U.S. Congress to amend its charter opening the league to "young people." The bill was signed into law by President Gerald R. Ford on Christmas Day.

75

There is legal basis—plenty of it—for filing suits. And not all of it has to do with Title IX of the Education Amendments of 1972. In fact, there are *five* federal laws under which a woman may sue if she thinks that she is being discriminated against in her pursuit of school sports: Title VII of the 1964 Civil Rights Act; Executive Order 11246; the Equal Pay Act; the equal protection clause of the 14th Amendment to the Constitution; and Title IX of the Education Amendments of 1972. A sixth, the equal rights amendment, has yet to be ratified by the requisite number of states.

But the law that's getting the most publicity these days is Title IX. The wording of the provision is worth repeating, since the clincher is in the last sentence (keep in mind that the word *recipient* used throughout means any school or college that receives federal funds):

---

**Title IX Regulations Affecting Athletics**

**Sec. 86.38 ATHLETICS.**

*(a)* GENERAL.

No person shall, on the basis of sex, be excluded from participation in, be denied the benefits of, be treated differently from another person or otherwise be discriminated against in any physical education or athletic program operated by a recipient, and no recipient shall provide any physical education or athletic program separately on such basis; provided, however, that a recipient may operate or sponsor separate teams for members of each sex where selection for such teams is based upon competitive skill.

*(b)* DETERMINATION OF STUDENT INTEREST.

A recipient which operates or sponsors athletics shall determine at least annually, using a method to be selected by the recipient which is acceptable to the Director, in which sports members of each sex would desire to compete.

*(c)* AFFIRMATIVE EFFORTS.

A recipient which operates or sponsors athletic activities shall, with regard to members of a sex for which athletic opportunities previously have been limited, make affirmative efforts to:

*(1)* inform members of such sex of the availability for them of athletic opportunities equal to those available for members of the other sex and of the nature of those opportunities, and

*(2)* provide support and training activities for members of such sex designed to improve and expand their capabilities and interests to participate in such opportunities.

*(d)* EQUAL OPPORTUNITY.

A recipient which operates or sponsors athletics shall make affirmative efforts to provide athletic opportunities in such sports and through such teams as will most effectively equalize such opportunities for members of both sexes, taking into consideration the determination made pursuant to paragraph *(b)* of this section.

*(e)* SEPARATE TEAMS.

A recipient which operates or sponsors separate teams for members of each sex shall not discriminate on the basis of sex therein in the provision of necessary equipment or supplies for each team, or in any other manner.

*(f)* EXPENDITURES.

Nothing in this section shall be interpreted to require equal aggregate expenditures for athletics for members of each sex.

---

"Physical education is one of the most discriminatory areas in the American educational system. Sports programs for boys start as early as the fourth grade in some areas but don't begin, even in limited form, for the girls until the seventh through tenth grades. By the time a girl reaches high school or college, she is often well programmed to think of sports as extraneous. She doesn't take pride in active and strenuous use of her body. Boys, in the meantime, are encouraged to keep in condition, both to maintain their health and to enjoy their athletic abilities.

"Why is it that such benefits are extended to only forty-nine percent of the population, except in rare cases? Why is it that women's sports programs in the public schools receive only about one percent of what the men's programs receive?

"I feel that the potential developed by our educational system can be greatly enhanced by... providing the opportunities that women deserve and have been denied in physical education."

—Statement from Billie Jean King before the Senate Subcommittee on Education

So this means that schools must allow a woman to go out for whatever sport she chooses. If no women's team exists, she may join the men's team, or they must create a team for her. But alas, there is no provision for equal funding. So, the fanfare may be in vain; women may be in for a rip-off again unless the ambiguity of that last sentence is cleared up once and for all.

It's obvious that the big schools, which depend on football revenue, are very upset about Title IX and are trying every ploy in the game book to try to subvert its intention. They'd like to see "revenue producing sports" (meaning football and basketball) excluded from the provisions of Title IX.

Some of the big schools, however, have acted in anticipation of Title IX. At the University of California at Los Angeles (UCLA), for example, a new female athletic director was hired, its women's athletic budget was tripled to $180,000, and it opened its formerly all male varsity teams to women.

The University of Kansas raised its women's athletic budget from $9,000 to $121,000 in one year. At the University of Washington, the women's budget jumped from $35,000 to $200,000, with $1.5 million approved for a women's sports facility. All of these measures, although taken in anticipation of Title IX, would have happened anyway. There has been such a strong ground swell on the part of college women for athletic facilities that their pleas and pressure tactics had to work.

One of the most unexpected sources of conservatism toward the women's sports movement has come from within the ranks of the women physical educators. For many years, these women had the phys ed departments all to themselves. They were accustomed to being ignored, downtrodden, and ridiculed. Now, with the new emphasis on sports participation, they really don't know what to do. They are suddenly in the limelight. They've been asked to reexamine some of the most sacred tenets close to a gym teacher's heart—such as the ritual inspection for a spotless gym suit. Does it really matter? Is that what's been turning off women to sports all these years? Some athletic directors at some universities when offered the largest budgets they've ever seen can't imagine how to spend the money. They're so accustomed to the bake sales by which women had to earn transportation money to get from one meet to another that they have no idea of what to do with the pittance they've been awarded.

"The athletic director and the dean and the president [were] all anxious to give more, but the women haven't asked for anything big," says Mary Jo Haverbeck, recently hired by Penn State as sports information director. "They [the women in charge] didn't ask for scholarships and they didn't ask for uniforms; these new additions are being gently suggested to [them]."

And the question of scholarships is another thing that the parent organization—the National Affiliation for Girls and Women in Sport, a division of the American Alliance for Health, Physical Education, and Recreation—had always opposed. Their attitude was a throwback to Mrs. Herbert Hoover's philosophy: sports are

*Women were internationally represented at the first annual Dr. Martin Luther King, Jr., International Freedom Games held in Villanova, Pa., in May 1969.*

*Jockey Robyn Smith prepares to head for home after participating in the women's Superstars competition, the new counterpart to male Superstars competition and symbol of the strides made in the women's sports revolution.*

just for fun, not for serious competition. Also, they didn't want their girls *corrupted* by the the evils of recruitment that plague men's sports. As late as April 1973, athletic scholarships for women were outlawed by this group. But they bowed at that time to public pressure.

So, in many ways, women have been their own worst enemies in getting what's coming to them in the way of facilities and money in the sports world.

This is not to say that all the questions are answered. Nobody really knows if coed teams, for example, are a solution. One man who is trying to find out is Pennsylvania's Secretary of Education John Pittenger. With the help of Kathleen H. Larkin, the state's deputy attorney general, he has gone beyond Title IX by declaring that separate is not equal, that women will play on teams with men (excepting football and wrestling), and that the sports funds will be equally divided. Perhaps he'll have some concrete research on whether it works or not long before other schools do.

Coed teams are not all that new: there are women already on some men's teams. Susie Kincade, for example, is on the men's varsity diving team at UCLA. Ellen Feldmann, one of the two women on the University of Virginia swimming team, was the first woman to compete on a male varsity team. Laurel Brassey plays on the men's volleyball team at San Diego State.

Coed team sports are going to be great fun to watch. I know that mixed doubles is more interesting than ordinary doubles. And World Team Tennis, the first sport in which men and women compete as equals, has led the way for all kinds of professional coed competition.

In the individual sports, however, I think the only fair way to compete is in three classifications: a men's division, a women's division, and an open division. That way, the best woman has a chance to try her skill against the best man. Certainly, the best women will be better than many of the men. Shouldn't they have the right to compete on equal terms?

The jury's still out on the coed team question. Perhaps after 15 years, when today's young girls who are interested in sports and who are encouraged to pursue them over the years perform with and against men who have been involved in sport all of their lives too, we'll start to have some answers. There is scant physiological evidence to back up claims of athletic supremacy on either side. Yes, women are better in marathon swimming events. But the guys are bigger and stronger. Yes, if you match up male and female competitors who have roughly the same lean body weight (that is, body weight minus the fat) and the same training program, they will be equal competitors. But what does it all really mean? Not much. Because we're not fighting the battle to beat men. We really just want to be recognized as athletes in our own right, who deserve the facilities and our cut of the school-budget or prize-money pie.

Unfortunately, so much extraneous nonsense enters into the picture that we lose sight of our real goal. That is to provide women the information to get started in their sport and to offer them the support that what they're doing is good for them, no matter what social pressures are levied against them. In order to do this, I've started *WomenSports* magazine, partly with my winnings from my match with Bobby Riggs. In it, I hope to expose more women athletes to the public so that younger women will have models to look up to and emulate. I want to tell everybody about the good things sports can do for you. For the youngsters, I'd like to encourage them to pursue the sport that makes them happy. For the middle-aged, I'd like to encourage them to get back to the sport they left when they were told it was unladylike to perform in it. And the oldsters who've led physically active lives don't need me to tell them how good it is for them. For those who want to compete for the big prize money, let's equalize it so that more women can make a profession of sports if they want to. And if you just want to be a Sunday bowler, or run through a couple of sets of tennis a week, that's OK, too.

Hopefully, the women's sports revolution will make it easier for all women to take part in sport, giving them the benefits and joys that such participation can bring.

AISLIN.

# canada is not
# the 51st state

## by Gordon Sinclair

*Illustrations by Aislin*, The Montreal Gazette

**Gordon Sinclair**

Author of the broadcast editorial "Americans," which became a best-seller in recorded versions, Mr. Sinclair is a radio and TV commentator in Toronto, Ont. In his opinion, the U.S. is the most generous of countries. His eulogy to America was inserted in the Congressional Record.

In 1974 Canada was the only country in the free world to vote for stability by reelecting a government putting conservatives down and socialists to rout. Canada set a national energy policy, gave the French language additional clout, set up long-range plans for public transportation, almost proved that Olympic Games can be financed by stamps, coins, and lotteries, and in a variety of other ways its people reasserted that they are not now, and don't intend to become, the 51st state.

Canadians are constantly being told by their writers, politicians, dramatists, and academics that they are a colorless, nonpromoting people of no exciting history, so they import history by way of British royalty, the American West, or the stormy seas. This image is a lie, but Canadians seldom deny it.

Canada is still being described in many places as a pioneering land of Christmas trees, Mounties, blizzards, and wolves—whereas it has several of the most modern and progressive cities in the world and a combination of socialist and capitalist enterprise that seems to work and make it truly Canadian. Transport, electricity, and telephones are examples.

It's true that in many cities (Calgary, Alta., being typical) an American set down without knowing his location might think he was at home. Canadians see the same movies, TV shows, and magazines. The dollar is a different color, but it's still a dollar, and flashing signs pinpoint locations of food and drink identical to what you'd find in San Diego, Calif., or Salt Lake City, Utah. But when Calgary hired an American as chief of police, indignation swept the city, and the Board of Police Commissioners had to send him back to California with apologies and give the job to a Canadian.

Let that same American be dropped three aerial hours eastward and he'll come down in Montreal, Que., which is different from any other city on this continent and is currently enlarging the difference through the upgrading of the French language. Take him a bit further east and he will find not only that the provincial

PARLIAMENT·OTTAWA.

capital of Quebec is European in style but that some of its parts (city walls as a sample) are even medieval European in style. No observant American would consider this to be any part of a 51st state, nor would an intelligent Frenchman link it with his own Normandy or Brittany.

It's true that even in the city of Quebec franchise operations from Kentucky Fried Chicken to Holiday Inns, and even a few familiar U.S. television shows, can be found, but these stand out as exceptions and are declining.

American books, however, are at saturation level. Only in Quebec will one find the most coveted spots on paperback bookracks reserved for the homegrown product.

Musicwise, in the pop field, American stars dominate as they've always done, and such Canadians as Anne Murray and Gordon Lightfoot line up annual or biannual tours below the border—while Rich Little, the mimic, is practically an American institution. But who is the Down East Canadian who scorns the American scene and is storming toward the top of the box office? Stompin' Tom Connors, that's who.

Tom's passionate Canadian nationalism may be intemperate and his language coarse, but in concert after concert he draws the crowds, especially if he's out there in the meadow or pastureland. Most of Tom's fans know his numbers upside down and inside out, but they stomp along with him, and their theme is "We are Canadians, good or bad, right or wrong, we are what we are and don't forget it."

One of Tom's numbers is 'We Ain't, No We Ain't . . . No 51st State'. That gives an idea of his style and his attitude. But the negative or anti-American approach doesn't work.

### The Myth of Yankee Takeover

For a ten-year period that began to peter out by 1972, Canada's newspapers constantly warned about the great American takeover: the rape of irreplaceable natural resources by covetous Yanks hell-bent on making Canada part of their own land. Political parties, clubs, associations, and groups were formed to prevent this assault. None prospered. Few if any are left.

This doesn't mean that the fear of annexation to the United States has passed; it means, to most, that the fear was never real. It was an artificial fear.

For a hundred years it has been known that there was oil, perhaps vast quantities of oil, on the sandy banks of the Athabasca River in northern Alberta. Black crude could be seen oozing out of the ground. A few small operations were started to extract that oil but died for lack of imagination, know-how, and money. Then came American geologists and technicians who ordered German machinery and started to dig.

A Canadian company was formed, hundreds of millions in U.S. dollars were poured in, difficulties of countless kinds were overcome, and oil began to flow. Fortunes in taxes and royalties were collected from this enterprise whose officers agreed to share their

THE WEST AND QUEBEC

knowledge with others—Canadians, Americans, or Japanese—
who might want to further develop the sands.

When the energy crunch came, it was seen that this company,
started with American money and men, was planning not to pipe
the oil stateside but to put it into a general pool. That was one of
the reasons why talk of American takeover began to ebb, one of
the reasons why rich Alberta is the only Canadian province without a sales tax. In 1974, for the first time, the oil sands gave up a
profit. But even in Alberta, which on a percentage basis has more
U.S.-born Canadians than any other province, they don't even
whisper that Canada is or might be the 51st state.

### "Insiders" and "Outsiders"

Some Canadians feel that because of increasing provincialism,
there is greater possibility of the breakup of confederation than of
any political merger with the United States, be that to create a
51st state or for any other reason. During the 1970's more prov-
ince-to-province barriers went up than in any previous generation.

Quebec made French the only official language. Prince Edward
Island, the smallest province and the birthplace of Canada as a

nation, not only set up a land bank against outside purchase but also defined "outside" as anyone not a resident of the province. Not only were American, British, or other outsiders banned from buying more than ten acres, but the restriction also applied to mainland Canadians.

British Columbia, under one of the three existing provincial socialist governments, put heavy new taxes on mines, most of the stock in those mines being owned by Canadians in other provinces. Alberta imposed no restrictions but had and still has vocal groups demanding that it separate from the rest of the country because it is contributing too much of its income to support poorer provinces.

Don't take this seriously. It's political hogwash like those standard clichés "granary of Empire" (what empire?), "longest undefended border in the world," "storehouse of mineral wealth," and so on. Such timeworn oldies still pop up but with less frequency.

Canada has an abundance of what the world needs from metals to meal, from fish to fruit, from gas to grain, but to this home-grown Canadian the greatest asset of all will one day be fresh water. Canada has often been listed as having more nickel than any other country in the world, but you can do without nickel. Canada also has the most fresh water of any land on earth, and this—for power, irrigation, and human use—is beyond measure in value.

In a military sense, Canadians have more than pulled their weight in two world wars and in separate skirmishes in between, but there is underlying mistrust in the feeling that the so-called heroes have been outsiders.

Canada never has had a five-star general, but it had two five-letter generals, James Wolfe and Isaac Brock, who managed to get themselves killed in "battles" that by modern standards were no more than petty skirmishes—the first against the French in Quebec, and the second against the Americans at Niagara.

As in most wars, the apparent losers eventually came out on top. After Wolfe had won but died on the Plains of Abraham, the French were supposedly vanquished. They are today the most durably determined and possibly the most politically astute force in Canada. After the Americans were picturesquely put to rout by a woman and a cow (if you believe junior histories), they later developed and owned the area's automobile and petroleum industries and much of its chemical, rubber, electronic, and furniture production. They were moving toward controlling banks and communications when stopped by law.

As Canadians realized how much of their production and distribution was in outside hands, there came nationalistic calls to "buy back Canada." That turned out to be unnecessary. In the market slump of 1974, cut-rate ownership of hundreds of Canadian corporations was on the line for any outsider.

Only in banking and communications did the government take exception. They banned outsiders from ownership of Canada's

♪

O YAKUSHEV,
WHY MUST WE BE SO BLAND?
TRITE AND CONTENT,
WITH CAMPBELL AND HIS BAND!

ON HOCKEY NIGHT,
WE'LL ALL GET TIGHT,
AND WATCH THE C.B.C.

SEE ROUSTABOUTS,
'TWEEN K.C. SCOUTS,
AND WASHINGTON, D.C!

O YAKUSHEV,
DESPITE YOUR REFEREE,
O YAKUSHEV, PLEASE LISTEN TO MY PLEA!

O YAKUSHEV,
WON'T YOU DEFECT FOR ME?!!

A NEW ANTHEM

banks, radio and TV stations, newspapers, and magazines.

Warehouses, factories, trucking lines, canneries, fisheries, paper and flour mills, breweries, and more were up for grabs. When they remained untouched, talk of greedy American takeover collapsed like a limp balloon.

### Unions and Sports

Greatest industrial cooperation between the United States and Canada is in the building of cars and trucks by the big four—Ford, General Motors, Chrysler, and American, all U.S.-owned. Parts and whole cars are moved back and forth across the border according to demand. United Auto Workers controls the labor force and thus to a large extent the industry on both sides. Each country claims that the other is getting the best of this, so it must be a tolerably fair deal.

If there is any one way in which the United States has already taken over Canada and shown no inclination of releasing even one man or one contract, it is in labor unions, a sore point with Canadians that is causing more and more irritation. Of the 15 biggest unions in Canada in terms of membership and assets, 11 are controlled and operated in and from the United States. Of the second 15 unions, 13 are directed from the United States.

Nor is this token control. There have been frequent examples of settlements worked out by Canadians for Canadians working in Canada that have been vetoed by the powerful parent below the border. Do it this way . . . or else!

This has worked in both directions, of which two recent examples are typical. United Auto Workers at McDonald-Douglas in Ontario refused a company offer after several weeks of strike. The local was controlled by militant Scots who said the offer was not good enough. The local was ordered from union headquarters in Michigan to accept.

On the other side of the coin the local of International Typographical Union, after bitter argument, worked out an agreement with the *Toronto Star*. It was rejected from union headquarters in Colorado, the strike was lost, and Canada's largest newspaper today has no printers' union.

There is cynical bitterness over these decisions imposed from without the country. Even worse is the fact that some Canadians, anxious to be part of a Canadian union (I'm one), often find that they must also join an American union.

An example is the Association of Canadian Television and Radio Artists, a solid, all-Canadian union. Its authority ends with the electronic medium. If its members step on a stage they must belong to Actors' Equity Association, American Guild of Variety Artists, or the Screen Actors Guild. Not only are these U.S. controlled, but also there is little evidence that they have ever been of any benefit to any Canadian in his own country. Several Canadians who have done well in the United States, without becoming Americans, offer salute to these U.S. unions and say they have been of help. But for the Canadian in his homeland who is compelled to join a U.S. union, even though he never takes a step across the border, it is one more example of how he feels ensnared.

Canadians have long been resigned to the realization that the best baseball, basketball, and football players come from the United States, so much so that a quota has been put on the number of imported football players who can turn up with Canadian teams. There is no similar quota against Canadian hockey players on U.S. teams, and if the Canadians were dropped, both attendance and interest would sharply decline.

Not until 1974 did the Canadian government attempt to totally ban a whole team and its league, even though the team was organized and financed by two of the country's most aggressive and youthful tycoons. John Craig Eaton and John Bassett, Jr., put up the money and promptly worked out a $3-million package for stars Larry Csonka, Jim Kiick, and Paul Warfield of the Miami Dolphins.

Into this picture stepped Marc Lalonde, Canada's minister of health and welfare, to declare that the World Football League (including the Toronto Northmen) would never play in Canada because it would ruin the Canadian Football League. Since a national election was just over the hill, promoters confidently expected that fans would rise up en masse to object to this sort of athletic censorship. Nothing came of it.

The Northmen found a home in Memphis, Tenn., and the young entrepreneurs later signed Vaclav Nedomansky and Richard Farda of the Czechoslovakian National Hockey Team for their Toronto Toros. There was no government objection because hockey was well established, whereas football was not. A precedent had been set.

There are, of course, athletic areas where free crossing of the border is a reality even though Canadians seldom win their own titles. Golf is probably the best example. Not since the 1950's has a Canadian won the Canadian Open, yet in 1974 the biggest

UNIONS AND SPORTS

crowds in the records of the game turned out to watch American stars compete for Canadian money.

To a lesser extent this is true in tennis and skiing. Rodeo riders, a breed apart, compete in their bone-crunching specialty and results come out nearly even. Jockeys and harness horse drivers move freely back and forth across the border in search of reward.

### Sanctuary, Cuban Trade, and Tourism

Major indications that Canada was no 51st state came in the sheltering and protection of U.S. draft dodgers and deserters and in continued trade with Cuba—especially in live animals and birds. Pressure to stop such trade with Cuba was never pushy or blunt, but it was mentioned at most international conventions. Despite this, a shuttle service of foam-padded and air-cooled airplanes carried a continuous stream of hogs, cattle, and chickens, with an occasional brood mare, to the island.

The situation in regard to the young Americans anxious to

avoid military service was one of the most clouded because it remained difficult to make a head count. Estimates of the number of these Americans taking sanctuary in Canada ranged from 10,-000 to ten times that many, and since no combination of investigative groups came up with anything accurate, "about 50,000" was settled on.

Technically these young men were in limbo so far as work was concerned. Unless they entered Canada as landed immigrants, they couldn't legally take work. But since native workers were scarce in some fields in which the young Americans had skill, they were employed by the thousands—with their employers and the government looking the other way.

The academic field became a shadow land when thousands of American teachers, lecturers, and professors moved into Canadian universities and colleges. Some places of higher learning had staffs that were up to 80% American, and many of the schools used American textbooks.

Occasionally there would be a glaring example of U.S. indoctrination so that a historic condition open to two or more interpretations usually took the American stance because that's what the teachers knew. Now and again it came as an astonishment to

PRIME MINISTER TRUDEAU AND CONSERVATIVE
OPPOSITION LEADER ROBERT STANFIELD

them that there was any other view. Most of these teachers above the high school level have remained.

Like most of the world's countries, Canada and her separate provinces have set up substantial budgets to attract American tourists. If these visitors misbehave, however, or take unfair advantage of the hospitality (which few do), they are advised in the name of "Our Sovereign Lady the Queen" that they are not welcome and must leave.

There is sometimes dispute as to how many American tourists do enter Canada and how much they spend. A fair yardstick with which to judge is the total revenue of the 13 toll bridges and one tunnel that connect the two countries. After writing off everything they could, these entry points showed record profit in the 1973–74 season.

Here and there Canadians are smug about their national appearance, and the Niagara frontier is a case in point. Canadians self-righteously declare that the American side of the river is made up of honky-tonk dives and a littered shoreline while maintaining that the Canadian side is a tidily groomed parkland. This is partly true, but not to the credit of any present Canadian. The making of the shoreline into Crown Land (anything not privately owned is held in the name of the Queen) was decided more than 100 years ago.

### Political Forecast: Stable

Canada was the first part of North America to have a socialist government, and that government was the first to introduce Medicare—despite noisy and prolonged objection by the medical profession and the hospitals.

By the early 1970's that government, in Saskatchewan, had been voted out, then voted in again. The one-term premier who had been scathing in his attack on "crippling socialism" died as a young man. Now there are three socialist governments in the ten provinces, and Medicare, with slight variations province by province, is nationwide and universal.

Like the old-age pension or the baby bonus, there is no qualifying test. Benefits are automatic and, while there are continued opposition in some areas and occasional outcries about socialist hordes at the gate, no politician with concern for his own future would suggest that any of the welfare measures be cut back. In fact, Ontario, the most industrialized of the provinces, is advertising for citizens with less than $2,600 a year to step forward and collect a guaranteed annual income up to that sum.

While Ontario is considered by many to be the most capitalistic of all the provinces, it is one of the few with a Criminal Compensations Act whereby the victims of crime get redress. In 1974 a man from New York state was paid under that act because of the murder, in Ontario, of his daughter—even though victim and killer and beneficiary were all Americans.

Canada's Prime Minister Pierre Elliott Trudeau—author, lawyer, and professor—has never lost an election. As member of Par-

liament for the Montreal constituency of Mount Royal, leader of the Liberal party, and prime minister he has consistently scored.

Trudeau's first try as a prime minister was no contest. He swept to success as "the swinging bachelor millionaire" on personality, charisma, chutzpah, or whatever you choose to call it. But four years later, in 1972, he lost the seats on the great plains and was set back in other areas, coming home with a minority. Bolstered by the left-wing New Democratic party (NDP), Trudeau continued in office as chief of government, putting much useful legislation together but leaving the country with a feeling of insecurity.

David Lewis, the NDP (socialist) leader, had added to his support and authority on a slogan against "Corporate Welfare Bums." Coming in with 31 seats, the most ever gained by his party, Lewis held the balance of power between the traditional old-line parties, Liberals and Conservatives, and was in the heady position of being able to topple the government any time he chose to crack the whip.

Although Lewis himself was temperate in his use of the balance of power, others of press and party struck poses of grandeur and repeatedly referred to the time when it would be convenient to "bring Trudeau to his knees." Occasionally arrogance or political euphoria touched Lewis himself, but he was clearly aswarm with misgivings in the uneasy fact that he was collecting much of his financial support from American-controlled labor unions.

While he was the oldest of four party leaders, Lewis looked fit in his almost daily appearances on television, usually spoke with restraint, and clearly held respect for the Parliament of the country but not the government, a distinction that many Canadians misunderstand. He could have had little inkling of what was in store for himself and his party, because this poised, articulate man oozed confidence.

In the same Parliament where Lewis was calling for price and profit controls, Robert Stanfield, an "honest John" style of Conservative leader, called for temporary controls on wages and prices but was fuzzy in explaining how they would work.

In the spring of 1974 John Napier Turner, Trudeau's minister of finance, brought in a budget that largely ignored both proposals —thus inviting an election that the Trudeau-Turner team won with an overall majority. Soon afterwards Conservative leader Stanfield, leader of Her Majesty's loyal opposition, said that he'd step down within two years. Except for unforeseen crises, this gives Canada stable government until at least 1978.

The campaign—described as dull by the press, which had helped to bring it on—was notable in that a prime minister's wife, Margaret Sinclair Trudeau, took an active and effective part and the socialists lost their national leader to a first-time campaigner, a woman of no political experience and of Italian background.

Another odd situation was repudiation by the Conservative chieftain of a chosen son. Leonard Jones, mayor of Moncton, second largest city in New Brunswick, thought that the French language was intruding too much into his province and took a stand against it. His national Conservative leader—Stanfield, who had taken a crash course in French, followed by another of more sophistication—knew that if he made no gains in French-speaking Quebec, he had little chance of winning a national mandate. So Stanfield disowned Jones in a face-to-face confrontation. The leader said that regardless of the fact that Jones had been democratically chosen as a Conservative, he would not accept him and would provide another candidate. Should Jones win he would not be welcome at meetings of the Conservative caucus.

Jones did win, handily, and now sits as the only independent in Canada's Parliament. With nearly four years in which to maneuver, Trudeau, a far-thinking man, is likely to change some of Canada's directions, and this could mean less of a chip-on-the-shoulder attitude against the United States.

In 1967, during his final visit to Canada, French President Charles de Gaulle had helped enhance nationalism by speaking from a balcony to the people of Canada on the subject of Quebec independence, or as he put it "freedom." This was such a breach of etiquette that a planned visit to the Canadian capital of Ottawa, which was to have been made the next day, was canceled and De Gaulle flew home from Montreal, never to visit Canada again.

During his brief term as secretary of the treasury of the United States, John Connally was in Ottawa, and he too said things that rubbed the wrong way and brought visible indignation. Since Connally was not a head of state, the tough talk, as it was called, didn't attract the attention that De Gaulle drew, but it did rankle many and outraged hair-trigger nationalists. In the stable air that has followed, return of majority government under a bilingual leader heading toward 12 years of office, Connally's opinions on what Canadians could and should do would go unheeded. It would be thought, "That's his opinion; so what?"

Canada is in a solid, even lucky position. The country has most of the things it needs and, corny as it sounds through overuse, one of the most friendly borders on earth. During the Edwardian period and up to the middle of World War I, many Canadians hoped and expected that the country would become part of the United States. Had there been a plebiscite, especially at times when the Canadian dollar was discounted as much as 12% by U.S. banks, the people might even have voted in favor of political union.

Not now! Within limitations, Canada is a contented land, and not many lands are in that happy position today. So let's conclude with an anecdote that shows, literally, how the wind blows.

Flags often silently tell part of a country's feelings, and Canada, having flown a British flag for most of its national life, still has many citizens who fly only the Union Jack on their property or boat, especially at their summering places. A few even demean the official flag by sneeringly calling it "Pearson's pennant."

Three of the ten provinces—Ontario, which has the most summer cottages, being one—also adopted the Union Jack as part of their provincial flag, and this is hard to distinguish from the old colonial banner.

But this might indicate the way things are going. Between Toronto and the northern resorts, a superhighway was opened about 20 years ago. Various names were suggested, notably Simcoe or Yonge, but since they were English no name was chosen—and there is no name to this day, just a number.

Of four service stations in the first 60 miles, a pair on each side, two chose to decorate their premises with 16 flags each. In the beginning there were seven red ensigns (the semiofficial Canadian flag), seven union jacks, and a stars and stripes of the United States at each end.

When the red maple leaf, which is now Canada's official flag, came in, there were five maple leafs, five union jacks, five red ensigns, and one American flag. The next change was to eight maple leafs and eight red ensigns, but these had a small but subtle change. Ontario had adopted the red ensign as its provincial banner with the union jack upper left and provincial coat of arms lower right. So there were eight provincial flags and eight national flags—none from Great Britain or the United States.

Now, as I finish this article, I notice another change. All 16 flags are the red maple leaf of Canada. It tells you something.

Canada is a land mass of 3,851,809 square miles and because of its Arctic Islands has the longest shoreline in the world—but only 22.5 million people. About 85% of these people live within 400 miles of the U.S. border, and half of these pretend that they enjoy being misunderstood.

The French, claiming to be the last bastion of their tongue in North or South America, say the Anglos don't understand them. The Anglos say the government constantly caters to the French at the expense of all others. Canadians of Italian, German, and Ukrainian background, who make up large parts of the total population, claim that neither the French nor the Anglos understand them, and increasing numbers of Canadians of Caribbean origin say nobody can figure them out, least of all other blacks from other parts of the world.

There is one point on which all (French or Anglo, Jamaican or Japanese) agree: Canada is not the 51st state. Anybody who claims it is can expect to be hedged in by noisy opponents, each giving a different reason as to why Canadians are Canadians and not carbon-copy Americans. The fact that they say this so loudly, so often, and in so many places, however, indicates that they aren't quite sure of it themselves.

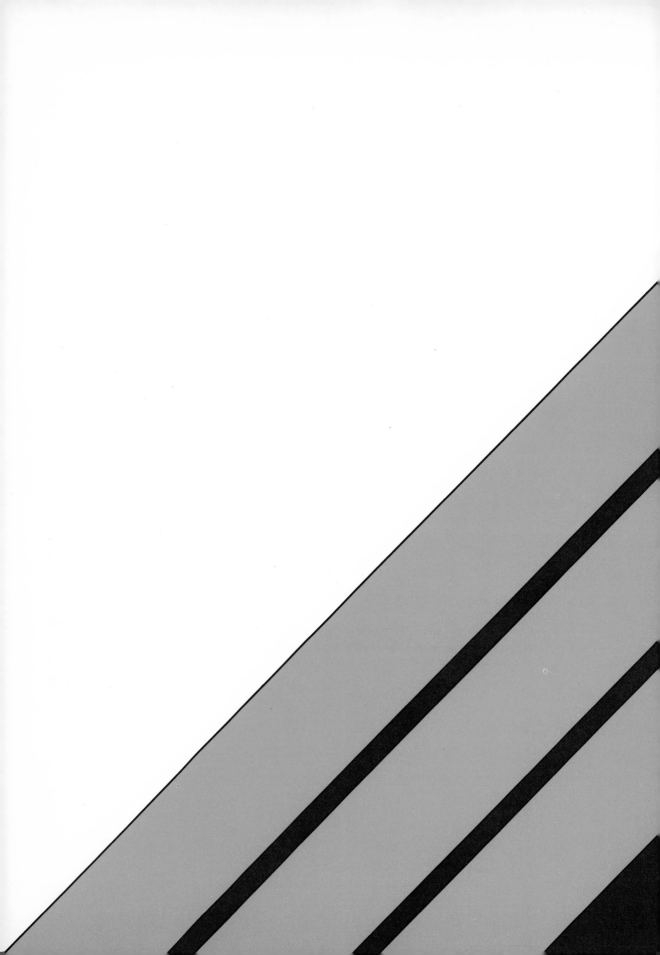

# events of the year

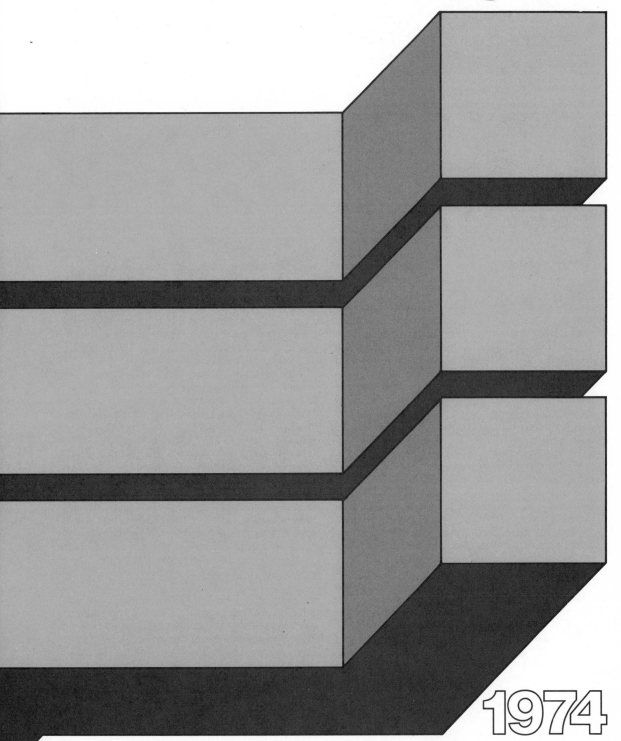

1974

*Stone books crumble in a February television advertisement, giving way to the new, long-awaited 15th edition of* Encyclopaedia Britannica, *the first really new idea in encyclopedias in 200 years. The use of television to announce and market a new major reference set was an advertising breakthrough, with the spot campaign appearing on 78 stations in 23 markets and reaching 91% of TV homes.*

**ADVERTISING.** Expenditures on advertising were up in 1974, but advertising, like much of the business world, was in a state of uncertainty. Shortages, inflation, and a recession restricted all business growth somewhat, although the problems of business created new opportunities for advertising used to promote companies' images to the public. Oil companies, for example, used large advertising campaigns in 1974 to explain their position on the energy crisis. To many people, their advertising seemed to be aimed solely at justifying high oil profits and getting laws and government policies changed to benefit the industry. Government agencies, however, upheld the oil industry's right to image and advocacy advertising.

On the other hand, advertising continued to feel the effects of the "truth-in-advertising" movement. The Federal Trade Commission (FTC) in 1974 proposed a ban on television advertising that used premiums such as trinkets, toys, games, puzzles, and box-top offers to sell cereals and other products to children. There was also discussion of banning the use of "hero figures" such as athletes and cartoon characters, banning vitamin, drug, and hazardous toy ads, and requiring disclaimers to be spoken as well as printed in ads aimed at preschoolers. The advertising industry itself began a formal program to monitor children's ads in 1974.

The FTC also objected to advertisements that claimed fuel savings for certain automobiles. The FTC contended that the tests used were not adequate or that the results were not fully reported. The FTC prohibited pesticide manufacturers in 1974 from advertising their products as "safe" when the government-required labels on the containers said that they were dangerous.

Women complained in 1974 about the sexism of National Airlines' "Fly me" and Continental Airlines' "We really move our tail for you" ads. The airlines were generally unsympathetic to the complaints. Some blacks objected to advertising for the movie 'Uptown Saturday Night' that implied that Harlem was a dangerous place. In the ad, which was later withdrawn, Bill Cosby, one of the stars of the movie, said, "Well, you can still go uptown without gettin' your head beat in by going downtown to see 'Uptown Saturday Night'."

Advertisers of tobacco products and alcoholic drinks came under criticism in Europe. In Great Britain both groups agreed to accept tight controls that would outlaw advertisement of alcohol aimed at young people and any suggestion that smoking improved the quality of life. In addition, all cigarette ads had to quote the official tar content.

In Norway, advertising of cigarettes was banned entirely. But perhaps the most extravagant development took place in the Netherlands, where legislation was introduced forbidding advertising that encouraged increased consumption of candy and requiring that all advertisements for candy carry a symbol of a toothbrush.

In the U.S. the movie 'The Great Gatsby' was promoted in 1974 by what was probably the most ambitious campaign in the history of U.S. advertising. Capitalizing on people's nostalgia for the 1920's, the producers of the movie signed agreements with such products as clothing, cookware, and beauty salons that promised to create the Gatsby look for buyers. The fashions of the 1920's did have a revival in 1974, perhaps because of the advertising campaign. But the advertising apparently was more successful than the movie itself, which received mixed reviews from critics and a cool reception from the public. (*See also* Fashion.)

*Two Jaguar aircraft prepare to land at Lossiemouth, Scotland, after the initial display of the first operational squadron and show of its paces on June 5. The Anglo-French Jaguar, a new frontline fighter, was the latest addition to the British Royal Air Force's weapon system.*

**AEROSPACE.** The worst air disaster in history shook commercial aviation in 1974 and brought official rebukes to U.S. regulatory agencies as well as to the airplane's manufacturer. The crash of a Turkish Airlines DC-10 jumbo jet on March 3 near Paris killed all 346 persons aboard. The cause appeared to be the sudden loss of the rear cargo door—the same type of mishap that had caused a near crash two years previously. At question was the improvement of the locking mechanism. A U.S. Senate subcommittee criticized the Federal Aviation Administration, the National Transportation Safety Board, and the plane's manufacturer, the McDonnell Douglas Corp., for the company's failure to deal more urgently with the suggestion for design change that followed the incident near Detroit, Mich., in 1972.

Despite the energy crisis, which made fuel a premium commodity, passenger traffic on U.S. airlines increased in 1974. In the first six months of the year, jet fuel prices soared 91.54% over those of the same period in 1973. Mounting fuel costs were cited as the cause of two major U.S. international flag carriers—Pan American World Airways (Pan Am) and Trans World Airlines, Inc. (TWA)—seeking financial aid. In October Pan Am and TWA proposed a plan for the reallocation of several international travel routes in order to eliminate costly direct competition. Legislation designed to help U.S. international carriers compete with foreign airlines was passed by Congress in December.

### New Developments

Costs for development of the Concorde supersonic airliner hit a startling $2.5 billion in 1974, and the only firm customers by midyear were the state-owned airlines of Great Britain and France, the two countries financing the Concorde program. Public opinion in both countries ran strongly in favor of abandoning the project.

The Soviet Union continued to test the Tu-144 supersonic transport following the crash of one of its prototypes at the 1973 Paris Air Show. A Tu-144 training flight in 1974 was reported to have covered 1,360 statute miles between Murmansk and Kiev in slightly more than an hour.

In 1974 the wide-bodied A300B airbus made by the Paris-based multinational Airbus Industrie went into commercial service on Air France between Paris and London. Round-trip runs were also scheduled for Nice, Marseilles, and Algiers.

Europe's biggest airport—l'Aéroport de Charles de Gaulle—was inaugurated on March 8, 1974. It spread over 75,000 acres about 15 miles northeast of Paris. The airport, which was expected to be finished between 1985 and 1990, had a planned capacity of 60 million passengers and 2 million tons of freight. The cylindrical terminal featured drive-in registration. Passengers were to board and deplane in seven satellite buildings attached to the main terminal by subterranean moving walkways.

A high point of the Farnborough International Air Show held in England in September was a new speed record set by a U.S. Air Force reconnaissance plane flying from New York to London at an average speed of 1,817 mph. The SR-71 jet made the 3,490-mile crossing in 1 hour 55 minutes 42 seconds, breaking the record of 4 hours 46 minutes set in 1969 by a British Royal Navy Phantom fighter. On its return trip from London to Los Angeles, the SR-71 flew 5,645 miles in 3 hours 48 minutes, for an average speed of 1,480 mph.

At the Hanover Air Show in West Germany, the Soviet Union displayed a new version of its Yak-40, configured for 32 passengers and capable of conversion for freight or mail service in less than 20 minutes. The Soviets also introduced the An-30, which had a fuselage designed to accommodate camera ports. The new plane had a 1,500-mile range in its photographic configuration. Its primary mission was said to be mapping and surveying.

### Military Aircraft

The Grumman Corp. found a way in 1974 to keep up its costly F-14A Tomcat fighter program. Under an agreement announced in October, nine U.S. banks and Bank Melli Iran would provide Grumman with up to $200 million in loans over a four-year period. After the U.S. Senate earlier voted down a proposal to have the U.S. Navy lend Grumman $100 million, the shah of Iran offered a $100-million loan against Iran's order for 80 of the $17.8-million planes. In October Grumman received a $154.9-million award for continuing work on the Navy's order of 50 F-14's.

The U.S. Department of Defense invited prospective European customers in 1974 to take part in evaluating the new YF-16 and YF-17 combat fighter aircraft, one of which would replace the Lockheed F-104G Starfighter. The General Dynamics YF-16 was powered by a Pratt & Whitney F-100 turbofan engine. The aircraft was said to have a potential combat radius about three times that of first-line fighters in the U.S. inventory in 1974. The fast, lightweight plane accommodated a pilot only. Its cockpit seat was tilted to increase pi-

lot tolerance of gravitational forces during combat maneuvering. Northrop said that its YF-17, with two turbojet engines and a new concept in wing design, was 40% to 50% more maneuverable than any other aircraft in operation.

The first Northrop F-5F fighter-trainer, a two-seat version of the F-5E, became the latest member of the company's F-5 low-cost fighters in 1974.

The controversial and expensive B-1 bomber was successfully tested on December 24. The estimated total program cost including research and development of the B-1 had risen another $4.3 billion to $18 billion.

In 1974 the U.S. Navy's Pacific fleet received the first of the Lockheed S-3A carrier-based jet aircraft to increase the Navy's capability of hunting down and destroying nuclear submarines. The Viking aircraft were described as ten times as effective as the Grumman S-2, which was for almost 20 years the mainstay of the Navy's antisubmarine defenses.

### Helicopters

Industry officials were making expansion plans in 1974 because of the increasing demand for helicopters in resources development and conservation programs. Bell Helicopter Co. planned to introduce a new business-and-utility helicopter in 1975.

A powered model helicopter rotor designed by Fairchild Republic was successfully wind tested in 1974 at speeds exceeding 400 mph. The model was a part of Fairchild's reverse velocity rotor concept.

U.S. Army helicopter training in 1974 emphasized low-altitude flight. Antiaircraft fire and electronic countermeasures in Vietnam combat proved the need for low-level flying. (*See also* Armed Forces, U.S.; Space Exploration; Transportation; Travel.)

**AFRICA.** Portugal's 400-year-old empire finally collapsed in 1974 following a military coup in Lisbon in April; this development presaged far-reaching changes in southern Africa. Guinea-Bissau (formerly Portuguese Guinea) became Africa's 44th independent state in September. (*See* Guinea-Bissau.) Mozambique was promised full independence as of June 1975, but no definite date was set for Angola's freedom. Another momentous event was a military coup in Ethiopia that ended the historic rule of Emperor Haile Selassie.

The drought of 1973 continued unrelieved; when the rains came to some parts, floods resulted, which brought new disaster as it became even more difficult to move food and medical supplies. In Wallo Province, Ethiopia, where more than 3 million people were afflicted by famine, locusts followed the rains bringing further ruin. Apart from Ethiopia, the worst affected region was the Sahel—the sub-Saharan region embracing Mali, Mauritania, Upper Volta, Chad, Niger, and Senegal, six of the world's poorest countries. Altogether, an area of some 5.5 million square miles was affected. The logistical

*The U.S. Air Force SR-71 Blackbird set a New York-to-London speed record in September with a flying time of 1 hour 55 minutes 42 seconds for the 3,490-mile crossing. The Blackbird, made of titanium, cruises at over three times the speed of sound or about 2,000 mph.*

KEYSTONE

*Leaders from 25 black and Arab African nations attended the June meeting in Mogadishu, Somalia, of the Organization of African Unity.*

problems of transportation and distribution, along with carelessness in local administration, prevented much of the emergency food supply from reaching the neediest drought victims. A controversial study released in March charged the U.S. government and international relief agencies with gross neglect that had contributed to 100,000 deaths in Africa. The study said it had been known for five years that a long-term drought was developing, yet no emergency relief plans had been made. (*See* Food.)

The colonial wars in Angola, Mozambique, and Portuguese Guinea were officially ended with promises of independence by the ruling Portuguese junta, although the initial transfer of power in Mozambique—to leaders of the black nationalist Front for the Liberation of Mozambique (Frelimo)—was marked by several outbreaks of racial violence. And in Angola, rival black independence groups engaged in a bitter struggle for supremacy.

Guerrilla groups were still active in Ethiopia, Chad, Rhodesia, and Namibia (South West Africa). In addition to the coup in Ethiopia, the government of Niger's President Hamani Diori was overthrown by a military group. In Upper Volta and Nigeria, promises by the military regimes to return power to civilian governments were withdrawn. Troops of Mali and Upper Volta clashed in a water-rights dispute.

The prospect of an independent black government in Mozambique brought new pressures to its white-ruled neighbors, Rhodesia and South

Africa. As a result of these pressures, Rhodesia's white prime minister, Ian Smith, announced to his stunned countrymen in December that his government would eventually yield to black-majority rule.

The 11th annual summit conference of the Organization of African Unity (OAU) was held in Mogadishu, Somalia, in June. The group endorsed the so-called Yaoundé Declaration adopted earlier by the African Liberation Committee (ALC); the declaration's two main points were a promise of friendship to Portugal on the condition that it negotiated independence of its African colonies only with liberation movements recognized by the OAU, and a commitment to increase financial and military support for guerrilla movements in Rhodesia, South Africa, and Namibia. Other items on the agenda at Mogadishu were the long-standing border dispute between Somalia and Ethiopia and the impact of increased energy costs on African economies. Agreement had been reached in February on the establishment of an Arab Bank for Economic Development in Africa (ABEDA) with initial capital of $200 million. This agreement followed protracted negotiations between the OAU's Committee of Seven and the Arab League.

Harmonizing relations between Arab and non-Arab African nations was a major activity during 1974. Somalia followed Mauritania to become the second non-Arab Muslim state to join the Arab League. The Sudan played a leading role in mediat-

HENRI BUREAU/SYGMA

*A West German airlift of food and medicine is awaited by Danakil tribesmen in northern Ethiopia, one of the areas hardest hit by the summer drought that spread to 16 African countries.*

ing between the African and Arab worlds. All the black African states (with the exceptions of Malawi and Lesotho), having suspended their relations with Israel in 1973, expected that the Arab oil producers would ensure continuing oil supplies to the continent while, for the first time, imposing a total embargo on Rhodesia; they also hoped that a special effort would be made to help cushion African countries against sharply rising oil prices. The Arabs refused these concessions, but they did agree to set up an Arab Bank for Agricultural and Industrial Development, with initial capital of $500 million and a technical assistance fund of $15 million.

Efforts continued during the year to bring anglophone and francophone states into a single West African Economic Community (CEAO). Although 15 states indicated their interest in establishing this new trading and customs community, some francophone African countries (supported by France) continued to express misgivings about the possible dominance of Nigeria in such an association.

### Foreign Relations

The Soviet Union, on the whole, maintained a low-profile presence in Africa, except in Somalia, which it continued to supply with weapons. The Soviets also continued to provide support for the liberation movements in southern Africa, a policy favored by black African governments, but the strengthening of the Soviet fleet in the Mediterranean Sea and Indian Ocean was not welcomed by any African state.

China's effective aid programs, support for liberation movements, and careful nonintervention in African affairs continued to win friends in the continent. The leaders of two countries previously hostile to China, President Mobutu Sese Seko of Zaire and

President Omar Bongo of Gabon, visited Peking and established cordial relations. As a result of Mobutu's visit, the Chinese agreed to help train Angolan liberationists headquartered in Zaire.

Africans were critical of British policies toward Rhodesia, South Africa, and Namibia, especially regarding joint British-South African military exercises at the Simonstown naval base. The disclosure of a U.S. policy document favoring a more conciliatory attitude toward South Africa produced predictably angry responses.

French policy was marked by demands from francophone African countries for revision of their special treaty relations with France. French arms sales to South Africa and expanding trade with the apartheid republic attracted criticism from black Africa, but French arms and Middle East policies won favor with the North African Arab states. (*See also* individual country articles; Middle East.)

**AGRICULTURE.** A wet spring, a dry summer, and an early frost in 1974 changed what was planned to be a year of bumper harvests into the worst growing season that the U.S. had experienced since the 1930's. Farmers, processors, and consumers all suffered from the consequent shortages and cost of feed grains. Early in July the U.S. Department of Agriculture (USDA) expected the corn harvest to yield 6.4 billion bushels, but after the drought and the freeze, forecasts for that principal feed grain dropped to about 4.7 billion bushels.

Livestock producers were caught between record feed prices and low returns for their animals. Cattlemen were losing $100 to $150 a head at market. To call attention to the soaring beef and pork production costs, in October Wisconsin members of the National Farmers Organization killed and buried more than 650 calves—before network television cameras. The voice of U.S. President Gerald R. Ford was heard in the following outcry. Among other protests another 1,000 calves were slaughtered, but they were processed and sent to hurricane victims in Honduras.

Early in October the administration asked grain exporters to seek USDA approval before closing sales exceeding 50,000 tons on one day or 100,000 tons in one week. The guideline came in reaction to the sale to the Soviet Union of 3.4 million tons of corn and wheat worth $500 million when U.S. supplies were short. President Ford persuaded the firms involved to cancel the deal, but some grain was expected to be delivered over a protracted period.

Low farm prices in the second quarter of 1974—especially for livestock—and rising farm expenses reduced the net income in that period to $23.9 billion—far below the $32.3-billion bonanza that the farm community earned in 1973. Farm production expenses in the second quarter of 1974 hit a record high of $74.5 billion, up from $62.9 billion a year earlier.

When the USDA encouraged farmers to go all out in 1974, many farm supply companies were not ready. They were still gauging production to farm policy that kept land out of production. A fertilizer shortage was critical, and fertilizer prices rose 81% in five months after federal controls were removed in October 1973. Federal disaster payments to growers, available for the first time in 1974, tided over a number of desperate farmers whose crops were ruined. An emergency guaranteed loan program for troubled livestock growers was rushed through the U.S. Congress in July 1974. The bill authorized the USDA to promise to repay 80% of an eligible loan if the borrower defaulted.

*An experimental lettuce harvester uses X rays to select ripe heads from irregularly maturing lettuce fields, reducing the costs and increasing the efficiency of harvesting previously done by hand.*
COURTESY, U.S. DEPARTMENT OF AGRICULTURE

VANCOUVER SUN

*Ken Davie of Delta, B.C., displays a beefalo, a newly developed crossbreed of two types of cattle and a buffalo, which does not feed on grain and may reduce beef prices.*

### Crops and Livestock

Wheat, rye, and rice production rose 5% from 1973. The wheat crop, forecast at 1,780,594,000 bushels, was up 4%. Rice production reached a record high, but the price of rice doubled between September 1973 and September 1974 because severe shortages in importing countries made the export market lucrative. Corn was 16% below the 1973 crop, and the soybean crop was down from about 1.6 billion bushels in 1973 to less than 1.3 billion in 1974 because of the destructive weather.

As the price of sugar rose 400% in one year, U.S. Attorney General William B. Saxbe sought an investigation into the industry's practices. World consumption of sugar had reduced inventories drastically. In June 1974 Congress killed the Sugar Act of 1948, thus ending quotas for domestic production and foreign imports and ending subsidies for U.S. producers. Industry expansion did not follow, however, because of the fear that countries with lower costs would flood the market and drive down the price.

There were a record number of cattle on farms and ranches in 1974, but the number on feed lots was down as 90% fed on grass and other roughage. Milk production dropped in 1974. Dairymen caught in the cost-price squeeze asked for higher supports.

Pork production rose by about 7% from 1973. The U.S. sheep and lamb industry declined again with an 8% drop in the lamb crop to 10,607,000 head in 1974. Egg production continued downward.

### Canadian Agriculture

Canada experienced the same growing conditions as the U.S. in 1974. The estimate of 16 million metric tons of wheat was reduced to one of 14.2 million metric tons. Canadian wheat sales to the People's Republic of China totaled 3,050,000 metric tons for 1974.

Protective measures for Canadian cattle producers seriously affected the U.S. livestock export trade. The importation of meat and meat animals fed with the growth hormone diethylstilbestrol was banned in April, and a 12-month import quota system began in August. (*See also* Food; Textiles.)

**ALBANIA.** On Jan. 16, 1974, the official Soviet news agency TASS distributed an article from the foreign affairs weekly review *Novoye Vremya* claiming that it was high time to end the abnormal situation existing between Albania and the U.S.S.R. The invitation to renew Soviet-Albanian diplomatic relations, by no means the first since the rupture of 1961, suggested that mutual respect of national sovereignty, territorial integrity, nonintervention in domestic affairs, and economic cooperation could heal the wounds. Albanian Communist Party First Secretary Enver Hoxha, according to a Belgrade, Yugoslavia, report, rejected the invitation just as he had done on all previous occasions. He stated that relations between the two countries could be restored only when the people of the Soviet Union would set up a true Marxist-Leninist regime again. Diplomatic observers in the Balkan capitals did not fail to connect the Soviet approaches to Albania with similar approaches by Bulgaria. Both had probably been prompted by a consideration of the effects of possible domestic difficulties in Yugoslavia after 82-year-old President Tito's ultimate departure from the political scene.

It was reported in May that the 80-year-old Monsignor Damian, head of the Albanian Orthodox church and archbishop of Tirana, had died in November 1973. He had been in prison since 1967, when all churches and mosques in Albania were closed compulsorily, in order that Albania should become "the first atheist state in the world." Early in September it was reported that Col. Gen. Beqir Balluku, defense minister since 1953, had been removed from his post. (*See also* Europe.)

**ALGERIA.** Celebrating in November the 20th anniversary of the start of their struggle for independence from the French, Algerians could look with some pride at the lead President Houari Boumé-

dienne was giving to other new nations to achieve what they saw as economic rights; at the new authority of their foreign minister, Abdelaziz Bouteflika, in his role as president of the United Nations (UN) General Assembly; at the evolution of a Palestinian Arab entity along the lines long advocated by Algeria; and at the newly won independence of African territories, in which Algeria had helped. If it was still a time of austerity at home and there was still massive rural underemployment, at least the effects of Algeria's attempt at an industrial revolution were beginning to be felt.

Early in 1974 Boumédienne had taken the initiative in calling for a meeting at the UN on raw materials, and in April a special session of the General Assembly was held on the subject, with Boumédienne making the keynote speech. His advice to the primary producers, to nationalize their resources and band together to show their strength in the face of what he saw as an inflexible attitude by the industrialized states, appeared pertinent, if somewhat alarming, economic good sense. Boumédienne, nevertheless, saw Algeria's role as a catalyst of cooperation as its first aim. At the end of October he called for a summit conference of oil producers in face of the mounting financial problems that sharp oil price rises were causing and in November urged the formation of a cartel of iron-ore producers.

The expansion of the hydrocarbons industry went ahead, and a contract for the supply of the first 5 in a proposed fleet of 13 methane tankers was, significantly, awarded to a French shipyard. The restoration of good relations with France, both political and economic, seemed assured. (*See also* Africa; Europe; France; Middle East.)

**ANIMALS AND WILDLIFE.** Just as it was largely through the efforts of thousands of young people in 1971 that a law was passed to save America's wild horses, it was a similar campaign that was effective in 1974 in securing an international agreement that may prevent extinction of the world's whales. Although the United Nations Conference on Human Environment at Stockholm, Sweden, in 1972 called for a ten-year moratorium on whale hunting (by a vote of 53 to 0), Japan and the Soviet Union ignored the resolution and allowed their whaling industries to continue operations. The two countries accounted for 85% of the world's whale catch even though eight species including the blue, humpback, and fin whales were approaching extinction. Early in 1974 a whale conservation organization known as Project Jonah launched a worldwide campaign to urge children to appeal to the governments of Japan and the U.S.S.R. to "stop whaling."

Three girls aged 10 to 13 from Sweden, Canada, and the U.S. went to Japan in June armed with letters from 75,000 young people around the world urging that Prime Minister Kakuei Tanaka join them in saving whales. The Japanese fishing indus-

*English youth on the Thames River help publicize the international campaign to prevent extinction of the world's whale population.*

LONDON EVENING NEWS/
PICTORIAL PARADE

try countered efforts of the save-the-whale movement with claims that the industry supplied employment to some 50,000 people and that whale meat constituted about 7% of the country's meat consumption. Project Jonah officials pointed out that this was only about 1% of the population's protein intake and that it was diminishing so rapidly that substitutes would have to be found.

That the efforts of the young people and Project Jonah did not go unheeded was indicated a short time afterward by action at a meeting of the International Whaling Commission. Although representatives from Japan and the U.S.S.R. refused to accept it, a ban on the hunting of a selective number of endangered species was agreed upon, this decision to be reviewed annually.

Meanwhile, the friends of wild horses who had fought and won passage of the Wild Free-Roaming Horses and Burros Act of 1971 discovered that continual vigilance was necessary to make the law effective. In Idaho a group of ranchers trapped about 50 wild horses in a canyon on protected public land, sewed hog rings in the nostrils of several of the animals to make them easier to handle, and drove some off a cliff to their deaths. The American Horse Protection Association and the Humane Society traced about 30 of the remaining animals to a slaughterhouse in Nebraska and managed to save 18 with a court order.

### Birds: Too Many and Too Few

An over-concentration of bird populations in a 60-acre pine forest near Graceham, Md., created a problem for residents of the area during late winter and early spring. What ornithologists described as a quirk in migrating patterns brought in thousands of starlings, grackles, red-winged blackbirds, and brown-headed cowbirds. In mid-March their numbers increased to millions. Each day the number of birds increased, the constant fluttering of their wings frightening children, dogs, and livestock, their nocturnal shrieks making sleep impossible without earplugs, their massive carpet of droppings creating a health hazard and an unbearable stench, and their appetites threatening spring-planted crops.

After enduring several weeks of harassment, the community began fighting back with aerial bombs, propane guns, shotguns, firecrackers, and high-pitched electronic whistles. By late April most of the birds were gone, but whether their departure was hastened by the noise assaults or was only a re-sumption of their normal migration patterns, no one could say for certain. Similarly huge winter concentrations of starlings were reported from Hopkinsville and Frankfort, Ky., and Albany, N.Y.

Other birds in the news were the almost extinct whooping cranes that spend their winters on the Gulf Coast of Texas, near a Matagorda Island area used by the U.S. Department of Defense for bombing practice. As the result of persistent protests from wildlife groups, the bombing runs were restricted to the summer months, which the cranes spend in Canada. In 1974 the U.S. Fish and Wildlife Service's official count of whooping cranes in the wild dropped to 45. Pepper, one of three cranes born and bred in captivity, died at the age of 18.

Other bird species whose survival was in growing jeopardy included the peregrine falcon, bald eagle, Mexican duck, and prairie chicken. Threatened for years by pesticides, which caused them to lay thin-shelled eggs that broke before hatching, the falcons faced a new hazard from the sudden revival of falconry as a sport. Disregarding state and federal laws, devotees of the sport were illegally capturing numerous young falcons in the wild.

In an effort to rebuild the vanishing stocks of bald eagles in the northeastern states—a decline that was also caused by pesticide-thinned eggshells —wildlife experts transplanted viable eagle eggs from nests in Minnesota to nests in Maine. To reestablish the Mexican duck as a breeding species in the Bosque del Apache National Wildlife Refuge in New Mexico, the Fish and Wildlife Service released 18 more of the endangered birds that had been raised in captivity. This brought the total released in nine years to 127.

Although several hundred thousand prairie chickens still survived in the Midwest, one species in Texas dropped in numbers to about 2,000, and another in Minnesota to about 4,000. Because of the rapid disappearance of nesting sites and the resulting inbreeding, zoologists warned that prairie chickens were becoming genetically weaker, thus endangering one of America's most distinctive native birds. Hopes for survival of the world's rarest bird—the Mauritius kestrel—were revived when two breeding pairs were sighted in 1974.

The first new genus and species of bird to be discovered in ten years, a member of the Hawaiian honeycreeper family, was reported from Hawaii. It was sparrow-sized, colored brown and beige, and its population was estimated at about 150.

*Wild horses roam the West in what federal officials called a population explosion since the 1971 protective legislation.*

## Other Happenings

Agricultural statisticians counted more than 50,-000 horses, the highest concentration in the U.S., in three Texas counties that included the Dallas-Fort Worth area. Although the number of horses was increasing in most states, mules were disappearing so rapidly that Benson, N.C., had to import several for its annual Mule Day celebration. An estimate of mules in the U.S. indicated a decline from about 4 million in 1930 to about 60,000 in 1974.

Because Smokey the Bear reached the advanced age of 24, a young bear named Little Smokey was brought from New Mexico and assigned to an adjoining cage in the Washington, D.C., zoo. Although Smokey walked with a stiff-legged limp and spent most of his days dozing, his coat was still glossy and he showed no indication of giving up his public relations job.

As the result of a lawsuit brought by a national conservation group, the U.S. Department of the Interior agreed to prepare an environmental program designed to guarantee the survival of Yellowstone National Park's last remaining grizzly bears. Within the past century grizzlies had declined from more than a million to less than a thousand. Their last major refuge was Yellowstone, but because of serious incidents with careless tourists, Interior Department officials had closed the park's garbage dumps, which had been the animals' main source of food. Grizzlies considered dangerous were trapped, marked, and removed to remote areas of the park. If they returned to camping areas, they were often killed. Conservationists opposed the program, claiming that the sudden removal of the bears disoriented them, threatened them with starvation, and caused them to be dangerous to hikers in wilderness areas. Since initiation of the policy, the conservationists charged, the grizzlies' death rate had increased to more than double the birthrate.

One of the last unspoiled desert grassland and brushland areas in the Rio Grande Valley of New Mexico was transferred to the U.S. Fish and Wildlife Service by a private family foundation. Formerly used as a ranch, the 220,000 acres formed the largest tract ever donated for use as a wildlife refuge. The most remote national wildlife refuge operated by the U.S. was established on Rose Atoll in American Samoa in the Pacific. Its purpose was to protect sea turtles, terns, and marine wildlife.

As a result of protection laws passed in 1963 and 1966, the Louisiana alligator was reported to be thriving again, and that state's wildlife commission agreed to transfer 500 of the reptiles to Mississippi and Arkansas for restoration programs. Another transfer project for an endangered species involved two pairs of timber wolves flown from a wilderness area of Minnesota to the Huron Mountains of Michigan. Because wolves had become nearly extinct in the Huron Mountains, deer, moose, and elk herds were becoming overpopulated. Biological scientists directing the transfer said the wolves were needed to cull out the weaker animals. From radio transmitters fixed to collars, the scientists were able to track the positions of the four wolves.

In November a species of Sinai leopard thought to have become extinct was located in Israel. The first photographs ever to be taken of the species were released at that time. (*See also* Environment; Fish and Fisheries; Pets; Zoos.)

*Swarms of migrating birds, estimated at 10 million, invade the western Maryland town of Graceham in March, creating numerous problems for residents.*

**Animals and Wildlife**

# Special Report:
# Birding – A Living Heritage

by Leif J. Robinson

Flight, striking plumage, and arresting behavior have endeared birds to societies that have had the leisure and education for aesthetic appreciation. A sympathy for birds is easily acquired, for the human mannerisms of each species soon become evident to an attentive witness. Traditionally, the British have been avid bird-watchers, and the current surge of interest in the United States is a reflection both of that heritage and of contemporary life.

"Sales of wild-bird feeders and foods have probably tripled in the past decade," says the president of Hyde Bird Feeder Co. "In suburbia there seems to be a status element: if someone has a cardinal, they don't want a neighbor to entice it away." This proliferation of backyard feeders has induced some formerly southern species to spread northward; the cardinal, mockingbird, and tufted titmouse are colorful and fascinating birds that now winter in New England because of the guaranteed food supply.

Much of the growing popularity of bird-watching, or birding, stems from local clubs that sponsor field trips to choice locations, usually under the direction of an experienced leader who can aid novices in identifying the birds sighted. The club that claims to be "America's most active" scheduled 240 field trips in 1973, ranging from two-hour quickies to weekend excursions that included all-day boat trips for oceanic species that are rarely seen from land. The environment-study programs now offered in many public schools have also stimulated much interest among young people, an interest that temporarily may be put aside but will seldom be forgotten.

The culmination of a birder's year rides on the southerly winds of spring that carry millions of migrants to their northern breeding grounds. Millions of Americans wait to glimpse the brilliant nuptial colors that speed by. Morning's first light finds businessman and student, housewife and secretary, worker and pensioner watching these avian all-stars at favored haunts. Observers in the southern tier of states command one of the best vantages on earth for viewing this annual migration, for the narrows of Central America act as a natural funnel through which the perennial hordes flow from their winter quarters.

## American Birders, Past and Present

Though descriptions of American birds were recorded by conquistadors as early as the 16th century, it was not until around 1800 that the United States felt the impact of its first major ornithologist, Alexander Wilson. Fortunately, his erudition was soon complemented by the artist John James Audubon, whose avant-garde paintings of birds in lifelike settings captured the attention of a young nation that was to make his name synonymous with nature appreciation and study. Yet Audubon's most enduring contribution was his stimulation of Spencer Baird and Robert Ridgway, who carried American ornithology into the 20th century and developed it into a mature science.

The pivotal figure in American bird study and appreciation was Frank M. Chapman at the American Museum of Natural History in New York City. During the first quarter of this century, as

*A team of bird-watchers conducts a dawn-to-dusk vigil at Point Lookout, Long Island, N.Y., logging 121 species in the annual count held by teams throughout the U.S. and in parts of Canada.*
WIDE WORLD

most scientific research passed from amateur hands to those of the professional, Chapman motivated many young people to become ornithologists. Simultaneously, his extensive program of public lectures, illustrated with his pioneering photographs of the living bird, carried wildlife and conservation to an extremely wide public. In 1899 Chapman founded *Bird-Lore*, which eventually became *Audubon* magazine, the standard today for superior nature articles and photographs.

The Chapman legacy also lives on in the first bird-watching sport, the annual Christmas Bird Count (CBC), which he established in 1900 as an alternative to a traditional wildlife slaughter. The objective of the CBC is to census every bird species within 15-mile-diameter circular areas. From an original 27 persons who scrutinized 25 areas, the CBC has burgeoned to about 25,000 enthusiasts and more than 1,000 areas that blanket the continent. Each year the competition is keen to better previous records and to outdo neighboring areas.

The explosive growth of bird-watching over the past several decades can be attributed largely to the publication in 1934 of *A Field Guide to the Birds* by Roger Tory Peterson, who has stimulated more interest in birds than any other living person. His revolutionary approach to field identification, the direct comparison of similar-appearing species in a pocket-sized collection of portraits augmented with a layman's text, permitted beginners to gain confidence quickly. To date, 2 million copies of the inexpensive Peterson bird guides have been sold. Equally important was the concomitant development of bird-watching aids: inexpensive high-quality binoculars, fast photographic lenses and emulsions, and portable high-fidelity tape recorders.

For more experienced birders, a second pinnacle in field guides appeared in 1966. Under the senior authorship of Chandler S. Robbins, *Birds of North America* included descriptions of about 700 species and such innovations as range maps and voiceprints, making it a handy reference for jet-set aficionados.

### Science, Sport, and Hobby

Ornithology is the science; bird-watching is the hobby. Yet these worlds often blend, and today's amateurs continue to make substantial contributions. Since 1951, for example, Harold Mayfield has censused the rare and endangered Kirtland's warbler on its Michigan breeding grounds. Not only has he documented their decline to a meager 400 individuals in 1973; he has led the drive to relieve these birds of their worst enemy, the brown-headed cowbird, which lays its parasitic eggs in the warblers' nests.

On a broader front, every year thousands of amateurs report migration statistics and rare-bird sightings. Recently, hundreds of volunteers in Massachusetts have undertaken the most ambitious project yet attempted—a five-year survey to map the geographical distribution of all bird species that nest in their state. This study will provide a standard for assessing changes in avian nesting populations due to natural or man-made alterations of habitat. Furthermore, since birds are extremely sensitive to environmental change, this project might provide a standard for future generations to judge the quality of their human habitat.

If sport means competition, bird-watchers have few equals—they compete against themselves, other birders, and nature! Their scoreboard is a "list." Most prized is the life list, a tally of every species a birder has identified. Almost equally valued is the North American list, including all birds seen north of Mexico as well as those sighted in Baja California, Bermuda, and Greenland. Then come accountings by state and by calendar year.

### Keeping Score

As a birder gains experience, his sophistication in field identification grows. At first, one is satisfied to learn the plumages of adult males and females. Then come the equally important calls and songs that are used in courting, establishing territory, and communicating with young and other individuals. After these basics, one can concentrate on juvenile plumages (some species require several years to attain adult attire), habitat and nesting preference, and the natural history of the species.

The top lister of North American birds is Joseph Taylor of New York with 707 species. Birders unable to travel continent-wide at the drop of a feather can look to Thomas Imhof, who has seen a record 96% (337 species) of the birds on the Alabama state list. The highest state total is held by Guy McCaskie with 486 species in California. Remarkably, in our smallest state, Frances Perry has seen 324 species, which accounts for only 87% of the total number known to have visited Rhode Island. Perhaps the most impressive record is held by McCaskie, who with three companions logged 227 species in a single day!

Records such as these are maintained by the American Birding Association. Its official checklist indicates that the most productive state is Texas, with 550 species seen at one time or another. On the other side of the coin are Idaho and West Virginia, with only 300 each.

Why watch birds? The answers are as varied as the birders, though most will agree to the enticements of beauty and the fun of the hunt. The enthusiasm can be incredible, such as that of one lister who drove 2,700 miles around Massachusetts in midwinter for a glimpse of a great gray owl, a species that had been seen in that state only six other times this century. The real frontier of birding, however, probably lies not with the lister and his personal records, but with the patient observer who gleans new and hard-won information about the life histories of birds, their behavior, and their interaction with man.

**ANTARCTICA.** During 1974 Argentina, Australia, Chile, France, Great Britain, Japan, New Zealand, South Africa, the U.S.S.R., and the U.S. continued scientific study of the Antarctic and the Southern Ocean from 34 stations in the Antarctic Treaty Area and 9 on outlying islands. One of the notable scientific achievements of the year was a publication of a map showing, for a large area of the Antarctic, detailed contours of the land lying below the immensely thick ice cover. This result of many years of fruitful cooperation between the U.S. and Great Britain in airborne radio-echo sounding of the ice sheet is an example of the trend toward closer international cooperation on scientific projects that were too big for any one country to undertake.

There were three major meetings during the year associated with Antarctica. The Polar Oceans Conference held in Montreal, Que., in May passed a number of recommendations about the need for international cooperation in the study of the Southern Ocean, particularly of its living resources. These were endorsed by the meeting of the Intergovernmental Oceanographic Commission's International Coordination Group for the Southern Ocean held in Buenos Aires, Argentina, in July. The 13th meeting of the Scientific Committee on Antarctic Research was held in Jackson Hole, Wyo., in September.

Tourism in the Antarctic increased with the addition of an Argentine cruise ship, the *Cabo San Rocque*, to the long-time activities of the *Lindblad Explorer*. David Lewis, whose *Ice Bird* was dismasted last year in an attempt to circumnavigate the Antarctic, started out from the U.S. Palmer Station, where his yacht had spent the winter, and was dismasted again in February 800 miles southwest of Cape Town, which he reached after 25 days under jury rig.

## ARCHAEOLOGY AND ANTHROPOLOGY.

Both the Arab-Israeli and the Greek-Turkish conflicts upset the normal pace of archaeological activities in the eastern Mediterranean region in 1974. Otherwise, the archaeological year was a productive one. Pressure against illegal traffic in antiquities persisted, and the U.S. Customs Service began an intensified campaign against the smuggling of plundered objects. Italian investigators continued to press inquiry into the true circumstances around the acquisition of the controversial $1-million Greek vase purchased by New York's Metropolitan Museum of Art in 1972. A head of a figure from a Roman mosaic found at Apamea, Syria, that had been stolen from Aleppo was returned during the year.

Passage of the Moss-Bennett archaeological conservation act was welcomed by American archaeologists. The act provided that funds amounting to up to 1% of the cost of a proposed federal construction project may be used to mitigate any unavoidable adverse impact upon archaeological or historic resources. The need for protection of archaeological sites was pointed up by the heavy damage to fragile rock formations in the California Desert, caused by

*Harvard University's Museum of Comparative Zoology staffers display a 6-million-year-old, six-foot by eight-foot turtle shell, the largest ever found, that they finished piecing together in February.*
UPI COMPIX

the increasing use of off-road recreational vehicles.

In one of the year's most significant North American discoveries, it was reported that the alignment of rock cairns making up the Big Horn Medicine Wheel in northern Wyoming showed specific correlations with the summer solstice. The Medicine Wheel was probably constructed to predict the event, thus helping to mark the time of the annual Plains Indian Sun Dance.

In Italy excavation continued at Oplontis, near Pompeii. A sumptuous villa with colorful wall paintings was one of the first structures exposed. In Rome itself, the ruins of a fine villa were encountered in probes beneath the Baths of Caracalla. The tomb of a woman, containing rich ornaments of gold and silver, was opened at Castel di Decima just south of Rome; it dated to the time of Rome's founding and is one of four tombs in the site to have been equipped with funeral chariots, considered indicative of noble status. The body was covered with a stole of silver thread and amber beads.

New excavations in Ch'ang-sha, China, yielded a hoard of manuscripts from the Han Dynasty, including the oldest maps ever found in China; and Soviet archaeologists working in Kamchatka on the U.S.S.R.'s Pacific coast reported the discovery of 9,000-year-old Aleut artifacts—beads, belts, and other items—that previously had been found only on the North American continent. The objects were said to be the first direct evidence to support the theory that America's original inhabitants migrated from Siberia, across the Bering land bridge.

The question of North American man's origins became more complicated, however, with the application of a recently developed technique for dating fossils, which revealed that human life in North America may go back nearly 50,000 years, or more than twice as long as the previously established date. The technique, called racemization, involved the study of the light-rotating properties of amino acids and when applied to two skulls, found in California around 1930, determined the human fossils to be 48,000 and 44,000 years old. Preliminary finds released in October from more than 18 fossil sites discovered in the Baja California peninsula provided further support for the new dating.

A new find in northern Ethiopia placed the date of upright man's origin another one million years earlier. Bone fragments found by U.S. anthropologist Donald C. Johanson were said to be evidence that *Homo erectus* lived in Africa as much as 4 million years ago. Also in Africa, a team from the University of California reported finding Acheulean hand axes about 1.5 million years old and thus presumably made by the early hominid called *Australopithecus*. Previously, such tools were believed to be no more than 500,000 years old. At the same time, French prehistorian Henry de Lumley produced evidence that a similar hominid inhabited caves on France's Riviera at least one million years ago. De Lumley recovered stone tools of the simple "pebble" type that is associated with *Australopithecus* in Africa. (*See also* Painting and Sculpture.)

## ARCHITECTURE.

In 1974 a number of architects and engineers experimented with methods designed to conserve energy in their buildings. The General Services Administration (GSA), a federal agency, commissioned a low-rise office building powered by solar energy in Manchester, N.H. Dubin, Mendel, and Bloom, engineering consultants retained by the GSA, found that the glass area of the building's surface could be reduced to 10% of the total area, as long as large amounts of glass were concentrated on the south wall—to take advantage of the winter sun.

Another federal agency, the National Aeronautics and Space Administration, began constructing a test facility for solar energy at its Langley Research Center in Hampton, Va. Four business corporations announced in August that they were cooperating to construct a commercial complex of buildings near Pittsburgh, Pa.; the complex would cost more to build than conventional buildings but it was hoped that this extra investment would be justified through economical use of solar energy for heating and cooling.

Charles Moore Associates constructed an unusual house in Guilford, Conn., designed to utilize solar energy. The south roof was covered entirely by a solar collector, and the walls of the house were designed as a kind of reverse thermos bottle—with heated water stored in the perimeter walls.

Another sign of the times could be seen at Expo '74, the world's fair in Spokane, Wash., where em-

*Archaeologists unearth graves in the cemetery of the Avars in Szekszard, western Hungary. The Avars were a nomadic people who migrated from the present-day Soviet Union and resided in the Carpathian Basin from A.D. 550 to 800.*

KEYSTONE

POWELL AND MOYA

*Designed by the British firm Powell and Moya, the Cripps building at St. John's College, Cambridge, England, features a roof-walk and terrace among the treetops and was built to last 500 years. It was the 1974 choice for the Royal Institute of British Architects' Gold Medal.*

phasis was placed on permanent long-term environmental considerations, rather than on spectacular but temporary exhibition design. The Washington State Pavilion, for example, was a permanent structure to be used as an opera house and convention center. (*See* Environment Special Report.)

In November in Kensington, Md., the Church of Jesus Christ of Latter-day Saints (Mormons) dedicated its newest and largest temple. The impressive edifice, which cost approximately $15 million to build, was a hexagon made of white marble. Six spires rose from the structure, with the tallest topped by an angel with a trumpet. (*See* Religion.)

The Hirshhorn Museum opened in Washington, D.C., amid controversy about its design. The museum was a circular building of reinforced concrete, with no windows on the outside exterior but with an open inner core. Detractors termed the museum "the biggest marble doughnut in the world." Architects Skidmore, Owings & Merrill adopted the circular design for functional reasons—mainly to ease the transition from room to room, exhibit to exhibit. (*See* Museums.)

The new Oxon Run Educational Center in Washington, D.C., was the first school in the capital to accommodate both primary and secondary grades. The school, designed by Perkins & Will, featured an open plan incorporating 35,000 square feet on three levels. It was planned with community activities in mind for "after school" hours.

The state of Colorado held a competition for a major new public building, the Colorado State Judicial/Heritage Center Complex. The competition, open to Colorado architects, was won by Rogers-

Nagel-Langhart. Their design featured a six-story structure for judicial functions, with a neighboring terraced building for the Heritage Center.

In Chicago a new U.S. Courthouse Annex was under construction, with completion scheduled for 1975. The 27-story correctional facility was designed by Harry Weese & Associates. The three-sided building featured slit windows only five inches wide—eliminating the need for bars on windows, traditionally seen in correctional facilities.

The new Charles de Gaulle Airport, near Roissy, France, featured a dramatic terminal building designed by architect Paul Andreu. The circular cast-concrete structure was supported by Y-shaped pillars; it had a central well open to the outdoors and crossed by futuristic moving walks. The new airport was the largest in Europe and one of the largest in the world. (*See* Transportation.)

*Progressive Architecture* magazine gave only one top design award in 1974, for the "recycling" of a 19th-century mill complex in Massachusetts into a community center; Michael and Susan Southworth of Boston, Mass., were the architects. The Royal Institute of British Architects awarded its Gold Medal for 1974 to the firm of Powell & Moya.

"A Humane Architecture" was the theme of the annual convention of the American Institute of Architects (AIA), held in Washington, D.C., in May. As examples of inhumane architecture and design, AIA delegates cited windows that could not be opened, closet doors that bang into furniture—anything designed without human needs in mind.

The death of U.S. architect Louis I. Kahn in March, at age 73, was mourned around the world by those concerned with architecture. Kahn was generally considered one of the most influential architects of the past 25 years. (*See* Obituaries.)

## ARCTIC.
After four years of debate over environmental and economic issues, the building of the pipeline to take oil from Alaska's north coast to the port of Valdez began in the spring of 1974. About 1,200 workers began by building a road, to be used for construction of the pipeline itself, from the Yukon River to the Prudhoe Bay oil fields. Plans called for laying pipe south of the Yukon River in 1975 and north of the river in 1976. Initially, the line was expected to supply about 4% of the current daily U.S. consumption of oil. Later the supply should increase.

In April the Alaskan Arctic Gas Pipeline Co. and the Canadian Arctic Gas Pipeline Ltd. asked the U.S. and Canadian governments to approve construction of a $5.7-billion pipeline to carry natural gas from the North Slope of Alaska and the Mackenzie River delta of northern Canada into the major consuming areas of North America. Later in the year, Alberta Gas Trunk Line Co. announced plans for a smaller but similar pipeline to serve Canada.

U.S. Secretary of the Interior Rogers C. B. Morton withdrew the remaining 15 million acres of "un-classified" land in Alaska from homesteading. Secretary Morton also designated 2 million acres, including Cape Krusenstern, the alleged land bridge between Asia and Alaska, with marine beach ridges showing evidence of nearly every major cultural period of man in Arctic history for the past 5,000 years, as a national historical landmark.

Soviet scientists reported that they had discovered evidence supporting the theory that ancient Asian tribes migrated to the American continent over the Bering Strait. An expedition to the Soviet Union's Pacific coast discovered objects such as beads and belts that previously had been found only in North America. One scientist called the objects the forerunners of the American Indians' "wampum." (*See* Archaeology and Anthropology.)

*In March, workers in the Arctic Ocean remove blocks of ice, replacing them with gravel to construct an artificial island as the base for a drilling rig searching for oil and gas.*
WIDE WORLD

One week after her husband's death, Isabel Perón enters the Casa Rosada on July 7 as the new president of Argentina for her first meeting with government officials.

ALAIN NOGUES—SYGMA

**ARGENTINA.** Juan Domingo Perón, who had returned from an 18-year exile in 1973 to resume the presidency of Argentina, died on July 1, 1974, after only nine months in office. (*See* Obituaries.) He was succeeded by his wife, Vice-President Isabel Martínez de Perón, who became the Americas' first female head of state.

During his exile Juan Perón had wooed the left wing of the Peronist movement and supported the most militant wing of the Argentine labor movement. Once back in power he increasingly revealed his close links with the armed forces and other right-wing groups. He still managed, however, by the force of his personality and the ability to appear as everyone's friend, to hold together his huge and diverse following. It was feared, however, that Isabel Perón, without the great respect commanded by her husband, would be unable to govern Argentina.

Even while Juan Perón was alive, splits were openly developing in both the government and the Peronist movement. In February, for example, rebelling police and right-wing trade unionists overthrew Ricardo Obregón Cano, the elected leftist Peronist governor in Córdoba. Perón, accused of complicity in the revolt, named a conservative to replace him.

Political kidnappings and assassinations, a chronic part of Argentine life, increased even more after Perón's death. In one week of September alone, 14 persons were killed. While the hitherto obscure right-wing group, the Argentine Anti-Communist Alliance, claimed responsibility for a number of killings, the terrorism was primarily seen as a result of the declaration early in the month by Mario Firmenich, a leader of the Montoneros, a left-wing Peronist guerrilla movement, of a "people's war" against the government of Isabel Perón. He hinted at joint action with the outlawed People's Revolutionary Army (ERP).

The Montoneros were backed by leftist students at Buenos Aires University, 800 of whom on August 14 had occupied the university to protest the dismissal of Education Minister Jorge Taiana by Isabel Perón in a major cabinet reorganization the day before. On September 17 the university was closed

down as a nest of "subversion." In August the ERP suffered a major setback when 16 guerrillas were killed in a running battle with police in Catamarca. *El Mundo*, a leftist newspaper accused of being the mouthpiece of the ERP, was banned in March. By September the only remaining leftist journals, *Noticias* and *La Causa Peronista*, were shut down. In late September in response to the wave of terrorism, Perón rushed through Congress a stiff new antisubversion law that provided mandatory jail terms for those trying to unconstitutionally change the country's political, economic, or social life. In November she declared Argentina under a state of siege and in hopes of effecting national unity had the body of Eva, Perón's much admired first wife, returned from Spain to Buenos Aires.

Despite the rightward trend domestically, Argentina moved leftward abroad. In May a trade mission was sent to the U.S.S.R. and other Communist countries in Europe. As a result Argentina received a promise of Soviet aid for hydroelectric development. Poland, Czechoslovakia, and Hungary agreed to help with coal mining, transportation, and communications projects. Earlier in the year Argentina had begun the first shipments of goods in a $1.2-billion trade agreement with Cuba.

A growth rate of 6.2% in Argentina's gross domestic product was reported by the government for the first half of 1974 as compared with only 4.8% for 1973. This was due in part to excellent crop harvests, to increased industrial output (especially of automobiles and farm machinery), and to the high level of exports.

A degree of price stability was achieved early in 1974, largely by the squeezing of company profits. This contributed to a notable decline in private investment, however, and by early October the annual rate of inflation, reduced in 1973 from 80% to about 20%, had climbed back up to about 40%. In March a nuclear plant, the first in Latin America, was inaugurated at Atucha. In August the government moved to nationalize the 1,600 gasoline service stations of three foreign-owned oil companies —Exxon, Cities Service, and Shell. (*See also* Latin America; Paraguay.)

Emmet Kay, the last known American prisoner of war in Indochina, shakes hands with one of his captors in Samneua, Laos, shortly before his release on September 18 after 16 months of imprisonment.

WIDE WORLD

# ARMED FORCES, UNITED STATES.

Air Force Gen. George S. Brown succeeded Adm. Thomas H. Moorer as chairman of the Joint Chiefs of Staff in 1974. A federal court overturned the conviction of William L. Calley for the My Lai massacre and ordered him released from prison. In Cleveland, Ohio, eight National Guard members involved in the 1970 shootings at Kent State University went on trial in October and were acquitted on November 8. The U.S. and the U.S.S.R. continued the Strategic Arms Limitation Talks (SALT), reaching a tentative agreement in November. (*See* Colleges; Law.)

When U.S. President Gerald R. Ford announced in September 1974 the details of his conditional amnesty plan for draft evaders and military deserters, requiring up to two years of alternative work in public service jobs, most veterans' groups were opposed, although a poll showed that 59% of all Americans approved. Many men affected argued that only unconditional amnesty or an apology would be acceptable. By year-end, only a small number had chosen conditional amnesty.

## Air Force

Gen. David C. Jones became chief of staff of the Air Force in 1974. Although other branches of the armed forces had some difficulty meeting their quotas through the volunteer system, the Air Force had so many volunteers that it could be selective.

The Air Force continued to modernize weapons by developing and testing many types of aircraft. Among other projects, the Air Force made structural changes on B-52's and continued development of the B-1 strategic bomber. Development and procurement of the F-15 fighter, designed for high maneuverability in air-to-air combat, also continued.

## Army

Gen. Creighton W. Abrams, Army chief of staff, died on Sept. 4, 1974. In 1968 U.S. President Lyndon B. Johnson appointed General Abrams as U.S. commander in Vietnam, where he presided over the American withdrawal. As chief of staff, General Abrams restructured the Army and worked to make a volunteer Army viable. (*See* Obituaries.)

The Army reported that its effort to recruit under the all-volunteer system was working successfully in 1974 in spite of criticism that it was taking a disproportionate number of blacks and a high number of poorly educated, mentally unfit men. The Women's Army Corps became fully integrated with the regular Army, apart from combat-related operations, and positions open to women were expanded. Enlistments of women were up 79% in 1974.

## Coast Guard

For the first time the Coast Guard accepted women into regular service in 1974. A study by the National Urban League, however, claimed that there was widespread racial bias in the Coast Guard.

More than 14,000 cases of pollution were reported to the Coast Guard during 1974. Coast Guard teams of the National Science Foundation helped clean up 26 spills. The Coast Guard continued to police fisheries, resulting in more than $1 million in fines against foreign violators.

### Marine Corps

U.S. Marines participated in several crises around the world in 1974. During the Cyprus crisis, Marines evacuated foreign civilians, and later a Marine guard defended the American embassy at Nicosia when it was attacked and the U.S. ambassador, Rodger Davies, killed. (*See* Obituaries.)

Marine officers served on a truce supervision team in the Middle East in 1974 and joined other countries in clearing the Suez Canal. In the Philippines Marines did rescue and relief work following floods in central Luzon. (*See* Middle East.)

### Navy

Adm. Elmo R. Zumwalt, chief of naval operations, retired in June 1974 and was replaced by Adm. James L. Holloway. During his four-year tenure, Admiral Zumwalt initiated many changes, including a completely new uniform, an assault on racism, alcoholism, and drugs, a new emphasis on education, and new kinds of ships and weapons.

The U.S. Navy continued to modernize but not to expand in 1974. Many new types of craft were being planned and built. The Navy continued its controversial Trident submarine program, although critics argued that the program was unnecessary, potentially obsolete, and too expensive. (*See also* Aerospace; Arms Control and Disarmament; Congress, United States; Defense.)

## ARMS CONTROL AND DISARMAMENT.
Negotiations on arms control continued during 1974, and the U.S. worked for an agreement on nuclear arms limitation with the U.S.S.R. To that end, both U.S. President Richard M. Nixon and U.S. President Gerald R. Ford traveled to the Soviet Union in 1974. Meanwhile, directors of the *Bulletin of the Atomic Scientists* set ahead the hands of the "doomsday clock," which is shown on the magazine's cover. Since completion in June 1972 of the first round of U.S.-Soviet talks to limit the nuclear arms race, the hands had stood at 12 minutes to midnight. On the September 1974 *Bulletin* the hands were set three minutes ahead—to where they were in 1947—because of failure to reach further significant agreements, development of new weaponry, and prospective introduction of nuclear reactors into the Middle East.

Arms control groups lobbied against the treaty, signed by Nixon in July 1974, which limited underground explosions to those below 150 kilotons—the force of 150,000 tons of TNT—but exempted nuclear tests for peaceful purposes. India justified its

first explosion of a nuclear device in May on the grounds that it was for peaceful purposes. Another awesome effect of nuclear war was described in 1974. There was general agreement among scientists that large-scale nuclear blasts could deplete the protective ozone layer in the stratosphere.

A breakthrough was made in November in the seemingly deadlocked second phase of Strategic Arms Limitation Talks. Meeting in Vladivostok, U.S.S.R., President Ford and Soviet leader Leonid Brezhnev tentatively agreed to limit through 1985 each country's offensive nuclear arsenal to 2,400 long-range missiles and bombers, including 1,320 multiple warhead missiles. A later amendment provided for arms reductions before 1985.

In a December meeting in Brussels, Belgium, ten European members of the North Atlantic Treaty Organization announced plans for an arms increase in 1975 to improve the alliance's military capacity. At the same time eight Latin American nations meeting in Peru issued an agreement to limit armaments and stop acquisition of offensive weapons. (*See also* Defense.)

**ASIA.** Much of the news in 1974—a time of violence and anxiety in Southeast Asia—was made by big powers from far and near. Superpower moves in the Indian Ocean were deeply disturbing to the Asian countries. There were reports that U.S. defense authorities were considering the establishment of major military facilities on the British-owned island of Diego Garcia. The reason officially given was that the Soviet Union was expanding its naval strength in the area. While U.S. reports concentrated on purported Soviet intentions in the Mediterranean-Arabian Sea sector, the People's Republic of China accused the Soviet Union of military expansion in Southeast Asia.

A string of archipelagic islands in the South China Sea became the subject of contention early in the year. In September 1973 South Vietnam had announced the incorporation of some of the islands and the granting of oil exploration rights to foreign companies. In a sudden military action in January, China took possession of the Paracel Islands, 165 miles southeast of the Chinese island of Hainan, driving away South Vietnamese aircraft and patrol boats. China also claimed sovereignty over the Spratly Islands, about 400 miles farther south, and over all the natural resources in the surrounding sea. The Philippines and Taiwan, as well as South Vietnam, claimed islands in the Spratly group.

The Chinese military action brought forth no public pronouncements from Southeast Asian governments except that of South Vietnam. But reports from various capitals showed clearly that it had caused dismay in the region. The Soviet Union's strict hands-off attitude and the stated U.S. position that the Chinese move did not indicate any desire to dominate the region were interpreted as signs that the big powers would permit one another to pursue

JEHANGIR GAZDAR—WOODFIN CAMP

*Foreign Ministers (left to right) Hossein of Bangladesh, Singh of India, and Ahmed of Pakistan join hands in New Delhi, India, after the April signing of a tripartite agreement.*

their interests in the area without interference.

Japan contributed another element to Asian tensions during the year. With Japanese business in a dominant position all over the region, particularly in Indonesia and Thailand, Prime Minister Kakuei Tanaka had decided to embark on a five-nation Asian goodwill tour in January. Weeks earlier, student representatives from various Southeast Asian countries had announced their decision to protest foreign exploitation of their countries. It was clear that there would be an organized attempt to make Tanaka's tour eventful. With the exception of the Philippines, under martial law, and Singapore, where authorities kept the lid on dissent, Tanaka's tour provided an occasion for massive public demonstrations of resentment and bitterness. In Malaysia, students organized public demonstrations and burned Tanaka in effigy. In Thailand, massive student rallies dogged the footsteps of Tanaka from the minute his aircraft landed at the Bangkok airport. In Indonesia, rampaging student mobs brought on Jakarta's first curfew since the Suharto government came to power in 1965. Japanese-made cars were damaged and business establishments ransacked. Several persons were killed and many injured before police could restore order.

Partly, it appeared the Japanese were being used as foils for local resentment against the respective governments and the failure of those governments to achieve either economic progress or democratic systems. The governments themselves seemed sensitive to their freshly demonstrated unpopularity; there was a new emphasis on security precautions in many countries, while Indonesia closed down the national press almost entirely and took severe measures against critics of the Tanaka visit.

Further anti-Japanese demonstrations took place in Seoul, South Korea, in September. Koreans blamed the Japanese for the death of President Park Chung Hee's wife, who was killed during an assassination attempt on President Park himself. Pro-North Korean sentiments in Japan—and rumors that Japan might establish diplomatic relations with the North—also stirred anger in Seoul.

One regional story receiving worldwide attention was the internationalization of the Muslim uprising in the Philippines. The Manila government used its full military power to put down the rebellion in its southern provinces but failed. In the process, international Muslim solidarity developed over the issue, and relations between Malaysia and the Philippines deteriorated. The extent of it became clear when representatives of 37 countries and the Palestine Liberation Organization (PLO) met in Kuala Lumpur, Malaysia, in June for the fifth Islamic Conference of Foreign Ministers. The Philippine question dominated the meeting. In the end the foreign ministers issued what amounted to a condemnation of the Philippine government. Indonesia pleaded for moderation, and Malaysia supported the plea. The Philippines, nevertheless, accused the Kuala Lumpur government of aiding the Muslim insurgency.

Developments in two Himalayan kingdoms drew international attention in 1974. In Bhutan, 18-year-old King Jigme Singye Wangchuk, one of the world's last absolute monarchs, was officially crowned on June 2. In nearby Sikkim, more than 300 years of monarchical rule came to an end. The ruler, Chogyal (King) Palden Thondup Namgyal, lost his base of power after the April elections; a new constitution, adopted in June, reduced the chogyal to the position of titular chief of state. Later in the year Sikkim officially became an associate state of India.

An accord signed in April by India, Pakistan, and Bangladesh resolved the last unsettled issues of the 1971 India-Pakistan war, clearing the way for normalization of relations between the three countries. Bangladesh agreed to repatriate the Pakistani prisoners who were being held for war-crimes trials. The future of several hundred thousand Biharis (non-Bengali Muslims) in Bangladesh remained uncertain, however. Most were in refugee camps.

In the light of the Philippines-Malaysia dispute, the Association of South-East Asian Nations (ASEAN) appeared somewhat shaky during 1974.

But its very attempt to help negotiate between the disputants was cited by some as proof of its usefulness. While mediation efforts produced no immediate result, ASEAN turned its attention to economic issues, with a slightly keener sense of urgency than in the past.

Economic cooperation was the dominant theme when ASEAN foreign ministers met in Jakarta, Indonesia, in May for their seventh annual meeting. Inaugurating the meeting, President Suharto stated that the only way ASEAN could remain master of its own political destiny was for each member country to improve its political and economic condition. He called for more efforts for the joint industrial development of the area. It was understood that the true test of solidarity among member countries would come in such sensitive areas as oil sharing. In 1973 Indonesia had caused dismay by telling Thailand and the Philippines that its considerable oil supplies were already committed to developed countries. Subsequently, Indonesian officials said they were seriously interested in supplying oil to ASEAN neighbors. At Jakarta the Singapore foreign minister announced that the five ASEAN countries would consider cooperating to alleviate shortages. His own country took the position that ASEAN members prepared to pay market prices for raw materials should be given priority.

*April election slogans in Gantok, Sikkim, urge a vote for the spade, symbol of the independent candidate and changing times as Sikkim prepared for the first popular election of its assembly.*
WIDE WORLD

As if to follow up its resolutions for achieving results, ASEAN decided to give itself a permanent home; Jakarta was agreed upon as a site for the new secretariat. The meeting also decided to set up procedures to settle disputes among member countries and to look into the possibilities of adopting a formal constitution. The question of the group's membership remained as confused as ever. It was no secret that ASEAN was quite interested in adding the Indochina countries to its fold. However, North Vietnam bluntly refused an invitation to sit as an observer at the 1974 meeting. South Vietnam, an observer in 1973, was not invited. Cambodia and Laos sent observers, but Burma did not. Clearly, political affiliations were decisive factors.

The dispute within ASEAN over relations with the People's Republic of China edged toward resolution following Malaysia's diplomatic recognition of China in May. Other Southeast Asian countries seemed to be responding approvingly to the Malaysian initiative. The secretary of the Southeast Asia Treaty Organization (SEATO) contended that China's friendly attitude was merely aimed to demonstrate to the Soviets "that it has the support of many friends." But the secretary's statement, asserting that SEATO was still committed to fighting subversion, was weakened by the fact that the United States—the main supporter of SEATO—had become a vigorous promoter of friendship with China, and also by the fact that the only Southeast Asian members of SEATO, Thailand and the Philippines, were actively seeking formal diplomatic relations with China.

The big news of 1974 about the United Nations Economic Commission for Asia and the Far East (ECAFE) was its decision to rename itself the Economic and Social Commission for Asia and the Pacific (ESCAP). The change signified abandonment of the term Far East, which was deemed to have colonial connotations, as well as a shift in emphasis from the strictly economic to the broader, and hopefully deeper, socioeconomic. (*See also* individual country articles; Pacific Islands.)

## ASTRONOMY.

Major advances were made along two extremely diverse fronts in 1974. On one hand, several of Earth's companions in the solar system yielded many of their secrets, mainly as a result of flybys by spacecraft. On the other, theoreticians and observational scientists critically assessed the evidence for the existence of black holes, portals in our universe through which a body may pass into another universe and another time.

### The Solar System

For centuries, Earth-based studies revealed little about the surface of Mercury, primarily because the innermost planet always remains near the sun, making it difficult to observe. In March and again in September, however, as the Mariner 10 space probe skimmed within 440 miles of Mercury's surface, it obtained extremely detailed photographs of this small world.

The surface of Mercury was discovered to be similar to that of the moon. Over vast areas it was densely pockmarked with craters, some young with

*A March photomosaic of Mercury, made from 18 pictures taken at 42-second intervals by Mariner 10 while at a 124,000-mile distance from the planet, displays the cratered, lunarlike surface of Mercury's southern hemisphere.*

COURTESY, NASA

*The Cerro Tololo Inter-American Observatory in the Chilean Andes produced its first photograph in late October after installation of the 13-foot 2-inch primary mirror in its telescope, the largest in the Southern Hemisphere.*

sharp rims, others ancient with crumbled walls. In contrast, there were smooth basins and plains, some hundreds of miles across, which also resembled their lunar counterparts. Some of the Mercurian plains were crossed by gigantic fracture patterns, and the planet's surface was covered with a porous soil having thermal properties similar to the lunar soil.

Though scientists had anticipated a moonlike topography for Mercury, they were surprised when Mariner 10 detected a very tenuous atmosphere around the planet, composed mainly of helium. Equally unexpected was the discovery of Mercury's relatively strong magnetic field.

Venus had been explored previously with space probes sent by the United States and the Soviet Union, but Mariner 10 made an unprecedented survey of the cloud-shrouded planet. Discovered above the 70-kilometer-deep atmosphere, composed largely of sulfuric acid droplets, was a 10-kilometer-thick stratified layer of haze. Overall, the appearance of Venus' lower atmosphere was symmetrical, with streaks of cirruslike clouds in the polar and temperate regions and round mottlings in the tropics. The latter were reminiscent of convection cells in Earth's atmosphere.

After a 21-month, half-billion-mile journey, Pioneer 10 accomplished man's deepest venture into space. The 550-pound spacecraft swept 81,000 miles above Jupiter's cloudtops; for two weeks its camera obtained more than 300 images. The best of them, released early in the year, revealed atmospheric features many times smaller than those previously recorded from Earth. Equally important were Pioneer's measurements of Jupiter's space environment. The bow shock wave produced by Jupiter's magnetic field as it plowed through the solar wind was first encountered at a distance of about 5 million miles, which was unexpectedly far from the planet. Later in the flight Pioneer discovered an intense concentration of trapped radiation near the plane of Jupiter's magnetic equator.

Pioneer 10 confirmed that Jupiter radiated about twice as much energy as it received from the sun, simulating a feeble star. The planet's chemical composition was also found to be starlike, being mainly hydrogen and helium. The evidence indicated that about 600 miles below Jupiter's cloudtops was a spinning ball of liquid hydrogen. At a depth of 15,-000 miles, about a third of the way to the center of the planet, the atmospheric pressure was 3 million times greater than that experienced on Earth, and the hydrogen was converted to its liquid metallic state. At the center of the planet the temperature probably reached 54,000° F., much hotter than previously believed. Scientists envisioned Jupiter as a ball of gas simply not massive enough to begin nuclear reactions that would turn it into a star.

On September 14, Charles Kowal of Hale Observatories in California added a 13th moon to those already known to circle Jupiter. This was the first addition to that planet's retinue since 1951. The new satellite, which may be only three to five miles in diameter, travels around Jupiter every 282 days at an average distance of 7.7 million miles.

On December 3 the 570-pound Pioneer 11, launched April 6, 1973, approached Jupiter from the planet's south pole, crossed the Jovian equator within 27,000 miles of the cloud cover, and swept up over the north pole and back out into space. This trajectory was designed to utilize Jupiter's gravitational force as a slingshot to hurl the spacecraft (nearing Jupiter at one third the distance of Pioneer 10) through the planet's severe radiation belts, most intense at the equator. As it passed through these radiation belts, sparks due to a buildup of electrical charges on the craft caused several instruments to go haywire, performing uncommanded operations, and had to be shut off by signals from Earth with an hour's loss of scientific data. Not lost, however, were the first pictures of Jupiter's poles, whose mottled red appearance, in contrast with the regularly striped equatorial region, was believed

**119**

caused by convection cells or vents for gases rising beneath the cloud cover. A closer look was taken at the vast Red Spot, now thought to be a centuries-old storm still in progress. Pioneer also provided the best pictures ever of Callisto, second largest of Jupiter's 13 moons, revealing an apparent south polar icecap and possible landing base for future manned flight.

Though Comet Kohoutek never became the awesome celestial spectacle some astronomers had forecast, it still proved to be an important object. The rapid development of technology during the past decade permitted observations at wavelengths and resolutions previously unattainable. Comet Kohoutek was the most intensely observed of any such visitor and was also the first comet to be seen by man from space, during the final Skylab mission.

The discovery of water in the comet was, perhaps, the most far-reaching new information obtained. It confirmed a model for comets advocated a quarter century ago by F. L. Whipple, who described the objects as "dirty snowballs," composed of ices and dust.

Comet Kohoutek was slowing down as it moved away from the sun, not to return again for about 75,000 years. To scientists Comet Kohoutek answered many questions, to newsmen it taught prudence, and to the Children of God and some other sects it provided a brief opportunity to prophesy the end of the world.

In October U.S. astronomers Joseph Taylor and Russell Hulse announced the important discovery of the first pulsar identified in orbit around an extremely dense object. And in the Netherlands scientists released a radio-emitted "photograph," produced by the Westerbork observatory's synthesis radio telescope, of the largest object yet discovered in the universe. The massive structure was almost 19 million light-years wide, or three times greater than the largest galaxy clusters, previously the largest known objects in the universe.

In November scientists began transmitting from the Arecibo, Puerto Rico, giant radio telescope the first deliberate radio message to space in hopes of initiating communication with life believed to exist in the target Messier 13 galaxy. The mathematically coded message was to take 24,000 years to reach its intended listeners.

### Black Holes

During the year the concept of black holes jumped off the mathematician's scratch pad into the imagination of observational astronomers. Though black holes were predicted as early as 1917, they had not yet been observed conclusively by the end of 1974. The recent discovery of objects that did not yield to conventional interpretation, however, led many astronomers to anticipate the imminent confirmation of the exotic objects.

What are black holes? Though their properties are amazing, their origin is mundane and a normal consequence of stellar evolution: black holes are the collapsed state of a star at least two or three times more massive than the sun. When any star exhausts its nuclear fuel, it must shrink to remain in equilibrium. For a star such as the sun, the process ends at the well-known white dwarf stage, stars about the size of Earth. In these objects, the contraction is halted by the repulsive forces among the star's electrons as they are squeezed together.

Slightly more massive stars have more exciting terminal histories. The electron pressure is insufficient to arrest the contraction, and the star continues to shrink until it is only 15 or 20 miles in diameter. Its matter becomes so compacted that the electrons and protons combine to yield neutrons. Ultimately, the very strong nuclear forces between the neutrons halt the contraction. The discovery of pulsars in 1967 gave the first observational evidence for these neutron stars.

Yet, many stars are known to be much more massive than the sun. What happens to them at the end of their lives? Again contraction occurs, but it never stops. The ever growing density of the star yields an ever stronger gravitational field. This process feeds on itself until gravity, normally the weakest force in nature, dominates all others. Light and particles can no longer escape from the star—all matter inside remains inside; all matter entering can never leave. Space and time fold over themselves, and the one-time star disappears, leaving a black hole.

The most compelling evidence for the existence of black holes came from observations of binary star systems in which one component was detectable only by its X-ray emission. (X rays would be emitted by matter from the ordinary star as it is drawn into the black hole.) The prime candidate was an object called Cygnus X-1. One of its components was an optically visible supergiant star with a mass of 15 to 35 suns. An X-ray source traveled around this star every 5.6 days, allowing astronomers to calculate that the mass of the source was at least that of six suns, well over the minimum necessary to form a black hole. Furthermore, rapid variations in the strength of the X-ray emission indicated that the source was a very compact object. (*See also* Chemistry; Space Exploration.)

**AUSTRALIA.** Prime Minister Gough Whitlam, who headed Australia's first Labor Party government in 23 years, dissolved Parliament on April 11, 1974, midway through his term, and called for new elections. Many of his proposed domestic reforms had been blocked by the Senate, in which the Liberal and Country parties had a majority. Labor won a narrow victory in the elections held on May 18. Whitlam pledged to continue his program, which included a state-controlled health insurance plan and a petroleum and mineral resources authority run by the government.

It was the third time in the country's history since federation in 1901 that both houses of Parliament

As Queen Elizabeth II arrives in Canberra, Australia, in late February to open the legislature, aborigines demonstrate to gain title to land rather than accepting settlement on government-owned reserves.
WIDE WORLD

were dissolved together. Besides the opposition to Whitlam's programs, the constitutional crisis was generated by what was described as one of the most daring gambles in Australian political history: Whitlam created a Senate vacancy by appointing a longtime foe, Vincent C. Gair, as ambassador to Ireland. The plan failed. Instead of Gair's seat going to a Whitlam supporter, the premier of Queensland state used a loophole in the law to put in another conservative. When the opposition in the Senate started to carry out its threat to defeat a money supply bill for providing funds for the day-to-day workings of the government, Whitlam called for new elections.

During the campaign, Opposition Leader Billy Snedden concentrated on the issue of Australia's 14% inflation rate. He promised to restore the incentives to foreign investment that Whitlam took away. Farmers berated Whitlam because his party abolished their longstanding tax concessions.

The election result was a victory for Whitlam. His party had a majority of five in the new House of Representatives and, though it failed to gain control of the Senate, Whitlam had the numbers to get his programs passed through a joint sitting of the houses.

Inflation and increased unemployment were major problems of the reelected Labor government. The administration came under strong pressure to avoid anti-inflation measures that might aggravate unemployment, which rose by 18.7% in July. A 17% rise in earnings in a 12-month period, noted early in the year, was the highest recorded in Australia. Prices rose by about 14% in the same period, however, and that was the biggest increase since the early 1950's. To help fight inflation, Whitlam's government revalued the currency upward, reduced excessive liquidity, lowered tariffs in order to make imports cheaper, and established a Prices Justifica-

tion Tribunal. In September the Australian dollar was devalued by 12%.

On August 8 the Labor government abandoned its heavy restrictions on the entry of foreign capital into Australia by slashing the Variable Deposit Requirement from 25% to 5%. This clamp on foreign capital inflow had been imposed three weeks after the government took office in December 1972. It was raised to 33⅓% from October 1973 to June 1974. As a result, net capital inflow in 1973–74 was reduced by $289 million from the previous year.

Federal Treasurer Frank Crean introduced a "social progress" budget in September 1974. It proposed a 32.4% increase in expenditures for a wide range of social services and reductions in personal income tax. Also proposed were a new capital gains tax, a 10% property surcharge, cessation of tax concessions to mining companies (except gold mining), and income tax deductibles for education. Australia also cut back immigration in 1974 as an anti-inflation procedure.

The Westralian Secessionist party, a group of western Australians, began to gain ground in 1974. The possibility was remote that Australia's largest state would become a separate country, but the secessionist movement was considered to be a measure of the opposition to Whitlam's policies.

Several hundred aborigines demonstrated when Queen Elizabeth arrived at Parliament House in February 1974. The queen said in her speech that the government would eliminate discrimination and would pass legislation to grant land rights to aborigines in the Northern Territory.

Whitlam called upon the U.S. and the Soviet Union in 1974 to exercise mutual restraint lest their rivalry lead to a large-scale buildup of their Indian Ocean forces. The appeal followed disapproval within the Australian government of plans by the United States to expand the naval facility at Diego

Garcia, a British-ruled island in the Indian Ocean.

In 1974 Whitlam was determined to ensure that Australia was accepted as a good neighbor in the Asian and Pacific region. He toured southeast Asia and continued Australia's dialogue with North Korea, with which diplomatic relations were established on July 31. Australia also recognized the annexation of the Baltic states of Latvia, Estonia, and Lithuania by the Soviet Union. A greatly expanded scheme of tariff preferences for less developed countries went into force in January 1974. In September Australia withdrew from the sterling area system upon the decline of its sterling holdings.

The Australian government continued in 1974 to protest nuclear testing in the Pacific. Whitlam followed a strong criticism of the French tests with a denouncement of the Chinese nuclear blast.

On Christmas Day the northern city of Darwin was devastated by a cyclone that killed 49 persons and damaged or destroyed 90% of the city. The government began immediate evacuation of survivors and pledged to rebuild the port city.

## AUSTRIA.

The death of President Franz Jonas on April 24, 1974, led to a presidential election in June. (*See* Obituaries.) The winner was Socialist Party of Austria (SPÖ) candidate Foreign Minister Rudolf Kirchschläger, who—although not an SPÖ member—was nevertheless the personal choice of Chancellor Bruno Kreisky. In a series of regional

elections held in Vienna, Upper Austria, Salzburg, and Lower Austria, the Austrian People's party (ÖVP) gained nine seats and the Austrian Freedom party (FPÖ) lost two. The position of the SPÖ remained unchanged.

As a nonpermanent member of the United Nations (UN) Security Council, Austria was particularly concerned with UN peacekeeping operations, especially in the Middle East, where its contingent was increased to more than 600 persons. In March Chancellor Kreisky led a delegation of the Socialist International on a tour of the Middle East. The visit provided an opportunity to improve relations between Austria and Israel, which had been seriously affected by the closure in 1973 of the Schönau transit camp.

Measures to combat oil shortages and price rises that occurred during the winter of 1973–74 included the introduction of a "motorless day" (discontinued in February) and speed limits on the roads. Apart from these temporary difficulties, the economic outlook was good. A continued rise in the gross national product compared favorably with other leading European industrial countries. Prices increased at a rate of less than 10%, and there was a marked expansion in exports. The floating of the Austrian schilling in May brought an upward revaluation of 3% against the West German mark, designed to promote stability and reduce the effect of "imported inflation." (*See also* Europe.)

*The body of Austrian President Franz Jonas is carried from the parliament building in Vienna, Austria, during the April 29 state funeral procession.*
WIDE WORLD

*The world's safest medium-sized family car, a modified Morris Marina equipped with rubber and fabric bumpers and capable of withstanding a 40-mph crash, is unveiled in England in June.*

**AUTOMOBILES.** Price increases and plummeting sales afflicted the automobile industry in 1974. Sales were slow except for fuel-saving small cars, which accounted for just under 50% of the receipts. Sales of domestic cars were expected to drop to 9 million for the year, from 11.5 million in the previous one. At year's end layoffs in the industry mounted to nearly 200,000, with the Chrysler Corp., which was hit the hardest, shutting down five of its six U.S. car-assembly plants at Thanksgiving for at least five weeks. Industry officials announced that only 1.6 million cars would be produced in the first quarter of 1975, a 14-year low for first-quarter production.

A number of mechanical innovations designed to help cars run more cleanly and efficiently were introduced in the 1975 models. The industry brought out the controversial catalytic converter to clean up engine exhaust.

Attributed to general inflation, price increases came at a relentless pace during 1974. Each of the big three automakers—General Motors (GM), the Ford Motor Co., and Chrysler Corp.—announced half a dozen price boosts during the 1974 model year, averaging in all about $500 to $600 per car. By July it was reported that buyers who had traded in their cars every two years were thinking about waiting another two, and that the usual four-year traders were looking at used cars.

The price spiral reached a climax in mid-August when GM announced a jump of over 9% in the price of the 1975 models. Even with a slight rollback that resulted when U.S. President Gerald R. Ford objected to the GM increase, the hikes were substantial. A 1975 Vega was priced almost 20% higher than its equivalent model a year earlier.

Equipment changes in the new cars were partly responsible for the price increases. Engines differing from 1974 models were used in some 1975's, and optional equipment was made standard in some cases. The overall effect of the announced increases was felt almost immediately as buyers emptied auto showrooms of the lower priced 1974 models. Big-car sales in particular picked up. The resulting shortage of 1974 cars forced late buyers to accept the higher price tags on the 1975's.

The new models reflected the industry's determination to switch to smaller cars. GM added a new series of small sporty models built on a 97-inch wheelbase and powered by 4-cylinder, V6, and V8 engines. With sharply declining sales of the Japanese Wankel-powered Mazda and unresolved fuel emission problems, however, GM indefinitely postponed the planned fall introduction of its first rotary-engine compact. At Ford the news was the addition of two new luxury compacts, the Granada and the Mercury Monarch, available in 2- and 4-door sedans. Chrysler introduced two new personal luxury cars, the Dodge Charger SE and the Cordoba, both variations of their intermediate coupes. American Motors discontinued the Ambassador and the Javelin at the end of the 1974 run and planned to introduce a 1975 luxury version of its Gremlin subcompact.

The catalytic converter introduced on most 1975 models was designed to treat exhaust gases so that they met emission control standards for unburned hydrocarbons and carbon monoxide. The converter

*Touted by its creator, Malcolm Bricklin, as the "safest and most advanced production car ever built," the Bricklin features a vacuum-formed acrylic body, a box steel frame rather than the conventional U steel frame, an individually enclosed engine, and integral roll cage protection.*

COURTESY, BRICKLIN VEHICLE CORP.

was said to be so thorough that automotive engineers were able to redesign the engines to regain all the efficiency lost when earlier clean-air changes were made. The converter cost an estimated $120 to $150 per car. The converter systems, which weighed about 50 pounds, fit into the front end of the exhaust system like an additional muffler. Minimum life of a converter as required by emission control laws was 50,000 miles, but auto engineers expected the converters to be effective for the life of the car.

The biggest threat to the longevity of the converter system was lead used in gasoline. Buyers of 1975 models were warned to use only unleaded fuel. The use of unleaded fuel, combined with the effectiveness of the electronic ignitions available on most 1975 models, was expected to extend the life of engine parts and accessories and to lengthen the interval between maintenance jobs. Spark plug changes on GM cars, for example, were recommended after every 22,500 miles instead of the previously recommended 6,000 miles.

The first major recall of autos for environmental reasons was ordered in 1974. The Environmental Protection Agency (EPA) told Chrysler to recall 825,000 of its 1973 models because of a defect in the pollution control system. The EPA said a sensor that controlled the exhaust-gas recirculation system was defective on about half of those cars.

### Fuel Economy Measures

New smaller engines designed to fit in the smaller car models made their debut in the 1975 lines. The small engines delivered better fuel economy. Many other new features of the 1975 models reflected the auto industry's concern for fuel conservation. Fuel-conscious buyers were offered lower axle ratios, slower running engines, recalibrated carburetors, faster acting chokes, vacuum gauges that monitored fuel consumption, and overdrive gearboxes.

The EPA stated in September 1974 that 1975 autos would get about 13.5% better gasoline mileage on the average than the previous models. The best fuel mileage performance was achieved by the Datsun B-210, which got 27 miles per gallon in simulated city driving and 39 miles per gallon in simulated highway driving in the EPA tests. The small U.S. cars were about even in their ratings, getting on the average 21 miles per gallon in the city and 29 on the road.

### A New Mass-Market Auto

The Bricklin—the first new commercial quantity auto since Kaiser's Henry J came out in 1946—went into production in 1974. The Bricklin had a wheelbase of 96 inches, a 360-cubic-inch V8 engine, and a four-barrel carburetor. Malcolm Bricklin announced that his company, General Vehicle, Inc., of Phoenix, Ariz., expected to produce about 1,000 Bricklins per month by October 1974 in a plant at St. John, N.B.

The aerodynamically styled two-seat sports car was designed with many safety features. Notable was a bumper system for withstanding impacts in excess of federal standards.

### Foreign Car Sales and Innovations

The sales slump in the first half of 1974 had a severe effect on imported cars. Their share of the total U.S. market dropped from about 16% to less than 14% by mid-1974. By the end of the year, however, sales were improving. Top sellers were Volkswagen, Toyota, Datsun, and Capri.

In Amsterdam, Netherlands, a 1974 advance for inner-city transportation was a two-seat electric vehicle that traveled up to 20 mph between strategically placed stations where it could be recharged in five minutes. Renters of the Witkar (Dutch for "white car") found that three of the drive-it-yourself vehicles occupied the parking space of a standard-sized European sedan and cost less than half as much as a taxi for an average trip. (*See also* Business and Industry; Employment; Safety.)

**AUTO RACING.** The year 1974 was a strange one for American motor sports. Conceived in the depths of the energy crisis and plagued by the specter of inflation-reduced sponsorships, the programs of the respective sanctioning organizations within and outside the Auto Competition Committee of the U.S. carried forward with more success than might have been expected.

The names of the champions and the major winners were distressingly familiar, if the sport can be viewed as something that needs new faces to remain vital. Richard Petty drove his STP Dodge to his fifth National Association for Stock Car Auto Racing (NASCAR) season crown, dueling for the dollar winnings crown with David Pearson and his Purolator Mercury and Chevrolet-mounted Cale Yarborough. Petty also won the classic Daytona 500 for an unprecedented fifth time.

Johnny Rutherford of Texas won two legs of the U.S. Auto Club (USAC) Triple Crown, taking the Indianapolis 500 and the Pocono Schaefer 500; he also captured the Rex Mays 150 in Milwaukee, Wis.

Rutherford, who won at Indianapolis in his 11th attempt, led 122 of the 200 laps in what proved to be a safe but noncompetitive race. Known for a propensity to drive cars harder than they can stand, he completed the race for the first time, earning $245,031 of a record $1,015,686 purse. What competition there was came from pole winner A. J. Foyt, who led 70 laps before exiting on the 142d with a broken oil line. Bobby Unser finished second, and Bill Vukovich came in third. The 1973 winner, Gordon Johncock, finished fourth, and David Hobbs of Great Britain came in fifth. Rutherford, who averaged 158.589 mph, made eight pit stops (a record for a winning driver) because the cars were limited to 285 gallons of methanol fuel.

Rutherford also won the Schaefer 500 and another $92,000, but Unser's fifth place finish assured him of the best record in the Triple Crown. Unser had previously won the California 500 by an

*In the preliminaries of the June 16 Can-Am race at Mosport, Ont., George Follmer in UOP Shadow (1) tightly trails his teammate Jackie Oliver in UOP Shadow (101). Oliver later won the Can-Am feature race of the day.*

CANADIAN PRESS

eyelash over his brother Al. He added winning points from Trenton, N.J., and Phoenix, Ariz., to wrap up the season title early in the season, due to steady high finishes in other races.

Although the ending changed occasionally, the players in the NASCAR biweekly heroics remained pretty much the same. Richard Petty won ten, including Daytona's 500, the Talladega 500, the Carolina 500, the Capital City 500, the Motor State 400, and the Atlanta Dixie 500. David Pearson, who edged Petty at the Charlotte World 600, won the Daytona Firecracker 400, the Yankee 400, and the Charlotte National 500. Cale Yarborough won ten races in his Carling Beer Chevrolet, including the 25th running of the Southern 500 at Darlington, S.C., the Mason-Dixon 500 at Dover, Del., the Winston Western 500 at Riverside, Calif., the Nashville 420, and the Bristol 500. The latter two were protested victories, the Nashville race producing the strange rule that Bobby Allison—who the judges admitted ran one lap more than Cale—protested too late because he had not spotted the discrepancy during the contest. Petty and Yarborough finished one-two in the season's standings and in money winnings. They and Pearson easily passed $200,000 in season winnings.

In Grand Prix (Formula One) racing, the winner of the world drivers' championship was Emerson Fittipaldi of Brazil. He captured the title when he finished first in the U.S. Grand Prix at Watkins Glen, N.Y.

## AWARDS AND PRIZES.

The 1974 Nobel peace prize was awarded jointly to Sean MacBride, a diplomat from Ireland, and Eisaku Sato, former prime minister of Japan. MacBride, United Nations (UN) commissioner for South West Africa (Namibia), was foreign minister of the Republic of Ireland from 1948 to 1951; in 1961 he became chairman of the board of Amnesty International, a private group that monitors the rights of political dissenters and political refugees.

Sato was cited for working toward nonproliferation of nuclear weapons; the peace prize committee also noted that Sato "has consistently demanded that Japan not acquire nuclear weapons." Sato, a founder of Japan's ruling Liberal Democratic party, served as prime minister from 1964 to 1972. The awarding of the peace prize to Sato aroused some criticism among the left in Japan—announcement of the award followed soon after revelations that while Sato was prime minister, U.S. ships had been entering Japanese ports without off-loading nuclear weapons. Agreements between Japan and the U.S. forbid the introduction of any nuclear weapons into Japan. (*See* Japan.)

The Nobel prize for literature was awarded jointly to Swedish authors Eyvind Johnson and Harry Martinson. The two men, both in their 70's, were revered in Sweden but little known internationally. Johnson, author of the anti-Nazi trilogy 'Krilon', was cited for his "narrative art, far-seeing in lands and ages, in the service of freedom." Martin-

LEFT: FRANK LEONARDO—
KEYSTONE;
RIGHT: WIDE WORLD

*Former Japanese Prime Minister Eisaku Sato and former Irish Foreign Minister Sean MacBride, who also served as UN commissioner for Namibia (South-West Africa), shared the 1974 Nobel peace prize.*

son was best known for his poem about a space trip that was used as a basis for the opera 'Aniara'; the citation noted that his literary works "catch the dewdrop and reflect the cosmos." Exiled Soviet author Alexsandr Solzhenitsyn accepted his 1970 Nobel prize for literature at the December 10 ceremonies in Stockholm, Sweden.

Gunnar Myrdal and Friedrich von Hayek shared the Nobel prize for economics. Von Hayek, born in Austria, had taught in Europe, the U.S., and Asia. Myrdal, born in Sweden, was a visiting professor at the City University of New York in 1974.

The Nobel prize for physiology or medicine was awarded to three scientists cited as being "largely responsible for the creation of modern cell biology." The three were Albert Claude, Christian de Duve, and George E. Palade. Claude, a naturalized U.S. citizen, was director of the Jules Bordet Institute in Brussels, Belgium. De Duve, a Belgian by birth, was on the faculty of Rockefeller University and the University of Louvain in Belgium. Palade, who was born in Romania and later became a U.S. citizen, taught at Yale University. Claude and Palade had formerly worked at Rockefeller University—when it was known as Rockefeller Institute—and Claude cited the institute as an important factor in the success of his work. (*See* Medicine.)

Paul J. Flory was awarded the Nobel prize for chemistry. Flory, born in Illinois, taught at Stanford University in California. He was cited for his research on the physical chemistry of macromolecules.

Two radio astronomers shared the 1974 Nobel prize for physics; they were the first radio astronomers to win a Nobel. Sir Martin Ryle and Antony Hewish, both working at the Cavendish Laboratory of Cambridge University in England, were cited for pioneering research in radioastrophysics. Ryle was cited for his advances in techniques of astronomical data-gathering. Hewish was probably best known for his work with pulsars. (*See* Physics.)

### Pulitzer Prizes

Robert Lowell won the Pulitzer prize for poetry, for his book 'The Dolphin'; it was Lowell's second such award. No Pulitzer was awarded for drama or fiction in 1974. The fiction jury had voted to recommend the prize for Thomas Pynchon, author of the novel 'Gravity's Rainbow', but the advisory board vetoed a prize for the book.

The Pulitzer for general nonfiction went to Ernest Becker posthumously, for his book 'The Denial of Death'; Becker had died March 6. The history prize was given to Daniel J. Boorstin for 'The Americans: The Democratic Experience'; biography prize, to Louis Sheaffer for 'O'Neill, Son and Artist'.

Donald Martino was awarded the Pulitzer prize for music, in honor of his chamber music composition 'Notturno'. A special citation in music was voted for the distinguished composer Roger Sessions, for the body of his work.

The Pulitzer prize for national affairs reporting

WIDE WORLD

*Arthur Petacque and Hugh Hough of the* Chicago Sun-Times *won the Pulitzer prize for general reporting with their investigative series on the 1966 murder of Valerie Percy.*

was shared by two journalists who had independently developed stories on the personal and political finances of then President Richard M. Nixon. James R. Polk of the *Washington Star News* was cited for a series of disclosures that included a secret Nixon campaign contribution of $200,000 from financier Robert Vesco. Jack White of the *Providence Journal-Bulletin* was cited for his stories on Nixon's 1970 and 1971 income tax returns. White's stories triggered a chain of events that culminated in Nixon's paying about $500,000 in back taxes.

Hedrick Smith of *The New York Times* won the prize for international affairs reporting for his coverage of the Soviet Union and its Warsaw Pact allies. *Newsday* received the gold medal for meritorious service by a newspaper for its series on heroin traffic in the New York City metropolitan area.

A series on Medicaid irregularities won the Pulitzer for investigative local reporting for William Sherman of the *New York Daily News*. The Pulitzer prize for general local reporting was awarded jointly to Arthur Petacque and Hugh Hough of the *Chicago Sun-Times* for a series on the unsolved murder of Valerie Percy, daughter of Senator Charles H. Percy (R, Ill.).

The Pulitzer prize for feature photography was received by Slava Veder of the Associated Press, for his photo of the homecoming of a U.S. prisoner of war returned from Vietnam. Anthony K. Roberts, a free-lance photographer, won the Pulitzer for spot news photography, for pictures of the killing of a kidnapping suspect. (*See* Photography.)

*Paul Szep of the* Boston Globe *received the Pulitzer prize for editorial cartoons.*

## Other Awards

The 16th annual Magsaysay awards for service to the Asian people were announced in August. The awards, which carry a cash prize of $10,000 for each recipient, commemorate the late Ramon Magsaysay, president of the Philippines. The Rev. William Masterson, an American Jesuit priest, won an award for international rural leadership training. Hiroshi Kuroki, governor of Japan's Miyasaka prefecture, won an award for promoting agricultural and industrial development while protecting the environment. Fusaye Ichikawa, a Japanese legislator, was cited for work in women's liberation and electoral ethics. Two other awards went to Zacarias Sarian, an agricultural editor in the Philippines, and Shrimati Sublakshmi, a devotional singer in India whose fees were donated to charity.

The prestigious Albert Lasker Medical Research Awards for 1974 were announced in November. John Charnley, a British orthopedic surgeon, won the clinical research award for his operation restoring the ability to walk in crippled persons by the construction of an artificial hipjoint. At the ceremony announcing the awards, one of Charnley's patients, ballet dancer Maria Gambarelli, dramatically demonstrated a few dance steps; her ability to walk had been impaired, and her ability to dance and participate in sports destroyed, by crippling arthritis—until her operation.

Four scientists won the Lasker award for basic research. They were: Ludwig Gross of the Bronx

Veterans Administration Hospital, New York City; Howard Skipper of the Southern Research Institute, Birmingham, Ala.; Sol Spiegelman of Columbia College of Physicians and Surgeons, New York City; and Howard Temin of the University of Wisconsin. The four were honored for research involving cancer.

The Vetlesen prize—often referred to as the "Nobel prize of the earth sciences"—was awarded to Chaim Leib Pekeris in 1974. Pekeris, a mathematician at the Weizmann Institute in Israel, was honored for his computations of the frequencies at which the earth vibrates during earthquakes. Pekeris' work has been crucial to scientists' determining whether an earthquake or an atomic explosion is taking place.

The National Cartoonists' Society gave awards to cartoonists in 12 categories in April. Patrick Oliphant of the *Denver Post*, whose work is syndicated, won the award for editorial cartooning. Other winners included Johnny Hart, creator of the syndicated strips "B.C." and "The Wizard of Id," for animation; Mell Lazarus, creator of the syndicated strip "Miss Peach," for humor; and George Lichty, creator of "Grin and Bear It," for a syndicated panel. (*See also* Architecture; Flowers and Gardens; Literature; Literature for Children; Motion Pictures; Music; Television and Radio; Theater; Women; Youth Organizations.)

**BAHAMAS.** The Bahamas' first year of independence ended with reports of a revival of outside and expatriate confidence in the political and investment spheres. Strict immigration controls were abated, and essential skilled foreign personnel gained admittance more smoothly. On the other hand, moves were reported in June to repatriate or deport a number of the 40,000 illegal immigrants or exiles from Haiti. The property market remained quiet, but industrial development was reported in Freeport. The adverse image created earlier by the presence of a number of questionable banking institutions among the more than 300 banks functioning in the Bahamas was dispelled by the closing down of most of them. The popularity of Prime Minister Lynden O. Pindling's Progressive Liberal party government among working-class voters was somewhat eroded by inflation and unemployment. Abaco, a dollar-earning Out Island with a roughly equal population of whites and blacks totaling 6,500, continued to agitate for home rule.

Tourism statistics showed some decrease in 1974, but tourism from Western Europe continued to rise. Food and transport were the major contributors to the rising cost of living. Some neglect of the social services was reported, not surprising in a society where most members were under the age of 25. Registration under the government's national insurance scheme started in November. A first Five-Year Economic and Social Development Plan (1974–78) was also announced. (*See also* West Indies.)

WIDE WORLD

*A mother and her son row to safety in Mymensingh, Bangladesh, where August floods claimed at least 2,000 lives.*

## BANGLADESH.

Early in 1974 Bangladesh announced a five-year development plan amid indications that good crop harvests, oil and gas exploration, and rising jute prices might enable the country to begin to raise itself out of its extreme poverty. The devastating floods of July and August 1974, however, dealt a severe blow to the development efforts. Enormous areas of the country, estimates of 50% or more, were under water. About 80% of the summer crops and the seedlings for the main winter crops were destroyed with a resulting loss of 40% of the annual food output. Many persons were killed by the floods or threatened by epidemics and famine. Other countries aided Bangladesh with food, supplies, and loans.

World inflation, rises in oil prices, and a general internal breakdown in law and order compounded the country's problems. Industrial output for 1973–74 was up 20% over the previous year but 10% below the government's target. Prices of staples rose as much as 400%. Violence that stemmed from political dissent and economic turmoil had claimed 3,000 lives since 1971 and continued to mount. On December 28 a national state of emergency was declared in an effort to curb the internal chaos that threatened the country.

Pakistan recognized Bangladesh in February 1974. Bangladesh signed an agreement with Pakistan and India in April concerning repatriation of Pakistani prisoners of war, Bengalis stranded in Pakistan, and Biharis in Bangladesh who wanted to go to Pakistan. Prime Minister Sheikh Mujibur Rahman and Pakistani Prime Minister Zulfikar Ali Bhutto, however, could not agree on division of assets or on the number of Pakistani nationals to be repatriated from Bangladesh to Pakistan. (*See also* Asia; Disasters of 1974; India; Pakistan.)

## BANKS.

The year 1974 was a tense one for U.S. banks and bankers. The prime rate spiral that had begun in 1973 continued in 1974. By the end of the year, the prime rate had leveled off from its 12-week peak of a record 12% to about 10½%.

Inflation was a major cause of the rise in the prime rate (the rate that the banks charge their biggest commercial customers for loans). A related cause was a systematic effort by the Federal Reserve Board to fight inflation by tightening the money supply. In September, however, the Federal Reserve Board announced a technical change in bank reserve requirements, indicating an easing of its tight monetary policy. (*See* United States.)

As the prime rate rose, consumer lending rates also reached historic highs. Defaults on bank installment loans accelerated. The cost of housing was rising rapidly; at the same time, the supply of money available for mortgages was shrinking. Interest rates for mortgages climbed. (*See* Housing.)

Though money was increasingly tight in the U.S. in 1974, banks increased their foreign loans dramatically. Andrew F. Brimmer, ex-governor of the Federal Reserve Board, in July noted that foreign lending had jumped by about $8.5 billion in the preceding six months.

Some banks suffered financial difficulties, for a variety of reasons. One was the decline of the stock

*"Same thing every morning—they all want to see their money."*

WAITE—LONDON DAILY MIRROR/ROTHCO

*First National Bank of Chicago's $8,000 investment in a popcorn machine showed a gross profit margin of 62%, the largest of the bank's profits on nearly $12 billion in loans.*
WIDE WORLD

market, which affected banks' investment portfolios adversely. (*See* Money and International Finance.)

One bank that encountered massive problems was the Franklin National Bank of New York City. The Franklin National overextended itself and was obliged to borrow about $1 billion from the Federal Reserve System. Also, in June, 11 large New York banks agreed to make secured loans to the Franklin National totaling about $250 million. In October Franklin National was declared insolvent and sold to a New York state institution owned by six large European banks. Earlier in the year, another big bank—the U.S. National of San Diego, Calif.—had to merge with another bank to avoid financial ruin.

In April the Supreme Court of the U.S. ruled constitutional the Bank Secrecy Act of 1970. That controversial law required banks to keep detailed records of a variety of transactions, including all checks over $100, and to make these records available to certain government agencies on demand. Civil libertarians had challenged the law as an unwarranted invasion of privacy.

No secret at all was the shortage of pennies in the U.S. The Firestone Bank of Akron, Ohio, advertised an offer to trade $1.10 for 100 pennies and was deluged with coins. Hoarders were holding the pennies because they were made of copper, a metal of increasing scarcity. Banks and retailers alike felt the penny pinch. Congressional action enabled the 41-year-old ban on private gold ownership by U.S. citizens to be lifted at year's end. (*See also* Business and Industry; Coins and Medals; Metals; Stocks and Bonds; World Trade.)

**BASEBALL.** The Oakland A's, continuing to thrive on a combination of mutinous tendencies and brutally efficient skills, won the World Series of baseball for the third successive time in 1974. Prospering despite clubhouse fights, legal infringements, and assorted other inner turmoils, the A's beat the Los Angeles Dodgers, four games to one, to make a shambles of the first all-California Series on record.

### Prominent Newsmakers

It was a year in which three of baseball's individual barriers, two statistical and one sociological, fell by the wayside. Hank Aaron of the Atlanta Braves shattered Babe Ruth's home run record; Lou Brock of the St. Louis Cardinals broke Maury Wills's stolen base record; and Frank Robinson was named baseball's first black manager by the Cleveland Indians.

Aaron entered the season-opening three-game series at Cincinnati, Ohio, with 713 home runs, one behind Ruth's lifetime total. In his first swing in the first inning of the first game, he smashed his 714th off the Reds' Jack Billingham to tie the record. He sat out the second game, and went 0 for 3 in the third game. That brought Aaron and the Braves back to Atlanta, Ga., for their nationally televised home opener on April 8. Against left-hander Al Downing of the Los Angeles Dodgers, the 40-year-old slugger hit his 715th home run over the left-center-field fence for a new record.

Brock stole 118 bases in 1974, wiping out Wills's mark of 104 set in 1962. Brock's 105th steal came against Philadelphia at Busch Stadium in St. Louis,

Mo., on September 10. Brock wound up the year with a lifetime total of 753, surpassing Max Carey's modern National League record of 738. Ty Cobb held the major league high of 892.

Frank Robinson got the Cleveland managerial job on October 3, replacing Ken Aspromonte. Robinson, a 19-year veteran in the majors, was the only man ever to win Most Valuable Player honors in both the American and National leagues. He signed a reported $180,000 one-year contract with the Indians and announced his intentions to be a player-manager in a bid to collect the 100 hits he needed to reach 3,000 and the 26 home runs he needed to reach 600. The signing of the first black manager came 27 years after Jackie Robinson (no relation to Frank) became the first black player with the Brooklyn Dodgers in 1947.

Al Kaline, the Detroit Tigers' superstar, collected his 3,000th hit in a game at Baltimore on September 24. He was the 12th man to reach that magic number and the first in the American League since Eddie Collins made the grade in 1925.

California Angels' fireballer Nolan Ryan pitched his third career no-hitter on September 28, striking

*Hank Aaron of the Atlanta Braves slugs his 715th home run on April 8 in Atlanta, Ga., breaking Babe Ruth's 39-year record.*

KEN REGAN—CAMERA 5

out 15 and walking 8 in a 4–0 conquest of the Minnesota Twins. Sandy Koufax of the Dodgers held the record for no-hitters with four. Ryan's feat came three weeks after four Rockwell International scientists had clocked his fastball at a record 100.8 mph.

Bob Gibson of the St. Louis Cardinals turned in his 3,000th strikeout on July 17. Only Walter Johnson, with 3,508, had previously reached that milestone. Ironically, Gibson's feat came on the same day that former Cardinals' pitching great Dizzy Dean died. (*See* Obituaries.)

Relief star Mike Marshall of the Dodgers pitched in a record 106 games, including another record 13 straight. Cleveland pitcher Gaylord Perry won 15 games in a row, one shy of the American League record. After Oakland's breach of contract, star pitcher Jim (Catfish) hunter was declared a free agent and at year's end signed a $3.75-million, five-year contract with the New York Yankees.

The Hall of Fame at Cooperstown, N.Y., added six members. Present for induction ceremonies were Mickey Mantle and Edward (Whitey) Ford of the New York Yankees, umpire John (Jocko) Conlan, and James (Cool Papa) Bell, the Ty Cobb of the old Negro Leagues. Sam Thompson and James (Sunny Jim) Bottomley were honored posthumously.

**Pennant Races and World Series**

Three of the four divisional races in the major leagues went down to the wire. In the National League, Pittsburgh won East Division laurels on the final night of the regular season, beating the Cubs, 5–4, in ten innings to oust St. Louis by 1½ games. Los Angeles clinched the West Division on the next-to-last night of the season. Cincinnati finished second, four games out. The Dodgers then went on to defeat the Pirates in the National League play-offs, three games to one.

In the American League, Baltimore beat out the New York Yankees by two games in the East Division in another race that went down to the next-to-last night. Oakland captured the West Division by five games over the surprising Texas Rangers. In the American League play-offs Oakland downed Baltimore three games to one.

The World Series opened at Dodger Stadium in Los Angeles, and the Oakland A's beat the Dodgers 3–2. Jim (Catfish) Hunter, the ace Oakland starter, was summoned in relief to record the final out after Jim Wynn's two-out solo home run and a subsequent single had put the tying run on first. The Dodgers outhit Oakland 11–6, but on a frustrating afternoon stranded 12 runners.

Los Angeles evened the Series in the second game by the same 3–2 score. Mike Marshall came on in relief for the Dodgers after a hit batsman and Reggie Jackson's double had imperiled winning pitcher Don Sutton's 3–0 lead. Joe Rudi singled for two runs, but Marshall then proceeded to pick off Herb Washington, pinch-running for Rudi at first. The Series switched to the Oakland Coliseum for the third game, and the habit-forming trend of 3–2 final scores continued for the third straight time. Oakland won by that now familiar tally to pull in front, two games to one. Hunter and Rollie Fingers were the ringleaders again on a combined seven-hitter.

Pitcher Ken Holtzman was the big star of the fourth game. His bat and arm triggered Oakland to a 5–2 triumph and a commanding Series margin of three games to one. Holtzman homered off loser Andy Messersmith for the game's first run in the third inning and checked the Dodgers on six hits prior to giving way to Fingers in the eighth.

Oakland clinched its third world title, four games to one, by staving off Los Angeles by that customary 3–2 score in the fifth game. A seventh-inning home run by Rudi off reliever Marshall snapped a 2–2 tie. The blast came right after the game had been held up temporarily to clear off debris thrown by unruly Oakland fans. Fingers, who pitched in relief in all four wins by the A's, was voted Most Valuable Player of the Series.

### Individual Stars

The Most Valuable Player awards went to Los Angeles Dodger Steve Garvey in the National League and Texas Ranger Jeff Burroughs in the American. Cy Young pitching awards were given to Jim (Catfish) Hunter of Oakland and Dodger Mike Marshall. Walton Alston of the Dodgers and Billy Martin of the Texas Rangers were named best managers of the year, while Texas Ranger Mike Hargrove and Bake McBride of St. Louis captured rookie-of-the-year honors.

Rod Carew of the Minnesota Twins captured his fourth career American League batting title and third straight by hitting .364 in 1974. Carew had 218 hits. Richie Allen of the Chicago White Sox topped the home run list with 32 despite his retirement before the end of the season. Jeff Burroughs of the Texas Rangers led the league in runs batted in, 118.

Nine American League pitchers won 20 or more games. Hunter of Oakland and Fergie Jenkins of Texas showed the way with 25 each. Four 22-game winners were Mike Cuellar of Baltimore, Luis Tiant of Boston, Steve Busby of Kansas City, and Ryan of California. Gaylord Perry of Cleveland and Jim Kaat of the White Sox posted 21, and Wilbur Wood of the White Sox wound up with 20.

Ralph Garr of the Atlanta Braves collected 214 hits en route to winning the National League batting championship with a .353 average. Philadelphia's Mike Schmidt grabbed home run honors with 36. Johnny Bench of Cincinnati led in runs batted in with 129. The only 20-game winners in the National League were Messersmith of the Dodgers and Phil Niekro of Atlanta.

The National League whipped the American League in the All-Star game for the 11th time in the past 12 outings. The score was 7–2 at Three Rivers Stadium in Pittsburgh, Pa. Steve Garvey of the Dodgers was voted Most Valuable Player for his two hits and fine defensive play. The Cardinals' Reggie Smith hit the only home run of the game. The winning pitcher was Ken Brett of the Pittsburgh Pirates, the loser Luis Tiant of the Boston Red Sox. The Nationals led the series, 26 to 18.

*During the fourth game of the World Series at the Oakland, Calif., Coliseum on October 16, Sal Bando (6) of the Oakland A's mimics the umpire's safe call on teammate Reggie Jackson (9) in a close play at the plate. Oakland went on to beat the Los Angeles Dodgers in that game, 5–2.*

UPI COMPIX

Nine-year-old Amy Dickinson practices sliding during a March workout of a Tenafly, N.J., Little League team. Pressure by feminist groups to open Little League baseball to girls had earlier resulted in the suspension of play by most of New Jersey's 2,000 Little League teams, but a subsequent April ruling of the New Jersey Supreme Court banned sex discrimination by the teams.
EDWARD HAUSNER—THE NEW YORK TIMES

## Amateur Baseball

The University of Southern California won its tenth national championship and fifth straight by beating the University of Miami, 7–3, in the finale of the National Collegiate Athletic Association College World Series at Omaha, Neb. The mighty Taiwanese took their fourth straight Little League World Series championship, defeating Red Bluff, Calif., 12–1, in the championship finals at Williamsport, Pa., in August. Teams from the island Republic of China made a clean sweep of the Little League's three boys' divisions in 1974. In addition to the series crown for boys 11 to 12 years old, they won the Senior series for boys 13 to 15 years old, played at Gary, Ind., and the Big League for boys, ages 16 to 18, played at Fort Lauderdale, Fla. It was the third Senior division title in a row for the Taiwanese when they defeated East Mecklenburg, N.C., 5–1. A 2–0 victory over San Antonio, Tex., produced Taiwan's first win in the Big League.

**BASKETBALL.** North Carolina State won the National Collegiate Athletic Association (NCAA) championship in 1974, defeating the University of California at Los Angeles (UCLA) on the way to the title. But because of the previous record seven consecutive championships for UCLA, 1974 might be remembered as the year UCLA lost as much as the year North Carolina State won.

UCLA, which had set another NCAA record with 75 consecutive wins, added 13 more wins in the season, including an 84–66 victory over North Carolina State during regular season play, before they were defeated by Notre Dame. Later UCLA was upset in consecutive games by Oregon State and by Oregon. It was the first such defeat for

Milwaukee Bucks' Kareem Abdul-Jabbar (33) makes a jump shot over Chicago Bulls' Clifford Ray (14) in the NBA series play-offs.
WIDE WORLD

Utah Stars' Gerald Govan, New York Nets' Wendell Ladner (4), and teammate Julius Erving eye the rebounding ball during the first game of the ABA championship series in New York City on April 30. Erving scored a season high of 47 points in the game to lead the Nets to an 89–85 win.

UPI COMPIX

UCLA since 1966 but did not prevent their winning the Pacific Eight conference championship.

During the season North Carolina State proved it was as good as its 27–0 record in 1973, when it was barred from postseason play for recruiting violations. The season's only loss was to UCLA, and the team was undefeated in its Atlantic Coast conference, which had two other teams, Maryland and North Carolina, in the top ten.

In the NCAA's Eastern regionals, North Carolina State's 6-foot 4-inch David Thompson led the team over Providence 92–78. Thompson was injured in the game against Pittsburgh, but North Carolina State won 100–72. In the Mideast regionals Notre Dame was upset by Michigan 77–68; Marquette then upset Michigan 72–70. In the Midwest regionals Oral Roberts, in only its third year of NCAA play, sprang a surprise by defeating Louisville 96–63. Kansas then defeated Oral Roberts 93–90 in overtime. As expected, UCLA won the Western regionals, but not without difficulty against Dayton, who took the game into three overtimes before losing 111–100. Against San Francisco, however, with sharpshooter Keith Wilkes and 6-foot 11-inch Bill Walton leading the scoring, UCLA won 83–60.

In the NCAA semifinals, when UCLA and North Carolina State played for the second time of the season, North Carolina State defeated UCLA 80–77. In the championship game against Marquette, who had defeated Kansas 64–51, North Carolina State won 76–64. UCLA took third place.

In the first Collegiate Commissioners Association runner-up tournament, Indiana won the championship by defeating Southern California 85–60. Purdue defeated Utah 87–81 to win the National Invitational Tournament. Morgan State beat Southwest Missouri 67–52 to win the NCAA college division championship. West Georgia upset Alcorn State 97–79 to win the championship of the National Association of Intercollegiate Athletics.

### College Stars

North Carolina State's success won many honors in 1974. Wire services, sports publications, and several athletic associations named Norm Sloan coach of the year and David Thompson player of the year. *Sporting News* selected Thompson for its All-American team, putting him at forward with Marvin Barnes of Providence. The team's center was UCLA's Walton, and the guards were Tom Hen-

derson, Hawaii, and Dennis DuVal, Syracuse.

Barnes led in rebounds with 18.7 a game. Leading the scorers was Larry Fogle of Canisius with a 33.4 average. From the foul line, the best shot was Rickey Medlock of Arkansas, who made 87 of 95 free throw attempts. The most accurate shooter from the field was Al Fleming of Arizona, successful in 136 of 204 attempts for a .667 percentage that tied the NCAA record held by UCLA's Lew Alcindor (Kareem Abdul-Jabbar) and Abilene Christian's Kent Martens.

**Professional Basketball**

The Boston Celtics won the championship of the National Basketball Association (NBA) in 1974, a record 12th title for the Celtics but their first since 1969. In the play-offs in the East, Boston won the series with the Buffalo Braves four games to two and defeated the New York Knickerbockers, the defending champions, in five games.

Boston's opponent in the finals, the Milwaukee Bucks, lost just one play-off game in nine in the West against the Los Angeles Lakers and the Chicago Bulls. When Milwaukee met Boston in the finals, it took Boston seven games to win the championship. Kareem Abdul-Jabbar, Milwaukee's 7-foot 2-inch center, scored 35, 36, 26, 34, 37, 34, and 26 points in the seven games of the series and was the key to a defense that kept the normally high-scoring Boston team under 100 in five games.

Abdul-Jabbar, who averaged 27 points and 14.5 rebounds a game, was named the NBA's most valuable player in 1974 for the third time. He was also named center on the NBA all-star team, with John Havlicek of Boston and Spencer Haywood of Seattle at forward and Walt Frazier of New York and Dave Bung of Detroit at guard.

Buffalo's Bob McAdoo became, at age 22, the youngest player ever to win an NBA scoring title. He averaged 30.6 points a game and also topped the league with a .547 field goal percentage, the first leading scorer to do that since Wilt Chamberlain in 1966. Ernie DiGregorio, a guard from Buffalo who was voted rookie of the year, led in assists with 8.2 a game and free throw percentages with .902. The best rebounder was Elvin Hayes of the Capital Bullets with an 18.1 average.

Age and injuries forced long-time NBA stars Oscar Robertson of Milwaukee, Jerry West of Los Angeles, and Willis Reed and Jerry Lucas of New York into retirement. Dave DeBusschere of New York gave up playing to become the general manager of the New York Nets of the American Basketball Association (ABA). Simon P. Gourdine became deputy commissioner of the NBA in 1974, the highest-ranking black in professional sports in the U.S.

New Orleans was awarded an NBA franchise, named the Jazz, in 1974. The possibility of NBA merger with the ABA was killed in 1974 when NBA club owners rejected a modification of players' con-

*Rich Kelly (23), of Stanford, passes the ball away from U.S.S.R.'S Ivan Yedeshko in the September 9 game in Greensboro, N.C., between the U.S.S.R. team and the U.S. college team. The U.S. won a 67–66 victory.*

tracts that would have ended the reserve-option system. Change in the system was thought to be necessary to avoid antitrust action if a merger were to take place.

In the ABA the domination by the Indiana Pacers ended. The New York Nets defeated the Utah Stars four games to one to capture the championship. New York's Julius Erving was named to the ABA all-star team as forward. Kentucky center Artis Gilmore, Indiana forward George McGinnis, Utah guard Jimmy Jones, and Carolina guard Mack Calvin made up the rest of the team. The ABA's rookie of the year was Larry Kenon of New York. One franchise, the Carolina Cougars, moved to St. Louis to become the Spirits. Wilt Chamberlain retired from his $600,000-a-year job as coach of the San Diego Conquistadors. But 6-foot 11-inch Moses Malone, the object of a recruiting war among the country's universities, agreed to a five-year million-dollar contract with the Utah Stars. Malone became the first player in 26 years to move directly from high school to professional basketball.

**BELGIUM.** The tripartite coalition government of Belgium—composed of Socialists, Social Christians, and Liberals under the leadership of Prime Minister Edmond Leburton—collapsed on Jan. 19, 1974, the reason, ostensibly, being Iran's withdrawal from a joint Belgian–Iranian oil refinery project near Liège. At King Baudouin's request, Deputy Prime Minister Léo Tindemans, leader of the Flemish wing of the Social Christians, tried forming a new government but failed. Subsequently, parliament was dissolved, and in the general election held March 10 Tindemans' party won the largest number of Chamber seats.

Serious disagreements on vital national issues, however, resulted in the failure of Prime Minister-designate Tindemans' efforts to form a coalition cabinet of Social Christians and Socialists. But later, on April 19, a marathon 23-hour conference paved the way for a minority government of Social Christians and Liberals. The new cabinet, sworn in on April 25, consisted initially of 13 Social Christian ministers and 6 Liberals, with 3 Social Christian and 3 Liberal secretaries of state.

On July 20, after long debate on the controversial issue of political autonomy for Belgium's French- and Dutch-speaking regions, a law was adopted setting up regional assemblies for French-speaking Wallonia, Dutch-speaking Flanders, and bilingual Brussels. Though Tindemans had pushed for full legislative power for the new assemblies, they would be empowered only to advise the national parliament on regional matters. Another bill was also passed to establish by October 1 three ministerial councils, one for each of Belgium's three regions.

Inflation, worsened by an oil production stoppage occasioned by the outgoing government's freeze on oil prices, became a major concern for the new government. Farmers' dissatisfaction with the agricultural policies of the European Economic Community and the rising cost of oil products and feedstuffs led to a series of demonstrations in September. (*See also* Europe.)

**BIOLOGY.** Developments in experimental biology produced some sensational news stories in 1974. One of these was the announcement of a bacteria-altering method that carried the potential threat of wiping out the human race. Microbiologists at Stanford University and the University of California Medical School reported the discovery of a way to insert "foreign" deoxyribonucleic acid (DNA) from viruses, other bacteria, plants, animals, and human beings into the common intestinal bacterium *Escherichia coli*. They reported successful transplants of DNA snippets from *Staphylococcus* bacteria and from a particular species of toad. It would theoretically be equally possible to transfer snippets of disease-causing viral DNA or antibiotic-resisting genes into rapidly multiplying *E. coli* germs with a resulting *E. coli* "supergerm"—immune to known antibiotics—that could kill millions.

UPI COMPIX

*A mouse and a goldfish thrive in a breathable liquid invented by onlooking Leland Clark. Possible uses of the silicone oil-based liquid include treatment of sickle-cell anemia.*

In a historic action scientists who were involved proposed an embargo on further *E. coli* gene manipulation. With the approval of the National Academy of Sciences (NAS), they published in *Science* (Washington, D.C.), *Nature* (London), and in the NAS *Proceedings* their call for a voluntary ban on certain types of genetic manipulation of bacteria until a 1975 conference could decide how to prevent possible harmful consequences to humanity.

Another highly publicized controversy involved the announcement by a respected British gynecologist, Douglas Bevis of Leeds University, that the world's first "test-tube" babies had been born. Prior to an appearance before the British Medical Association, Bevis presented a surprise press release in which he claimed that techniques of test-tube conception and embryo implantation had led to the births of three apparently healthy, normal babies. The announcement generated a storm of scientific and religious debate. Bevis was criticized by other scientists both for the unprofessional manner of his disclosure and for making claims unsupported by scientific evidence. Although pressed—specifically for the names of those involved in the experiments

—Bevis refused to present supportive evidence or details. Later he declared that he was abandoning the research, disgusted by the publicity his disclosure had generated.

Still another, more public controversy arose over the subject of fetal research, beginning with the prosecution of a Boston physician, Frederic D. Frigoletto, who claimed that his experimental prenatal surgery had saved the lives of numerous babies suffering from Rh incompatibility. Subsequently, on July 12, President Richard M. Nixon signed the U.S. National Research Act, which called for a specific Commission for the Protection of Human Subjects of Biomedical and Behavioral Research. The Department of Health, Education, and Welfare was forbidden to finance research on "living" fetuses before or after induced abortion, and the new commission was to recommend alternatives to fulfill research needs.

It was revealed during the year that William T. Summerlin, a scientist with the prestigious Memorial Sloan-Kettering Cancer Center, New York City, had falsified his research results. The "Summerlin scandal"—and reports of similar incidents in psychological and biochemical research—raised questions about the pressures of life in the scientific community. (*See also* Animals and Wildlife; Flowers; Pets; Psychology; Zoos.)

**BIRTHS.** Among the births that drew public attention in 1974 were:

To Elizabeth McAlister, former nun, and Philip Berrigan, former priest, on April 1, a daughter.

*Sheila and Al Hansen of San Antonio, Tex., admire their identical quadruplet daughters, born in October.*

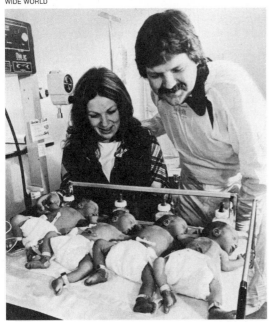

To Annette Funicello, actress and former Mouseketeer, and talent agent Jack Gilardi, on Oct. 23, a son.

To Princess Irene, daughter of Queen Juliana of the Netherlands, and Prince Carlos Hugo de Bourbon-Parma, on June 23, a daughter.

To Carole King, singer-composer ('Tapestry') and Charles Larkey, musician and her bass accompanist, on April 23, a son.

To Meredith MacRae, actress and daughter of singers Gordon and Sheila MacRae, and Greg Mullavey, actor, on Aug. 12, a daughter.

To Rick Nelson, singer and actor, and his wife, Kristin, on Sept. 12, a son.

To Luci Baines Nugent, daughter of the late President Lyndon B. Johnson, and her husband, Patrick, on July 10, a daughter.

To Seiji Ozawa, vibrant conductor of the Boston and San Francisco symphonies, and his wife, Vera, in June, a son.

To Tony Perkins, actor ('Psycho') and scriptwriter ('The Last of Sheila'), and Berinthia (Berry) Berenson, photographer, on Feb. 2, a son.

To Jason Robards, Jr., stage and film actor ('A Thousand Clowns'), and his wife, Lois, on Aug. 22, a son.

To Secretariat, horse racing's 1973 Triple Crown winner, and Leola, an Appaloosa mare, on Nov. 16, a red chestnut colt, the stallion's first offspring.

To singing stars Carly Simon ('You're So Vain') and James Taylor ('Fire and Rain'), on Jan. 7, a daughter.

To Nancy Sinatra, singer, and Hugh Lambert, television director, on May 22, a daughter.

To film stars Natalie Wood and Robert Wagner, on March 9, a daughter.

**BOATS AND BOATING.** The fuel shortages of early 1974 threatened to seriously curtail pleasure boating, and it was suggested that the sport be outlawed for at least one year. The industry responded by showing that the estimated 9½ million boats consumed approximately 800 million gallons of fuel per year—only about 0.5% of the country's total, yet all aspects of the business employed 300 thousand people. The government decided against outlawing boating, and the end of the Arab oil embargo provided sufficient—but much more expensive—fuel for a normal season.

The preliminary trials in August for the America's Cup quickly reduced the field to the new *Courageous* and the dowager queen *Intrepid*, with little to choose between them as far as speed was concerned. The wooden-hulled boat had beaten its newer rival six out of nine times and was a great sentimental favorite throughout the country. In the final days of the selection process the score was 4–4; Robert N. (Bob) Bavier had stepped aside as skipper of *Courageous* in favor of sailmaker Ted Hood; members of the eliminated *Valiant* and *Mariner* crews had been recruited; and the new aluminum

*The U.S. boat* Courageous *easily won four consecutive races over Australia's challenging* Southern Cross *in the best of seven series to defend the America's Cup in September.*

boat was chosen to defend the cup. The final event was an anticlimax, with *Courageous* winning four in a row to defeat the Australian *Southern Cross.* Many observers credited the victory to the hotly contested selection of the U.S. boat as compared to the "no contest" of choosing the challenger.

Sumner A. (Huey) Long's radically designed new *Ondine* set a new record for the Newport, R.I., to Bermuda race of 2 days 19 hours 47 minutes, but was moved back to eighth in fleet on corrected time. The winner was class B *Scaramouche,* owned by Charles E. Kirsch of Sturgis, Mich. Other Great Lakes skippers fared well in the race, and third place went to Carlos A. Corna, a visitor from Argentina. A precedent may have been set when M. J. Fisher's *Osprey* went to the aid of a sinking fiberglass boat that had been holed after striking two coral heads in the middle of a stormy night. After rescuing the crew of B. Temple Brown's *Wimoweh,* the 41-footer completed the Miami, Fla., to Nassau, Bahamas, race and was declared the winner, partly due to the time allowance for the slowing effects of the additional 11 members of her crew, no doubt granted in recognition of the first-rate rescue job.

On Aug. 4, 1974, in Seattle, Wash., George Henley won the American Power Boat Association (APBA) Gold Cup, top prize in American powerboat racing. He drove the unlimited hydro-plane *Pride of Pay 'n Pack,* owned by Dave Heerensperger, to a perfect score of four straight first places. Bob Hering won the Union of International Motorboating OZ class outboard world championship in St. Louis, Mo., using a Mercury motor and Molinari hull. Art (Snapper) Norris won the APBA inboard offshore championship in *Slap Shot.*

**BOLIVIA.** It was a year of political crises for Bolivia, but President Hugo Banzer Suárez stayed in control of the government. Late in January a state of emergency was declared by Banzer as thousands of peasants blocked roads around the agricultural center of Cochabamba. The peasants were protesting a government decree doubling the prices of food staples, and demanded Banzer's resignation. Assisted by tanks and planes, troops reopened the roads, but it was reported that at least 13 persons had been killed. Banzer charged that the uprising was part of an international left-wing plot.

Also provoked by the price increases, a series of brief work stoppages hit the country. In one walkout, about 5,000 tin miners declared their "solidarity with the peasants of Cochabamba." On February 3 the bishops of Bolivia's Roman Catholic church denounced the government's economic policies and criticized Banzer for labeling "as extremist or subversive any dissenting opinion."

On June 5, troops loyal to Banzer put down an attempted coup by a group of young army officers who had demanded Banzer's resignation and general elections. Apparently in response to the increasing pressure, Banzer announced in July that elections would be held in 1975 and that the country would be "constitutionalized." After quashing another military rebellion on November 7, however, Banzer announced a new government of "national reconstruction," banned all political activity until 1980, and indefinitely postponed the elections planned for 1975.

Unlike the country's inflation-ridden domestic economy, the external economic picture appeared bright, with record exports of more than $260 million in 1973. The government also succeeded in attracting major foreign loans, including $35 million for road improvements and $46 million for oil-refining facilities from the Inter-American Development Bank. In return for Bolivian natural gas, Brazil agreed to aid that country's industrial development. (*See also* Latin America.)

**BOWLING.** In 1974, bowling tournaments thrived throughout the U.S., and the men's and as usual the women's national events highlighted the year. Olympia Beer of Omaha, Neb., became the first team from that midwestern state to win the American Bowling Congress (ABC) regular team championship, with a score of 3,186. Gene Krause, Cleveland, Ohio, came within two pins of the all-time record in winning the regular singles with 773. The rest of the regular titles belonged to Chuck Sunseri and Bob Hart, both of Detroit, Mich. In regular doubles, they won with 1,419; Hart won in all-events with 2,087; and their Goebel Beer team took the all-events with 9,574, second highest in history. There were 6,105 teams, 12,904 doubles, 25,-840 singles, and 23,682 all-events entrants in regular and booster competition, plus 33 classic (professional) teams, 164 classic doubles, 272 singles, and 258 all-events entries shooting for part of the record

$781,415 prize fund. Classic division, champions were Ebonite Corp., Hopkinsville, Ky., 3,117; Bob Perry, Paterson, N.J., and Tye Critchlow, Claremont, Calif., in doubles with 1,359; Ed DiTolla, Hackensack, N.J., in singles with 747; and Jim Godman, Vero Beach, Fla., 2,184 in all-events, an all-time ABC tournament record. Elliott's Jesters, Peoria, Ill., hit 2,839 for the booster crown.

The Women's International Bowling Congress (WIBC) major champions in the Houston, Tex., tourney were Kalicak International Construction, Kansas City, Mo., with 2,973; Carol Miller and Janie Leszczynski of Milwaukee, Wis., in open doubles with 1,313; Hall of Famer Shirley Garms of Chicago in open singles with 702; and Judy (Cook) Soutar, Kansas City, Mo., in open all-events with 1,944. Soutar, of the Kalicak team, also won her first Queens crown, topping runner-up Betty Morris 939–705, the 939 the best ever in the title match.

Paul Colwell, Tucson, Ariz., posted a 7–0 match game record and defeated Steve Neff, Sarasota, Fla., 967–905 in four games to capture the coveted ABC Masters crown and $5,620. Colwell averaged a record 234.17 for 28 games.

Increased membership resulted in more ABC and WIBC high-score awards than ever before. Men bowled 1,377 perfect games, up 199 from the record total the preceding year; women added another 19 300's. Significant increases in 800 series by men resulted also, with 202, up 65. Two women reached 800, bringing WIBC's all-time total to four.

American Junior Bowling Congress (AJBC) awards also increased. A record 28 perfect games were bowled, and six rolled 800 series, the highest (859) by Frank Smillie, Cupertino, Calif.

The WIBC Hall of Fame increased by three in 1974. Joan Holm, Chicago, became the sixth Superior Performance electee, while Merle Matthews, Los Angeles, was the 25th bowler to be elected to the Star of Yesteryear category. Meritorious service membership went to the late Georgia Veatch, Chicago, the 11th member so elected. ABC hon-

*Larry Laub of San Francisco, Calif., takes aim on February 16 at New York City's Madison Square Garden, where he took first place in the U.S. Open Bowling Tournament.*
WIDE WORLD

ored Dick Hoover, Akron, Ohio, and the late Claude (Pat) Patterson, St. Louis, Mo., as the 56th and 57th players to make the Hall of Fame. Two were honored posthumously for meritorious service: Mort Luby, Sr., Chicago, and Dennis J. Sweeney, St. Louis.

Earl Anthony, a lefthander from Tacoma, Wash., won the $25,000 first prize in the Professional Bowlers Association (PBA) Tournament of Champions and repeated as PBA National champion, while Larry Laub of San Francisco, Calif., won the U.S. Open. Darrell Miller, Buffalo, N.Y., won the year's top prize of $47,000 for first place in the Petersen Classic in Chicago with 1,698. Ralph Welborn, Mt. Hood College, Portland, Ore., sophomore, won the Association of College Unions-International all-events championship on ABC tournament lanes with 1,987 for ten games. Dale Glockley, a senior from Clarion State College in Pennsylvania, won the National Association of Intercollegiate Athletics all-events crown with a 197 average for 15 games and led Clarion to the team championship over Bryant College, Smithfield, R.I.

## BOXING.

Muhammad Ali regained the world heavyweight championship in 1974, ten years after he had first won the title, by knocking out George Foreman in eight rounds at Kinshasa, Zaire, on October 30. Ali became, at age 32, only the second heavyweight in history to recapture the world title, a feat previously achieved by Floyd Patterson in 1960 at the age of 25.

The fight, the first heavyweight title match to be held in Africa, was heavily promoted, and the nation of Zaire made extensive, elaborate prepara-

### WORLD BOXING CHAMPIONS
As of Dec. 31, 1974

| Division | Boxer |
|---|---|
| Heavyweight | Muhammad Ali, U.S. |
| Light Heavyweight | John Conteh, England |
| | Víctor Galíndez, Argentina * |
| Middleweight | Rodrigo Valdés, Colombia |
| | Carlos Monzón, Argentina * |
| Junior Middleweight | Oscar Alvarado, U.S. |
| Welterweight | José Nápoles, Mexico |
| Junior Welterweight | Perico Fernández, Spain |
| | Antonio Cervantes, Colombia * |
| Lightweight | Gattu (Guts) Ishimatsu, Japan |
| | Roberto Durán, Panama * |
| Junior Lightweight | Kuniaki Shibata, Japan |
| | Ben Villaflor, Philippines * |
| Featherweight | Bobby Chacon, U.S. |
| | Alexis Argüello, Nicaragua * |
| Bantamweight | Rodolfo Martínez, Mexico |
| | Soo Hwan-Hong, South Korea * |
| Flyweight | Shoji Oguma, Japan |
| | Susumu Hanagata, Japan * |

* Recognized as champion by the World Boxing Association.

tions for the match. When Foreman suffered a cut above his right eye in training, the fight was postponed for five weeks. Foreman, who had won the world title in 1973 from Joe Frazier and who was undefeated in 40 professional matches, with 37 knockouts, was the heavy favorite to win. Ali, however, won the match by outfighting Foreman throughout nearly every round, and in the eighth round he floored Foreman. The win was Ali's 45th

*Muhammad Ali aims a right at George Foreman during the world heavyweight title bout October 30 in Kinshasa, Zaire. Ali regained the title with an eighth-round knockout of Foreman.*
UPI COMPIX

LONDON DAILY MAIL / PICTORIAL PARADE

*Britain's John Conteh lands a devastating right to Tom Bogs of Denmark to end the sixth round and retain the European light-heavyweight title on March 12.*

victory in 47 bouts with 31 knockouts. There was controversy after the fight over an alleged fast count on Foreman and the condition of the ring.

The world light-heavyweight championship changed hands in 1974. Bob Foster of the U.S., champion for six years, was held to a draw by Jorge Ahumada of Argentina at Albuquerque, N.M. Foster then declined to defend the title against John Conteh of England. Both the World Boxing Council (WBC) and the World Boxing Association (WBA) declared the title vacant. The WBC recognized Conteh as the new champion when he outpointed Ahumada in London. The WBA nominated Víctor Galíndez of Argentina as the champion. Galíndez later defeated Len Hutchins of the U.S. in Buenos Aires, Argentina, to retain the crown.

In Europe in 1974 Joe Bugner of England continued to dominate the heavyweights, stopping Mario Baruzzi of Italy in nine rounds in Copenha-gen, Denmark. Conteh held the European light-heavyweight title with wins over Tom Bogs of Denmark and Chris Finnegan of England, but relin-quished it after becoming WBC world champion.

**BRAZIL.** Gen. Ernesto Geisel, choice of Bra-zil's ruling military junta, became the nation's presi-dent in 1974. Geisel had been selected as the candi-date of the junta's National Renovation Alliance and was overwhelmingly elected on January 15 by a vote of the electoral college. Token opposition was offered by Ulysses Guimarães, candidate of the Brazilian Democratic Movement (MDB). His sym-bolic "countercampaign" protested the indirect sys-tem of presidential elections and called for the full restoration of democratic rights.

Geisel, who succeeded Gen. Emílio G. Médici, was sworn in as president on March 15 for a five-year term. In his brief inaugural speech he pledged to continue the "development" and "security" poli-cies followed since the overthrow of Brazil's last civilian government in 1964.

The tenth anniversary of the 1964 coup d'état was celebrated on March 31. A few days later the ten-year ban on political activities by pre-junta leaders was lifted. Other gestures of possible reconciliation by Geisel, reputed to be one of the junta's more liberal leaders, included consultations by his aides with leading critics of the government in the Roman Catholic church and in the press. The November 15 elections were termed by many the freest in a decade, with the MDB winning a substantial num-ber of seats in the national congress. But the November disclosure of new reports alleging torture of many persons for political reasons cast doubt on the seeming liberalization of the government.

With some 75% of its oil needs being met by im-ports, Brazil's economy, which had been growing at more than 9% per year for six years, was hard hit by the oil crisis. Even after the Arab oil embargo was lifted, a steep rise in the price of imported oil was leading to a general rise in all prices. To ensure its oil supplies and guard against further price in-creases, the Brazilian government sought to enter into long-term contracts with the Arab oil-produc-ing countries. (*See also* Latin America; Paraguay.)

## BURMA, SOCIALIST REPUBLIC OF THE UNION OF.

In the long-awaited general election held early in 1974, the candidates of Ne Win's Burma Socialist Program party won 99% of the seats in the 451-member unicameral People's Assembly, the few remaining seats going to govern-ment-backed Independents. The election, provided for in the new socialist constitution popularly ap-proved in a referendum in 1973, was the first since Ne Win seized power in 1962. At its first session the Assembly elected, on March 2, a 28-member State Council, which in turn chose Ne Win as the first president. The election of the State Council was widely publicized because the constitution designated it as the supreme authority of the state. Ne Win also made the formal gesture of transferring state authority to the People's Assembly.

There was awareness that the union's future stability would depend on how the new team tackled the economic morass into which Burma had sunk. The people ventilated their wrath in May and June, when what began as food riots against the inadequate rice rations turned into widespread student and worker demonstrations and strikes in factories. At least 22 people were killed before the army and police restored order. Presenting the 1974–75 budget to the Assembly, Deputy Prime Minister U Lwin warned that an all-out effort was needed to rescue the economy. He proposed to limit imports to essential items, reorganize unprofitable state enterprises, and curtail government spending. International agencies—including the World Bank, Asian Development Bank, and International Development Agency—provided aid for projects such as dam construction, improvement of water and power supply, fishing industry development, and irrigation facilities. U Thant, former United Nations secretary general, died on November 25. (*See also* Asia; Obituaries.)

## BURUNDI.
President Michel Micombero, after an April 1974 cabinet reshuffle, maintained control of the government by the Tutsi ethnic minority through the massive suppression of the Hutu (85% of the population). A study of the situation by the Minority Rights Group, London, estimated that more than 3% of the population had been killed.

By May the compensation due to Tanzania for the 1973 border troubles had been paid in full, though the problem of Hutu refugees in Tanzania remained. Landlocked Burundi depended on Tanzanian outlets for about 80% of its exports. A World Bank loan to finance a joint rail link to facilitate Burundi nickel exports was initiated during the year. A National Trade Office was established by presidential order to oversee trade agreements, such as the January economic and technical agreement with Romania, to carry out government commercial policy, and to ensure the country's supply of commodities for state administrations. Burundi signed a trade agreement with the U.S.S.R. in May.

The government improved Burundi's relations with its neighbors Rwanda and Zaire at a June summit meeting. The republic's first constitution was promulgated on July 11, widest power remaining vested in the president as head of the sole political party and supreme commander of the armed forces. The 1974 budget spent heavily on national security, while revenue, mainly from taxation and customs duty, showed the country's continued dependence on foreign aid, largely Belgian. Britain provided $11,750 for fishing development, and the International Development Association granted $5 million for road development under the 1974–78 maintenance and development plan. (*See also* Africa.)

## BUSINESS AND INDUSTRY.
From start to finish, 1974 was a year of crisis for U.S. business. Starting with the oil crunch in the opening months, U.S. industry wrestled with successive crises in materials shortages, capital drought, strikes, record-high interest rates, farm disasters, bank failures, and uncontrollable prices.

It was a year in which a mighty utility—Consolidated Edison Co.—was unable, for the first time in 89 years, to pay its regular dividend; two once great airlines—Pan American World Airways and Trans World Airlines, Inc.—begged for subsidies in order to survive; a former aerospace giant—Grumman Corp.—was willing to accept a capital transfusion from the shah of Iran in order to remain a viable business; the nation's 20th largest commercial bank—Franklin National Bank—was declared insolvent after a series of imprudent international monetary ventures. It was a year, in short, when one could no longer even "be sure" of Westinghouse Electric Corp., as that giant industrial combine found itself awash in operating losses. To boot, the government filed in November the biggest antitrust suit in history, against American Telephone and Telegraph Co., the country's largest privately owned corporation. (*See* Communications.)

The Arab oil embargo early in the year was followed by a quadrupling of oil prices that affected everyone, and the cost of producing everything went through the roof. From February through August the usually slow-moving industrial wholesale price index shot up at the almost unbelievable annual rate of 37%.

Year-to-year gains in wholesale prices of individual commodity groups looked like this: cotton products, 23%; fuels and power, 67%; industrial chemicals, 62%; tires and tubes, 25%; paper, 32%. In no month of 1974 was the increase in industrial wholesale prices—which comprises about two thirds of all wholesale prices—less than 2%. In August the overall wholesale price index (which includes farm commodities) soared a record 3.9%, following a leap almost as big in July.

### The Consumer Price Battle

Consumer price increases naturally reflected the turmoil in industrial markets. By November, the consumer price index (CPI) was 12.1% higher than a year earlier, representing the highest annual inflation rate since 1947.

Hourly earnings, many of them pegged to hikes in the CPI, rose rapidly—at an annual rate of 12% through most of the year—and that, too, inevitably fed the inflationary fires. Total personal income rose only about 10% through the summer, however, and was not enough to keep pace with rising prices.

The greatest blow to consumers came at the supermarket checkout counter as food prices roared upward at a faster rate than anyone had ever seen in the U.S. Spring floods, summer drought, and fall frost clobbered U.S. farmers and had a devastating effect on crop output. Corn production, for example, fell more than 20% below initial forecasts. (Corn is the key feed used in producing meat, milk, and poultry.) The drop in corn yield per acre from 91.4 bushels in 1973 to 77.8 bushels in 1974 was the sharpest year-to-year decline since the 1940's.

Sugar prices spurted late in 1973 and kept climbing through 1974. It was the fourth consecutive year in which world consumption of sugar outpaced production. The result was that the U.S. price of raw sugar jumped about 400% in a year. The increase was reflected in the prices of baked goods, candy bars, soft drinks, canned fruits, and hundreds of other items. Major producers of sugarcane saw their profits triple during 1974.

Consumers paid at least $500 more for 1974 model cars than for their 1973 counterparts, and 1975 models introduced in September carried price tags typically $400 higher than the 1974 models. But the longtime U.S. love affair with the automobile cooled markedly during 1974. First-quarter gasoline shortages sent millions of people back to mass transit or car pools. Later price increases of 40% at the pump caused people to drive much less and, in many cases, to hang onto earlier models that lacked the gas-guzzling "refinements" of the 1974 models. During August and September, however, there was a run on leftover 1974 models as buyers raced to avoid both 1975 price increases and the now-mandated catalytic converter designed to remove pollutants from car exhaust.

All those price increases heaped on 1974 models served only to keep the auto industry's poor profits performance from being horrible. General Motors Corp. (GM), for example, reported an 85% profit plunge in the first quarter, followed by a 62% drop in the company's worst second quarter in 13 years. Other auto company profits followed suit. By year's end layoffs in the industry reached 200,000, and planned first-quarter production was the lowest in 14 years. (*See* Automobiles.)

## Energy Crisis and Raw Materials Shortage

Oil company earnings skyrocketed throughout the first half of 1974, but most of the big companies cited sales of large crude oil inventories purchased earlier at lower prices as the major reason for the gains. As these low-cost inventories were replaced by sharply higher priced crude, and profit margins in European operations narrowed markedly, most industry analysts anticipated profits for the second half of the year that would fall short of the comparable period in 1973.

The energy crunch had a visible impact on gasoline retailing. Faced with fuel shortages, proliferating price increases, and consumer dissatisfaction, nearly 20,000 gas stations closed during 1974, reducing the national count of such outlets by 10%. Major oil producers were charged with putting pressure on independent operators and, in some cases, refusing to renew leases in order to strengthen the position of company-owned-and-operated stations. Federal and state regulators moved to reduce such practices.

Steel mills ran at their effective capacity through most of 1974 but still were unable to keep pace with demand. Steel for construction, auto production, containers, and countless other uses was in short supply, and stretched-out delivery dates curtailed production of many products. In August, Chrysler Corp. bought a Detroit company simply to obtain for its own use the large quantity of sheet steel stored in that company's warehouse.

Shortages of structural steel were only partially responsible for so many companies cutting back their capital spending plans during 1974. Cash shortages plagued almost every company, and no one wanted to borrow with the prime rate at 12%. Earlier methods of raising capital—through sales of stock or corporate debt—became either impossible or unattractive. So, despite high demand and the obvious need for greater capacity, many com-

panies were unwilling or unable to pay the price.

Xerox Corp. shelved "indefinitely" its plans for a new corporate headquarters originally slated to have begun construction in August. GM postponed plans to build a 3.2-million-square-foot plant in Oklahoma City, Okla., and deferred conversion of a 1.2-million-square-foot plant in Memphis, Tenn., purchased earlier from RCA Corp. (At the same time, however, GM announced plans for a $100-million assembly plant in Saudi Arabia, where it would build 8,000 cars a year for oil-rich Arabs.) Goodyear Tire and Rubber Co. cut its 1974 capital spending by 10%. Ford Motor Co. revealed that it would cut about $230 million out of its capital spending plans for 1975 because of falling profits and rising costs. At year's end auto plant shutdowns or closings had become daily headlines.

The drop in housing starts that began in 1973 worsened in 1974. By year-end the housing industry was in big trouble, with no improvement even hoped for earlier than mid-1975. The drop in starts was reflected quickly in sales of building materials, household appliances, and furnishings. By late summer, output of construction products was running more than 5% below 1973, and production of consumer durables was down about 1.5%. Both were expected to drop further later in the year.

Overall industrial production flattened out in July and August and headed downward. August strikes in coal and iron mines, copper-fabricating plants, telephone equipment factories, and other industries were the largest contributing factor, but government economists said production probably would have shown a modest decline even without strikes.

One industry running full out throughout the year was machine tools—a small but barometric industry whose new orders generally mirrored the expansion plans of the metalworking industries. During 1974, however, much of its order volume came from companies either seeking to increase productivity as a cost-cutting measure or rushing to beat greater price increases they knew had to come. As a result, some tool builders had order backlogs stretching out as long as two years.

The most depressed industry in the U.S. probably was the securities business. Stock prices rallied briefly with the ending of the oil embargo and price controls, the renewal of confidence that followed the succession of U.S. President Gerald R. Ford, and the fall dip in the prime interest rate; but the bad news so outweighed the good that stock prices continued to tumble through the year. By the fourth quarter, the Dow-Jones index of 30 industrial stocks had broken through the 600 floor, only a few years after penetrating the magic 1000 level in better days. Trading volume was down. Brokerage house profits dwindled and disappeared. New York Stock Exchange firms, alone, posted $45.9 million in losses in the first half. More than 100 firms were expected to merge or go out of business by the end of 1974. The price of a seat on the New York Stock Exchange fell to $65,000, little more than one tenth of the going price a few years earlier.

Ironically, while U.S. investors' disenchantment with the securities market grew, foreign investors' interest grew markedly. Foreign investments in U.S. securities soared to almost $90 billion during 1973, with another $17.7 billion in direct investments. The influx of foreign capital increased sharply during 1974 as money from oil-rich Arab countries poured into the U.S., thereby coining a new word: petrodollars. The First National City Bank of New York estimated that oil-exporting nations would generate more than $100 billion in oil revenues in 1974, compared with only $30 billion in 1973; about $65 billion of that was available for investment. By September, the U.S. Treasury Department was estimating that some $7 billion in petrodollars had already been invested in the U.S. during 1974, including roughly $4 billion in various types of U.S. government securities.

Early in the year, the federal government removed the restrictions on foreign investment by Americans, some of which had been imposed 11 years earlier in an effort to check the imbalance in U.S. international payments. At the time, U.S. Treasury spokesmen hoped the relaxation would encourage more foreign investment in this country. By year-end, however, some economists had begun to worry about a foreign takeover of U.S. industry. (*See also* Banks; Employment; Fuel and Power; Stocks and Bonds; Transportation; World Trade.)

*Sewing machines remain idle in a New York City garment factory when workers joined the June strike by about 110,000 members of the Amalgamated Clothing Workers of America, the union's first major work stoppage in 53 years.*
PAUL HOSEFROS—THE NEW YORK TIMES

*A weary Cambodian government soldier takes a break from patrol duty in May along Highway 9 north of Phnom Penh.*

UPI COMPIX

**CAMBODIA.** The government of President Lon Nol hung on for another year as the four-year-old Cambodian civil war raged on. Backed by increasing supplies of U.S. arms, government troops beat back Communist Khmer Rouge attacks on the capital city of Phnom Penh, where in January and February some of the war's heaviest bombardments killed more than 300 persons. Oudong, the old royal capital, was lost to the Khmer Rouge in March, but it was retaken in July, many of its historic temples and monuments almost totally destroyed. U.S. aircraft were used to provide government forces with military intelligence information.

Little was changed strategically in Cambodia during the year. The government continued following a defensive strategy of holding the vital enclaves of Phnom Penh, the provincial capitals, and several key highways and waterways. The Khmer Rouge tightened its hold on the countryside but failed to mount an all-out offensive on the capital.

Meanwhile, there was growing popular unrest in Phnom Penh as living costs soared and official corruption grew more widespread. Antigovernment student demonstrations, growing out of a long teachers' strike for higher wages, jarred the capital early in the year. In June students protesting emergency laws prohibiting public meetings occupied a high school and took as hostages Cambodia's edu-

cation minister and his assistant who were killed when police stormed the school.

In the menacing disquiet that followed, Premier Long Boret's cabinet disintegrated as opposition Republican party members resigned. President Lon Nol then resorted to his familiar crisis technique of reshuffling cabinet posts. Long Boret was retained as prime minister, with a cabinet consisting of seven members of Lon Nol's Social Republican party, seven independents, and two from the military.

After the recapture of Oudong in July, Lon Nol proposed peace talks with the rebel forces and their leader, Prince Norodom Sihanouk, who had been ousted as Cambodia's chief in 1970. The offer followed talks between government leaders and U.S. Ambassador John Gunther Dean and differed from the one made in 1973 that insisted first on a ceasefire. From his exile in Peking, China, however, Sihanouk said there could be no negotiations with the "traitors." Late in August Sihanouk appealed to U.S. President Gerald Ford for an end to U.S. aid to Lon Nol. Predicting a military victory for his forces "in one or two years," he said that he would then be satisfied as a figurehead leader, with actual running of the country left to Communist leader Khieu Samphan. A November effort in the United Nations to oust the Lon Nol delegates and seat Sihanouk's failed narrowly. (*See also* Asia.)

RENAULT—MC CLATCHY NEWSPAPERS, CALIF./ROTHCO

*"We're full. Did you make reservations?"*

**CAMPING.** Gasoline, the economy, and legislation were the big news makers in the realm of camping in 1974. Perhaps the biggest news out of Washington, D.C., was the action taken by Congress to reinstate camping fees in federal campgrounds, thus reversing the action taken in 1973 that made camping free in all federal areas. The new bill went into effect on June 22, just as the camping season was getting under way. The action restored fees in approximately 2,000 of the 5,000 Forest Service campgrounds and in 280 campgrounds operated by various agencies of the Department of the Interior. It was estimated that the 1973 action resulted in a revenue loss of up to $7 million. The action taken by Congress was lauded by operators of private campgrounds who had charged "unfair practice" when the fees had been discontinued.

In 1974 the National Park Service increased from 6 to 21 the number of National Parks where campers could reserve campsites in advance. The heart of the system was a computerized center using a toll-free telephone number. Toward the end of the summer season the National Park Service terminated the service because it was plagued with problems of overloaded telephone circuits. Although the system was advertised as an "instantaneous" reservation service, it was reported that on just one day a total of 29,464 persons called to make reservations, and 25,000 of them got only a busy signal. It was not known if the Park Service would make another attempt at a reservation system in 1975.

During the height of the fuel crisis early in 1974, some dire predictions were made concerning vacation camping for the 1974 season. In retrospect, Sunday gas station closings and spiraling gasoline prices had little effect on vacation camping. State parks, however, reported a larger than usual use by in-state residents, coupled with longer stays. It appeared that campers during the summer traveled shorter distances and tended to stay at one place rather than tour about.

The question was again raised in popular vacation states concerning the relationship between the cost of park facilities and the use made of them by the people of the state who paid taxes. In some states, use of state parks by out-of-state tourists was greater than that by residents of the state. Park officials in Idaho attempted to lure greater use by state residents by offering discount camping rates. To encourage new campers, the state also offered, for an additional fee, a 9-foot × 12-foot tent set up on the site plus a cookstove, utensils, two cots, mattresses, and a kerosene lantern.

Condominium camping continued its slow but steady development in 1974, primarily by large franchises. Most continued to reserve some of the sites for the conventional rentals. Prices varied considerably, depending upon size and location. On April 2 the National Committee on Camping Consumers, a cooperative effort of the five largest camping clubs, was formed. The committee stated that "We are concerned conservationists, dedicated to the esthetics of natural wilderness areas and the education of our constituent camping members to the preservation and wise use of such areas."

Children's summer camps felt the economic crisis even more than vacation family camping. Enrollments in camps across the country were down as parents felt they simply could not afford the cost of sending their children to camp even though camps did their best to hold down their fees in the face of rapidly increasing costs. (*See also* National Park Service.)

**CANADA.** As the only industrialized Western country that produces more oil than it consumes, Canada managed to make economic gains in a year when most other countries were slipping backward. The value of the Canadian dollar hit a 14-year high —a reflection of the basic strength of the economy —but inflation was also high, running at about 11%. The worst threat to Canada's economic growth in 1974 was the possibility that recession or depression elsewhere would reduce the foreign market for Canadian products.

In the wake of the worldwide fuel crisis, Ottawa raised the export tax on crude oil to $6.40 per barrel in order to compensate for the higher price being paid for imported oil in eastern Canada. It was calculated that Canada would earn $6 million per day as a result of increases in the price of oil sold to the United States. In November, however, the government revealed a long-range national energy program that called for drastic reductions in U.S. oil exports beginning Jan. 1, 1975, and culminating in a complete termination of such exports by 1982. Later, in talks with U.S. President Gerald R. Ford, Trudeau stood firm on his government's policy.

Trudeau introduced in May the Liberal minority government's $23.95-billion budget for 1974–75,

*Canadian Prime Minister Pierre Trudeau speaks from the platform of his campaign train in Port Hawksbury, N.S., on May 28 while Nova Scotia Premier Gerald Regan and Margaret Trudeau look on. Trudeau's Liberal party won an easy victory in the July 8 election, gaining 32 seats for a total 141 of the 264 seats in the House of Commons.*

CANADIAN PRESS

calling for stiff corporate taxes, particularly in the mineral and petroleum industries, as a chief means of combating inflation. The response in the House of Commons was a vote of no confidence backed by two opposition parties, the Progressive Conservatives and the New Democratic party (NDP). Trudeau's Liberal party was defeated 137 to 123, thus forcing a new national election, which was scheduled for July 8.

Inflation was the main issue of the 1974 campaign, with Progressive Conservative leader Robert Stanfield asking for "a mandate to put our economy back in order" and proposing a system of wage and price controls. The highly emotional language issue and the associated problem of minority rights were also subjects of concern to voters. Despite most predictions, Trudeau's Liberal party won a substantial victory. Liberals gained 32 seats, giving them a total of 141 of the 264 seats in the House of Commons; the Conservatives lost 12 seats and the NDP—which had precipitated the election—fell from 31 seats to 16. With his new majority Trudeau was expected to have at least five more years in office. Shortly after the election, Stanfield, 60, announced he was retiring from the post of Conservative party head. The failure of the Conservatives was blamed largely on his advocacy of economic controls.

Following India's test of an atomic device, Canadian Foreign Minister Mitchell Sharp announced the suspension of nuclear aid to India. Later, similar aid to Taiwan was also withdrawn,

apparently in consideration of Canadian relations with the People's Republic of China. At the same time, Canadian and British nuclear agencies drafted an agreement for Anglo-Canadian cooperation.

A Canadian-Soviet dispute over fishing rights erupted in June, when Newfoundland's fisheries minister accused the Soviets of overfishing off the province's coast. The Soviets had previously agreed to limit their catch but were found to be substantially exceeding the restrictions. Norwegian ships were also found to be violating fishing agreements.

Roland Michener, governor-general of Canada for nearly seven years, was succeeded in January by Jules Léger, a French-Canadian career diplomat.

### The Cabinet

Through the unconventional "firing" of five ministers, Prime Minister Trudeau opened the way to 12 changes in the Canadian Cabinet after his 1974 election victory. No minister had been demoted by Trudeau in this manner during his first six years in office, and there were few historical precedents for such action. But Trudeau had little choice if he was to change his team significantly in preparing to exercise a strong new mandate following the election, and only one Cabinet member—Environment Minister Jack Davis—had been defeated. Denied the traditional openings created by defeat or retirement, Trudeau was nevertheless reluctant to use another maneuver for dropping unwanted colleagues—an appointment to the Canadian Senate.

Instead, the prime minister simply demoted to the back benches of the House of Commons Consumer and Corporate Affairs Minister Herbert Gray; Robert Stanbury, revenue minister; Stanley Haidasz, minister of state for multiculturalism; and

Jean-Eudes Dubé, public works minister. Trudeau defended his moves publicly by saying that he wanted to begin a new pattern of "flexibility" that would permit a "rotation" of MP's in and out of Cabinet. However, most observers concluded that lackluster or trouble-prone performances accounted for the demotions.

Two ministers stepped down from positions of prestige or power to less impressive posts. Mitchell Sharp, once a candidate against Trudeau for the leadership of the Liberal party, left the prestigious External Affairs portfolio to become privy council president, which is the title of the government leader in the House of Commons. Sharp traded with Allan MacEachen, who was expected to pursue a more active foreign policy role for Canada. Another veteran, Charles Drury, left the presidency of the treasury board to take on the double portfolio of public works and science and technology. Jean Chrétien, 41, a French-speaking minister enjoying a steady rise in influence, succeeded Drury as the government's watchdog on spending and management.

Four men entered the Cabinet for the first time. Senator Ray Perrault, who headed the Liberals' successful July 8 campaign in the province of British Columbia, was made leader of the government in the Senate. Barnett Danson, plastics manufacturer and former parliamentary secretary to Trudeau, became minister of state for urban affairs, in charge of the government's housing programs. Judd Buchanan took over Chrétien's former job as minister of Indian affairs and northern development, having served previously as parliamentary secretary to Chrétien. Romeo LeBlanc, once Trudeau's press secretary, was made minister of state (fisheries).

**The Economy**

Canada experienced a fourth consecutive year of substantial growth in 1974, but the rate of expansion dropped sharply as a result of slumping markets for exports, strikes and shortages across the country, and the distorting impact of inflation. The real growth of output in the economy—after eliminating price increases—slipped below 5%. It had been 5.6% in 1971, 5.8% in 1972, and 7.1% in 1973. Capacity restraints in the steel industry and in other key sectors became increasingly acute, limiting the potential of the economy as a whole for further major increases in production. Capacity utilization of the nation's productive facilities—an important measure of the tempo of the economy—inched up to 96% early in the year.

Signs of the abrupt weakening at mid-year were a flattening of construction expenditures by business and industry, together with a 25% drop in the rate of housing starts between the first and second quarters. In part, the weakness in construction reflected a shortage of mortgage money and unprecedented mortgage rates in the area of 12%. But it was also a result of widespread strikes among construction workers, particularly in Quebec and British Columbia, which accounted in large part for a record of 5.2 million man-days of work lost during the first half of the year.

Unemployment in Canada had passed the 6% level in 1970—reaching 6.9% in 1972—and preoccupied public policy until early 1973, when it dipped again below 6%. In 1974, it crept below 5% at midyear, but the hesitation in growth and the secondary effects of strikes were pushing unemployment back toward 6% at year-end.

The remarkable growth in both the labor force and new jobs in the Canadian economy continued during the year at rates matched by few other industrialized countries in the world. The broad measures of labor income showed that increases in the paychecks of workers were starting to fall behind the rate of inflation during 1974, signaling a wave of labor unrest and launching a series of catch-up wage settlements that threatened to exert serious pressure on prices. From an annual increase in base rates of wage settlements averaging 9.2% in 1972, the level went to 11.3% in 1973, and to 15.5% in the second quarter of 1974. Another effect of inflation was the substantial increase in the number of cost-of-living adjustment clauses in recently negotiated contracts. Major strikes disrupted air and ship traffic and virtually paralyzed mail service.

Canada continued to be a strong buyer from its trading partners, but the slowdown in the economies of the United States, Japan, and Britain caused Canadian exports to fall off slightly. Nevertheless, Trade Minister Alastair Gillespie announced in October that exports had risen 26% during 1974, despite the weakening of foreign economies. A balance of payments deficit of $1 billion was in prospect for the year, more than double that of 1973. The annual rate of increase in Canada's consumer price index passed the 10% level during the year, with food prices running at a rate of 15% to 20%.

No other industrialized nation was as well protected from the fourfold increase in oil prices that confronted the world in 1974. Although eastern Canada is a substantial importer of crude oil from Venezuela and other countries, Canada has exported about the same amount of oil to the United States by pipeline from its own rich basins in the west. The federal government chose to deal with this situation by negotiating with provincial governments a wellhead price for Canadian crude oil of $6.50 per barrel, far below the international price. On exports to the U.S., the federal government collected an export tax yielding about $1.5 billion annually, and this revenue was used to reduce prices paid by eastern consumers for imported oil. As a result, the direct impact of the world explosion in oil prices was minimal in Canada, although there were many secondary effects as higher fuel costs around the world resulted in sharp price increases for goods imported by Canada. In September, the National Energy Board (NEB) suggested that the oil tax

VANCOUVER SUN

*One of 500 striking grainhandlers in Vancouver, B.C., combines sanding with September picketing of Vancouver's Burrard Terminal.*

structure be revised in favor of a multi-tier system which would lower export taxes on certain oils in order to make the products more competitive. However, the subsequent decision to curtail oil exports to the U.S. posed a threat of adverse effects on future U.S.-Canadian trade relations.

Following the U.S. lead, stock and bond markets slumped badly and major corporations were beginning to face difficulty in meeting their expansion plans, despite year-over-year increases in profits averaging 35%–40%. Investor confidence waned, and even with unprecedentedly high interest rates, few savers were realizing a net gain in income on their investments after accounting for inflation and taxes.

Some tax measures were proposed by the federal government to ease tax burdens on savings, but defeat of the federal budget of May 6 in a House of Commons vote delayed implementation of the proposals. Other provisions of the defeated May

*Demonstrators on Parliament Hill in Ottawa, Ont., take a break from their September 30 protest in support of the simultaneous protest by native Indians against construction of the James Bay hydroelectric project in Quebec.*

CANADIAN PRESS

budget called for increasing corporate taxes, ending sales tax on such items as clothing and footwear, and levying a special excise tax on luxury automobiles, powerboats, and private aircraft. On September 30, the government introduced a new legislative program to control inflation, expand production, and regulate foreign business and investments.

### The Provinces

The escalation of oil prices by producing nations late in 1973 created enormous problems for countries around the world in 1974, but it was a bonanza for Canada's oil-rich province of Alberta. Alberta began planning to use increased petroleum revenues to develop a broadly based economy and to improve the quality of life of its 1.7 million citizens.

Alberta produces 85% of Canada's conventional oil and 80% of its natural gas; within its borders lies the world's largest future source of petroleum, the Alberta oil sands. The sands contain 900 billion barrels of crude bitumen, which could yield a volume of synthetic crude oil equal to the known oil reserves of the entire Middle East. Hundreds of millions of dollars will be required for research and development to find methods to extract the oil from the sands economically. The magnitude of this impending investment, with the economic, social, and environmental challenges it will present, posed critical policy questions for the provincial government of Premier Peter Lougheed.

Early in 1974, Lougheed accepted a national agreement to keep the wellhead price of oil for consumption within Canada at $6.50 a barrel, compared with an international price exceeding $10. But even at this level, Alberta government revenues from royalties and other charges jumped by almost $1 billion annually. At current rates of production, Alberta stood to exhaust its existing conventional sources of crude oil in 13 years. Lougheed resolved publicly to use this precious time for wise investment of the additional government revenues, in part to secure development of the oil sands and in part to broaden the Alberta economy from its narrow base of petroleum, natural gas, and grain and dairy farming. He introduced special legislation controlling the timing of major developments within the province, and entered a further negotiation with the federal government over the sharing of corporation taxes on petroleum company profits.

In one form or another, almost all of Canada's ten provinces experienced the common issue of claims from the country's 295,000 native Indians. In 1974, Indian leaders were assisted with their legal costs by the federal government in demanding payment for lands given over to the multibillion-dollar hydroelectric power development in the James Bay area of Northern Quebec. The Indian-Eskimo lawsuit against the James Bay Energy Corporation had been headed for the Supreme Court, but in November an accord was reached between Indian chiefs and representatives of local and provincial governments. The Indians were granted a $150-million settlement, plus exclusive hunting, fishing, and trapping rights in a 25,000-square-mile area. The agreement also provided that in any future development of the area, a minimum of 25% of revenues would go to the local people. It was regarded as an important precedent for the settlement of similar claims against mineral developments throughout northern Canada.

Indian frustrations continued to produce occasional violence; in summer 1974 attention focused on developments in Ontario, where militant Indian leaders formed a "Warriors Society" within the Ojibwa tribe and seized Acininabe Park in the resort town of Kenora. The young Indians defended the park at gunpoint for weeks, after the earlier American model of Wounded Knee, claiming the land had been taken away from them illegally in 1959. They demanded better housing, health services, and schooling, new Indian-operated industries, and reforms of the judicial system. On September 30, when the government met in Ottawa to consider Prime Minister Trudeau's new legislative program, more than 200 Indians demonstrated outside the Parliament building. Earlier they had occupied an empty government building.

In the French-speaking province of Quebec, a government move to legislate the use of that language was the overwhelming public issue of 1974. The Liberal administration of Premier Robert Bourassa used its huge majority in the legislature to force through a bill declaring the supremacy of French as the only "official" language of the province. The legislation decreed French to be the ordinary language of communication in the government and its agencies and the language of schooling for all children except those who already speak English. (Under the previous bilingual system, immigrants settling in Montreal had been choosing English-speaking schools over French at a rate of eight to one.) Public utilities and professional bodies were obliged to use French in communication with the government and public, and business firms to have a French capability. This capability was made sub-

ject to a government test, and it was a condition of receiving government grants or contracts.

The language bill was fought unsuccessfully by the substantial English-speaking minority in Quebec, and many spokesmen of both cultures expressed fears that businesses would either leave the province or carry out future expansions in English-speaking provinces. (*See also* Trudeau.)

**CHEMISTRY.** Several firsts in chemistry marked the year 1974. A novel kind of chemical compound was synthesized. A new vitamin was added to the list of food supplements. Minerals in the asteroid belt between Mars and Jupiter were identified. Processes were developed for converting cellulose wastes to sugar and for using chemicals to fracture coal. And a new chemical element, number 106, was identified.

The novel compound synthesized contains a xenon-nitrogen bond. Darryl D. DesMarteau of Kansas State University synthesized the compound fluoroxenonimidobis(sulfuryl fluoride), which has the formula $FXeN(SO_2F)_2$. The white crystalline

A new phosphor powder that glows under ultraviolet light was put into use early in the year in Canadian post offices to trigger machines that hourly cancel 25,000 letters.

COURTESY, GENERAL ELECTRIC RESEARCH AND DEVELOPMENT CENTER

solid slowly decomposes to form xenon, xenon difluoride, and tetrakis(fluorosulfuryl)hydrazine.

Thomas B. McCord and Michael J. Gaffey of Massachusetts Institute of Technology identified minerals in the asteroid belt by comparing visible and near-infrared reflectivities of asteroids in space with reflectivities of meteorites on Earth. Most common in asteroids is carbonaceous chondrite, with enstatite (magnesium silicate) and nickel-iron metals present.

Two separate teams of scientists—one U.S., one Soviet—announced the synthesis of a new chemical element, number 106, which had a half-life of only $\frac{9}{10}$ of one second. The joint discovery precipitated the usual controversy over which country deserved the credit and, therefore, the right to bestow a name upon the new element.

At the U.S. Army's research laboratories in Natick, Mass., development of a process to convert cellulose to sugar seemed to point to conversion of newspapers and wood pulp into foodstuffs or raw materials for the chemical industry. The process depends on the activity of enzymes produced by the fungus *Trichoderma viride*.

Vitamin Q was discovered by Armand J. Quick of the Medical College of Wisconsin in Milwaukee. He obtained a phospholipid, extracted from soybeans, which is essential to proper functioning of the blood clotting mechanism.

Investigators at Syracuse University Research Corporation developed a process for fracturing coal with low molecular weight compounds such as liquid ammonia and methanol, which penetrate the coal faults. Blood flow in the eye's choroid—the section that supports the retinal metabolic functions—can be viewed by a new technique combining indocyanine green dye with infrared radiation. The technique was developed at Johns Hopkins Applied Physics Laboratory in Baltimore, Md.

Many scientists consider Aug. 1, 1774, a red-letter day in experimental chemistry. On that day Joseph Priestley produced oxygen by decomposing mercuric oxide with sunlight and a simple lens. This experiment led to the rise of modern chemistry. The bicentennial was celebrated at Priestley's Northumberland, Pa., home. (*See also* Awards and Prizes; Consumer Affairs; Earth Sciences; Environment; Medicine.)

**CHESS.** In 1974 the world chess champion, Bobby Fischer of the U.S., did not play in public. In June, during the International Chess Federation (FIDE) congress, Fischer sent a telegram resigning his title in a dispute over rules. FIDE asked him to reconsider and to play the match for the championship in 1975. Fischer gave no answer, and it seemed doubtful that he would defend the title. Preparations went on, nevertheless, and the U.S.S.R.'s Anatoly Karpov won a lengthy 24-game match to become the challenger for the title.

At the 21st Olympiad of chess at Nice, France, the Soviet Union had little difficulty retaining the World Team Championship. Yugoslavia was second, and the U.S. third. The U.S.S.R. was also first in the World Students Team Championship tournament at Thornaby, England. In the World Cadet Championship, for players under 16 years of age, at Pont-Sainte-Maxence, France, A. J. Mestel from England won first place. The first prize at the second World Open Tournament in New York City was won by Bent Larsen of Denmark. The 23d U.S. Championship at Chicago was won by Walter Browne of the U.S. The World Junior Championship at Manila, Philippines, was won by Tony Miles of England.

A Soviet computer beat a U.S. computer in a chess match in 1974. Scientists said that computers had reached a rating of 1750 in chess, as compared with a rating of 2810 for Bobby Fischer, and that there was no chance of computers beating humans at chess in the near future. The sponsor of the tournament claimed that using computers to play chess would help scientists understand how the human mind worked and how humans could use computers. The next International Chess Tournament to be played by computer was planned for 1977.

*Anatoly Karpov paces while waiting for Viktor Korchnoi's move in a September round of the World Chess Challengers match in Moscow.*
WIDE WORLD

ALAIN KELLER—SYGMA

*Chile's leaders, including President Gen. Augusto Pinochet Ugarte, attend mass in Santiago on September 11, the first anniversary of the Chilean military coup.*

**CHILE.** The right-wing military junta that in September 1973 overthrew Marxist President Salvador Allende Gossens dominated Chilean life in 1974. Congress remained dissolved; the country lived under martial law. Strikes and protests, and even informal criticism, were forbidden. Censorship and a curfew continued, although foreign correspondents were less severely restricted and the curfew hours were eased. Critics charged the junta with complete suppression of civil liberties and with political arrests, torture, and executions.

The Chilean officers, led by President Gen. Augusto Pinochet Ugarte, allowed absolutely no Marxist activity, although some of the Allende officials were released and sent into exile. Some political refugees were allowed to leave Chile, although they often had difficulty finding asylum. Several military officers and civilians sympathetic to Allende were put on trial; others remained in prison.

The traditional non-Marxist parties were mostly inactive. The Christian Democratic party, Chile's largest, as well as lawyers, judges, and the clergy, did dare, however, to criticize the government's policies. Some observers said that no more than 20% of the population supported the junta at the end of the year.

Other countries also began to take a more critical attitude toward the military government. The U.S. Congress voted to cut off all military aid to Chile, Great Britain canceled all aid and military agreements, and Mexico cut diplomatic ties.

It became apparent in 1974 that the military leadership had no intention of handing control of the nation back to the electorate in the near future but that it would retain control for as many years as it deemed necessary to restore political stability.

It became known in 1974 that the U.S. Central Intelligence Agency (CIA), with the approval of Henry A. Kissinger, then the presidential adviser on national security, had carried out an $8-million clandestine campaign against Allende by making payments to anti-Allende politicians and newspapers and radio stations. There was no evidence that the CIA or Kissinger had had any role in the revolution itself. Furthermore, it was revealed that because of pressure from the U.S., Chile had received almost no aid from international lending groups. Later it was learned that money from Latin American business interests had also funded the attempt to undermine Allende's government.

In spite of austerity programs by the government, Chile in 1974 still had to contend with a horrifying rate of inflation, estimated as high as 300%, although far below the rate under Allende. Unemployment in 1974 reached 12%. Although Chile imported much more food than usual during the year, food shortages were severe.

Chile settled claims by copper companies expropriated by Allende and initiated compensatory negotiations with the International Telephone & Telegraph Corp. A new foreign investment law was decreed to lure investors to Chile. Guaranteeing remittance of profits and insuring that investments would not be jeopardized by internal political changes, the government hoped to attract enough foreign investment to stimulate its slow economy. The policy seemed to work, for several nations, including the U.S., indicated they were willing to invest in Chilean copper mines, although low copper prices later caused the government to shut down a major mine. Nevertheless, renewed faith in the political order helped the junta obtain foreign credit, something that Allende had found difficult. (*See also* Intelligence Operations; Latin America.)

**CHINA.** Early in 1974 China appeared to be renewing its traumatic Cultural Revolution of the 1960's. Under the initiative of Communist Party Chairman Mao Tse-tung, the new movement was ostensibly aimed at the ancient Chinese philosopher Confucius and his "counterrevolutionary" teachings of caution and restraint. Lin Piao, Mao's heir apparent who died in 1971 after an unsuccessful attempt to seize power, was accused of being a "disciple" of Confucius. The frenzy of the Cultural Revolution was never reached, however, and the anti-Lin-Confucius movement later subsided.

The initial movement seemed hostile to Premier Chou En-lai and his moderate leadership, but Chou typically diverted the attack onto Lin Piao and placed the movement under the firm control of the Communist party. The mass rallies and criticism sessions were the largest since the Cultural Revolution, and countless wall posters appeared airing grievances and criticizing leaders.

A major move to strengthen central civilian control over the military was announced at the beginning of the year. Commanders in 8 of China's 11 military regions were reshuffled. Among them were two powerful Communist party Politburo members, Hsu Shih-yu and Chen Hsi-lien, who were transferred from commands they had held for many years. Another Politburo member, Li Teh-sheng, also was shifted. Significantly, the three untouched military commanders were the only ones appointed recently—since the death of Lin Piao.

Teng Hsiao-ping, newly restored to the Politburo and named deputy premier after years of obscurity, began acting in place of Chou En-lai at many official functions in May. At first it was speculated that Chou had suffered a political setback. But in July it was officially revealed that the 76-year-old premier had been hospitalized with a heart ailment.

Chou made his first major public appearance in two months on September 30 as host at an official reception commemorating the 25th anniversary of the founding of the People's Republic of China. In a speech to about 5,000 guests Chou backed the anti-Lin-Confucius movement, saying that China would "advance bravely along Chairman Mao's revolutionary line." There were reports that the 80-year-old Mao had suffered a stroke in September, but Danish Prime Minister Poul Hartling, who met with Mao on October 20, found him in good health.

Relations with the Soviet Union were hostile during the year as territorial disputes remained unresolved and rivalry for leadership in the Communist world continued. In January five Soviet citizens, including a senior diplomat, were expelled from China on charges of espionage. A Chinese diplomat, accused of spying, was expelled from the Soviet Union. In March the Chinese captured a Soviet military helicopter that had strayed over the

WIDE WORLD

*Named to replace David Bruce as U.S. envoy to Peking, George Bush (left) talks with Ambassador Huang Chen, head of China's liaison office in Washington, D.C., prior to his October 17 departure for Peking.*

*Crowds gather in July in Peking to study wall posters denouncing high party officials accused of reactionary tactics.*

border and charged that it had been on a spy mission. At the United Nations (UN), the Chinese called the Soviets hypocritical for proposing world disarmament while continuing their development of nuclear weapons. Nevertheless, a $300-million trade agreement was signed between China and the Soviet Union in May. At year's end, however, both countries were busy rejecting each other's suggestions for negotiations of their mutual disputes. A Chinese nonagression proposal was flatly turned down by Soviet leader Leonid I. Brezhnev.

China backed off from its long-held supernationalist doctrine by advising some 15 million overseas Chinese in the countries of Southeast Asia to be loyal to their adopted countries. China also muted its policy of inciting worldwide people's liberation wars, increasingly adopting conventional diplomacy with other countries. A full-scale trade agreement between China and Japan was signed in January, and regular air service between Peking and Tokyo was begun in September.

During the year many heads of government paid state visits to China. Included were President Houari Boumédienne of Algeria, President Julius K. Nyerere of Tanzania, President Kenneth D. Kaunda of Zambia, President Léopold S. Senghor of Senegal, Prime Minister Zulfikar Ali Bhutto of Pakistan, Archbishop Makarios of Cyprus, Prime Minister Tun Abdul Razak of Malaysia, and Gen. Yakubu Gowon of Nigeria.

In August the Peking government was reassured by the new administration of U.S. President Gerald

R. Ford that there would be no change in the United States' commitment to improving relations with China. Although Peking protested the appointment of a senior U.S. diplomat as ambassador to the Chinese Nationalist government on Taiwan, it restated its policy of accommodation with Washington. (*See* Taiwan.)

In September a top-level bipartisan U.S. Congressional delegation made a two-week tour of China. In October George Bush, Republican party national chairman, replaced David Bruce as U.S. envoy to Peking. In November Chiao Kuan-hua, chief of China's UN delegation and a loyal supporter of Premier Chou's outgoing foreign policy, replaced Chi Peng-fei as China's foreign minister. This all led to speculation that full U.S.-Chinese diplomatic relations might soon be established.

Along with claims that China had achieved self-sufficiency in its food supplies, the government announced in September that a record grain crop of 250 million metric tons had been harvested in 1973. Output for 1974 was expected to be even higher. At the same time, visiting farm experts from the U.S. praised China's agricultural gains. They reported that China was "well prepared" to meet the problem of feeding its 800 million people.

Helping to meet the world energy crisis, China began supplying large amounts of oil to Japan, Thailand, and the Philippines during the year. Chinese oil production was reported at a record 50 million tons (about 350 million barrels) for 1973, up by some two thirds over 1972. (*See also* Asia.)

*Balloons are released during the October 25 dedication ceremony for Alexander Calder's stabile 'Flamingo' in Chicago's Federal Center Plaza.*

**CITIES AND URBAN AFFAIRS.** In 1974, U.S. cities continued to face a constellation of serious problems, including financing difficulties, strikes, racial unrest, and corruption. At the same time, efforts were being made to create new programs to alleviate old ills.

Baltimore, Md., was virtually crippled by a 15-day strike in July. Policemen, sanitation workers, and other municipal workers struck for higher wages. The sanitation strike presented a grave health hazard in view of Baltimore's summer heat. When the police went on strike, violent incidents in the city multiplied rapidly, and Maryland's governor called in state troopers to restore order.

City office and hospital workers went on strike in San Francisco, Calif., in March; at first, it appeared that the strike would not halt the entire city. Business was brought to a standstill, however, when municipal transportation workers decided to honor picket lines set up by the office workers; the city's public transportation system was shut down. The city's teachers joined the strike, also. After nine days a wage settlement was reached with the original groups of striking workers.

A number of municipalities began the first year of programs to reward efficiency and improved productivity among city workers. In Orange, Calif., for example, policemen were to be rewarded with bonus pay if the crime rate dropped appreciably. Sanitation workers in Detroit, Mich., agreed to speed up garbage collection in return for bonuses.

Disturbances occurred in a predominantly Puerto Rican area of Newark, N.J., in September. Puerto Rican leaders enlisted black nationalist Imamu Amiri Baraka as one of their spokesmen. Discriminatory treatment of blacks and Latins by Newark's police was offered as the cause of the violence.

Racial disorders began in Boston, Mass., at the

MARK JOSEPH—THE FIRST NATIONAL BANK OF CHICAGO

*Dedicated September 27, Marc Chagall's mosaic mural 'The Four Seasons' graces the First National Bank of Chicago plaza, adding to the city's growing collection of outdoor art.*

opening of the new school year in September and continued to the end of the year. White students and parents used violence to resist court-ordered busing of black students into white neighborhoods, particularly in South Boston. (*See* Education; Supreme Court of the U.S.)

The Pennsylvania Crime Commission issued a massive report in March, detailing evidence of widespread corruption in the Philadelphia police force. Graft and extortion· were uncovered on a grand scale. According to the report, Mayor Frank L. Rizzo and his administration had tried to stifle the inquiry into the city's police department. Rizzo, a former police chief who had run for mayor on a "law and order" platform, defended the police even after the report was issued. Richard G. Lugar, mayor of Indianapolis, Ind., fired the top two police officials after similar revelations of corruption.

The City Planning Commission of New York City, in attempting to deal with urban problems, decided to take a new approach and emphasize the needs of local communities. The commission dropped its "master plan" for the entire city and instituted "miniplans" for neighborhoods. The solution to the rising costs of city government, however, was not new; in December New York City Mayor Abraham Beame, faced with a $430-million deficit budget, ordered 7,000 municipal workers dropped from the city's payroll. Other cities were also faced with the need for massive cutbacks of employees as the year ended.

In December federal revenue-sharing funds to Chicago were ordered temporarily halted after a federal court found the city guilty of discrimination in its minority hiring practices. Other cities charged with discrimination were threatened with a similar cutoff of federal funds. (*See also* Crime; State Governments, U.S.)

## Cities and Urban Affairs

# Special Report:
# Safety in the Streets

by Patricia Dragisic

"Two things stand out about the [American] Revolution. The first, of course, is that it was successful and immediately became enshrined in our tradition and history. The second is that the meanest and most squalid sort of violence was from the very beginning to the very last put to the service of Revolutionary ideals and objectives."

The violence of the times in 1776 is made clear in the above quotation from 'Violence in America', a staff report to the National Commission on the Causes and Prevention of Violence. The same report goes on to point out that it was routine for street thugs to be recruited for such now hallowed skirmishes in the revolutionary struggle as the Boston Tea Party.

Two hundred years later, Americans were strongly concerned—some were obsessed—with violence and "crime in the streets." Crime rates, rising steadily in the 1960's and 1970's, received much attention in the media. Emotional currents ran high, with strong racial overtones. A number of state legislatures began to restore the death penalty for certain crimes, attempting to tailor their statutes to fit the Supreme Court's restrictions on capital punishment. In this atmosphere, a government study was released in 1974 that attacked some of the commonly circulating notions about crime.

The study, based on surveys conducted by the U.S. Bureau of the Census for the Law Enforcement Assistance Administration (LEAA), concluded surprisingly that New York City was the safest of 13 major cities studied. New York had long endured a nationwide, even a worldwide, reputation as a crime-infested jungle where life and property were under constant threat.

Such motion pictures as 'The Out-of-Towners' gained popularity by exploiting the idea that the Big City was a maze of dangers for the unwary Mr. and Mrs. Middle America. Guests and hosts on TV talk shows found muggings and other crimes in New York a source of seemingly endless jokes and anecdotes. How could it be possible that New York City is one of America's safest?

### Crime Statistics: Figures Can Lie

A novel approach to gathering figures was used for the LEAA study. The standard approach to crime statistics is as follows: the Federal Bureau of Investigation (FBI) collects figures on crimes from individual police departments in U.S. cities, then publishes those figures as received.

The traditional FBI method has been criticized as inaccurate on many occasions. Some police departments may underreport crime in order to make their cities look better and safer. Another problem is that individual citizens may fail to report to the police when they become victims of crime, in fear of retaliation; the LEAA study found this latter syndrome to be widespread.

In a note preceding the FBI crime statistics, the 'Statistical Abstract of the United States', a publication of the Census Bureau, says straightforwardly: "In summarizing and publishing crime data, the FBI does not vouch for the validity of the reports it receives, but presents the data as information useful to persons concerned with the problem of crime and criminal-law enforcement."

How "useful" can such figures be if they are not accurate? Or if they do not reflect life as it is lived and experienced by the average citizen in a U.S. city? More is involved here than nit-picking or quibbling over a few numbers. Facts about crime and emotional reaction to crime have become influential in people's decisions about where to live and work, about whom and what to vote for at the polls, and in various other matters of choice.

Concerned by such considerations, LEAA officials wanted to approach the problem in a new way. They hoped to present information on crime that citizens would find useful in dealing with their public officials and agencies responsible for public safety and law enforcement.

It was decided, therefore, to go directly to residents of various cities. The Census Bureau used its proven methods to select a sample of persons to interview. Census Bureau interviewers talked to residents in each of the 13 cities under study (persons 12 years of age and over) and asked each subject if he or she had been the victim of a serious crime in the period under study (1972 in some cities, 1971 in others).

The LEAA study found that the ratio of unreported crime to reported crime averaged almost three to one for 12 of the 13 cities. Much of this unreported crime had to be attributed to citizens' failing to report, rather than any such action on the part of a police department. For the city of Philadelphia, Pa., however, the ratio of unreported crime to reported rose to 5.1 to 1. Some sources questioned the policies of the Philadelphia police department and the administration of Mayor Frank Rizzo in reporting crimes.

## More Details of the LEAA Study

The surveys for the LEAA covered three major crimes against persons—rape, robbery, and assault—as well as crimes against property (both residential and commercial). Murder was not included in the study because the number of homicides is statistically insignificant in relation to other crimes against persons. Also, the method used for the surveys ruled out inclusion of homicides: no victims are on hand to be interviewed.

Thirty-six New Yorkers out of every 1,000 reported that they had been victims of serious crime in the period under study. Detroit, Mich., fared worst of the group of 13 cities, with a rate of 68 per 1,000.

The breakdown for crimes against persons per 1,000 persons in the group of 13 was as follows:

| | |
|---|---|
| New York City | 36 |
| St. Louis, Mo. | 42 |
| Newark, N.J. | 42 |
| Dallas, Tex. | 43 |
| Atlanta, Ga. | 48 |
| Los Angeles | 53 |
| Cleveland, Ohio | 54 |
| Chicago | 56 |
| Baltimore, Md. | 56 |
| Portland, Ore. | 59 |
| Philadelphia | 63 |
| Denver, Colo. | 67 |
| Detroit | 68 |

In terms of robbery, Dallas proved safest of the group, with 10 per 1,000 persons (ranging up to 32 per 1,000 for Detroit). New York City took honors as safest in the assault category, with

159

11 per 1,000 residents—in contrast to 46 per 1,000 for Denver. Dallas rated safest on auto thefts (24 per 1,000); Cleveland least safe, with 76 per 1,000.

Even in the category of burglary against "households," including apartments and single-family dwellings alike, New York City came up safest. Sixty-eight New Yorkers out of each 1,000 reported that they had been victims of burglary, as against the figures of 161 for Atlanta and 174 for Detroit.

In terms of crimes against businesses, Los Angeles and Chicago vied for honors as safest cities (L.A. reported 311 burglaries per 1,000 business establishments; Chicago, 317). New York City scored mid-range in this category, at 328 per 1,000. Newark (631 per 1,000) and Atlanta (741 per 1,000) brought up the rear on commercial burglaries.

## Who Are the Victims of Crime?

The LEAA study upset the applecart of cherished notions on another important point—just exactly who the victims of crime are. Many of the people fearful of crime are white, and they fall in middle-income or upper-income groups.

According to LEAA figures, blacks are more often the victims of crime than whites, men more often than women, and lower-income persons ($3,000 to $7,499) more often than upper-income ($15,000 and up). In addition, persons under 35 years old find themselves victims more often than those over 35. In fact, a "composite victim" was said to be a young black man with an income of less than $10,000 per year.

A 1965 study by the National Opinion Research Center of the University of Chicago had showed the same conclusion: that blacks are crime victims more often than whites. According to that study, based on a nationwide sampling, white persons were victims of serious crimes in a ratio of 1,860 per 100,000 population. Black persons were victimized at a rate of 2,592 per 100,000. For rape victims, the ratio was 22 per 100,000 for white women and 82 per 100,000 for black women.

Similarly, a number of studies have established the fact that if you are going to become a homicide victim, chances are better than one in two that your murderer will be a friend, acquaintance, or loved one. And that he or she will live in your neighborhood or area.

## Future Studies and the LEAA Results

By mid-1974 LEAA-commissioned surveys had begun in another group of 13 cities. These were Boston, Mass.; Buffalo, N.Y.; Cincinnati, Ohio; Houston, Tex.; Miami, Fla.; Milwaukee, Wis.; Minneapolis, Minn.; New Orleans, La.; Pittsburgh, Pa.; San Diego, Calif.; Oakland, Calif.; San Francisco, Calif.; and Washington, D.C. The LEAA planned to update the figures regularly for each of the two groups of 13. Eventually, all the cities in the U.S. were to be studied along the same lines.

A possible criticism of the methodology used by the LEAA and the Census Bureau involves the selection of cities for study. Washington, D.C., probably should have been included in the original group of 13 because its crime problems appear to be similar to those of New York City, Philadelphia, Chicago, and Detroit.

In playing any "numbers game," it is important to look not only at what is being included but what is not. The LEAA figures are, in effect, percentages. Though New York City residents suffer "only" 36 serious crimes per 1,000 persons, one must take into account the fact that New York has the largest population of any U.S. city. The *number* of crimes, therefore, is probably greater in New York City than elsewhere, even though the *rate* is lower. Still, the figures are valid for an individual asking himself, "If I plan to live in Denver, what will be my chances of becoming a crime victim?"

The LEAA results seemed not incompatible with existing homicide statistics—generally thought to be the most reliable of locally gathered figures. In 1973 New York City recorded 21.9 homicides per 1,000 residents, as against 48.2 homicides per 1,000 in Detroit. Other figures included 17.7 per 1,000 for Los Angeles and 26.9 per 1,000 for Chicago.

Of course, crime rates for cities have long been higher than those for suburbs or rural areas. The LEAA studies did not include suburban residents who might have been victimized in the city—but if such inclusion would have raised the New York figures, it surely would have affected the other figures, too.

The LEAA study hopefully will help bring more factual analysis and less emotional bias to the scrutiny of crime in U.S. cities. Only when an accurate picture of crime is obtained will it be possible to think seriously about controlling crime and eliminating its causes.

COURTESY, U.S. MINT

*Bicentennial designs for the reverse of the quarter, half-dollar, and dollar were unveiled in March. The obverse of each coin will bear the commemorative dating "1776–1976."*

**COINS AND MEDALS.** The numismatic highlight of 1974 was the selection of the three winning designs for use on the U.S. Bicentennial quarters, half-dollars, and dollars. The winning designs were chosen by a committee of five artist/sculptors under the supervision of U.S. Mint Director Mary T. Brooks. The entirely new designs will be used on the reverses of the coins, with no changes on the faces except that all will bear the double date "1776–1976." It was planned to put the coins in circulation on July 4, 1975, and to produce large quantities of each. Special strikings for collectors will be available, at premium prices, from the Bureau of the Mint through 1975.

One of each coin was struck at the Philadelphia, Pa., Mint on Aug. 12, 1974, and flown to Bal Harbour, Fla., for exhibition at the annual American Numismatic Association (ANA) convention. The growing interest in numismatics was indicated by an attendance of over 10,000 at the convention and by new price records set in the sale of a number of numismatic items bought and sold there. The ANA reported that it had accepted nearly 3,700 new members during its past fiscal year.

While coin collectors had been permitted to hold gold coins as collectors' items, with some restrictions, they as well as the general public looked forward to removal of the federal ban on the buying, selling, and ownership of gold as of December 31. The demand for and price of rare coins and other numismatic items were being influenced by the progress of inflation, causing more and more interest in them as investments.

In connection with the coming observance of the Bicentennial of the American Revolutionary War, the U.S. Mint commenced the issuance of ten pewter reproductions of America's earliest medals. The original medals were struck in recognition of outstanding commanders and successful Revolutionary War battles. In addition to previously issued state medals observing the Bicentennial, several new state medals were issued during 1974. These were produced by private minting firms.

Canada issued the first four coins (dated 1976) of a 28-coin set in observance of the 1976 Olympic Games to be held in Montreal, Que. Private mints issued many commemorative medals, including ones honoring Pablo Casals, Sigmund Freud, Charles Ives, General William Tecumseh Sherman, the bicentennial of the arrival of the Shakers in America, and the centennial of the invention of the telephone. (*See also* U.S. Special Report.)

**COLLEGES AND UNIVERSITIES.** A combination of problems continued to plague U.S. institutions of higher education in 1974: soaring costs, declining college-age population, reduced government aid, fewer private grants, and changing attitudes about the value of a college education.

Despite the reduction in the general population of college-age persons, overall enrollment in colleges and universities was up in 1974. A report issued in January by the U.S. Office of Education's National Center for Educational Statistics gave total enrollment as 9,662,763, an increase of 3.9% over the previous year's figure of 9,297,787. The larger number was due primarily to the increased enrollments of women and part-time students.

Enrollments at agricultural colleges were up sharply, more than doubling in the past ten years, and increasing at about 13% per year. Students from urban backgrounds and women students accounted for a large part of the increase. Administrators cited environmental concerns and increased interest in natural resources as explanations for the trend. Also increasing were enrollments at the country's military service academies—West Point, Annapolis, and the Air Force Academy—which offer free education and postgraduate job security. The surviving women's colleges, having resisted the tide of coeducation, saw applications rise again.

With economics dominating other concerns, the institution of tenure—traditionally almost a guaranteed position for life—was shaken on campus. Inflation-hit budgets and stabilizing (or in some cases, declining) student populations combined to reduce the need for some senior, tenured staff. The Carnegie Commission on Higher Education estimated that under present patterns, 90% of all U.S. professors would have tenure by 1990. These patterns seemed to be changing during 1974, however, as hundreds of professors were denied tenure or dismissed in spite of it. In another attempt to control expenditures, many schools offered early-retirement options and others were considering mandatory-retirement rules. Austerity budgets also affected junior professors and new graduates seeking faculty appointments, particularly at regional universities and state colleges.

For students entering college in 1974, the greatest concern—after the high cost of tuition—was whether they would find jobs following graduation. As a result, there was increased emphasis on professions such as law and medicine, and on courses providing business training. Surprisingly, a Gallup Poll showed that 25% of college students intended to enter the already overcrowded field of teaching, where applicants outnumbered jobs by two to one.

The Department of Health, Education, and Welfare issued its long-awaited recommendations for equal treatment of the sexes in educational institutions, foreshadowing far-reaching changes in campus routine. One proposal, for example, was that male students must abide by the same curfews as female students. Another forbade quotas on the basis of sex in law and medical school admissions. The proposals governing intercollegiate athletics permitted—but did not require—mixed teams and called upon schools to provide women with "comparable" athletic opportunities. But the rules forbidding discrimination in recruiting students and awarding scholarships promised to bring even more opposi-

tion from athletic departments than those bearing directly on sports. (*See also* Education; Law.)

**COLOMBIA.** Presidential and congressional elections were held in April 1974, the first since 1958 in which the result was not determined by the National Front arrangement, whereby the two major parties agreed to alternate in the presidency and to maintain parity in the Congress. The election was a decisive victory for the Liberal candidate, Alfonso López Michelsen, who received 56% of the vote, leading the Conservative candidate by more than a million votes. The Liberal party also gained control of the Congress. Parity between the two parties was to continue in the cabinet for four years.

Michelsen in his campaign was particularly critical of U.S. involvement in the Colombian economy and of U.S. trade practices; he advocated Colombian trade with Cuba. Michelsen also campaigned for agrarian reform, redistribution of wealth, separation of church and state, constitutional reform, women's rights, and new divorce laws.

Serious problems faced the new president, who took office in August, among them the unequal distribution of wealth and the failure of the 12-year-old agrarian reform plan. Eleven million Colombians, about half of the population, earned their meager livings from farming, but few owned their land; only about 20,000 peasant farmers had received land under the reform program. Many peasants boycotted the election out of cynicism over the possibility of meaningful political change, and many became more militant and continued to take over the property of large landholders.

The most immediate economic problem for Colombia in 1974 was inflation, which reached 30%

*Jurors in the trial of eight former Ohio National Guardsmen indicted in the 1970 Kent State University shootings visit the site of the incident on October 30. On November 8 Federal District Court Judge Frank Battisti acquitted the men, charged with denial of the students' civil rights, on the grounds of insufficient evidence.*
WIDE WORLD

COMITI—SYGMA

*On May 11, after a number of short flights within Colombia, a skyjacked Avianca Airlines plane with 94 passengers and crew landed at Bogota, and police moved in minutes later, killing one and capturing the two other skyjackers in the ensuing gun battle.*

during the year. The government introduced several measures to control inflation, and in September President Michelsen declared a 45-day state of emergency, which empowered him to conduct economic policy by decree. (*See also* Latin America.)

**COMMUNICATIONS.** Western Union put two domestic commercial communications satellites, Westar 1 and 2, into orbit in 1974, completing the initial phase of a U.S. network to be used primarily to relay television and telephone signals. By 1976, three additional U.S. systems were to be created by other companies. On its own system, Western Union inaugurated mailgram service, less expensive than telegrams, during the year. The "mail" traveled at the speed of light from New York City to Los Angeles where the U.S. Postal Service provided next-day delivery.

The first message sent over a telegraph system—Samuel Morse's "What hath God wrought?"—opened a new era in communications. Scientists said that the beginning of communication by satellite was comparable to other enormous developments in communications—speech, writing, printing, and telephone and radio. Satellite communication

would, scientists said, provide a quantum jump in people's ability to talk to and see one another. Because the cost of long-distance communication should go down, its use should rise dramatically. Communication by satellite, scientists thought, might replace much business travel and alter people's living patterns.

The National Aeronautics and Space Administration launched the Applications Technology Satellite-6 (ATS-6) in May. One of the most important purposes of ATS-6 was providing medical care to areas of Appalachia and the Rocky Mountains and to the states of Washington and Alaska through the use of two-way voice and picture communication between patients and doctors. ATS-6 was to be used also to provide health and educational programs, family planning information, and cultural programs to rural regions of India.

The Federal Communications Commission allotted some unused high frequencies to the land-mobile industry during the year. The additional frequencies were expected to markedly increase the development and sales of equipment such as mobile telephones and two-way radios.

At Senate hearings in June, many witnesses testi-

*The first tethered-balloon communications relay facility "aerostat," designed to provide civil TV, telephone, and radio service, is tested in April on Grand Bahama Island prior to being shipped to South Korea for installation there.*

COURTESY, TCOM CORPORATION

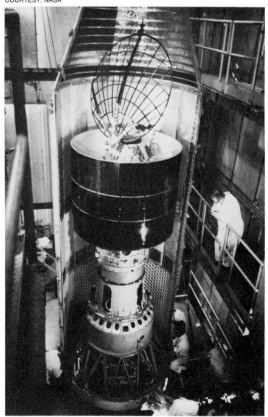

*Engineers at the Kennedy Space Center in Florida encapsulate on April 9 Westar 1, the first U.S. domestic communications satellite, in preparation for its April 13 launching into a hovering orbit 22,300 miles above the Equator.*

COURTESY, NASA

fied against unfair marketing practices by American Telephone & Telegraph Co. (AT & T) and its subsidiaries that together controlled 80% of the U.S. telephone business. In November, the Department of Justice announced antitrust proceedings against AT & T, asking among other things that AT & T divest itself of its Western Electric division.

A Bell Telephone Laboratories scientist was granted a patent for a process that would allow transmission of telephone calls over beams of light. The Bell Telephone System completed the highest capacity underground cable in the world in 1974. Cincinnati Bell became the first Bell system to charge customers for directory assistance calls, a practice that was expected to be used in other areas of the U.S. in the future.

Something traditional in communications disappeared in 1974. Western Union discontinued the singing telegram in California, the last state in which the service was offered. It was still possible, however, to send Raggedy Ann dolls and boxes of candy by Western Union. (*See also* Magazines; Newspapers; Space Exploration; Television and Radio.)

## CONGRESS, UNITED STATES. A 93d

Congress preoccupied during the first half of 1974 with the possible impeachment of President Richard M. Nixon nevertheless achieved a substantial legislative record. It passed a pension reform measure hailed as a measure as important as the Social Security system. It made new rules for political campaigns and set up machinery for more orderly handling of the federal budget—and some legislation was passed dealing with inflation, unemployment, and the energy crisis.

Congress became directly involved with the impeachment process when resolutions calling for an investigation of possible cause for such action were introduced after President Nixon removed Special Prosecutor Archibald Cox from office in October 1973. The resolutions were referred to the House Judiciary Committee, which spent the first half of 1974 building an impeachment staff and amassing evidence. The committee voted three articles of impeachment in July, charging obstruction of justice in the Watergate case, repeated misuse of office to violate the constitutional rights of citizens, and unconstitutional defiance of committee subpoenas.

In working through the impeachment procedure, the House Judiciary Committee necessarily established precedents for judging the powers and limitations of the presidency. Throughout the proceedings, however, the committee was never able to reach a precise definition of what constitutes an impeachable presidential offense.

The committee's vote on the articles of impeachment, however, provided significant elements of that definition. Failure to see that laws are faithfully executed, abuse of the presidency to violate civil rights, and defiance of Congressional demands for information needed in the course of its legal activities can be regarded as valid grounds for possible impeachment of future presidents. There also were decisions on the amount of proof the House needs

to pass a bill of impeachment and just how specific articles of impeachment must be. Resignation of President Nixon August 9 ended the proceedings, except for the final Judiciary Committee report, which was approved by the House on August 20.

A landmark measure to revamp the country's private pension system was passed in August. The law, which affects an estimated 30 million workers, does not require companies to set up pension plans. It does require companies with plans in existence and those that will set up new plans to adhere to federal standards. Church, government, and union retirement plans were exempted. For new plans the measure was made effective at the beginning of the plan year after the bill was enacted. The effective date for participation standards of existing plans was the start of the next plan year after Dec. 31, 1975.

A key provision was that employees be "vested" in their pension rights—that is, guaranteed that money was being held to provide their pensions. Employers could guarantee full benefits for employees with 10 years of service; or 25% of full benefits after 5 years, increasing 5% a year for the next 5 years and 10% for each of the next 5 years, to provide full vesting after 15 years; or use the Rule of 45, which would require 50% vesting when an employee's age and years of service equaled 45.

It required that all pension plans be currently

*James St. Clair (foreground), President Nixon's chief lawyer, takes notes during the opening public session on May 9 of the House Judiciary Committee's hearing on the question of the president's impeachment.*

UPI COMPIX

GEORGE TAMES—THE NEW YORK TIMES

*Senator James Buckley (Cons. R, N.Y.), right, became in March the first conservative in Congress to call upon President Nixon to resign. Rep. Harold D. Donohue (D, Mass.), left, introduced the formal motion for impeachment on July 24 to the House Judiciary Committee.*

funded, but the secretary of labor was given the power to grant waivers for hardship cases. Employers who failed to comply would suffer a severe tax penalty. A surviving spouse would be entitled to half of an employee's pension, unless the employee had specifically waived that right. A government-run insurance program, financed by employers, would guarantee workers against loss of benefits if a pension plan failed.

The bill also provided important tax benefits for many persons planning provisions for their own retirements. Employees not covered by a company pension plan can receive tax deductions on up to 15% of their earned income, up to $1,500 a year, to set up their own retirement annuity accounts. Self-employed individuals would be allowed tax deductions of 15% of earnings, up to $7,500 a year, for such retirement accounts. The previous limit was 10%, up to $2,500. The amount of tax-deductible contributions that can be placed in a profit-sharing plan was limited to 25% of an employee's income, up to $25,000. In a separate action, Congress overrode a veto by the new U.S. president, Gerald R. Ford, and voted more than $7 billion to subsidize the bankrupt railroad retirement system.

Congress made its first comprehensive attempt to establish an orderly procedure for dealing with the federal budget. In the past, presidential requests for spending authority were dealt with individually and were increased or decreased without much regard to total federal spending. Under the new plan, House and Senate committees were set up to get advice from experts on how individual actions affect the overall budget. Congress was to be required to set target figures for total spending through a budget resolution. To allow time for the new process to work, the start of the federal fiscal year was to be moved from July 1 to October 1, beginning in 1976.

The House of Representatives made a mild effort to reform its own procedures. It increased staff appointments for the minority party; banned committee voting by proxy; ordered establishment of subcommittees in very large committees; gave the speaker new power over referring of bills, including power to refer parts of the same bill to different committees; and required that committee reports on bills state effect upon inflation. All standing House committees were given power to subpoena evidence. Congress provided for the first time a system of public financing of presidential campaigns.

Economic problems occupied much attention during the 1974 session. Near the close of the session, Congress began working on legislation recommended by the Democratic party convention in December—legislation that shifted the emphasis from control of inflation to countering effects of recession. A $5.5-billion program was authorized to create over 300,000 new jobs in public agencies, to extend by 13 weeks the current unemployment benefits, and to provide 26 weeks of unemployment compensation to workers not previously covered. It also provided funds for public and private works projects to create jobs.

Wage and price controls were allowed to expire on April 30, as was funding for the Cost of Living Council on June 30. In August, however, Congress acceded to President Ford's request to establish a Council on Wage and Price Stability to monitor economic developments through Aug. 15, 1975. A mass-transit aid bill, authorizing $11.9 billion for mass-transit operating expenses and capital improvements for the fiscal years 1975–80, was cleared in November. Private ownership of gold was authorized for U.S. citizens, effective December 31, for the first time since the 1930's.

An Energy Research and Development Administration (ERDA) was set up, a measure that envisioned the abolition of the Atomic Energy Commission. Most of its functions would be transferred to ERDA, but safety, licensing, and regulatory powers would be vested in a new Nuclear Regulatory Commission. ERDA was to take over geothermal and solar heating projects from the National Science Foundation and development of an alternative auto engine from the Environmental Protection Agency. To cope with immediate fuel shortages, the Congress established a Federal Energy Administration early in the year.

The federal government was given the right to seek injunctions against abuses in commodity-futures trading and to intervene directly in commodity exchanges during an actual or threatened market manipulation or if an act of the U.S. or a foreign government threatened a major market upset. Two billion dollars was earmarked for a program of emergency federally guaranteed loans to livestock producers. The minimum wage for most nonfarm workers was raised to $2 an hour on May 1. It was to go to $2.10 an hour at the start of 1975 and $2.30 an hour at the start of 1976. Additional domestic workers were brought under the act at somewhat lower rates. A somewhat lower scale also was applied to previously covered farm workers. Minimum wage and overtime provisions were extended to federal, state, and local government employees, with overtime for police and firemen to be phased in gradually. The number of retail store employees covered by the minimum wage law was increased, and employment of full-time students at 85% of the minimum wage was authorized.

Congress overrode a presidential veto late in the session to increase educational allowances for veterans by 22.7%. Congress also passed a measure that allowed veterans serving since the start of World War II to reuse their GI home loan benefits,

provided previous loans were paid off. The amount of federal guarantee was increased to $17,500.

Federal aid to education was extended, with all programs substantially unchanged. The education bill provided that no student could be ordered bused further than the district next to his own, unless courts ruled it was necessary to prevent civil rights violations. It also paved the way for parents to challenge existing busing orders in court if they felt their children's health or education was being endangered. Bilingual programs were expanded, and reading improvement programs were made eligible for federal aid. Congress ordered that districts must abide by federal standards for student privacy to qualify for federal aid. Parents were guaranteed access to students' records, and in most situations access of others to the records without parents' consent was forbidden.

In a lame-duck session Congress passed a $2.7-billion foreign aid bill that included a $1.1-billion Mideast appropriation, imposed ceilings and restrictions on aid to South Vietnam and Cambodia, and eliminated military assistance to Chile. A major foreign trade bill was also approved, giving trade concessions to the U.S.S.R. in exchange for the easing of Soviet emigration policies. Major legislation not enacted by the 93d Congress included bills for comprehensive tax reform, national health insurance, and a consumer protection agency.

President Ford nominated Nelson A. Rockefeller on Aug. 20, 1974, to be his vice-president. Under provisions of the 25th Amendment to the Constitution, it was necessary for Congress to confirm him. After intensive hearings, both houses voted confirmation, and Rockefeller took the oath of office on December 19 in the Senate chamber, where he would preside. (*See also* Elections; Environment; Ford; Fuel and Power; Labor Unions; Nixon; Rockefeller; Transportation; United States.)

*Senator Henry Jackson (D, Wash.), left, briefs executives of the seven largest U.S. oil companies before the January 21 Senate hearing to investigate whether the energy crisis was real or contrived.*

GEORGE TAMES – THE NEW YORK TIMES

# Members of the Congress of the United States

## 1st Session, 94th Congress*

## THE SENATE

### President of the Senate: Nelson A. Rockefeller

| State | Senator | Current Service Began | Current Term Expires | State | Senator | Current Service Began | Current Term Expires |
|---|---|---|---|---|---|---|---|
| Ala. | John J. Sparkman (D) | 1946 | 1979 | Mont. | Mike Mansfield (D) | 1953 | 1977 |
|  | James B. Allen (D) | 1969 | 1981 |  | Lee Metcalf (D) | 1961 | 1979 |
| Alaska | Ted Stevens (R) | 1968 | 1979 | Neb. | Roman L. Hruska (R) | 1954 | 1977 |
|  | Mike Gravel (D) | 1969 | 1981 |  | Carl T. Curtis (R) | 1955 | 1979 |
| Ariz. | Paul J. Fannin (R) | 1965 | 1977 | Nev. | Howard W. Cannon (D) | 1959 | 1977 |
|  | Barry Goldwater (R) | 1969 | 1981 |  | Paul Laxalt (R) | 1974 | 1981 |
| Ark. | John L. McClellan (D) | 1943 | 1979 | N.H. | Thomas J. McIntyre (D) | 1962 | 1979 |
|  | Dale Bumpers (D) | 1975 | 1981 |  | Vacancy† | — | — |
| Calif. | Alan Cranston (D) | 1969 | 1981 | N.J. | Clifford P. Case (R) | 1955 | 1979 |
|  | John V. Tunney (D) | 1971 | 1977 |  | Harrison A. Williams, Jr. (D) | 1959 | 1977 |
| Colo. | Floyd K. Haskell (D) | 1973 | 1979 | N.M. | Joseph M. Montoya (D) | 1964 | 1977 |
|  | Gary W. Hart (D) | 1975 | 1981 |  | Pete V. Domenici (R) | 1973 | 1979 |
| Conn. | Abraham A. Ribicoff (D) | 1963 | 1981 | N.Y. | Jacob K. Javits (R) | 1957 | 1981 |
|  | Lowell P. Weicker, Jr. (R) | 1971 | 1977 |  | James L. Buckley (C)‡ | 1971 | 1977 |
| Del. | William V. Roth, Jr. (R) | 1971 | 1977 | N.C. | Jesse A. Helms (R) | 1973 | 1979 |
|  | Joseph R. Biden, Jr. (D) | 1973 | 1979 |  | Robert B. Morgan (D) | 1975 | 1981 |
| Fla. | Lawton Chiles (D) | 1971 | 1977 | N.D. | Milton R. Young (R) | 1945 | 1981 |
|  | Richard Stone (D) | 1975 | 1981 |  | Quentin N. Burdick (D) | 1960 | 1977 |
| Ga. | Herman E. Talmadge (D) | 1957 | 1981 | Ohio | Robert Taft, Jr. (R) | 1971 | 1977 |
|  | Samuel A. Nunn (D) | 1972 | 1979 |  | John H. Glenn, Jr. (D) | 1974 | 1981 |
| Hawaii | Hiram L. Fong (R) | 1959 | 1977 | Okla. | Henry L. Bellmon (R) | 1969 | 1981 |
|  | Daniel K. Inouye (D) | 1963 | 1981 |  | Dewey F. Bartlett (R) | 1973 | 1979 |
| Idaho | Frank Church (D) | 1957 | 1981 | Ore. | Mark O. Hatfield (R) | 1967 | 1979 |
|  | James A. McClure (R) | 1973 | 1979 |  | Bob Packwood (R) | 1969 | 1981 |
| Ill. | Charles H. Percy (R) | 1967 | 1979 | Pa. | Hugh Scott (R) | 1959 | 1977 |
|  | Adlai E. Stevenson III (D) | 1970 | 1981 |  | Richard S. Schweiker (R) | 1969 | 1981 |
| Ind. | Vance Hartke (D) | 1959 | 1977 | R.I. | John O. Pastore (D) | 1950 | 1977 |
|  | Birch Bayh (D) | 1963 | 1981 |  | Claiborne Pell (D) | 1961 | 1979 |
| Iowa | Dick Clark (D) | 1973 | 1979 | S.C. | Strom Thurmond (R) | 1956 | 1979 |
|  | John C. Culver (D) | 1975 | 1981 |  | Ernest F. Hollings (D) | 1966 | 1981 |
| Kan. | James B. Pearson (R) | 1962 | 1979 | S.D. | George S. McGovern (D) | 1963 | 1981 |
|  | Bob Dole (R) | 1969 | 1981 |  | James Abourezk (D) | 1973 | 1979 |
| Ky. | Walter (Dee) Huddleston (D) | 1973 | 1979 | Tenn. | Howard H. Baker, Jr. (R) | 1967 | 1979 |
|  | Wendell H. Ford (D) | 1974 | 1981 |  | William E. Brock III (R) | 1971 | 1977 |
| La. | Russell B. Long (D) | 1948 | 1981 | Tex. | John G. Tower (R) | 1961 | 1979 |
|  | J. Bennett Johnston, Jr. (D) | 1972 | 1979 |  | Lloyd M. Bentsen (D) | 1971 | 1977 |
| Me. | Edmund S. Muskie (D) | 1959 | 1977 | Utah | Frank E. Moss (D) | 1959 | 1977 |
|  | William D. Hathaway (D) | 1973 | 1979 |  | Jake Garn (R) | 1974 | 1981 |
| Md. | Charles McC. Mathias, Jr. (R) | 1969 | 1981 | Vt. | Robert T. Stafford (R) | 1971 | 1977 |
|  | J. Glenn Beall, Jr. (R) | 1971 | 1977 |  | Patrick J. Leahy (D) | 1975 | 1981 |
| Mass. | Edward M. Kennedy (D) | 1962 | 1977 | Va. | Harry F. Byrd, Jr.§ | 1965 | 1977 |
|  | Edward W. Brooke (R) | 1967 | 1979 |  | William L. Scott (R) | 1973 | 1979 |
| Mich. | Philip A. Hart (D) | 1959 | 1977 | Wash. | Warren G. Magnuson (D) | 1944 | 1981 |
|  | Robert P. Griffin (R) | 1966 | 1979 |  | Henry M. Jackson (D) | 1953 | 1977 |
| Minn. | Walter F. Mondale (D) | 1964 | 1979 | W.Va. | Jennings Randolph (D) | 1958 | 1979 |
|  | Hubert H. Humphrey (D) | 1971 | 1977 |  | Robert C. Byrd (D) | 1959 | 1977 |
| Miss. | James O. Eastland (D) | 1943 | 1979 | Wis. | William Proxmire (D) | 1957 | 1977 |
|  | John C. Stennis (D) | 1947 | 1977 |  | Gaylord Nelson (D) | 1963 | 1981 |
| Mo. | Stuart Symington (D) | 1953 | 1977 | Wyo. | Gale W. McGee (D) | 1959 | 1977 |
|  | Thomas F. Eagleton (D) | 1968 | 1981 |  | Clifford P. Hansen (R) | 1967 | 1979 |

*Convened January 14, 1975.
†Election of Louis C. Wyman (R) challenged by John A. Durkin (D).

‡Party designation: Conservative party (of New York).
§No party designation (Independent).

# THE HOUSE OF REPRESENTATIVES*

## Speaker of the House: Carl Albert

### Alabama
Jack Edwards, 1 (R)
William L. Dickinson, 2 (R)
Bill Nichols, 3 (D)
Tom Bevill, 4 (D)
Robert E. Jones, 5 (D)
John Buchanan, 6 (R)
Walter Flowers, 7 (D)

### Alaska
Donald E. Young (R)

### Arizona
John J. Rhodes, 1 (R)
Morris K. Udall, 2 (D)
Sam Steiger, 3 (R)
John B. Conlan, 4 (R)

### Arkansas
Bill Alexander, 1 (D)
Wilbur D. Mills, 2 (D)
John P. Hammerschmidt, 3 (R)
Ray Thornton, 4 (D)

### California
Harold T. Johnson, 1 (D)
Don H. Clausen, 2 (R)
John E. Moss, 3 (D)
Robert L. Leggett, 4 (D)
John L. Burton, 5 (D)
Phillip Burton, 6 (D)
George Miller, 7 (D)
Ronald V. Dellums, 8 (D)
Fortney H. (Pete) Stark, 9 (D)
Don Edwards, 10 (D)
Leo J. Ryan, 11 (D)
Paul N. (Pete) McCloskey, Jr., 12 (R)
Norman Y. Mineta, 13 (D)
John J. McFall, 14 (D)
B. F. Sisk, 15 (D)
Burt L. Talcott, 16 (R)
John Krebs, 17 (D)
William M. Ketchum, 18 (R)
Robert J. Lagomarsino, 19 (R)
Barry Goldwater, Jr., 20 (R)
James C. Corman, 21 (D)
Carlos J. Moorhead, 22 (R)
Thomas M. Rees, 23 (D)
Henry A. Waxman, 24 (D)
Edward R. Roybal, 25 (D)
John H. Rousselot, 26 (R)
Alphonzo Bell, 27 (D)
Yvonne B. Burke, 28 (D)
Augustus F. Hawkins, 29 (D)
George E. Danielson, 30 (D)
Charles H. Wilson, 31 (D)
Glenn M. Anderson, 32 (D)
Del Clawson, 33 (R)
Mark W. Hannaford, 34 (D)
Jim Lloyd, 35 (D)
George E. Brown, Jr., 36 (D)
Jerry L. Pettis, 37 (R)
Jerry M. Patterson, 38 (D)
Charles E. Wiggins, 39 (R)
Andrew J. Hinshaw, 40 (R)
Bob Wilson, 41 (R)
Lionel Van Deerlin, 42 (D)
Clair W. Burgener, 43 (R)

### Colorado
Patricia Schroeder, 1 (D)
Timothy E. Wirth, 2 (D)
Frank E. Evans, 3 (D)
James P. (Jim) Johnson, 4 (R)
William L. Armstrong, 5 (R)

### Connecticut
William R. Cotter, 1 (D)
Christopher J. Dodd, 2 (D)
Robert N. Giaimo, 3 (D)
Stewart B. McKinney, 4 (R)
Ronald A. Sarasin, 5 (R)
Anthony J. Moffett, 6 (D)

### Delaware
Pierre S. du Pont IV (R)

### District of Columbia
Walter E. Fauntroy (D)†

### Florida
Robert L. F. Sikes, 1 (D)
Don Fuqua, 2 (D)
Charles E. Bennett, 3 (D)
Bill Chappell, Jr., 4 (D)
Richard Kelly, 5 (R)
C. W. Bill Young, 6 (R)
Sam M. Gibbons, 7 (D)
James A. Haley, 8 (D)
Louis Frey, Jr., 9 (R)
L. A. (Skip) Bafalis, 10 (R)
Paul G. Rogers, 11 (D)
J. Herbert Burke, 12 (R)
William Lehman, 13 (D)
Claude D. Pepper, 14 (D)
Dante B. Fascell, 15 (D)

### Georgia
Bo Ginn, 1 (D)
Dawson Mathis, 2 (D)
Jack Brinkley, 3 (D)
Elliott H. Levitas, 4 (D)
Andrew Young, 5 (D)
John J. Flynt, Jr., 6 (D)
Lawrence P. McDonald, 7 (D)
W. S. (Bill) Stuckey, Jr., 8 (D)
Phil M. Landrum, 9 (D)
Robert G. Stephens, Jr., 10 (D)

### Hawaii
Spark M. Matsunaga, 1 (D)
Patsy T. Mink, 2 (D)

### Idaho
Steven D. Symms, 1 (R)
George V. Hansen, 2 (R)

### Illinois
Ralph H. Metcalfe, 1 (D)
Morgan F. Murphy, 2 (D)
Martin A. Russo, 3 (D)
Edward J. Derwinski, 4 (R)
John C. Kluczynski, 5 (D)
Henry J. Hyde, 6 (R)
Cardiss Collins, 7 (D)
Dan Rostenkowski, 8 (D)
Sidney R. Yates, 9 (D)
Abner J. Mikva, 10 (D)
Frank Annunzio, 11 (D)
Philip M. Crane, 12 (R)
Robert McClory, 13 (R)
John N. Erlenborn, 14 (R)
Tim L. Hall, 15 (D)
John B. Anderson, 16 (R)
George M. O'Brien, 17 (R)
Robert H. Michel, 18 (R)
Thomas F. Railsback, 19 (R)
Paul Findley, 20 (R)
Edward R. Madigan, 21 (R)
George E. Shipley, 22 (D)
Melvin Price, 23 (D)
Paul Simon, 24 (D)

### Indiana
Ray J. Madden, 1 (D)
Floyd J. Fithian, 2 (D)
John Brademas, 3 (D)
J. Edward Roush, 4 (D)
Elwood Hillis, 5 (R)
David W. Evans, 6 (D)
John T. Myers, 7 (R)
Philip H. Hayes, 8 (D)
Lee H. Hamilton, 9 (D)
Philip R. Sharp, 10 (D)
Andrew Jacobs, Jr., 11 (D)

### Iowa
Edward Mezvinsky, 1 (D)
Michael T. Blouin, 2 (D)
Charles E. Grassley, 3 (R)
Neal Smith, 4 (D)
Tom Harkin, 5 (D)
Berkley Bedell, 6 (D)

### Kansas
Keith G. Sebelius, 1 (R)
Martha E. Keys, 2 (D)
Larry Winn, Jr., 3 (R)
Garner E. Shriver, 4 (R)
Joe Skubitz, 5 (R)

### Kentucky
Carroll Hubbard, Jr., 1 (D)
William H. Natcher, 2 (D)
Romano L. Mazzoli, 3 (D)
M. G. (Gene) Snyder, 4 (R)
Tim Lee Carter, 5 (R)
John Breckinridge, 6 (D)
Carl D. Perkins, 7 (D)

### Louisiana
F. Edward Hebert, 1 (D)
Lindy Boggs, 2 (D)
David C. Treen, 3 (R)
Joe D. Waggonner, Jr., 4 (D)
Otto E. Passman, 5 (D)
W. Henson Moore III, 6 (R)
John B. Breaux, 7 (D)
Gillis W. Long, 8 (D)

### Maine
David F. Emery, 1 (R)
William S. Cohen, 2 (R)

### Maryland
Robert E. Bauman, 1 (R)
Clarence D. Long, 2 (D)
Paul S. Sarbanes, 3 (D)
Marjorie S. Holt, 4 (R)
Gladys N. Spellman, 5 (D)
Goodloe E. Byron, 6 (D)
Parren J. Mitchell, 7 (D)
Gilbert Gude, 8 (R)

### Massachusetts
Silvio O. Conte, 1 (R)
Edward P. Boland, 2 (D)
Joseph D. Early, 3 (D)
Robert F. Drinan, 4 (D)
Paul E. Tsongas, 5 (D)
Michael J. Harrington, 6 (D)
Torbert H. Macdonald, 7 (D)
Thomas P. O'Neill, Jr., 8 (D)
John Joseph Moakley, 9 (D)
Margaret M. Heckler, 10 (R)
James A. Burke, 11 (D)
Gerry E. Studds, 12 (D)

### Michigan
John Conyers, Jr., 1 (D)
Marvin L. Esch, 2 (R)
Garry E. Brown, 3 (R)
Edward Hutchinson, 4 (R)
Richard F. Vander Veen, 5 (D)
Bob Carr, 6 (D)
Donald W. Riegle, Jr., 7 (D)
Bob Traxler, 8 (D)
Guy Vander Jagt, 9 (R)
Elford A. Cederberg, 10 (R)
Philip E. Ruppe, 11 (R)
James G. O'Hara, 12 (D)
Charles C. Diggs, Jr., 13 (D)
Lucien N. Nedzi, 14 (D)
William D. Ford, 15 (D)
John D. Dingell, 16 (D)
William M. Brodhead, 17 (D)
James J. Blanchard, 18 (D)
William S. Broomfield, 19 (R)

### Minnesota
Albert H. Quie, 1 (R)
Tom Hagedorn, 2 (R)
Bill Frenzel, 3 (R)
Joseph E. Karth, 4 (D)
Donald M. Fraser, 5 (D)
Richard Nolan, 6 (D)
Bob Bergland, 7 (D)
James L. Oberstar, 8 (D)

### Mississippi
Jamie L. Whitten, 1 (D)
David R. Bowen, 2 (D)
G. V. (Sonny) Montgomery, 3 (D)
Thad Cochran, 4 (R)
Trent Lott, 5 (R)

### Missouri
William (Bill) Clay, 1 (D)
James W. Symington, 2 (D)

*Numbers after names indicate Congressional districts; where no number is given, congressman is elected at large.
†Nonvoting elected delegate.

Leonor K. (Mrs. John B.) Sullivan, 3 (D)
Wm. J. Randall, 4 (D)
Richard Bolling, 5 (D)
Jerry Litton, 6 (D)
Gene Taylor, 7 (R)
Richard H. Ichord, 8 (D)
William L. Hungate, 9 (D)
Bill D. Burlison, 10 (D)

**Montana**
Max S. Baucus, 1 (D)
John Melcher, 2 (D)

**Nebraska**
Charles Thone, 1 (R)
John Y. McCollister, 2 (R)
Virginia Smith, 3 (R)

**Nevada**
James Santini (D)

**New Hampshire**
Norman E. D'Amours, 1 (D)
James C. Cleveland, 2 (R)

**New Jersey**
James J. Florio, 1 (D)
William J. Hughes, 2 (D)
James J. Howard, 3 (D)
Frank Thompson, Jr., 4 (D)
Millicent Fenwick, 5 (R)
Edwin B. Forsythe, 6 (R)
Andrew Maguire, 7 (D)
Robert A. Roe, 8 (D)
Henry Helstoski, 9 (D)
Peter W. Rodino, Jr., 10 (D)
Joseph G. Minish, 11 (D)
Matthew J. Rinaldo, 12 (R)
Helen S. Meyner, 13 (D)
Dominick V. Daniels, 14 (D)
Edward J. Patten, 15 (D)

**New Mexico**
Manuel Lujan, Jr., 1 (R)
Harold Runnels, 2 (D)

**New York**
Otis G. Pike, 1 (D)
Thomas J. Downey, 2 (D)
Jerome A. Ambro, Jr., 3 (D)
Norman F. Lent, 4 (R)
John W. Wydler, 5 (R)
Lester L. Wolff, 6 (D)
Joseph P. Addabbo, 7 (D)
Benjamin S. Rosenthal, 8 (D)
James J. Delaney, 9 (D)
Mario Biaggi, 10 (D)
James H. Scheuer, 11 (D)
Shirley Chisholm, 12 (D)
Stephen J. Solarz, 13 (D)
Frederick W. Richmond, 14 (D)
Leo C. Zeferetti, 15 (D)
Elizabeth Holtzman, 16 (D)
John M. Murphy, 17 (D)
Edward I. Koch, 18 (D)
Charles B. Rangel, 19 (D)
Bella S. Abzug, 20 (D)
Herman Badillo, 21 (D)

Jonathan B. Bingham, 22 (D)
Peter A. Peyser, 23 (R)
Richard L. Ottinger, 24 (D)
Hamilton Fish, Jr., 25 (R)
Benjamin A. Gilman, 26 (R)
Matthew F. McHugh, 27 (D)
Samuel S. Stratton, 28 (D)
Edward W. Pattison, 29 (D)
Robert C. McEwen, 30 (R)
Donald J. Mitchell, 31 (R)
James M. Hanley, 32 (D)
William F. Walsh, 33 (R)
Frank Horton, 34 (R)
Barber B. Conable, Jr., 35 (R)
John J. LaFalce, 36 (D)
Henry J. Nowak, 37 (D)
Jack Kemp, 38 (R)
James F. Hastings, 39 (R)

**North Carolina**
Walter B. Jones, 1 (D)
L. H. Fountain, 2 (D)
David N. Henderson, 3 (D)
Ike F. Andrews, 4 (D)
Stephen L. Neal, 5 (D)
Richardson Preyer, 6 (D)
Charles Rose III, 7 (D)
W. G. (Bill) Hefner, 8 (D)
James G. Martin, 9 (R)
James T. Broyhill, 10 (R)
Roy A. Taylor, 11 (D)

**North Dakota**
Mark Andrews (R)

**Ohio**
Willis D. Gradison, Jr., 1 (R)
Donald D. Clancy, 2 (R)
Charles W. Whalen, Jr., 3 (R)
Tennyson Guyer, 4 (R)
Delbert L. Latta, 5 (R)
William H. Harsha, 6 (R)
Clarence J. Brown, 7 (R)
Thomas N. Kindness, 8 (R)
Thomas L. Ashley, 9 (D)
Clarence E. Miller, 10 (R)
J. William Stanton, 11 (R)
Samuel L. Devine, 12 (R)
Charles A. Mosher, 13 (R)
John F. Seiberling, 14 (D)
Chalmers P. Wylie, 15 (R)
Ralph S. Regula, 16 (R)
John M. Ashbrook, 17 (R)
Wayne L. Hays, 18 (D)
Charles J. Carney, 19 (D)
James V. Stanton, 20 (D)
Louis Stokes, 21 (D)
Charles A. Vanik, 22 (D)
Ronald M. Mottl, 23 (D)

**Oklahoma**
James Rogers Jones, 1 (D)
Theodore M. Risenhoover, 2 (D)
Carl Albert, 3 (D)
Tom Steed, 4 (D)

John Jarman, 5 (D)
Glenn English, 6 (D)

**Oregon**
Les AuCoin, 1 (D)
Al Ullman, 2 (D)
Robert Duncan, 3 (D)
James Weaver, 4 (D)

**Pennsylvania**
William A. Barrett, 1 (D)
Robert N. C. Nix, 2 (D)
William J. Green, 3 (D)
Joshua Eilberg, 4 (D)
Richard T. Schulze, 5 (R)
Gus Yatron, 6 (D)
Robert W. Edgar, 7 (D)
Edward G. Biester, Jr., 8 (R)
E. G. Shuster, 9 (R)
Joseph M. McDade, 10 (R)
Daniel J. Flood, 11 (D)
John P. Murtha, 12 (D)
R. Lawrence Coughlin, 13 (R)
William S. Moorhead, 14 (D)
Fred B. Rooney, 15 (D)
Edwin D. Eshleman, 16 (R)
Herman T. Schneebeli, 17 (R)
H. John Heinz III, 18 (R)
William F. Goodling, 19 (R)
Joseph M. Gaydos, 20 (D)
John H. Dent, 21 (D)
Thomas E. Morgan, 22 (D)
Albert W. Johnson, 23 (R)
Joseph P. Vigorito, 24 (D)
Gary A. Myers, 25 (R)

**Rhode Island**
Fernand J. St. Germain, 1 (D)
Edward P. Beard, 2 (D)

**South Carolina**
Mendel J. Davis, 1 (D)
Floyd Spence, 2 (R)
Butler C. Derrick, Jr., 3 (D)
James R. Mann, 4 (D)
Kenneth L. Holland, 5 (D)
John W. Jenrette, Jr., 6 (D)

**South Dakota**
Larry Pressler, 1 (R)
James Abdnor, 2 (R)

**Tennessee**
James H. Quillen, 1 (R)
John J. Duncan, 2 (R)
Marilyn Lloyd, 3 (D)
Joe L. Evins, 4 (D)
Richard H. Fulton, 5 (D)
Robin L. Beard, 6 (R)
Ed Jones, 7 (D)
Harold E. Ford, 8 (D)

**Texas**
Wright Patman, 1 (D)
Charles Wilson, 2 (D)
James M. Collins, 3 (R)
Ray Roberts, 4 (D)

Alan Steelman, 5 (R)
Olin E. Teague, 6 (D)
Bill Archer, 7 (R)
Bob Eckhardt, 8 (D)
Jack Brooks, 9 (D)
J. J. (Jake) Pickle, 10 (D)
W. R. Poage, 11 (D)
James C. Wright, Jr., 12 (D)
John Hightower, 13 (D)
John Young, 14 (D)
E. (Kika) de la Garza, 15 (D)
Richard C. White, 16 (D)
Omar Burleson, 17 (D)
Barbara Jordan, 18 (D)
George H. Mahon, 19 (D)
Henry B. Gonzalez, 20 (D)
Robert Krueger, 21 (D)
Bob Casey, 22 (D)
Abraham Kazen, Jr., 23 (D)
Dale Milford, 24 (D)

**Utah**
K. Gunn McKay, 1 (D)
Allan T. Howe, 2 (D)

**Vermont**
James M. Jeffords (R)

**Virginia**
Thomas N. Downing, 1 (D)
G. William Whitehurst, 2 (R)
David E. Satterfield III, 3 (D)
Robert W. Daniel, Jr., 4 (R)
W. C. (Dan) Daniel, 5 (D)
M. Caldwell Butler, 6 (R)
J. Kenneth Robinson, 7 (R)
Herbert E. Harris, 8 (D)
William C. Wampler, 9 (R)
Joseph L. Fisher, 10 (D)

**Washington**
Joel Pritchard, 1 (R)
Lloyd Meeds, 2 (D)
Don Bonker, 3 (D)
Mike McCormack, 4 (D)
Thomas S. Foley, 5 (D)
Floyd V. Hicks, 6 (D)
Brock Adams, 7 (D)

**West Virginia**
Robert H. Mollohan, 1 (D)
Harley O. Staggers, 2 (D)
John Slack, 3 (D)
Ken Hechler, 4 (D)

**Wisconsin**
Les Aspin, 1 (D)
Robert W. Kastenmeier, 2 (D)
Alvin J. Baldus, 3 (D)
Clement J. Zablocki, 4 (D)
Henry S. Reuss, 5 (D)
William A. Steiger, 6 (R)
David R. Obey, 7 (D)
Robert J. Cornell, 8 (D)
Robert W. Kasten, Jr., 9 (R)

**Wyoming**
Teno Roncalio (D)

LODGE—THE AUSTRALIAN, SYDNEY/ROTHCO

*"I don't suppose you've heard about consumer protection...."*

**CONSUMER AFFAIRS.** In 1974, legislation to create a consumer protection agency died in the U.S. Congress. The measure would have created an independent federal agency to represent consumer interests before federal courts and regulatory agencies. A coalition of large firms and business organizations had fought a similar bill for more than five years.

Another setback to consumerism was a U.S. Supreme Court ruling in May that restricted certain kinds of class-action suits. The court ruled that a class-action suit could not be filed on behalf of a large number of persons unless all those who could be identified were notified of the suit, with the cost of notification borne by the person bringing suit.

The growing influence of consumerism throughout the country resulted in the formation of a national organization of state, county, and city consumer officials. The conference delegates had voted to support the legislation establishing a federal consumer protection agency.

The first National Conference on Product Safety was held in May, with delegates from all 50 states discussing ways to enforce the Consumer Product Safety Act. In its first year, the Consumer Product Safety Commission (CPSC) investigated a wide range of products that included aerosol spray cans, bicycles, lamps, television sets, ovens, aluminum wiring, and lawn care equipment.

Household products in aerosol cans using vinyl chloride as the propellant were banned by the CPSC, because the chemical was linked to a rare form of liver cancer among industrial workers. Contents of the cans were chiefly paints, solvents, and degreasers. The Environmental Protection Agency suspended further sales of all pesticide aerosols containing vinyl chloride for use in enclosed areas. Public health officials studied the possibility that the cancer hazard might extend to the general public, especially those living near the manufacturing plants.

The Federal Food and Drug Administration (FDA) proposed new regulations to protect the consumer from nutritionally substandard foods and those fortified with nutrients for which there was no nutritional logic. The FDA also ordered the antacid industry to stop making exaggerated claims about their products and to use only safe and proven ingredients. New labels were to include warnings about possible conflicts with other medication.

In July the federal government issued mandatory safety standards for bicycles. The CPSC planned to impose minimum strength and performance requirements on brakes, steering systems, and other parts.

The FDA published rules in late July that were designed to prevent unnecessary dosages of medical and dental X rays. The first federal standards were set for diagnostic medical and dental equipment, which involve the main sources of exposure to manmade radiation.

The Health Research Group, a subsidiary of consumer advocate Ralph Nader's Public Citizen, Inc., published the first consumer directory of physicians in 1974. It contained such information about the doctors in a Washington, D.C., suburb as office hours, fees, and willingness to make house calls. In San Francisco, Calif., the Group Legal Institute of California published a survey of lawyers' fees. It was mailed to about 46,000 California organizations—such as labor unions and church and fraternal groups—that are potential users of group legal services.

New regulations intended to discourage false and misleading advertising about recreation land were adopted by the U.S. Department of Housing and Urban Development (HUD). The rules strengthened the Interstate Sales Full Disclosure Act of 1968, which basically required interstate sellers of more than 50 lots to register with HUD and give property reports to buyers.

In March 1974, the Federal Energy Administration (FEA) set up a consumer affairs unit to counter criticism that the agency seemed to be more concerned with the welfare of the oil industry than of the consumer. In August, complaining that the unit had been ignored by the FEA, its director quit.

Products containing lead were under scrutiny in 1974. The FDA ordered the recall of about 5,000 imported silver-plated baby cups that it said contained excessive amounts of lead. The cups were made in India and sold in the U.S. from January 1974 until August.

In Canada, where up to 98% of the homes use electric teakettles, it was discovered that the solder used in making them was releasing dangerous levels of lead into the boiling water. The Canadian Cabinet prepared in June to ban kettles that exceeded safety standards and to review all products used in food storage, preparation, or service. (*See also* Environment; Food; Safety.)

## COSTA RICA.
The presidential election held in February 1974 was won by Daniel Oduber Quirós, who received 43% of the vote, defeating seven opposition candidates. For the first time since 1949, however, the president's National Liberation party lost its overall majority in the Legislative Assembly. At his inauguration on May 8, President Oduber outlined his economic policy for the following four years. The country's mineral resources were to be actively developed and basic industries expanded. To stimulate agricultural growth, Costa Rica hoped to join other Central American countries in seeking export markets outside the region.

The additional cost of oil imports in 1974, other pressures on the balance of payments, and, more particularly, the deteriorating fiscal situation led to the introduction on April 25 of a comprehensive exchange reform, accompanied by measures to control external indebtedness and to tax exports. Agricultural products continued to account for the majority of exports, and the attempt to find new markets met with some success. In the first quarter of the 1973–74 season, the Soviet Union bought more Costa Rican coffee than any other country except the U.S. Venezuela imported 25,000 beef cattle in 1974, and Israel showed interest in buying both meat and sugar.

A tax of one dollar per crate, imposed by Costa Rica and others in the newly formed Union of Banana Exporting Countries, was opposed by the Standard Fruit & Steamship Company. Costa Rica obtained notice when the matter was raised before

WIDE WORLD

*National Liberation party candidate Daniel Oduber Quirós was elected the new president of Costa Rica in February.*

the United Nations and the Organization of American States. Subsequently, the tax was lowered to 25 cents, and Standard Fruit announced that it would continue operations in Costa Rica. There were protests during the year against the government's modification of the extradition law to permit fugitive U.S. financier Robert L. Vesco, a friend of outgoing President José Figueres Ferrer, to remain in Costa Rica. (*See also* Latin America.)

## CRIME.
Serious crimes rose 6% in the U.S. during 1973, the Federal Bureau of Investigation (FBI) disclosed in 1974. Crime increased by 15% during the first three months of 1974, continuing the trend evidenced in the last three months of 1973. Since 1968, violent crimes had increased by 47% and property crimes by 28%. Figures from the National Center for Health Statistics set the 1973 U.S. homicide death rate at 9.7 per 100,000, a peak rate for the 20th century. Crimes by juveniles were also on the increase. In New York City, for example, there were an average of 37 gang incidents and 62 arrests every week in 1973. Moreover, a poll sponsored by the Law Enforcement Assistance Administration showed that the U.S. experienced twice as much crime as official figures reflected. (*See* Cities and Urban Affairs Special Report.)

There was a sharp increase in kidnappings in the U.S. during 1974 following the bizarre abduction on February 4 of Patricia Hearst, 19, daughter of newspaper executive Randolph A. Hearst. Through a letter sent to a radio station, the Symbionese Liberation Army (SLA) took responsibility for the kidnapping. The SLA demanded that Patricia's father provide free food for a month for each poor person in California. Hearst declared himself unable to meet the initial demand, which would have cost $400 million, but he arranged to have $2 million in food distributed to the poor. When the kidnappers demanded $4 million more in food, the Hearst Corporation agreed, provided the SLA release Patricia unharmed. More than a month after her abduction, in a tape-recorded message to her parents, Patricia asserted that not enough had been done to bring about her release. Early in April, in another taped message, Patricia announced that she had joined the SLA and had taken the name Tania.

Members of the SLA robbed a San Francisco bank on April 15. Photographs taken during the robbery showed Patricia holding a semiautomatic rifle. A few days later, in another tape-recorded message, Patricia said she had taken part willingly. Six SLA members died on May 17 in a police raid on their Los Angeles hideout. Patricia and others continued to evade authorities. On June 6 a federal grand jury in San Francisco indicted Patricia Hearst on charges of armed bank robbery. She was also wanted in Los Angeles on 19 charges ranging from kidnapping to robbery.

On February 20 J. Reginald Murphy, editorial page editor of the *Atlanta Constitution*, became the victim of the second shocking abduction of 1974. Telephone calls identified his kidnapper as a colonel of the "American Revolutionary Army." Two days after his abduction, Murphy was released unharmed when his newspaper paid $700,000 in ransom. A few hours later William A. H. Williams and his wife were arrested in suburban Atlanta.

Two Minnesota women, both married to bank presidents, were kidnapped early in 1974. On March 15 Eunice Kronholm of South St. Paul was kidnapped. She was released on March 18. A Minnesota man, James W. Johnson, was arrested in connection with the kidnapping, in which a $200,-000 ransom was paid. On May 14 Ardis Graham of Waverly was kidnapped from the family home, held hostage for almost 35 hours, and released after a $50,000 ransom was paid. Arrested and charged with the abduction was Charles H. Ward. Officers found the money in his apartment.

Sydney Gans, 64, a Florida businessman, and his wife were abducted on July 17 and ordered to draw $50,000 out of a Miami bank. When police gave chase, the kidnapper shot and killed the couple and abandoned the car. A man identified as Thomas Knight was arrested hours later.

Another bizarre extortion plot involved not kidnapping but bombing. From September to November, in a region east of Portland, Ore., 11 electrical-transmission towers were rocked by dynamite blasts, threatening the power supply of much of Oregon, Washington, Idaho, and Montana. A typed letter sent to the Portland FBI office demanded a $1-million payment and threatened wider sabotage of the region's power facilities. But before any further damage occurred, the FBI arrested a 34-year-old unemployed trucker and his wife; the couple pleaded guilty to charges of extortion.

**Murder Cases**

By April 16, 1974, 12 persons in San Francisco had been slain in random shootings that had begun late in 1973 and became known as the Zebra killings. Four Black Muslims were indicted in May and

Bank surveillance photos recorded the April 15 robbery of San Francisco bank allegedly executed by the SLA. The FBI identified the woman in the center as kidnapped heiress Patricia Hearst, who later stated on a tape recording that she had taken part willingly.
UPI COMPIX

*A policeman searches Marcus Wayne Chenault before his arraignment on July 1 in Atlanta, Ga., on charges of murder in connection with the June 30 slaying of Mrs. Martin Luther King, Sr.*
WIDE WORLD

charged with murdering three white persons and with conspiring to kill whites at random. An informer asserted that a black militant group known as Death Angels was responsible for the murders.

In San Antonio, Tex., Elmer Wayne Henley, Jr., 18, was found guilty of taking part in a torture ring that claimed the lives of 27 teenage boys in Houston. Henley was brought to trial in connection with six slayings. On July 16, 1974, he was sentenced to six 99-year prison terms.

Mrs. Martin Luther King, Sr., 69-year-old mother of the slain civil rights leader, was fatally wounded June 30 when a young black shot her as she played the organ at the Ebenezer Baptist Church in Atlanta, Ga. Also killed in the fusillade of shots was a church deacon, Edward Boykin. Police identified the assailant as Marcus Wayne Chenault, 21, a college student from Dayton, Ohio. He was convicted in Atlanta on September 12 and was sentenced to die in the electric chair.

In an October bid for a new trial in the 1968 murder of Martin Luther King, Jr., James Earl Ray sought to reverse his original guilty plea. Ray contended the plea was entered under pressure by his lawyers and hinted at conspiracy in the murder. Possibility of conspiracy was also being suggested in the 1968 slaying of Robert F. Kennedy, and plans for an appeal were announced by lawyers for the convicted assassin, Sirhan Sirhan.

W. A. (Tony) Boyle, former president of the United Mine Workers of America (UMW), was found guilty in April of first-degree murder in ordering the assassination of Joseph A. Yablonski, a reform-minded union election rival. Yablonski, his wife, and daughter were killed in 1969 by gunmen, paid with UMW money, authorized by Boyle.

One man's attempt to avoid the violence of urban America produced a poignant news story in 1974. Walter B. Strauss, 52, who drove a taxi in New York City for 27 years, moved to California in August 1973 to escape the crime of New York. He bought a store in Glendale in December 1973. In May 1974 he was shot and killed during a holdup.

**Airports and Airlines**

The worst civil airport bombing in U.S. history started the "alphabet bombings," which terrorized Los Angeles in August. Three persons were killed August 6 when a bomb exploded in a locker in the Pan American World Airways lobby at Los Angeles International Airport. In a series of messages to the news media, a man demanding better treatment for aliens said that his bombings would spell out "Aliens of America." Ten days after the bombing at the airport (which stood for "a"), police located and dismantled a bomb in a locker at the Los Angeles Greyhound Bus station. That took care of the "l" (locker). While fears mounted in regard to what damage would result from the "i" bombing, police arrested a Yugoslavian man on August 20. He was identified as Muharelm Kuregovic, who had been in the U.S. since 1967.

In March 1974, in Brooklyn, N.Y., 19 persons were indicted in federal district court and were charged with the theft of more than 7,000 blank airline tickets. The thefts resulted in a loss to carriers of more than $2 million.

There were no hijackings of scheduled U.S. aircraft in 1973, as compared with 29 in 1972. In February 1974, however, a gunman fatally shot an airport policeman and the copilot of a Delta Airlines jet while trying to hijack a plane at Baltimore-Washington International Airport. (*See also* Colombia; Tunisia.)

In June 1974 the U.S. Marshals ended their involvement in the Anti-Air Piracy program. The four-year effort accounted for more than 4,400 arrests and the seizure of $18.6 million in narcotics.

### A Major Theft and a Counterfeit Ring

In October 1974, thieves took an estimated $4.4 million from a locked vault of an armored car company in Chicago. The robbery ranked among the highest cash thefts in history. The theft was discovered when a fire inside the vault set off a smoke sensor alarm. Police and FBI agents speculated that the fire was set to cover the theft.

Two of the burglars were arrested shortly after the theft as they carried suitcases full of money at the Grand Cayman Island airport in the British West Indies. More than $1.5 million was believed to be on deposit with various banks on the island, and on November 21 another $1.5 million was found buried in the basement of the unoccupied home of one suspect's grandmother. Six men were under indictment in November.

In October U.S. Secret Service agents made what they termed the largest seizure of counterfeit money in the country's history. More than $8 million in $100 bills was seized in Los Angeles, and four California men were arrested.

### Narcotics

Attorney General William B. Saxbe reported in January 1974 that narcotics cases had increased by 37% to a record 9,755 in 1973 and were estimated to make up about 20% of the total federal criminal case load. Heroin traffic was on the upswing in the U.S. in 1974 after two years of decline. Mexico was replacing Europe as the primary source.

In New York City, federal narcotics officials seized 170 pounds of heroin worth $112 million. It had been concealed in a shipment of simulated antique furniture from France. Four French citizens and an Argentine were arrested.

In a drug raid in Chicago, $20 million worth of heroin was seized in October 1974. It had been hidden in a gas tank in a car driven from Mexico.

Officials in Georgia revealed in April an intensive investigation into the criminal activities of the so-called Dixie Mafia, a loosely knit group of traveling narcotics dealers, burglars, and others operating in the South. Attributed to the group were 74 deaths, the victims ranging from police officers to informers to innocent bystanders killed during gun battles. (*See also* Drugs; Turkey.)

### Crimes by Public Officials

Crimes that involved misconduct in office attracted major public attention in 1974. Many for-

WIDE WORLD

*Texas highway patrolmen killed Richard Magnum and seized two accomplices in August, ending the escaped convicts' week of revenge against those who had helped put them in prison.*

mer aides of Richard M. Nixon were under indictment or serving terms in jail. Former Attorney General John Mitchell, John Ehrlichman, and H. R. Haldeman, principal defendants in the Watergate cover-up trial, were found guilty on several counts. One former Nixon attorney, Edward L. Morgan, pleaded guilty to criminal conspiracy for backdating documents that enabled Nixon to claim a $576,-000 tax deduction for papers donated to the National Archives. And in an outgrowth of the Milk Fund scandal, two ex-officers of a large dairy cooperative were convicted of making illegal campaign contributions and other improper payments to government officials. On Feb. 19, 1974, the U.S. Court of Appeals upheld the convictions of former Illinois Gov. Otto Kerner and a close associate in connection with racetrack stock dealings. (*See* Law.)

N. Dale Anderson, the successor to former U.S. Vice-President Spiro T. Agnew as Baltimore County Executive, was convicted by a federal court jury in 1974 on 32 counts of extortion, conspiracy, and tax evasion. Other public figures found guilty in court proceedings included Tim M. Babcock, former governor of Montana; California Lieut. Gov. Edward Reiecke; and Chicago Alderman Thomas E. Keane. (*See also* Museums; Police; Prisons; State Governments; United States.)

# CUBA.

Some economic progress, political liberalization, and changes in foreign policy characterized the government of Premier Fidel Castro in 1974. Cuba's ties with the Soviet Union remained firm, but both countries seemed disposed to end Cuba's estrangement with the United States.

At his first press conference in August, U.S. President Gerald R. Ford hinted that his administration was studying a renewal of ties with Cuba. In April the U.S. Senate Foreign Relations Committee had unanimously approved a resolution calling for an end to the embargo and a resumption of relations with Cuba. Two U.S. senators, Jacob K. Javits (R, N.Y.) and Claiborne Pell (D, R.I.), visited Cuba in September. Afterward they reported, "There is a thaw ... the ice has been broken." The senators were the first congressmen to visit there since the U.S. severed relations with Cuba in January 1961.

Several developments hinted that a reversal of of-

*The first congressmen to visit Cuba since the U.S. severed relations with that country in 1961, Senators Jacob K. Javits (right) and Claiborne Pell (left) flank Cuban Premier Fidel Castro during a September 29 meeting with the press in Havana, Cuba.*

UPI COMPIX

ficial hemispheric policy toward Cuba was imminent, and it appeared for a time that the United States might take a leading role in the process. In April 1974 the U.S. government lifted its ban on the sale of motor vehicles to Cuba by U.S.-owned companies in Argentina. Soon the Argentine subsidiaries of General Motors Corp., the Ford Motor Co., and Chrysler Corp. concluded transactions valued at $75 million. Cuba's trade with Latin American countries was expected to reach $100 million in 1974, up nearly 500% since 1969. Clearly, reevaluation of the ten-year-old sanctions imposed against Cuba by the Organization of American States (OAS) was becoming inevitable. Already six Latin American nations were in defiance of the sanctions, and they were joined in 1974 by Panama and Venezuela, which reestablished relations with Cuba.

As a step toward discussions on Cuba's return to the OAS, foreign ministers from OAS countries agreed at an April meeting in Washington, D.C., to poll member nations as to whether to invite Cuba to participate in their next meeting. Castro indicated that he would send representatives "in a constructive spirit" to the meeting scheduled for March 1975 in Buenos Aires, Argentina. But in a surprise development in November, at a meeting of OAS foreign ministers in Quito, Ecuador, a motion to end the sanctions against Cuba fell two votes short of the needed two-thirds majority.

Formation of a Cuban-Mexican shipping line was announced early in May 1974. (Mexico never cut its ties with Cuba.) Cuba planned to buy five tuna boats valued at more than $8 million from a Peruvian company. From Argentine sources, Cuba contracted for motor vehicles, railway equipment, cargo vessels and tugs, and a meat-packing plant.

Leonid I. Brezhnev, general secretary of the Soviet Communist party, visited Havana in January. Under the terms of an agreement signed in Moscow in February, Cuban-Soviet trade was to reach $1.8 billion—an increase of 18% over the 1973 figure. The U.S.S.R. undertook to meet Cuba's requirements for petroleum and its byproducts and to increase shipments of machinery and equipment for modernizing the sugar industry in Cuba.

Improvement was being shown in overall agricultural and industrial output in Cuba in 1974. The tremendous increase in the world price of sugar, Cuba's main agricultural product—was providing Castro with a major source of foreign exchange. Even though he delivered half of the country's sugar to the Soviet Union, there was still upwards of $1.5 billion worth to sell elsewhere. Emphasizing the need to link wages more closely to productivity, the secretary general of Cuba's labor union announced on May 1 that workers who exceeded their production targets would get cash bonuses. Castro said in May that private farmers' cooperatives would be given more scope for their activities. (*See also* Latin America.)

*The Presidential Palace suffered heavy damage in the July military coup that ousted Archbishop Makarios as president of Cyprus.*

**CYPRUS.** In 1974 Archbishop Makarios was ousted as president of Cyprus in a military coup. Turkish troops then occupied the northern part of the island country. As a result there were far-reaching international repercussions, including the fall of the military regime in Greece and a crisis within the North Atlantic Treaty Organization, to which both Greece and Turkey belonged.

As the year began, talks were continuing in Cyprus between representatives of its Greek majority and Turkish minority communities as to how much autonomy the Turkish Cypriots would have in running their affairs. President Makarios took a middle ground, supporting neither the partition of Cyprus advocated by Turkish Cypriot nationalists nor the union of Cyprus with Greece desired by Greek Cypriot nationalists. To him Cyprus was "an independent, sovereign, and unitary state" of both Greeks and Turks. The talks were broken off in April, with both sides deadlocked, but thanks to efforts of the United Nations (UN), which had a peacekeeping force on Cyprus, the talks were reopened in June.

Gen. Georgios Grivas, leader of the Greek extremist guerrilla movement known as EOKA B, died on January 27. A hero of the patriotic struggle for Cyprus' independence from Great Britain in the 1950's, Grivas had come out of retirement in 1971 to lead terrorist attacks on the moderate Makarios government. Makarios denounced EOKA B's terrorist tactics for promoting partition and weakening his attempts to unify Cyprus.

Increased terrorism by EOKA B after Grivas'

death caused Makarios in April to outlaw the organization and later mount an all-out campaign to destroy it. In June he moved to purge the Cypriot national guard (army) of its Greek officers, under contract with the Greek government, who were increasingly hostile to him because of his opposition to *enosis*, or union with Greece.

On July 15, Cypriot national guard troops overthrew Makarios, quickly crushing any opposition by his private presidential guard. Makarios fled from the capital city of Nicosia to his native town of Paphos. After taking refuge at a British air base in southern Cyprus, he was flown to Malta and then to London. In New York City a few days later, he spoke before the UN Security Council, which received him with the full honors accorded a head of state. He appealed for UN intervention to restore him to the presidency of Cyprus and to compel the Greek government to recall its military officers from Cyprus. He accused the Greek military regime of having "extended its dictatorship to Cyprus."

The Cypriot rebels meanwhile named Nikos Giorgiades Sampson, newspaper publisher and one-time gunman for EOKA B, president of Cyprus. Sampson called Makarios a "traitor" and accused his government of torturing its political opponents. Alarmed at the prospect of annexation by Greece, Rauf Denktash, vice-president of Cyprus and leader of its Turkish community, demanded the reinstatement of Makarios. Then, on July 20, Turkish troops landed at Kyrenia, on Cyprus' northern coast. The Turkish invasion served to unite the Greek Cypriots, but their troops received little assistance from Greece and were driven back by the Turks.

Three days later Sampson resigned the presidency. He turned the office over to Glafkos Clerides, who as president of the Cypriot House of Representatives was the constitutional successor to Makarios. On the same day the military regime of Greece itself fell. Clerides, who had been the chief negotiator in the talks with the Turkish Cypriots, proclaimed a cease-fire.

As guarantors of the 1960 treaty by which Cyprus had won its independence, the British, Greek, and Turkish governments after talks in Geneva, Switzerland, agreed on July 30 on conditions for an end to the fighting. By the time a firm cease-fire took effect, on August 16, the Turkish army controlled the northern third of Cyprus and more than 200,000 Greek Cypriots had become refugees. Many Greek Cypriots blamed the United States for the invasion. During a protest demonstration at the U.S. embassy in Nicosia on August 19, U.S. ambassador Rodger Davies was shot. (*See* Obituaries.)

On August 22 the Soviet Union proposed an international conference on Cyprus, to include the 15 members of the UN Security Council as well as Greece, Turkey, and the Greek and Turkish Cypriots. The new civilian government of Greece agreed, but Turkey called instead for a resumption of the Geneva talks, and Clerides and Denktash began preliminary meetings again in September. The new discussions were broken off by the Turks after the discovery of a mass grave with the bodies of more than 80 massacred Turkish Cypriots. After a few days the talks again resumed and led to a prisoner-of-war exchange, but no settlement of the key refugee problem was achieved.

Makarios again addressed the UN on October 1. He denounced repeated proposals for setting up a federation of distinct Greek and Turkish areas in Cyprus, likening this to partition that would lead to annexation of the separate areas by Greece and Turkey and the destruction of Cyprus as an independent nation. He called for an end to "foreign military occupation" of Cyprus and the return of Greek Cypriot refugees to their homes in the north. In November 5,000 Turkish troops were withdrawn from Cyprus, presumably in an effort to delay the planned December cutoff of U.S. military aid to Turkey. Congress later extended the cutoff date to Feb. 5, 1975.

On December 7, Makarios returned to Cyprus and a joyful welcome from tens of thousands of Greek Cypriots. He still rejected partition, but said he was willing to consider the creation of a small, autonomous Turkish zone on the island, provided no forcible "transfer of populations" was involved. Clerides, who was conducting useful talks with Denktash, threatened to resign if Makarios did not give him a fresh mandate for negotiations.

The economy of Cyprus was in trouble even before the ouster of Makarios and the Turkish invasion. A drought in 1973 had severely hurt the country's agriculture. Grain production was way down, and the resulting fodder shortage led to a decline in milk production and widespread slaughter of cattle. Also down was the output of vegetables, olives, and tobacco. Payment for increased imports of food caused a deficit in the country's trade balance and a decline in its foreign monetary reserves.

To counter the effects of the drought the government accepted a 30-year $6.5-million loan from West Germany, and the World Bank agreed to a long-term loan of $33 million for a water development project. The government had to impose price controls on some items to fight growing inflation.

With the general disruption of the country's economy by the Turkish invasion, the future looked bleak—at least for Greek Cypriots. Some 70% of the country's wealth was produced in areas occupied by the Turks, and economic losses to the Greek community, just between July 15 and September 6, were estimated by the government of Cyprus at more than $800 million. Moreover, unemployment was expected to rise to as high as 10% by the end of the year as a result of the dislocation of so many people. For Turkish Cypriots, however, the year ended more happily, and Turkey's long-sought partition of Cyprus was, in effect, an accomplished fact. (*See also* Greece; Middle East; Turkey; United Nations.)

**CZECHOSLOVAKIA.** Normal relations between Czechoslovakia and the West seemed closer in 1974. The ratification of the 1973 Czech–West German treaty on the normalizing of relations paved the way for a German visit by Czech Foreign Minister Bohuslav Chnoupek in July. Communist Party General Secretary Gustav Husak visited Finland in September. During his trip, an agreement on the gradual removal of trade barriers between the two countries was signed. An agreement settling long-standing mutual financial claims between Czechoslovakia and the United States was reached in Prague on July 6. Under the terms of the agreement, the U.S. would relinquish Czech gold seized during World War II in return for compensation for U.S. property nationalized in Czechoslovakia in 1948.

Relations with the Vatican took a turn for the worse as a result of the sudden death on April 6 of Stepan Cardinal Trochta, archbishop of Litomerice. The cardinal had died of a heart attack after a long interview with a government official on the same day, and Catholic circles in the West claimed that the official had abused and threatened the cardinal, an accusation denied by the Czech government. Hopes for greater tolerance of political opposition remained unfulfilled in 1974. Pavel Kohout, a prominent dissident writer, told West German correspondents visiting Prague that the literary atmosphere there bore comparison to Stalin's U.S.S.R. Deteriorating conditions of political prisoners in Czechoslovakia were condemned by Amnesty International, and a new law that came into force on July 1 gave the Czech security forces extended powers to "override" civil rights if necessary to protect the state or the public order.

In January, at the time of the funeral of Josef Smrkovsky, one of the most popular leaders of the 1968 reform movement, police prevented the attendance of a number of Smrkovsky's friends. World attention focused on Czechoslovakia when an Italian Communist weekly published the text of a condolence letter written to Smrkovsky's widow by Alexander Dubcek, former party leader and a close colleague of the deceased. In the letter, Dubcek complained that he and his wife were "dishonored and defenseless" under the present political system. He attacked Gustav Husak, who succeeded him as party secretary, for Husak's role in Smrkovsky's downfall.

In contrast to the rather depressed political atmosphere, the economic outlook was bright. Industrial output in the first half of the year increased by more than 6% over that of the same period in 1973. The 10-million-ton grain harvest was a record, and other economic indicators were also positive. But Czechoslovakia continued to suffer from an acute labor shortage, and the campaign for greater saving of men and materials continued. The volume of foreign trade increased, and imports from the West were 55% higher than in 1973. To offset the effects

*Czechoslovakia's new TV transmitter tower located atop Jested Hill in the Lusatian Mountains doubles as the chief tourist attraction in northern Bohemia, offering a spectacular view and elegant tourist accommodations.*

KEYSTONE

of international inflation, Czechoslovakia earmarked about $482 million to cover increased prices of raw materials and fuels imported from abroad. (*See also* Europe.)

**DANCE.** In June 1974 Valery Panov, Soviet-Jewish ballet star, and his non-Jewish wife, Galina Ragozina, were finally allowed to emigrate to Israel, ending two years of persecution that included the couple's dismissal from their positions with Leningrad's Kirov Ballet and an attempt by the Soviet government to make Panov depart without his wife. The arrival of the Panovs in the West and the earlier cancellation—for obviously political reasons—of a long-awaited U.S. tour by the Kirov was the biggest news of the year in the dance world.

Almost simultaneously, another Kirov dancer captured the headlines. Mikhail Baryshnikov, 26, defected while on tour in Canada with members of the Bolshoi Ballet. Baryshnikov had been the leading male dancer of the Kirov, the same company from which Rudolf Nureyev had defected in 1961. Hailed as the "finest classical male stylist" ever produced by the U.S.S.R., Baryshnikov was enthusiastically received in his U.S. debut.

**American Dance**

One of the most commented-on events in the dance year 1974 was the opening in April of the Harkness Theater in New York City. The building itself, a former movie-vaudeville house and later a television studio, was purchased for more than $1 million and totally renovated especially for dance at a cost of more than $5 million by benefactress Rebekah Harkness, founder-director of the Harkness Ballet company. Unfortunately, most reviewers attending opening night in the new house were more impressed with its marble floors, Daliesque proscenium mural, and gold rest room fixtures than with the quality of the performance.

Despite the failures of several established companies—including the National Ballet of Washington, D.C., and the Radio City Music Hall Ballet Company—as a result of mounting financial costs and insufficient grants, one new company did come into being during the year. The Eliot Feld Ballet owed its existence to the tireless efforts of director Feld as well as to grants from the Rockefeller Foundation and theater space from the New York Shakespeare Festival's Public Theater. Two new works, both on Jewish themes, 'Sephardic Song' and 'The Tzaddik', were created for the first season, and the initial reception was so favorable that the company extended its debut season from three to five weeks.

The Dance Theater of Harlem, following several successful seasons of touring, made its Broadway debut in the spring. Repertory included the traditional 'Le Corsaire' pas de deux, George Balan-

**Dance**

BIL LEIDERSDORF

*Rebekah Harkness takes a bow with her company after the Harkness Ballet's April 9 gala opening performance in the new Harkness Theater in New York City. The lavish, 1,277-seat theater, built originally in 1905, was renovated at a cost of more than $5 million, becoming the first U.S. theater designed specifically for dance.*

chine's 'Concerto Barocco' and 'Agon', other works in classical idiom, as well as ballets with Afro-jazz roots. Among the new works offered were Geoffrey Holder's revised 'Dougla', Talley Beatty's 'Caravanserai', and Milko Sparemblek's 'Ancient Voices of Children'.

The City Center Joffrey Ballet, directed by Robert Joffrey and resident at the New York City Center, included among its new works Gerald Arpino's 'The Relativity of Icarus' (Gerhard Samuel) and Jonathan Watts's 'Evening Dialogues' (Robert Schumann); the Joffrey also presented new produc-

*In their first performance since emigrating from the U.S.S.R., Valery and Galina Panov (left) appear in Tel Aviv, Israel, on November 10. New York City Ballet's Patricia McBride and Helgi Tomasson (right) dance in the May world premiere of Jerome Robbins' 'Dybbuk' at New York City's Lincoln Center.*

WIDE WORLD  MARTHA SWOPE

tions of Michel Fokine's 'Petrouchka' (Igor Stravinsky), Sir Frederick Ashton's 'Monotones' (Erik Satie), and Jerome Robbins' 'New York Export, Op. Jazz' (Robert Prince) with decor by Ben Shahn.

The New York City Ballet, with directors Lincoln Kirstein and George Balanchine, presented several new works during its season at its home theater in Lincoln Center and one notable new production—'Coppélia'—in its summer home at Saratoga Springs, N.Y. Other new pieces included Robbins' 'Dybbuk' (Leonard Bernstein), based on a classic Yiddish drama about possession and exorcism; Balanchine's 'Variations pour une porte et un soupir' (Pierre Henry); and Jacques d'Amboise's 'Saltarelli' (Antonio Vivaldi).

The American Ballet Theater (ABT) opened its season with Alvin Ailey's 'The River', dedicated to the memory of its late composer, Duke Ellington. (*See* Obituaries.) New productions included the U.S. premiere of John Neumeier's 'Le Baiser de la fée' (Stravinsky); 'Divertissements from Napoli', extracts from the August Bournonville Danish ballet; and Lar Lubovitch's 'Three Essays' (Charles Ives). In July ABT introduced Baryshnikov to New York audiences. The Soviet star danced 'Giselle', 'La Bayadère', and the 'Don Quixote' grand pas de deux with an earlier Kirov defector, Natalia Makarova. Ballerina Gelsey Kirkland left the New York City Ballet to join ABT in the fall to dance with Baryshnikov at his request.

Martha Graham, who celebrated her 80th birthday on May 11, directed her company in a New York City repertory season, and traveled with her dancers on a national tour and on a tour of the Orient sponsored by the U.S. State Department. (*See* Women.) The Alvin Ailey City Center Dance Theater added several new works to its repertory—among them Janet Collins' new 'Canticle of the Elements' and John Jones's 'Nocturnes'—and presented revivals of historic works by pioneer black dancers Katherine Dunham and Pearl Primus.

### Visiting Companies from Abroad

Among the major visiting companies was Britain's Royal Ballet, which was celebrating the 25th anniversary of its first New York appearance. The repertory featured the U.S. premiere of director Kenneth MacMillan's 'Manon' and presented Rudolf Nureyev as guest star. Another U.S. visitor was the National Ballet of Canada, also with Nureyev as guest artist. A traveling Soviet troupe, "Stars of the Bolshoi Ballet," showcased Maya Plisetskaya in a repertory of divertissements and extracts. Both the Royal Swedish Ballet and the Norwegian National Ballet made their U.S. debuts in 1974.

Ethnic dance groups and solo artists included Slask (Poland), Moiseyev Dance Company (U.S.S.R.), Ritha Devi and Bhaskar (India), the Armenian State Dance Ensemble (U.S.S.R.), and representatives of Sri Lanka, Senegal, Hungary, Jamaica, Brazil, Spain, Japan, and Korea.

**DEFENSE.** Defense expenditures in the U.S. in 1974 were about 6% of the gross national product (GNP), the lowest percentage since before the Korean War. In comparison, defense expenditures in the Soviet Union in 1974 were estimated at less than 6% of its GNP. But because Soviet defense figures were not always reliable and did not always include related spending, it was possible that the U.S.S.R. spent substantially more of its GNP on defense in 1974 than did the U.S.

The U.S. continued to reduce its conventional forces in 1974. By the end of the fiscal year in June, the armed forces had decreased by 89,800 to 2,163,000. The U.S.S.R., however, increased its forces in 1974 by 150,000 to 3,175,000.

The U.S. Congress passed an $82.6-billion defense appropriations bill in 1974, the largest single funding package ever enacted. The appropriations for weapons development, procurement, and military and civilian payrolls were $4.5 billion lower than administration requests but over $3 billion more than appropriated in 1973.

High inflation in the U.S. complicated the problem of the Department of Defense in getting what it thought were adequate funds. In the second quarter of 1974 alone, the cost of 42 major weapons programs increased $16.9 billion. The increase in the cost of producing the B-1 bomber was the most spectacular. When the Air Force began the B-1 program in 1970, it estimated the cost to be $45 million a plane. By 1974 the cost was estimated at $76 million a plane. There was a possibility that Congress might eventually scrap some of the programs rather than vote more funds for them at such inflationary rates.

Part of the money requested for the 1974–75 fiscal year was for research, development, and testing to improve the accuracy and striking power of U.S. nuclear missiles against foreign military targets, particularly Soviet missile sites. U.S. missiles in the past were trained primarily on Soviet cities and on other relatively large targets such as industrial areas, their function being primarily to deter a first strike by the Soviet Union against the U.S. Recently, however, Soviet warheads had become more accurate, giving the U.S.S.R. for the first time the

*"All God's chillun got N-power."*

OLIPHANT, THE DENVER POST 1974 © THE LOS ANGELES TIMES SYNDICATE

capability of destroying U.S. missile sites. Congress agreed after some debate that the U.S. should work to achieve equally sophisticated weapons.

Improved, more versatile nuclear weapons were a part of what was perhaps the most significant change in U.S. defense policy in recent years. U.S. Secretary of Defense James R. Schlesinger worked to convince Congress to reject the policies of the 1960's and early 1970's that U.S. nuclear strength should primarily be defensive. The official policy had been that U.S. nuclear strength should be developed in a way to deter a deliberate attack on the U.S. or its allies.

Schlesinger proposed that the U.S. not allow the Soviet Union to acquire an advantage in the sophistication of its weapons. He also proposed that U.S. presidents have options for retaliation to a limited Soviet attack and not be confined to striking only Soviet cities, industries, and large military installations. Schlesinger's proposals met with considerable criticism, particularly from Congress. Several senators argued that research and development to give the U.S. improved nuclear weapons would be interpreted by the Soviet Union as a desire for the U.S. to develop the ability to strike first and would therefore only accelerate the arms race.

At a meeting in Vladivostok, U.S.S.R., U.S. President Gerald R. Ford and Soviet leader Leonid Brezhnev reached a tentative agreement in November, limiting offensive nuclear arms through 1985. A later rewording of the accord provided for arms reduction by both countries before 1985.

The U.S. announced plans in 1974 to establish a permanent naval and air base on the British-owned island of Diego Garcia in the Indian Ocean. Officials said that the base would balance increased Soviet military influence in the area and that it would be used primarily for refueling and for logistic support. Several countries—including India, New Zealand, and Australia—fearing that Diego Garcia would become a nuclear base, strongly protested the U.S. action. The U.S. and Japan announced that some of the U.S. bases remaining on the island of Okinawa would be reduced in size or relocated. U.S. officials were concerned that changes in Greek government policy might jeopardize continued U.S. use of Greek naval and air facilities.

A realignment of military bases and headquarters in the U.S. was announced in November. It would eliminate 11,600 civilian jobs and put 11,500 military personnel in other jobs at an annual $300-million savings, expected to begin in 1977. The defense budget would not be reduced; the savings would be used to increase combat strength. (*See also* Armed Forces, U.S.; Arms Control and Disarmament.)

**DENMARK.** The economic and political instability of Denmark continued in 1974. Inflationary rises in prices, a feature of Danish life for a decade, were widely blamed on the country's system of automatic wage increases based on the consumer price index, but a proposal to abolish the system was defeated. Denmark continued in 1974 to hold European records for high interest rates and taxes. Government spending consumed almost 50% of the country's gross national product. Despite a sharp rise in unemployment during the year, there was growing sentiment that public expenditures be cut and some public services dropped.

The government introduced a compulsory savings plan whereby persons with incomes above a certain amount were required to deposit a percentage of their income in banks for five years. Al-

*The U.S. Army has expressed interest in buying Ireland's Short Brothers' "Skyspy," a flying saucer reconnaissance vehicle capable of flying 100 mph and fitted with TV cameras to provide critical battlefield data.*

LONDON DAILY EXPRESS/PICTORIAL PARADE

*About 40,000 striking workers rally on May 13 in front of Christianborg Castle, seat of parliament in Copenhagen, Denmark, to protest the government's proposed sales tax increase.*

though the action was widely protested by workers, the government increased indirect taxation.

The Liberal government under Prime Minister Poul Hartling ruled with only 22 seats in the 179-member, 10-party parliament. The special parliamentary session called in September to deal with new economic proposals was highly dramatic, the government surviving no fewer than four no-confidence motions. The Progress party, founded by tax lawyer Mogens Glistrup, whose trial on charges of tax evasion began in October, increased in popularity in 1974. The party, holding the second largest number of seats in parliament, advocated the abolition of income tax, a simplified legislature, and drastic cuts in public spending. Hartling called in December for general elections to be held on Jan. 9, 1975, after a majority of the parties in the parliament opposed his crisis plan to freeze wages and prices and to extend all labor agreements for 1975. (*See also* Europe.)

## DENTISTRY.
Dentists continued to investigate the possible involvement of the body's immunity system on periodontal (gum) disease and on tooth decay itself. Dental researchers found that the tissue inflammation of periodontal disease could be linked to the body's immunological attack against the products of bacteria living in a film of dental plaque—a sticky, colorless substance—at the base of the teeth. An immunological approach to the prevention of dental caries (tooth decay) bore some fruit in 1974. Researchers were able to devise a vaccine that lessened the number of decay-causing bacteria in laboratory monkeys. It would still be some time, however, before an effective vaccine for humans emerged.

The American Dental Association (ADA) called for a national educational program to improve the food intake of children. The ADA favored pending legislation—the child nutrition education bill—that would regulate the sale of sugar-rich foods in schools. Health-food devotees believed that unprocessed sweetening agents were better for bodily health than processed sugar, but findings in 1974 failed to discern any difference between processed sugar and molasses, raw sugar, or honey on the development of tooth decay.

In September the Los Angeles City Council opted to fluoridate the water of the city's 3 million inhabitants. As a result, more than 100 million persons in the United States resided in areas having fluoridated water supplies. Experimental evidence indicated that fluorides might alter the chemical processes of tooth decay as well as strengthen tooth enamel. Fluorides appear to intercept acid production in bacterial plaque that forms on teeth.

*Dentists in Stony Brook, N.Y., examine a new ultraviolet cavity camera that detects cavities before they are visible on the surface.*

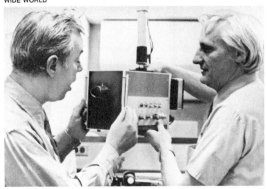

# Dentistry

## Special Report:
## Preventistry –
## The Dentist as Teacher

by Robert Barkley, D.D.S., and John Dennis

"The worst thing you can have in your mouth is no teeth!"

George Washington, the first president of the United States, would have disagreed with this typically double-negatived old Newfoundland saying. Trying to eat, smile, or kiss his wife with his mouthful of hand carved wooden teeth was worse. Bad as that was, the agonies he suffered while losing his own teeth were far worse. With no anesthetics yet invented to kill pain, George had one horrible bout after another until all 32 of his teeth had been pulled. Furthermore, none of his dentists had ever gone to dental school. During the country's infancy, barbers, jewelers, and other tradesmen moonlighted as dentists repairing and removing teeth and making false teeth. By the time Abraham Lincoln left Springfield, Ill., for the presidency, dentistry had advanced somewhat. Abe's dentist, A. W. French, boasted of having attended a course of 30 private lectures and demonstrations and was a full-time "dental surgeon" who regularly advertised in Springfield newspapers. Some medical doctors also practiced dentistry, although their dental and medical schooling was rather skimpy.

### The Growth of Modern Dentistry

After Baltimore Dental College was formed in 1840 in Maryland, dental schools began springing up all over the country. In 1867, two years after Lincoln's death, his former dentist took a year's leave from his practice to complete a formal course at Missouri Dental College in St. Louis (now Washington University) and became *Doctor* French. He later became one of the early leaders of the Illinois State Dental Society. By this time states were beginning to feel a need to protect the public from untrained men working as dentists. State licensing boards were formed to test those who had never attended dental school. It was not until the turn of the century, however, that these boards actually tested graduates of dental schools. Today every graduate, in spite of six to eight years of college and dental school, must pass a state board examination before receiving a license to practice.

It was only natural that along with the development of dentistry as a profession went all of the usual power struggles for prestige and leadership of the profession. During the 1800's simply being "painless" gave a dentist great prestige. By the century's turn, the best maker of false teeth (prosthodontics) seemed to be the most influential. During the first two decades of this century, local anesthetics were developed to kill pain. X rays were also refined to identify and locate smaller cavities, abscesses, and diseases of the bone. Electric motors replaced the foot pedal drill, and the filling of teeth

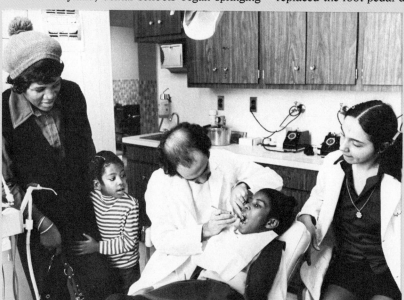

*Entire families enroll in the Comprehensive Approach to Child Health Community Service program conducted by New York City's Brooklyn Jewish Hospital; here a family watches as a young patient is treated in the program's dental department.*

CHRISTA ARMSTRONG – RAPHO GUILLUMETTE

became commonplace and well within the financial reach of the average working man. As dental surgery became highly sophisticated, the oral surgeon became the envied specialist and remained so past mid-century. During the past 25 years there has been an increasing development in the area of complete mouth rehabilitation. Restorative dentists developed outstanding skill in treating mouths badly damaged by disease or accident, and these men have gained high stature.

Now the era of the preventive dentist seems imminent. Not that dentists haven't always tried to be preventive. "Cut down sweets" has long been a battle cry. Dentists have worked hard to teach people to brush after meals, and some people have. Far more haven't, however, and surprisingly it hasn't seemed to make much difference. The people who had serious decay or gum involvement have continued to have trouble in spite of all of their brushing. This is one of the areas of different approach. The new preventive dentists are busy learning to apply research that fairly well proves the toothbrush to be a weak, ineffective tool for avoiding either tooth decay or the dread gum disease pyorrhea.

Independent research at the Tulane University Medical School, the University of Texas Dental School, and the Royal Dental College in Denmark agree that bacterial plaque seems to be the primary cause of both tooth decay and gum disease. This germ-filled plaque grows on teeth as a thin scum near and beneath the gums and between the teeth. If removed once a day, the plaque seems relatively harmless, but it cannot be removed from between the teeth with a toothbrush, and that's where most decay happens. And so unwaxed dental floss becomes the primary tool, and the brush is used to follow up at the gumlines.

### The Management of Learning

While most of the preventive knowledge in dentistry is not new, recent knowledge in the psychology of teaching and learning has had a big influence on the changing practice methods employed by the newer breed of preventive dentists to best utilize the knowledge. These dentists attempt to combine all of the technical skills of their predecessors with the best skills of an effective teacher. They attempt to remake their offices into good learning environments for children and adults alike.

Perhaps one of the most noticeable changes is the manner in which children's dental health is promoted. Traditional sound preventive practice has seen children going to their dentist twice a year to have their teeth professionally cleaned, fluorides applied, their mouths examined, and instructions given in adequate home care. The new approach operates on the premise that dentists have been naive in trying to teach a skill by demonstration. Passive learning is not usually pervasive or long lasting. For this reason the new preventive approach has the child do his own cleaning and fluoride applications, under supervision. In the event the child is too small to do this for himself, the parent cleans the child's teeth and applies the fluorides. The interval between cleanings is usually three months, thereby providing twice the topical fluoride as in the traditional six-month program. If decay still becomes a problem, the interval is often reduced to 60 days or even one month to provide additional fluoride and reinforce home cleaning skills. Since the child cleans his mouth exactly as he should be doing at home, he learns over the years to become skillful at becoming independently healthy. The preventive dentists avoid ever having the child in a passive role in the office insofar as his preventive work is concerned. The dentist realizes that the child still may not be as regular and thorough at home as desirable, but over the years the possibility that he will become so is far greater when the child's responsibility for plaque control is never infringed upon.

Adults are handled basically the same way except that the new preventive dentist takes considerable time with the new adult patient to learn about his attitudes toward and awareness of dentistry, his family's dental disease patterns, and his own personal dental disease history. The dentist tries to help the patient identify his own dental problems and the solutions to these problems. By helping the adult establish his own long-term preventive and rehabilitative goals, including the keeping of his own teeth forever, the preventive dentists help patients plan for long-term success. In the past, few people thought about future goals for dental health, but it is too risky trying to become and remain healthy just by accident. If dental disease is a serious problem for a patient, its underlying causes will be identified by the dentist. Serious decay in adults is associated with food habits. Decay is not usually severe in adults unless they eat sugar several times a day, perhaps as breath mints or other sweet foods. Unless these habits are identified, plaque control alone will not usually control the decay. Gum and bone involvement are much more common in adults, especially with those people who never had many cavities. For gum problems, plaque control is the most important single objective.

Research in Denmark by Harald Löe revealed that when germ-filled plaque is allowed to remain against gums for ten days or so (very common in tooth brushers), the gums will bleed if probed. On the other hand, if plaque is removed for five or six consecutive days, bleeding will cease. This research, for the first time, offers a visible level of health for adults to achieve and maintain. The new preventive dentist will likely have those people with serious disease repeat this experiment of daily plaque removal for five or six consecutive days at the dental office. This concentrated supervised learning experience allows an adult to become healthy to the point where his gums no longer bleed upon probing—he learns for himself that Löe's research is valid, he learns that he can become independently healthy at his own hand, and he gets past the first three or four clumsy, often uncomfortable days of plaque removal.

For the patient to learn cleaning skills is not enough. The preventive dentist realizes that habit change takes time, even in sincere people who have serious dental disease. For this reason, the adult patient at first returns every three or four months to the dental office for a health control check. He is usually later able to go at least a year between professional cleanings instead of the traditional six months. Quite often two or three years pass before being healthy becomes a firm habit, although some people never relapse from the beginning. The new preventive dentist usually has a more tolerant, less authoritarian approach than his predecessors. He feels that there are no failures—only people who haven't learned yet. His job is to help them until they do learn, however many years that may take. Once the adult patient feels health to be within reach, he can progress into any dental treatment he needs with considerably* more confidence that his dentistry will be long lasting. If disease is reasonably controlled, the time of rehabilitative treatment is largely at the patient's discretion; therefore, the finest dental care available, formerly affordable only by the wealthy, can now, over a period of years, be obtained by most people of average means.

The new look in preventive dentistry, then, is one of management of learning. The dentist as a teacher is a new, and sometimes startling, idea for people. It will, however, lead dentistry to a new plateau and help children and adults of the world to achieve a level of health unequaled in the history of the world. Best of all, it can someday make false teeth, from George Washington's wooden ones to the newest modern porcelain ones, museum pieces—no longer needed to help man eat, smile, or kiss his wife.

*In a preventive dentistry program, a mother and her child learn the proper use of unwaxed dental floss to remove plaque between teeth.*

DOUG WILSON—BLACK STAR

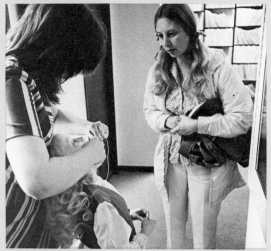

## DISASTERS OF 1974.

Among the fatal catastrophes occurring in the world in 1974 were:

### Air Disasters

**Jan. 26** Izmir, Turkey. A Turkish jetliner crashes on takeoff after rising 400 feet above the airport runway; 65 persons are killed, 8 survive.

**Jan. 31** Pago Pago, American Samoa. A passenger jet landing during a severe thunderstorm crashes short of the airport runway and bursts into flames; 96 die, 5 survive.

**March 3** Near Paris. A Turkish Airlines DC-10 crashes into a forest northeast of Paris shortly after taking off from Orly Airport; 346 persons perish in the worst aviation disaster in history.

**April 4** Francistown, Botswana. An airliner transporting gold miners home to Malawi from work in South Africa catches fire shortly after takeoff and crashes; 77 persons die, but 7, thrown clear by the crash, survive.

**April 22** Bali, Indonesia. A passenger jet crashes into a mountain as it begins its approach to the airport at Denpasar; rescue teams eventually recover all 107 bodies.

**April 27** Leningrad, U.S.S.R. An Aeroflot turboprop crashes shortly after leaving the runway at Leningrad Airport; all 118 passengers and crew reportedly die in the flaming wreckage.

**Sept. 8** Near Athens, Greece. A jet en route to Rome plunges into the Ionian Sea after the pilot reports engine failure; all 88 persons aboard perish.

**Sept. 11** Near Charlotte, N.C. A jetliner preparing to land crashes into woods minutes from the airport; 71 die, 11 survive.

**Sept. 15** Near Saigon, South Vietnam. A passenger plane is blown up in midair by three South Vietnamese hijackers, killing all 70 persons aboard.

**Nov. 20** Nairobi, Kenya. A West German jumbo jet crashes and explodes shortly after takeoff from the Nairobi airport; 59 of the 157 passengers and crew die in the first fatal crash of a 747 jet.

**Dec. 1** Upperville, Va. A 727 jetliner, battling a driving rainstorm on its approach to Washington, D.C., crashes in a wooded area on Mount Weather, near a secret government installation; all 92 persons aboard perish.

**Dec. 4** Near Colombo, Sri Lanka. A chartered Dutch jet carrying Indonesian Muslims on a pilgrimage to Mecca crashes in a rainstorm minutes before landing in Colombo for refueling; all 191 persons aboard are killed.

**Dec. 22** Maturín, Venezuela. A passenger jet carrying Christmas travelers to Caracas explodes and crashes shortly after take-off, killing all 77 persons aboard.

### Fires and Explosions

**Jan. 23** Heusden, Belgium. A dormitory in a Roman Catholic boys' school is swept by fire; the lack of emergency exits prevents many boys from escaping; 23 die, two others are seriously burned.

*Black smoke billows from the remains of a chemical factory near Flixborough, England, that exploded in early June, causing 29 deaths and damage to a five-mile radius.*

**Feb. 1** São Paulo, Brazil. A fire engulfs the upper 14 stories of a newly constructed 25-story office building; at least 227 persons lose their lives.

**June 1** Flixborough, England. A violent explosion completely destroys a recently completed chemical plant about 180 miles north of London; 29 persons die, victims of raging fire and toxic fumes.

**June 30** Port Chester, N.Y. A flash fire sweeps through a crowded singles bar trapping scores of dancers in dense smoke; during the ensuing panic many are unable to reach the narrow stairs leading to the exit; 24 young people die, 32 are injured.

**Oct. 31** Near Allahabad, India. A cigarette dropped in a crowded train sets off firecrackers carried in a passenger's luggage, and the resulting fire kills 52 persons and injures about 60 more.

**Nov. 3** Seoul, South Korea. An early morning fire breaks out in a hotel housing a discotheque whose exits are locked to ensure that customers pay their checks; 88 persons perish.

**Dec. 27** Lievin, France. An explosion in a mine shaft, nearly half a mile below ground, kills 42 miners.

## Marine Disasters

**Feb. 8** Arctic Ocean. The ultramodern 1,106-ton British trawler *Gaul* founders and sinks in stormy seas off Norway; after an eight-day air and sea search, all 36 crew members are presumed dead.

**Feb. 22** Off Chungmu, South Korea. A South Korean navy tugboat capsizes while trying to effect a turn; 15 sailors are known to have perished, 144 are missing and presumed dead, and 157 survive.

**April 23** Near Rangoon, Burma. A fishing schooner sinks some 155 miles from Rangoon; 100 lives are feared lost.

**September** Bay of Bengal. A passenger boat capsizes, and 160 people are feared drowned.

**September** Black Sea. A Soviet destroyer, equipped with guided missiles, explodes and sinks, drowning the entire crew, estimated at 225, in one of the worst peacetime naval disasters in history.

## Natural Disasters

**January** Eastern Australia. Prolonged storms cause record flooding over large areas of the eastern half of Australia; Queensland, the most devastated region, reports at least 15 deaths and damage to property in excess of $100 million.

**Jan. 17** English Channel. Winds of 100 mph and 50-foot waves sweep the English Channel in the channel's worst storm in 20 years; all told, at least 34 persons die when the storm sinks two freighters and causes a number of related mishaps.

**February** Northwestern Argentina. Torrential rains inundate half of Santiago del Estero Province, virtually destroying the cotton harvest; similar destruction occurs in ten other provinces; in all, at least 100 persons are killed and 100,000 homeless.

**March** Brazil. One of the country's worst floods in modern times hits a ten-state area in northern Brazil, leaving thousands of people dead or missing and about 250,000 homeless. In southern

*A fireman surveys the debris of the June 30 flash fire in a Port Chester, N.Y., singles bar that trapped and killed 24 panic-stricken patrons and employees who stampeded a narrow stairway leading to the exit.*

Brazil torrential rains cause the Tubarão River to rise 36 feet within hours and overflow its banks, virtually destroying the city of Tubarão; 1,000 to 1,500 persons are reported killed, and 60,000 of the city's 70,000 people are made homeless.

**April 3–4** Southern and midwestern U.S. and Ontario, Canada. In a single eight-hour period, a series of nearly 100 tornadoes sweeps an 11-state area extending from Georgia to Michigan, hitting hardest in Kentucky and Ohio, and swirls into Canada; at least 320 persons are killed, the highest tornado death toll in 49 years.

**April 25** Central Andes, Peru. Heavy rains and earth tremors cause parts of three mountains to shear loose in huge landslides, obliterating several villages; more than 1,000 are believed dead.

**May** Northeastern Brazil. Heavy rains cause landslides that kill 91 persons; all told, floods claim about 200 victims, mostly in the state of Ceára.

**June** Chittagong, Bangladesh. Heavy rains, followed by landslides, kill at least 40 persons and render 50,000 homeless.

**June 28** Quebradablanca, Colombia. A huge avalanche of rocks and mud thunders onto 800 yards of twisting highway engulfing 6 crowded buses and more than 20 other vehicles; officials estimate more than 200 dead and 100 injured.

**July 7** Southwestern Japan and South Korea. Typhoon Gilda sweeps through, leaving some 100 dead and 24 missing.

*Police investigate the site of the March 3 crash of a Turkish Airlines jet, 26 miles northeast of Paris, that took 346 lives in the worst aviation disaster in history.*

Sept. 18–20 Central America. Hurricane Fifi rips through Nicaragua, Honduras, El Salvador, Guatemala, and Belize causing widespread floods and landslides, millions of dollars in damage, and leaving an estimated 7,000 to 8,000 persons dead and 10,000 missing.

Oct. 3 Peru. An earthquake hits the southern coast, followed by more than 130 sharp aftershocks; in Lima streets are flooded, windows shattered, and many historic buildings damaged; at least 73 persons die, and 2,000 suffer injury.

Oct. 6 Betulia, Colombia. Floodwaters cause a major landslide, the region's second in a week, and partially bury the small town of Betulia; at least 90 persons are reported killed in the two slides.

Dec. 25 Darwin, Australia. Cyclone Tracy strikes with 125-mph winds, destroying or damaging 90% of the city, killing at least 45 persons, leaving 20,000 of the 37,000 residents homeless, and threatening survivors with disease from polluted water supplies.

Dec. 28–29 Northern Pakistan. An earthquake hits a remote section of the Karakoram Mountains, followed by a day of aftershocks; officials report the virtual destruction of the village of Patan and estimate at least 5,200 dead, 16,000 injured, and countless rendered homeless in the nine villages that were hit.

### Railroad Disasters and Traffic Accidents

Jan. 7 Zeytinlik, Turkey. Two trains are accidentally routed onto the same track and collide in a railroad station; 25 people die, some 50 are injured.

Jan. 28 Peru. A bus plunges into a river in the Andes and is swirled 400 yards downstream; at least 35 persons perish.

March 11 Near Indramayu, Indonesia. An overloaded bus tumbles into a ravine and catches fire; 61 persons die, 4 are injured.

March 27 Near Lourenço Marques, Mozambique. A Mozambique freight train, loaded with petroleum products, collides with a Rhodesian passenger train about 31 miles north of the Mozam-

bique capital; an estimated 60 persons are burned to death, and about 50 others are seriously injured.

Aug. 30 Zagreb, Yugoslavia. An express train speeds through a red light and jumps the tracks in Zagreb's main station, killing 124 persons.

Oct. 23 Aragon, Ga. A maintenance train backs up into a school bus at a railroad crossing; 7 children perish, 73 are injured.

### Miscellaneous

Feb. 17 Cairo, Egypt. Thousands of soccer fans, unable to gain entry to a packed stadium, rush the gates and set off a stampede of frightened people inside the stadium; 49 people are crushed to death or suffocate, and 47 others are injured.

June India. In the worst smallpox epidemic of the century, an estimated 20,000 persons are reported to have died in the state of Bihar alone.

October Bangladesh. Massive famine takes the lives of a reported 5,000 Bengalis with little hope of preventing thousands of other deaths before emergency foreign food shipments arrive in November and the country's rice crop can be harvested.

October São Paulo, Brazil. After several months of an epidemic of meningitis, a toll of at least 1,500 lives is reported.

## DOMINICAN REPUBLIC.

The presidential election in May dominated political events in the Dominican Republic in 1974. The principal opposition to the Reformist party, led by President Joaquín Balaguer, was the Santiago Agreement, a coalition formed by five parties with widely differing politics. The coalition withdrew from the race two days before the election, charging lack of guarantees for a free election. President Balaguer was easily reelected to a third term.

To answer the opposition's charges against his staying in office, President Balaguer in August proposed a constitutional amendment that in the future a person not be permitted to succeed himself as president for more than two consecutive terms. He

*A couple wheels away salvaged belongings amidst wrecked buildings in Xenia, Ohio, one of 11 states hit on April 3 and 4 by a series of about 100 tornadoes, leaving at least 320 persons dead and causing $1 billion in damage.*

THE NEW YORK TIMES

also returned the right of freedom of speech to several opposition leaders.

In September 1974, members of the leftist 12th of January Freedom Movement kidnapped seven persons and held them hostage. All their demands, except their request for safe exit from the country, were refused, but the kidnappers released their hostages unharmed.

The Dominican Republic continued economic diversification in 1974, opening a free port and an industrial park in the city of Santiago. In February and March the city of Santo Domingo was host for the 12th Central American and Caribbean Games. The country continued to develop areas as tourist attractions and restored several colonial buildings. The Dominican Republic also increased food production in 1974. Recently, agricultural production fell behind demands generated by a rapidly growing urban population. Large migration from the country to the cities aggravated the problem. The city of Santo Domingo grew 12% per year during the last decade, but only 3% of its growth was attributable to increased births. (*See also* West Indies.)

**DRUGS.** The Food and Drug Administration (FDA) was under fire in 1974 for its alleged inability to execute a mandate to protect U.S. drug consumers. Also, no real abatement of drug abuse was noted during the year. The FDA was assailed by one of its own biochemists, Jacqueline Verrett, who claimed that the FDA was too deferential to drug manufacturers. The FDA biochemist charged the agency with incompetence in, for example, the some 15 years it took to investigate the safety of cycla-

mate artificial sweeteners, eventually banned in 1970.

The U.S. Senate in September thwarted the FDA's plan to regulate certain vitamins. By considering them drugs, the FDA wanted to control the production of vitamins marketed in portions exceeding 150% of their nutritionally recommended daily allowances. Senator William Proxmire (D, Wis.), a Senate leader against vitamin regulations, felt the FDA had no right to dictate anyone's vitamin intake, so long as the vitamins were not toxic. House action on the FDA proposal was pending.

The FDA was attacked again when some critics asserted that the agency bore some responsibility for the medical profession's overprescribing of antibiotics. In an article in the *Journal of the American Medical Association*, U.S. Deputy Assistant Secretary for Health Henry E. Simmons and Paul D. Stolley of Johns Hopkins University suggested that up to 100,000 U.S. hospital deaths each year might be caused by the gram-negative bacteria that have been thriving during the more than 30-year reign of antibiotics. Through the wholesale use of antibiotics against bacteria and viruses over which the drugs had no influence, doctors have been unwitting allies of the dangerous gram-negative bacteria that flourished while antibiotics were knocking out their gram-positive cousins. Simmons, former chief of the FDA's Bureau of Drugs, said that the FDA had done all it legally could in regulating drug use.

In June the FDA presented tentative rules over the amounts of food additive vitamins and minerals to prevent "an irrational nutritional horsepower race." The regulations would stop food manufac-

*Women harvesters return to Turkish poppy fields in July when Turkey canceled its 1971 accord with the U.S. prohibiting the growing of poppies. American officials expressed great concern over the potentially revived flow of Turkish opium to the U.S. drug market.*

LOREN JENKINS—NEWSWEEK

turers from adding additional vitamins and minerals to their products merely for promotional reasons. Also, the FDA guidelines would require labeling of vegetable protein "meat extenders" as to their vitamin and mineral content to ensure it was the equivalent of the meat protein replaced. If not, the additives would have to be labeled "imitation."

Twenty-five states had laws prohibiting druggists from advertising prescription drug prices. In mid-1974, however, the Federal Trade Commission (FTC) considered superseding state laws by requiring that pharmacists throughout the country post their drug prices. The FTC justified such a questionable tactic by alluding to the wide range of prices consumers paid for any specific medication in certain locales.

The Department of Health, Education, and Welfare (HEW) announced a plan in November to save at least $89 million annually in prescription drug costs. The plan would limit the payment for drugs under Medicaid and Medicare programs to the lowest price at which they were available.

Also in November, a fourth HEW report, entitled "Marijuana and Health," was released. The report cited evidence that marijuana use might interfere with the body's immune mechanisms and may also have the effect of lowering the level of the male hormone testosterone. These conclusions were disputed by independent researchers.

Turkey incited U.S. ire when it rescinded its three-year ban on the farming of opium poppies, a ban subsidized by the U.S. government. Narcotics agents expected a resulting rise in heroin flow into the U.S. A decade had passed since methadone maintenance programs went into effect as a treatment of heroin addiction. Methadone is a synthetic narcotic that maintains its effect for two or three days, compared with the six hour or so "high" of heroin. Proponents of methadone maintenance argued that in contrast to heroin addicts, methadone addicts could hold down responsible jobs because of the longer intervals between their need for more methadone. But methadone, too, was finding its way to the streets, according to critics, because of poor security measures at dispersing clinics. Methadone abuse in New York City in 1973 caused twice as many deaths as heroin.

A September crackdown by the Federal Drug Enforcement Administration and Mexican officials resulted in more than 125 arrests of persons dealing in illegal amphetamines.

The U.S. Coast Guard took part in a year-end maritime blockade in southeast Florida waters to stop dope smugglers who apparently had hijacked boats and murdered the crews. (*See also* Medicine.)

**EARTH SCIENCES.** By 1974 the results of one of man's successful attempts to combat a natural disaster had become clear. During 1973 a volcano on Heimaey Island off the coast of Iceland erupted, pouring out millions of cubic yards of lava and volcanic material. Because the eruption threatened the harbor of the island, seawater was used to form a frozen wall to divert the flow. The diverted lava added a square mile to the area of the island, increasing its size by about 20%. The ash that had nearly buried the town was cleared with bulldozers and used to extend the island's airport.

Droughts, floods, and killing frosts in many areas of the world during 1974 seriously damaged or completely destroyed crops and drastically reduced the world's food supply. Research reported by the National Center for Atmospheric Research in Boulder, Colo., supported the views of many climatologists that the slightly higher temperatures over the earth during the first half of the 20th century, which reached a peak during 1945-49, had been replaced by a trend toward lower average temperatures that might reach the level of the cool years of 1850-1900. Some scientists believed that weather was more variable during cool periods, with greater extremes of hot and cold, worse droughts, and more storms producing floods. Although the statistics were too fragmentary to provide definite proof, the erratic weather of 1974 and the all-time record number of tornadoes in the U.S. in 1973 and 1974 —about 2,100—tended to support the theory.

Scientists throughout the world continued experimenting in 1974 with techniques for predicting earthquakes. One of the latest experiments began at the California Institute of Technology in conjunction with the National Aeronautics and Space Administration (NASA). By calculating changes in distance between two points on the earth's surface through measurement of differences in the times of radio signal arrival from quasars, scientists believed that they could detect changes in the earth's surface occurring before earthquakes. If correct, they would have techniques to make long-range, extremely accurate predictions of quakes.

Geologists in 1974 believed that they had found the missing land link that would satisfactorily confirm the theory that South America and Africa were at one time a single continent that later broke apart. Scientists found a region off the coast of Argentina that was once part of the continent of South America but that long ago had sunk two miles beneath the ocean. The nature of the rock, its age, and its fossil specimens supported the theory and made the structural fit between South America and Africa an almost perfect one.

There was more evidence in 1974 that the layer of ozone shielding the earth from the sun's lethal ultraviolet radiation was being destroyed. In addition to previous evidence that supersonic airplanes gave off in their exhausts oxides of nitrogen that depleted the ozone, there was new evidence that nuclear explosions also had the same effect. In addition, some scientists argued that gas used in the common household aerosol spray can could also destroy the ozone layer.

An astronomer at the U.S. Naval Observatory

THEODORE L. SULLIVAN—THE NEW YORK TIMES

*Scientific measurement showed a one- to two-inch widening in recent years of the fissured Thingvellir rift zone near Reykjavik, Iceland, contributing evidence that continental drift may be due to a vast volcanic structure in the North Atlantic centered in Iceland.*

measured the orbital speed of the moon with the precision of an atomic clock and announced in April that the force of gravity was decreasing at the rate of 1 part in 10 billion per year. The finding supported a theory proposed two years previously by the British astronomer Fred Hoyle. The weakening of gravity would allow the moon to move away from the earth 4 centimeters (about 1½ inches) a year and to increase its orbital period one two-thousandths of a second a year. It would also mean that a person weighing 70 kilograms (about 150 pounds) on the earth would lose seven millionths of a gram a year, or about seven millionths of the weight of a paper clip.

Interplanetary probes in 1974 provided scientists with significant new information on other planets. Mariner 10 reached Venus early in the year and then passed by Mercury in March and again in September. Data from Pioneer 10's December 1973 probe of Jupiter were released during the year and were augmented by Pioneer 11's Jovian rendezvous in early December. The U.S.S.R. probed Mars in July and August and made a lunar study in May. (*See also* Astronomy; Awards; Disasters; Environment; Oceanography; Space Exploration; Weather.)

**ECUADOR.** Though the gains that Ecuador had experienced since the commencement of oil exports in recent years were undeniable, the government failed in 1974 to avoid the concomitant social pressures. They had come to the fore with the gradual realization that despite admirable plans the government had been unable or unwilling to channel the massive oil revenues into productive uses, resulting in growing inequality in favor of the coastal traders and businessmen—not to mention the government and the armed forces—and against the peasant population, who suffered great hardship because of high prices and shortages of foodstuffs.

During the year the government took steps to extend the life of proven oil reserves by establishing maximum production levels. Following a revision of the oil companies' contracts, government revenue from oil was expected to reach nearly $1 billion in 1974. On the advice of the Organization of Petroleum Exporting Countries (OPEC), in which Ecuador had been accorded full membership, negotiations were being speeded up to acquire large shares in the operation of the oil companies.

The crucial importance of oil both economically and politically was demonstrated later in the year by the dismissal of the strongly nationalist minister of energy and natural resources, Capt. Gustavo Jarrín Ampudia, who had long been a critic of "excessive profits" by the oil companies and a militant voice in OPEC. His dismissal followed a denunciation of U.S. President Gerald R. Ford's alleged "imperialist threats" against oil-producing countries; Ecuadorian President Guillermo Rodríguez Lara hastened to express a conciliatory attitude toward the U.S. It was reported, though not officially announced, that the U.S. had quietly resumed military sales to Ecuador during the year. (*See also* Latin America.)

**EDUCATION.** Inflation touched most aspects of American life in 1974, and education was no exception. In addition to the financial difficulties facing nearly every school district were the problems of increased student violence and vandalism, growing racial imbalance, and increasing teacher militancy.

Elementary school enrollments dropped slightly more than 2% in 1974, the third year of decline. The 1974 elementary enrollment was 31.5 million, contrasted with the high of 34 million in 1970. Total private and public enrollments in 1974 at all levels dropped from a total of 60.1 million in 1973 to 59.4 million in 1974. The downward trend was expected to continue until at least 1980.

Some 3 million teachers, supervisors, and administrators staffed the country's schools. Education cost $108 billion, or 8% of the gross national product (GNP). Costs escalated $11 billion over those of 1973, despite the decrease in enrollments.

### Federal and State Financing

After a two-month delay in a House-Senate conference committee, the $25.2-billion Education Amendments of 1974 finally cleared the U.S. Congress in August and received the president's signature. The amendments were to run through fiscal 1978. The reason for the bill's delay was the controversial issue of busing. The House version of the bill, backed by President Richard M. Nixon, had contained stiff antibusing language, while the Senate version maintained the authority of the federal courts to order busing when it was necessary to protect the constitutional rights of black students. The resulting compromise act forbade court-ordered busing past a student's second-nearest school unless constitutional rights of minority group children were violated.

The new legislation authorized an Advisory Council on Women's Educational Programs and directed that a comprehensive review of sex discrimination in education be undertaken. The amendments also created provisions for career education, metric education, community schools, and gifted children. Spending on programs for the handicapped was increased from $47.5 million annually to more than $1 billion for a three-year period.

Bilingual, multicultural education also was boosted by the new act. Dual-language instruction was expected to promote learning as well as dignity and self-respect among students for whom English is a second language. Early in 1974 the Supreme Court ruled that Chinese students in San Francisco, Calif., who do not speak English must receive positive action to alleviate learning problems. The ruling was likely to have impact on other bilingual groups, which commonly have high drop-out rates, lower standardized test scores, and below-average collegiate entry rates. Later in the year the Board of Education of New York City agreed in federal court to establish new programs for Spanish-speaking students. The agreement was the result of a class-action suit by two Puerto Rican organizations against the city's school system.

Finances emerged as the chief state education topic. Efforts were made to maintain fiscal stability, but the energy crisis brought escalated fuel costs, and galloping inflation created financial crises in public schools and colleges. Costs of school supplies, particularly books and paper, nearly doubled in 1974. In order to reduce costs, local school dis-

*This building is designated as one meeting site for protesters in Kanawha County, W.Va., where Fundamentalist parents' groups, in sometimes violent demonstrations, objected to several books included in the high school English curriculum.*

UPI COMPIX

*A St. Louis, Mo., resident responds to the November defeat of a proposed school tax increase that may result in the closing of 11 schools and a 15% reduction of teachers.*

tricts resorted to such measures as reducing janitorial services, pruning administrative staffs, curtailing after-school activities, and eliminating classes for handicapped and retarded pupils.

A California State Superior Court judge ruled

*Preschool children are shown the difference between short and tall in the new 'Sesame Street Book of Opposites with Zero Mostel'.*

that the state must find alternatives to district-by-district property tax financing of public schools. The ruling was the first following last year's Supreme Court decision that Texas school inequities could be ended only by statewide action. A report entitled "Financial Status of the Public Schools, 1974," issued in July in conjunction with the annual National Education Association (NEA) meeting, pointed out wide disparity among the states in the funding of public schools. New York State's average school year expenditure per pupil was $1,809 in 1973–74, as compared with $716 in Alabama. Wide variances in teachers' salaries were also cited.

## Desegregation

With the advent in May of the 20th anniversary of the Supreme Court's historic Brown *vs.* Board of Education ruling, desegregation—and its associated issues of busing and "quality education"—was still making news. Since the passage ten years previously of the U.S. Civil Rights Act, the number of black students attending school with whites in the South had risen from 2% to 90%; fewer than 9% were still in all-black schools. In the northern and western states, however, 11% of black students were still attending all-black schools, and 70% attended schools where blacks were a majority. A report issued during the year by the Center for National Policy Review charged the Department of Health, Education, and Welfare (HEW) with violating the civil rights of hundreds of thousands of children by failing to desegregate schools in Northern and Western states. The study also charged that millions of tax dollars were going to segregated schools.

In one of its most important decisions of 1974, the Supreme Court, in a 5–4 ruling, banned the busing of school children across school district lines for desegregation. At issue was a 1972 District Court ruling that authorized the purchase of $3 million worth of school buses to facilitate integration of Detroit, Mich., schools (65% black) with those of nearby suburbs (80% white). Supporters of integration regarded the court's decision as a defeat almost equal in impact to the victory of the 1954 Brown ruling. In his dissenting opinion, Justice Thurgood Marshall charged "emasculation" of the equal protection doctrine and deemed the decision "a giant step backward."

As schools opened in the fall, there was calm in most states. Denver, Colo., schools integrated without incident, with enrollment running at 93% of the predicted total. But in Boston, where court-ordered integration took effect in September, emotions ran high. In all-white, predominantly Catholic South Boston, white students boycotted classes, and buses carrying blacks were stoned. An interracial stabbing at South Boston High School set off a new wave of violence and strengthened white resistance to desegregation. After losing in the U.S. Circuit Court of Appeals, the all-white Boston School Committee voted to take its case to the Supreme Court. Mean-

CH. SIMONPIETRI—SYGMA

*Waving to crowds along the route, U.S. President Nixon during his June visit to Egypt accompanies Egyptian President Sadat on a train trip from Cairo to Alexandria.*

while, the committee's defiance of a federal court order to approve a city-wide desegregation plan for 1975 resulted in the suspension of a $1.9-million HEW grant to the city's school system.

### Other Developments

Two years after the Education Act Amendments of 1972, which forbade discrimination by sex in educational institutions, HEW finally issued draft proposals to implement the legislation. Under the new regulations, physical education classes would have to be coeducational and courses such as home economics and industrial arts would have to be open to both sexes. Major changes in vocational counseling were also called for, along with equalization of teacher hiring and firing practices. College admissions quotas and policies for intercollegiate athletics were also touched upon. (*See* Colleges.)

Violence erupted in Kanawha County, W.Va., and neighboring counties in a dispute over high school English books that were alleged by white, Fundamentalist parents' groups to be obscene, irreligious, and unpatriotic. There were protest marches, school boycotts, shootings, and firebombings of empty schools. After agreeing to recall the controversial materials, the county board of education voted in November to reinstate nearly all of the books—with the provision that no pupil would be forced to read them. The decision, however, touched off new protests. (*See also* Race Relations; Supreme Court of the U.S.)

**EGYPT.** Israeli withdrawal from Egyptian territory and liberalization of the country's economy and political life were the main concerns in Egypt during 1974. Through the intervention of U.S. Secretary of State Henry Kissinger an agreement on the disengagement of Egyptian and Israeli military forces was reached on January 18. The Egyptians took up positions along both banks of the Suez Canal following a final Israeli withdrawal on March 4.

Work then began on clearing bombs and sunken ships from the canal. But even with the help of the U.S., British, and French navies, and a $50-million loan from the World Bank, the canal was not expected to reopen until spring of 1975. Work began also on rebuilding the shattered canal cities of Suez, Ismailia, and Port Said.

Though Egyptian President Anwar el-Sadat reassured other Arab leaders that he would not make a separate peace with Israel, there was speculation that Israel might agree to withdraw from all of the Sinai peninsula in return for full navigation rights in the Suez Canal and an Egyptian declaration of nonbelligerency. But Israel reportedly refused to give up the Sinai oil fields, and Egypt said it would not reopen the canal while the Israelis remained on the Gulf of Suez.

Diplomatic relations between Egypt and the United States were resumed on February 28 after a seven-year break. U.S. President Richard M. Nixon visited Egypt in June and received a great popular welcome. The United States encouraged Egypt's moves toward opening its economy to foreign investments.

With the upturn in U.S.-Egyptian relations, those with the Soviet Union quickly deteriorated. Despite an exchange of visits by the Egyptian and Soviet foreign ministers, there was little improvement at first. Sadat was openly critical of the Soviet Union for failing to match U.S. support of Israel. The Soviet press, in turn, criticized Egypt's drift away from the socialist program of Sadat's predecessor, President Gamal Abdel Nasser. During June and July, however, Sadat visited Romania and Bulgaria, and by September there were clear signs of a rapprochement with the Communist countries. In December Egyptian-Soviet relations appeared on the decline again; a January 1975 visit by Soviet leader Leonid I. Brezhnev was canceled; Brezhnev's health was given as an official reason.

Sadat was fairly successful in cultivating relations with other Arab states, visiting 11 of them in January. In February President Gaafar al-Nimeiry of Sudan visited Egypt and agreed on measures for "political and economic integration" of the two countries. During the summer King Faisal of Saudi Arabia visited Egypt and pledged $300 million in aid. In August Egypt and Iraq agreed on joint economic ventures worth $1 billion. Despite a visit by Libyan President Muammar el-Qaddafi in February, Egyptian-Libyan relations worsened. In April Egypt accused Libya of implication in an armed attack on the Egyptian Military Technical Academy near Cairo, in which 11 persons were killed. There were reports of an assassination attempt on Sadat.

Censorship of the press was relaxed in February, and an open debate emerged on the Nasser era. A major step in "de-Nasserization" was taken when the country's highest court ruled in May that confiscation of private property during the Nasser administration was illegal. In January and again in October several prisoners convicted of plotting against Nasser were released.

Mindful of Nasser's powerful hold on the memories of the Egyptian people, Sadat made clear that his aim was to correct the defects of the Nasser era but to keep its achievements. Sadat kept the presidency but relinquished the premiership on September 26 to First Deputy Premier Abdel Aziz Higazi, a strong advocate of opening up the Egyptian economy. There was popular discontent with shortages of some basic commodities during the year, and in October industrial workers at Helwan went on strike. Heavy military expenditures continued to put pressure on the country's balance of payments. (*See also* Middle East.)

## ELECTIONS.

The November 1974 elections, first since full disclosure of the Watergate scandal and resignation of U.S. President Richard M. Nixon, resulted in substantial gains for the Democratic party. There were moderate gains for women and for blacks, especially on state and local levels.

UPI COMPIX

*Rep. Ella T. Grasso (D, Conn.) became the first woman in the country to be elected governor on her own merit.*

The gains of the Democrats were about normal for the party opposing the president in an off-year election. They gained 43 seats in the House—the normal is 30; three Senate seats—the normal is four; and four governorships—the normal is six.

The situation was far from normal, however. In 1972, President Nixon had chosen to keep his campaign effort largely separate from Congressional and gubernatorial campaigns. While he scored a landslide victory, Republicans failed to make substantial gains on the Congressional and state levels. Thus, the Democrats were defending many more incumbencies than the Republicans were in 1974. Nevertheless, the Democrats captured five Senate seats and lost only one. They unseated 36 incumbent Republican U.S. representatives and failed to reelect only four incumbent Democrats who were candidates.

The Democratic margin in the House was the biggest since 1967, when the Congress elected with President Lyndon B. Johnson in 1964 went out of office. The Senate also had the largest Democratic majority since the Johnson Administration; the number of governorships held by the Democrats was the largest since the 1930's.

The Democratic sweep extended to state legislatures. The party increased the number of legislatures it controlled from 28 to 37. The number controlled by the Republicans fell from 16 to only 4. Six states had divided legislative control. (One legislature—Nebraska—was nonpartisan.) The Democrats polled almost 60% of the Congressional vote nationwide. But only 38% of those eligible had voted.

The economy was perhaps the most decisive issue in the election campaign, with the implications of Watergate a close second. President Gerald R. Ford, who as vice-president had taken office in August, pledged wholehearted cooperation with the enlarged Democratic majority in Congress in coping with the nation's troubled economy. Robert S. Strauss, Democratic party chairman, hailed the vote as a mandate for the party to formulate a program to solve the nation's problems. George Meany, president of the AFL-CIO, disagreed: "I don't think it was a mandate for the Democratic party. It was a vote against the party that happened to be in the White House."

### Gains by Women, and New Personalities

Women scored dramatic breakthroughs in politics in 1974. The 12 female members of the House of Representatives who sought reelection were all returned to Congress. Six other women were elected to their first terms in the House. They were Democrats Martha Keys, Kan.; Gladys N. Spellman, Md.; Helen S. Meyner, N.J.; and Marilyn Lloyd, Tenn.; and Republicans Virginia Smith, Neb.; and Millicent Fenwick, N.J.

Most dramatic was the election victory of U.S. Rep. Ella T. Grasso as governor of Connecticut. While other women had been elected governors, all the previous ones were elected after their husbands had held the office. Other notable women election victors included Susie Sharp, N.C., first woman elected chief justice of a state supreme court; Janet Gray Hayes, elected mayor of San Jose, Calif., the largest U.S. city yet to have a woman as mayor; and March Fong, a Democrat of Oriental ancestry, elected secretary of state in California. Women were

elected to about 595 seats in state legislatures, an apparent increase of 129 over 1974 totals.

All 15 black incumbents in the House won reelection. A 16th black, Democrat Harold E. Ford, was elected in Tennessee. Blacks also increased the number of seats held in state legislatures, including a gain of 34 in the South.

The elections catapulted a number of winners into positions of national prominence. Most surprising single victory was that of James B. Longley, who won the governorship of Maine. Although a Democrat personally, he ran as an independent, polling 40% of the vote to the Democratic 37% and the Republican 23%.

Two Republicans gained attention by thwarting Democratic hopes of capturing the governorships of the ten most populous states. James A. Rhodes, governor of Ohio from 1963 to 1971, defeated incumbent Gov. John J. Gilligan. Gov. William G. Milliken of Michigan won his second consecutive election from Democrat Sander M. Levin.

In Utah, Edwin J. Garn, former mayor of Salt Lake City, kept the Republicans in control of the U.S. senate seat formerly held by Wallace F. Bennett. In Alaska, Republican Jay S. Hammond, a former state senator, defeated incumbent Democratic Gov. William A. Egan by a few hundred votes. Former Gov. Paul Laxalt of Nevada took the only Senate seat lost by the Democrats, that of retiring Senator Alan Bible. Republican Robert F. Bennett, ex-mayor of Kansas City and longtime state legislator, took the governorship of Kansas from the Democrats. In the South one bright spot for the Republicans was South Carolina, where James B. Edwards won a previously Democratic governorship.

One Senate seat remained in dispute at year's end. In New Hampshire, Rep. Louis C. Wyman (R) appeared to be the winner by 542 votes in original election returns. Recounts gave the election to John

*North Carolina Associate Justice Susie Sharp was elected chief justice of the state supreme court, the country's first woman to hold that position. In New York Mary Anne Krupsak was voted in as the nation's first woman lieutenant governor with Rep. Hugh Carey (D, N.Y.) defeating incumbent Gov. Malcolm Wilson.*

PHOTOS, WIDE WORLD

A. Durkin (D) and then back to Wyman. The results were challenged, with the final decision apparently a matter for the courts or for the Senate, which has constitutional authority on whom it seats. In neighboring Vermont, Democrats elected a senator for the first time since the Republican party was founded in 1854. He was Patrick J. Leahy, who campaigned on economic issues, the energy shortage, and a pledge to remain independent, like outgoing Senator George D. Aiken (R).

Two Democrats, former Gov. Wendell H. Ford of Kentucky and Gary W. Hart of Colorado, defeated Republican Senate incumbents. Hart was manager of George McGovern's presidential campaign in 1972. In Florida, Secretary of State Richard Stone (D) won the Senate seat of Edward J. Gurney (R), who did not seek reelection after a grand jury indicted him in a case involving election contributions. Stone had promised to take the door off his office as a symbol of open government.

The Democrats elected two Spanish-surname governors, Raul Castro of Arizona and Jerry Apodaca of New Mexico. In Hawaii, Democrat George R. Ariyoshi became the first Japanese-American to gain the governorship.

In Colorado, Democrat Richard D. Lamm stressed environmental issues and defeated Republican Gov. John D. Vanderhoof. Democrat Michael S. Dukakis, who campaigned on the issue of efficiency in government, won in Massachusetts, defeating Republican Gov. Francis W. Sargent. In Oklahoma, Democrat David L. Boren captured a formerly Republican governorship by trudging the state's roads with a broom, promising to sweep out the old guard and its scandals. Also replacing Republican governors were Democrats Ray Blanton of Tennessee, Robert Straub of Oregon, and Ed Herschler of Wyoming. (*See also* Cities and Urban Affairs; Congress; Political Parties; State Governments; United States.)

## ELECTRONICS.
Electronics technology was influencing fields as dissimilar as transportation, food marketing, and medicine in 1974. A reason was that electronic components were becoming cheaper to make, while their range of abilities was growing. A new component in electronics technology was the microprocessor, a small semiconductor integrated circuit that acts as the central processing unit of a digital computer. By using microprocessors, engineers could build small computers into equipment without the need for a cumbersome central unit, thus reducing costs and accelerating data handling. Other proposed control activities of microprocessors included monitoring of brakes and other automobile systems, inventory control and check-out of supermarket goods by means of computerlike cash registers, and computer supervision of the vital signs of hospital patients.

Semiconductor circuits capable of storing large amounts of computer information were still fairly

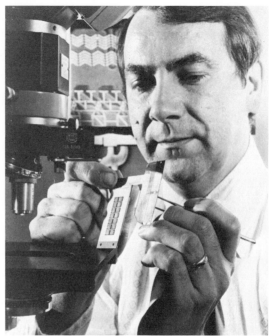

AUTHENTICATED NEWS INTERNATIONAL

*A scientist examines a new "magnetic bubble" memory that can store information equivalent to 27,000 telephone numbers and was designed for use in telephone switching systems.*

costly items to make. University of Utah electronics engineers, however, devised a relatively inexpensive way of producing semiconductor circuits capable of storing more than 16,000 "bits" of information. Each chip contained some 19,000 transistors in less than half a square inch.

It was easier to buy a modestly priced pocket-size electronic calculator in 1974. Not only were the handy calculators cheaper but some were almost portable computers. One, the Hewlett-Packard Model 65, used a magnetized program strip, which when inserted into the calculator could perform complex mathematics. The introductory price of the calculator was $795. Electronic wristwatches were also less expensive in 1974. Only one of every four or so watch buyers, however, would choose an electronic model, at least until 1980. The lower cost of the mechanical watches would be a major factor.

Coast-to-coast electronic communications in the United States were aided with the advent of Westar 1, Western Union's communications satellite put into geostationary orbit 22,300 miles above the equator, on a line south of Dallas, Tex. Functioning as a private "telephone" line, Westar 1 could carry either 14,400 voice conversations or 12 color-TV signals.

The U.S.S.R. and the U.S. decided to establish satellite communications because the "hot line" telephone system between Moscow and Washington, D.C., was plagued with breakdowns. It seemed that U.S. and European farmers as well as others often dug into the telephone lines and disrupted the system.

The trend was toward more solid-state color TV's in 1974. One unusual feature was in the Magnavox STAR (silent tuning at random) system. A viewer could select any vhf or uhf channel, and the set would tune directly to it without going through in-between channels. The new channel number becomes briefly visible on the screen. Semiconductor varactor diodes were at the core of the novel system.

Another 1974 innovation was a variable speed playback device for equipment such as magnetic tapes and long-playing records. The device adjusted the speech signal—stretched or compacted it—to eliminate "Donald Duck" sounds in speedup and rumbled noises in slowdown. Sped-up tapes or records would yield more information. Conversely, slowed speech would enable the transcription of involved material, say by a secretary typing a complicated letter from a dictated tape recording.

## EL SALVADOR.
The effects of the 1969 war between El Salvador and Honduras continued to be reflected in the Salvadorean economy in 1974. The border between the two countries remained closed to each other's trade, which was especially detrimental to El Salvador—the most densely populated, industrialized, and trade dependent of the Central American republics. Efforts to restore traditional trade between the estranged countries were unsuccessful. As the economic situation worsened in El Salvador—where the unemployment rate was at least 20%, the underemployment rate twice that, and inflation running at an annual rate of 60%—the government found itself pressured by opposition parties to resolve differences with Honduras. The economic news was particularly dispiriting for El Salvador because of a substantial price drop of the country's key commodity, coffee, which usually accounted for more than one third of its foreign exchange earnings.

A token gesture toward agrarian reform was made at the beginning of the year by President Arturo Armando Molina in an effort to avoid serious unrest as a consequence of inflation and the diminished strength of the Central American Common Market. Molina issued a decree to alleviate rural poverty by promising a minimum wage of $1.10 per day and a minimum daily food ration of corn, beans, and salt. The proposals were refused by the ruling landowners, however, and the president abandoned his efforts. In spite of these problems, the ruling National Conciliation Party won congressional and mayoral elections on March 10.

The Inter-American Development Bank approved two loans in 1974 for El Salvador. One, for $18.4 million, was earmarked for improving the water system of San Salvador, the capital; the other, for $15 million, was for expanding health services throughout the country. (*See also* Latin America.)

## EMPLOYMENT.
Under the impact of the winter 1973–74 energy crisis, January unemployment figures showed the largest monthly increase in four years. Unemployment was at 5.2%, and it was estimated that 9% of those receiving unemployment benefits were victims of the energy squeeze.

Despite its optimistic pronouncements, the administration of President Richard M. Nixon—trying simultaneously to combat inflation, recession, and unemployment—achieved no notable economic success. Unemployment figures that had remained fairly stable through June began a steady month-by-month rise. By year's end, labor leaders' predictions that the U.S. was headed for another full-scale depression began to seem justified. In December, when unemployment reached 7%, joblessness replaced inflation as the country's prime concern; for the first time since the Great Depression, 6 million Americans were without jobs. An Emergency Unemployment Act, originally proposed in August, finally became law in December. The act extended jobless benefits, created about 300,000 public-service jobs, and provided $500 million for public works projects.

The vagaries of the economy seemed to strike hardest at the automobile industry. January layoffs were prompted by the energy crisis, but the real trouble came in the fall as new car sales plummeted and inventories swelled. During November and December, major auto manufacturers announced massive layoffs, extended holiday plant closings, and reduced production. The construction industry also suffered acutely with an estimated one eighth of its workers unemployed. Other industries forced to lay off huge numbers of workers included rubber, textiles, lumber, glass, home appliances, and electrical equipment. (*See* Automobiles; Housing.)

In addition to the December emergency bill, two major pieces of employment legislation were signed

*"The monetarists assure us that as unemployed we're helping fight inflation. Pass it on."*

DAVID LANGDON—PUNCH/ROTHCO

during 1974. The first was a bill providing for gradual increase of the minimum wage from the current $1.60 to $2.30 an hour by 1976. The second important bill, the Employee Retirement Income Security Act of 1974, was aimed at regulating private pension and retirement plans and ensuring that the retired would receive all earned benefits.

The National Association for the Advancement of Colored People and other minority-rights groups continued to focus attention on the building trades. In July the Labor Department imposed mandatory minority-hiring goals on all federally funded construction in 21 areas of the country. About 100 locals from most of the 17 building trades were affected. And for the fifth time in four years, the Civil Rights Commission accused the federal government of failure to end discrimination in hiring. The Congressional Office of Placement and Office Management admitted complying with requests from some Congressional offices that only white candidates be considered for staff positions. Economic decline and massive layoffs threatened a potentially explosive legal issue for members of minorities: they contended that traditional seniority-based layoffs perpetuated discrimination against groups that had been unfairly denied employment.

In a landmark settlement involving age bias, the U.S. Labor Department won an agreement from Standard Oil of California to pay $2 million in back wages to "over-40" employees laid off in 1971–73. It was announced that more than 200 companies that had resisted compliance with the 1967 age discrimination law were being sued for millions in damages, the largest being a $20-million suit against the Chessie System Inc.'s two railroads. (*See also* Congress, U.S.; Labor Unions; United States.)

# ENGINEERING PROJECTS.

A number of large-scale engineering projects were undertaken throughout the world during 1974:

## Bridges

Brazil's 8.7-mile bridge across the Bay of Guanabara, the first direct connection between Rio de Janeiro and Niterói, was opened to traffic in March. A key link in Brazil's 2,500-mile coastal highway, the bridge crossed the channel in three spans (two of 656 feet and one of 984 feet). In England the newly completed Avonmouth bridge over the Avon River had three main spans (two of 370 feet and one of 570 feet) extended by 17 approach spans from 100 feet to 240 feet in length.

In Japan the Nanko cantilever bridge across Osaka Bay neared completion. With a central span of 1,683 feet set between two bankside spans of 776 feet each, it was to be the third longest of its type in the world. Nanhae Island was linked to Hadong on the South Korean mainland by a 2,165-foot suspension bridge.

Work neared completion on a cable-styled bridge across the Loire estuary in France, between Saint-Nazaire and Saint-Brévin. It had a central span of 1,325 feet flanked by two spans of 518 feet each. In West Germany the Deggenau bridge near Deggendorf on the Danube River, consisting of two cable-stayed metal spans of 476 feet and 951 feet, was under construction. Work continued on the Kiev bridge (984-foot main span) in the U.S.S.R. and on the Suehiro bridge, with three spans, in Japan.

In France work began on the Meules bridge over the Seine River, downstream from Rouen. It was to have three cable-stayed spans, of which the 1,050-foot center span would set a world record. In the United States, mobile rigs were used to build the Pine Valley Creek Bridge in California. The bridge had a 450-foot main span with a deck consisting of two uniform 19-foot depth box girders, each supporting a 42-foot roadway. The same construction method was used for the four-span Felsenau viaduct crossing the Aare River in Switzerland.

The main innovation in the construction of concrete bridges during 1974 lay in the use of lightweight aggregates. Dutch engineers appeared to have established a lead in this field, and three identical structures spanning the Meuse-Waal canal near Nijmegen, Netherlands, were brought into service. (*See also* Sudan.)

## Dams

Two dams were completed in Spain—the Guadalhorce-Guadalteba rockfill dam (height 272 feet) and the Arenos rockfill dam (height 344 feet) on the Mijares River. In Italy the Piastra concrete gravity dam on the Gesso River and the Passante solid gravity dam on the Passante River were both under construction. Work continued on the Kardamakis earth and rockfill dam on the Aliakmon River in Greece. In the U.S.S.R. the Zeya buttress dam (height 367 feet) was completed, and work continued on two others—the Serebryansk earth and rockfill dam on the Voronya River and the Sayano-Shushenshoye dam (height 700 feet) in Siberia.

The Tarbela earth and rockfill dam (height 470 feet) on the Indus River in Pakistan, the world's largest of its kind, neared completion. In India the Idikki parabolic arch dam (height 555 feet) on the Periyar River was completed. Work continued in Indonesia on the Karangkates rockfill dam on the Brantas River. Construction started on the Ban Chao Nen rockfill dam on the Quae Yai River in Thailand and on the Temengor rockfill dam on the Upper Perak River in Malaysia.

About 60 dams, each over 130 feet high, were under construction in Japan. Dams completed during 1974 included the Oto concrete gravity dam (height 328 feet) on the Niyodo River, the Kajigawa concrete gravity dam (height 351 feet) on the Kaji River, the Sameura concrete gravity dam (height 348 feet) on the Yoshino River, and the Nikappu rockfill dam (height 338 feet) on the Nikappu River.

In the U.S. the Pueblo massive-head concrete buttress and earthfill dam (height 190 feet) was

UPI COMPIX

*Opened in September, the Koehlbrand Bridge in Hamburg, West Germany, which spans the Elbe River and links the city with its harbor area, was expected to carry 31,000 vehicles daily.*

completed on the Arkansas River in Colorado. Construction continued on the Crystal double-curvature arch dam on the Gunnison River, in Colorado; on the New Melones rockfill dam on the Stanislaus River, California; and on the Back Creek rockfill dam on the Little Back Creek, Missouri.

In Brazil the Passo Real earth and rockfill dam (height 184 feet) on the Jacuí River was completed. Four other dams were under construction in that country: the São Simão and Itumbiara dams on the Paranaíba River, the Foz do Areia dam on the Iguaçú River, and the Itaipu solid gravity dam on the Paraná River. Two earth and rockfill dams, Futaleufú and Los Reyunos, were under construction in Argentina; while on the Rio Diamante, the Agua del Toro double-curvature arch dam neared completion. In Morocco the Bou-Regreg earth and rockfill dam (height 328 feet) on the Oued Bou-Regreg (watercourse) was completed. Under construction in South Africa, the Le Roux arch dam on the Orange River would have the highest concrete arch in that country.

## Roads

In the planning of road systems, two concepts gained increasing recognition in 1974: one being that of the pioneer road thrust into a developing region; the other being that the development of any road system should be planned in conformity with the overall development plans for the region it was designed to serve. Brazil offered perhaps the best example of how to utilize these concepts successfully when it constructed the Belém–Brasília high-

way as part of its Trans-Brazilian Highway and then, with the southern section of the road still not completed, undertook to build yet a second major highway from its Atlantic Coast that would connect with roads leading to Peru and Bolivia.

The Asian Highway Network, extending about 40,000 miles overall, was connected to the European Highway Network at the Iran-Turkey border and to the Middle East Highway Network at the Iran-Iraq border. In Greece a new 28-mile freeway, linking the Greek-Yugoslav frontier post of Evzoni with the Athens–Thessalonica national road, was put into service. The newly opened 97-mile Chemaia–Agadir road in Morocco cut one hour off the trip time between Casablanca and Agadir. The 70-mile Guidam-Romji and Madaoua section of the Niamey-Zinder road opened in Niger. In Thailand a new 60-mile road was built through the mountainous country between Sri Satchanalai and Phrae, and a 40-mile length of new construction opened on the Rong Kwang–Song–Nagao Highway. In the U.S. the 1,060-mile Baja California Peninsular Highway was opened.

France planned to build 335 miles of expressway by 1978, which would extend its national network to 3,750 miles. An additional 20-mile section of the A8 expressway between Aix-en-Provence and Nice was finished, linking together the Paris–Marseille and the Esterel–Côte d'Azur expressways. The Paris–Orleans expressway and the Les Pennes–Mirabeau–Martiques expressway also opened. Nearly 57 miles of new expressway opened in Great Britain, with an additional 397 miles under construction and another 547 miles being planned.

The opening up of continental road networks in Africa, South America, and Asia meant an increased world expenditure on road building—amounting to more than $50 billion yearly. Despite dramatic increases in prices of oil products, it appeared that road building programs in Europe and North America would continue, but at a slower pace. In less developed countries, however, where transport is an essential key to primary production, expenditure on new roads would increase.

## Tunnels

In April representatives from 19 countries met in Oslo, Norway, to form the International Tunneling Association. It was an event of major significance for furthering international cooperation on tunneling matters. The association established a permanent secretariat at Bron, France, and scheduled its first meeting for 1975 in West Germany.

On both sides of the English Channel trial borings got under way for the 32-mile-long Channel Tunnel that would link England and France. In Switzerland work continued on the St. Gotthard Tunnel, which, when completed, would be the longest road tunnel in the world. Work also went ahead on the twin-bore, 3.5-mile-long Seelisberg tunnel that would eventually form part of the N2 highway linking Switzerland and Italy. Work began on the Furka Railway system, including 7.7 miles of tunnel. In Austria construction was started on the world's second longest road tunnel, consisting of 4.6-mile-long twin bores through the Arlberg massif.

The Dutch maintained their lead in the construction of immersed tube tunnels by constructing four of them. In Amsterdam, Netherlands, work continued on the underground section of that city's first subway line, a project that was proving to be one of the most difficult underground railways ever constructed. Construction of a subway system in Oslo, Norway, introduced technically interesting new methods for using explosives in urban areas.

In Hong Kong there was considerable tunneling activity. Work proceeded on three trial tunnels for a 20.2-mile-long subway system. At Kai Tak International Airport a cut-and-cover tunnel under the airport's main runway was being constructed. Inland, work progressed on the tunneling of 15.4 miles of hard rock, required for Hong Kong's High Island water system. In Japan excavation began on the tunnels to be part of the 32.3-mile-long Seikan crossing. Scheduled for completion in 1979, it would be the longest railway tunnel in the world. Tunneling began in Peru on a massive irrigation project that would include driving approximately 29 miles of tunnel to irrigate the Pampas de Majes. In Rio de Janeiro work continued on the first section of the world's first sea-level subway in a tropical locale.

In the U.S., in September, San Francisco, Calif., opened the last major segment of its $1.6-billion Bay Area Rapid Transit system—a four-mile-long tunnel under San Francisco Bay that connected with other segments already in operation. In New York City 8.5 miles of hard rock tunnel were being driven as part of the largest municipal water supply contracts ever let in the hemisphere. (*See also* Transportation.)

*Work proceeds on a Soviet hydroelectric power station in Siberia on the River Angara. The system's projected power output was to equal that of all other Soviet systems combined.*
V. CHERNOV—CAMERA PRESS/PHOTO TRENDS

**ENVIRONMENT.** In 1974 the conflict between the world energy crisis and the need for environmental protection continued to loom as one of mankind's most difficult dilemmas. During the height of the oil shortage in early 1974, some leaders of U.S. conservation groups expressed fears that much of the hard-won federal and state environmental legislation might be swept away.

Other conservationists saw benefits in the fuel shortage because it corroborated their long-standing position on conserving resources and might speed up public demand for alternative sources of power, such as solar energy. Traditional antagonists of the environmental movement considered the ecologists at least partly responsible for the fuel shortage; however, in a national poll during the severe shortage, only 2% blamed the ecology movement—25% tended to blame the oil companies.

Shortly after Gerald R. Ford took office as U.S. president, he made a speech suggesting the broad outline of energy-environment policies to be pursued by his administration. President Ford said that the energy crisis had demonstrated that the country must use more coal, search for more oil on the ocean's continental shelf, develop oil shale resources, and build more nuclear power plants. He rejected "zero growth" policies as lacking in creativity and declared that it is possible to have both environmental protection and economic growth.

In October, however, Ford removed John C. Sawhill as head of the Federal Energy Administration. Sawhill reportedly favored stringent controls on energy use. He was to be replaced by Andrew E. Gibson, an oil company executive, but when Gibson's confirmation in the Senate looked doubtful, Ford selected Frank G. Zarb, of the Office of Management and Budget, to head the agency.

Earlier in the year Russell E. Train, head of the Environmental Protection Agency (EPA), urged his fellow citizens not to "panic and trade off short-term energy gains for long-term environmental values." By year-end, however, environmentalists had suffered several setbacks—including postponements for enforcing pollution standards, relaxation of offshore drilling restrictions, and relaxation of water-discharge regulations for steam electric plants.

### Economics Versus Environmental Protection

Ambivalence and confusion over the energy-environment dilemma were reflected in the long debate in Congress on a new federal strip-mining law. Before the fuel shortage reached its acute stage, the Senate passed a tough strip-mining bill, totally barring mining on private lands for which the government owns only the mineral rights—a situation prevailing for at least 35% of the surface coal reserves in the western states. By the time House of Representatives hearings on the bill opened, however, the fuel shortage was at a peak. Power shortages and pressure from coal lobbyists brought on acrimonious debates. A compromise bill finally

UPI COMPIX

*The remains of a defunct streetcar system, several decaying buildings, and tons of junk were recycled into this multimillion-dollar shopping center in Salt Lake City, Utah.*

emerged from a House-Senate conference committee in December; however, a pocket veto by President Ford prevented the bill from becoming law.

Because most strip mining in the U.S. was expected to shift from Appalachia to the Northern Great Plains and Mountain states in the future, considerable opposition to the practice came from ranchers, wheat growers, American Indians on reservations, and others who felt their way of life threatened by coal stripping. Opponents of stripping argued that the delicate ecosystems of the thin-soiled High Plains and the prevalent low rainfall would require complex plans for reclamation and safeguards to protect streams and water tables.

In June the U.S. celebrated the 50th anniversary of the designation of its first wilderness area, the Gila Wilderness in southwestern New Mexico. Since the establishment of Gila, 90 similar areas had been set aside, totaling about 11 million acres. Conservationists warned against incursions into wilderness areas; they pointed to current examples such as efforts by commercial interests to open two thirds of Idaho's wilderness areas for mining and lumbering and a revival of proposals by power companies to build a dam in the Grand Canyon.

Minnesota conservationists fought a long battle

to stop pollution of Lake Superior along the Silver Bay–Duluth shoreline by a taconite mining company. A federal district court judge ruled that the company was guilty of pollution and ordered the plant closed until fouling of the lake was discontinued. A U.S. appeals court ruling, however, allowed the company to resume operations while searching for an alternate means of disposing of polluting wastes. In late August the company submitted a proposal for on-land waste disposal.

For 18 years the taconite plant had poured millions of tons of iron-mining wastes into Lake Superior, but only recently was it discovered that the wastes contained asbestos fibers, a proven cancer-producing agent. It was a classic example of the conflict between environmental protection and economic security, because the employment of more than 3,000 workers was affected. The district court judge noted, however, that the general public should not be "continuously and indefinitely exposed to a known human carcinogen in order that the people in Silver Bay can continue working."

In Gary, Ind., some 2,500 workers were laid off when U.S. Steel Corp. was ordered to either close its remaining open-hearth furnaces or pay a $2,300-a-day fine. The company, which had been granted previous deadline extensions, chose to cease open-hearth operations rather than pay the fine.

Passage of an effective land-use planning law was blocked again when the House, by a narrow vote of 211–204, rejected a measure that would have appropriated $800 million over eight years to the states for use in land planning under federal guidance. After the Senate had twice passed similar bills and the administration had backed them, strong lobbying from land developers and industrial corporations prevented passage in the House.

### Threat from Pesticides

For the first time since the banning of DDT from general use (Dec. 31, 1972), the EPA permitted use of the insecticide in a battle against tree-killing tussock moths infesting at least 750,000 acres of fir forests in Washington, Oregon, and Idaho. The EPA insisted that it approved the use of DDT only after other control methods had proved ineffective against the infestation. Many environmentalists claimed, however, that DDT was ineffective against the moths and that other materials were preferable. Naturalists credited the general DDT ban with increasing the number of birds reappearing in areas from which they had almost vanished. Bald eagles, for example, were sighted in the Chesapeake Bay region and in Florida, Michigan, and Wisconsin.

The EPA ordered a halt in the production of aldrin and dieldrin, two of the most widely used pesticides in the U.S. The Environmental Defense Fund had gathered evidence that aldrin and dieldrin are long-lived in the environment, cause mental impairment in monkeys, cause birth defects and tumors in mice, and may cause cancer in mankind.

In September a group of botanists announced that 10% of the floral species found in the U.S. were in danger of extinction. Some 266 species were endangered in Hawaii alone, the state with the largest total. The list of endangered plants was drawn up at the request of the Smithsonian Institution under a provision of the Endangered Species Act. A U.S.-Soviet accord for preservation of disappearing plant species was also signed during the year.

### Oil Spills and Water Pollution

Remembering the disastrous oil spill off Santa Barbara, Calif., in 1969, seven cities along the California coast joined forces to oppose the federal government's decision to permit immediate offshore drilling only a few miles from some of the region's choicest beaches. Geological surveys indicated that 2 billion–8 billion barrels of oil could be gained from the offshore area in question, but the seven cities asked for a delay in issuing new leases until a draft environmental statement and a state conservation plan could be properly completed.

Damaging U.S. oil spills in 1974 included one from a grounded barge in the Hudson River below Albany, N.Y., and another from a pumping leak off Port Jefferson, N.Y., that closed 24 miles of beaches off Long Island Sound. Other major spills were a 60-mile-long crude-oil slick in the Mississippi River near New Orleans, La., and one resulting from a ship collision that poured 16,000 gallons of fuel oil into the Pacific Ocean off Big Sur, Calif.

One of the largest tanker spills in international waters occurred near the Strait of Magellan in September. About 14 million gallons poured out of a grounded ship, coating 18 miles of shoreline. A massive leak in western Japan spilled more than 260,000 barrels of heavy oil into the Inland Sea.

The U.S.-Canadian International Joint Commission reported some progress in its long, arduous struggle to clean up the polluted Great Lakes. Lake Erie, which biologists had described as a "dead" lake a few years ago, lost its green scum after the amount of phosphorus flowing into its waters was reduced. Beaches were cleaner, with no summer closings because of dangerous bacteria counts in the waters.

Progress was also reported in cleaning up the Miami River in Florida. Three years earlier the river had been so filled with debris and pollutants that no marine species could live in its waters. A cleanup program sponsored by local conservationists brought out more than 2,000 volunteers to remove debris. Though the cleanup program was only 60% completed, most of the Miami's waters were already clean enough for swimming. Pelicans—which had departed years ago—returned to the river.

Water pollution made news in November when it was learned that earlier EPA tests had shown that chlorination of drinking water could produce numerous cancer-causing compounds. Ironically, Congress in December approved a long-delayed safe-water bill, which authorized the EPA to establish national minimum standards for drinking water.

### Lead-Free Gas and Other Developments

A report of the National Academy of Sciences emphasized the continuing dangers in urban areas from air pollution, especially from automobile exhausts. A yearlong study made by the agency estimated that as many as 4,000 persons a year were dying in the U.S. from exhaust poisons. Beginning July 1, 1974, the country's largest gas stations began selling lead-free gasoline, under orders from the EPA. Gas stations with annual sales of more than 200,000 gallons were required to sell the lead-free gas under the government's clean-air program.

The release of other harmful gases into the atmosphere also aroused concern in 1974. One report revealed that fluorocarbons, widely used as propellants in aerosol cans, are contributing to the destruction of the earth's vital ozone shield. (*See* Earth Sciences.) And an EPA report indicated that industry may annually be emitting more than 200 million pounds of vinyl chloride, a gas linked to certain forms of cancer. (*See* Medicine.)

Acting on the theory that younger Americans have a greater stake in environmental protection than do older segments of the population, the EPA and the Office of Environmental Education (OEE) made available funds for local school and college study groups willing to leave their classrooms to engage in practical projects. The OEE offered grants for specific projects: using polluted streams as laboratories, combating soil erosion, and making on-site studies for sewage treatment plants.

A university study of Oregon's controversial bottle deposit law showed that during the first year of enforcement the decline in litter and waste resulted in cleanup savings of about $700,000. The Oregon law required deposits on all beverage containers and prohibited pull-tab cans. Brewers and bottlers saved about $8 million on container costs, the study found, and about 365 additional jobs were created in the industry. The most significant savings were in energy and raw materials that would have been used to make new throwaway containers. In Vermont, where a similar bottle-deposit law was adopted in 1973, attempts at repeal failed. South Dakota passed a similar law in 1974, but opponents of such legislation were successful in 15 other states.

The California League of Conservation Voters flexed its political muscles and took credit for the victories of two candidates involved in very close primary races for Congressional seats. Statewide the league tallied 19 primary winners among 25 candidates whom it had backed. (*See also* Animals and Wildlife; Arms Control and Disarmament; Automobiles; Fuel and Power; Oceanography; Weather.)

*The dumping of wastes into Lake Superior by the Reserve Mining Company's taconite plant at Silver Bay, Minn., continued to be a prime target of environmentalists' protests.*
WIDE WORLD

# Special Report:
# Expo '74

by Edith Wasserman

"Do as I say, and do as I do" is the message from Spokane, Wash., site of Expo '74, the 1974 World's Fair. Expo's theme, "Celebrating Tomorrow's Fresh, New Environment," generated an amplitude of talk about ways to achieve it; and the host city itself was an object lesson. Spokane cleared away a maze of railroad tracks and rundown buildings in the heart of town to prepare the fairground. Now the site is a riverside park. An opera house and convention center remain there as a legacy of the fair. Expo '74 was the first event of the United States bicentennial celebration and the only international exposition scheduled for the U.S. during the 1970's. A stocktaking and guidepost combined, it was a good start for the country's third hundred years.

Expo '74 was the first international exposition in the U.S. since it joined the Bureau of International Expositions (BIE) in 1968. The BIE regulates and schedules such events to the best advantage of its member countries. More than 5.1 million visitors saw Expo '74 between its opening on May 4 and its closing on November 3. That attendance figure exceeded the original prediction by 380,000 visitors.

### A Century of Fairs

Most international fairs in the U.S. have celebrated an important historical event or summed up a period of accomplishment. The U.S. marked its first centennial in Philadelphia, Pa., birthplace of the Declaration of Independence. Crowd stoppers at the 1876 festivities included the telephone, Thomas Edison's duplex telegraph, the typewriter, and the sewing machine.

The World's Columbian Exposition of 1893 in Chicago observed (a little late) the 400th anniversary of America's discovery by Columbus. The classical facades of the exhibition halls spurred a neoclassic movement in architecture. Behind the

*In keeping with its theme of "Celebrating Tomorrow's Fresh, New Environment," Expo '74 in Spokane, Wash., provided the city with a form of instant urban renewal by redeveloping for its site a shabby, dying downtown section of the city on the Spokane River's edge.*
DOUG WILSON—THE NEW YORK TIMES

*Visitors on a skyride trundle past Expo '74's U.S.S.R. Pavilion, which offers a display of environmental problems and socialist state solutions.*
WIDE WORLD

plaster fronts, visitors were treated to something still unfamiliar to most of them—electricity. The first big display of automobiles beguiled the crowds when St. Louis, Mo., was host to the Louisiana Purchase Exposition in 1904. That fair commemorated the 100th anniversary of the U.S. acquisition of the Louisiana Territory in 1803. (People like fairs. If the dates were off by a year or so, there is no record of mass protests.)

Motion pictures and airplane rides were attractions at a fair for the first time when the Panama-Pacific International Exposition of 1915 took place in San Francisco, Calif. That fair observed a contemporary event, the opening of the Panama Canal. In 1933–34, A Century of Progress International Exposition at Chicago hailed the scientific achievements made during that city's first hundred years. An eight-acre Hall of Science was a focal point. The New York World's Fair of 1939-40 honored the 150th anniversary of George Washington's inauguration as the first U.S. president, but the fair's theme was "The World of Tomorrow." Although television was still in an experimental stage, regular television programs were inaugurated in March 1939, when the National Broadcasting Co. telecast the opening of the New York World's Fair. The famous landmarks of that fair—the Trylon, a triangular shaft that tapered to a point 728 feet high, and the Perisphere, a true sphere 180 feet in diameter—were said to symbolize "the shape of things to come."

The Century 21 Exposition in Seattle, Wash., in 1962 emphasized technical and scientific progress. Visitors liked the elevated monorail train, which moved them from downtown to the fairground in 94 seconds, and the Space Needle, a 600-foot steel tripod topped by a revolving restaurant. The Space Needle became part of a Seattle civic center after the fair. The New York World's Fair of 1964-65 drew the largest single day's attendance in the history of U.S. fairs. On its closing day there were 446,953 visitors at the 646-acre site.

Many expositions of lesser status have been a source of enjoyment. The popularity of state and county fairs continues in the U.S.; about 2,000 fairs and festivals take place annually. Industrial and trade shows also have burgeoned in the second half of the 20th century.

## Sights and Sounds of '74

Expo '74 was centered on Havermale and Cannon islands in the Spokane River. Exhibits covered 50 acres of the 100-acre downtown site, and the other 50 were occupied by the clear, cascading river—the prize exhibit of them all. A new sewage treatment plant upstream and settling ponds in nearby mining areas transformed the polluted waters that now sparkle and run with trout.

On the site, which survives as a park for the people of Spokane, four Expo buildings remain. They are the Washington State Pavilion, which includes a 2,700-seat opera house and a convention center; the U.S. Pavilion; the Boeing International Amphitheater; and the Bavarian Gardens, a German restaurant for fairgoers, which will house an antique carousel.

Among the myriad multimedia sights and sounds that lured Expo visitors, the motion picture at the U.S. Pavilion was the favorite. Projected onto a curved 65-foot-high screen, the film took viewers on a swooping airplane ride into the Grand Canyon and on a raft ride down the churning Colorado River. In contrast to the scenic grandeur were close-ups of strip-mining machinery clawing at the earth and of a lettuce grower plowing under a crop that was ruined by smog. Among the exhibits under the huge vinyl canopy of the U.S. Pavilion was a fountain made of old bathtubs, sinks, washbasins, and

207

shower heads. It called attention to personal responsibility for the prodigal use of water. Rest assured that the fountain's waters were recycled.

The Soviet Pavilion was the largest, costliest, and most popular of the foreign exhibits. Its interior was a stylized "biosphere" centered by a massive electric sun. Detailed mock-ups of Soviet cities, air and water purification systems, environmental movies, a mineral display, and archaeological treasures dazzled the throngs milling in the multilevel pavilion.

Other countries exhibiting at Expo '74 included Australia, Canada, West Germany, Iran, Japan, Korea, Mexico, the Philippines, and Taiwan. Canada made a lasting contribution to Spokane by turning one-acre Cannon Island (renamed Canada Island) into an oasis of flowers and tree species from all parts of Canada. Now part of the riverside park, it is a delightful place for viewing the river falls.

A traditional Japanese garden beautified the grounds of Japan's pavilion, one of Expo's largest. Inside, motion pictures and exhibits described Japanese life from the serene to the frenetic. As visitors walked along mirrored halls of the Australian exhibit, they felt surrounded by Australia's environment. The effect was created with the help of photographs, slides, recordings, and mounted animal displays. Australia was praised for its frankness in pointing out environmental disasters that included Sydney's slums and depredations of unique wildlife species.

Expo '74 presented several engaging domestic exhibits, too. A nursery for young specimens of endangered species attracted crowds to Spokane County's Vanishing Animals Exhibit. A Folk Life Festival presented "live," with their music and arts and crafts, the folk who settled and developed the Pacific Northwest. The Affiliated Tribes of Northwest Indians took an active part. The Afro-American Pavilion concentrated on black culture and achievement. Passing through a "heritage tunnel," visitors heard a narrator describe the exhibits, which were spotlighted one by one. Paintings and sculpture by black artists were also on display. An unusual art exhibit at Expo '74—"Our Earth, Our Sea, Our Sky"—brought together a selection of works by U.S. and Canadian artists, past and present. The scenery that they painted ranged from arctic Canada's stark wilderness to the warm Hawaiian landscape.

An open construction of timber and Douglas fir trees made an appropriate setting for displays on forest management in the American Forest Pavilion. In the Energy Pavilion, problems of fuel supply were defined. During its run, Expo '74 was host to a series of international symposia on environmental matters.

On the lighter side, Expo '74 provided an amusement park and a calendar of professional entertainment. The fairground was embellished with gardens, winding walks, trees, and benches. Overhead gondolas took fairgoers on a spectacular ride across the river below the falls. Another aerial ride offered a panoramic view of the grounds. Tempting food of many lands attracted visitors to the outdoor stands near umbrella-shaded tables.

How did Spokane, with a population of about 172,400, become a world's fair city? The idea sprang from a decision made in 1969 by the Spokane County Historical Society to celebrate the city's centennial. The centennial year was set arbitrarily at 1974. (A settlement was established at Spokane Falls in 1871; a village by that name was incorporated in 1881 and chartered in 1882; and "Falls" was dropped from the name in 1890.)

Local businessmen and officials decided to use the occasion as an economic vehicle for rejuvenating the city's blighted heart. When they found that the centennial celebration would not be broad enough to support the project, the idea for a world's fair evolved. The business community levied a tax on itself to raise seed money. This was matched by state and federal grants. The railroads donated 13 acres on Havermale Island, and the city bought adjacent property. Finally, plans were approved by the BIE in November 1971. Before Expo '74 was opened, it had already generated widespread urban improvements and new businesses for Spokane.

*A gondola ride crosses above the once badly polluted Spokane River, now Expo '74's showcase exhibit on environmental cleanup.*

BLACK STAR

Lieut. Gen. Aman Michael Andom, Ethiopian army chief of staff and minister of defense, became head of the ruling military council upon the deposition of Emperor Haile Selassie on September 12, but was later killed in the November mass executions by the military government.

A.F.P./PICTORIAL PARADE

**ETHIOPIA.** In 1974 the revolt against the long-established feudal order in the empire of Ethiopia finally gained sufficient force and popular backing to initiate a series of fundamental changes. The movement began in mid-February when strikes and demonstrations by students, taxi drivers, and trade unions paralyzed life in the capital. Civilian demonstrators in Addis Ababa, Asmara, and Harar were joined by the armed forces, who were motivated by a number of issues including demands for higher pay. On February 27 the cabinet of Prime Minister Aklilu Habte-wold resigned.

A series of events, including minor cabinet changes and nationwide arrests of corrupt officials, culminated in a proclamation on September 12 that ended the imperial rule and led to the deposing and imprisonment of Emperor Haile Selassie I. The throne was offered by the Provisional Military Administrative Council, known commonly as the Dirgue, to Haile Selassie's named heir, 57-year-old Crown Prince Asfa Wossen, who was recuperating in Geneva, Switzerland, from a serious stroke.

The changes at the top were accompanied by measures against the ruling group of aristocratic families and palace appointees. Habte-wold's cabinet had already been arrested, and his successor, Endalkachew Makonnen, was arrested in July. On August 16 the emperor's Crown Council, Imperial Court, and Private Cabinet were abolished. On November 23, when 60 of the country's imprisoned aristocrats and officials were executed, one of Selassie's grandsons was reportedly killed.

Parliament was suspended effective September 12, as was the 1955 revised constitution. A civilian Technical Advisory Council began work in October on a new constitution it would propose to the Dirgue. That 120-member body, composed of representatives of the armed forces and the police, was under the chairmanship of Lieut. Gen. Aman Michael Andom. General Aman, as chairman, became Ethiopia's nominal head of state but was killed during the mass execution of November 23. Major Mengistu Haile Miriam was reported to have succeeded Aman as military strongman.

A commission of inquiry began investigating the backgrounds of those officials in detention. Carefully timed publicity was given to initial findings that implicated the emperor and the royal family in financial scandals involving government property, holdings in local firms, and the awarding of scholarships abroad to children of influential families. In November the government announced that the deposed emperor had signed a letter authorizing the transfer of his fortune to aid the country's drought and famine victims, At year's end the Dirgue declared its plan to reconstruct Ethiopia into a one-party socialist country and to modernize the agricultural system. The new government also announced willingness to negotiate with the Eritrean separatists. (*See also* Africa.)

*Angry over falling agricultural prices, French farmers man a protest roadblock on the main Paris–Chantilly route. The September 16 demonstration was one of many throughout the European community.*

UPI COMPIX

**EUROPE.** The 35 nations of the Conference on Security and Cooperation in Europe tried during 1974 to formalize détente between Eastern and Western European countries. The meetings, however, made little progress, primarily because of the West's reluctance to concede the legitimacy of some of the existing boundaries between Communist and non-Communist countries and the Soviet Union's refusal to modify its internal politics to allow Western-style freedom of thought and movement.

Within individual Western European nations, national Communist parties enjoyed increasing popularity and participation in government in 1974, particularly in Italy, Portugal, and France. Most national parties had modified their positions to accommodate themselves to local issues and to adopt a European, rather than a strictly international, Communist outlook. In some countries Communist parties had formed temporary working alliances with other leftists and socialists on certain issues.

Western Europe's relations with the U.S. remained strained in 1974, particularly over oil and defense policies. The North Atlantic Treaty Organization (NATO) adopted guidelines promising joint consultation on military policy but allowing for unilateral action in emergencies, a matter that had been a source of contention between Europe and the U.S. in the past. Fighting in Cyprus between two NATO members, Turkey and Greece, and political instability in Greece and its withdrawal from the military alliance threatened NATO. Although opposed by some Europeans, U.S. Army Gen. Alex-

ander M. Haig, formerly White House chief of staff, was accepted as the supreme allied commander of NATO. (*See* Arms Control and Disarmament.)

In Western Europe the progress of the European Economic Community (EEC) was undramatic, and the unity of European nations remained somewhat precarious. French President Valéry Giscard d'Estaing and West German Chancellor Helmut Schmidt met during the year, however, and called for a strengthening of the EEC. The new alliance of France and Germany and their desire and need to revitalize the EEC's plans for interdependence among European nations gave hope that greater unity might be achieved in the future.

### Great Britain, the EEC, and Energy

Britain's foreign secretary, James Callaghan, announced in April that the new Labour government intended to renegotiate the terms of Britain's entry into the EEC. Callaghan attacked the ambitious plans for economic, monetary, and political union. He also objected to the Common Agricultural Policy (CAP) that many British blamed for rising food prices and asked for a reduction in Britain's contribution to the EEC's budget.

Callaghan estimated that by 1980 Britain, using the present formula, would be providing 24% of the EEC's resources, although Britain's share of the EEC's gross domestic product (GDP) would be only 14%. Later in the year, however, the EEC produced figures showing that, in its first 18 months of membership, Britain had benefited to the extent of

$601 million, with $752 million received in loans and grants and $478 million in subsidies on food imports, against a contribution of $652 million to the EEC budget. Britain later narrowed its demands for renegotiation—that apparently could eventually be resolved with the other eight EEC countries.

Europe's quarrel with the U.S. grew serious over the refusal of EEC members, primarily because of French pressure, to consult the U.S. about an offer for long-range cooperation with the Arab nations. In March their relations seemed at a breaking point. U.S. President Richard M. Nixon responded by threatening cuts in the number of U.S. troops in Europe, an action that apparently influenced the EEC to agree to consult with the U.S. in the future. In July the EEC and the Arab League countries decided to work out economic agreements.

In November, at the urging of the U.S., 16 oil-consuming countries formed the International Energy Agency (IEA) to provide for the pooling of energy resources in emergencies and for cooperative energy conservation and development programs. Opposed to U.S. leadership of the IEA and hesitant to jeopardize relations with the Arab oil nations, France steadfastly refused to join. French President Giscard, meeting with U.S. President Gerald R. Ford in December, however, agreed on the desirability of convening a conference of oil exporting and importing nations in 1975 and on "the importance of solidarity among oil importing nations."

## Monetary Union and the Economy

World inflation had an uneven effect on EEC countries in 1974, widening the gap between those countries whose currencies were floating jointly (including West Germany) and those that had free-floating currencies—Britain, France, and Italy. Virtually no progress was made during the year toward economic and monetary union.

Consumer prices rose by 15% to 20% in Britain and Italy during 1974, but by less than 10% in West Germany and the Netherlands. Although growth rates had been remarkably even in 1973, within a range of 5% to 6%, they also varied widely in 1974. Britain's GDP declined by about 1% during the year. Those of West Germany and Denmark grew slowly, by about 2%. Those of France, Italy, Belgium, and Luxembourg grew rapidly, by between 4% and 5%. Unemployment, which had been very low in most EEC countries, grew substantially.

Balance of payments problems of the EEC countries became acute during the year. The total deficit amounted to about $20 billion, compared with a surplus of $1 billion in 1973. The deficits of Britain and Italy were each about $10 billion. West Germany, however, recorded a huge surplus, as did the Netherlands. The halt in the rise of the cost of most raw materials by midyear, as well as the decision by the EEC to raise loans of up to $3 billion to help member countries in balance of payments difficulties, indicated an alleviation of the problem in the future. At year's end, under the auspices of the Organization for Economic Cooperation and Development (OECD), plans were made to set up a $25-billion revolving loan fund for mutual support among members in balance of payments crises.

## Agriculture and Restrictive Practices

The CAP continued to play a major part in ensuring stability of food prices in EEC countries in spite of large increases in world prices. EEC farm prices, however, were increased twice during 1974. The first increase averaged 8¾%. The second was a 5% increase, accompanied by a 5% increase in premiums for delaying slaughter of beef cattle and an extension of an earlier ban on beef imports. Both the British and the West Germans wanted to reduce the cost to them of the CAP.

By October, export subsidies, to which the U.S. and other countries had objected, were suspended

*Common Market employees demonstrate for higher wages at the opening of the foreign ministers' meeting in Luxembourg on April 1.*
WIDE WORLD

*Italian Treasury Minister Ugo La Malfa presides over a January meeting in Rome of finance ministers and central bank governors called to discuss monetary system reform.*

by the EEC on most farm products. The EEC imposed tight export restrictions on cereals, rice, and sugar and imposed levies on the limited amount of cereals and sugar allowed to be exported. There was pressure for the EEC to retain stockpiles of beef, butter, and other commodities to prevent shortages that would raise prices.

The EEC in 1974 continued its action against restrictive practices and monopolies, and in two key cases its decisions were upheld by the Court of Justice in Luxembourg. In one case the court found that a U.S. firm was abusing its position by withholding supplies of an essential ingredient of a drug from one of its competitors in Italy. The EEC for the first time used its powers to impose daily penalties for as long as the practice continued.

In the other judgment the court upheld a decision that a company producing decaffeinated coffee was abusing trademark rights by preventing the import of its products from one EEC country to another in an attempt to divide the market. Other abuses by automobile and oil companies, a computer firm, and a radio manufacturer were investigated in 1974.

### Social Programs and Foreign Relations

In January the EEC adopted a social program for 1974–76. The first set of seven projects was presented soon afterward, and in June the EEC adopted three projects covering aid for migrant workers, aid for disabled workers, and establishment of an EEC industrial safety committee.

The EEC was in various stages of considering a wide range of other social programs. These included equal pay for men and women, a 40-hour work week, four weeks of annual paid vacation, environmental control, legislation on collective dismissal of

workers, a European vocational training center, and protection of workers' rights in mergers and takeovers. Proposals for equal access to employment, vocational training, and promotion and programs for promoting health and safety at work and for combating poverty were also on the agenda.

In one of its most positive achievements of the year, the EEC in July reached an agreement on trade and aid with 44 African, Caribbean, and Pacific (ACP) countries. The ACP won broader trading rights. The EEC eased its rules of origin for ACP exports and eliminated some barriers to ACP agricultural exports to EEC countries.

The EEC promised to promote industrial development in ACP countries. The EEC offered $500 million toward a $3-billion fund, to be made up partly by oil-producing nations, to aid less developed countries. In October the EEC released $150 million as a grant to ACP nations. (*See also* individual countries by name; Money; World Trade.)

## FAMILIES.
In 1974 the birthrate in the U.S. continued on a downward slide that left experts on family life puzzled. For the first time in U.S. history, the birthrate dropped below the so-called replacement level—the number of children necessary to replace their parents statistically, 2.1 per couple. In 1973 each couple was producing only 1.9 children. If that rate continued or dropped further, the country would realize zero population growth in the first half of the 21st century. (*See* Population.)

A number of theories were put forth to explain the drop in births—changes in life-style, a general concern for world overpopulation, easier access to birth control means and abortion facilities, and concern over a sagging economy. Some experts thought that another baby boom was inevitable, that the trend would reverse and as many as 85% of the postponed babies would be "made up" by 1979.

In the six-year period mid-1967–mid-1973, the number of U.S. women obtaining birth control information from family planning clinics increased by almost 500%. This dramatic figure was contained in a report prepared by Planned Parenthood-World Population, one of the best-known sources of family planning aid. The report stressed that millions of low-income women were not being reached by existing programs of family planning information.

Sterilization was the birth control method of choice for an increasing number of couples in the prime childbearing years (ages 20 to 39). About one couple in six in that age group had had a sterilization operation by mid-1974. The Association for Voluntary Sterilization estimated that the number of such operations for women had been increasing for four years. Sterilization for men, on the other hand, apparently reached a high point in 1971.

*Families of men still listed as missing in Southeast Asia demonstrate near the White House on November 11, urging the administration to press harder for an accounting of their missing sons, husbands, and fathers.*

WIDE WORLD

Abortion continued to be a controversial issue in the U.S., in the wake of the 1973 decision by the Supreme Court liberalizing state abortion laws. A number of antiabortion amendments to the U.S. Constitution were offered in Congress, and the amendments were promoted vigorously by lobbyists from the National Right to Life Committee, Inc., a group made up mostly of Roman Catholics. The Senate Judiciary Subcommittee on Constitutional Amendments heard complex scientific testimony from a number of expert witnesses on questions such as when life begins and whether a fetus can feel pain.

A "nonfertility" rite—featuring a dance by three women in white—was held in New York City's Central Park in August by the National Organization for Non-Parents. Speakers included Alvin Toffler, author of 'Future Shock', science writer Isaac Asimov, and feminist Claudia Dreifus.

Government figures showed that the U.S. divorce rate per 1,000 married women rose 73.6% in the decade 1962–71. By 1973 there were approximately 455 divorces for every 1,000 new marriages, and the trend showed no letup in 1974.

In a 1974 survey by the Roper Organization, nine out of ten respondents said that they still believed in marriage but that they wanted it redefined. About half the women polled said that they considered children "very important" to a good marriage; only 40% of the female respondents under age 30 would agree with that proposition.

Two studies prepared at the University of Michigan showed that married people are the happiest in U.S. society. Among married people, childless couples tended to be happiest. Divorced or separated people were identified as the unhappiest group in the U.S., followed closely by the "never marrieds" over age 29. (*See also* Biology; Women.)

## FASHION AND COSMETICS.
Clothes that had an easy fit and swingy motion made news in 1974. Skirts were a focus of fashion as an important part of the moving silhouette. Longer lengths were winning acceptance, partly because they were offered as a choice and not by dictum. What made them differ from the rejected long skirts of 1970 was the graceful width. Along with the animated skirt—gored, biased, or softly gathered—the cape was a key to the "big" look of the year. Many women of all ages made their first autumn purchase a wool cape that was wide, swinging, and bulkless.

The dress reentered the fashion scene in the fall after many efforts to bring it back had been rebuffed by pacesetters who preferred the multilayered look. Many new dresses were loose enough to allow for a blouse or sweater underneath. In the roomy shape of the chemise, the dress dominated fall fashion shows in both New York City and Paris. Some chemises were tiered or flounced. Some resembled smocks.

In keeping with the wide-at-the-top silhouette,

soft blouses were gaining favor over the tailored shirt. They were worn not only with skirts but also with pants, which retained their popularity.

The knit look was a strong favorite in 1974. It was seen in long self-belted sweaters for street wear and in snug caps that matched the single most important accessory of the fall—the long, long scarf. Scarves were worn wound around the neck with ends falling to the hem or worn knotted low on the chest or even worn two at a time. Many dresses and coats had matching scarves.

Boots—not sleekly fitted but crumpled at the ankle—were worn with the "bigger" clothes, but so were graceful instep strap or T-strap shoes. Most fashion authorities held that high heels were necessary to balance the longer skirts, but Halston had some of his willowy models wear ballet slippers.

Nostalgic films, such as 'The Great Gatsby', continued to influence fashion. Crepe de chine and drawn-thread work were rediscovered. The vogue for art deco jewelry also was reminiscent of the 1920's. Its simple elegance looked right with the 1974 evening clothes, such as bias cut gowns and flowing satin pajamas. (*See* Interior Design.)

In cosmetics, lustrous eyes and vivid lips were recommended for those who wanted to look like Gatsby's Daisy. Luminous and smoky eyeshadow and black mascara helped to achieve the look.

Nail polish matched lipstick in 1974 with the same revival of blazing reds or the more subdued brandy and copper shades. Young women took up the use of cheek rouge in the fall to accent the "pale and pretty" mood.

To balance the new clothes and to wear with the rage of fall hats—the simple beret—stylish heads looked smaller. They were bobbed, waved, frizzed, or shingled. Bangs were in again.

## Menswear

The classic two-piece suit remained the foundation of male fashion in 1974. Emphasis tended to be on fabrics, including woolens, mohairs, and blends of natural and man-made fibers. Knitted fabrics presented no serious challenge to the woven materials for suits.

Subtly colored shirts still outsold plain whites nearly everywhere. Ties were somewhat narrower than they had been, and they were brightly colored. The bigger bow tie gained in popularity for both day and evening wear. In topcoats and raincoats, the trend was toward shorter lengths. (*See also* Advertising.)

*New on the 1974 fashion scene was the "Gatsby look," such as the offerings at left shown by Selfridge's, London. Old and unlamented in passing was the extreme platform shoe, blamed for many injuries and accidents.*

**FINLAND.** During 1974 the world energy crisis dominated trade developments in Finland—with massive price increases, especially for Soviet oil (65% of Finland's supply)—and seriously threatened the economic stability of the country. Throughout the year Finland continued to negotiate with Eastern European states on the progressive abolition of tariffs and barriers to trade, to bring those countries into line with its terms of trade with the Soviet Union and Western Europe. Agreements were reached with Hungary, Czechoslovakia, and Bulgaria during 1974, and negotiations continued with Poland and Romania.

On March 19 Prime Minister Kalevi Sorsa's four-party coalition government reached a significant wage and price agreement with the trade unions and industry designed to limit wage increases to 10% over a two-year period. With a 20% inflation rate forecast for 1974, the government in June announced a massive program to combat inflation and improve the short-term balance of trade, including a high export surcharge on the paper industry, Finland's leading foreign currency earner.

On March 22 the Soviet Union, Poland, East and West Germany, Denmark, Sweden, and Finland signed a convention on the protection of the Baltic Sea from all forms of pollution. Relations with the two German states were further consolidated following the previous year's long-awaited establishment of diplomatic relations. Foreign Minister Ahti Karjalainen made the first official post-World War

II visit by a Finnish cabinet minister to East Berlin on May 27 and a similar visit to Bonn on September 18.

Finland's constitution came under attack during 1974, and a government committee was set up to study its reform. The key question was the status of the president, the powerful central figure in Finnish politics, and there were calls for subjecting the presidency to Parliament. No real progress was made as President Urho Kekkonen authoritatively blocked advocates of reform. (*See also* Europe.)

**FISH AND FISHERIES.** The world fishing industry faced a threefold problem in 1974: high operating costs caused by increased fuel prices; a surplus fish supply in cold storage; and the threat of strict new international fishing regulations. At the third United Nations Conference on the Law of the Sea, held June–August in Caracas, Venezuela, most countries favored the creation of a 200-mile "exclusive economic zone" and a 12-mile exclusive fishing zone. No firm decision was reached by the conferees, although the U.S., Canada, Iceland, and Norway announced independent decisions to establish a 200-mile zone. (*See* Oceanography.) U.S. tuna fleet operators—who for years had fished illegally in Latin American coastal waters—and Gulf coast shrimpers angrily opposed the concept of a 200-mile limit. On the New England coast, however, where competition from foreign trawlers had been putting local fishermen out of business, the prospect of new

THE NEW YORK TIMES

*A Louisiana shrimp fisherman, caught in a tightening price squeeze, hauls in a netful of diminishing returns.*

restrictions was welcomed. Elsewhere, reaction was equally mixed. Norwegian small-boat cod fishermen feared the incursion of British deep-sea trawlers. The large British fishing companies—fearing restrictions on their distant fleets off Iceland, Canada, and Norway—began to invest in smaller coastal vessels, to the chagrin of the Scottish small-boat fleet. (*See* Iceland.)

The fuel crisis had serious repercussions for the fishing industry. With consumer spending power cut, fish prices went down; and with large stocks of fish, bought when prices were high, still choking cold storage, no price rise was foreseen. Increased fuel costs were a particularly heavy burden on fleets that had traditionally fished far from home ports. One logical answer was for countries with large fishing industries to set up bases in countries with rich fisheries. Negotiations of this sort were undertaken by Spain, Poland, and Japan in an attempt to set up agreements with Ireland, Canada, and African countries. "Trash" fish, those previously considered unsalable, attained new value in 1974 as a result of two developments. First, the price of fish meal rose because of the 1972–73 failure of the Peruvian anchovy catch. Secondly, a new deboning machine was introduced that produced a highly marketable "minced" fish from those unmarketable in whole form or too small to be filleted economically. (*See* Food.)

# FLOWERS AND GARDENS.
There was a big upsurge in home gardening throughout the U.S. in 1974, mostly because of high prices and the fear of food shortages. Families that never before had grown vegetables dug up parts of lawns and flower beds to plant tomatoes, beans, and squash, and salad greens. Community gardens were started in many cities so that persons with little or no land also could grow food.

Every year wind-thrown trees, weakened by decay, have caused deaths, injuries, and property damage. Until 1974 there was no easy, safe, and inexpensive way to determine whether a tree was sound or not. After seven years of studies and tests, a portable electronic meter was developed that permitted on-site measurements of trees for strength and safety. The "Shigometer"—named for one of its originators, plant pathologist Alex L. Shigo—sends a short series of electric currents through a tree. Since the resistance to a pulsed current is much less in decayed wood than in sound, deterioration could be readily detected.

In a paper presented at the annual meeting of the American Society of Plant Physiologists in June, Cornell University researchers reported major progress in efforts to find an artificial way to increase hardiness in plants, permitting them to be grown outdoors in areas where ordinarily they would winter-kill. The researchers, finding that when the membrane of the chloroplast is frozen and thawed at a slow rate certain proteins break loose, stopping biological activity, had succeeded in bringing these proteins back to the membrane and restoring organ function.

The International Convention of the World Federation of Rose Societies was held in Chicago, September 7–12, the third worldwide rose convention but the first under the aegis of the World Federation that had been formed in 1971 in New Zealand. The next convention was scheduled for 1977 at Oxford, England.

A plant sciences delegation spent nearly a month of late summer in the People's Republic of China arranging with Chinese scientists for exchange of information about advancements in crop and forestry research and of genetic resources. In December the U.S. and the Soviet Union agreed to work together to preserve endangered plant species—both wild and cultivated—in the two countries. Seeds and young plants were to be exchanged for experimental cultivation.

All-America selections for 1974's best new flower and vegetable varieties were: Scarlet Ruffles and Peter Pan Orange, zinnias; Showboat, a marigold; Red Fox, a celosia; Magic Charms, a dianthus; Diablo, a cosmos; Table King, a bush acorn squash; and Goldcrop, a wax bean. The 1975 All-America rose award winners were Oregold, a new pure-yellow hybrid tea; Arizona, a bronze and copper grandiflora; and Rose Parade, a light coral-pink floribunda.

**FOOD.** Rising food prices added 7 million persons to the poverty rolls in the first six months of 1974, according to a midyear report by the U.S. Senate Select Committee on Nutrition and Human Needs. The elderly and others living on low incomes were forced to eat less, to incur heavier debts, and in some cases to eat pet foods. Substituting traditionally cheaper protein sources for meat became a major problem as prices rose sharply for dried beans, peanut butter, and fish.

The world food situation in 1974 was the worst since World War II, the United Nations Food and Agriculture Organization (FAO) concluded in a report for the World Food Conference held in Rome in November 1974. World food stocks fell to their lowest level in 20 years. Fears of excessive price fluctuations and more famine in less developed countries led the FAO to push for a world food reserve plan in which each country would maintain its own stockpile of cereals. Agriculture officials in the U.S. were resisting a return to the grain storage business after turning farmers back to the free market and urging full production. The officials thought that such a reserve might discourage output.

Food prices soared throughout 1974. In late August, on the basis of reduced crop estimates, retail food prices for all of 1974 were expected to average as much as 17% above 1973. Compared with a 10.7% increase for retail prices of all goods and services in the Consumer Price Index, food prices in the U.S. rose 15.5% between mid-1973 and mid-1974. Criticism was directed primarily at retailers.

The November 1974 issue of *Consumer Reports* magazine disclosed that rodent hairs, insect parts, and pieces of feather contaminated most canned tuna. The magazine tested 52 brands of tuna from 16 major distributors. Filth was found in at least one sample from all except three distributors, but only small amounts of products from those distributors were tested. The magazine called for tighter government standards for tuna.

Famine in the African Sahel, which contributed to the death of more than 100,000 in 1973, continued into 1974. Drought in Ethiopia affected hundreds of thousands. Poor crops and maldistribution set off food riots and widespread famine in India. Flooding in Pakistan and Bangladesh resulted in high prices and shortages. (*See* Africa; Asia.)

Food assistance in the U.S. totaled more than $5 million in the year ending June 30, 1974—an increase of about 20% over 1973. Approximately 14 million U.S. citizens received food stamps during 1974. The U.S. Department of Agriculture announced in October that a low-income family of four would have its food stamp benefits raised by about $4 a month beginning Jan. 1, 1975. About 25 million school children were served by the government-assisted school lunch programs in 1974. (*See also* Agriculture; Chemistry; Fish and Fisheries; Oceanography; United Nations.)

WIDE WORLD

*As sugar prices soared this Omaha, Neb., supermarket joined hundreds across the country urging shoppers to boycott sugar and use more substitute sweeteners. The price of sugar rose about 400% in one year.*

# Special Report:
# Good-bye, Frozen Rhubarb

by Erma Bombeck

It would probably shock no one that last year 83 million youngsters sent Colonel Sanders a Mother's Day card.

That in a survey among six-year-olds, 183,000 said their dish pattern was cardboard with two golden arches with an "M" insignia.

And that Mom's apple pie isn't apple pie at all unless it has a red light over it to keep it warm.

The home-cooked meal is dead! Plagued by shortages of food, high prices, and the competition of carryout prepared foods, it deteriorated into a leftover and eventually expired of apathy and circulation failure.

Happily, the survivors have a choice of substitutes: the carryout hamburgers, the drive-in chickens, the take-home tacos, the all-you-can-eat pizzerias, the come-as-you-are fish and chips, and the stop-and-burp six-legged hot dog and 64-ounce gas-filled cola.

Who killed the home-cooked meal? Who knows? Some say "Mom" in her white starched apron and her headband let it die. Intimidated by galloping chefs, home economists, and shelves of cookbooks, she bustled about to serve the well-balanced meal to her family. It was boring.

Mom just couldn't compete with the fun clown where you yelled an order into his mouth and two seconds later picked up your bagful of food.

As one mother explained, "I didn't realize what a failure I had become until one night I served a meal that had taken me all day to prepare. I had a lean meat, one leafy yellow vegetable, one stringy green one, a starch, and a dessert. I put it on a plate and set it before my preschooler. The child turned on me, propped my mouth open with a fork and yelled into it, 'You weren't paying attention, clown. I ordered a Happyburger, a frostee malted, and two fries!'"

Mothers tried to simulate the excitement of drive-ins and takeouts, but it was too late. One mother installed a scoreboard over her stove that tallied the hamburgers she served. (She was up to 105,000.)

Another woman wore a straw hat, carried a cane, and played ricky-tick piano whenever she served pizza.

A mother in Norfolk, Va., actually painted her garbage cans orange to make the children believe they were eating at Howard Johnson's. None of it worked.

Some say the home-cooked meal faltered the day 43% of the women in the country decided to go back to work. Some of these were women who, as housewives, had been eating leftovers for 15 or 20 years. Eating out was not only a new experience but a revealing one.

An office worker would pick up a piece of fresh bread and ask, "What's wrong with it? It's soft." The newness of cold cuts astounded her as did the absence from the menu of cold pork chops with a child's teeth marks on them.

The inevitable happened. You cannot send a woman back to a peanut butter world when she has moved up to a Diner's Card any more than you can send a boy back to the farm after he's seen John Wayne's horse. No siree!

The most popular theory, however, is that American women got sick of the battle of long lines at the supermarket, empty shelves, high prices, and the

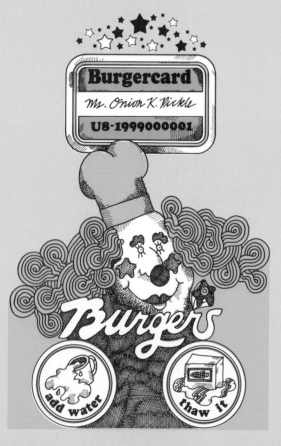

futility of pulling together a meal while a naturalist like Euell Gibbons just grazed for lunch on his front lawn.

The housewife felt shortages more acutely than any other single group. Overnight, chickens stopped laying eggs, floods ruined bean crops, tuna stopped biting, strikers refused to unload chocolate, toilet tissue stopped growing, cattle formed unions, truckers couldn't move potato chips because of the gas shortage, and there was a plague on all of the country's lemon-scented houses.

It was not unnatural for the American housewife to spend entire days groveling and scraping, begging, and crawling around on her hands and knees. That was only for her car keys. Then it was an uphill battle to get gas, stand in lines, take what was available, and arrive home wondering what she could make out of a box of tapioca and a small jar of mustard.

Finally, the incongruity became apparent. More than 137 million dogs were eating gourmet home-cooked meals while millions of Americans were eating their meals out of doggie bags and boxes.

This created a fair amount of frustration.

### Hold the Chutney

First, with thousands of hamburger drive-ins all over the country, it is virtually impossible to get a plain hamburger anymore. Everyone, in an effort to top his competitor, can assemble anything between a sesame seed bun with the exception of a plain hamburger.

You walk up to the counter and a man in a little white two-cornered hat asks, "What'll it be, sir?"

"I'll have a plain hamburger."

"Don't make trouble. All of our hamburgers come broiled over a kerosene-flavored flame, topped by a pound of shredded lettuce, floating in a current of our magic secret sauce, topped by a slice of onion, and held captive by two sesame seed buns."

"Just a plain hamburger."

"How about a Miniburger?" he suggests, "For people who have just eaten but want to watch girls."

"No, just a. . . ."

"Or a Fatsoburger for fat people with fat appetites."

"No really . . . a plain. . . . '

"Got it! A Gluttonburger. This is our big one for people who are depressed because they are overweight. Or perhaps you'd like to try our newest . . . the Orgyburger."

"What's an Orgyburger?"

"It's 85 pounds of hamburger under a 25-pound bun, topped with a giant pickle that feeds a family of 15 for a week."

"Just a plain hamburger."

"Tell you what. I could take a Whammyburger and leave off the sauce and put the lettuce on a Beefrigger, hold the mayonnaise and the tomato,

transfer the cheese from the Charbeef to the Brawney Brute, scrape off the chopped onion and the poached egg, and give it to you in a plain brown bag."

"What do you call it?"

"A plain hamburger."

### Future Shock

Secondly, cars were never built to dine in. If the Good Lord had meant for families to eat in cars, he would have invented disposable children.

This form of dining will eventually rip the American family apart. Recently, a father of four was found wandering incoherently around a Mexican food carryout parking lot with a French fry hanging out of his ear.

When he was apprehended and quieted, he told of a bizarre story in which two of his children had a lettuce fight in the back seat, two colas were spilled down his neck, the dog ate half of his taco and threw up, and the trade-in value of his car decreased $500 when a toastada fell behind the seat—giving the car terminal pollution.

Of course, the obvious problem of families eating out is an economic one. With stoves, ovens, disposals, cookware, china, and grocery stores obsolete, we are saying good-bye to a billion-dollar industry.

Good-bye to the scores of little boxes that wanted to help our hamburger.

Good-bye to frozen rhubarb.

Good-bye to dripless spouts and imitation oleo.

Good-bye to the three most beautiful words in the English language: "Just add water."

Food, like the evolution of man, has had its ages. In the 1940's, women went through the Stone age, where the flour was ground for bread, and cakes were made from scratch.

During the 1950's, aluminum and cardboard flourished as prepared foods lined the pantries of every cook in the country.

During the 1960's, homemakers moved into the Ice Age, where anything that deserved to be eaten deserved to be quick-frozen and thawed.

It was inevitable that the 1970's would be influenced by flight, where meals were grabbed on the run, preferably from a speeding car.

The future of food is more predictable than you think.

It is clearly a matter of time before drive-ins will exhaust their supply of ideas on what you can do with a hamburger (even going to the desperation of adding meat).

A special holiday treat will be eating with the cat.

Someone will discover that plastic forks are not biodegradable in the stomach.

The energy crisis will force the lights to go out over the apple turnovers.

And one day a small child will jump up and down and whine, "Why can't we stay at home and eat?"

And the stoves will go on again all over the world.

*Two Honolulu Hawaiians tackle a Southern California Sun in a July game as the fledgling World Football League battles for survival.*

**FOOTBALL.** After 42 years of frustration, Art Rooney's Pittsburgh Steelers finally won it all with a 16–6 victory over the Minnesota Vikings in Super Bowl IX at New Orleans, La. The tough Steeler defense played a near-perfect game, smothering the Viking offensive assault, which managed only 17 net yards rushing. The only Viking score came in the fourth quarter when their defense blocked a punt and recovered in the Steeler end zone for a touchdown. Similarly, the Steeler defense brought the only first-half score, downing Fran Tarkenton for a two-point safety. It was not until the second half that the Steeler offense came through, scoring two touchdowns. The irrepressible Franco Harris scored the first of these on a nine-yard run. Harris eventually totaled 158 yards in 34 carries, both Super Bowl records. Terry Bradshaw threw a four-yard pass to Larry Brown for the final touchdown.

In the Canadian Football League, the Montreal Alouettes defeated the Edmonton Eskimos 20–7 in the Grey Cup championship game. Quarterback Sonny Wade guided the Alouettes to victory.

The Pittsburgh Steelers and the Minnesota Vikings fought their way to the Super Bowl in a year when the National Football League (NFL) was having trouble off the field. A players' strike, soaring expenses, declining fan interest, and a federal court ruling that the player-reserve system was illegal helped mar the season. Perhaps of greatest future significance was the court ruling, which meant that a player who has fulfilled the option clause of his contract becomes a free agent and can sign with another team in the league without that team's having to compensate the one he left.

In 1974, attendance dropped to fewer than 10 million, the NFL's tacit goal, and more than a million advance ticket buyers became "no shows" when they failed to attend games. Reasons for the decline revolved mainly around the tight economy and the abundance of free football on television.

Despite these problems, there were still some happy people in the NFL. The happiest of all may have been in Pittsburgh, because the Steelers finally won a championship. The Steelers, however, had their rough moments during the season. Their offense was often sporadic, and coach Chuck Noll was split over whom he wanted as a starting quarterback—Terry Bradshaw or Joe Gilliam.

By the time Pittsburgh won the American Football Conference (AFC) Central Division title, Bradshaw was playing ahead of Gilliam. He proved equal to that position when he directed the Steelers to a 32–14 play-off victory over the Buffalo Bills, completing 12 of 19 passes for 203 yards and one touchdown. The Pittsburgh defense shackled Buffalo's O. J. Simpson, who finished third in rushing behind the San Diego Chargers' Don Woods and the Denver Broncos' league-leader Otis Armstrong. In the AFC championship game against the Oakland Raiders, the Steeler defense reached its zenith. A fierce line, led by tackle "Mean" Joe Greene and end L. C. Greenwood, held the Raiders to only 29 yards rushing, while defensive backs intercepted three Oakland passes. On offense, Rocky Bleier and Franco Harris ran for 98 and 111 yards, respectively, leading Pittsburgh to a 24–13 victory.

The satisfaction felt by the Steelers' 73-year-old owner, Art Rooney, must have been as great as the Raiders' disappointment. Although Oakland had made the play-offs six times in the last seven seasons, the Raiders had not been to the Super Bowl since 1967. Moreover, in 1974 they had the best regular-season record in pro football (12–2), and they reached the finals only after defeating the Miami Dolphins 28–26 in a game of classic proportions. The Dolphins appeared to have it won, 26–21, with about two minutes left. But Oakland quarterback Ken Stabler, who had already thrown for three touchdowns, coolly directed the Raiders down the field and, with 26 seconds remaining, passed to Clarence Davis for the victory.

The Minnesota Vikings made it to their third Super Bowl and second in a row with two easy play-off wins. The Vikings won the National Football Conference (NFC) Central Division title handily and defeated their first play-off opponents, the St. Louis Cardinals, 30–14. The game was tied 7–7 when the Vikings broke it open with 16 points in the third quarter. The Los Angeles Rams, who won their first play-off game over the Washington Redskins 19–10, gave Minnesota more of a struggle, but lost because of mistakes. Los Angeles lost three fumbles, had two passes intercepted, and was pressured into other mistakes by Minnesota defenders Carl Eller, Jim Marshall, and Alan Page. Their work was enough to make a Tarkenton touchdown pass to Jim Lash and a scoring plunge by Dave Osborn stand up for a 14–10 win and the NFC title.

The World Football League (WFL) was in constant trouble during its first year. Early on, it was disclosed that some of the WFL's 12 teams were inflating attendance figures. By the end of the season, there were only 10 teams left as the Detroit Wheels and the Jacksonville Sharks went out of business. The Internal Revenue Service filed liens against the holdings of both Jacksonville and the Portland Storm. According to estimates, the WFL was $20 million in debt after its four month season. The debt was partly salaries owed to players on seven teams, including the two in the league's championship game, the Birmingham Americans and the Florida Blazers. Players from both teams threatened to boycott the first World Bowl, which Birmingham won, 22–21. At year's end the plan seemed to be to wait until the arrival of about 60 NFL players who had signed with WFL teams. But Oakland's Stabler found a way out of his contract with Birmingham, and others seemed sure to follow. Larry Csonka, Jim Kiick, and Paul Warfield of Miami, however, appeared committed to their $3-million deal with the Memphis Southmen.

## College Football

Oklahoma would have been the undisputed number-one college football team of 1974 except for one problem: the Sooners were on probation for violating the National Collegiate Athletic Association (NCAA) recruiting regulations. As a result, Oklahoma was banned from national television appearances and postseason bowl games. United Press International (UPI), which reflected the sentiments of 35 college coaches, refused to mention Oklahoma in its weekly poll and selected the once-beaten University of Southern California (USC) as its top team. However, the Associated Press (AP), relying on the opinions of 63 sportswriters, ranked Oklahoma all season and made the Sooners number one when they emerged unbeaten and untied.

The Sooners, who had a 29-game winning streak, were intimidating offensively and defensively. The offense was easier to see—as when All-American running back Joe Washington led the way to romps of 63–0 over Kansas State and 72–3 over Utah State. The Oklahoma defense had its sternest test against Nebraska. The Cornhuskers led 14–7 in the third quarter, but the Sooner defense held thereafter while the offense clicked for a 28–14 win.

The logical bowl-game opponent for Oklahoma would have been Alabama, which went 11–0 in regular-season play. By defeating Notre Dame in the Orange Bowl, Alabama conceivably could have been number one in both polls. But the Fighting Irish, playing their last game for resigning coach Ara Parseghian, spoiled that dream 13–11.

USC used that upset and one of its own making

*Unrelenting "Mean" Joe Greene (75) of the Pittsburgh Steelers tracks the fleeing Minnesota Viking Fran Tarkenton (10), who frantically searches for a receiver. It was an oft-repeated scene of Super Bowl IX, in which the charge of "Mean" Joe and his fellow linemen was a key factor in the Steeler 16–6 victory.*

on New Year's Day to catapult to first place in the UPI rankings and second in the AP. The Trojans capped their season with a stunning 55–24 victory over Notre Dame on the strength of four Anthony Davis touchdowns. But USC had to be better against Ohio State in the Rose Bowl, and they were. With barely two minutes to play, quarterback Pat Haden threw a touchdown pass to John McKay and a two-point conversion pass to Shelton Diggs, giving USC an 18–17 victory.

Ohio State's Archie Griffin, who ran a record 100 yards or more in 22 consecutive games, led the Buckeyes through eight wins before they tripped over Michigan State 16–13. Then they came back to beat previously undefeated Michigan 12–10 on four field goals by Tom Klaban. Michigan and Ohio State had identical 10–1 records, but the Big Ten athletic directors voted to send the Buckeyes to the Rose Bowl for the third straight year.

Yale had a chance to win the Lambert Trophy as the best team in the East until it came up against Harvard and its All-American receiver, Pat Mc-Inally. He caught six passes, one for a touchdown, and the Crimson upset Yale 21–16, giving the Lambert Trophy to Penn State. In the country's other major traditional game, Bob Jackson scored two touchdowns to lead Navy 19–0 over Army.

Following up Oklahoma in the Big Eight Conference, Nebraska tied for second place with Missouri,

*Spider Lockhart pickets outside the New York Giants' rookie training camp in Fairfield, Conn., during the July NFL players' strike.*

ROGER W. STRONG—THE NEW YORK TIMES

but the Cornhuskers' overall 8–3 record was good enough to place them in the Sugar Bowl, where they won 13–10 over Florida. Maryland took the Atlantic Coast Conference and wound up in the Liberty Bowl, losing to Tennessee 7–3. Baylor was a surprise winner in the Southwest Conference but a big loser, 41–20, to Penn State in the Cotton Bowl. Auburn, runner-up to Alabama in the Southeastern Conference, landed in the Gator Bowl with Texas, whom they whipped 27–3. Other conference winners were Miami (Ohio) in the Mid-American, Tulsa in the Missouri Valley, Brigham Young in the Western Athletic, San Diego State in the Pacific Coast, and Yale and Harvard tied in the Ivy League. In the NCAA's Division II championship game, Central Michigan crushed Delaware 54–14.

Griffin of Ohio State, whose 1,620 total rushing yards led major colleges, won the Heisman Trophy as the year's top player. The Outland Trophy, for the outstanding lineman, went to Maryland's defensive tackle Randy White. Despite Griffin's superior yardage total, Louie Giammona of Utah State averaged 153.4 yards for ten games to lead major college runners in that category. Temple quarterback Steve Joachim led major colleges in total offense with 222.7 yards a game passing and running. The leading passer, Steve Bartkowski of California, connected 182 times in 325 attempts, but his .560 completion average was behind that of North Carolina's Chris Kupec, whose .693 (104 of 150) established an NCAA record. Dwight McDonald of San Diego State averaged 7.8 pass receptions a game to lead the nation, and Wisconsin runner Bill Marek paced all scorers with 12.7 points a game.

The Oklahoma Sooners led in total offense (507.7 yards a game), rushing offense (438.8 yards), and points per game (43). The top defensive team was Michigan, which surrendered 6.8 points a game.

## FORD, GERALD R. 

A situation unprecedented in the country's history made Gerald R. Ford the 38th president of the U.S. on Aug. 9, 1974. He assumed leadership when U.S. President Richard M. Nixon resigned as the result of Watergate scandals. (*See* Nixon.) Under provisions of the 25th Amendment to the Constitution, Ford took office as the country's first unelected chief executive. His oath was administered in the East Room of the White House by U.S. Supreme Court Chief Justice Warren E. Burger. In a short address, Ford asked the people to bind up the wounds of Watergate. "Our long national nightmare is over," he said. "Our Constitution works. Our great republic is a government of laws and not of men."

Eight months earlier, Ford had become vice-president under extraordinary conditions. He had been minority leader of the House of Representatives when Nixon named him vice-president designate on Oct. 12, 1973, after Vice-President Spiro T. Agnew resigned. Ford was confirmed by the required majority in both houses of Congress.

WIDE WORLD

*President Ford, solaced by his golden retriever, Liberty, studies his proposed federal budget in the Oval Office of the White House.*

To a country shaken by revelations of crime and deceit in the highest places of government, Ford brought candor and a reputation for integrity. The people of the U.S. looked to him to find relief from soaring inflation, mounting unemployment, food shortages, and the energy crisis with its far-flung ramifications. Through the years, Ford had described himself as a moderate in domestic affairs, a conservative in fiscal affairs, and an internationalist in foreign policy. Reassuring the country and the world that he sought continuity in foreign policy, Ford asked Secretary of State Henry Kissinger to remain in office. On the domestic side, Ford called inflation Public Enemy Number One.

Inflation was the keynote of Ford's first address to Congress. He vowed to hold down federal spending, and he called for reactivation of the Cost of Living Council to monitor wages and prices. He asked for "communication, conciliation, compromise, and cooperation" between the White House and the Congress, where for 25 years he had represented Michigan's 5th Congressional district.

Ford moved to reestablish White House rapport with the news media, blacks, labor, and city and state officials. He promised an ethical administration, and he began to thin out the White House bureaucracy. Ford said he "probably" would run for the presidency in 1976. Shortly after his accession, Ford asked Republican officials and Democratic Congressional leaders to let him know their choices for vice-president. On August 20, Ford announced his selection, former Gov. Nelson A. Rockefeller of New York. (*See* Rockefeller.)

A condition widely described as euphoria prevailed in the early days of the Ford Administration. That happy state ended abruptly on Sunday, Sept. 8, 1974, when Ford granted full pardon to Nixon for all offenses against the U.S. that he might have committed while president. Ford's own press secretary, Jerald F. terHorst, resigned in protest. Strong opposition was voiced in Congress and in public opinion polls. Many persons saw unfairness in precluding trial for Nixon while his associates served or faced prison sentences. (*See* Law.)

Soon Ford endorsed conditional amnesty for men who had evaded or fled service in Vietnam. Inevitably, he was asked why he gave full pardon to Nixon and only conditional amnesty to the others. He said that he saw no real connection.

Late in September, a House Judiciary subcommittee began hearings into circumstances of the pardon and the arrangements made with Nixon concerning disposition of tape recordings and documents related to Watergate. Attempting to defuse the pardon issue, Ford appeared voluntarily before the committee on October 17 to explain his reasoning.

His formal appearance before a committee of Congress was another first for a sitting U.S. president. Ford emphasized that he had made no pre-resignation "deal" with Nixon and that the pardon was issued to change the national focus from Watergate to more pressing issues. On December 19 Ford signed legislation giving custody of the Nixon tapes and documents to the General Services Administration, thereby nullifying an earlier agreement granting Nixon ownership of the material.

To face the biggest problem at hand, Ford called an economic "summit meeting" for September 27 and 28. Economists, government officials, businessmen, labor leaders, and consumer advocates attended. Predictably, they reached no consensus about how to rescue the economy from the unprecedented mixture of inflation and recession.

With pressure building for action, the Ford Administration worked hard and fast to produce an effective program. The key proposals that Ford presented to Congress on October 8 were: a one-year temporary surcharge of 5% on corporate and "upper level" adjusted gross incomes of $15,000 or more for families and $7,500 for individuals; bigger investment tax credits for business; tax relief for low-income families; windfall profits taxes on oil companies; an expanded public-service program; financial aid for the mortgage market; a voluntary fuel conservation program; enforcement of antitrust laws; and a budget cut of about $5 million. Ford also appealed to the citizenry to conserve food and fuel. Addressing Congress, Ford wore a button bearing the acronym WIN, for "Whip Inflation Now," and he invited others to wear one as a symbol of determination. Although Ford was committed to reductions in spending, some economic policymakers thought that rising unemployment and a business slump might call for more instead of less federal spending. Early in November, Ford conceded that the U.S. economy was moving into a recession. The tax surcharge proposal was dropped in December, and a new economic approach— aimed more toward combating recession than whipping inflation—was under consideration.

Personal distress beset Ford in the fall. His wife, Betty, underwent surgery on September 28 after cancer was found in her right breast.

On October 15, Ford signed a bill that provided for the most sweeping campaign reforms in U.S. history. It radically overhauled future election campaign financing. As he had done earlier in 1974 as vice-president, Ford campaigned hard for fellow Republicans before the November 5 elections. The Democratic party, however, enjoyed a landslide vote. (*See* Elections; Political Parties.)

Congress overrode a Ford veto for the first time on October 17, passing into law a controversial $7-billion railroad retirement bill that he regarded as inflationary. On November 21, Congress overrode two Ford vetoes—one concerning legislation expanding public access to government-held information and one authorizing $850 million for vocational rehabilitation programs in fiscal 1976. (*See* Congress, U.S.)

In the first week of his presidency, Ford faced a crisis with the Greek government, which resented what it believed to be U.S. favoritism toward Turkey in hostilities on Cyprus. Ford later assailed Congress when it voted a cutoff of military aid to Turkey because it used U.S.-made arms in the Cyprus invasion. A compromise measure delayed the cutoff. (*See* Greece; Turkey; United Nations.)

Ford told the United Nations General Assembly in September that the U.S. would not use its food supply as a political weapon, and he suggested that oil-producing countries follow a similar course with their strategic commodity. He warned, however, that the U.S. could no longer be expected to feed all the world's hungry people. Citing domestic considerations, the administration turned down a request for an immediate increase of one million tons in world food aid. The request was made at a World Food Conference in Rome early in November. (*See* Agriculture; Food.)

Ford met with Mexican President Luis Echeverría late in October at sessions conducted on both sides of the border. The Mexican leader stressed that the U.S. would have to pay the high world market price to share in Mexico's newly discovered oil.

On his first presidential journey overseas, Ford became the first U.S. president to visit Japan. The trip was designed to relieve the tensions that followed what Japan considered to be neglect by the Nixon Administration. Ford paid a one-day visit to South Korea, where he promised to maintain U.S. military forces. From Korea, he flew to his first meeting with Leonid Brezhnev, Soviet Communist party general secretary. The occasion was planned to introduce the leaders and to lay the groundwork for a summit meeting in 1975 in Washington, D.C. A tentative new arms limitation agreement resulted from the meeting. (*See* Arms Control and Disarmament.)

In December, Ford met with President Valéry Giscard d'Estaing of France on the island of Martinique in the Caribbean to discuss international energy and economic concerns. (*See also* Employment; Money; United States.)

**FOREST PRODUCTS.** In 1974 U.S. President Richard M. Nixon proclaimed March 21 World Forestry Day and proposed that the event be made an annual one. The international holiday had the endorsement of the European Federation of Agriculture as well as the Food and Agriculture Organization (FAO) of the United Nations.

The FAO announced that 1973 had been the most favorable year for all sectors of the forest products market for a long time and that the trend was continuing through 1974. After a period of several years with rising costs but static prices, production reached peak levels and prices rose sharply— resulting in better profits. World roundwood production had increased 4%, for example, in 1973— an appreciably higher rate of increase than that of previous years. Growth in the production of roundwood resulted in sharp increases in trade, with substantial price increases also reported worldwide. The volume in trade of coniferous roundwood had increased by 16% and of nonconiferous by 20%. World production of sawn softwood had increased by 3%, mainly in Western Europe, but the estimated production of sawn wood in the U.S. for the first quarter of 1974 indicated a 5.3% drop from the corresponding period of the year before. The decrease was attributed to a slump in housing construction.

Though the production of woodpulp was increased, it was still not sufficient to meet the demands of the papermaking industry. Difficulty in obtaining pulp and paper supplies was experienced worldwide with the result that prices of pulp increased 50% between July 1973 and July 1974, with similar increases for paper and paperboard following. Pulp and paper mills were operating at near capacity in sharp contrast to earlier years.

A ruling banning log exports from national forest lands west of the 100th meridian was put into effect by the U.S. Department of Agriculture in March. It also stipulated that timber from western national forests would no longer be sold to replace timber cut from private lands for export. The ruling particularly affected Japan, which had received 85% of U.S. log exports. Japan was expected to turn to Canada and the U.S.S.R. for more of its future needs. (*See also* Chemistry; Magazines; Newspapers.)

**FRANCE.** The most momentous event of 1974 in France was the sudden and unexpected death of President Georges Pompidou on April 2. Finance Minister Valéry Giscard d'Estaing, a conservative but not a Gaullist, was elected Pompidou's successor on May 19. Giscard defeated François Mitterrand, the United Left candidate, by a narrow margin; both candidates based their campaigns on the voters' intense desire for change and progress.

For the first three months of 1974, Pompidou attempted to deal with the economic crisis brought on by the phenomenal rise in the price of oil from the Middle East. The Council of Ministers voted on January 19 to float the franc for six months, in opposition to an existing international agreement. The left attempted to bring down Pompidou's government with a censure motion in the National Assembly, but the motion failed by a wide margin. Amid this economic and political tension, Foreign Minister Michel Jobert visited Saudi Arabia in January; he reportedly offered arms to the Saudis in exchange for a guarantee that France would receive oil from them.

A strike at the Lip watch factory in Besançon, in progress for almost a year, was settled in January 1974; however, that settlement was practically the only bright spot in industrial relations during the year. The stock exchange and banks in Paris were paralyzed by strikes lasting several weeks, and industrial disputes also affected the Atlantic dockyards, the major hotels in Paris, Air France, and the newspapers.

At the end of February, Pompidou reorganized his cabinet. Beyond a reduction in its size, no substantive changes were made, however.

Pompidou was widely eulogized at his death. On April 6, a day of national mourning, a solemn memorial service in his honor was held at the Cathedral of Notre Dame and attended by many heads of state. Alain Poher, the president of the Senate, duly assumed the duties of interim head of state. (*See* Obituaries.)

Twelve candidates ran for president in the first round, held May 5. Because none of the 12 received a majority of the votes cast, a runoff was scheduled between the top two contenders, Mitterrand and Giscard. Mitterrand's vote-getting power was expected; Giscard's garnering of the conservative vote away from Jacques Chaban-Delmas, however, was surprising.

In the two-week interval before the runoff election, Giscard and Mitterrand conducted intensive campaigns, a novelty in France in recent times. A record 86.17% of the electorate turned out for the runoff; Giscard took 50.81% of the total vote and Mitterrand took 49.19%. Despite Mitterrand's defeat, the French left scored a success by obtaining the greatest percentage of total votes since 1946.

Giscard began his presidency on May 27; symbolically, he discarded the traditional ceremonial pomp of the occasion for the most part and even walked to the Elysée Palace. The president's desire for change only started with the inauguration ceremony, however. Jacques Chirac was named premier of the new government. Giscard's government was formed with a strong contingent of reformers and centrists. Jean-Jacques Servan-Schreiber, appointed minister for reforms, was fired abruptly in June for criticizing the government's decision to continue nuclear tests in the Pacific.

In his early speeches as president, Giscard defined his three immediate concerns as social welfare,

*Construction of a trade center on the former site of Les Halles in Paris was interrupted in September while authorities explored a plan to make the area a huge green park.*

*Newly elected President Giscard (right) of France meets with Alain Poher, interim president, at the Elysée Palace on May 20.*

the battle against inflation, and the political unification of Europe. Under his leadership, France became the first Roman Catholic country to legalize abortion and to liberalize birth control laws. During the summer, prison riots led to several deaths; the government responded by preparing plans for "humanizing" the penal system.

The number of persons unemployed exceeded 500,000 in September, a record for postwar France and an increase of about 30% over that of the preceding year. In October a landmark bill was passed guaranteeing one year's wages to any worker laid off because of economic pressures.

A series of strikes occurred in the autumn; the postal strike paralyzed mail service for weeks. Sporadic strikes occurred in the coal mining and transportation industries.

To promote European unity and the economic health of Europe, Giscard began to cultivate a close relationship with West Germany's Chancellor Helmut Schmidt. Relations with Great Britain remained problematic, as Giscard firmly opposed Britain's attempt to renegotiate its terms of membership in the European Economic Community.

Though firmly committed to European unity, Giscard also worked to strengthen France's alliance with the United States. Giscard and U.S. President Gerald R. Ford met for three days in December in Martinique. They agreed to cooperate in their future negotiations with the oil-producing countries. France was considered strongly conciliatory toward the Arab oil producers; in August France had removed a long-standing ban on arms sales to Israel or the Arabs—which, in effect, was a decision to sell arms to the Arabs. (*See also* Algeria; Europe; Fuel and Power; Money and International Finance; World Trade.)

**FUEL AND POWER.** In 1974 world events involving fuel and power were again dominated by the Organization of Petroleum Exporting Countries (OPEC) and by the Arab members of that body, the Organization of Arab Petroleum Exporting Countries (OAPEC). In reaction to the Arab-Israeli war of October 1973, the OAPEC instituted an oil embargo against nations it considered pro-Israel; these nations included the United States, the Netherlands, Portugal, South Africa, and Rhodesia. Production cutbacks were also instituted as a general measure, to raise prices and to put pressure on "good" countries to put pressure in turn on the U.S. to drop its military commitments to Israel.

The winter of 1973–74 in Europe, Japan, and the U.S. thus was characterized by a shortage of gasoline, spiraling prices for gasoline when available, and a state of near panic among governments and civilian populations. In the U.S., the effect of the embargo on heating-oil supplies was minimized fortuitously by an unusually mild winter. The effect on gasoline supply was severe; during February and March it was common, especially in the Northeast, to see long lines of cars at the few service stations open at any one time. Waits of several hours in line were the rule, and once at the pump, the unfortunate motorist was generally limited to only a few gallons or a dollar's worth of gas. In an effort to ease the situation, several states adopted "alternate day" programs in which motorists could get gasoline only on odd- or even-numbered days, according to their license plate numbers.

The general oil embargo against the U.S. was lifted on March 18 by all OAPEC members except Libya and Syria. The embargo against the Netherlands was lifted July 10, but for Portugal, Rhodesia, and South Africa, it remained in effect throughout the year. Between November 1973 and January 1974 it became clear that the previous pricing system was no longer operative, despite Teheran and Geneva agreements on petroleum. In less than two months, the posted price of Arabian light crude oil rose from $5.11 a barrel to $11.65 a barrel.

The OPEC members, heady with their newly wielded power, announced in 1974 that production would be strictly controlled to maintain the higher price levels; changes in taxation were also devised to boost oil prices. At a year-end meeting in Vienna, Austria, OPEC leaders announced additional price increases that brought price-per-barrel to five times the October 1973 level. And, in what seemed a calculated attempt to undermine the British economy, it was announced that British pounds would no longer be accepted in payment for oil.

These actions stunned the oil-importing countries of the world—including all industrialized nations except the U.S.S.R. Oil was the largest single item in international trade, and never before in history had the price of a basic raw material risen so much so fast. For some of the oil countries the additional annual income during 1974 was larger than the country's entire gross national product (GNP) in the preceding year. For Europe the higher prices posed grave balance of payments problems; the U.S., dependent on imports for only one third of its total oil supply, was more fortunate but still felt the shock. U.S. Secretary of State Henry Kissinger tried throughout 1974 to convince the Western European nations—France, in particular—and Japan that a joint strategy by oil-consuming nations was crucial. By December, the idea of united action finally seemed to be gaining acceptance. A 16-nation International Energy Agency was established, with emergency energy-sharing and cooperative conservation programs among its first priorities. (*See* Europe.)

The new level of oil prices was a powerful stimulus to the search for new oil resources throughout the world. Additional discoveries were made in the North Sea and in Indonesia (both offshore and onshore). More surprising was the discovery of a large oil field in the Aegean Sea, ten miles off the coast of northeastern Greece.

In the U.S. a new world depth record of 31,441 feet was set by a well drilled in western Oklahoma. Construction on the long-delayed trans-Alaska pipeline began in October, with first delivery through the pipeline expected in 1977.

### Oil Companies Scrutinized

Huge profits were rolled up by U.S. oil companies in the last quarter of 1973 and the first quarter of 1974. Standard Oil of California, for example, showed an increase in profits of 92% for the first quarter of 1974—in comparison with the first quarter of 1973. Texaco boosted its profits 123% for the same period; Occidental topped all comers with 718%. Exxon, largest of the oil companies, claimed a profit of 39%—but some analysts claimed that Exxon had understated its profits by putting aside moneys into a "reserve" fund for future contingencies; counting the "reserve" funds as profits, the true profit figure would be 118%.

Consumerists and officials of the Federal Energy Administration (FEA) were concerned that the companies might be maneuvering to take advantage of the OPEC situation. It appeared, for example, that some companies were buying oil from their own foreign subsidiaries at a nominal price but charging for that same oil at the higher prices commanded by the Arab nations.

In late May the FEA announced new regulations to limit severely the price increase in such intracompany oil "sales." U.S. companies were specifically prohibited, also, from charging "posted" prices—that is, the artificial figures used to compute taxes in producing nations.

As of mid-1974, U.S. companies had a larger crude oil inventory than they did in mid-1973, but they were keeping down gasoline production. The industry claimed that a large inventory of crude was needed because of government allocation programs, but critics felt that the companies wanted to keep

D.P.A./PICTORIAL PARADE

*The completed block A of the world's largest nuclear power station, under construction on the Rhine River near Biblis, West Germany, is shown from the block B site.*

the gasoline supply down in order to keep prices up.

As the winter of 1974–75 began, an adequate supply of gasoline was predicted for U.S. motorists. Gasoline consumption had declined somewhat during the first ten months of 1974 because of the 55-mph speed limit and higher gas prices.

### Natural Gas

The Colorado School of Mines estimated that there is enough natural gas potentially available to meet U.S. needs for 60 years. About 60% of the undeveloped gas resources is in Alaska, deeper than 15,000 feet below ground, or offshore under the ocean. It is generally estimated that offshore gas costs three times as much to produce as other gas and Alaskan gas possibly nine times more.

The demand for gas was growing faster than reserves were increasing. Slower industrial growth meant, however, that the demand for gas was not increasing as rapidly as might be expected. The price of gas continued in an upward spiral.

In 1974 the American Gas Association estimated proved reserves (including Alaska) at 250 trillion cubic feet, down from 266.1 trillion cubic feet a year earlier—and the lowest level since 1957.

The Federal Power Commission (FPC) proposed regulations that would require all companies to report proved domestic gas reserves. The FPC said that existing industry surveys failed to provide an adequate picture of the supply situation. Disclosure of gas reserves and of ability to meet consumer demand was sought by the Securities and Exchange Commission, also.

### Coal and Electric Utilities

Coal prices moved up sharply during the year in response to increased demand related to the oil embargo. For the first time in memory, U.S. electric utilities and steel companies began importing coal and coke from such sources as Canada, Europe, and South Africa.

The coal industry had suffered a declining demand for a number of years in the face of competition from alternative fuels and nuclear power; thus, the industry was unprepared for the sudden upsurge in demand. Short-term supply difficulties were intensified by a United Mine Workers strike in November and a December walkout by mine construction workers. (*See* Labor Unions; Mines and Mining.)

Readily accessible coal reserves in the U.S. were estimated at more than 190 billion tons—capable of producing at least four times as much energy as the total lifetime capacity of the Arabian oil reserves. Nevertheless, there were serious environmental problems involved in coal mining, including the level of air pollution produced by burning the coal. Although a tough strip-mining law regulating production of coal in the western states was passed by Congress, the bill was pocket-vetoed by President Gerald R. Ford in consideration of the nation's acute energy needs. (*See* Congress, U.S.; Environment.)

The U.S. electric utility industry, plagued by higher prices for its fuels and high interest rates, experienced severe financing difficulties. State regulatory commissions were deluged with requests for rate increases, which were vigorously contested by industrial and individual consumers alike.

Although the number and size of rate increases granted during the year set a record, the rate relief was not sufficient to forestall a wave of postponements and cancellations of construction projects for new generating capacity, both fossil and nuclear. These financing problems did not, however, affect the industry's ability to meet current system loads.

### Alternative Energy Sources

Attention was focused more and more frequently on solar energy as the wave of the future. H. Guyford Stever, director of the National Science Foundation, estimated that solar heating and cooling systems might be available within five years. Rep. Chet Holifield (D, Calif.), ranking House member of the Joint Committee on Atomic Energy,

*Syllac, a $10-million apparatus at the Los Alamos Scientific Laboratory in New Mexico, is considered to be a possible key to the development of a practical reactor that draws on the energy of nuclear fusion. Syllac is shown from above the inner circle of the machine, where superheated gas or plasma is held in a magnetic field.*

UPI COMPIX

UPI COMPIX

*With a month of spare time and $90 worth of wood and sheet metal, Ted Strunck of Okemos, Mich., built a windmill to use along with an auto generator for home heating.*

disputed Stever's estimate as too optimistic, pointing out that such a change would require not only advanced technology but also ready financing, changes in attitudes, and availability of materials.

Early in the year oil-shale development was touted as an important step toward self-sufficiency in energy needs for the U.S. By October, however, the Colony Development Operation announced that it was suspending indefinitely its pioneer experiment with oil shale, mainly because of inflation. (*See also* individual country articles; Arctic; Middle East.)

**GERMANY.** The Federal Republic of (West) Germany was rocked by the resignation of Chancellor Willy Brandt on May 6, 1974. Less than two weeks earlier, one of Brandt's personal aides, Günter Guillaume, had been arrested on suspicion of being a spy for the (East) German Democratic Republic. Brandt was succeeded by Finance Minister Helmut Schmidt, who was sworn in as the new chancellor on May 16.

In his letter of resignation Brandt accepted political responsibility for the Guillaume affair. It became clear, however, after a special commission accused West German security services of being negligent, that Brandt had probably used the case to step down from a post that was an increasing burden to him. Meanwhile, Brandt remained chairman of the Social Democratic party (SPD).

Electoral support for the SPD seriously sagged

during the year. In March the party lost its longtime absolute majority in the Hamburg state parliament and suffered heavy losses in local elections in Schleswig-Holstein and the Rhineland-Palatinate. The SPD vote also went down in the Lower Saxony state election in June, and the trend toward the conservative Christian Democratic Union (CDU) and its Bavarian ally the Christian Social Union (CSU) continued in state elections in Hesse and Bavaria in October. The conservative vote increased not only in rural areas but also in the big cities and among young voters. To a large extent the electoral losses of the SPD and its junior partner, the Free Democratic party (FDP), were attributed to the nation's economic problems.

Walter Scheel, former foreign minister and a leader of the Free Democrats, was elected to the ceremonial office of president on May 15. He succeeded Gustav Heinemann, who retired at the end of June. In a continuation of the SPD-FDP government coalition, Free Democrat Hans-Dietrich Genscher replaced Scheel as foreign minister and Social Democrat Hans Apel, a former foreign ministry official, took over the finance ministry.

In the face of continued inflation and rising unemployment—although lower than in most other industrialized nations—Chancellor Schmidt instituted a program of economic stability based on

*Chancellor Brandt (center) walks with his aide, Günter Guillaume (right), before the latter's arrest in April as a suspected spy.*

SVEN SIMON/KATHERINE YOUNG PHOTOGRAPHY

*The U.S. and East Germany established diplomatic relations in September, ending 24 years of cold war enmity. Signing the agreement in Washington, D.C., is Herbert Suess (left), representing East Germany, and Arthur Hartmann, of the U.S.*
UPI COMPIX

big cuts in public spending. But as unemployment climbed at year's end, large sums of money were made available for local hospital, school, and road projects.

A leader of an urban guerrilla group, Roger Meins, died in prison on November 9 after a two-month hunger strike. There were protest demonstrations in several West German cities. The next day a leading West Berlin judge, Günter von Drenkmann, was assassinated, and the government ordered special protection for all judges and prosecutors.

While continuing Willy Brandt's *Ostpolitik* of seeking better relations with the Soviet Union and its allies, the Schmidt government placed the main emphasis of its foreign policy on strengthening ties with the countries of Western Europe. Helpful to this aim were talks between Schmidt and French President Valéry Giscard d'Estaing, who visited West Germany in July. Relations with the United States, strained as a result of differences over the October 1973 war in the Middle East, improved sharply in December, when Schmidt visited Washington, D.C., and talked with President Gerald R. Ford. A joint statement by the two men hinted at a new U.S.-German global partnership.

Schmidt had headed a delegation to Moscow in October and talked with Soviet leader Leonid Brezhnev. As a result a West German industrial consortium was to help the Soviet Union build a pipeline that would supply Soviet natural gas to West Germany. Agreement was also reached on West German aid in the construction of a nuclear power plant in the Soviet Union that would supply electricity to West Berlin.

West Berlin continued as a center of political tension during the year. In July the West German government opened an environmental protection office in West Berlin over East German protest that this was a violation of the four-power agreement that

West Berlin was not part of West Germany. In July the East German TV and press denounced Scheel for making an official visit to West Berlin.

The 25th anniversary of the founding of the German Democratic Republic was celebrated in East Berlin in October. The East German government's march toward worldwide recognition was climaxed in September when diplomatic relations were finally established with the United States. At the anniversary celebrations Erich Honecker, first secretary of the Socialist Unity (Communist) party, boasted that East Germany had reached tenth place among the nations of the world in industrial production.

In September the East German parliament amended the nation's constitution, extending the parliamentary term from four to five years and reducing the voting age to 18 years. More significant, all reference to Germany as one nation was dropped from the constitution, thus underlining Communist abandonment of the goal of a reunified Germany. Earlier in the year, representatives of the two German states had signed an agreement to set up permanent missions in each other's capitals. Although they were de facto embassies, the missions were not referred to as such because of West Germany's insistence that there was still but one German nation. (*See also* Europe; Iceland.)

**GHANA.** Col. Ignatius K. Acheampong, head of the National Redemption Council (NRC) military regime, tightened his personal control in 1974, adding finance to his defense portfolio. In his speech on January 13, the second anniversary of the NRC revolution, Col. Acheampong, though making no reference to return to civilian rule, announced the setting up of a civilian National Advisory Council on political affairs. He further announced the "demilitarization of economic life" and the inauguration of a 33-member National Economic Planning Council, to be charged with evolving a system to involve every Ghanaian in the second stage of the self-reliance program, and with the launching of a second Five-Year Plan to increase diversification (from cocoa, timber, and gold), develop mining of bauxite and other minerals, and encourage light industry for export. The universities were closed from February 11 to March 15 following "unruly demonstrations," and several Soviet officials were deported for spying.

Ghana's foreign trade figures continued to move upward, with a record trade surplus, though rocketing prices accounted for much of this, particularly in the case of Ghana's cocoa, which contributed 70% of the country's foreign exchange reserves, 30% of its national revenue, and 60% of its exports; prices soared to $2,250 a ton by March. Apart from the danger of a price fall, the cocoa industry faced disease problems, labor dissatisfaction from farmers, and large-scale smuggling. Timber, the second largest export, likewise benefited from world demand and rising prices, but by March the high price of hardwoods had already led to a large oversupply. Ashanti gold prices rose to a record $170 a fine ounce. By mid-1974, however, the impact of oil and world inflation were affecting Ghana's boom. In June a government decree unified import and export control with stiff punishment for evasion, and similar central coordination was established for home and overseas investment. In September Shirley Temple Black, retired movie actress, was sworn in as U.S. ambassador to Ghana. (*See also* Africa.)

Shirley Temple Black, appointed ambassador to Ghana in September, is greeted at the United Nations during an October visit.

Tension shows as Lee Trevino birdies the ninth hole on his way to victory in the PGA championship at Clemmons, N.C., in August.

**GOLF.** Johnny Miller won eight tournaments in 1974 and the top prize money of $353,030. Miller equaled Arnold Palmer's total of eight victories in 1960, the highest number since Byron Nelson's record in 1945. Miller did not, however, win any major championships. He was never in contention in any one of the four, and his best finish was tenth place in the British Open. Miller did, nonetheless, establish himself as one of the world's finest golfers.

Gary Player won the U.S. Masters and the British Open in 1974. Player built his victory in the Masters on a great third-round score of 66, followed by steady, unfaltering play on the final day. The British Open was a resounding triumph for Player, who led throughout. Player's major championships—three British Opens, two Masters, two Professional Golfers' Association of America (PGA) championships, and one U.S. Open—had been surpassed only by Jack Nicklaus, Walter Hagen, and Ben Hogan.

Hale Irwin won the U.S. Open in 1974, played on the extremely demanding Winged Foot course near New York City, with an unusually high score of 287. Only Player matched par, with a 70 on the first day of play. Palmer shared the lead with Irwin after 36 holes, but disastrous play the following day took Palmer out of contention.

Not since 1970 had Nicklaus failed to win a major title. Lee Trevino spoiled Nicklaus' final chance in 1974 when he beat Nicklaus by one stroke in the

PGA championship. Nicklaus, however, did win the first Tournament Players Championship, and Trevino also won the World Series of Golf after seven sudden-death holes with Player. Trevino and Irwin were third in the World Cup behind the South Africans and the Japanese.

U.S. teams dominated the amateur internationals in 1974. In the world championships, the U.S. men's team won the Eisenhower Trophy by ten strokes over Japan. The U.S. women's team won the Espirito Santo Trophy by the overwhelming margin of 16 strokes over tied South Africa and Great Britain.

U.S. women won their 14th victory in the Curtis Cup match by defeating Great Britain by one point. Several women professional golfers were very successful in 1974. JoAnne Carner set a new record for winnings. Sandra Haynie won both the U.S. Open and the PGA championships. Jo Ann Prentice won the year's biggest prize of $32,000 in the Colgate-Dinah Shore Winners Circle. Colgate also promoted the first professional tournament for women in Europe. Judy Rankin won the tournament, held at Sunningdale, England, by five strokes.

## GREAT BRITAIN AND NORTHERN IRELAND, UNITED KINGDOM OF. Economic and political crises dominated life in Great Britain for most of 1974. In the political arena, there were two general elections and a change of government. In January 1974 the country's economy began to stagger from the effect of the three-day workweek instituted late in 1973—in the wake of cutbacks in oil from the Middle East and slowdowns by British coal miners and railway workers. Religious and political strife in Northern Ireland continued to be a major problem, with Irish terrorists striking in England itself.

In February the National Union of Mineworkers voted to strike, more than 75% of the membership turning down the wage increase offered by the government of Prime Minister Edward Heath. Shortly thereafter, Heath called for a general election on February 28 in order to seek a mandate from the voters for his Conservative party's tough stance on unions and wage increases.

The Labour party, led by former Prime Minister Harold Wilson, campaigned on a comprehensive program drawn up in 1973. Labour's priorities included renegotiation of the terms of British membership in the European Economic Community (EEC), a wide-ranging program of social programs to help low-income groups, extension of public ownership of industry, and the repeal of the Conservatives' Industrial Relations Act of 1971, which had set up a system for the regulation of trade unions. The Liberal party, long a weak third party, also offered a plan to curb inflation and to assist low-income groups.

In the February 28 election, Labour emerged with a narrow victory. Labour party candidates

UPI COMPIX

*'The Guitar Player', by the Dutch master Jan Vermeer, was stolen from Kenwood House in London on February 23. Several unrelated ransom demands were made for the painting, which was valued at $2.3 million. A tip led police to a London churchyard, where they found the art work on May 6.*

won 301 seats in Parliament's House of Commons, versus 296 for Conservative party candidates. Labour did not have an absolute majority of the seats in Commons, however, because of the number of seats held by the Liberals and other small parties. Heath's attempt to form a coalition with the Liberals was unsuccessful; he therefore resigned and Wilson again became prime minister.

Wilson's new Cabinet, which came into power on March 4, included James Callaghan, foreign affairs; Roy Jenkins, home secretary; Denis Healey, chancellor of the exchequer; and Anthony Wedgwood Benn, industry. The government, though insecure in the House of Commons on a numerical basis, was able to effect some controversial legislation—including the repeal of the Industrial Relations Act and the abolition of the Pay Board.

Wilson's government settled the coal strike by making an exception to existing counterinflationary provisions and offering wage increases more than double those offered by Heath. The state of emergency that began in November 1973 was ended on March 11; the five-day work week had been resumed two days earlier.

Statutory wage controls ended in July. Meanwhile, Labour was negotiating with the Trades Union Congress (TUC) for voluntary restraint on wage increases. The TUC evolved a position calling for maintaining real income, rather than increasing it, in the face of spiraling inflation; this would involve "catch up" raises for the previous 12 months of inflation. The TUC also asked for raises for anticipated inflation, a controversial request in some quarters thought likely to promote inflation even further.

To strengthen his hand in dealing with the economy and other issues, Wilson called a general election for October 10. Labour retained control of the government, gaining an edge of 43 seats over the Conservatives (with 319 to 276). In the October election Labour finally produced an absolute majority of the Commons' seats, but with a slim margin.

## The Economy

Inflation had been building up rapidly in 1973, fed by increases in world commodity prices (especially for oil) and by an increase in the domestic money supply. In December 1973 the Conservatives introduced measures to cut public expenditure drastically and dampen demand. Controls were reimposed on consumer credit, and restrictions placed on bank lending.

Within three weeks of being appointed Labour's chancellor of the exchequer, Healey brought in his first budget on March 26. At that point the government had to balance and weigh the opposing risks of continuing inflation with recession and high unemployment. Healey's March budget increased taxation by over $3 billion. About $1.2 billion was provided for food subsidies. The balance of payments deficit was growing rapidly (reaching $1 billion for the month of October), largely because of oil prices; Healey proposed to finance that deficit by overseas borrowing, rather than by cutting imports.

In July Healey announced a supplementary package of budgetary measures. He sought to hold back price increases by reducing the value-added tax (VAT) from 10% to 8%. The July measures also included relief for domestic ratepayers, increased rent rebates and allowances, and additional food subsidies.

By the time Healey brought in the autumn budget on November 12, the financial difficulties of many industrial companies had become critical. He chose to divert more than $3 billion to industry by changes in price controls and by easing taxes on corporation profits arising from inflation of stock values. Despite the earlier reductive measures, the VAT was raised to 25% on gasoline.

Late in the year the government came to the financial rescue of British Leyland, the country's largest automobile manufacturer—employing about 165,000 workers. Earlier in the year the government had provided subsidies for Ferranti, a major supplier of electronic defense equipment; Rolls-Royce, the auto company that also produced airplane engines; and the bankrupt Court Line, a major company involved in shipbuilding and package vacations.

WIDE WORLD

*A fireman directs a stream of water onto Westminster Hall in London, where fire followed a terrorist bombing in June.*

Even the largest banks in Britain were affected by a drastic decrease in property values and stock market prices; some suffered huge losses in foreign currency exchange transactions. The Bank of England's minimum lending rate eased only a little during the year, from 12½% to 11½%.

In Britain, as in the U.S., it was a traumatic year for the stock market. The *Financial Times* industrial ordinary shares index, which stood at 500 in January 1973, had dropped to around 320 in January 1974. By August the index slipped below 200 for the first time since 1958 and continued its plunge to 150 by mid-December. This was a more drastic decline than that of the 1930's.

High interest rates were a cause of difficulty in the housing market. The demand for mortgage loans was inflated by the rapidly rising cost of houses in the preceding two or three years; however, building society funds were hit by competitive interest rates, even as the government pressured the societies not to increase mortgage rates. In April the government made available a loan of more than $225 million to the building societies. The March budget included plans to enable local authorities to purchase unsold houses.

### Foreign Policy

The Wilson government, elected in part because of its pledge to renegotiate the terms of EEC membership, sent Foreign Minister Callaghan to a meeting of the European Council of Ministers on April 1 to begin that negotiation. Wilson's government hoped for more favorable terms in a number of areas, one of the most important being agricultural policy. Britain, a major food importer, felt the current policy unfair.

Negotiations with the EEC and its member countries continued throughout the year. West Germany's Chancellor Helmut Schmidt visited England in November and told a Labour party conference that the countries on the Continent warmly supported British membership in the EEC.

European union was considered a premature objective for Great Britain, even for 1980. In his various negotiations, Callaghan stressed that his

*Soldiers surrounded London's Heathrow Airport early in 1974 to guard against the threat of Palestinian terrorists.*

country wanted to maintain an effective Atlantic alliance with the U.S.

### Northern Ireland

Strife between the Roman Catholic and Protestant communities in Northern Ireland became even more murderous after the breakdown of the power-sharing formula devised by a conference of leaders from Britain, Northern Ireland, and Ireland in late 1973. The executive body created at that meeting, and headed by Brian Faulkner, was brought down by the hostility of militant Protestants; that hostility culminated in a general strike by Protestant trade unions in May 1974. When Faulkner's rule toppled, the British government resumed direct rule from London.

A judge and a magistrate, both Catholics, were assassinated at their homes in Belfast, the capital of Northern Ireland, in September. The outlawed Provisional wing of the Irish Republic Army (IRA) acknowledged responsibility for the killings.

By the end of November there had been at least 90 murders of Catholics or Protestants during the year; by year-end the five-year total of murders approached 1,200. There was a decline in the number of bombings in Northern Ireland in 1974, but this form of terrorism was accelerated in England. An IRA bomb damaged the Houses of Parliament in June, and at least ten persons were injured.

One person died and many were injured by a bomb placed in the White Tower of the Tower of London. Twelve persons were killed when a bomb wrecked a bus on a highway in Yorkshire. Bombs planted in public houses (pubs) killed 5 in Guildford, 2 in Woolwich, and 20 persons in Birmingham. The Birmingham bombings, which occurred on November 21, led the British government to rush through Parliament legislation for new powers of arrest, detention, and expulsion to deal with the terrorism, including the banning of the IRA (including a ban on traditional IRA emblems such as the black beret). In December, however, a move to restore the death penalty for terrorism was defeated in Parliament. Late in December a bomb was exploded at the London home of former Prime Minister Heath, presumably by the IRA; Heath was not at home, and no one was injured. (*See also* Europe; Ireland.)

**GREECE.** For Greece, 1974 was a momentous year, culminating in the restoration of democracy and in the first free elections since 1964. The year began, however, under the junta of Brig. Gen. Demetrios Ioannidis that had toppled Georgios Papadopoulos in November 1973 and had set up a new government under Prime Minister Adamantios Androutsopoulos. The new regime continued repressive domestic policies.

Hostility with Turkey began in 1974 with a dispute over rights to explore for oil in the Aegean Sea. It seemed for a time that there might be fighting over the issue. Although negotiations were agreed

*When the reigning Greek military junta relinquished power in July, former Prime Minister Constantine Caramanlis (left) returned home from exile to head the government. Archbishop Serafim of Athens administers the oath of office in the presence of President Phaidon Gizikis.*

CAMERA PRESS / PICTORIAL PARADE

to, Greece broke them off, and the matter remained unresolved. Relations with the U.S. deteriorated in 1974. Negotiations for an extension of U.S. use of Greek bases were unsuccessful because of U.S. unwillingness to meet the Greek demand that the U.S. completely reequip the Greek air force. Relations with Great Britain also were unfriendly. At midyear Greece declared its intention to withdraw from the North Atlantic Treaty Organization (NATO).

Cyprus, however, was the most serious foreign problem for Greece in 1974, and transformed its domestic politics as well. On July 15 the Greek Cypriot national guard, led by Greek officers and supported by the Greek army contingent stationed on Cyprus, under orders from Greece, deposed Archbishop Makarios III, the president of Cyprus. Turkey invaded Cyprus on July 20, and Greece underwent a general mobilization. On July 21 the Greek government ordered the military to attack the Turkish invasion forces on Cyprus and to shell the Turkish border. The military objected to the orders, declaring that it was equipped to defend but not to attack, but it did fly troops to Cyprus, who landed with heavy losses. Turkey eventually took control of 40% of Cyprus.

On July 23 the Greek military told political leaders that the armed forces could no longer rule and would surrender power. Constantine Caramanlis was asked to return from exile to become prime minister of a civilian government. Caramanlis began talks on Cyprus that later broke down but did result in an uneasy cease-fire.

The Caramanlis government stripped the military of its political power, freed political prisoners, reinstated the 1952 constitution, and asked for a referendum on the future of the monarchy. By October martial law had been lifted in all except a few border areas. Ex-dictator Papadopoulos and four associates were banished. Judicial proceedings began against more than 100 junta collaborators.

Shortly after Caramanlis took office, preparations began for elections. Several political parties and coalitions were formed. In September, Caramanlis lifted the 27-year-old ban on the Greek Communist party. Retribution against the junta and its followers, guarantees against military coups in the future, resolution of the problems on Cyprus, and effective ways to deal with high inflation became the principal election issues.

On November 17, voters gave Caramanlis a majority of greater than 54%, empowering him to make constitutional reforms he had advocated. Only one other political group won substantial power. Caramanlis announced new efforts to settle the Cyprus dispute, including his willingness to consider a division of the island into separate Greek and Turkish states that would be joined in a national federal government. Archbishop Makarios visited Greece for talks in late November and then returned to Cyprus. On December 8 Greece voted to abolish its 142-year-old monarch, President Phaidon Gizikis resigned, and Michael Stassinopoulos was elected provisional president by a new parliament. (*See also* Cyprus; Europe; Turkey.)

**GRENADA.** On Feb. 7, 1974, in an atmosphere of extreme unrest, Grenada became an independent state, the 34th member of the Commonwealth of Nations. The ceremony was boycotted by the prime ministers of the independent Caribbean countries and by the queen's representative, who did not attend for security reasons.

The opposition to independence was largely based on opposition to Prime Minister Eric M. Gairy, whose support had traditionally come from the rural areas. Gairy was opposed by the Committee of 22, a broad spectrum ranging from the business and professional communities and urban white-collar workers to radical intellectuals. On Jan. 1, 1974, the Committee of 22 called a general strike in protest of police brutality. The government countered with legislation making it illegal for business premises to close their doors during normal trading hours. In the weeks before independence there were daily anti-Gairy demonstrations and marches, a general strike and business shutdown, and a cutoff of fuel and utilities. Looting and violence were common, and a prominent trade union leader was killed. Efforts by Caribbean trade unions, church groups, and others to mediate failed, as did appeals to the British government to defer independence.

A new wave of arrests occurred after independence, and the strikers returned to work on February 23. Many Grenadians fled the island. The economy—based on tourism, cocoa, nutmeg, and bananas—was reported to be in a shambles, with up to 90% of usual revenue lost. By May some normality had returned to the island, but the economy remained precarious. Grenada joined the Caribbean Common Market, and on September 17 the United Nations General Assembly elected Grenada as its 137th member. (*See also* West Indies.)

**GUATEMALA.** Following the presidential elections held on March 3, 1974, Kjell Eugenio Laugerud García, the candidate of the ruling conservative coalition, was declared the winner. The left-leaning opposition front, whose candidate was widely believed to have polled the most votes, voiced strong protests. President Laugerud took office on July 1 for four years. In his inaugural speech Laugerud referred to the need for social reform; his first major policy step, however, was the announcement on August 13 of an action plan to deal with inflation—a problem attributed to a shortage of staple foods, an excess of monetary liquidity arising from high prices received for commodity exports, and the high cost of some imports, particularly petroleum. The official figure for the increase in the cost of living for the first eight months of the year was 17%, but unofficial sources estimated that the inflation rate for the year was near 30%.

There was a decline in activity in the construction industry because of sharp rises in the cost of building materials. Hotel construction expanded, however, reflecting a rapid growth of tourism. Unofficial figures for the number of tourists in the first quarter of 1974 were higher than for the whole of 1973, and it was expected that income from tourism would exceed $200 million for the year. Production was adversely affected by two natural disasters that caused serious damage. In mid-September Hurricane Fifi struck the northern part of the country, destroying banana plantations and staple crops. (*See* Disasters; Weather.) Two weeks later, volcanic eruptions occurred in the southwest, causing widespread damage to cotton, coffee, and cereal crops. These setbacks—coupled with the decline in world prices of coffee, cotton, and meat—harmed the agricultural sector, still the mainstay of the economy. (*See also* Latin America.)

**GUINEA.** At a meeting in the capital city of Conakry in early March 1974, an International Bauxite Association was formally established by the world's leading bauxite-producing countries. Guinea holds two thirds of the world's bauxite reserves. Drought conditions were reported throughout the country in April. Also in April the government arranged to purchase special drawing rights from the International Monetary Fund to ease an adverse balance of payments arising from diminished exports. The economy was also helped by an African Development Bank loan to improve Conakry's water supply, agreements with Egypt and Libya for economic and technical cooperation, announced prospecting for offshore oil by a U.S. company with Guinea's participation, the building of a new dam at Koutoutamba to bring electric power to the southeast, and the agreement for the building of a trans-Guinea railway by a Canadian company at a cost of about $555 million.

In a continuing quarrel with Senegal and the Ivory Coast, President Sékou Touré was persuaded by the chairman of the Organization of African Unity (OAU) to withdraw the matter from the United Nations and settle it amicably within the OAU. In November it was announced that presidential and general elections would be held on December 27 and that the Central Committee of the Democratic Party of Guinea (the single, governing party) would raise the number of parliamentary seats from 100 to 150. (*See also* Africa.)

**GUINEA-BISSAU.** On Sept. 10, 1974, Portugal granted formal independence to its West African colony of Guinea-Bissau, known formerly as Portuguese Guinea. A brief ceremony in Lisbon, attended by leaders of the anti-Portuguese nationalist movement, ended 13 years of fighting in which an unknown number of Portuguese and black soldiers on both sides had been killed. A week later, on September 17, Guinea-Bissau became the 138th member nation of the United Nations.

In Guinea-Bissau, however, leaders of the African Party for the Independence of Guinea and Cape Verde (PAIGC), the rebel movement that made up the government of the new republic, dated their country's independence from September 1973. It was then, with African guerrilla forces in control of most of the country, that the PAIGC had first proclaimed the territory free of Portuguese rule.

The independence agreement with Portugal was signed August 26 in Algiers, Algeria, following several months of negotiations there and in London between Portuguese and PAIGC representatives. Under the terms of this agreement, Portugal was to continue supplying Guinea-Bissau with doctors, teachers, and other essential personnel. The agreement, however, did not meet one of the PAIGC's main demands—that the new country also include the Cape Verde Islands, which are about 400 miles northwest of Guinea-Bissau. Portugal agreed, in-

THOMAS A. JOHNSON—THE NEW YORK TIMES

*Soldiers of the African Party for the Independence of Guinea and Cape Verde line up for flag-raising ceremonies in Guinea-Bissau, formerly Portuguese Guinea, which became independent on September 10. Portuguese troops began to depart late in August.*

stead, to grant self-determination to the people there in a referendum sometime in the future.

Luis Cabral—who had assumed PAIGC leadership after his half brother, Amilcar Cabral, the party's philosopher-founder—was assassinated in January 1973, became Guinea-Bissau's first president. Among the immediate problems facing the Cabral government were the economic pressures of a poor agricultural economy, tribal rivalries, and the distrust of some mainland Africans for leaders with mixed African-European ancestries such as Cabral's. (*See also* Africa; Portugal.)

**HAITI.** President Jean-Claude Duvalier's support in the cabinet and among the armed forces was further consolidated in 1974 after a reshuffle on March 19, which reflected a compromise, with some old-guard Duvalierists remaining in power together with several respected "technocrats" chosen by the president. An economic recovery had brought about an annual gross national product growth rate of about 5% since Duvalier assumed the presidency. New manufacturing industries fared best, and exports of assembled products reached an annual total of more than $32 million by the first of the year. Tourism also showed considerable growth,

with receipts at a near 50% increase over those of 1973 and hotel construction rushing to keep up. Remittances from Haitians living abroad increased to about $20 million a year with many "economic exiles" keen to invest in Haiti's growth.

The boom occurred exclusively in Port-au-Prince, the capital, however, and involved only a tiny proportion of the urban population. New jobs were created in factories, in hotels, and on numerous building sites, but the increased economic activity was taking place entirely in the services and export industries and did not result in expanded output for the home market. For the 80% of Haiti's inhabitants living in remote overcrowded valleys or on badly eroded mountain slopes conditions deteriorated. With the population growing at 2.1% annually and agricultural production stagnant or shrinking, a sharp rise in inflation caused added grief. Even if agricultural production were to be stimulated, a basic problem remained in the lack of an adequate road system. The government therefore obtained a World Bank loan for $10 million to improve the Port-au-Prince to Cap-Haitien highway and a more than $22-million Inter-American Development Bank loan to modernize the road west to Les Cayes. (*See also* West Indies.)

*Stanley Hopgood of Andover, England, puts finishing touches on his replica of the Tower Bridge in Wuppertal, West Germany, which he built with 4,000 matchsticks in 2½ years.*

**HOBBIES.** As both avocation and industry, hobbies continued to flourish in 1974. At the annual hobby industry show in Chicago, 300 manufacturers exhibited, exceeding by 50 the number who displayed their goods the previous year.

Radio-controlled planes, helicopters, and boats were leaders among the hobby wares in 1974. Other favorites included historical, military, and mythological figures and miniatures; plastic kits, especially the diorama type; wood and plastic ship models, including boats powered by steam or gas; and science-oriented hobbies.

At a time of soaring food prices, the food hobby kits sold well. Space Age Gardens were preseeded planters for growing corn and tomato plants, cucumbers, and even pumpkins. Kits for making wine, cheese, candy, and soap were also popular.

A wide variety of kits on the market ranged in price from a few dollars to hundreds. Automobile hobbyists liked the Wankel Rotary Engine kit. More than one million of the model Mazda car kits had been produced since 1971, spurred by the rotary engine's popularity. A new model engine was the Ford turbine; some engineers predicted that the Ford turbine would supersede existing types of auto engines by 1980.

The Ford Model T and the Rolls Royce Silver Ghost were popular car models in 1974. Museum quality cars by Pocher d'Italia were designed from original factory blueprints and prototype drawings. The kits contained up to 2,200 parts, and the models were priced from $100 to $200.

The United States Postal Service, which claimed to be the world's largest manufacturer of hobby goods, became a new member of the Hobby Industries of America Association. Its products engaged 16 million stamp collectors in the United States.

Licensed to market toys, dolls, games, hobbies, and crafts bearing approval of the Smithsonian Institution, the Tonka Corp. brought out the first of these products in 1974. They were four dioramas of the museum type in which objects are displayed against a realistic background to recreate a moment in time. Each diorama came with a booklet written in cooperation with the Smithsonian.

Time Capsules came in kits that contained military miniatures, battlefield artifacts, color background scenes, clear plastic display containers, and diaries of events. With these diorama components, hobbyists could recreate major battles of World War II.

Among the art hobbies favored in 1974 were

*Carefully detailed military miniatures, available from every historical period, are the current choice of many collectors.*

Wire Art Mosaics, in which silver-toned wire was used to create ships, bridges, buildings, and animals framed against a black velour background. Blockit held the makings of a three-dimensional painting suitable for hanging or free-standing display. With the Casting Ivory Classics kit, ministatues were fashioned in simulated ivory and then given an antique finish. For rockhounds three new rock-polishing tumblers were available in 3-, 6-, and 12-pound capacities.

A crafts festival lasted all during the summer of 1974 at Toronto, Ont., in conjunction with the tenth anniversary conference of the World Crafts Council. Objects displayed at the Ontario Science Centre represented work done by master craftsmen and anonymous ones as well.

A hobby that caught on with the young, young set in 1974 was bubblegum card collecting. The cards, stickers in this case, were parodies of well-advertised products. (*See also* Coins and Medals; Stamps; Toys and Games.)

**HONDURAS.** The country's most devastating natural calamity of the century occurred September 18 and 19 when Hurricane Fifi struck the north coast, killing at least 5,000 people and damaging or destroying 182 communities through flooding and landslides. The valleys drained by the Aguán, León,

*Hurricane Fifi visited death and destruction on Honduras in September. Here floodwaters pour over twisted tracks of the Tela Railroad Co. in northern Honduras.*

and Ulúa rivers were hardest hit. One town, Choloma, lost 2,800 inhabitants when they were buried by an avalanche of debris that left the community under 12 feet of mud. Disaster aid was rapidly forthcoming from the International Red Cross, and through private efforts from many countries in the Americas and from Europe, for the more than 100,000 rendered homeless and on the verge of starvation. Poor roads, inadequate organization, and fuel shortages slowed assistance efforts. The hurricane's damage to the economy was widespread. About 60% of the country's bananas, the leading source of export revenue; 40% of its cattle, a growing export resource; and more than half of the rice and corn, both staples in the Honduran diet, were lost. (*See* Disasters; Weather.)

In January, President Oswaldo López Arellano announced a 15-year development plan effecting significant changes in several areas, among them agriculture, industry, and labor. The plan called for cooperative agricultural communities designed to abolish the extremes of large and small landholdings, government support for trade unions' collective bargaining, a minimum wage scale, a gradual nationalization of forest resources, and an end to lucrative mining concessions to foreign companies. Honduras joined the new Union of Banana Exporting Countries designed to protect their economic interests; however, when the union decided in March to impose an export tax of up to $1 per 40-pound crate on the producing companies, the companies retaliated. Though Honduras imposed only a 50¢-a-crate charge on April 25, the Standard Fruit and Steamship Co. halted exports and cut production. When the company resumed exports in May at one third its normal output, the exports went to new markets where the tax did not apply. (*See also* El Salvador; Latin America.)

**HORSE RACING.** There was no Triple Crown winner in thoroughbred horse racing in 1974, as there was in 1973 when Secretariat won all three of the most important races held on U.S. tracks. Nevertheless, Little Current managed to capture two of the three and look very good in doing so.

At Churchill Downs in Louisville, Ky., on May 4, a record crowd of over 150,000 persons, including Princess Margaret of Great Britain, packed the historic enclosure for the 100th running of the Kentucky Derby. The 1¼-mile race was taken by Cannonade, who gathered in the first-prize money of $274,000 for owner John Olin. Ridden by jockey Angel Cordero, the horse was clocked at 2:04. Another record was established on Derby day when 23 horses made up the starting field, which eclipsed the old mark of 22 horses in 1928. Finishing behind Cannonade were Hudson County and Agitate.

Little Current, owned by John Galbreath and ridden by Miguel Rivera, won the Preakness Stakes at Pimlico in Baltimore, Md., in powerful fashion, after finishing fifth in the above mentioned stampede at Churchill Downs. The three-year-old horse then went on to take the Belmont Stakes at Elmont, N.Y., earning $101,970, with a time of 2:29.2. Jolly Johu was second; Cannonade, third.

In Canada the 1974 thoroughbred racing season was replete with outstanding performances, and some of the brightest stars emerged from the two-year-old division. J. L. Levesque's homebred L'Enjoleur, a son of champions Buckpasser and Fanfreluche, won five stakes and established himself as one of the best juvenile runners in Canadian history. At sprint distances, however, W. P. Gilbride's Greek Answer was almost invincible. The colt's blazing speed carried him to victory in three Canadian stakes and in the rich Arlington-Washington Futurity at Chicago.

*Almost flying across the finish line, Little Current, with jockey Miguel Rivera, wins the Belmont Stakes by seven lengths. The horse also won the Preakness but finished fifth in the Kentucky Derby.*

UPI COMPIX

TONY ROLLO—NEWSWEEK

*Medical investigators have discovered that bacteria on the stems of flowers given to hospital patients present a serious threat of infection, particularly to burn victims.*

**HOSPITALS.** The freedom of hospitals to manage their own affairs gave way again in 1974 to increased federal regulation, designed primarily to curb the cost of health care. Hospitals were forced in 1974 to balance federal economic control against the need to maintain quality health-care standards in an inflationary economy.

By the time the Economic Stabilization Program (ESP) of the administration of U.S. President Richard M. Nixon ended in April 1974, the hospital industry was one of only a few industries still controlled. Throughout the 990 days of ESP controls, the hospital industry had set a record of inflation fighting perhaps unmatched by any other segment of the economy. Beginning in early 1973, the rate of inflation in the economy was greater than that of hospitals. The trend continued throughout 1973, and by May 1974 economy-wide inflation had reached 11.1% while hospital service charges had risen only 7.9%.

This accomplishment was not made without some sacrifices. American Hospital Association (AHA) surveys indicated that hospital operating margins fell to less than 1% in 1973 from 2.2% in 1971, a trend that appeared to continue into 1974. Money spent for expansion and improvement of services also decreased. In addition, other federal regulations aimed at further reducing costs began to take effect. The establishment of boards to review professional standards, requirements for approval of capital expenditures, and limitations on reimbursement for services to Medicare and Medicaid patients were expected to have a significant impact on hospital economy.

Hospitals entered a catch-up period of higher charges following the end of ESP in 1974 in order to cover the increased costs of goods and services they had to buy—notably food, fuel, and plastics. Higher charges also reflected wage adjustments made for hospital employees, many covered for the first time under an extension of the minimum wage law that went into effect on May 1, 1974. Furthermore, passage of a law lifting the exemption of employees of not-for-profit hospitals from provisions of the National Labor Relations Act was expected to lead to an increase in collective bargaining among more than 1.5 million employees in nearly 3,500 hospitals.

Economic and legislative pressures notwithstanding, hospitals in 1974 tried to improve delivery of health-care services through extension, or introduction of new facilities and services. There was an increase in hospital programs emphasizing improved management techniques, shared services, and joint purchasing arrangements. Besides one-day and twilight surgery, hospitals accelerated development of extended, home, and self-care programs, emergency medical care systems, alcoholism programs, health maintenance organizations, multifacility units, and ambulatory care facilities.

In another development, a study by Charles E. Butterworth, Jr., chairman of the American Medical Association's Council on Foods and Nutrition, strongly suggested that doctors and hospitals are ignoring patients' nutritional needs. Hospitals, the study claimed, often ignored good nutrition both before and after surgery, failed to diagnose and treat malnutrition, and sometimes, in fact, caused malnutrition. One patient included in Butterworth's study died from irreversible malnutrition after 35 days in the intensive-care unit of a hospital after heart surgery. At the other extreme, a new British hospital, built for the affluent, offered vintage wine as well as delicacies such as chicken liver pâté, poached trout, and braised duck with cherries. (*See also* Medicine; Nursing.)

**HOUSING.** No single element of the U.S. economy suffered more in 1974 from inflation, materials shortages, tight money, and the decline of consumer confidence than residential construction. The chief economist of the National Association of Home Builders characterized the situation as the worst housing slump since the depression.

Higher yields available from other investments siphoned money out of thrift institutions at an alarming rate, reducing funds available for mortgages and sending interest rates on new mortgages as high as 12% in some states. Housing starts fell throughout the year, most sharply in the last half. The year topped out with less than 1.4 million starts, down one third from 1973 and one million fewer than the all-time peak of 2.42 million in 1972. New housing volume did not even keep up with the average rate of new household formation, esti-

UPI COMPIX

*A New York City apartment house for Soviets serving at the UN is constructed from the top down. Each floor is assembled on the ground, then jacked into place on two core pillars, a technique expected to save months in construction time and about $1 million in costs.*

mated at 1.48 million per year for the 1970's.

In September the Federal Reserve Board eased up slightly on its tight money policy and, as a result,

*"It was rather naive of me to think that was the cost of the house."*

ULUSCHAK – EDMONTON JOURNAL, CANADA / ROTHCO

commercial lending rates softened a bit. In turn, the basic interest rate on government insured or guaranteed home mortgages was reduced to 9% in November with further reductions expected.

The shortage of mortgage funds would have been worse were it not for federal programs that bought record amounts of mortgages or participation in mortgage portfolios from the country's lenders and subsidized interest rates above a certain level for needy families. In August 1974 U.S. President Gerald R. Ford signed into law a bill that authorized housing and community development subsidies of more than $11 billion payable over the following three years. The law also lowered down-payment requirements and boosted the ceilings allowable on most mortgage loans purchased under the program.

The new law called for the federal government to pay the difference between local fair market rents and 15% to 25% of the gross income of eligible low-income families leasing new or existing apartments. Another housing aid bill was signed into law on October 18, providing $3 billion to finance up to 100,000 home purchases through conventional loans rather than via existing government-assisted plans.

Vacancies in modern units in most major markets were the lowest in several years. In many cities the rental stock was depleted by conversions of rental units to condominiums. Meanwhile, the normal apartment demand was swollen everywhere by the thousands of families priced out of the single-family home market. The widespread extending of construction deadlines due to materials shortages further aggravated the situation.

Only about 475,000 apartment units were started during 1974, with only 325,000 of them slated for rentals; the rest were condominiums. That total compared with about 610,000 rental starts in 1973.

Soaring prices and interest rates squeezed more and more would-be buyers out of the market for housing. The median sales price of new homes jumped 17.8% from 1972 to 1973—from $27,600 to $32,500—and at least that much again in 1974. Total home-buying costs rose 3½ times faster than average personal income. Those who could meet the high costs were often unable to find a lender for mortgage money.

Even the mobile home business suffered during 1974. Sales dropped 25% to 425,000 units.

Builders, big and small, were hit hard in 1974. During the first seven months, more than 1,000 builders collapsed into bankruptcy. By late summer about one eighth of the industry's more than 4,000,000 workers were unemployed, and another 200,000 had left construction work. (*See also* Banks; Business and Industry; Employment.)

**HUNGARY.** A reshuffle in the party leadership as well as in the government, initiated by the Central Committee of the Hungarian Socialist Workers' party in March 1974, forecast changes in the functioning of the New Economic Mechanism (NEM), the only economic system within the Comecon group allowing some freedom of decision to state enterprise managers and a range of fair market prices. Rezso Nyers, principal architect of NEM, was removed from the post of party secretary and relegated to virtual obscurity as director of the Economic Institute of the Academy of Sciences. He was succeeded by Karoly Nemeth, a member of the Politburo and head of the Budapest party organization. Gyorgy Aczel, another party secretary and supporter of Nyers, in charge of Hungary's relatively liberal cultural policy for the previous seven years, was made deputy premier, and his job in the secretariat was given to Imre Gyori. Lajos Feher, one of the five deputy prime ministers and also a supporter of Nyers, was retired and succeeded by Janos Borbandi. Both Gyori and Borbandi were members of the Central Committee.

Hungarian Socialist Workers' (Communist) Party First Secretary Janos Kadar visited Czechoslovakia in April and met Communist Party General Secretary Leonid I. Brezhnev of the U.S.S.R. in the Crimea at the beginning of August. A party and government delegation led by Kadar paid an official visit to the U.S.S.R. in late September. Premier Jeno Fock of Hungary paid a visit to East Berlin, and both Polish Premier Piotr Jaroszewicz and Yugoslavian President Tito paid friendly visits to Budapest during the year.

In October internationally known writer Gyorgy Konrad, sociologist Ivan Szelenyi, and poet Tamas Szentjoby were arrested and charged with subversive activity. The arrests caused a wave of foreign protests, and the three were released on October 28 and offered the chance to emigrate. (*See also* Europe.)

**ICE HOCKEY.** Another summit series against the U.S.S.R. surpassed all the intramural rivalries and franchise shuffling in the World Hockey Association (WHA) and the National Hockey League (NHL) in 1974. The Soviets won the rancorous eight-game series against Team Canada, a WHA all-star team—four wins, one loss, and three ties. The first four games were played in the Canadian cities of Quebec, Toronto, Winnipeg, and Vancouver, the last four in Moscow. Two years before, in the fall of 1972, an NHL all-star team narrowly beat the Soviets in a similar series.

The Toronto Maple Leafs of the NHL recruited Borje Salming, the premier defenseman in Sweden. In his rookie season, Salming ranked among the four or five best rear guards in North America's oldest established hockey league. The Toronto Toros of the WHA encouraged two impressive players, Vaclav Nedomansky and Richard Farda, to defect from the Czechoslovak national team. Their clandestine departures from Prague were arranged through agents operating in Switzerland and Sweden. The Winnipeg Jets of the WHA imported Scandinavian players in carload lots, beginning the 1974–75 season with four Swedes and two Finns in the lineup.

The Philadelphia Flyers won the Stanley Cup, the first expansion team to capture the major team prize in the NHL. The Flyers, led by Bobby Clarke at center and Bernie Parent in goal, beat the Boston Bruins four games to two. But the Bruins' center Phil Esposito won the 1974 Hart Trophy—his second—for most valuable NHL player.

Philadelphia was one of six clubs added to the NHL when the league expanded to 12 teams in 1967. Four teams were subsequently added and, in 1974, the Kansas City Scouts and the Washington Capitals were admitted to the NHL lodge. This increased NHL membership to 18 and resulted in a radical rearranging of the divisions. The former East and West alignment was broken up into four divisions—the Lester Patrick, the Conn Smythe, the James Norris, and the Charles F. Adams. Patrick, Smythe, Norris, and Adams were NHL pioneers, all deceased except Smythe, the founder of the Toronto Maple Leafs. Teams in Denver and Seattle were franchised to join the NHL in 1976.

Massive realignment also occurred in the WHA, the addition of the Indianapolis Racers and the Phoenix Roadrunners boosting league membership to 14 teams. The WHA regrouped in three divisions—Eastern, Western, and Canadian, the latter containing teams in Toronto, Quebec, Winnipeg, Edmonton, and Vancouver. WHA franchises continued to fold in one community and resurface elsewhere, the New Jersey Knights abandoning

*A healthy and plentiful crop of fall barley is harvested in the fields of a cooperative farm in Kisapostag, Hungary.*

UPI COMPIX

*Philadelphia Flyers' goalie Bernie Parent blocks the puck as Boston Bruins' Wayne Cashman moves in for a possible rebound during the sixth game of the Stanley Cup series in May. The Flyers won the series four games to two.*
WIDE WORLD

Cherry Hill to become the San Diego Mariners, and the Los Angeles Sharks leaving California to be reincarnated in Detroit as the Michigan Stags.

The Houston Aeros won the Avco Cup, representative of the WHA championship, defeating the Chicago Cougars in the final series, four games to none. Gordie Howe, a distinguished right wing for 25 years in the NHL, was a Houston star at 46. Howe came out of retirement to play for Houston with his two sons, 19-year-old Mark and 20-year-old Marty. Their family compact represented the first time in hockey history that a father-son combination played on the same team at the same time in the same pro league.

**ICELAND.** Early in 1974 the three-year-old coalition of leftist parties under Prime Minister Olafur Johannesson began to show signs of discord, mainly over economic issues. On May 9 parliament was dissolved, a full year before its term was to have run out. A new election was held on June 30, producing gains for the Independence party, which received 42.8% of the vote and 25 out of 60 seats in the legislature. On August 28 a new coalition government was formed under the premiership of Independence party leader Geir Hallgrimsson.

On October 22, negotiations to revise Iceland's defense pact with the U.S. were formally terminated. The change of government had led to a reversal of that policy, and the new government decided that it would allow the U.S. troops at Keflavik air base to remain for the time being.

The "cod war" with West Germany and the United Kingdom over fishing rights within the claimed 12- to 50-mile fishing zone continued, but skirmishes between Icelandic coast guard boats and fishing trawlers were on a reduced scale. In July the International Court of Justice, though not recog-nized as competent by Iceland, ruled that Iceland was not entitled to exclude West German and British vessels from the disputed area. The Hallgrimsson government later stated that it aimed to extend the limit to 200 miles by the end of 1975.

Iceland's worst avalanche in more than 50 years struck an east-coast fishing town in late December. At least nine persons died.

Economic matters took a turn for the worse during the year. Export prices, mainly for fish meal and oil, declined from their high 1973 level, and import prices rose. The balance of payments became unfavorable, and real national income ceased to increase. The forces of world inflation, combined with heavy cost increases at home, produced an inflation rate of 40% for 1974. The krona was twice devalued (by 4% and further by 17%) in the light of inflationary pressures. (*See also* Oceanography.)

**ICE SKATING.** The appeal of ice skating was reflected in 1974 by an increase of television coverage consequent upon favorable audience research figures. Another trend, the growing demand for municipally owned rinks, was prompted by a realization that overall operating costs could be much reduced by putting a swimming pool and an ice rink in adjacent buildings and designing a common power plant on a complementary basis. Prominent among several new rinks in warm-climate countries was South Africa's first truly international-sized rink, opened July 4 in Johannesburg. The popularity of ice dancing was recognized by the conferring of Olympic status on this branch of ice skating, to take effect from 1976. Technical progress was demonstrated by Gordon McKellen of the U.S., during training, when he became the first person to achieve a triple axel jump, requiring three and a half midair rotations.

New singles champions emerged when 22 nations were represented by 128 skaters in the world ice figure and dance championships held in Munich, West Germany, March 5–9. Jan Hoffmann of Dresden, East Germany, took the undefended men's title with three great triple leaps—Lutz, Salchow, and toe loop—but really owed his victory to a vital lead in the figures. The Soviet Union's Sergei Volkov narrowly hung onto second place, edging out Toller Cranston of Canada, who was by far the best free-skater, producing two triple Salchows in a superbly original performance, grinning impudently throughout, and receiving two well-deserved sixes for artistic presentation.

Nine judges split 6–3 in favor of Christine Errath when the East German from Berlin gained the vacant women's crown. Thanks to her earlier advantage in the figures, she was able to thwart a last-ditch stand by the runner-up, Dorothy Hamill of the U.S., who outpointed the new champion in the free skating and scored a six for artistic presentation. Dianne de Leeuw, a Dutch skater living in the U.S., took the bronze medal.

In the pairs competition, mockery was made of the once-revered six mark—meant to denote perfection—when one judge gave it for technical merit to Aleksandr Zaitsev and Irina Rodnina of the Soviet Union. The couple from Moscow decisively retained the title but made three blatant errors. It was Rodnina's sixth successive pairs title, a record; she had been partnered the first four times with Aleksei Ulanov, who was on this occasion a worthy runner-up with his wife Ludmila Smirnova. Third were Wolf Östereich and Romy Kermer of East Germany.

Perhaps inspired by the news of the forthcoming Olympic inclusion of their event, Aleksandr Gorshkov and Ludmila Pakhomova of the Soviet Union gained a record fifth successive ice dance victory. Skating with admirable cohesion and slick changes of tempo, the couple reached new heights in the best performance of their linked careers, scoring seven sixes for artistic presentation and another for technical merit. Only runners-up Glyn Watts and Hilary Green of Great Britain seemed to be in a comparable class, comfortably ahead of the third-place finishers, Genadi Karponosov and Natalya Linicuk of the U.S.S.R.

Sten Stensen of Norway took the overall title in the men's world ice speed championship at Inzell, West Germany, February 9–10. He won both the long-distance events—5,000 meter and 10,000 meter. Harm Kuipers of the Netherlands and Göran Claesson of Sweden were second and third overall, but neither won an individual event. Hans van Helden, another competitor from the Netherlands, took the 1,500 meter, and Masaki Suzuki of Japan won the 500-meter sprint.

In the women's world speed championship at Heerenveen, Netherlands, February 23–24, Atje Keulen-Deelstra of the Netherlands won the overall title for a third successive year and equaled the record total of four victories attained nine years previously by Inga Voronina of the Soviet Union.

*U.S.S.R.'s Irina Rodnina and Aleksandr Zaitsev perform in the March preliminaries of the world figure skating championships in Munich, later winning the world title for the pairs event.*
TONY DUFFY

Keulen-Deelstra was first in three of the four events; Sheila Young of the U.S. won the 500 meter; but Tatjana Averina and Nina Statkevich, both of the U.S.S.R., took second and third overall places. Separate world sprint titles for men and women were won by Per Bjørang of Norway and Leah Poulos of the U.S. at Innsbruck, Austria, February 16–17.

Two women's world records were improved in April, both by Averina at Medeo, U.S.S.R. She set a new time of 1 minute 26.4 seconds for the 1,000 meter (a distance to be added to the next Olympic men's schedule) and lowered the 1,500-meter mark to 2 minutes 14 seconds.

Gordon McKellen of Lake Placid, N.Y., won the U.S. male figure-skating championship, and Dorothy Hamill won the women's title. The events were held in Providence, R.I., in February.

**INDIA.** Despite India's growing economic and political troubles during 1974, Prime Minister Indira Gandhi's supremacy remained unshaken. In legislative elections in February, Gandhi's Congress party eked out an absolute majority in the state of Uttar Pradesh, India's most populous. The Congress also won in the state of Orissa, where it came close to a majority. In both states, however, the government was expected to rely on an alliance with the Communist party to stay in power.

Four major non-Communist opposition political groups and several minor parties merged in August to form the Bharatiya Lok Dal, or People's Party of India. They included the Bharatiya Kranti Dal (Indian Revolutionary party), the Swatantra (Freedom) party, and the Samyukta Socialist party. The new party ran a candidate for the largely figurehead post of president in August, but Congress candidate

Fakhruddin Ali Ahmed was overwhelmingly elected by India's electoral college, which consists of members of Parliament and the state legislatures. Ahmed succeeded President V. V. Giri, who was stepping down after five years in office.

Early in January students in the western state of Gujarat went on strike demanding lower food prices. The action quickly grew into a broad anti-government movement against food shortages, rising prices, and alleged corruption. After weeks of rioting, the chief minister was forced to resign, the legislative assembly was dissolved, and Gujarat was placed under rule of the central government. Similar trouble then flared up in the eastern state of Bihar, where veteran political leader Jayaprakash Narayan took charge of the agitation and demanded dissolution of the state legislative assembly there. Police and demonstrators clashed repeatedly.

In another challenge to the government, the 2 million workers on the state-owned railways went out on strike for higher wages in May. Refusing to negotiate, Prime Minister Gandhi had thousands of strikers jailed, including almost the entire leadership of the rail union. The strike collapsed after 20 days.

At the heart of the country's political storms was the poor state of the economy. The 1974 monsoon rains were far below normal over large parts of northern and central India, and some areas were hit by severe floods. In addition there was a shortage of fertilizers. A 7-million-ton decline in the summer grain crop was feared. Many growers hoarded their food stocks, leading to hunger and even starvation in some areas.

To help meet the country's economic crisis, drastic cabinet shifts were made by the prime minister in October. Defense Minister Jagjivan Ram was named to replace Agricultural Minister Chidam-

*January state election posters in Calcutta, India, featuring portraits of Prime Minister Indira Gandhi and Congress party election symbols, the cow and the calf, urge a vote for the ruling Congress party.*
KEYSTONE

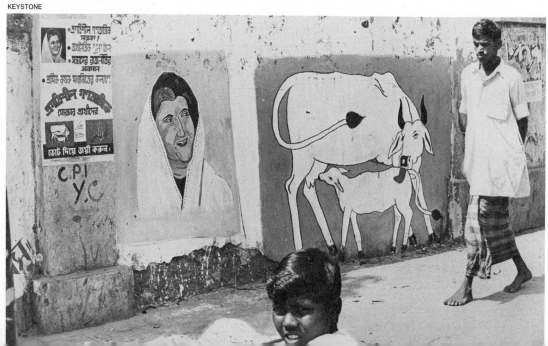

*Doctors and public health officials vaccinate patients for smallpox in the state of Uttar Pradesh, India, where visits are made to about 14,000 villages a month in an effort to contain the perennial smallpox epidemics.*

NIK WHEELER—SYGMA

baram Subramaniam, who was named to replace Finance Minister Y. B. Chavan, who was named to replace Foreign Minister Swaran Singh, who was named to replace Ram as defense minister. K. Brahmananda Reddy was made home affairs minister. Some commentators and politicians saw the move as "merely a game of musical chairs," while others viewed it as an effort to put those with quick, practical solutions in charge of key ministries. Critics from the left accused Gandhi of backing away from long-range socialist planning principles.

India became the sixth country (after the United States, the Soviet Union, Great Britain, France, and China) to join the world's "nuclear club" when it exploded an underground nuclear device in the Rajasthan desert on May 18. There was widespread world criticism of what the Indian government called "a peaceful experiment." In June Prime Minister Gandhi explained that India had opposed the 1968 nuclear nonproliferation treaty as being "discriminatory and unequal," but would now agree to a ban on "all atomic tests if everybody else agrees."

United States Secretary of State Henry Kissinger visited India in October in an effort to improve relations between the two nations, severely strained since the U.S. supported Pakistan against India in the 1971 war that created Bangladesh. There were reports that India would receive some 500,000 tons of low-priced food from the U.S.

The last of some 93,000 Pakistani prisoners from the 1971 war were repatriated by India in April, an agreement to resume telecommunications and travel was reached in September, and a nine-year trade ban ended in December. After a visit to India by Sheikh Mujibur Rahman, prime minister of Bangladesh, the two countries agreed to exchange some territorial enclaves and to work out an equitable sharing of the waters of the Ganges River. Prime Minister Gandhi and the shah of Iran exchanged visits during the year and set up a program for expansion of Indo-Iranian economic cooperation. The Himalayan protectorate of Sikkim was made an associated state of India during the year. China and Pakistan accused India of annexing Sikkim. (*See also* Asia.)

**INDIANS, AMERICAN.** In September 1974 the eight-month trial of Dennis J. Banks and Russell C. Means ended when all charges against them were dismissed. The two leaders of the American Indian Movement (AIM) were tried on ten felony counts, including assault on federal officers, in connection with the armed occupation of a trading post at Wounded Knee, S.D., in 1973.

Federal District Court Judge Fred J. Nichol said that he was "ashamed" of the conduct of the prosecution. Judge Nichol criticized prosecutor R. D. Hurd for resisting a unanimous verdict of acquittal by 11 jurors after the 12th became too ill to continue on the case. Commenting on Federal Bureau of Investigation (FBI) participation in the prosecution, Judge Nichol said that the FBI had "stooped to a new low."

Hurd and the FBI came under severe criticism for their handling of the chief prosecution witness, Louis Moves Camp, a former AIM member. Judge Nichol suggested that the FBI had used its influence to suppress a rape charge against Moves Camp in order to preserve his credibility as a witness. Also, the federal government paid Moves Camp a considerable sum to testify, allegedly for "relocation" expenses. Moves Camp's colorful testimony included statements that he had seen Means lead an attack on an armored personnel carrier and that he had seen Means and Banks confer with secret foreign backers from a variety of nations including East Germany and West Germany. A dramatic challenge to Moves Camp's credibility occurred when

*After years of efforts to obtain satisfaction from the federal government, the Kootenai Indian tribe near Bonners Ferry, Idaho, declared war on the U.S. in September and closed the boundaries on land they claim in Idaho and Montana, demanding a toll for those passing through.*

his mother left her seat in the courtroom to interrupt him and accuse him of lying. In the resultant uproar, a federal marshal used chemical Mace to subdue spectators.

Defense attorneys William Kunstler and Mark Lane were jailed overnight by the judge on that occasion for improper conduct. At the end of the case, however, Judge Nichol congratulated Kunstler and Lane for their even-handed conduct of the defense. At the conclusion of the Wounded Knee trial, U.S. Attorney General William B. Saxbe appointed a task force to study government handling of cases in which the defendants are "political." The acquittal of Banks and Means apparently was being considered with that of other defendants in federal cases, including the Berrigan brothers.

In January the U.S. Department of Justice filed a suit accusing the state of Arizona of depriving Indians of equal voting rights. The suit was the first of its kind on behalf of American Indians, previous voters' rights cases having involved blacks and Latinos. The government, in effect, accused the state of gerrymandering to reduce Indian influence. The Justice Department stated that the population of Apache County, Ariz., included 23,994 Indians and only 8,304 non-Indians; yet of the three voting districts in the county, Indians formed a majority in only one.

Morris Thompson, an Athabascan Indian from

*A cousin of Calvin and Ruth Gibson salvages metal from the remains of the family home on the Onondaga Indian reservation near Syracuse, N.Y., in July. The Onondagas had forced the Gibsons to leave their home because Ruth is white, but the Gibsons chose to burn down the house rather than surrender it to the tribe.*

BOB LORENZ—THE NEW YORK TIMES

Alaska, completed his first year as commissioner of Indian affairs, and thus head of the U.S. Bureau of Indian Affairs (BIA), in 1974. Thompson, 34, joined the BIA in 1969 and was appointed commissioner as of Dec. 3, 1973.

A conflict developed during the year between the Navajo drive for economic development and the need for environmental protection. The Navajo tribal council was negotiating with the Exxon Corp. over the sale of uranium-mining rights on Navajo trust land in northwestern New Mexico. Exxon would pay the tribal council $6 million as soon as prospecting began, and eventual profits to the Indians could be hundreds of millions of dollars. The BIA refused, however, to approve the agreement with Exxon until the U.S. Department of the Interior could conduct an environmental impact study on the uranium situation. Water supply was thought to be a critical issue, because great quantities of water are needed for uranium mining, and water was already in short supply for farmers in the area.

The Sierra Club, a power environmental lobbying group, opposed a bill before Congress that would give the Havasupai Indian tribe control of more than 180,000 acres on the rim of the Grand Canyon. The Sierra Club claimed that the tribe might permit economic exploitation, with unsightly buildings, on the land. As the controversy developed, about 400 Havasupai were living on the floor of the canyon, cut off from all supplies and all civilization during the winter. Indian leaders pledged that they would use their homeland on the canyon rim only for "traditional" purposes and would not sell out to developers. Two U.S. senators not ordinarily considered allies—Edward M. Kennedy (D, Mass.) and Barry Goldwater (R, Ariz.)—supported the Havasupai and criticized the Sierra Club.

Onondaga Indians in New York State used violence in their attempts to evict white families from reservation land. The whites had in most cases purchased houses on the land years before; some of the homeowners termed "white" by the Onondaga Indian Council were in fact Indians. The Onondaga entered homes and attacked the residents, setting fires in some cases. Calvin, a full-blooded Onondaga, and Ruth Gibson burned their house to the ground rather than surrender it to the tribe. (*See also* Race Relations.)

# INDONESIA.

At the beginning of 1974 the lengthy political honeymoon between the administration of President Suharto and the country's students and intellectuals collapsed in widespread rioting in the capital. For the first time under Suharto, Indonesia appeared to lose confidence and direction, entering a period of political uncertainty. By the close of the year, however, the domestic stability that had been a trademark of the Suharto government seemed to have been restored.

Three days of rioting, known as the January 15 incident, were touched off by students who massed around the presidential palace while Suharto conferred with visiting Japanese Prime Minister Kakuei Tanaka. The student mob, joined by unemployed youths and other dissidents, roamed through Jakarta's business quarter smashing Japanese-made automobiles and ransacking shops and office buildings in what appeared to be a protest against excessive Japanese influence in the Indonesian economy. Part of the resentment was directed at alleged unscrupulous and exploitative Japanese business practices. Behind the anti-Japanese sentiments, however, were profound frustration over the inequitable distribution of Indonesia's growing wealth and increasing anger at corruption among high officials.

The army restored order, and in the aftermath of the riots a curfew was imposed, some 800 persons were arrested, and the publishing permits of several crusading newspapers were canceled. Suharto prohibited army officers from acquiring controlling shares in companies, authorized a crackdown on graft, raised the salaries of civil servants, and revised the new five-year plan to provide for a more even distribution of wealth.

The surfacing of political stresses notwithstanding, Indonesia's economy continued its brisk upward movement, due mostly to the country's position as the principal oil producer of the Far East. During the first five-year plan (1969–74) Indonesia's oil production rose by 53.2%, reaching 1.5 million barrels per day. Within the next five-year plan (1974–79), production was expected to double.

Following the Arab oil embargo early in the year and the quadrupling of oil prices, Indonesia earned about $3.8 billion in foreign exchange from oil sales alone. Politically astute, however, the government in Jakarta pegged the price of its oil lower than Arab prices in an adroit maneuver to win friends among less developed Afro-Asian countries and to maintain an atmosphere of accommodation with developed nations, which were a principal source of capital investment for Indonesia's expanding economy.

Despite internal political turmoil, Indonesia maintained a strong position in Asia. Responding to Chinese military action against islets claimed by South Vietnam, Indonesia officially claimed that its territorial boundary in the South China Sea extended to the Natuna Islands. Later it was reported that offshore oil deposits had been discovered in the Natunas. In May Indonesia expressed "alarm" over the detonation by India of a nuclear device. There was a feeling that India's action may have put strong pressure on Indonesia to join the nuclear club at the expense of socioeconomic development.

A completely unanticipated problem developed when the new Portuguese government announced plans to give its overseas territories—including Timor, half an island (the other half is Indonesian)—the right of self-determination. Indonesia announced that it would respect the decision of the 600,000 people of Portuguese Timor, who were to

During Japanese Prime Minister Kakuei Tanaka's January visit to Jakarta, Indonesian youths rampage through the city in violent anti-Japanese demonstrations to protest Japanese economic "imperialism" in Indonesia.

PHILIPPE LEDRU—SYGMA

vote on their future in 1975. Some observers felt that Indonesia could not remain neutral over the prospect of an independent Timor—with a substantial Chinese minority—which might inject an element of instability into the Indonesian archipelago. (*See also* Asia; Japan; Pacific Islands; Philippines.)

**INSURANCE.** High interest rates and tight money in the U.S. caused heavy borrowing against life insurance policies in 1974. Total policy loans outstanding at the end of June were up 14% from a year earlier; as a percentage of life insurers' assets, policy loans rose to 8.3% from 7.7% a year earlier —the highest since the 10% recorded in 1940. The record of 18.3% was set in 1932.

The Equity Funding Life Insurance Co. was liquidated in 1974, and a plan was implemented to restore full benefits to its policyholders. Since the Equity scandal broke in March 1973, the policyholders had been eligible for death benefits only. The company had collapsed after the revelation that it had created millions of dollars in fraudulent assets by issuing bogus insurance policies and selling them to other companies.

At the end of 1973 about 145 million persons in the U.S. owned life insurance policies with legal reserve life insurance companies. This insurance accounted for about $1.8 trillion of protection, an increase of $150 billion of coverage over 1972. The average amount of life insurance carried by the insured U.S. family increased by $1,900 over the previous year to a total of $28,800. Life insurance benefit payments grew to $20.3 billion in 1973, an increase of $1.7 billion over the year before. Of that total, benefits to living policyholders amounted to $11.7 billion. Life insurance sold in the U.S. in 1973 totaled $233.8 billion.

Five years after the concept of variable life insurance was introduced, not a single policy had been sold. The policy was designed to pay benefits (above a guaranteed minimum) that would rise or fall depending on the result of the investment of its premiums in the stock market. Negotiations as to regulation kept the policy off the market.

The debate about national health insurance continued in 1974. U.S. President Gerald R. Ford urged quick passage of a health insurance bill. During 1973, health benefit payments totaled $22.8 billion, of which $2 billion was issued in disability benefits. Insurance companies paid $11.3 billion to persons under 65 years of age, including all of the disability benefits, while the rest came from Blue Cross, Blue Shield, and other plans.

Businesses that carried professional or liability policies faced sharply increased rates while the insurers struggled to overcome mounting losses on liability policies. With the growth of the consumer movement, the number of claims rose from 35,000 in 1960 to more than 500,000 in 1973.

In May 1974 the U.S. Senate passed (53–42) and sent to the House a national no-fault auto insurance bill. About 20 states had instituted some form of no-fault plan since 1971.

**INTELLIGENCE OPERATIONS.** The thrust of U.S. covert activities was under scrutiny in 1974. Controversy over the purpose of the Central Intelligence Agency (CIA) arose with the revelation that more than $8 million had been authorized for the CIA to undermine the government of Marxist President Salvador Allende Gossens of Chile. Allende died in a military coup on Sept. 11, 1973. At a top-secret Congressional hearing in April 1974, CIA Director William E. Colby gave the report to the House Armed Services Subcommittee of Intelligence. The account was made public in September.

Colby's testimony indicated that high officials in the administration of U.S. President Richard M. Nixon repeatedly misled the U.S. Congress about the extent of involvement in Chile's affairs during Allende's three years in office. Colby said that all of the CIA activities in Chile were approved in advance by the 40 Committee, a secret intelligence panel headed by Henry Kissinger, who was then Nixon's national security adviser.

U.S. President Gerald R. Ford acknowledged in September that the U.S. had channeled millions of dollars into Chile to aid newspapers and political leaders who opposed Allende. It was done, he said, "in the best interest of the people of Chile." Nevertheless, the controversy grew as intelligence sources reported that most of the $8 million was used to subsidize strikes that plunged Chile into chaos. Further fueling the debate were reports in 1974 by former intelligence agents about the toppling of governments.

Citing national security as the reason, the CIA censored the first printed account of some of the agency's clandestine activities in Chile. 'The CIA and the Cult of Intelligence' was published in June with blank spaces where 168 passages had been deleted. A former CIA agent living in England revealed in 1974 that he had been involved in bringing down Ecuador's governments in 1961 and 1963. Meanwhile, Colby sought legislation to strengthen his power to enforce CIA secrecy regulations.

Kissinger was questioned at his own request in July 1974 in connection with his role in the wiretapping of 17 officials and newsmen from 1969 to 1971. He threatened to quit as secretary of state unless his reputation was cleared. In response, the Senate Foreign Relations Committee members asked him in closed session about reports suggesting that he had not been completely candid with them in September 1973, when he was confirmed as secretary of state. He insisted that he did not initiate the wiretaps. The committee concluded that Kissinger's role did not constitute grounds for barring his confirmation.

The Senate Armed Services Committee investigated a bizarre story of military spying that surfaced early in 1974. A U.S. Navy yeoman, working

*FBI Director Clarence Kelly stated in January that he would seek to revive counterintelligence tactics in the event of a national emergency.*
WIDE WORLD

as a military clerk inside the White House for 15 months, said he was instructed by two admirals to funnel top-secret documents from the White House to the Pentagon office of Adm. Thomas H. Moorer, then chairman of the joint chiefs of staff. Admiral Moorer acknowledged receiving some White House documents but denied knowing then that they had been obtained improperly. He denied also that a spy ring had functioned with his knowledge to keep the chiefs of staff informed of Kissinger's secret negotiations in 1971 with North Vietnam, China, and the Soviet Union.

A White House investigation into the leak of sensitive documents on the India-Pakistan war led to discovery of the pilfering in December 1971. The liaison office was abolished at once. Moorer and administration officials minimized the breach of security as a matter of "overexuberance."

In November U.S. Attorney General William Saxbe made public an investigation of secret counterintelligence programs conducted from 1956 to 1971 by the Federal Bureau of Investigation (FBI) against "subversive" groups. Cointelpro, code name for the programs authorized by then FBI Director J. Edgar Hoover, reportedly carried out more than 2,300 operations designed to disrupt the activities of both left- and right-wing groups. At year's end there were newspaper reports of further CIA malfeasance. During the Nixon Administration the CIA allegedly expanded its surveillance to thousands of U.S. citizens, including antiwar activists and other dissidents. The illegal activities involved break-ins, wiretaps, and taped dossiers. Top members of CIA counterintelligence, including the man described as the head of the domestic spy operation, resigned. (*See also* Chile; United States.)

**INTERIOR DESIGN.** In spite of inflation, the decorative arts managed to hold their own in 1974. Buyers poured into Chicago's Merchandise Mart for the International Home Furnishings and National Floor Covering markets, which ran simultaneously from January 6 to January 11. Manufacturers reported even heavier buying than had been expected. Twenty-eight countries were represented at the Mart's International Furnishing Week, June 16–21; they attended primarily for the sixth annual National Exposition of Contract Interior Furnishings (NEOCON)—a forum for designers, manufacturers, dealers, and consumers involved in office, school, hospital, hotel, restaurant, and other nonresidential interiors. The home furnishings market sales for 1974 were, according to industry figures, close to $14 billion, and floor covering was estimated at another $6 billion.

The most important single event of the year for the American interior designer was the merger of the two professional organizations—the American Institute of Interior Designers (AID) and the National Society of Interior Designers (NSID). Although there had been violent disagreements in the past between AID and NSID, the purpose of both organizations was essentially the same: the creation of a society to represent the best interests of professional interior designers. The differences between the groups had become increasingly academic, and the existence of two organizations performing in effect the same functions seemed redundant. For several years there had been sessions of both groups to work out the details of unification. Finally, in July at a joint conference held in Denver, Colo., AID and NSID voted to consolidate; the new organization was to be called the American Society of Interior Designers (ASID) and to become effective on Jan. 1, 1975. The merger was regarded by most members as both sensible and practical.

There were no startling new trends in 1974; the American interior continued to be eclectic, that is, a blend of various styles and periods, juxtaposing radically different elements in the same setting. There was a shift away from the strong, vibrant colors of the past five years and a return to subtlety in fabrics, floor coverings, and wallpapers. The hot colors such as yellow, orange, and brilliant pink, as well as parrot green, continued to be popular, but the trend toward natural tones and pastels, a reflection of the colors in women's clothing, dominated the new lines. Colors such as peach and the paler blues were much in vogue.

The most interesting and original influence in furniture—but especially in accessories, fabrics, and wallpapers—came from the recent past in the form of the art deco revival. Art deco, or simply deco as it was sometimes called, was a term popularized in the late 1960's by London art critic Bevis Hillier in his book 'Art Deco' and at an exhibition that he supervised at the Minneapolis Institute of Arts in Minnesota in 1971. The term was an abbreviation of the name of the 1925 Paris exhibition of radical modern designs called "Exposition internationale des arts décoratifs et industriels modernes"; in the United States in the 1930's the style had been called modernistic, modern, moderne, or streamlined. Its new popularity made *deco* the word and fad of the year. (*See also* Fashion and Cosmetics.)

Displaying the current interior design trend to combine various styles and periods, art deco lamps, flooring, fabric, and accessories blend with oriental and contemporary pieces to create a harmonious eclectic deco interior.
COURTESY, BLOOMINGDALE'S, NEW YORK

**Interior Design**

# Special Report:
# Decorating with Green Plants

by Naomi Suloway

Well-formed, vigorously growing plants can't be anything but decorative. Once their needs are recognized and served, they should be displayed to their best advantage. A solitary plant on a windowsill is not always aesthetically pleasing, unless the plant is a whopper. A large plant by itself, however, is attractive anywhere—on a windowsill or tabletop, or standing on the floor.

The leaves of most plants move in the direction of the source of the brightest light, which is usually a window. Unless you are willing to look only at the backs of the leaves, you'll want to turn the pots regularly so that all sides of the plant are exposed to light. The best-shaped plants are grown with almost equally bright light coming from several directions, a condition usually difficult to create. The effect of a single source of bright light is less obvious in certain plants: plants in which the leaves spring directly from a central stem, such as the dracaenas, aspidistras, and palms; plants that grow from common points at the soil line, such as the ferns and spider plants; and most cacti. These are the plants that will look best, with a minimum of turning, on a windowsill, assuming, of course, that the growing conditions needed by the plants are available there.

Where else should plants be put? Anywhere they look good. Other than tall plants that must stand on the floor, many other plants do, indeed, look good on the floor. Of course the position must be chosen for adequate light. Not only is the floor usually cooler, which is better for most plants than tabletop height, but some plants look better when viewed from above rather than from straight on.

Trailing or sprawling plants look best in pots hanging either from the ceiling or from wall brackets. They should be positioned out of drafts and out of the major traffic paths. The most beautiful plant that snags you as you pass by is a nuisance. I've found that hanging plants look especially handsome when suspended a few feet over a table. A most unusual combination is made by hanging a trailing plant directly above a pot of the same variety that sits on a table. Tending a hanging pot is more time-consuming than tending one at a lower level. The plant may have to be taken down for watering, and watering and misting may be required more often because room air is usually warmer and drier closer to the ceiling. The pots chosen for hanging plants should be the kind with attached saucers to catch the drips.

### Easy-to-Grow House Plants

The 30 plants in the list that follows are easy to grow. Flowering plants are not included, although some of the plants listed produce small, inconsequential blossoms. The plants are in alphabetical order under what seem to be their most commonly used names. Other common names for the same plant are in parentheses. Names in italics are the "proper" botanical names.

Light conditions are expressed in terms of windowsill light from windows facing east, west, north, and south. None of these plants requires southern exposures; in fact, many cannot survive in the continuous sun of a south window. If you have only south windows and a west exposure is called for, the plant can be grown set back from the window five to ten feet; similarly, if an east exposure is called for, set the plant as far back from the window as possible. Light of a north exposure can be approximated at a south window if the window is curtained or covered with a light-filtering shade. In all cases, the amount of light called for in the table is approximate. You must experiment with your own plants using the light from your own windows to find the position in which your plants will thrive.

Temperatures are shown in two ranges: warm, which is a minimum of 70° F., and cool, which is 60° F.

*"Well, now, who will have a little water, who will have some plant food, and who would like conversation this morning?"*
BOOTH—THE NEW YORKER

| PLANT | SHAPE OF PLANT; LEAVES; GROWTH HABIT | PREFERRED LIGHT CONDITIONS | BEST TEMPERATURE; SPECIAL REQUIREMENTS |
|---|---|---|---|
| **arrow plant** (goosefoot) *Syngonium Nephthytis* several varieties | upright, but eventually drooping; arrow-shaped leaves, some with "ears" at their base, all green, several shades of green, or blotched | east, west, or north window, except not west window in summer in hot climates | warm; will grow in water or damp sand; extremely easy to overwater unless in bright light |
| **asparagus fern** *Asparagus plumosus* | upright and umbrellalike; stiff, short, threadlike needles; growth arises as a clump | east or west window, except not west window in summer in hot climates | warm; soil must be damp most of the time; misting the plant in winter helps appearance |
| *Asparagus sprengeri* | trailing; soft pinelike needles on long stems, which are at least 1 foot long; new growth arises from the roots | east or west window, except not west window in summer in hot climates | warm; soil must be damp most of the time; misting the plant in winter helps appearance |
| **aspidistra** (cast-iron plant) *Aspidistra elatior Aspidistra elatior variegata* | upright; arching lance-shaped leaves, *elatior* is all green, *elatior variegata* is striped cream-colored; new growth from a central stalk | east or north window, except not east window in summer in hot climates | warm to cool; will tolerate dusty leaves, extreme dryness, low light |
| **begonia** (fancy-leaf begonia) *Begonia rex* hundreds of varieties | upright to sprawling; varied shape and color leaves, some spotted or blotched; growth from underground rhizome may hang over pot | east, west, or north window, except not west window in summer in hot climates | warm; soil must be damp most of the time; avoid wetting the leaves except with fine mist |
| **cactus** thousands of varieties | usually upright, frequently squat; with prickly spines; new growth comes from plant rather than from roots | any exposure, except not south window in hot climates | warm, but will survive cool; soil must dry out completely to the bottom of the pot before rewatering |
| **citrus plants** lemon, lime, orange, grapefruit many varieties | upright, bushy; shiny, dark green, oval leaves; branching and, depending on kind, eventually will bear fruit | any exposure, except not south window in summer | warm; mature plants frequently bear fruit; plants can be started from seeds removed from fruit |
| **coleus** (flame nettle) hundreds of varieties | upright; leaves of all colors; branching and bushy if cut back regularly | any exposure, except not south window in summer | warm; plant gets leggy and unattractive in low light; cut off flower stems as they appear |
| **dieffenbachia** (dumb cane) dozens of varieties | upright; large leaves spotted and blotched with white, cream, or yellow; growth from central stem | east, west, or north window, except not west window in summer in hot climates | warm; needs high humidity; lower leaves frequently drop off in low humidity |
| **dracaena** (dragon plant) *Dracaena marginata* | upright; long, slender, arching dark green leaves edged with dark red; growth from central stem; can grow 1 foot per year | east, west, or north window, except not west window in summer in hot climates | warm; lower leaves frequently fall, leaving a treelike plant with leaves only at the top |
| (corn plant) *Dracaena fragrans massangeana* | upright; broad, long leaves marked with yellow center stripe, resembling corn plant; growth from central stem | east, west, or north window, except not west window in summer in hot climates | warm; lower leaves frequently fall, leaving a treelike plant with leaves only at the top |
| **fern** (Boston fern and sword fern) *Nephrolepsis exaltata bostoniensis* | initially upright, eventually sprawling; dark green, tapering, cut, swordlike fronds; growth spreads from original clump and from runners | east or north window, except not east window in summer in hot climates | warm; must be misted regularly; will tolerate limited sun; soil at top of pot must always be damp |
| **fern, footed** (deer's-foot fern) *Davallia canariensis* | upright, bushy; finely cut triangular swordlike fronds; furry rhizomes eventually appear above the soil and grow over the pot | east or north window, except not east window in summer in hot climates | warm; must be misted regularly; will burn up in bright sun; soil at top of pot must always be damp |
| **fig** (fiddle-leaf fig) *Ficus lyrata* | upright; fiddle-shaped, deeply veined, light green leaves; branching if top growth is removed, otherwise all new growth comes from top of plant | east or north window | warm; sensitive to abrupt changes in temperature, light, or humidity; will lose leaves with changes; mist to encourage new growth |
| (weeping fig) *Ficus benjamina* | upright, treelike; small oval leaves, some slightly rippled; freely branching downward ("weeping") | east or north window | warm; sensitive to abrupt changes in temperature, light, or humidity; will lose leaves with changes; mist to encourage new growth |

| | | | |
|---|---|---|---|
| **ivy**<br>(common ivy)<br>*Hedera*<br>    dozens of varieties | climbing or trailing; small, 3- or 5-pointed leaves with whitish veins; vines will adhere to plaster, wood, or brick | east or west window, except not in west window in summer in hot climates | cool;<br>needs misting in dry air, usually all winter |
| **ivy, grape**<br>*Cissus rhombifolia* | climbing, or bushy and eventually trailing; serrated, downy leaves in groups of 3 | east or north window | warm to cool;<br>vigorous growth with minimum light |
| **ivy, swedish**<br>*Plectranthus australis* | trailing; round, serrated, thick leaves, pinkish when young; new growth arises from many points on the vines | east or north window | warm;<br>tiny inconsequential white flowers, usually in autumn |
| **jade plant**<br>(jade tree)<br>*Crassula argentea* | upright; thick paddle-shaped leaves, in bright light are pinkish underneath; branches freely if top growth is removed | east or north window | warm;<br>must dry out between waterings; readily rots if overwatered; older plants have heavy "trunks" |
| **kangaroo vine**<br>*Cissus antarctica* | climbing, or bushy and eventually trailing; dark green, serrated, heavily ribbed leaves; freely branching vines | east, west, or north window, except not west window in summer | cool;<br>will stand temperature changes well; grows best in cool spot; can grow extremely large |
| **monster plant**<br>(cut-leaf philodendron and swiss-cheese plant)<br>*Philodendron pertusum,*<br>or *Monstera deliciosa* | upright, large leaves, often 1 foot long, cut from the edges almost to the center; new growth arises from the top | east or north window, except not east window in summer in hot climates | warm;<br>can grow 10 feet or taller in bright light |
| **palm**<br>(dwarf palm)<br>*Chamaedorea elegans,*<br>or *Neanthe bella* | upright single stalk; grows to height of several feet; broad arching fronds with feather-shaped leaves; new growth usually arises from top | east or north window, except not east window in summer in hot climates | warm to cool;<br>can survive for several months with minimum of light, but must have good light for at least several months each year |
| **peperomia**<br>*Peperomia caperata* | mound shape; small leaves rippled like spinach, stems almost at center of underside of leaves; with age, plant will mound over edges of pot | east, west, or north window, except not west window in summer in hot climates | warm;<br>tiny, yellow "flowers" closely spaced along a thin spike that rises above mound of leaves several times a year |
| **philodendron**<br>(heart-leaf vine)<br>*Philodendron cordatum*<br>*Philodendron scandens* | trailing; heart-shaped leaves; sprawling and rambling; new growth arises from many points on vine, often with new roots at the same point | east or north window, except not east window in summer in hot climates | warm;<br>tolerant of some shade, but needs more light if new leaves get progressively smaller; can grow 4 feet or more per year |
| **pothos**<br>(ivy-arum, devil's ivy)<br>*Scindapsus aureus* | trailing; heart-shaped leaves, some speckled or marbled white or yellow; new growth arises from many points | east, west, or north window, except not west window in summer in hot climates | warm;<br>can grow 4 feet or more in length in a year in good light |
| **rubber plant**<br>*Ficus elastica* | upright; large waxy, dark oval leaves, pinkish underneath; branching if top growth is removed, otherwise all new growth comes from top of plant | east or north window | warm;<br>sensitive to abrupt changes in temperature, light, or humidity; will lose leaves with changes; mist to encourage new growth |
| **sansevieria**<br>(snake plant and mother-in-law's tongue)<br>*Sansevieria trifasciata*<br>    *laurentii*<br>*Sansevieria trifasciata*<br>    *hahnii* | upright; long, thick, fleshy, narrow marbled leaves, *laurentii* has yellow edge; plants may grow several feet tall, except *hahnii,* which has short broad leaves; new growth arises from center of rosette of leaves and from the rootstock | east, west, or north window, except not west window in summer in hot climates | warm to cool;<br>tolerant of low light and little water; marbling is more prominent in bright light |
| **schefflera**<br>(umbrella tree and octopus tree)<br>*Brassaia actinophylla* | upright, umbrellalike; banana-shaped, glossy leaves; 3 to 11 or more leaves on each stem arise usually from top of stalk | east, west, or north window, except north only in summer in hot climates | warm to cool;<br>must dry out between waterings; can grow 10 feet or more in bright light |
| **spider plant**<br>*Chlorophytum*<br>    *cosmosum*<br>*Chlorophytum*<br>    *cosmosum*<br>    *variegatum* | upright and trailing; grasslike leaves, *variegatum* is white striped; leaves are produced at the soil line in clumps, from the center of which slender, flexible, arching stalks arise | east, west, or north window, except not west window in summer in hot climates | warm to cool;<br>new plants along stems may be cut off, rooted in water, and planted |
| **wandering jew**<br>*Tradescantia*<br>    *fluminensis*<br>*Zebrina pendula*<br>    several varieties | trailing; oval, pointed leaves, striped silverish, white, pink, or purple, some downy; most new growth arises from points on the freely branching vines | east or north window | warm to cool;<br>colors are most intense in bright light |

*"Guess what, everybody. Mrs. Fancher is going to visit her daughter in Florida, and her Cissus rhombifolia is coming to stay with us for a few weeks."*

## The Grouping of Plants

If you don't have a large plant, you can improvise one by grouping several small plants of the same variety. Put the pots relatively close together into a large, decorative container. Stand the small pots on sand, pebbles, jars, upturned pots, almost anything that will bring them up at least to the level of the rim of the container. As an alternative the plants can be staged, that is, one or more can be raised higher than the others. As another alternative, the smaller pots can be placed on a shallow tray filled with water and pebbles or gravel. The tray becomes the unifying element of the group and conveniently can be used to supply humidity to the plants. The tray should ideally be as large as the leaf spread of the mass of plants, but a tray just large enough to contain all the pots is better than nothing. The tray collects splashes that can result from watering the pots through a mass of foliage and also the drip from leaves that have been misted.

One need not be limited to masses of the same kind of plants grouped together. Combining more than one kind of plant can produce a pleasing display. Here are a few ideas:

Group one or two tall plants with shorter ones. Plants can be made to appear taller by placing them on different levels. If the plants are chosen for their growth habits, the tall one upright, the shorter ones trailing or sprawling, less-than-beautiful pots and staging supports can be completely obscured.

Combine fine-leaved plants with those that have broad leaves. A palm, with its narrow, long leaves, for example, combines well with the foliage of one or more pots of philodendron. Another good combination is the long, arching leaves of the aspidistra and the round, notched leaves of the Swedish ivy.

Plants with multicolored leaves—one variety only —combine well with those that have plain green leaves. Particularly good combinations are a schefflera or a mostly green sansevieria with several rex begonias or wandering Jews. Not only is dumb cane, or dieffenbachia, with grape ivy a handsome combination, but the upward, vining growth of the ivy covers the bare stalk of the mature dumb cane, a plant that frequently loses its lower leaves—despite the best of care.

All the groupings, needless to say, must be made with the plant's needs for light and temperature foremost. Plants that need shade, for example, must be grouped with others that have the same requirements—in the shade. A trickier arrangement combines plants that need bright light in such a way that their foliage shades other plants below or behind that need less bright light.

## The Necessity of Light

Eventually, one is faced with the compulsion to put plants where they won't get enough natural light. Artificial light is an obvious answer; a dark corner illuminated by a spotlighted green plant is a dramatic sight. If artificial light is not available, some plants can be made to survive in dimly lighted positions. Three conditions are needed, and, unless they are provided, the plants will be spindly with few, widely spaced leaves.

The temperature of the dimly lighted area must be kept cool, below 70° F., which rules out plants that need much warmth. Dimly lighted plants must be supplied with as much humidity as possible. The third requirement is an unusual amount of restraint on your part: the plant needs much less water than it would if it were in brighter light. When the plant is first put into its dimly lighted home, water it as if it were in brighter light. Then gradually lengthen the intervals between waterings. Don't let the leaves wilt. This is an instance where determining the need for water can be made by the feel of the leaves. Particularly if the plants have proper humidity, the feel is an accurate indicator, and a limp leaf means that water is needed. When fertilizer is used, it should be used sparingly—one quarter to one third of the amount recommended for the plant when grown under better conditions.

While the plant is becoming accustomed to its new location, a few leaves may yellow and drop. As it becomes acclimatized, this should stop. Ideally, a plant growing under such adverse conditions should be periodically brought into bright light for short periods. Do this gradually—don't move it suddenly into bright light. Move it a few feet each day toward the bright light, where of course it will need more watering. When it is returned to its dim corner, its water needs decrease.

**IRAN.** Oil-rich Iran was busy during 1974 taking advantage of the general rise in world oil prices. Using its huge oil revenues, expected to total $20.9 billion for the year, Iran was investing in Western technology to promote its own economic development. This accorded with the warning by Shah Mohammed Reza Pahlavi that Iran must industrialize.

At the conclusion of a state visit to France in June, the shah announced a $5-billion industrial-development agreement whereby his country would purchase five 1,000-megawatt nuclear reactors and 12 large oil tankers. Iran, in turn, would get assistance in railway electrification, building a subway in the capital city of Teheran, establishing a petrochemical industry, and constructing a steel plant and gas liquefaction plant and pipeline.

It was announced in July that Iran was buying a 25% interest in West Germany's giant Krupp steel works, one of the biggest direct investments ever of money from an oil-producing country into Western industry. At the same time, Iran negotiated for $4 billion of communications equipment from the U.S. and contracted for advanced U.S. military hardware to equip its modern 200,000-man army and air force. In December Iran announced plans to provide $5-billion credit for the foundering Italian economy in exchange for technological aid.

Meanwhile, the governing New Iran party, under Prime Minister Emir Abbas Hoveida, was moving ahead with a program for building a modern road network and establishing farm cooperatives. Domestic political opposition seemed to be waning, although early in the year 12 persons were convicted of terrorist activities and plotting to kill the shah.

More of the periodic border fights between Iran and Iraq broke out in February and March. At dispute were navigation rights in the Shatt al-Arab waterway, the outlet of the Tigris and Euphrates rivers to the Persian Gulf. Part of the hostility between the two Muslim countries was because of Iraq's support of a separatist movement of the Baluchi people in northeastern Iran. (*See also* Iraq; Middle East.)

**IRAQ.** In February and March 1974 Iraq and Iran fought along their borders. The two countries had a history of disagreements over control of land and navigation rights in the Persian Gulf area of the Middle East. The clashes were renewed in August and September. In March 1974 the Ba'athist (Arab Socialist) government proclaimed self-rule for the Kurdish minority in the northern part of the country, the region that contained the major oil fields of Iraq and the important city of Kirkuk. The plan, announced by President Ahmed Hassan al-Bakr, did not meet all of the demands of the Kurds, a non-Arab Muslim group who made up one fourth of the country's population and who had wanted veto power over legislation pertaining to Kurdistan. The self-rule plan did grant the Kurdish language official status, allow a regional budget, and provide for a regional legislative council.

When the Kurds, led by Gen. Mulla Mustafa al-Barzani and the Kurdish Democratic party, did not accept the plan, although it automatically went into effect, fighting broke out between the Kurds and government troops. Fighting continued throughout the year in spite of various moves by the Ba'athist government to placate the Kurds. Results of the fighting were somewhat inconclusive, although the Kurds at times occupied large areas and did well against the Iraqi government's superior technology.

Iraq improved foreign relations with other Arab states during 1974, signing economic agreements with Egypt, Syria, and Turkey; but U.S.-Iraqi relations continued to be hostile. Oil production increased during 1974 to 2 million barrels a day and was expected to reach 3.5 million barrels a day by 1975. Oil revenues in 1974 were estimated at more than $7 billion. (*See also* Iran; Middle East.)

*Gen. Mulla Mustafa al-Barzani, Kurdish army leader, rests between clashes with the forces of Iraq. The Kurds rejected an Iraqi offer of limited autonomy in March.*

J. R. WILTON–SIPA/REX FEATURES LTD.

*Empty frames remain at Sir Alfred Beit's home in County Wicklow, Ireland, after a five-member gang stole 19 paintings valued at $20 million in April in the biggest art theft on record. The thieves later demanded $1.2 million in cash and the transfer from English to Irish prisons of four persons serving life sentences for bombings in London. Police recovered the paintings from a rented cottage in County Cork on May 4.*

UPI COMPIX

**IRELAND.** In November 1974, only 17 months after taking office for a seven-year term, Irish President Erskine Childers, 68, died of a heart attack. (*See* Obituaries.) A new president, Carroll O'Daly, a former Irish attorney general and chief justice of the Supreme Court, was sworn in December 19.

The main concern of the republic's coalition government during its second year in office was the situation in Northern Ireland and, especially, the failure there of power sharing. Ireland had contributed substantially to the working out of the Sunningdale agreement at the end of 1973 and had given wholehearted support to the power-sharing Northern Ireland Executive, an 11-member governing board in which Roman Catholics had, for the first time, been allowed to share in political power. Early in 1974 Irish Prime Minister Liam Cosgrave met with Northern Ireland's Chief Minister Brian Faulkner to clarify the terms of agreement. But two events in May—a 15-day general strike led by Ulster's militant Protestants and Faulkner's subsequent resignation—caused the collapse of the power-sharing Executive. The result was keen disappointment in the republic, followed by a cool reaction toward North-South cooperation on the part of Cosgrave, who blamed violence in the North for "killing the desire for unity in the republic."

Nor was violence confined to the North. In addition to prison breaks, hijackings, and minor aerial bombings, the worst single act of violence ever known in the republic—and the worst in the whole of Ireland since the beginning of the recent troubles in 1969—occurred in 1974. On Friday, May 17, four massive bombs exploded, three of them in downtown Dublin at the height of the rush hour. Thirty persons were killed, and nearly 200 were injured. The next day, the recall of Ireland's contingent of soldiers serving with the United Nations in the Sinai and Cyprus was announced.

An attempt was made by the government to legalize the sale of contraceptives to married couples. This was made necessary by a Supreme Court decision overturning a ban on mail-order importation of contraceptives. Prime Minister Cosgrave decided on a free, conscience vote and then voted against his own government's bill. The measure was defeated.

The Irish economy suffered from continuing inflation, with unemployment rising steeply. Although exports continued to expand, imports outstripped them substantially; and with a poor tourist season —due in part to the political situation in the North —the country was expected to have a balance of payments deficit in the region of $700 million. Economic uncertainty was aggravated by a taxation white paper that proposed the introduction of capital gains tax and wealth tax. The government's April budget introduced a form of income tax for farmers—who had previously been exempt—and this, coupled with the poor return to small farmers in Ireland from the common agricultural policy of the European Economic Community during the year, caused considerable controversy. There were further difficulties in the fall when British farmers prevented the import of Irish cattle and also disrupted container traffic through Britain to Europe.

In May President Childers made a state visit to Belgium, the first to a European country by an Irish chief of state. Earlier in the year Ireland and the Soviet Union exchanged ambassadors for the first time. Diplomatic relations were established with Japan and Libya during the year. In October, Sean MacBride became the first Irishman to win the Nobel peace prize. (*See also* Europe; Great Britain and Northern Ireland.)

*Lebanese children watch an Israeli put up a section of barbed-wire fence in July at Avivim on Israel's border with Lebanon. The fence was part of a system on Israel's northern frontier to seal it against infiltration by Arab guerrillas.*
MICHA BAR-AM—THE NEW YORK TIMES

**ISRAEL.** The last weeks of 1973 and the first six months of 1974 were dominated by the course and cost of the October 1973 war; the second half of 1974 was shaped largely by the consequences—political, economic, and psychological—of that war. It was a year during which Israel sought to restore the equilibrium that the war's impact, rather than the war itself, had upset.

A series of political crises plagued the country, and Israelis seemed to be suffering from collective psychological shock. A kind of witch-hunt was unleashed in the press, among the public, and even in the government against those who were said to have been responsible for the lack of military preparedness in the face of the surprise Arab attack on Yom Kippur of 1973. Principal targets of criticism were Defense Minister Moshe Dayan and, to a lesser degree, Prime Minister Golda Meir. The attack was accompanied by an emotional campaign to win the release of Israeli prisoners of war in Egyptian and Syrian hands, ultimately forcing the government to trade some 8,000 Egyptian prisoners for 241 Israelis and to make large concessions to Syria in return for fewer than 100 Israelis. In order to assuage the public mood and political discontent, the government appointed a commission under Chief Justice Shimon Agranat to investigate the causes that led to the initial setback for Israeli forces on Oct. 6, 1973.

The postponed general election was held on Dec. 31, 1973, and served only to add to the political disorientation. The Labor alignment, headed by Mrs. Meir, remained the largest single faction but won no outright majority. On the contrary, it lost a number of seats to the Likud, the combined right-wing opposition that had been formed by the Herut, Liberal, State List, and Free Center parties. Mrs. Meir's Labor alignment won 39.9% of the votes and

51 of the 120 seats in the Knesset. Likud, the largest opposition group, won 27.4% of the votes and 39 seats. The National Religious party lost 2 seats for a total of 10 in the new Knesset.

The election produced a political stalemate that resulted in a nine-week domestic crisis. Mrs. Meir faced serious difficulties in forming a coalition government and had to ask for an extension beyond the 21-day postelection deadline. The National Religious party, traditionally an ally of Labor in coalition governments, refused to join with the prime minister. After five weeks of political bargaining, she stunned her party by announcing the abandonment of the coalition effort and her own resignation; she was shortly persuaded to reverse these decisions. On March 6, largely under pressure of a Syrian buildup on the Golan Heights cease-fire line, she formed a government and convinced both Dayan and Communications Minister Shimon Peres to rejoin it despite their previous refusals to do so. Both the border crisis and the new government were short-lived, however.

Meanwhile, Mrs. Meir had had talks in Washington, D.C., with President Richard M. Nixon; U.S. Secretary of State Henry Kissinger had come and gone; and the talks with the Egyptians continued. In January Lieut. Gen. David Elazar for Israel and Lieut. Gen. Mohammed Gamasy for Egypt had signed the disengagement agreement and the accord on the U.S. proposal for limited deployment of forces in the forward zone. Mrs. Meir supported the agreement but met opposition from the right-wing Likud, whose leader characterized the accord as unilateral withdrawal and retreat. After a bitter debate, the Knesset approved the agreement on January 22 by 76 votes to 35, and on February 21 the withdrawal of all Israeli troops from "Africa," the bridgehead on the western bank of the Suez Canal, was completed.

The preliminary report of the Agranat committee was released in early April. It blamed the chief of staff, General Elazar, for some of the military shortcomings of the October war and recommended that he be replaced. It also criticized the chief of Israel's military intelligence, Maj. Gen. Eliahu Zeira, and three of his principal assistants for a mistaken doctrine that led them to misread the warnings of the Israeli secret service about Arab preparations for war. Zeira and the assistants were also to be replaced. The committee made a number of important recommendations with regard to the reorganization of the intelligence services. Mrs. Meir accepted all the recommendations. The chief of staff was replaced by Maj. Gen. Mordechai Gur.

Although the Agranat report cleared Dayan and Mrs. Meir of responsibility, accusations persisted against them and other members of the government. Finally, on April 10 Mrs. Meir resigned again —this time irrevocably. In the balloting for succession to head of the Labor party, Yitzhak Rabin, 52, former chief of staff and ambassador in Washington, D.C., won 298 votes against the 254 of the runner-up, Shimon Peres, who initiated a spirit of cooperation by declaring to work loyally with Rabin.

Instead of moving for new elections, the Labor party decided to try to form a new coalition government—a task that proved to be more difficult than had been expected; and it seemed for a while as if Rabin would have to exchange one set of recriminations for another. This arose from his desire to re-shape the face of the government and from the determination of some former members not to serve under him. Finance Minister Pinhas Sapir, kingmaker of Labor cabinets since the resignation of David Ben-Gurion, became chairman of the Jewish Agency rather than serve under Rabin. Abba Eban, foreign minister for nine years, would continue to serve only as foreign minister, a position preempted by Rabin's colleague Yigal Allon. It was not easy for Rabin to negotiate a new coalition while the Meir government continued to function.

The last act of the Meir government was to request the Knesset on May 30 to ratify the Golan Heights disengagement agreement with Syria. The Knesset approved with a 76–36 vote, and then Mrs. Meir's "October government" stepped down. Rabin presented his new government to the Knesset on June 3 and received a vote of confidence of 61–51 (5 abstentions). The religious parties had refused to join Rabin's government, but the liberal Citizen's Rights Movement supported Rabin, and its leader, Shulamit Aloni, joined the cabinet. Peres became minister of defense and Allon foreign minister.

The first priority for the new government was to overhaul and reequip the country's defense forces, with the aid of massive U.S. financial support and supplies; the U.S. Congress voted a $2.2-million grant, and President Gerald R. Ford ordered new weapons to be taken from U.S. stocks to reequip Israeli troops. By the end of November, Israel's forces were proportionately larger than in October 1973 and qualitatively greatly improved. Delivery of U.S. arms was speeded up in November in the face of a new Soviet airlift to Syria; the high priority

*Israeli soldiers evacuate children on May 15 from a schoolhouse at Ma'alot where Palestinian terrorists had held them hostage. In the shootout 20 children were killed.*
N. GUTMAN–SIPA/LIAISON

assigned to defense was reflected in the partial mobilization and general alert ordered by the government on November 14 when Israel observed unexplained military activity by Syrian forces.

In early December meetings with Kissinger, Allon hinted at Israel's willingness to cede another section of the Sinai Peninsula to Egypt to further Mideast peace negotiations. Egyptian President Sadat, however, insisting on the return of Sinai land holding rich oil fields and strategic passes, rejected the offer as meaningless. By year's end peace negotiations had reached an impasse, Mideast tension was building rapidly, and Israel's reluctance to make significant concessions to the Arab states was straining its relations with the U.S.

A number of murderous raids—many by Lebanese-based Palestinian liberation groups, including the Popular Democratic Front for the Liberation of Palestine and the General Command—inflicted grievous casualties on civilians in border towns inhabited largely by Jewish immigrants from Arab countries. Mainly women and children were killed in the more than 25 attacks on such settlements as Qiryat Shemona (April 11), Ma'alot (May 15), Kibbutz Shamir (June 13), Nahariya (June 24), and Bet She'an (November 19). Israel pursued a policy of reprisal against acts of terrorism, bombing guerrilla targets in Lebanon and shelling Lebanese fishing ports. Public anger at the terrorists was matched by resentment against the Israeli government, which seemed powerless to stop such attacks. A Palestinian spokesman characterized the terrorist activities as "legal military actions" and vowed that they would continue until Israel agreed to negotiate with the Palestine Liberation Organization (PLO).

The Palestinian issue became more acute after the Arab summit meeting in Rabat, Morocco, at which the PLO was recognized as the only legitimate representative of Palestinian interests. The problem took on new dimensions when the United Nations (UN) General Assembly voted on November 22 that the Palestinians should be entitled to return to their land and property. Rabin—with massive national support—reaffirmed that Israel would never negotiate with the PLO. Rabin's difficulties were not lessened when he finally brought the National Religious party into the government at the end of October, at the cost of losing the support of Mrs. Aloni—who resigned her cabinet post—and the Citizen's Rights Movement. Information Minister Aharon Yariv joined Defense Minister Peres in calling for a government of national unity as the country's response to the acceptance of the PLO and its leader, Yasir Arafat, by the UN General Assembly. Speaking in the Knesset, Foreign Minister Allon denounced the UN as an organization controlled by a Soviet-Arab bloc.

As the year drew to a close, economic problems began to demand attention. Tourism and trade were down sharply, resulting in a record $3.5-million balance of payments deficit; inflation was running at 40%. On November 9 the cabinet ordered a drastic devaluation of the Israeli pound by more than 40%, accompanied by austerity measures including sharp increases in the prices of basic commodities and a six-month ban on imports of various nonessential consumer goods. Initial public reaction to the measures included angry demonstrations in some sectors. (*See also* Middle East; United Nations.)

**ITALY.** The year 1974 for Italy was a succession of government crises, a series of politically motivated acts of violence, and an outburst of kidnappings that put the keenly awaited and controversial referendum on the divorce law in the shade. The oil crisis, an inflation rate of about 25%, and the urgent need to secure oil supplies and foreign loans dictated every aspect of Italian foreign and economic policy.

On February 28 the resignation of the treasury minister, Republican Ugo La Malfa—in open disagreement with the terms of a $1.2 billion loan to Italy, which he had himself negotiated in Washington, D.C.—brought the first crisis of the year. Premier Mariano Rumor offered his resignation on March 2, but four days later he was asked by President Giovanni Leone to form a new government on the same lines as the previous one (a four-party coalition of Christian Democrats, Socialists, Social Democrats, and Republicans). The new cabinet was practically the continuation of its forerunner.

Great controversy was generated by the approval of a bill for the financing of political parties from public funds, at a cost of $68 million a year, and an extra $23 million in election years. Later, signatures were collected all over Italy in an attempt to force a referendum on the matter. *Referendum* seemed to be the "in" word: such an initiative had already been taken by opposers of the 1970 divorce law. The leading Christian Democrats and the neofascist Italian Social Movement-National Right (MSI-DN) campaigned for a vote to repeal the law. On May 12–13, it was retained by a majority of 59.1% of the votes.

The Christian Democrats' standing was greatly weakened by their losing campaign, and a month later Premier Rumor again offered his resignation, although his decision was officially caused by cabinet disagreement over economic measures. This time President Leone rejected the resignation, and after compromise was reached among the coalition partners, parliament gave its vote of confidence to the Rumor government on June 28. Local elections in Sardinia June 16–17 further emphasized the difficulties of the Christian Democrats: their majority decreased from 44.6% (1969) to 38.3%.

Premier Rumor again resigned on October 3, after the Social Democrats walked out of the coalition. Christian Democrat Secretary Amintore Fanfani, the former premier, was asked on October 14 to form a new government, but after a series of unsuccessful consultations he gave up on October

An exhortation to vote Communist tops the party banners on a street in Rome. As Italy was almost bankrupted by oil prices and was beset by political crises, Communist gains were spectacular in 1974.

KEYSTONE

25. The choice then fell on Aldo Moro, who was foreign minister in the Rumor cabinet and himself a former premier. On November 23 he formed a new two-party government (a coalition of Christian Democrats and Republicans) with the outside support of Socialists and Social Democrats.

Episodes of political violence, mainly attributed to right-wing movements, renewed fears of a coup d'etat in 1974. A right-wing organization based in Padua was investigated and several persons were arrested, including industrialist Andrea Piaggio.

Kidnappings were rife in 1974. Most were carried out for extortion, some for political purposes. There was intense speculation about the disappearance of Judge Mario Sossi of Genoa on April 18. He was freed on May 23 by the Red Brigades—a Communist-oriented group disowned by the Communist party—after the Genoa tribunal had agreed to set free eight followers of the left-wing October 22 group. The promise was not kept; the chief judge refused to sign the release order.

Italian foreign involvement was aimed at securing oil supplies and credit. At the end of January Foreign Minister Aldo Moro went to Egypt, Abu Dhabi, Kuwait, Iran, and Saudi Arabia shortly after receiving in Rome the oil ministers of Algeria and Saudi Arabia. After a visit to President Leone by Mexican President Luis Echeverría Álvarez and by Soviet Foreign Minister Andrei A. Gromyko in

February, the oil search was resumed when Premier Rumor received Libyan Premier Abdul Salam Jalloud in Rome on February 25. Argentine Vice-President Isabel Martínez de Perón's talks with Leone and Rumor on June 17 were followed by Moro's trip to Poland in the same month. On September 25, Leone began an official visit with U.S. President Gerald R. Ford. Leone visited Shah Mohammed Reza Pahlavi of Iran in December.

In order to contain the trade deficit within $11.2 billion, as estimated at the beginning of 1974, a series of economic plans were suggested, also taking into account the increased cost of oil imports. Tax reform came into effect on January 1; later, limits were set to the export and import of currency, and a special deposit fund was established against all imported goods (50% of their value, for six months and no interest paid). The price of gasoline was increased in two stages from $1.25 to $1.85 a gallon. A once-only tax was charged on cars, according to size, and on houses, payable by owners. Value-added tax rates were increased; electricity, water, rail, postage, and public transport cost more.

By the end of November, prices had increased by 26.2% as compared with November 1973. Industrial production had shown encouraging signs at the beginning of the year, but the increase had fallen to 7.4% by November. This was largely a result of the crisis in the car industry. (*See also* Europe.)

**JAMAICA.** In 1974 Jamaica's serious economic and social problems were compounded by the world energy crisis and rocketing inflation. About 25% of the work force was unemployed, and the cost of living was rising at a rate of about 30% a year. The country's banana crop and tourist industry brought in increasing revenue; also, the price of sugar, another Jamaican crop, was increasing rapidly on world markets.

Fully 40% of the country's income, however, was derived from the mining of bauxite by U.S.-owned aluminum companies. In May Prime Minister Michael Manley set forth a comprehensive plan whereby the government would increase taxes and royalties on bauxite production by about 500%, would require the companies to meet production standards determined by the Jamaican government, and would eventually nationalize the companies—or some portion of the companies' assets. The tax increase then was duly passed in the Jamaican legislature. Another important point made by Prime Minister Manley was that taxation would be assessed with the value of the finished product in mind, not simply the raw materials involved; this, he predicted, would be a prime economic strategy of the future for all less developed nations selling their resources to industrial countries.

Symptomatic of a larger crime wave, four prominent businessmen were shot and killed in a 16-day period in March. The incidence of shootings had reportedly risen more than 1,000% in ten years. Two very strong anticrime measures were passed promptly by the legislature. The two laws, the Suppression of Crime Act and the Gun Court Act, permit searches and seizures for guns without warrants, secret trials, and indefinite detention of persons convicted of illegal possession of weapons. A Gun Court stockade for offenders was constructed in the heart of Kingston, the capital, as a visible warning and reminder. (*See also* West Indies.)

**JAPAN.** Like other major industrial countries, Japan was suffering from severe inflation in 1974 coupled with a drop in the economic growth rate. Political scandal forced Prime Minister Kakuei Tanaka to announce on November 25 that he would resign from office, and on December 9, Takeo Miki succeeded Tanaka as prime minister. Added to Japan's domestic woes, relations were tense with the U.S. and several Asian neighbors.

### Economic Affairs

In February the Economic Planning Agency announced that during 1973 Japan's rate of inflation

*Death and tremendous destruction resulted when a terrorist's bomb exploded at the Mitsubishi Co., which was heavily involved in military production, in Tokyo on August 30.*

KEYSTONE

*Demonstrators extend their fists in front of the U.S. embassy in Tokyo to protest a November visit by U.S. President Gerald R. Ford. The adverse reaction was caused in part by reports that U.S. warships had entered Japanese harbors with nuclear weapons aboard, despite agreements not to do so.*
UPI COMPIX

was the worst among the ten leading industrial nations. The West German Bureau of Statistics and the Bundesbank published statistics on inflation among the world's industrial countries; the highest rise in the cost of living was registered in Japan, 25.4% for the year ended August 1974.

The retail price index published by the government reached 152 in June (1970=100)—a staggering increase even when compared with rising U.S. prices. The Bank of Japan estimated that savers experienced an average per capita loss from inflation of 99,000 yen, or $370, in 1973.

Labor unions declared a "spring offensive" to secure wage hikes in the wake of price inflation. The result was the biggest strike in the country's history, in April. Transportation workers, postal workers, teachers, and doctors went on strike; business ground to a halt. The unions won wage increases averaging more than 30% for 35 million workers.

In February the Diet (parliament) held a special three-day session on price problems. Presidents of major trading firms admitted to price "irregularities" in their companies and promised corrective action, including recycling of excess profits.

In May the Tokyo High Public Prosecutor's office indicted the Petroleum Association of Japan, including 12 major petroleum refining companies and 17 of their executives, on charges of collusion in price fixing and production curtailment. Japan's economy, heavily based on external trade, is dependent on oil to a high degree.

The Japanese gross national product (GNP) declined in 1974 for the first time since World War II. According to figures released in December by the finance ministry, the 1974 GNP showed an apparent increase of 19%, but adjustments for the effects of inflation brought that figure to −1% or −2%.

Japan's balance of payments deficit increased by $1 billion in a single month, May 1974. The value of the country's exports continued to increase, but not as fast as the price of raw materials and essential imported goods.

## Political Developments

Japanese voters expressed their dissatisfaction with Tanaka and his Liberal Democratic party (LDP) at the polls in July. The 252 seats in Japan's upper house were at stake; the LDP lost 8 seats overall and ended up with 126. Japan's Socialist party won 28 new seats, for a total of 62. The Communist party won 13 new seats, for a total of 20.

Tanaka's power base was further weakened by the resignation of several cabinet members soon after the elections. Deputy Prime Minister Takeo Miki and Finance Minister Takeo Fukuda both made references in their resignation statements to reforming the conservative LDP. Fukuda had been a strong rival of Tanaka's for control of the LDP.

The shadow of scandal and political corruption fell across Tanaka's reputation. Japan's major newspapers provided extensive coverage of the developing story of how the prime minister had amassed his personal fortune. Allegations of kickbacks, bribes, and conflict of interest continued to mount, and on November 25 Tanaka announced that he would step down. On December 9 the Diet formally elected Miki prime minister, and he in turn named Fukuda, one of his chief rivals for the premiership, as deputy prime minister and also head of a new Economic Planning Agency. After the unprecedented action of revealing his total personal assets, Miki announced a new program to reform the LDP's handling of political contributions. In another unusual move, he met with the heads of four opposition parties; inflation was the main discussion topic.

A terrorist's bomb exploded near the entrance of the Mitsubishi building in Tokyo in August, killing 8 persons and injuring more than 300. Police speculated that the bomb was a protest against the Mitsubishi combine, thought to account for half the military production in Japan. In October a bomb was exploded at the Mitsui head office in Tokyo, injuring 16 persons.

The nuclear-powered ship *Mutsu* was the center of furious controversy. For two years the ship had been kept in its Honshu Island port by public reaction of the local fishermen, who feared that a radiation accident would poison the waters and kill their fish. Finally, on September 1, the *Mutsu* was put out for a test run and promptly developed a leak in its nuclear reactor. Public outrage was predictable, and the ship was not allowed to return to port for several weeks. Finally, the government promised funds for local fisheries development, and the *Mutsu* was allowed to return.

### Foreign Affairs

Relations between Japan and the U.S., nominally close allies, were increasingly strained—despite rosy public pronouncements. There was a six-month gap between the departure of U.S. Ambassador Robert S. Ingersoll and the arrival of the new U.S. ambassador, James D. Hodgson.

Prime Minister Tanaka visited Washington, D.C., in September and established a cordial relationship with U.S. President Gerald R. Ford. In November Ford became the first U.S. president to visit Japan while in office. His visit was preceded by massive protests from leftists and moderates, and by massive security measures.

Japan's famous "nuclear allergy," manifested in the *Mutsu* incident, was partly responsible for the adverse reaction to Ford's visit. Testimony before a U.S. Congressional committee by a retired U.S. admiral indicated that American warships regularly entered Japanese ports without off-loading their nuclear weapons—in violation of existing agreements. Opposition forces suspected that successive conservative governments of Japan had been duped by, or were in collusion with, the U.S. in circumventing Japan's prohibition of nuclear arms.

The U.S. government indirectly repudiated the admiral's testimony, and Tanaka pledged that Japan would reject any U.S. request to introduce nuclear weapons into the country. Fears of the Japanese citizenry were only slightly assuaged, however, and more than 300,000 persons demonstrated nationwide on International Antiwar Day in October. Against this background, Japan's intellectuals were not pleased with the news that former Prime Minister Eisaku Sato had been awarded the Nobel peace prize. (*See* Awards and Prizes.)

Tanaka's goodwill tour of neighboring Asian countries in January was marred by demonstrations in Thailand and riots in Indonesia. Relations with South Korea were in crisis after a Korean exile who had been living in Japan assassinated the wife of South Korea's President Park Chung Hee. (*See* Korea.)

In the spring Japan and the Soviet Union signed an agreement to develop coking coal in southern Yakutsk, U.S.S.R.; Japan would finance the project in return for 104 million tons of coking coal. In September Japan and the People's Republic of China inaugurated scheduled airline service between the two countries. (*See also* Asia; Taiwan.)

**JORDAN.** The West Bank—formerly Jordan's richest agricultural region, location of its major tourist areas, and site of Muslim religious shrines in East Jerusalem—continued in 1974 to be one of the principal problems of Jordan's foreign policy. Early in the year Jordan proposed that Israel withdraw from the Jordan River to the western edge of the Jordan Valley in the West Bank as the first step toward an Israeli-Jordanian settlement. It seemed certain that Israel would never agree to such terms and that Jordan would never accept the Israeli proposal to return to Jordan large numbers of Palestinians from the West Bank, many of whom were bitter enemies of King Hussein I.

Jordan had as much difficulty with other Arab countries in 1974 over the question of representation of the Palestinians in peace negotiations and over the status of the West Bank. King Hussein had insisted in the past that Palestinians should be represented only as members of the Jordanian delegation. King Hussein agreed with Egyptian President Anwar el-Sadat in July, however, that he would allow a separate Palestinian delegation, the Palestine Liberation Organization (PLO), to represent the Palestinian people living outside Jordan. Hussein's shift in position brought him into agreement with the other 17 members of the Arab League. The question of Jordan's claim to the Israeli-occupied West Bank, however, remained unclear. Jordan argued that the area should revert to Jordanian control. Palestinians and the other Arab nations favored establishment of a separate Palestinian state.

Protesting the September agreement between Egypt and Syria to work for the establishment of a Palestinian state on the West Bank, separate from Jordan, and in the Gaza Strip, King Hussein announced that Jordan was withdrawing from Middle East peace efforts and would boycott all negotiations. In October Jordan nonetheless took part in a 20-nation Arab summit that unanimously endorsed PLO chairman Yasir Arafat as the "sole legitimate" spokesman for all Palestinians, including those living in Jordan and on the West Bank; gave the PLO the exclusive right to set up an independent Palestinian state on any occupied Palestinian territory recovered from Israel; and provided the PLO with a $50-million annual military subsidy. Jordan was awarded an annual $300 million for arms by the summit and, while losing control of the West Bank, was thereby relieved of the agonizing Palestinian problem.

Adjusting to the altered reality of the West Bank, Hussein announced in November that Jordan's constitution would soon be rewritten and its cabinet and parliament reorganized to remove Palestinian representatives from the West Bank. Palestinian residents of the East Bank were to be given the choice of Jordanian or Palestinian citizenship.

Jordan announced plans in 1974 to reorganize and modernize its armed forces, including mechanization of the army and expansion of the air force. Jordan's aim reportedly was to protect itself against its leftist neighbors, Syria and Iraq, as well as against Israel. In addition to the Arab subsidy, Jordan received aid from the U.S. and from some Arab countries in 1974 out of appreciation for Jordan's role in the 1973 war with Israel.

U.S. President Richard M. Nixon received a warm welcome when he visited Amman in June. In August King Hussein visited Washington, D.C., for talks with President Gerald R. Ford and Defense Secretary James R. Schlesinger.

Early in 1974 some Jordanian army troops mutinied to protest wages and inequitable pay scales and to demand the dismissal of several government and military officials. King Hussein, whose ties to the Jordanian army had always been strong, responded sympathetically. He visited military garrisons, ordered pay increases, and shook up the military command. Although the king did not meet all its demands, the military seemed satisfied. (*See also* Middle East.)

**KENYA.** During 1974 Kenya pursued a domestic policy aimed at achieving the complete Africanization of trade within the country. In February all noncitizen traders who had received notices to quit the country were ordered to leave as soon as they handed over their businesses. A new five-year development plan costing $4.2 million was introduced in March, but Kenyans were warned that economies would be required if the plan was to be successful. Strikes caused problems in Kenya in 1974; one by bank workers in July resulted in the banning of all strikes until further notice. Also in July, Swahili replaced English as Kenya's official language.

Kenyans elected their third Parliament in a decade of independence in October. Unopposed for reelection, President Jomo Kenyatta was declared reelected to another five-year term. The elections took place amid accusations of corruption in high places and were marked by the imposing of restrictive measures that favored candidates of the Kenya

*Kenyan President Kenyatta joins in a January celebration that marks his turning over of a 1,313-acre farm to 106 landless families.*
WIDE WORLD

UPI COMPIX

*Police discharge tear gas near the Japanese embassy in Seoul, South Korea, where demonstrators protest the October attempted assassination of President Park by a Korean resident of Japan.*

African National Union, the ruling political party.

In the area of foreign relations, the government announced in March that Kenya's armed forces would not take part in the United Nations cease-fire patrols along the Suez Canal, a peacekeeping operation that might have brought Kenya prestige. Wary of developments in neighboring Uganda and beset by demands made by a group calling itself the United Liberation Front of Western Somalia, Kenya ordered six British aircraft and arranged for pilots to be trained in Great Britain. In December, Kenya sealed its borders with Tanzania in the face of growing economic and diplomatic disputes.

Kenya deported two American geologists who had discovered a rich ruby deposit in Kenya's Tsavo West National Park. Their ouster followed a pattern set earlier when an American oil company executive was summarily expelled after he tried to collect unpaid fuel bills for farms reportedly owned by President Kenyatta. (*See also* Africa.)

**KOREA.** President Park Chung Hee of South Korea announced measures in January 1974 that virtually banned all opposition to his government. The maximum punishment was 15 years in prison, but after student demonstrations in April, Park raised the maximum to death. By mid-1974 the government said that more than 1,000 persons had been arrested; opponents of the government put the number at four or five times the official figure.

Trials, many of them secret, began soon after the measures were announced, and by midyear nearly 100 persons had been found guilty and had been given sentences ranging from a few years in prison to death. Among those before the courts were students, professors, religious leaders, and politicians. Yun Po Sun, a former president of South Korea, was convicted and given a suspended sentence. South Korea's best known poet, Kim Chi Ha, was also convicted and sentenced to death, but his sentence was later commuted to life in prison. The conviction of a Roman Catholic bishop in August touched off demands by church groups and others that the official policy of repression end. Later in the year Park lifted two of the four decrees suppressing political activity, but he refused to release those in jail or on trial.

On August 15, South Korea's Independence Day, at a rare public appearance by Park, a 22-year-old Korean man who had been living in Japan fired shots at the president. The man missed Park, but a bullet struck his wife, Yook Young Soo, who died a few hours later. Although government officials charged that the assassin was under North Korean orders, massive demonstrations broke out in Seoul against Japan, and South Korea threatened diplomatic action. Japanese Prime Minister Kakuei Tanaka attended the first lady's funeral, and in September the two governments officially closed the incident. (*See* Obituaries.)

South Korea's domestic policies significantly alienated foreign support, particularly in the U.S., where some urged the government to cut off all aid to South Korea. Although committees in both the House and Senate proposed to end economic and military aid to South Korea, President Gerald R. Ford nevertheless made a scheduled one-day stop in Seoul after a visit to Japan. Ford assured Park that U.S. forces would remain in South Korea.

Rejecting a South Korean proposal for a nonaggression pact on the grounds that it would perpetuate U.S. presence in the South, as well as the division of the country, North Korean Premier Kim Il Sung proposed his own peace agreement. During the year Red Cross negotiators agreed to reopen preliminary meetings to establish full-scale talks. Renewal of unification negotiations was also discussed at the United Nations on November 29. Earlier in the month it had been discovered that North Korea was building tunnels through the demilitarized zone that separates North and South.

Although South Korea's sympathy from other countries declined in 1974, North Korea made diplomatic progress by establishing relations with Australia, Guinea-Bissau, and Libya. Several presidents and foreign ministers visited North Korea in 1974. General hostility between North Korea and the U.S. continued in 1974.

Although South Korea had serious inflation during the year, Premier Kim said that his government would reduce the prices of industrial goods in North Korea an average of 30%. Kim said that successes achieved in industry and agriculture had led to markedly increased production of mass consumption goods. The Supreme People's Assembly of North Korea abolished all taxes, which had constituted less than 2% of the government's revenue. (*See also* Asia.)

**KUWAIT.** In January 1974 Kuwait announced that it would buy 60% of Kuwait Oil Co., which produced more than 90% of the country's oil, from the Gulf Oil Corp. and British Petroleum Co., Ltd. Kuwait paid $112 million for the shares. The agreement allowed for the possibility of complete nationalization, but Kuwait's oil minister indicated that his country was not anxious for this step. He also stated that Kuwait's oil policy would be aimed toward protecting the interests of the countries where Kuwait had substantial investments.

In February members of two Palestinian guerrilla groups, cooperating with members of a leftist Japanese group, seized the Japanese ambassador to Kuwait and members of his staff. Although government officials and the press strongly criticized the terrorists, Kuwait met their demands to allow four fellow guerrillas from Singapore to be flown to Kuwait. The government refused, however, to allow any of the terrorists to remain in the country but did allow them to fly to the People's Democratic Republic of Yemen.

Kuwait's oil production of 2.6 million barrels a day in 1974 was lower than the 1973 level of 3 million barrels a day. There were pressures to reduce the supply further, primarily to conserve the country's oil reserves.

Kuwait's oil income in 1974 was nearly $10,000 per person, more than double the per capita income of the U.S. Affluence continued to transform its society into a modern social welfare state with universal education and virtually full employment.

Kuwait continued to invest large amounts of its oil revenues abroad. Kuwait made loans to other Arab countries and announced plans to buy British government and U.S. Treasury bonds. Kuwait offered $246 million for British real estate, primarily in London, and bought a second island 15 miles off the coast of Charleston, S.C., to be developed as a tourist resort. (*See also* Middle East.)

*U.S. Treasury Secretary William E. Simon visits with Kuwait's minister of finance and oil, Abdel Rahman al-Atiqi, as part of a July trip to the Middle East. Simon tried to persuade Persian Gulf oil producers to lower their prices and to invest their revenues in the U.S.*
WIDE WORLD

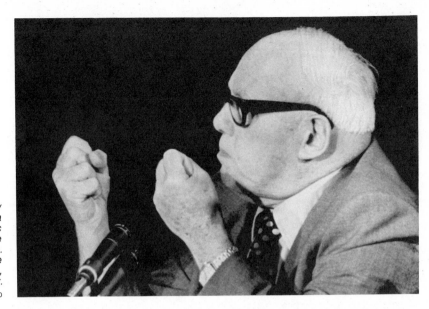

*President George Meany of the AFL-CIO makes a point at an economic summit meeting on the sore subject of inflation. The two-day conference was held in Washington, D.C., late in September.*

WIDE WORLD

## LABOR UNIONS.

Organized labor in the U.S. continued to grow slowly in 1974, the largest increases being in public employment and in the service industries. The latest available reports put union membership at 20,833,000—with about 8,928,000 in manufacturing, 9,444,000 in non-manufacturing, 1,356,000 in federal employment, and 1,105,000 in state and local governments. Because the U.S. labor force continued to grow faster than union membership, organized labor represented decreasing percentages of the total labor force (24.3% in the latest official count in 1972).

Some individual unions, however, made important gains in 1974. The Textile Workers Union of America won plant elections at J. P. Stevens & Co. in Roanoke Rapids, N.C., after trying unsuccessfully for ten years. The Amalgamated Clothing Workers of America won a long and difficult organizing strike in Texas plants of the Farah Manufacturing Co., and the United Mine Workers (UMW) won contract rights for coal miners in Harlan County, Ky., with the Eastover Mining Co. In Kannopolis, N.C., however, the textile union received a severe setback when workers at 15 Cannon Mills Co. plants voted to reject unionization.

### A Year of Strikes

Although strikes were averted in many large industries in 1974, strikes increased in small industries. For the first eight months of the year, the percentage of days lost through strikes was the highest in years, mostly as the result of the large number of strikes during the summer that exceeded records for any period since the 1940's. In votes on ratification, union members turned down 12.3% of all new contracts in 1974, or about one in eight, as compared with a rejection rate of 9.6% in 1973.

With the end of wage controls and with increased militancy in unions, settlements were substantially higher in 1974. The U.S. Department of Labor reported settlements in the first half of 1974 running at an average 8.7% for the first contract year and 7% over the life of the contract. These increases compared with 5.8% for the first year and 5.1% for the contract in 1973. Increases in the first quarter of 1974 averaged 6.2% for the first year while controls were in effect but rose to 9.2% in May and the following months of the second quarter. Continued inflation prompted unions to demand more protection of wages through cost-of-living "escalator" clauses.

Thousands of new contracts were negotiated during 1974, covering more than 5 million workers. The most important negotiations of the year—involving the United Steelworkers and the can, aluminum, basic steel, and steel fabricating industries—were uneventful. The Experimental Negotiating Agreement, established in 1973, worked effectively to bring about a quick settlement in 1974, without even the threat of a strike. Union and industry agreed to continue the arrangement for the next bargaining sessions in 1977.

After nine weeks of unsuccessful negotiations, on November 11—the last day of a three-year miners' contract—the country's 120,000 soft-coal miners walked out in a strike that ended with the December 5 ratification of a new contract, providing a 64% increase in wages and fringe benefits over three years. The contract included sick pay, a pension increase, stricter safety rules, and a new cost-of-living clause. A December walkout by 4,500 mine construction workers delayed reopening at many mines.

The Amalgamated Clothing Workers of America struck the men's and boys' clothing industry on a national basis for the first time in 53 years. More than 100,000 were out for 11 days at 750 plants before settling for $1 an hour over three years, their first cost-of-living clause.

In the city and county of San Francisco, Calif.,

four unions representing 15,000 public employees struck for nine days, partly to establish the right of collective bargaining. Among other strikes by public employees in 1974 was the strike of 3,000 employees in Baltimore, Md., which lasted for 14 days in spite of court injunctions.

Many strikes in the building trades erupted after wage controls ended and craft unions demanded large wage increases to make up for annual increases of about 5% during the period of controls. In one of the largest walkouts, construction unions in California slowed or stopped projects for 49 days before a settlement for an increase of about $3.75 an hour over three years was reached.

The Communications Workers of America (CWA) and other telephone unions negotiated settlements without strikes in the first nationwide bargaining with the Bell Telephone System, a subsidiary of American Telephone & Telegraph Co. (AT & T). International Brotherhood of Electrical Workers locals, however, struck 16 plants of AT & T's manufacturing division, Western Electric, for over a month before accepting terms similar to those in CWA's contract with the Bell system.

The energy crisis had an impact on union members' jobs in 1974. The United Auto Workers probably suffered more than any other union. Automobile and truck manufacturers cut production and layoffs spread throughout the industry. Unemployment in the industry rose to its highest level at year's end, and it was predicted that as many as 240,000 of the industry's hourly workers would be laid off in January 1975.

The trucking industry and the International Brotherhood of Teamsters also were hard hit, but the industry's independent truckers, most of them owner-drivers, were affected the most by rising fuel prices, fuel shortages, and the 55-mph speed limit. Drivers blocked highways, kept trucks idle, and sometimes demonstrated violently but had only limited support from the Teamsters.

## Labor and the Federal Government

Labor leaders were pleased with federal legislation in 1974 that reformed private and industrial pension plans and that provided alternatives for fee-for-service medical care, a possible basis for national health care in the future. Labor also successfully supported the enactment of minimum wage increases in 1974 that increased the earnings of an estimated 4.2 million workers. The bill added 7.4 million workers to coverage by the Fair Labor Standards (Wage-Hour) Act, including 1.5 million domestic workers. With some exceptions, the minimum wage allowed by federal law increased for most workers from $1.60 an hour to $2.00 in 1974, with future increases to $2.10 in 1975, and $2.30 in 1976.

Federal agencies and the courts toughened the enforcement of laws against bias in employment of blacks and other minorities and of women and the aged and ordered multimillion-dollar back payments to those discriminated against in the past. Apprenticeship rolls were opened to women. The first women got jobs in coal mines, overcoming not only male-only hiring practices but also a long tradition that women in mines brought bad luck.

Federal courts ruled against appeals by James R. Hoffa, former president of the International Brotherhood of Teamsters, by barring Hoffa from all union activities for the remainder of his parole from prison. A. Philip Randolph, one of the AFL-CIO's few major black leaders, retired as a vice-president in 1974 at the age of 85 after six decades of work in labor and civil rights. Albert Shanker, 46, the powerful leader of city and state teachers in New York and an AFL-CIO vice-president, won election as president of the American Federation of Teachers, becoming one of the strongest young leaders in the U.S. labor movement. (*See also* Business and Industry; Employment; Mines and Mining; Newspapers; United States.)

Truck drivers look over their slashed tires at an exit from a truck stop at Breezewood, Pa. The drivers parked there to block other trucks during a February independent drivers' dispute that was marked by violence.
WIDE WORLD

*A Roman-villa-style museum, built by multimillionaire J. Paul Getty on his Malibu, Calif., estate to house his collection of Greek and Roman antiquities, 18th-century French furnishings, and rare paintings, opened in January. A reflecting pool enhances the courtyard.*

## LANDMARKS AND MONUMENTS.

Governments, organizations, and individuals worked throughout the world in 1974 to save historic areas. In Egypt a cofferdam around the island of Philae was completed and pumping was begun to lower the Nile water level. Work was to begin by the end of the year to move the island's ancient temples to the island of Agilkia, which was being prepared to resemble ancient Philae.

In Peru restoration of Incan and Spanish colonial monuments began. In Senegal plans were drawn up to restore the historic fortress on Goree Island guarding the entrance to the port of Dakar and its old slave barracks. The government of Luxembourg worked to protect the abbey and gardens of Echternach from a highway into the city by building a costly tunnel underneath the gardens. The government also considered plans to close the historic city to automobile traffic.

In France President Valéry Giscard d'Estaing used his power of veto several times during 1974 to protect historic areas of Paris. Giscard vetoed a plan by municipal authorities for an expressway along the city's Left Bank, directly opposite Notre Dame. He also vetoed plans to demolish historic artists' studios built from material salvaged from the 1878 Paris Exhibition and plans to redevelop the area once occupied by the pavilions of Les Halles, also the site of the historic church of St. Eustache.

Work on rescuing Venice, however, was hampered by economic and political problems in Italy. Plans for a modern sewage system were ready, but construction awaited government funds. Regulations on atmospheric pollution were adopted, but regulations on industrial expansion and construction around Venice were not.

An alarming number of historic buildings in the U.S. continued to be destroyed in 1974, although plans for the bicentennial celebration in 1976 helped create interest in preserving buildings, including railroad stations, showing earlier traditions and architectural styles. When travel by passenger train declined in the U.S., most of the country's railroad stations, many of them monumental or at least interesting in design, fell into disuse. By 1974, many had been demolished or were threatened with destruction. A few cities—such as Duluth, Minn., Baltimore, Md., Chattanooga, Tenn., and Indianapolis, Ind.—did manage to save their stations for cultural or commercial centers. Residents of Cincinnati, Ohio, saved the magnificent murals of their station by moving them to a new airport terminal building, but the station itself appeared doomed.

Mutilation and theft of monuments continued to be a problem in 1974. During the height of London's tourist season, terrorist bombs exploded at two important historical sites—Westminster Hall and the Tower of London. In New York City, officials said that thieves were gradually dismantling the Riverside Bridge by stealing bronze decorations from the bridge's ornate lamps as well as sections of railing from the bridge itself. Also in New York City, thieves stole cast-iron facades from a building, considered one of the finest cast-iron structures in the world, which was being demolished. Police speculated that the thieves were narcotics addicts who wanted the metal to sell.

Chicago took extraordinary precautions to protect its newly installed Marc Chagall mosaic sculpture in a public plaza both from the atmosphere and from vandals. Officials announced that a plastic coating would protect the mural from weather, pollution, and graffiti. A barrier with electronic sensors, 24-hour guards, and closed-circuit television cameras also monitored the area. (*See also* Architecture; Cities and Urban Affairs; Environment Special Report; National Park Service; Painting and Sculpture; U.S. Special Report.)

**271**

**LAOS.** The third attempt in 20 years to establish a neutral Laos got under way in April 1974 with the formation of the long-awaited coalition government. For more than a year after the signing of the Indochina cease-fire agreement, the Vientiane government and the Pathet Lao argued about administrative details. The main stumbling block was the neutralization of the political and royal capitals, Vientiane and Luang Prabang, respectively. Agreement was finally reached in February on joint policing and neutral administration for the two towns. With the resolution of this last major dispute, the coalition was launched.

On April 3 the Pathet Lao leader, Prince Souphanouvong, landed in Vientiane. In an emotional airport welcome, he embraced his half-brother, Prince Souvanna Phouma, the prime minister, and was cheered by thousands of Laotians. Two days later the new cabinet (consisting of 12 members, five from each side and two neutrals) and the National Political Council (42 members, 16 from each side and 10 neutrals) were sworn in. Souvanna Phouma remained as prime minister, and Souphanouvong became president of the National Political Council. Well-known Pathet Lao leader Phoumi Vongvichit became minister of foreign affairs and one of two vice-premiers.

Despite meticulous efforts to balance political power, the Pathet Lao quickly emerged as the dominant partner in both cabinet and council. On May 11, Constitution Day, the National Assembly did not open its scheduled session. The Pathet Lao members of the cabinet argued that the old National Assembly (elected while the war was still in progress and mostly right-wing) was unrepresentative of the people. The rightist elements in the cabinet and outside grew more restive as Pathet Lao influence increased. On July 10, following public demonstrations by dissident rightists, the old assembly was dissolved.

Two days later, 72-year-old Prince Souvanna Phouma suffered a mild heart attack. In the absence of any specific order of governmental succession, the two vice-premiers were put in charge of day-to-day affairs. In August, when Souvanna Phouma went to France for ten weeks' recuperation, the Pathet Lao's vice-premier, Phoumi Vongvichit, was named acting prime minister.

The issue of withdrawal of foreign troops remained unresolved. Although Thai forces left before the June 4 deadline and U.S. troops were reduced, North Vietnamese troops reportedly remained covertly. Western sources estimated their numbers at between 30,000 and 55,000. Another foreign presence, never officially acknowledged, was that of Chinese soldiers and workers building a strategic road network in northwestern Laos. Estimates of their strength ranged from 3,000 to 30,000.

It was too early to say how the Laotian economy, long dependent on U.S. aid, was shaping under the new regime. Immediately after the coalition government was formed, the United States, Britain, France, Japan, and Australia renewed their budgetary aid to Laos. Rumors that the kip, the Laotian currency, might be devalued sent that currency on a downward spiral. But the cabinet decided against devaluation and planned to introduce foreign exchange control, import restrictions, a revised tax structure, and new export regulations. It was made clear that the new government intended to accept economic aid from both Communist and non-Communist countries.

In Washington, D.C., Senator Edward Kennedy (D, Mass.) expressed concern that U.S. economic aid, going exclusively to non-Communist villages and refugees in Laos, might perpetuate political divisions. U.S. government officials acknowledged that current plans called for most aid to go to the "Royal Laotian" side because the U.S. was continuing existing programs, which were naturally in areas controlled by the former non-Communist government. (*See also* Asia.)

*At their formal investiture in April, Prime Minister Souvanna Phouma (center right) and Pathet Lao Foreign Minister Phoumi Vongvichit (at his right), top members of the Laotian coalition government, listen to their national anthem.*

WIDE WORLD

**LATIN AMERICA.** The year opened on an optimistic note for U.S.-Latin American relations. In February, at a three-day conference in Mexico City, U.S. Secretary of State Henry Kissinger met with representatives of 24 Latin American and Caribbean countries. Kissinger called for the creation of a new "Western Hemisphere community" and a spirit of cooperation he dubbed the "spirit of Tlatelolco," for the name of the district where the meeting took place. A Declaration of Tlatelolco was issued, calling for the establishment of a framework for high-level talks and negotiations. Two major issues covered in the declaration were the promise of maximum effort by the administration of U.S. President Richard M. Nixon to secure legislation of preferential tariffs in 1974 and the avoidance of any new measures that would restrict access of Latin American goods to the U.S. market.

With the resignation of Nixon from the presidency in August, many observers felt that Latin America stood to benefit substantially. These expectations were seriously dampened, however, following the reports of U.S. intrigue and covert activity in Chile aimed at the overthrow of the Allende administration. Secretary Kissinger's responsibility in these matters did not enhance his credibility in Latin America as a whole and seemed likely to destroy much of the goodwill he had earned. (*See* Intelligence Operations.)

The Cuban question was a major topic at meetings of the Organization of American States (OAS) in April and November. Costa Rica, Colombia, and Venezuela led the faction calling for termination of economic and political sanctions against Cuba. There were many signs that the United States was also considering a renewal of relations with Cuba, including hints to that effect by newly installed President Gerald R. Ford and a unanimous resolution by the Senate Foreign Relations Committee calling for an end to economic sanctions.

A five-day ministerial meeting was convened in November at Quito, Ecuador, to discuss the status of the economic and political sanctions against Cuba. The 12 countries in favor of ending the sanctions were initially optimistic, but the final vote fell two short of the necessary two-thirds majority. The U.S., expected by several countries to vote with the 12, abstained, as did Haiti, Guatemala, Bolivia, Brazil, and Nicaragua. Seven members of the OAS already had diplomatic relations with Cuba, despite the ban, and Venezuela joined that group in December. The issue threatened future disunity among the already divided member states.

**Inter-American Finances**

The 15th meeting of the Board of Governors of the Inter-American Development Bank (IDB) was held in Santiago, Chile, in April. Despite record levels of activity, the bank needed new capital to maintain growth, and on terms that would enable it to maintain its ratio of concessional loans. The major items approved at the meeting were the Venezuelan proposal to establish a special trust fund to be administered by the IDB, a study of the bank's charter to verify whether there were impediments to financing exports to countries outside the region, and the acceptance, in advance, of applications for membership by Guyana and the Bahamas. The discussion of a project for 12 Western European and Pacific nations to join the bank as associate members and to provide $500 million in funds was postponed to the next meeting. In preparation for this discussion, the Committee of Governors met in June to study a report from the Executive Board on the possibility of increasing the bank's resources. The report stated that the bank planned to raise the annual level of loans from $884 million in 1973 to $1 billion by the end of 1974, and to exceed this volume after 1975.

The International Bank for Reconstruction and Development (IBRD) stated in its 1972–73 annual report that the combined gross national product (GNP) of the Latin American and Caribbean countries increased by an average annual rate of 5.6% during the 1962–73 decade and that the annual growth reached 7% in the last four years of the period. The increase in population, at a rate of 3% a year, was accompanied by a massive exodus from the rural areas, transforming basically rural societies into mainly urban ones, in which progress was not shared either by all the countries or by all the social levels. This change in population distribution coincided with the transformation of the economic structure; the share of agriculture in both the GNP and the labor force declined in view of the expansion of the industrial, construction, and transport sectors. Despite the large increase in population, per capita income rose substantially.

**Regional and Subregional Integration**

Notwithstanding the weaknesses and failures of the Latin American Free Trade Association (LAFTA) as a viable integration mechanism, some progress was recorded in the expansion of intraregional trade. LAFTA exports to, and imports from, the rest of the world were also increasing.

With regard to the Andean Group (Bolivia, Chile, Colombia, Ecuador, Peru, and—as of 1973—Venezuela), significant progress was made in 1974 to maintain the momentum of integration achieved since the group's founding in 1969. The all-important joint industrial planning mechanism was gradually getting under way, though there was dissension on the implementation of Decision 24, which restricts foreigners to minority interests in businesses operating within the region and also limits foreign profits. By 1974 Peru and Venezuela were the only members to have fully enforced Decision 24, and new foreign capital was unlikely to be attracted to the subregion until all the rules of the game had been clearly defined and translated by the individual member countries into legislation.

Venezuela, reaping billions of dollars from oil

*Entering the April OAS general assembly meeting in Atlanta, Ga., U.S. Secretary of State Kissinger encounters pickets protesting Cuba's possible return to that organization.*

sales, was less interested in foreign investment and more willing to enforce the decision. Chile, on the other hand, trying to recoup the economic losses of the Allende period, opposed Decision 24 and adopted a more liberal stance. The Chilean military junta issued a new foreign investment law that appeared to have little in common with the Andean legislation: the new law made no provision for the gradual transformation of a foreign company into a mixed or national concern, nor did it establish a maximum limit for the remittance of profits abroad. This attitude was perhaps understandable in view of the need to attract foreign investment at a time when local conditions were not propitious for large inflows of risk capital, but by making its own legal framework more attractive to foreign capital, Chile allowed national economic priorities to take precedence over group considerations.

Several sectorial industrial programs of the Andean group still had to be formulated and negotiated before the end-of-1975 deadline, when products reserved for sectorial development would automatically revert to the general trade liberalization procedure if they had not already been incorporated into individual programs. One program, metalworking, had already been approved. Dispersement of the automotive and petrochemical industries was proving more difficult to negotiate.

Venezuela was displeased with the decision that it would produce only heavy trucks and two categories of automobiles. The Venezuelans were also unhappy that Bolivia was assigned to produce certain pieces of oil-drilling equipment.

The Central American Common Market (CACM: Costa Rica, El Salvador, Guatemala, Honduras, and Nicaragua) saw a significant increase in the absolute value of regional trade, but its share of total trade was not growing. The high-level committee that was studying the restructuring of the CACM presented constructive plans for industrial development and tariff harmonization, but there was little doubt as to the extent of the political consensus needed to implement the proposals. The chief obstacle continued to be the unresolved dispute between El Salvador and Honduras stemming from the "soccer" war of 1969. Both countries faced domestic problems that hampered the granting of concessions. El Salvador was experiencing a very high level of unemployment, while the agrarian reform program in Honduras was making little headway. Elsewhere, too, more pressing difficulties drew attention away from the integration process. The reconstruction problems in the aftermath of the 1972 Managua, Nicaragua, earthquake and, in 1974, the severe damage caused by Hurricane Fifi in Honduras would further delay integration.

A new economic interest group, the Union of Banana Exporting Countries, was formed in 1974, including Ecuador, Costa Rica, Honduras, Panama, Guatemala, Colombia, and Nicaragua. Nine major coffee-producing countries also launched a joint effort to boost world coffee prices, and 20 sugar producers formed a similar cartel in December.

In one of the year's most promising events, eight nations—Peru, Chile, Bolivia, Ecuador, Venezuela, Argentina, Colombia, and Panama—produced a mutual arms limitation agreement. Further arms talks, which, it was hoped, would be attended by all Latin American countries, were being planned for 1975. (*See also* individual country articles.)

**LAW.** The Watergate case continued to dominate legal news throughout 1974. The most dramatic development occurred on August 9, when Richard M. Nixon resigned as president of the United States. His vice-president, Gerald R. Ford, was sworn in as his successor. On August 5 Nixon had released a statement and transcripts of tape recordings admitting that six days after the break-in at the Democratic National Committee's headquarters he had ordered the Federal Bureau of Investigation (FBI) to halt its investigation of the break-in. Nixon's statement destroyed what Congressional support he had, and within 48 hours the House Judiciary Committee had voted unanimously for impeachment. (*See* Congress, U.S.)

After assuming office, President Ford nominated former New York Gov. Nelson A. Rockefeller as his vice-presidential choice. On September 8 Ford granted Nixon a full pardon for all federal crimes committed during his terms in office. Ford's announcement was unexpected and evoked a great amount of controversy and protest. (*See* Ford; Nixon; Rockefeller.)

A number of the individuals caught up in the Watergate affair were attorneys. In addition to criminal prosecution, several of them faced disbarment. John W. Dean III, who had pleaded guilty to conspiracy charges in connection with the cover-up, was disbarred in Virginia; others disbarred included G. Gordon Liddy, Charles W. Colson, and Herbert W. Kalmbach. (Former Vice-President Spiro Agnew was also disbarred, but as a result of his no contest plea to a 1973 tax evasion charge.)

Of the five defendants in the cover-up conspiracy trial, John Mitchell, John Ehrlichman, H. R. Haldeman, and Robert Mardian were found guilty; Kenneth Parkinson was acquitted. Colson had pleaded guilty to earlier charges, and the Watergate indictments against him had been dropped.

On September 25 the U.S. District Court of Appeals overturned the Army's 1971 My Lai murder conviction of former Army Lieut. William Calley, Jr. On November 19, after serving one third of his ten-year term, Calley was paroled by the Army. Also in November, eight National Guardsmen accused in the 1970 Kent State killings were acquitted

in criminal court. (*See* Colleges and Universities.)

In other legal proceedings throughout the country, a number of officials were prosecuted for other criminal matters. On May 16 Richard G. Kleindienst, who had resigned as U.S. attorney general in April 1973, pleaded guilty in a federal district court in Washington, D.C., to a misdemeanor charge that he had refused to testify "accurately and fully" before a Congressional committee investigating the Nixon Administration's handling of the controversial International Telephone and Telegraph antitrust case. California Lieut. Gov. Ed Reinecke was convicted of perjury in connection with the same matter. Congress later in the year passed a bill substantially increasing the penalties for those guilty of antitrust violations.

The Supreme Court of the United States on June 17 refused to hear an appeal by Otto Kerner, former governor of Illinois and the first sitting federal appellate judge to be convicted of a felony. He had been convicted on Feb. 19, 1973, of conspiracy,

*Former Army Lieut. William Calley, Jr. (right), leaves the Ft. Benning stockade in June to ask a federal court to overturn his 1971 My Lai murder conviction.*

UPI COMPIX

Palestinians raise
their flag over ruins
of a Nabatieh, Lebanon,
refugee camp bombed
by Israeli planes in a
May 16 reprisal strike
for the Ma'alot
schoolhouse massacre.
UPI COMPIX

fraud, perjury, bribery, and income tax evasion in conjunction with the sale of racetrack stock. On July 29 Kerner entered prison to begin his three-year sentence.

Legislative enactments also made headlines during the year. On July 23 President Nixon signed a bill extending the National Cancer Act through fiscal 1977. The new law authorized $2.8 billion for cancer research over a three-year period. On September 2 President Ford signed a pension reform bill, the Employee Retirement Income Security Act of 1974, establishing federal standards for private pension plans. On September 16 he signed a proclamation offering Vietnam War-era deserters and draft evaders who had left the country an opportunity to earn reentry into the U.S. by swearing an oath of allegiance and by performing up to two years of alternate public service. The proclamation met with mixed reaction. (*See also* Consumer Affairs; Crime; Environment; Police; Prisons; Supreme Court of the U.S.; United States.)

## LEBANON.

The principal problem for Lebanon in 1974 was guerrilla raids against Israel by Palestinians living in the southern part of the country. Although the guerrillas had promised in 1973 to stop the attacks, they did not do so. Neither was the Lebanese government willing to risk arousing Palestinian hostility by preventing the attacks on Israel. As a result, Israel attacked Palestinian refugee camps and southern Lebanese villages, as well as the Lebanese ports of Sur, Sidon, and Ras a-Shak, sometimes causing heavy damage and casualties.

Lebanon turned more and more to Arab countries for military aid to strengthen its weak military force and to protect itself against Israel. At the same time, Lebanon tried to restrict the availability of more sophisticated weapons to the Palestinian guerrillas for fear that such weapons would only further antagonize the Israelis.

The presence and activities of the Palestinians led to serious domestic conflicts as well. Palestinians and right-wing Lebanese fought in the streets during the year. Attempts by the government to ban the carrying of firearms by citizens, as a way of preventing such clashes, helped lead to the fall of the government in September. Prime Minister Takieddin al-Solh resigned, and former Prime Minister Saeb Salam was asked to form a new government.

There were other serious domestic problems as well. Although Lebanon benefited from the rising incomes of Arab states and although manufacturing exports more than doubled in value over 1973 levels, inflation was high. Attempts by the government to control prices and profits were not wholly successful. In addition, police stormed the American University of Beirut in April to control student protests. The Roman Catholic community protested civil service reforms that took many key positions from them. (*See also* Israel; Middle East.)

**LIBRARIES.** Efforts in the area of library development were characterized in 1974 by a growing, worldwide emphasis on the need for an international standardization of library techniques. A meeting on the "national planning of documentation and library services," devoted to Arabic-speaking countries, was held at Cairo, Egypt, in February. It was the final meeting in a series of regional conferences that culminated in the International Conference on Planning of National Overall Documentation, Library, and Archives Infrastructures held in Paris in September, sponsored by the United Nations Educational, Scientific, and Cultural Organization (UNESCO).

At its annual General Council held in Washington, D.C., in November, the International Federation of Library Associations (IFLA) took up the theme of "national and international planning of libraries." Another agenda item, that of "universal bibliographical control" (UBC), adopted by IFLA in 1973, was developed further by IFLA's committee on cataloging, the international office for UBC.

Librarians in many countries pushed ahead in their efforts to arrive at one standard classification scheme for books and documents. In the U.S.S.R., Soviet librarians called for a one-volume edition of the "BBK" classification system, widely used in Eastern Europe, while in East Germany a five-volume edition was authorized. In East Germany, too, work proceeded on the coordinating of German and Russian thesauri for use in subject-indexing and mechanized information retrieval, and on multilingual coordination under UNESCO auspices. In West Germany plans were formulated for a centralized book selection service for libraries, to be administered by the Central Library Supply Center in Reutlingen.

In the public library field the U.S.S.R. reported steady progress during 1974, with a total of more than 126,000 libraries serving some 105 million readers—an increase of 20 million readers in ten years. In Canada the Toronto, Ont., Public Library undertook the development of a services-to-immigrants program, and a multicultural language and literature center was founded at the National Library in Ottawa, Ont.

There were developments, too, in the area of university libraries. In Africa, for example, where librarianship generally lacked academic recognition and where most university libraries lacked trained staffs, the University of Zambia completed construction of a new library incorporating such features as open planning and open access to subject sections. In West Germany the Library of Bochum opened its audiovisual center, and new buildings went up at Dortmund and Freiburg im Breisgau. Other notable library openings in 1974 included the Bibliothèque Universitaire de Poitiers, France; the National Library of Ivory Coast at Abidjan; and, in Moscow, the Fundamental Library of the Social Sciences of the U.S.S.R. Academy of Sciences. In Iran library training courses leading to B.A. and M.A. degrees were instituted at two universities.

In the United States both public and school libraries, coast to coast, continued to widen their range of activities. The increasing emphasis on audiovisual media, and on electronic and nonprint materials, sparked a growing debate over the value of reading and the place of the library.

**LIBYA.** Libya enjoyed a threefold increase in oil revenues in 1974 as a result of the world increase in oil prices. Libyan policy was not always in line with that of other Arab oil producers, notably Saudi Arabia. Col. Muammar el-Qaddafi, however, remained adamant about the importance of the continued political role of oil in Middle Eastern affairs —in the Palestinian question in particular—and was in addition in favor of further increases in price.

Most of the year was marked by poor relations between Libya and Egypt. Qaddafi accused President Anwar el-Sadat of Egypt of sabotaging the proposed federation of Egypt, Syria, and Libya, and relations reached a low level in April when Libyan involvement in an attack on the Egyptian Military Technical College near Cairo was suspected by

UPI COMPIX

*Libyan Colonel Qaddafi and Tunisian President Bourguiba discuss in January the planned merger of their two countries into one "Arab Islamic Republic." Two days after official proclamation of the union, however, it was indefinitely postponed by Tunisia.*

the Egyptians. Angry exchanges followed, including accusations that a Qaddafi-initiated submarine attack on the Jewish tourist cruise through the Mediterranean on the *Queen Elizabeth 2* in 1973 had been prevented only by a countermanding order from Sadat. The latter's revelation in early August of the presence in Egypt of Libyan French-made Mirage jets was embarrassing to both the Libyan and French governments. Meanwhile, early in July, President Gaafar al-Nimeiry had accused Libya of plotting against the Sudan. In a letter published in October, Qaddafi openly advocated overthrow of Sadat in favor of a "people's" government.

At the end of a six-day visit to France in March by the Libyan prime minister, Maj. Abdul Salam Jalloud, a long-term Franco-Libyan cooperative agreement was signed. Under it, in exchange for oil, France would assist Libya in the construction of nuclear power stations and in other industrial energy projects and also in banking and finance. In April it was announced that Qaddafi would lay aside political and administrative functions and devote himself to "ideological" work It was expected that more work would devolve upon Jalloud, who visited the U.S.S.R. in May; agreement on trade and economic, scientific, and technical cooperation was reached. (*See also* Middle East; Tunisia.)

**LITERATURE.** In stepping down as editor in chief at G. P. Putnam's Sons in 1974, William Targ warned the publishing industry in the United States that its practices were working against the survival of large publishing houses. Singling out in particular a current lack of care in book editing and production, large advances, and a tendency to endorse "one-shot" projects by nonprofessionals, Targ advocated a return to long and productive relationships between editor and author based on "courtesy, fair play, and publishing for a profit." Targ's remarks came in a year when economies seemed to have become the major factors in book publishing. Overall sales of new hardback books were down, costs were up, and fewer textbooks seemed destined for mass adoptions. Translators lobbied and editors struck for higher wages. Book publishing cooperatives were announced, and established writers went increasingly to small, marginal presses with their work. Some kind of reorganization appeared imminent as actual book editing and production continued to be damaged by understaffing and cheapened manufacture.

### Nonfiction

A large number of the books published in 1974 dealt with the happenings in Washington, D.C. Publishers went to newspaper and television reporters for "in depth" studies of the issues and personalities that were making news headlines. Among the books that dealt directly or indirectly with politics were 'Impeachment' by Charles L. Black, Jr., 'Executive Privilege' by Raoul Berger, 'The Mask of State' by Mary McCarthy, 'The Jaws of Victory' by the Ripon Society, 'Test of Loyalty' by Peter Schrag, 'The Watergate Hearings' by *The New York Times*, and the "infamous" official White House transcript of Watergate-related tapes. Leading the books dealing with the personalities involved was Carl Bernstein and Bob Woodward's 'All the President's Men'. Less successful in winning readers were television reporters Marvin Kalb and Bernard Kalb, who tried to come to terms with 'Kissinger'. Jeb Stuart Magruder contributed 'An American Life', and Richard M. Cohen and Jules Witcover wrote 'A Heartbeat Away: The Investigation and Resignation of Vice President Spiro T. Agnew'. Richard T. Johnson's 'Managing the White House' told of the problems involved with being U.S. president, and Andrew M. Greeley surveyed governmental policies in 'Building Coalitions'.

The whole problem of secrecy and of private and public access that colored much of the Watergate testimony was treated in 'State Secrets' by Paul Cowan, Nick Egleson, and Nat Hentoff; 'Private Lives and Public Surveillance' by James B. Rule; and 'None of Your Business', a collection of essays and comments edited by Norman Dorsen and Stephen Gillers. John C. Raines's 'Conspiracy' approached the Harrisburg trial and the attempt to control freedom of expression. If government attempts at censorship suffered a setback at Harrisburg, they suffered an even more embarrassing one when Victor Marchetti and John D. Marks's 'The CIA and the Cult of Intelligence' saw print. Marchetti, a former Central Intelligence Agency (CIA) official, and Marks, a former State Department employee, were allowed to restore nearly 200 passages cut by the CIA as "sensitive."

Suffering from the publishing industry's interests in government were its highly publicized efforts to give voice to the black, the American Indian, and women. Fewer overt "consciousness-raising" works appeared, and those few that dealt with blacks and women—such as Maya Angelou's 'Gather Together in My Name', Elizabeth Hardwick's 'Seduction and Betrayal', and Kate Millett's 'Flying'—did so with a new seriousness. Identity was still vitally important for Erik H. Erikson's 'Dimensions of a New Identity' and Juliet Mitchell's 'Psychoanalysis and Feminism'; and Watergate did not keep readers from a new treatment of evolution in Jacob Bronowski's 'The Ascent of Man'; Bruce Catton's 'Gettysburg: The Final Fury'; 'The Freud/Jung Letters'; Piers Paul Read's account of the survivors of a plane crash in the Andes, 'Alive'; Carlos Castaneda's 'Tales of Power'; Mary McCarthy's observations on Hanoi, Vietnam, and Captain Medina, 'The Seventeenth Degree'; or William F. Buckley, Jr.'s report as a UN delegate, "United Nations Journal'. The 1930's were treated in 'Stage Left' by Jay Williams, 'The Devil's Decade' by Claud Cockburn, and Anne Morrow Lindbergh's 'Locked Rooms and Open Doors'. World War II furnished

An Experiment in Literary Investigation
For years I have with reluctant heart withheld from publication this already completed book: my obligation to those still living outweighed my obligation to the dead. But now that State Security has seized the book anyway, I have no alternative but to publish it immediately.
THE AUTHOR

*Nobel laureate Aleksandr Solzhenitsyn's 'The Gulag Archipelago, 1918–1956' unveils a harsh portrait of the Soviet penal system and labor camps and was the first tome of what was expected to be a three-volume work.*

LEFT: KEYSTONE. RIGHT: COURTESY, HARPER & ROW PUBLISHERS, INC.

the subjects for Cornelius Ryan's 'A Bridge Too Far' and Jim Bishop's 'FDR's Last Year'. Alonzo L. Hamby went 'Beyond the New Deal'. The Kennedy interests were kept alive by Rose Fitzgerald Kennedy's 'Times to Remember' and David E. Koskoff's 'Joseph P. Kennedy'. Daniel P. Moynihan wrote of his experiences under three presidents in 'Coping'. 'Letters of Hart Crane and His Family' were edited by Thomas S. W. Lewis, and those of Alice B. Toklas by Edward Burns as 'Staying on Alone'. 'Engels, Manchester, and the Working Class' were the subjects of Steven Marcus' latest book, while both Dr. Benjamin Spock ('Raising Children in a Difficult Time') and educator John Holt ('Escape from Childhood') devoted themselves to matters of upbringing in the 1970's.

Readers were also treated to new biographies of 'Roger Casement' by Brian Inglis, 'Lincoln Steffens' by Justin Kaplan, 'Alfred Stieglitz' by Dorothy Norman, 'Pablo Casals' by H. L. Kirk, 'Eisenhower' by Peter Lyon, 'De Gaulle' by Brian Crozier, 'Hitler' by Joachim C. Fest, Hermann Goering by Leonard Mosley ('The Reich Marshal'), 'Faulkner' by Joseph Blotner, Robert Moses by Robert A. Caro ('The Power Broker'), 'Gesualdo' by Glenn Watkins, 'Thomas Jefferson' by Fawn M. Brodie, 'Brezhnev' by John Dornberg, 'Stalin' by Adam B. Ulam, Gertrude Stein by James R. Mellow ('Charmed Circle'), Harry S. Truman by Merle Miller ('Plain Speaking'), Bernard DeVoto by Wallace Stegner ('The Uneasy Chair'), 'Whistler' by Stanley Weintraub and by Roy McMullen ('Vic-

torian Outsider'), 'Evelyn Waugh and His World' by David Pryce-Jones, T. S. Eliot by T. S. Matthews ('Great Tom'), 'Oscar Wilde' by Martin Fido, Robert Browning by William Irvine and Park Honan ('The Book, the Ring, and the Poet'), Yukio Mishima by Henry Scott-Stokes ('The Life and Death of Yukio Mishima'), George Gissing by Gillian Tindall ('The Born Exile'), 'Arnold Bennet' by Margaret Drabble, 'Aldous Huxley' by Sybille Bedford, John Wilmot, Earl of Rochester, by Graham Greene ('Lord Rochester's Monkey'), and 'The Life of Emily Dickinson' by Richard B. Sewall. Dumas Malone published volume five of his definitive biography of Thomas Jefferson, 'Jefferson the President: Second Term, 1805–1809'.

Supreme Court Justice William O. Douglas wrote of his early life in 'Go East, Young Man', and Frank Sheed, cofounder of the Sheed & Ward publishing house, of his religious involvement in 'The Church and I'. Astronaut Michael Collins related his personal experiences in 'Carrying the Fire'. Volume five of Anaïs Nin's 'Diary' also appeared, covering the years 1947–55, and Malcolm Muggeridge issued the second installment of his 'Chronicles of Wasted Time'. Playwright-actor Emlyn Williams described his life from 1927 to 1935 in 'Emlyn', and novelist Louis Auchincloss his youth in 'A Writer's Capital'. Meyer Levin's troubles with the Frank family and his suit over the play version of 'The Diary of Anne Frank' formed the basis of his 'The Obsession'. Less overtly autobiographical were Stephen Spender's 'Love-Hate Relations' and

'If Beale Street Could Talk', James Baldwin's 13th book, is a first-person narrative novel of a traditional love story set in the Lower East Side of New York City.

LEFT: JILL KREMENTZ. RIGHT: COURTESY, THE DIAL PRESS

Robert Graves's 'Difficult Questions, Easy Answers'. The visionary experience in literature was the topic of Joyce Carol Oates's 'New Heaven, New Earth', and Jacques Barzun wrote of 'The Use and Abuse of Art'. I. A. Richards collected together his recent observations into 'Beyond'. F. R. Leavis' 'Letters in Criticism' was issued, and Francis Murphy edited 'The Uncollected Essays and Reviews of Yvor Winters'. Kurt Vonnegut, Jr., collected his comments on sundry issues into 'Wampeters, Foma & Granfalloons'. Bruno Bettelheim continued his analyses of conditions for emotional therapy in 'A Home for the Heart'.

## Fiction and Poetry

Outstanding fiction by Philip Roth ('My Life as a Man'), Dan McCall ('Jack the Bear'), Wendell Berry ('The Memory of Old Jack'), Jeff Fields ('A Cry of Angels'), Alison Lurie ('The War Between the Tates'), and Iris Murdoch ('The Sacred and Profane Love Machine') paced a strong list of new novels that included Vladimir Nabokov's 'Look at the Harlequins', James Baldwin's 'If Beale Street Could Talk', and John Hawkes's 'Death, Sleep & the Traveler'. Joseph Heller contributed his first novel since 'Catch-22' with 'Something Happened', and Tillie Olsen pieced together fragments from her writing in the 1930's for 'Yonnondio'. Richard Brautigan wrote a Gothic western in 'The Hawkline Monster'. 'The Messengers Will Come No More' marked Leslie A. Fiedler's entry into science fiction. Upset with the country's plans for the bicentennial,

James A. Michener celebrated in his own way with 'Centennial'. Louis Auchincloss looked at a Wall Street law firm in 'The Partners', and Sue Kaufman at housewives in 'Falling Bodies'. In one of the year's better-selling books ('Jaws'), Peter Benchley told of a white shark menacing a Long Island resort. Suspense was the key to Paul Gallico's 'The Boy Who Invented the Bubble Gun', John le Carré's 'Tinker, Tailor, Soldier, Spy', and Joseph Hayes's 'The Long Dark Night'. David Wagoner published 'The Road to Many a Wonder', R. V. Cassill 'The Goss Women', John Knowles 'Spreading Fires', and Anthony Burgess 'Napoleon Symphony'. Other interesting new novels included Maxine Kumin's 'The Designated Heir', Lois Gould's 'Final Analysis', Anthony Caputi's 'Loving Evie', Evan S. Connell's 'The Connoisseur', and Gore Vidal's 'Myron'.

Grace Paley returned to publishing after a long silence with a distinguished collection of stories, 'Enormous Changes at the Last Minute'. Other strong story collections were Shirley Ann Grau's 'The Wind Shifting West', Joyce Carol Oates's 'The Hungry Ghosts', Carol Emshwiller's 'Joy in Our Cause', Tennessee Williams' 'Eight Mortal Ladies Possessed', Roald Dahl's 'Switch Bitch', V. S. Pritchett's 'The Camberwell Beauty and Other Stories', and 'The Ebony Tower' by John Fowles.

Notable collections of poems included the posthumously edited 'Collected Poems' of Paul Goodman and 'Thank You, Fog: Last Poems' by W. H. Auden, as well as volumes of selected poems by

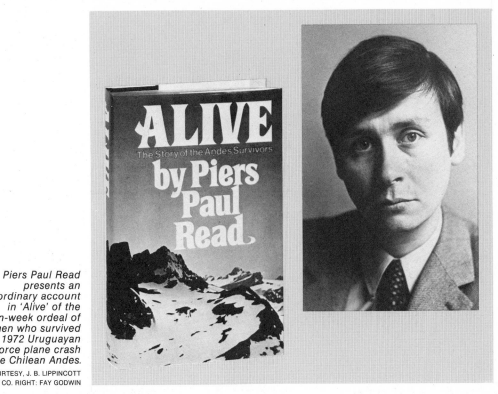

*Piers Paul Read presents an extraordinary account in 'Alive' of the ten-week ordeal of 16 men who survived the 1972 Uruguayan air force plane crash in the Chilean Andes.*

LEFT: COURTESY, J. B. LIPPINCOTT CO. RIGHT: FAY GODWIN

Galway Kinnell ('The Avenue Bearing the Initial of Christ into the New World'), Peter Davison ('Walking the Boundaries'), and David Ray ('Gathering Firewood'). New volumes included 'Residue of Song' by Marvin Bell, 'An Ordinary Woman' by Lucille Clifton, 'Looking for Holes in the Ceiling' by Stephen Dunn, 'Man-Fate: The Swan Song of Brother Antoninus' by William Everson, 'Noise in the Trees' by William Heyen, 'Two-Part Inventions' by Richard Howard, '1933' by Philip Levine, 'New Poems' by Kenneth Rexroth, 'Hymn to Life' by James Schuyler, 'The Death Notebooks' by Anne Sexton, 'Correspondences' by Anne Stevenson, 'Other Hand' by Dabney Stuart, 'The Secret Look' by Jessamyn West, and 'The Hidden Waterfall' by Marya Zaturenska. There were also distinguished first volumes of poems by Carl Dennis ('A House of My Own'), Anthony Petrosky ('Waiting Out the Rain'), and Joseph Stroud ('In the Sleep of Rivers').

## Literature Abroad

The expulsion of Nobel prize laureate Aleksandr I. Solzhenitsyn from his homeland in 1974 colored the literary news from the Soviet Union. The exile came as a result of the publication of 'The Gulag Archipelago, 1918–1956'. The government complained that the work was an inaccurate, pro-Nazi account of World War II rather than an indictment of the Soviet penal and labor camp system up to 1956. Solzhenitsyn, who had been under increasing attack since the appearance of 'The Cancer Ward' in 1968, had had only two books published in the Soviet Union: 'One Day in the Life of Ivan Denisovich' (1962) and a collection of four short stories (1966). These two works were removed from all Soviet public libraries except those with locked archives designated for materials considered objectionable. Support for Solzhenitsyn from fellow writers met with decisive counterpressure. Vladimir Voinovich, the first to speak in defense of the Nobel laureate, was expelled from the Soviet Writers Union. Less severe measures were taken against the poet Yevgeny Yevtushenko, who charged that the truth about Stalinist terror was being suppressed in Soviet literature and in history texts. Yevtushenko assailed writers who had signed the petition supporting the exile of Solzhenitsyn. Novelist Viktor Nekrasov complained of pressure from the Soviet Writers Union to force him to denounce Solzhenitsyn and applied for permission to leave the country. In a move toward conciliation, the Writers Union saw to it that Nekrasov's living conditions were improved. The poem 'There Is No Poet Outside the People' was interpreted by some Western critics as an effort by Yevtushenko to ease his own situation with the Writers Union. Yevtushenko hotly denied the work in any way attacks Solzhenitsyn. More in keeping with what the government wanted was Ivan Stadnyuk's novel 'War', which made a strong defense of Stalin's behavior during World War II.

In China, 'Whirling Snow Brings Spring', a first novel written by Chinese miners on their life and struggles, made it to the best-seller lists. The novel's main writers were reported to be a miner, an army

*The second volume of criticism by Joyce Carol Oates, 'New Heaven, New Earth', explores the critical duality experience by "visionary" writers— among them Franz Kafka, Virginia Woolf, and Samuel Beckett—in their search beyond the constraints of reality and society and their simultaneous need to function within that same society.*

LEFT: JACK ROBINSON. RIGHT: COURTESY, VANGUARD PRESS, INC.

veteran, and a young engineer, although four veteran miners were said to have acted as advisers, reading the work chapter by chapter, suggesting changes and additions, and making comments. The disclosure of multiple authorship refuted the idea of a single author, Chou Liang-szu, whose name had accompanied excerpts of the work in magazines.

In Italy and France, memoirs and diaries seemed to dominate as the distinguished Italian novelist Mario Soldati issued 'Un prato di papaveri', his diary from 1947 to 1964, book publisher Valentino Bompiani 'Via privata', writer-diplomat André Malraux 'La tête d'obsidienne', and poet Pierre Reverdy 'Note éternelle du présent', his writings on art from 1923 to 1960. Far less interesting were Giorgio Manganelli's newspaper contributions, collected into 'Lunario dell'orfano sannita'. Franco Codero's 'Viene il re' and Bruno Guy-Lussac's 'L'homme violet' were among the new novels published. Poets Mario Tobino ('L'asso di picche e Veleno e amore secondo'), Camillo Pennati ('Erosagonie'), Sandro Boccardi ('Ricercari'), Sebastiano Grasso ('Il giuoco della memoria'), and Roberto Pazzi ('L'esperienza anteriore') contributed new books of poems.

Uruguay's Juan Carlos Onetti, considered one of the top novelists writing in Latin America, was jailed when a story that he voted to give a literary prize to was declared obscene and subversive by Uruguay's right-wing military government. The story, 'The Bodyguard', by Winston Nelson Marra, was based on the killing of a police inspector by Uruguayan Tupamaro guerrillas. Presumably based on real life situations, it angered authorities who saw the story supportive of the Tupamaro movement. Before his release, Onetti suffered a nervous breakdown and spent 94 days in a clinic.

André P. Brink's 'Knowledge of the Night', judged last year's best work in Afrikaans, got into trouble with the government of South Africa. The 500-page novel treats two explosive topics: sex between races and police treatment of nonwhites. It was the first major work in the Dutch-derived first language of much of the political establishment to be attacked. Usually the books banned by the government for treating touchy issues had been in English. Nadine Gordimer, who had had more books banned than any other South African author, supported efforts to get the Brink novel circulated. She felt that a concerted effort by both English and Afrikaans writers might totally remove censorship.

No effort, however, was made by the Singapore government to control the sale of T. K. S. George's 'Lee Kuan Yew's Singapore'. The book, an attack on Prime Minister Lee Kuan Yew, quickly became a best-seller, though the work was not expected to cause any immediate changes. The people of Singapore seemed satisfied enough with their government to want inequities more serious than those George pointed out before seeking redress.

The world's record auction price for a manuscript set in 1966 was equaled in 1974 when Lew D. Feldman, a New York City dealer for the House of El Dieff, Inc., paid $216,000 for a copy of Geoffrey Chaucer's 'Canterbury Tales'. The manuscript dated to about 1440. (*See also* Awards and Prizes; Literature for Children; Magazines; Newspapers.)

# Literature

## Special Report:
# America's Contribution to World Literature

by Jerome Mazzaro

Ralph Waldo Emerson's "intellectual Declaration of Independence" of America from "the courtly muses of Europe" in "The American Scholar" (1837) has come to be the central document in an effort to fix America's unique contribution to Western literature. Before 1837, "the spirit of the American freeman" was "timid, imitative, tame." Edward Taylor, William Cullen Bryant, and Royall Tyler could be seen as derivative of an English tradition. Ben Franklin claimed Joseph Addison as his model, and even the "originality" of the political writers was tempered by traditional forms of expression. Only the early American tendency to experiment, to look toward the future rather than the past, and to focus on how things worked promised a basis for hoping that Emerson's "declaration" would succeed. Displaced from the settled towns and cultures of Europe, both Puritan and non-Puritan were forced to come to terms with "the inhuman remoteness of the landscape" they encountered by either imposing their wills upon it, letting the landscape shape them, or mutually interacting. If the writer wanted a complex and satisfying moral world, he had to build it, often at the cost of a subjectivism bordering on the psychological.

### American Contributions

By the end of the 19th century, American literature could boast of having contributed to Western literature three unmistakably American masterpieces: Herman Melville's 'Moby-Dick' (1851), Walt Whitman's 'Leaves of Grass' (1855), and Mark Twain's 'Adventures of Huckleberry Finn' (1885). The interlacing of "how to" material amid epic simile, Shakespearean language, and a Homeric confrontation of man and whale gives the Melville work its peculiarly American stamp. Its pragmatic realizations of metaphysical issues make classic its statement of America's willingness to tolerate any amount of violence in the monomaniacal pursuit of an ideal. 'Leaves of Grass' introduces a leveling expansiveness into world letters with its celebration of occupations, its embrace of contradictions, and its binding of an entire continent by love and understanding. Coming after the Civil War, Twain's novel deals with the difficulties of returning to innocence and, by a very refusal to accept closure, illustrates, in turn, America's unwillingness to grow up. Indeed, the sense of perpetual open-endedness, of "having come through," beginning again and being able to visualize a better world runs through the most typically American accomplishments. By the early 20th century, Sigmund Freud could say that the country's Rousseauistic optimism would prevent it from ever accepting his views about sex or the workings of the mind.

But America's unique contributions to Western literature extend beyond these three books to embrace as well the native geniuses of Edgar Allan Poe, Emily Dickinson, and Gertrude Stein. In his poetry, Poe raised the psychological into the metaphysical by making mystery central to his universe and by using language as a way of evoking instead of explaining mystery. His view of words as mne-

*The great white whale challenges a whaling crew in Melville's symbolic novel 'Moby-Dick' (1851).*

monic tokens prepared the way for the French symbolists later in the century. In contrast, he wrote "how to" essays on both the poem and the short story, indicating an accord at least with scientists who tried to explain mystery away. Emily Dickinson reversed the manner of Poe by turning the commonplace magically into metaphysical observations without exaggeration that might make her poetry comic. The very humbleness of her vision makes abstraction and religion immanent in a subjective and almost mystical way, and wit keeps her vision from becoming prolix or sentimental. To Gertrude Stein belongs the most successful effort to use contemporary experiments in psychology and break completely with the past and metaphysics. Her work concentrates on how to make language a "continuous present" and on the meaning of words —not their origins and histories, but the sums of their effects. Each of her works constitutes an advancement over its immediate predecessor so that the entirety of her writing, like a history of science, is made up of a series of experiments built one upon the other—successes, failures, but few repeats.

## The Battle of Tradition

Perhaps no character in American literature so successfully represents to non-Americans what settling the frontier was like as does 'Leatherstocking', or Natty Bumppo. As hero of a five-novel sequence that James Fenimore Cooper began to publish in 1823 with 'The Pioneers' and completed in 1841 with 'The Deerslayer', he upsets the process of his author and life by growing younger in the later volumes and establishing a theme of regression that becomes prevalent in the 20th century. The entire

*Mark Twain's late-19th-century fiction led American literature from romance to realism.*

sequence spans 60 years and half a continent before the protagonist dies in exile and honor among the Pawnee Indians. Equally successful at capturing the spirit of the country's past is Nathaniel Hawthorne's 'The Scarlet Letter' (1850), a novel modeled on the religious plays of the French dramatist Jean Racine and critical of the scientific imagination. For Hawthorne, man's character is so determined by his history and environment that the possibilities of choice are limited. Only the American Revolution with its break with political traditions offered any relief by assuming an eschatological aura.

In his looking backward, Hawthorne achieves the first significant wedding of individual innovation with a consciously adopted Western past. A second writer in this tradition is Henry Wadsworth Longfellow, whose 'Song of Hiawatha' (1855) is an epic on the American Indian written in a Finnish meter. Longfellow went repeatedly to Continental sources for his themes, forms, and subjects, and even more than Hawthorne is credited with having begun what is sometimes called "the metropolitan tradition." Also in this tradition is Henry James, whose novels of Americans abroad deal intimately with manners and often convert Hawthorne's preoccupations with evil into social and psychological referents. After James, the tradition is best seen in the writings of the expatriate writers of the 1920's: Ezra Pound, T. S. Eliot, Ernest Hemingway, and F. Scott Fitzgerald. Their work achieves an international coloring that anticipates the bridging of Europe by modern technology and the country's move out of isolationism in the 1940's.

At the same time, the greatest of America's playwrights, Eugene O'Neill, was using the Scandinavian dramatists August Strindberg and Henrik Ibsen and the Irish dramatists John Millington Synge and Sean O'Casey to fashion his plays about the betrayals of values and illusions. The openness of the American wilds was soon being pitted by William Faulkner against the oppressions of an inherited Christian culture. However heroic, those who were possessed by the past were as damned as those who were entirely outside Christian time. Life was no more than a losing battle with tradition.

## Underlying Philosophy

Supporting these writers was a distinctly American philosophy of pragmatism. Begun by Charles Peirce and continued by William James and John Dewey, pragmatism sought to define things in terms of response. For Peirce, the underlying motivation was a logic of science that he called "abduction." Peirce hoped that the correlation of a number of effects would secure definition in the same way that scientific experiments lead to hypotheses. For James, "truth" is what works in the long run. James's more subjective approach to conditions suits his interests in psychology and complements his notion of consciousness as a stream in which certain memories and sensations keep flowing into one another. Finally, Dewey converts this "stream of consciousness" into "contexts of experience" and in 'Art as Experience' (1934) develops a purely American aesthetics on the basis of a continuity of experience instead of formal principles. Unity becomes a system of fusions—including those with "fringe" elements outside the artwork—that exists so long as a problematic situation does not arise to force breakage by a discontinuous counter quality of discrimination or analysis.

The 1930's saw changes in these preoccupations. The "novel of initiation" became popular as protagonists entered the arenas of social interaction by way of injustice or sex. Richard Wright described the difficulties of American blacks in achieving notice in a "land of plenty," and John Steinbeck wrote of the hardships that weather, bad farming, and economics generated. After World War II the black became Ralph Ellison's "invisible man," and the "novel of initiation" was opposed by works of innocence like J. D. Salinger's 'Franny and Zooey'.

Increasingly, European ideas began to prevail. One of the most important new novelists, Vladimir Nabokov, had been born in Russia. Existentialism colored the vision of Norman Mailer, and in the writings of John Barth the critics of consciousness took precedence. Occasionally a writer like Joyce Carol Oates went back to a tradition of naturalism, but the majority of the writers continued the traditions of the 1920's. Robert Lowell succeeded Pound and Eliot as the mediator of "tradition" and "the individual talent," and Flannery O'Connor gave a new urgency to Faulkner's Christian burden. Allen Ginsberg showed the perverse realization of Whitman's America, and in an effort to come up with a new kind of lyric, Theodore Roethke combined nonsense, nursery rhyme, Elizabethan rant, depth psychology, mysticism, and the poetics of the German writer Rainer Maria Rilke.

### Constant Reinterpretation

Stein considered movement America's great contribution to world literature; it was "something strictly American to conceive a space that is filled with moving, a space of time that is filled always filled with moving." Others have seen the contribution as the tendency to look away from what is known toward what may be conjectured and tested by personal experience. This tendency has produced visionaries rather than craftsmen, and these visionaries show by their breaks with the past the authenticity of their visions and by their abilities to create fresh language that "they have used, and not been used by words."

Such a constant reinterpretation has kept American writers responsive to the changes technology has imposed, much as automobiles are redesigned annually so as to remain innovative and attractive. This ability to be flexible—often by moving with the surfaces of change—has become the dominant characteristic of recent American writing.

## LITERATURE FOR CHILDREN.

Rarely does a book for children become an instant classic, but the literary event of 1974 was certainly the acclaim received by Richard Adams for the fantasy 'Watership Down', which became a best-seller for both children and adults. Among the trends of the year were more books about feminine liberation and about the American Indian; there was a marked increase in the number of biographies and concept books for young independent readers.

### For Younger Readers

One of the most engaging of the year's picture books was 'Our Animal Friends at Maple Hill Farm' by Alice and Martin Provensen. Large pages gave the author-illustrators an opportunity to display lively drawings of many animals, their distinctive and amusing personalities clear in both pictures and text. Other books about animals were Eric Carle's 'All About Arthur', an alphabet book that stresses alliteration as Arthur, "an absolutely absurd ape," meets a series of animals: Ben the bear in Baltimore, Cindy the cat in Cincinnati, and so on; Lillian Hoban's beguiling 'Arthur's Honey Bear', in which a small monkey finds a way to give his sister a favorite toy without losing all vested interest; and Mercer Mayer's successful wordless picture book, 'Frog Goes to Dinner', a hilarious story about the upheaval in a restaurant caused by an amiable frog's leaping visits to unsuspecting diners.

There is humor also in Susan Jeschke's 'Firerose', a fantasy about a foundling child who has a delicate little green tail that creates a problem when she arrives at school age. Equally amusing and sophisticated is Russell Hoban's 'How Tom Beat Captain Najork and His Hired Sportsmen', a tall tale with an English setting and a hero who triumphs because of his experience in solitary play.

A gentle story of the love between a boy and his grandfather is unfolded some years after the latter's death, in a conversation between the boy and his mother in Charlotte Zolotow's 'My Grandson Lew', delectably illustrated by William Pène du Bois. Mary Ann Hoberman's 'Nuts to You and Nuts to Me' is a merry, breezy alphabet of poems. Trina Schart Hyman's illustrations vary from gaiety to serenity to fit the moods of the range of poems in Charles Causley's 'Figgie Hobbin'.

An alphabet book that shows many facets of African culture is 'Jambo Means Hello', a Swahili alphabet book written by Muriel Feelings and beautifully illustrated in black and white by Tom Feelings. Two excellent informational books are Aliki's 'Green Grass and White Milk', which describes the way cows digest grass and are milked and how milk is processed for consumers, and 'Shapes' by John Reiss, in which jewel-tone colors show geometric figures. A Pueblo Indian tale is retold in Gerald McDermott's 'Arrow to the Sun', and the stunning, stylized illustrations dramatically incorporate Indian art motifs.

Paula Fox's
'The Slave Dancer',
winner of the
Newbery Medal, is
a vivid account of
survival aboard a
slave ship in 1840.
COURTESY, BRADBURY PRESS, INC.

## For the 8-to-11 Group

Folk tales never lose their appeal, and one of the year's best collections was Dorothy Sharp Carter's 'Greedy Mariani'. Twenty tales from the Antilles are told in the cadenced style of the true oral tradition. Two other impressive anthologies were Hans Baumann's 'The Stolen Fire: Legends of Heroes and Rebels from Around the World', in which there is strong emphasis on ethical conduct, and 'Sea Magic and Other Stories of Enchantment' by Rosemary Harris, with ten legends, each from a different country, told in a rich, flowing style.

For this middle group, there was some fine fantasy: Susan Cooper's 'Greenwitch', third volume in a sequence of tales set in England, a series in which people have magical powers against the forces of evil, and Peter Dickinson's 'The Gift', in which a boy's mindreading ability involves him in an exciting and dangerous adventure. Verging on fantasy, Jonathan Gathorne-Hardy's entertaining 'Operation Peeg' describes a Scottish island that drifts off to sea with two schoolgirls, a housekeeper, and two British soldiers (who emerge from an intricate underground system where they've lived not knowing World War II was over) who cope with an arch-villain who wants to rule the world.

'The Ghost on Saturday Night' by Sid Fleischman is a tongue-in-cheek tale in which a small-town boy and his intrepid aunt play major roles in running a confidence man who raises "ghosts" out of town. The tales of Tom the Great Brain are peren-

nial favorites, and in John Fitzgerald's 'The Return of the Great Brain' the mercenary boy is as inventive as ever.

Bobbi Katz in 'The Manifesto and Me—Meg' struck a blow for feminine liberation as her organized group of girls is championed by an elderly woman who agrees that since they're too young to burn bras, they can (and do) burn their Taffy Teen dolls. Another doughty heroine is the teacher in Paula Danziger's 'The Cat Ate My Gymsuit'. Thirteen-year-old Marcy tells the story of a lively young English teacher whose students, and some parents, support her stand against a reactionary supervisor.

There is little humor in Eleanor Clymer's 'Luke Was There'. Fatherless, his mother in a hospital, Julius is in an institution when he meets Luke, a black social worker whose compassion and understanding give the boy much-needed security. Another good realistic book was Barbara Cohen's 'Thank You, Jackie Robinson', the story of another fatherless boy whose friendship with an elderly black man begins with their shared love of the Dodgers and ends with a touching demonstration of the child's love when the man lies dying.

'Our Fathers Had Powerful Songs', compiled by Natalia Belting, is a collection of poems from North American Indian tribes and is illustrated with quiet pictures that echo the reverence of the poetry. Another fine poetry collection, edited by Lilian Moore and Judith Thurman, is 'To See the World Afresh', and the care with which the editors have chosen the selections does indeed provide those

*Margot Zemach's whimsical illustrations for 'Duffy and the Devil', a version of the Rumpelstiltskin story, were awarded the Caldecott Medal.*
COURTESY, FARRAR, STRAUS & GIROUX, INC.

new perspectives that are the essence of poetry.

David Macaulay's 'City' is profusely illustrated with finely detailed drawings that extend the textual description of the planning and construction of an ancient Roman city. In 'How to Make Your Science Project Scientific' Thomas Moorman defines scientific attitudes and methods for investigation in a book that is lucid, objective, and sensible.

### For Older Adolescents

Each of Virginia Hamilton's books has shown some new facet of her talent. In 'M. C. Higgins, the Great' she writes about a black mountain family whose home is endangered by the spoil pile left by strip mining. The dialogue, setting, characters, mood, and theme are beautifully integrated in a story with depth and warmth.

Among the other outstanding realistic books of the year were Edward Fenton's 'Duffy's Rocks', the story of a Roman Catholic family in a grimy Pittsburgh suburb; Robert Cormier's 'The Chocolate War', a powerful depiction of bullying authoritarianism in a fund-raising drive held by a school; and Scott O'Dell's 'Child of Fire', the story of an idealistic young Chicano as told by his probation officer. The picture it draws is a perceptive and touching view of the dispossessed.

Two period pieces by distinguished English writers were 'The Sound of Coaches' by Leon Garfield and 'Midnight is a Place' by Joan Aiken. Both are rich in style, characterization, and dialect; both are essentially romantic. In Garfield's book a foundling

boy gives up a career as a coach driver to enter a Shakespearean touring company; in Aiken's story two orphaned children are forced into factory work when they lose their home and their guardian in a fire.

One of the best mystery stories of the year was Martin Cobalt's 'Pool of Swallows': it has humor, pace, suspense, a love interest, and a logical explanation for events that have seemed supernatural. One of the most interesting biographies of the year was James Haskins' 'Adam Clayton Powell', an admiring but candid account of the career of the controversial black political leader.

An outstanding anthology, 'Modern Poetry', was compiled by John Rowe Townsend. It contains the editor's favorite poems emanating from the 1930's through the 1960's. John FitzMaurice Mills's 'Treasure Keepers', an authoritative and fascinating book on the problems and practices of museum curators and their staffs, is lavishly illustrated with photographs of art objects. It describes forgeries, detection techniques, establishing credentials, caring for art objects, and the decisions a curator must make in displaying art treasures.

### Awards

The Newbery Medal, awarded by the American Library Association for the most distinguished contribution to children's literature in the preceding year, was won by Paula Fox for 'The Slave Dancer'; and the winner of the Caldecott Medal, given for the most distinguished picture book, was

Margot Zemach, for 'Duffy and the Devil' by Harve Zemach. The National Book Award went to Eleanor Cameron for 'The Court of the Stone Children'.

The Canadian Library Association's award for the best children's book of the year was given to Elizabeth Cleaver for 'The Miraculous Hind', and its award for the best picture book was given to William Kurelek for 'A Prairie Boy's Winter'. The Library Association of the United Kingdom chose Penelope Lively's 'The Ghost of Thomas Kempe' for the Carnegie Medal, given for the most outstanding children's book. The Greenaway Medal for the best picture book of the year went to Raymond Briggs for 'Father Christmas'.

The Hans Christian Andersen Medals, awarded biennially by an international jury to an author and to an illustrator for the body of their work, were given to Maria Gripe of Sweden for her writing and to Farshid Mesghali of Iran for his illustrations.

**MAGAZINES.** Besides inflation, two basic economic issues plagued magazine publishers in 1974—the rising cost of paper and the increase in postal rates. Slight gains in advertising revenue for most commercial titles were reported by the Publishers Information Bureau. More than $15 million was spent on product news in 1974 by leading magazine advertisers.

The U.S. Congress gave some relief to small-circulation magazines, which were especially hard hit by paper costs. Congress extended for three years the 127% postal rate increase approved in 1972, which originally was to be implemented over a five-year period. As an economy measure, several major publishers increased subscription prices, cut down on the number of pages per issue, and reduced the number of copies printed.

Challenging the current belief that general, mass circulation magazines are dead, Time Inc. introduced *People*, a national weekly. It was sold from newsstands and not by mail. Another national magazine launched in 1974 was tennis star Billie Jean King's *WomenSports*, devoted to all aspects of women in national and international sports.

More than 100 new alternative culture magazines were published in 1974. Magazines for special audiences—such as *Max*, for people over six feet tall—also proliferated. *Common Sense* was one of a number of new magazines dedicated to the observance of the country's bicentennial.

Among the magazines that failed in 1974 was *Architectural Forum*, which dated from 1892. *Intellectual Digest*, introduced in 1969, *Good Food*, a sister publication of *TV Guide*, and *Homelife*, which was just launched in the summer of 1973, also ceased publication during the year.

*Time* and *Newsweek* both published special issues on the resignation of U.S. President Richard M. Nixon. *Time*'s newsstand sale of 527,500 for that issue was believed to break all records for a news magazine. (*See also* Newspapers.)

*Editor Rosalie Wright (center) and staff members select cartoons for the first issue in May of WomenSports, a new magazine published by Billie Jean King.*
WIDE WORLD

*Her majesty the* raja permaisuri agong *of Malaysia arrives with Prince Philip, the duke of Edinburgh, at London's Buckingham Palace on July 9, beginning a four-day state visit to Great Britain with her husband, the* yang di-pertuan agong *of Malaysia.*

LONDON EVENING NEWS / PICTORIAL PARADE

## MALAGASY REPUBLIC.

On Jan. 1, 1974, Madagascar's seven agronomic research institutes were placed under a single Malagasy organization, with Malagasy-financed control. The institutes had previously been jointly financed by France and the Malagasy Republic. In similar circumstances the French-directed National Geographic Institute became the Cartographic Institute of Madagascar. The government also took a controlling share in various public utility companies. Later in January the republic signed two agreements, for trade and for economic and technical cooperation, with China in Peking. In February Gabriel Ramanjato, editor of the Tananarive newspaper *Bosy Vava*, was sentenced to a year's imprisonment for "defamation" of the army and police. In March the Social Democratic party merged with the Union Socialiste Malgache to form the Parti Socialiste Malgache.

President Gen. Gabriel Ramanantsoa's rural reorganization entered its second phase during the year. The essence of the scheme was the building up of a widespread economic and social pattern based on the self-organization of rural communities, which would sell their produce directly to a state company and avoid middlemen. The reorganization was attacked by the government's critics as creating a division in the island's life, under which the coastal people would work for the benefit of the Merinas of the plateau. In March lower wages and salaries in public and private sectors were raised to meet hardship in the face of steadily rising prices of basic foodstuffs, particularly rice.

In June closer relations were established with Tanzania. In August a new factory was opened to exploit Madagascar's deposits of marble, and in October the republic began to take its first population census, which was to be finished in 1975. (*See also* Africa.)

## MALAYSIA.

In the general elections held in August 1974, the National Front, a coalition led by Prime Minister Tun Abdul Razak and dominated by Malays but including some Chinese, won an overwhelming victory. One of the key domestic policies of the National Front was to continue to give the rural Malays preferential treatment in jobs and education over the urban Chinese, who in the past had prospered and had controlled large parts of the economy. Most Chinese viewed the policy as discriminatory. It was feared that the elections would incite racial violence between the Malays and the Chinese, who make up about one third of Malaysia's population, as had happened in the 1969 voting. The election was generally peaceful.

Earlier in the year Prime Minister Razak signed an agreement establishing full diplomatic relations with the People's Republic of China. As part of the agreement, China announced that it considered all Malaysian citizens of Chinese origins to have forfeited Chinese nationality and that all Chinese in Malaysia should abide by Malaysian law. The Malaysians apparently saw the agreement as strengthening their hand in their struggle against Communist insurgents.

Malaysia continued to enjoy a booming economy, although inflation continued and industrial growth showed some signs of slowing down. In 1973 export volume increased by 20% and export prices by 37%, and Malaysia had a large balance of payments surplus. These trends appeared to continue in 1974. Prime Minister Razak announced guidelines to restrict foreign acquisition of Malaysian companies through mergers and takeovers, and the national petroleum corporation began to take steps to end foreign domination of the country's oil industry. Industry was expected to become increasingly Malaysian in ownership. (*See also* Asia.)

**MALTA.** On Dec. 3, 1974, Malta became the 19th republic in the Commonwealth of Nations, and Gov. Gen. Sir Anthony Mamo took office as the first president. Earlier the government of Malta had taken steps to draw up a new constitution and held discussions on proposed amendments with the opposition. The country's highest court, which had not been in session since January 1972 except for three months in 1973, remained suspended. An opposition member submitted a complaint to the Council of Europe, whose Committee for Legal Affairs sent an investigator to report on the suspension.

As a result of talks with Great Britain, the government agreed in June to resume repayments of British loans, and Britain gave Malta substantial technical assistance. In July the European Economic Community (EEC) discussed Malta's request for a revision of the 1970 agreement intended to give preferential treatment for agricultural products exported by Malta to EEC countries. The EEC granted Malta additional concessions, but the government rejected them as inadequate.

In April the government wrote off a large liability incurred by the dry docks over the past few years. Work was started on the building of a 300,000-ton tanker dock, supervised by Chinese technicians, and a new shipbuilding complex was planned.

When national banks found themselves in difficulty, the government supplied capital and bought up to 60% of their equity. National insurance benefits and government employees' salaries were increased; the civil service started working a five-day week. In November family allowances for not more than three children were introduced. By the end of the year tourism had increased by about one third over 1973. Texaco Malta, Inc., was given the concession, for payment of $10 million, to drill for oil south of Malta. The government planned record expenditures for 1974–75 of $157.5 million, $32 million of which was for capital outlay.

# MARRIAGES. Among noteworthy marriages in 1974 were:

**Meredith Baxter,** 27, to David Birney, 34, stars of the now-defunct television series Bridget Loves Bernie; April 10, in New York City.

**Mariola Martínez Bordiu,** 21, granddaughter of Spanish chief of state Generalissimo Francisco Franco, to Rafael Ardid, 27, a Madrid lawyer; March 14, in Madrid, Spain.

**Bill Bradley,** 30, New York Knicks basketball star, to Ernestine Schlant, 38, a German-born professor at a New Jersey college; January 14, in Palm Beach, Fla.

**Eugene Chaplin,** 21, fifth of Charlie Chaplin's eight children, to Sandra Guignard, 20; August 10, in Brent, Switzerland.

**Faye Dunaway,** 37, film star ('Bonnie and Clyde', 'Chinatown'), to Peter Wolf, 28, composer and songwriter; August 7, in Beverly Hills, Calif.

**Julius Erving,** 24, New York Nets superstar, to

ARGUS/PHOTO TRENDS

*Princess Dlalisile, 17, daughter of King Sobhuza II of Swaziland, wed Vusi Tshabalala, son of a South African business tycoon, in Johannesburg, South Africa, on January 26.*

Turquoise Brown, 23; February 10, in New York City.

**Michael Ford,** 24, son of then Vice-President Gerald R. Ford, to Gayle Brumbaugh, 23; July 5, in Catonsville, Md.

**Paul Getty,** 17, grandson of millionaire J. Paul Getty, to Martine Zacher, 25, West German model-

*Baron David de Rothschild, 31, son of Baron Guy de Rothschild, and Olimpia Aldobrandini, daughter of an Italian businessman, were married in Reux, France, on June 29.*

A.F.P./PICTORIAL PARADE

UPI COMPIX

*Guru Maharaj Ji, 16, "perfect master" and spiritual leader of the Divine Light Mission, married his secretary, Marolyn Lois Johnson, 24, on May 20 in Denver, Colo.*

photographer; September 12, in Sovicille, Italy.

**Sanjay Gandhi,** 28, son of Indian Prime Minister Indira Gandhi, to Menaka Anand, 18; in September, in New Delhi, India.

**Huntington Hartford,** 63, heir to the A. & P. grocery fortune, to Elaine Kay, 21, former hairdresser; May 21, in New York City.

**Kenneth B. Keating,** 74, U.S. ambassador to Israel, to Mary Pitcairn Davis, 53; June 7, in Princeton, N.J.

**Henry Kissinger,** 51, U.S. secretary of state, to Nancy Maginnes, 39, staff director of Nelson Rockefeller's Commission on Critical Choices for Americans; March 30, in Arlington, Va.

**Marvin Mandel,** 54, governor of Maryland, to Jeanne Blackistone Dorsey, 37; August 13, in Baltimore, Md.

**Terry Anne Meeuwsen,** 25, Miss America of 1973, to Tom Camburn, 38, a sales manager; December 15, in Milwaukee, Wis.

**Liza Minnelli,** 28, superstar singer and actress ('Cabaret'), to Jack Haley, Jr., 40, film producer ('That's Entertainment'); September 15, in Montecito, Calif.

**Anna Moffo,** 39, Metropolitan Opera star soprano, to Robert Sarnoff, 56, board chairman of RCA; November 14, in New York City.

**Wayne Osmond,** 23, one of the singing Osmond brothers, to Kathlyn White, 21, reigning Miss Utah and Brigham Young University student; December 13, in Salt Lake City, Utah.

**Adm. Hyman Rickover,** 73, father of the nuclear submarine, to Comdr. Eleonore Bednowicz, 43, a Navy nurse; January 19, in Elmwood Park, Ill.

**Jane Russell,** 52, movie star of the 1940's, and John Peoples, 47, California real-estate broker; January 31, in Santa Barbara, Calif.

**Tommy Smothers,** 37, of the Smothers Brothers comedy act, to Rochelle Robley, 37; July 17, in Las Vegas, Nev.

**Sly Stone,** 30, rock superstar, to Kathy Silva, 20, actress, in a Madison Square Garden extravaganza before 21,000 fans; June 5, in New York City.

**Mary Wilson,** 30, only original member still singing with the Motown group The Supremes, to Pedro Antonio Ferrer, 30, road manager for the group; in May, in Las Vegas, Nev.

**Bob Woodward,** 31, *Washington Post*'s investigative Watergate reporter, to Frances Barnard, 28, Washington correspondent for the *Fort Worth Star-Telegram*; November 29, in Washington, D.C.

## MEDICINE.

Medical care in the United States cost more in 1974 than ever before. Caspar W. Weinberger—secretary of health, education, and welfare (HEW)—charged that doctors' fees and hospital bills provided "prominent fuel in the acceleration of the nation's inflation." In late fall the HEW secretary said that physician fees had gone up 19.1% in a year, while hospital costs rose 17.7%.

A Library of Congress research report, however, found that the median net income of office-based doctors, an estimated $42,700 a year, had not risen since 1970. Even so, leaders of the American Medical Association (AMA) urged physicians to practice "voluntary restraint." Malpractice insurance fees, clerical expenses for filing Medicare and Medicaid forms, and other rising costs were implicated in the great cost of U.S. health care. The Watergate controversy stalled attempts toward a national health insurance system. Congressional leaders predicted adoption of a plan by 1975.

### Doctor Shortage Abating Somewhat

A record 14,436 students entered 114 U.S. medical schools in 1974, bringing the total of future physicians in training to nearly 54,000. Teaching facilities were expanding: seven new medical schools opened in 1974; four others were to graduate their first class of doctors in 1975.

A National Health Service Corps (NHSC) was founded in 1970 to channel more doctors into regions sorely in need of health services, and to provide a military service alternative for medical students getting U.S. school aid. In late September the U.S. Senate stopped short of outright federal regulation of medical practice by rejecting a broad piece of legislation requiring all new physicians to serve in doctor-poor regions, under the NHSC program.

More than 200 Professional Standards Review Organizations (PSRO's) were scheduled to be functioning in the United States by early 1976. PSRO's were to monitor medical standards in all cases where federal tax money paid for care. This included care of patients under Medicare and Medicaid and, presumably, any future national health insurance plan. The AMA took a conciliatory stand on PSRO's, maintaining that peer review was all right as long as nondoctors were not involved in the process.

## Medical Advances in 1974

As U.S.-China relations improved, more medical experts visited China to observe the "wonders" of acupuncture firsthand. Many experts conceded, however, that too little research had been done to explain how, or even if, acupuncture really worked. A cooperative U.S.-Chinese effort not only might solve the acupuncture controversy but also might explain more about the puzzling nature of pain.

Perplexing, too, was the subject of fetal death. A National Foundation-March of Dimes study estimated that more than 38% of the more than 5.16 million conceptions in the U.S. in 1973 ended with the death of the fetus. Although induced abortions accounted for nearly a third of these ended pregnancies, some 1.34 million fetal deaths were unplanned. The causes of these spontaneous abortions were unknown, but scientists thought many were the result of flaws in the fetal genetic makeup.

The first known case of successful correction of a genetic flaw in an unborn child was recorded at Tufts–New England Medical Center in Boston. Doctors carefully tapped fetal amniotic fluid in the womb of a young mother to learn if her unborn child had a vitamin $B_{12}$-correctable enzymatic defect that killed another of her children. After finding the condition in the fetus, doctors gave the mother massive doses of vitamin $B_{12}$ in the last two months of pregnancy. Birth of a healthy child resulted.

The Middle Atlantic states suffered a brief, sharp attack of type B influenza in the early spring, but the flu "bug" was not as great a threat in early 1974 as in other years. A rare complication of flu called "Reye's syndrome" killed more than 300 children, however, principally in the Midwest. No available flu vaccine proved totally effective because the makeup of influenza viruses changed constantly. Late in 1974, however, about 2,000 New York area schoolchildren received a "hybrid" vaccine made of a potpourri of minor components of several past flu strains. It was hoped that the vaccine would inhibit production of a key viral protein.

A spinal meningitis vaccine was licensed by the Food and Drug Administration (FDA). The FDA allowed distribution of the vaccine to stem epidemics after the agency received convincing proof that the vaccine protected U.S. Army recruits against type C meningitis, a principal form.

The annoying "common cold" was yet unconquered, but Canadian and U.S. investigators cau-

*The Rodriguez sisters, Clara and Alta, of the Dominican Republic are examined three days after a team of 23 doctors and nurses at Children's Hospital of Philadelphia, Pa., separated the Siamese twins in a 10½-hour operation on September 18.*
UPI COMPIX

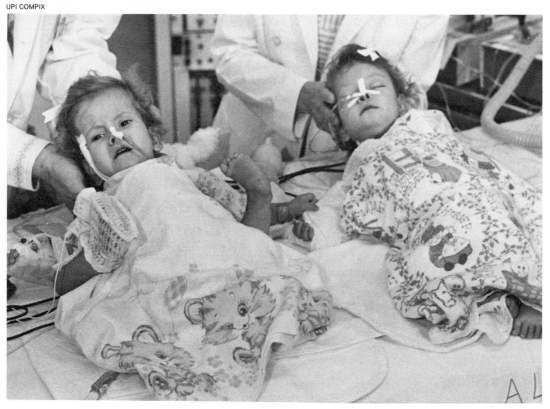

FROM LEFT: UPI COMPIX; WIDE WORLD; WIDE WORLD

*Three scientists (left to right)—Albert Claude, head of the Jules Bordet Institute in Brussels, Belgium, Christian de Duve of Rockefeller University in New York, and George Palade of Yale University in New Haven, Conn.—shared the 1974 Nobel prize for medicine.*

tiously endorsed vitamin C as a cold preventive, a role long advocated by Nobel laureate Linus Pauling. Nonetheless, prolonged intake of possibly harmful "megavitamin" doses was discouraged. A daily glass of orange juice or a cold tablet supplemented by the vitamin was innocuous and perhaps helpful, according to the scientists. A vaccine was thought to be on the way against serum hepatitis, an ailment that was striking more than 40,000 persons in the U.S. each year. With the virus associated with the disease uncovered at last, scientists in 1974 were trying to grow enough of it to make a vaccine.

Steps were taken to institute an all-volunteer blood donor system that would replace the old system of paid-for blood. The American Red Cross and others were trying to set up a donated-blood system, arguing that some of the purchased blood was infected by the hepatitis virus. Objections of some religious sects to blood transfusions were quelled through the application of autotransfusion. Hundreds of U.S. hospitals had the equipment to collect a person's own blood, filter and process it, and then return it to the body. Autotransfusion eliminated the hazards of crossmatching, allowed surgery on persons with rare blood types, and reduced transfusion costs.

### Cancer

About a quarter of the $2.6 billion in federal medical research funds went to the fight against cancer in 1974. Unfortunately, the American Cancer Society (ACS) said, this effort came too late to save the 355,000 victims of cancer during the year. An estimated 655,000 persons in the U.S. discovered that they had some form of cancer in 1974.

Awareness of breast cancer, a disease that killed some 33,000 persons, mostly women, in the U.S. each year, soared when two prominent women— Betty Ford, wife of the U.S. president, and "Happy" Rockefeller, wife of the vice-president-

designate—were found to have the disease. Both had radical mastectomy operations, removal of the afflicted breasts and surrounding tissue. Sparked anew was the surgical controversy over whether these extensive operations really improved cancer survival. Although many surgeons defended the technique, a study was underway to evaluate less disfiguring, simpler procedures.

Special brassieres fitted with tiny heat-sensing devices were also under study in 1974. By detecting the telltale hot spots in mammary tissue that could signal the presence of a malignant tumor, the bras could someday serve as an early-warning system.

Attempts continued to pinpoint a virus as a cause of human cancer. Viruses were known to produce animal cancers, but the viral role in human malignancies remained unproved. Albert B. Sabin, discoverer of an antipolio vaccine, coauthored a report claiming the cold sore-producing herpes simplex virus was also responsible for human cancers. Sabin later retracted the claim for want of evidence. Meanwhile, the National Cancer Institute (NCI) reorganized its efforts in the search for a viral cause of cancer, a ten-year-long, $250-million quest that produced few tangible results. The NCI wanted to open research to a greater number of qualified cancer experts, thus dulling criticism of the virus research programs as being "closed shops" for NCI-favored scientists.

The FDA approved a cancer test in 1974 that was fairly effective in discovering remissions of cancer. The test looked for the presence of a protein called carcinoembryonic antigen (CEA) in the blood of cancer patients under treatment. Disappointingly, the CEA test was not reliable enough for large-scale cancer screening programs. A new form of neutron radiation therapy extracted from a giant atom smasher was proving more effective and less damaging than conventional cobalt radiation treatment for cancer in patients considered hopeless.

## Heart Disease

About $334 million was spent on heart disease study in 1974. The American Heart Association (AHA) estimated that nearly 670,000 died of heart attacks in 1974, a quarter of all the year's deaths. The AHA and the National Heart and Lung Institute (NHLI) fed research money into studies on reducing the heart attack toll.

A finding that called for a switch in medical thinking held that heart muscle does not necessarily die an hour or so after being deprived of blood during a heart attack, as previously thought. In some instances it can live for hours or even days after. With this new knowledge, doctors could take quick steps to save damaged heart muscle. Such steps could include the administration of nitroglycerin and a careful lowering of blood pressure. Scientists in St. Louis, Mo., reported a test capable of showing the extent of heart damage after an attack. Noting that dying heart muscle cells gave off an enzyme called creatine phosphokinase (CPK), the researchers said measurement of a patient's CPK blood level could give a good idea of heart damage.

Boston heart surgeons devised a way of actually seeing how much heart muscle was damaged from a heart attack. Using a combination of radioactive technetium and tetracycline, an antibiotic that becomes uniquely attached to dying heart muscle cells, the doctors could view affected heart areas in bedridden patients by means of a portable scintillation camera.

In June General Electric Co. recalled 94 of its heart pacemakers implanted in persons whose own hearts were unable to maintain a normal beat. The faulty pacemakers were implicated in the deaths of two users. The coronary bypass operation was under study in 1974 to see if it was the blessing that advocates maintained. The operation involved shunting blood around blocked parts of a coronary artery through a vein removed from the leg and relocated in the heart area. Preliminary data from the study showed that persons subjected to the costly operation did not seem to live any longer than those whose heart condition was nonsurgically treated with drugs and diets.

On November 25 South African heart surgeon Dr. Christiaan Barnard scored a medical first when he implanted a second heart in a 58-year-old man whose own heart was severely diseased; on New Year's Eve he performed a second twin-heart operation. In each case the two hearts beat at their own rates, though pacemakers were being developed to synchronize them. In November Louis B. Russell, Jr., the world's longest-surviving heart transplant recipient, died in Richmond, Va. Russell had received a heart transplant in August 1968.

## Occupational Health

Cases of a rare liver cancer cropped up in Kentucky, New York, and Connecticut, prompting in-

dustrial doctors to investigate a material used in fabricating plastic products. Chronic exposure to the material—vinyl chloride—was thought to be the cause of the cancer, according to the Occupational Safety and Health Administration (OSHA). The chemical was used in making polyvinyl chloride, a widely employed plastic. Emergency measures were taken by the OSHA to reduce the "safe" levels of vinyl chloride in factories from 500 parts per million parts of air to 50 parts per million.

Fourteen employees of a garment factory in Oklahoma were hospitalized in mid-1974 with pesticide poisoning, according to the Atlanta-based Communicable Disease Center. The symptoms included headache, loss of control of extremities, and vertigo. The pesticides apparently infiltrated the factory from the outside, said investigators. In late summer several employees of an electronics plant suffered from the apparent symptoms of carbon monoxide poisoning. Inadequate ventilation was the culprit, but another finding was that cigarette smoking workers were the most seriously affected.

## Public Health

Two years of federal campaigning for venereal disease (VD) detection and treatment seemed to be paying off. The U.S. Public Health Service said that there was a decline in the number of cases of primary and secondary syphilis during the first half of 1974 as well as a leveling off of the decade-long rise in gonorrhea. Although the incidence of both forms of VD rose during the summer, public health officials were hopeful that their efforts would bring an

*A nurse in surgery prepares an Auto Suture, a surgical stapler for suturing, the use of which has become widespread since its introduction in the U.S. in 1966.*
UPI COMPIX

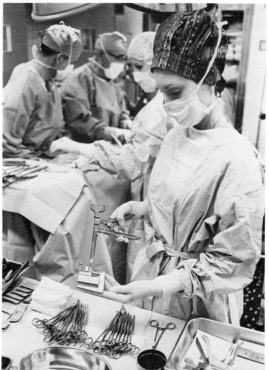

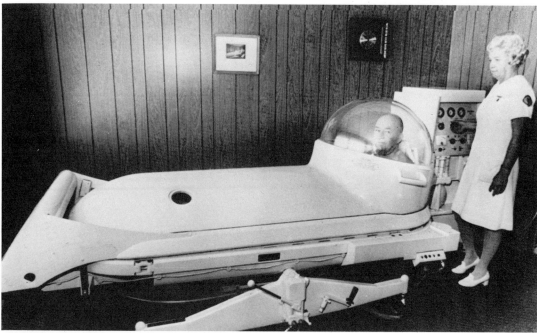

*The hyperbaric oxygenation pressure chamber is demonstrated at the Miami Heart Institute in Florida. The device, which introduces oxygen into the blood at high pressure in conjunction with a drug, results in improved brain functioning, and doctors think the process may provide a possible cure for memory loss and senility.*

overall decline by year's end. By late October some 717,000 new cases of gonorrhea and nearly 20,000 cases of syphilis had been reported.

Scientists at the Center for Disease Control fretted over the declining number of young persons immunized against such communicable diseases as polio, measles, whooping cough, and diphtheria, among others. Within ten years, for example, the immunization level of U.S. children vaccinated against polio had dropped enough for public health officials to contemplate future epidemics of the dread disease. Particularly worrisome was the low level of immunization evident in the inner cities.

International travel by jetliner has raised the chances of infectious organisms being transported all over the world, noted a number of epidemiologists. An outbreak of malaria in northern California during the summer, for instance, was probably triggered by Punjabi farmers settling in California. The area of northern India from which the Punjabis came was experiencing a rise in malaria cases. Better study of malaria, a disease that was killing at least a million persons in the world each year, was made possible by the discovery of a mutant form of the malaria parasite capable of infecting laboratory mice. Prior to the discovery by two New York University scientists, there was no ethical way of experimenting with malaria because the malaria organism infected only humans.

The World Health Organization (WHO) remained confident that international prevention programs would soon eradicate smallpox everywhere. The disease was still endemic, however, in four countries—Bangladesh, Ethiopia, India, and Pakistan. WHO officials felt, nonetheless, that the remaining "reservoirs" of the disease were drying up so well that by 1975 "the world will have seen its last case of smallpox."

## Surgery

In recent years a few doctors had contended that persons in the U.S. were sometimes subjected to needless surgery. In a 1974 report the same critics surprisingly found that physicians and their spouses submitted themselves to surgery more frequently than did their nonmedical peers. This seemed to indicate that as "enlightened consumers" the doctors chose surgery as a health need.

Year-old Siamese (conjoined) twins born in the Dominican Republic were successfully separated by surgeons at Philadelphia's Children's Hospital in September. The 10½-hour-long operation involved separating the twins at the waist and pelvis, constructing an artificial large intestine and rectum for one of the twins, and carefully redistributing blood vessels and other tissues. A Japanese surgeon successfully implanted an artificial long bone during the year. Faced with having to amputate a patient's leg, the surgeon replaced the cancerous femur with a titanium-polyethylene tube. (*See also* Consumer Affairs; Dentistry; Drugs; Hospitals; Mental Health; Nursing; Women.)

# Medicine

## Special Report:
# The Progress of Medicine

by Joseph A. Zullo

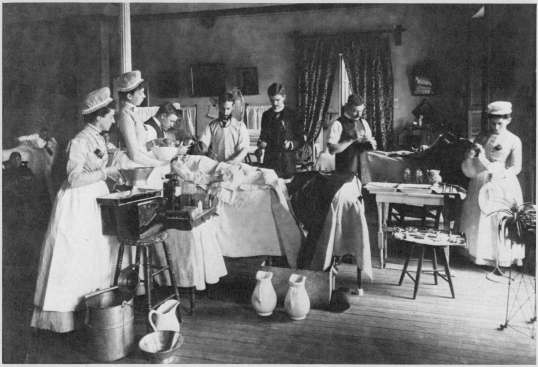

*Primitive surgical procedures of the 19th century were greatly advanced by the introduction in 1846 of the general anesthetic and the discovery in 1865 of the importance of antisepsis.*

As the United States approaches its 200th birthday, it boasts one of the finest health-care systems in the world, or so say the admirers of American medicine. Yet dissenters say that the practice of medicine in the U.S. provides excellent medical care only for suitably incomed citizens but disregards the needs of the urban poor and the rural population. In answer, defenders of the medical system say that anyone in the country can choose freely his or her doctor and get the best care on a fee-for-service basis without the governmental red tape found in countries where free or low-cost health care prevails. After 200 years of development, where does American medicine stand today?

Perhaps because of the unique health needs of frontier life, American medicine still maintains a doggedly individualistic stance. Surgery and medicine did not develop in different directions in the early days of the U.S. as they did in medieval Europe. Today's excellence of American surgery is undoubtedly attributable to this lack of differentiation. Because the U.S. was a young country with an expanding frontier, many early doctors had to practice their art under trying circumstances that demanded initiative and experimentation.

### Pre-20th-Century American Medicine

Physicians in colonial times were poorly armed to treat illness. They had to supplement their sparse scientific expertise with treatments derived from Indian folk medicine. Medical skills were usually learned from a preceptor, an older physician-teacher. In some cases colonial doctors furthered their education at the great European universities. It was not until 1765 that the first medical school in the pre-United States opened its doors. Eleven years later, several physicians would be among the signers of the Declaration of Independence.

Even during colonial days, efforts were made to ensure high-quality medical care in the young land.

In 1772 New Jersey was one of the earliest of the soon-to-be states to enact laws regulating the standards of medical practice.

Quality medical training in eastern and southern cities prior to the Civil War was usually the norm. After the war, however, a number of "diploma mills," schools that offered quick courses in medicine, cranked out doctors who were ill-prepared to carry out a conscientious medical practice. Quacks traveled the American frontier as well as other regions and sold useless nostrums and other cure-alls to a public desperate for medical help. As early as 1847 a group of eastern doctors formed the American Medical Association (AMA) to protect the professional, political, and financial interests of physicians.

One of the offshoots of orthodox medicine that the AMA fought for years was osteopathy. The osteopathic profession grew out of ideas and practices devised by Andrew T. Still, a midwestern medical practitioner, beginning in 1874. Still believed that the body contained within itself the best means for healing its own ills, and because of personal experience he came to reject most of the "poisonous" drugs commonly used at the time. He also believed in the strong interrelation of structure and function, and he used manual manipulation to correct the structural abnormalities he found in joints, muscles, or ligaments. Surgery was always part of his practice, as was some drug therapy, but the profession that grew from a small school in Kirksville, Mo., gradually adopted all the available tools of mainline medicine, as licensing legislation was worked out in each state. Today's doctors of osteopathy (D.O.'s) still include structural diagnosis and treatment in their practice, along with all the other forms of treatment employed by doctors of medicine (M.D.'s).

The medical educational system to which the reformers had objected was markedly changed as a result of the no-nonsense Flexner report of 1910. This resulted in accreditation of both medical and osteopathic schools along lines of a systematically scientific curriculum.

## Tests, Tests, and More Tests

The days of American doctors practicing largely by luck and guesswork are over. Multiphasic tests have been devised to eliminate much of the guesswork from diagnosis. Sophisticated electronic equipment can gauge heartbeat, blood pressure, electrical activity of the brain, and myriad other physiological processes that indicate the general state of health. The increasing automation of medicine, however, has triggered an outcry by concerned physicians and consumers who fear that doctors will eventually develop a disregard for the whole-person aspects of their patients and concentrate solely on malfunctioning body parts. A common plaint voiced by patients who are subjected to multiphasic testing techniques is that they are attended by "computer doctors" who send them off for tests without discussing the nature of the patients' ailments. And yet, few would downgrade the intrinsic worth of such testing—a way of getting a quick and relatively complete evaluation of the health of vital body systems. One task facing American doctors today, therefore, seems to be a demonstration of their concern and feeling for their patients.

## Peer Review and a Doctor Shortage

Physicians feel that they are threatened with substantial problems. Governmental control of medical practice is one. Even though doctors have long maintained a "hands off" attitude toward one another's practice, it has been argued that if the profession is unable to police itself and have more stringent control over fees and standards of care, it invites government interference. The federal government has already mandated Professional Standards Review Organizations (PSRO's), peer review groups composed of physicians who oversee the hospital care given to certain patients. The AMA has objected to PSRO's, saying that government standards for their operation are not precise enough to offset meddling by federal administrations.

The "doctor shortage" is another problem confronting American medicine. In the face of a pre-

*The shortage of doctors continues to be a problem throughout the U.S., but smaller communities like Tilden, Ill., are particularly hard pressed by the lack of trained professionals.*
WIDE WORLD

dicted shortage of physicians, medical schools are turning away some 60% of all qualified applicants because of lack of space. One proposal (rejected by the AMA) to relieve the shortage of doctors in rural areas, was for graduating physicians to spend two years practicing in towns with fewer than 20,000 residents.

### Doctors' Unions

One of the most surprising recent developments in American medicine has been the formation of doctors' unions for collective bargaining purposes. The first such union emerged in the mid-1950's; others, later. Union spokesmen state that doctors are not concerned with raising their incomes but are trying to prevent regulatory attempts from "reducing the doctor to the functionary level of the postman and schoolteacher." Many doctors are also concerned about their self-image and feel that through unions they can inform the public of their intention to help and serve. By 1974 perhaps more than 15,000 physicians, of a total of 350,000, were unionized.

Some doctors' unions, such as the Union of American Physicians in the San Francisco area, are solely local groups. Others are directly linked with labor unions, as is the Nevada Physicians Union, affiliated with the AFL-CIO. The AMA remains aloof to such unions, but the obvious discontentment of physicians, particularly younger ones, which goads them to organize, cannot be dismissed readily by the traditionalist AMA.

Maintenance of income is a key motivator of the organizing attempts of many older physicians. The extensive paperwork associated with public and private health insurance requires many doctors to enlarge their clerical staffs. As a result, the costs of maintaining a medical practice mount. Paltry reimbursement of medical fees by health insurance plans has also irked many doctors. And with some form of national health insurance certain to be enacted, union officials feel that doctors can better influence the content of such legislation with the weight of organized labor behind them.

But what effect does unionized medicine have upon the consumer—the patient? When a union affiliate—the Teamsters, for instance—goes on strike, must affiliated physicians walk off the job too? Will doctors demand overtime pay for emergency calls? Can a work stoppage by surgeons close down a hospital? These are not idle worries because strikes by doctors in Canada, Belgium, Portugal, and Italy have had a temporary effect on medical care in those countries.

Whether or not doctors will modify their age-old individualism by plunging into union activity remains to be seen. With growing governmental intrusion into the practice of medicine, however, it is likely that the second 200 years of American medicine will be conducted on a considerably less laissez-faire basis than the first.

### MENTAL HEALTH.

As in years before, governmental and private health agencies cited mental illness as the top U.S. health problem in 1974. Total state mental health expenditures for the year neared $4 billion, and more than 2 million Americans needed inpatient or outpatient treatment.

In recent years community-based mental health clinics were replacing large state-run institutions. More than 8,000 community mental health facilities operated in 1974, where alcoholism, drug abuse, and a wide range of other behavioral disorders were aided. Critics were pointing out, however, that the community concept of treatment was not achieving all expectations. They asserted that in many cases mental patients released from large institutions did not relocate in treatment-oriented "halfway houses" but gravitated to tawdry hotels and other substandard places from which they wandered their neighborhoods in search of food and help.

The trend toward deinstitutionalization essentially began a few years ago when California started to phase out its mental hospitals. Some states, however, in 1974 were rethinking the practice of wholesale release of the mentally ill to their communities. California, too, decided to maintain a few of its mental institutions.

The civil rights of mental patients were being championed with vigor in 1974. A paramount effort was for the legal establishment of a patient's right to treatment. Another was the attempt to apply fair labor standards to patients used as unpaid help in mental institutions.

A team of scientists reported at the start of 1974 that nearly a quarter of the adult U.S. population in 1970, the year of the survey, used psychotherapeutic drugs, mainly tranquilizers and sedatives. One of the survey findings was that "Americans believe that tranquilizers are effective but [the users] have serious questions about the morality of using them and doubts about their [the drugs'] physical safety." The report thus indicated that many users were aware of psychotherapeutic drug limitations.

Behavior modification—a psychological program of changing forms of behavior through rewards and punishments—was dropped early in the year, at least temporarily, by the U.S. government as a way of adjusting the behavior of "troublesome" convicts. Some inmates viewed the procedures, sometimes involving electroshock applications, as "cruel and unusual" punishment. The American Psychological Association voiced displeasure with the scrapping of the program for fear that "outmoded" and "inhuman" prison rehabilitation programs would resurface.

Psychologists had long known that disaster survivors sometimes suffered "survivor's syndrome," guilt over not having been killed with family or friends sufficient to warrant mental-health treatment. Recently noted, however, was the possibility that the syndrome could be experienced by persons

*A young girl, one of many children transferred by court order from the Willowbrook State School for the Mentally Retarded, suffers a different kind of neglect at the Wards Island, N.Y., center, which lacks trained staff and treatment programs for the retardates.*

who, although they were not physically present at the site of a disaster, had suffered the loss of close family members or friends. (*See also* Drugs; Medicine; Prisons; Psychology.)

**METALS.** A brisk demand for gold continued in 1974. "Record" prices for gold were set and the records broken repeatedly; there was considerable fluctuation in prices, but the general trend was upward. In January gold was traded in Paris for the record price of $136.58 per ounce; with a change of government in France, however, the price on the same market rose briefly to $197 per ounce in April.

Gold prices in London reached $163 per ounce in May but fell, as did silver futures in New York City, with the unfolding U.S. political crisis that led to President Richard M. Nixon's resignation. In August U.S. President Gerald R. Ford signed legislation permitting private citizens to buy and sell gold, a practice forbidden by law in the U.S. since the 1930's. In Europe gold prices soared to nearly $200 per ounce prior to December 31 when the law took effect, but early trading in the U.S. was slower than expected and prices declined.

Citing increased production costs, major U.S. steel companies announced spring price increases, averaging in some cases 23%. New price hikes in December were challenged by Ford, and partial rollbacks left average increases of 2.5%–8%.

Copper prices, meanwhile, dropped drastically.

Early in the year the price of copper reached $1.50 per pound on the London market. At that time the U.S. producers were unable to take advantage of the price bonanza; they were restricted, by price controls, to charging 68¢ per pound. In response to sagging prices Chile, Peru, Zaire, and Zambia, which account for 70% of the world's copper exports, announced in November that they would reduce shipments by 10%.

In July the Anaconda Co. announced a settlement with the government of Chile for the company's copper mining subsidiaries expropriated in 1971. Chile agreed to pay the U.S. headquarters of the subsidiaries about $65 million in cash and more than $185 million in notes. (*See also* Coins and Medals; Consumer Affairs; Mines and Mining.)

**MEXICO.** In 1974, year of the world oil crisis, the big news in Mexico was about the huge new oil discovery in the southern states of Chiapas and Tabasco. In July, Antonio Dovalí Jaime, director of Pemex, the state oil monopoly, said he believed the deposit to be the country's "richest yet" and that it would insure Mexico's self-sufficiency in oil. Mexico's natural resources minister, Horacio Flores de la Peña, said that the new oil would be marketed at the prevailing world market prices set by the Organization of Petroleum Exporting Countries, with preference given to other Latin American nations.

Another favorable economic development in

UPI COMPIX

*U.S. President Ford joins hands with Mexican President Echeverría amidst a crowd of spectators and photographers in Nogales, Mexico, on October 21.*

1974 was an increase in direct private investment over that of 1973. Mexico's economic expansion continued, with President Luis Echeverría Álvarez announcing in September that the country's gross domestic product for 1974 would be up 7%.

The economy was being hard hit, however, by growing inflation, with the price index rising by more than 22% from midyear 1973 to midyear 1974. Especially hurt were Mexico's millions of urban poor, who were paying 50% to 100% more than they were a year before for such food staples as beans, corn, rice, and cooking oil. The government ordered a temporary price freeze in June, but the powerful Confederation of Mexican Workers threatened to strike, and the government granted a general 22% pay increase in September.

Mexico's external trade position weakened during the year. While both exports and imports increased by about 50% from early 1973 to early 1974, the country's trade deficit was expected to rise from a high $1.7 billion in 1973 to an even higher $2.8 billion in 1974. Moreover, total foreign debts were estimated to be $10 billion at the end of June, a rise of $4 billion in just 12 months.

There was an upsurge in terrorist activity during the year. One spectacular case was the kidnapping in March of U.S. diplomat John Patterson. No ransom was ever paid, and his body was found in July. Millionaire labor leader Ruben Figueroa, widely considered as a possible successor to Echeverría in 1976, was kidnapped by a guerrilla band in May but was rescued in September. Echeverría's father-in-law, 83-year-old leftist leader José Zuno Hernández, was kidnapped in August by the Peo-

ple's Revolutionary Armed Forces. They demanded the release of three persons serving prison terms for the 1973 kidnapping of a U.S. official. Peaceably released by his captors after ten days, Zuno said, "I convinced them that their fight should be against imperialism and the CIA" (the U.S. Central Intelligence Agency) and not the Mexican government. In December several of the guerrillas responsible for the Figueroa kidnapping and their leader, Lucio Cabañas, revered by many as a folk hero, were slain in a battle with army troops.

In his September state of the union address Echeverría announced that the government was moving to end discrimination against women. In a swipe at "machismo" he said that "women must enjoy absolute equality with men in the exercise of their rights and obligations." He also called for an end to the economic blockade of Cuba.

Echeverría welcomed U.S. President Gerald R. Ford to Mexico in October. They discussed the problems of drug traffic and trade barriers between the two countries and regulation of the flow of migrant workers from Mexico to the United States. Echeverría paid official visits to West Germany, Austria, Italy, and Yugoslavia (in February) and to Costa Rica, Ecuador, Peru, Argentina, Brazil, Venezuela, and Jamaica (in July). His aim—to continue an independent policy of improving relations with countries other than the United States. Diplomatic relations with Chile, however, increasingly tense since the 1973 Chilean military coup, were broken in November. In early October two new states, the 30th and 31st, were admitted to the union—Baja California Sur and Quintana Roo. (*See also* Latin America.)

**MIDDLE EAST.** The first half of 1974 marked a distinct improvement in the Middle East situation as U.S. mediation helped to secure military disengagement; but failure to achieve further progress toward a settlement caused the atmosphere to deteriorate toward year's end, and both sides warned of the acute danger of renewed war.

As the year opened, the Egyptian-Israeli disengagement talks continued in a deadlock; it was clear that a new impetus was needed. This was provided by U.S. Secretary of State Henry Kissinger, who arrived in Egypt on January 11 and, after shuttling repeatedly between there and Jerusalem, arranged an agreement acceptable to both sides.

There was criticism of the accord in Syria, where it was feared that a separate Egyptian-Israeli agreement might endanger Syrian interests. Various Palestinian groups, including the Palestine Liberation Organization (PLO), also voiced disapproval of the agreement and of the Egyptian government for accepting it. However, PLO Chairman Yasir Arafat continued in close consultation with Egypt, which pressed for PLO participation in renewed Geneva peace talks.

Kissinger pursued his efforts to achieve a Syrian-

Israeli disengagement on a new Middle East trip in late February. The chief obstacles were the issues of Israeli prisoners of war and Syrian refugees. Serious Israeli-Syrian fighting occurred in the Golan Heights throughout March and April, and the military situation deteriorated. In April Kissinger began a new peace mission, but his task was complicated by Palestinian guerrilla attacks on two northern Israeli towns that caused many civilian casualties and hardened the Israeli mood. Kissinger, however, after shuttling between Middle Eastern capitals for 30 days, succeeded in bringing about a disengagement agreement on May 29.

The formation of a new Israeli government under Yitzhak Rabin—not including former Defense Minister Moshe Dayan—offered improved hope of a renewal of Geneva peace talks. The chief stumbling block was still the question of Palestinian representation. The PLO refused to recognize Israel, while Israel insisted it would negotiate the Palestinian problem only with Jordan's King Hussein.

Meanwhile, the PLO was making steady progress in its campaign to achieve international recognition. Early in the year, at the Islamic conference in Lahore, Pakistan, the PLO was declared "the sole legitimate representative of the Palestinian nation." On September 21 the United Nations (UN) General Assembly, overriding strong Israeli objections, included on its agenda for the first time "the Palestine question" as a subject for debate instead of as a part of the general Middle East problem. In a historic decision, the assembly invited the PLO to take part in its upcoming debate on the Palestine question. The vote was 105 in favor, 4 against (including Israel and the U.S.), with 20 abstentions. On November 13 PLO leader Arafat appeared before the assembly to present the Palestinian proposals, saying he had come "bearing an olive branch and a freedom-fighter's gun." Arafat flatly rejected the notion of a separate Palestinian state to coexist with Israel. Instead he called for the creation of a secular state of Palestine—to include what is now

*Oil ministers from the nations belonging to the Organization of Petroleum Exporting Countries meet in Geneva, Switzerland, in January to work for the establishment of new relations with the industrialized, oil-consuming nations.*
KEYSTONE

Israel—in which both Palestinian Arabs and Israeli Jews would live. (*See* United Nations.)

In December Israel reaffirmed its refusal to ever recognize or negotiate with the PLO. Meanwhile, as a condition for Mideast peace, Egyptian Foreign Minister Ismail Fahmy called for Israel to suspend immigration and "freeze" its population for 50 years. Kissinger's renewed efforts to negotiate a second stage of the Golan Heights disengagement were stalemated at year's end with Egypt, Syria, and Israel all refusing significant concessions and Mideast leaders foreseeing only renewed hostilities.

### Inter-Arab Relations

A large measure of the Arab solidarity that was a feature of the October 1973 war and its aftermath was maintained during 1974—as evidenced at an Arab summit in Rabat, Morocco, in October—although it was severely tested at many points. Heading the agenda was the question of Palestinian representation at future peace talks. Jordan's King Hussein, a longtime foe of the PLO, had previously insisted on his right to represent the Palestinians living on the West Bank. Under the combined influence of the other Arab nations and the recent UN invitation to the PLO, however, Hussein was persuaded to accept a resolution that any liberated Palestinian territory "should revert to its legitimate Palestinian owners under the leadership of the PLO." Thus Hussein prepared himself for the loss by Jordan of its West Bank. The Arab ministers also pledged more than $2 billion a year in oil revenue to Egypt, Syria, Jordan, and the PLO to finance the continuing campaign against Israel.

Egypt was the pivotal state in inter-Arab relations during 1974. It was helped by the new prestige acquired by President Anwar el-Sadat and by its close relations with both Saudi Arabia and Algeria, two key states at opposite ends of the political spectrum. Egypt, however, had to deal with Syrian and Palestinian suspicion of its new close relations with the U.S. and fears that it was preparing to reach a bilateral settlement with Israel. Its attempts to mediate between Palestinians and Jordanians sometimes aroused resentment from both sides. Libya's previously close relations with Egypt declined, while closer ties developed between Egypt and Sudan.

### International Relations

There was a marked improvement in Arab-U.S. relations, although some states, such as Syria, remained skeptical about U.S. intentions. President Richard M. Nixon's visit to four Arab countries and Israel in June symbolized the changing U.S. Middle East policy. Diplomatic relations were restored between Washington and Cairo and Damascus, and after the resumption of U.S. relations with Egypt, the two countries announced plans for a joint commission to improve economic, scientific, and cultural cooperation. The U.S. provided $250 million for reopening the Suez Canal and promised materials to help Egypt build a nuclear reactor.

There were signs in autumn of a thaw in Egyptian-Soviet relations, at least partly because of Egypt's need for arms and U.S. promises of large-scale military aid to Israel. Throughout the year the Soviet Union had made it clear that it would not abandon its role in the Middle East. The Soviet government evidenced some annoyance at having been left out of Kissinger's Egyptian-Israeli disengagement pact, and Foreign Minister Andrei Gromyko attempted to assert soviet influence over the later Syrian-Israeli settlement. The Soviets pressed continually for full-scale Geneva peace talks, attempting thereby to remove the entire Middle East issue to an arena of greater Soviet strength. Soviet leader Leonid Brezhnev's year-end cancellation of his planned January 1975 Mideast visit, however, further threatened resumption of the Geneva talks. (*See also* individual country articles.)

*A U.S. ship participates on August 30 in the combined Anglo-American-Egyptian-French operation, begun in April, to clear the Suez Canal of unexploded munitions.*
KEYSTONE

*UMW President Arnold Miller talks with union members in West Virginia prior to beginning contract bargaining with coal-mine owners in late August.*

## MINES AND MINING.

For the first half of 1974, earnings of U.S. mining companies were at record highs; many were 50% higher than profits for the same period in 1973. The increased profits were largely the result of record prices for metals and minerals. The year began with an energy shortage, but by midyear there was an adequate supply of petroleum—at higher prices. Cost inflation was at unprecedented levels, and this contributed to militancy among labor unions involved in mining. Copper company contracts with the United Steelworkers expired June 30; after several strikes a settlement was reached on new three-year contracts.

The United Mine Workers (UMW) of America staged a one-week, nationwide shutdown of coal mining operations in August, ostensibly in memory of 100,000 men who had died in U.S. coal mines since 1900. Coal miners converged for the commemoration in Harlan, Ky., for years the scene of violent struggles between companies and the union.

Mine safety was a major issue in regular contract negotiations between the UMW and industry. The three-year, industry-wide contract expired on November 11. The miners went on strike at midnight, despite lengthy negotiations beginning in September. A new contract, ratified December 5, provided significant salary and fringe benefit increases. A subsequent five-week walkout of mine construction workers, however, prevented full resumption of coal production until their December 23 approval of a new three-year contract.

In Michigan and Minnesota, seven new iron ore projects, along with expansions of existing projects, were expected to increase pellet capacity by about 50%, to a total of about 80 million tons a year by 1978. Badly needed zinc smelting facilities were in various stages of progress in Kentucky, Oklahoma, and Tennessee. In light of the need for increasing domestic energy production, President Gerald Ford used a pocket-veto on December 30 to kill a controversial strip-mining bill. (*See also* Environment; Labor Unions; Metals.)

## MONEY AND INTERNATIONAL FINANCE.

The tremendous increase in oil prices and the surge of oil money through financial markets staggered the international economic system in 1974. Monetary authorities sought to cope with rampant inflation, huge international payments imbalances, and weakening economic activity. Although the roots of the dilemma went deeper than the oil crisis, that crisis intensified cost inflation and caused unemployment as energy-related consumer expenditures fell. At the same time, the oil-exporting countries amassed current account surpluses totaling about $60 billion. The investment of those funds did not match the borrowing needs of the deficit countries. The industrial nations' payments deficit was $40 billion, the largest in history. The many uncertainties put an end for the time to efforts for working out an international monetary reform based on more stable exchange rates.

In a shift toward tight money, demand pressures gradually moderated, speculation was checked, and international raw material prices turned down; but the effects of earlier rises in the prices of foodstuffs, raw materials, and oil—together with a renewed wage spiral—pushed annual rates of consumer price increases up to as much as 25% in some industrial countries. Under those circumstances, monetary restraint drove short-term interest rates up to record highs, and long-term rates rose as well. High interest rates had a disproportionately severe effect on housing, and sharp drops in the prices of bonds and shares weakened the asset structures of some companies and financial institutions. Central banks took steps to tighten their supervisory practices, especially in regard to foreign exchange business, and in some cases they developed special new facilities for helping troubled banks.

In 1974, many banks faced a deluge of short-term deposits from the oil producers, which could not be safely reinvested or reloaned on a long-term basis for fear that the oil producers might pull out their funds. Banks in the U.S. and Eurodollar banks—

303

WIDE WORLD

*A no quotation sign in a Tokyo bank notes the closing of Tokyo's foreign exchange market on January 21 after floating of the French franc.*

Eurodollars are dollars on deposit outside the U.S. —were relending heavily to oil-importing countries, but the international banking system was uneasy about continuing its intermediary role at such a fast pace.

Thrift institutions in the U.S. experienced a sharp increase in withdrawals as consumers put their holdings into money market instruments that offered higher yields of interest. U.S. consumers began to cut back on plans to buy such key items as automobiles and major appliances. (*See* United States.)

The Middle Eastern oil producers invested or loaned most of their surplus funds in the industrial oil-consuming countries. The major impact of the oil crisis fell upon the poorest countries, and the trade deficit of the oil-importing, less developed countries was expected to more than double in 1974 to about $20 billion.

In August, the World Bank increased its interest rate on loans to 8% from 7¼%. The World Bank and its affiliates, including the International Development Association, which channels money into developing countries, were borrowing from the oil-rich Middle East. In December, Saudi Arabia disclosed that it had loaned $750 million to the World Bank, to be repaid over ten years. That sum was the largest ever loaned to the World Bank by one state.

On Dec. 10, 1974, market reports suggesting that Saudi Arabia was no longer willing to take sterling in payment for its oil forced the Bank of England to spend about $250 million in an effort to support the currency. The setback came as Great Britain's leaders were seeking cooperation in the recycling of oil money to deficit-running countries. Italy and Great Britain were in particularly bad straits in 1974.

The U.S. insisted in 1974 that oil-consuming industrial countries must present a united front instead of letting each country fend for itself in dealing with the Organization of Petroleum Exporting Countries (OPEC). Late in the year, the U.S., Japan, and all of the European Economic Community except France joined with other Western European countries in a new International Energy Agency proposed by the U.S. France had sought its own bilateral deals with OPEC and wanted to avoid an appearance of confrontation. At a meeting between U.S. President Gerald R. Ford and French President Valéry Giscard d'Estaing in December, it was agreed that the French would help to develop a joint policy.

The new energy agency planned a $25-billion fund for rescuing any country threatened with financial ruin due to selective Arab investment. The agency also planned to conserve, develop, and share the energy sources of member countries.

The International Monetary Fund (IMF) Committee of 20, negotiating world monetary reform, agreed in June to a package of interim arrangements. The old system had collapsed when the U.S. ceased in 1971 to convert the dollar into gold, and exchange rates began to float. The new IMF guidelines for floating stated that no country would be asked to hold any particular rate against strong market pressure.

The price of gold as part of the international monetary system had stood at $42.22 per ounce, and the countries that had reserves of gold were unwilling to exchange it among themselves at that low rate. At a monetary conference of the Group of Ten on June 11, leading finance ministers agreed that, henceforth, borrower and lender countries could negotiate a value for gold used as collateral in international loans at the current open market price, then $160 per ounce. After the December Ford-Giscard meeting that reaffirmed plans for the upward valuation of U.S. and French gold reserves, however, the shah of Iran warned that such action would annul OPEC's current nine-month oil price freeze and force oil prices to new highs.

Policymakers in the U.S. preferred to have gold removed altogether from the world monetary system, and a start in that direction was made when the Committee of 20 agreed to eliminate gold as one of the elements (the U.S. dollar was the other) that backed special drawing rights (SDR's), the IMF's reserve currency. The SDR's would be backed during an interim period, instead, by 16 currencies, with the dollar carrying about one third of the load.

In August, President Ford signed into law a bill ending the ban on private ownership of gold bullion by U.S. citizens as of Dec. 31, 1974. The U.S. planned to sell 2 million ounces of gold in 400-ounce bars early in 1975 to curb speculation.

In 1974, the U.S. also ended its controls over the outflow of dollars for lending and investment abroad. The improved U.S. balance of payments was cited as a reason when the controls were lifted in January, but the cost of oil upset the balance of trade in 1974, and the outflow of investment dollars worsened the deficit. (*See also* Banks; World Trade; individual countries and world areas by name.)

**MOROCCO.** The Spanish Sahara would be "liberated" and reintegrated in Morocco before the end of 1975, King Hassan II announced in a speech on July 8, 1974, and this remained the overriding theme of Morocco's policy, both domestic and external, for the rest of the year. Direct talks with Spain on the territory's future were held in Madrid, Spain, in mid-August, but after their failure Hassan threatened that he would resort to military action if necessary to regain "usurped territory." In November, more than 20 people were killed in clashes between Moroccans and Spanish troops in the Spanish Sahara. Within Morocco, attention was given to the development of Tarfaya Province, adjoining the Spanish-administered territory, and five refugee camps for those said to have fled across the border were set up. Two radio stations began to beam propaganda on the issue—one to the Sahara, the other toward Spain.

Rabat was the scene of the seventh Arab Summit Conference in October, which confirmed the Palestine Liberation Organization as the sole representative of the Palestinian Arabs and gave Hassan the opportunity to play mediator as well as host.

The Moroccan economy, still suffering from an imbalance in foreign trade, a fast-growing population, and the need for ever increasing foreign aid, received a boost from the world demand for phosphates. In a year in which food imports were up and earnings from citrus exports and tourism down, the announcement in March that deposits of oil-bearing shale had been discovered in the Atlas Mountains was welcome. Meanwhile Morocco remained heavily dependent on assistance from the U.S., West Germany, and France. Iran, Saudi Arabia, and the United Arab Emirates also pledged substantial help. (*See also* Africa; Middle East.)

**MOTION PICTURES.** To the delight of the film industry in Hollywood, paid attendance at motion pictures in the U.S. increased dramatically in 1974. The Motion Picture Association of America (MPAA) estimated that more than one billion customers attended movies during the calendar year ending Dec. 31, 1974; this total represented a 20% increase over the total for the preceding year. Jack Valenti, president of the MPAA, attributed much of the increase to the country's economic difficulties. Valenti pointed out that film attendance had also jumped during the depression, when people turned to the silver screen for escapist entertainment.

James Cagney, a longtime favorite actor with audiences and industry personnel alike, was honored at a televised ceremony in March with the Life Achievement Award of the American Film Institute —the first actor to win the award. The versatile Cagney, 74, had starred in dozens of movies including 'Public Enemy', 'The Roaring Twenties', 'Yankee Doodle Dandy', and '13 Rue Madeleine'.

### Academy and Other Awards

The Academy of Motion Picture Arts and Sciences presented its 46th annual Academy Awards, or Oscars, in April—honoring excellence in 1973 releases. 'The Sting', a box-office hit starring Paul Newman and Robert Redford, garnered a total of seven awards, including best picture. Other Oscars awarded for 'The Sting' went to George Roy Hill, best director; David S. Ward, best original story and screenplay; Marvin Hamlisch, best musical scoring; Edith Head, best costume design; and William Reynolds, best film editing. Hamlisch, who adapted the music for 'The Sting' from Scott Joplin piano rags, became the first person to win three Oscars in the same year. The other two were both for

*Paul Newman and Robert Redford (far right) paired up as 1930's con artists in the lightweight gangsterland film 'The Sting', which won seven Academy Awards, including the best picture of the year.*

CINEMA INTERNATIONAL CORP. (UK)

'The Great Ziegfeld', an Academy Award winner of 1936, was one of many spectacular musicals produced by MGM from the 1930's to the 1950's and included in the nostalgic MGM retrospective 'That's Entertainment!' in 1974.

'The Way We Were': best song and best original dramatic score.

Jack Lemmon received the Oscar for best actor for his starring role in 'Save the Tiger'. Glenda Jackson was named best actress for 'A Touch of Class'. John Houseman was named best supporting actor for his role in 'The Paper Chase'. Tatum O'-Neal, daughter of actor Ryan O'Neal, won the award for best supporting actress for her role in 'Paper Moon'; nine-year-old Tatum was the youngest person ever to win an Academy Award.

William Peter Blatty received the award for the best screenplay adapted from another medium, for 'The Exorcist'. That controversial motion picture received ten Oscar nominations originally—the same number as 'The Sting'—but won only two Oscars. The other was for best sound.

'Day for Night', a film about film making by French director François Truffaut, was named best foreign language film. The Irving G. Thalberg Memorial Award went to producer Lawrence Weingarten, whose pictures included 'A Day at the Races', 'Adam's Rib', and 'Cat on a Hot Tin Roof'.

Beloved comedian Groucho Marx received a special honorary award for the body of his work. In his acceptance remarks, he paid tribute to his late brothers Harpo and Chico Marx and to their co-star, Margaret Dumont, also deceased.

In January the National Society of Film Critics announced its awards for 1973 films. 'Day for Night' was voted picture of the year; Truffaut was voted best director, for that picture. Marlon Brando was named best actor for his starring role in 'Last Tango in Paris'. Liv Ullmann was named best actress for her starring role in the Swedish film 'The New Land'. Robert DeNiro was voted best supporting actor for his role in 'Mean Streets', a critically acclaimed film that failed to draw large audiences. Valentina Cortese was named best supporting actress, another victory for 'Day for Night'. The critics' society gave the award for best screenplay to George Lucas, Willard Huyck, and Gloria Katz for 'American Graffiti'.

The New York Film Critics Circle, announcing its awards in January, concurred in naming 'Day for Night' best film, Truffaut best director, and Brando best actor. The circle's members voted Joanne Woodward best actress for her role in 'Summer Wishes, Winter Dreams'. The margin of victory was very small on several of the circle's votes; Brando, for example, only narrowly defeated Al Pacino, nominated for his role in 'Serpico'.

## Films Released in 1974

The year's new pictures seemed to fall into a number of categories or trends, but there were some that proved elusive in terms of typing. A distinct trend did develop, for example, toward the "catastrophe" or disaster film—along the lines of the 1973 box-office winner 'The Poseidon Adventure'. The new crop of peril pictures included 'Airport 1975', depicting the horrifying adventures of the passengers on a heavily damaged airliner. In 'The Towering Inferno' a star-studded cast dealt with a major fire in a high-rise block of apartments. Ingenious special effects were used in 'Earthquake' to show what could happen during a major quake in the Los Angeles area. Richard Lester's 'Juggernaut' was the story of a doomed ocean liner.

Nostalgia generally characterized a number of films, in varying degrees of effectiveness. 'Badlands', a directorial debut by Terrence Malick, was loosely based on a mass-murder case of the 1950's. 'Buster and Billie' centered on teenage life in the late 1940's but was not romantic in terms of climax or conclusion. Director Robert Altman made 'Thieves Like Us', based on a novel of the Great Depression.

Roman Polanski directed 'Chinatown', a detective story set in the 1930's. 'Chinatown', starring Jack Nicholson and Faye Dunaway, was sometimes acclaimed as a nostalgia piece—particularly because of its period costumes and sets—but it was in the main a contemporary, ironic look at the conventions of detective movies.

Violence seemed to carry continuing appeal for many audiences. Sam Peckinpah, whose picture 'The Wild Bunch' had ushered in an era of bloody realism in Hollywood, completed 'Bring Me the Head of Alfredo Garcia' in 1974. 'Death Wish', directed by Michael Winner, represented a school of moviemaking that might be called "urban paranoia"; Charles Bronson played a man who, unhinged by the death of his wife, launches a spree of murdering possible muggers and rapists. Francis Ford Coppola provided a sequel to his highly successful 1973 film 'The Godfather' in 'The Godfather, Part II', a compelling view of power and corruption in America.

Violence for a cause was glorified in the exploitation picture 'The Trial of Billy Jack', a sequel to two previous pictures. Actor George C. Scott produced, directed, and starred in 'The Savage is Loose', a saga of primitive sexuality on a desert island.

'Blazing Saddles', directed by Mel Brooks, was a popular comedy that offended many sensibilities but evoked many laughs as did Brooks's parody 'Young Frankenstein'. 'Sleeper', a Woody Allen vehicle, was a more subtle, intellectualized comedy about a health food store owner who dies, is frozen indefinitely, and wakes up in the distant future.

In 1974 films for and about black people continued to improve from the low point of the late 1960's. 'Claudine', starring James Earl Jones and Diahann Carroll, was a bittersweet tale of the romance between a carefree sanitation worker and a harassed mother of a large family. Michael Campus directed 'The Education of Sonny Carson', a picture acclaimed for its realism in the portrayal of young black manhood. A lighter note was struck in 'Uptown Saturday Night', a comedy directed by Sidney Poitier and featuring performances by well-known black actors including Poitier and Bill Cosby.

'A Woman Under the Influence', directed by John Cassavetes, opened late in the year. Gena Rowlands and Peter Falk starred in the film, which carried a typical Cassavetes theme: two strong-

*Linda Blair starred as a young girl possessed by the devil in the controversial, Academy Award-winning film 'The Exorcist'.*

COPYRIGHT © BY WARNER BROS. INC.

minded characters trying to work out their marriage amidst the wife's identity crisis. Psychological insights were also apparent in Hal Ashby's comedy-drama 'The Last Detail', starring Jack Nicholson as a career sailor in the U.S. Navy. Prisoners and guards compete allegorically in a football game in 'The Longest Yard', directed by Robert Aldrich and starring Burt Reynolds.

Director Peter Bogdanovich made 'Daisy Miller', from the Henry James novel, as a vehicle for star Cybill Shepherd. Jack Clayton directed 'The Great Gatsby', from the novel by F. Scott Fitzgerald; 'Gatsby' the film was generally termed a success in recreating a period but a disappointment in terms of the value and meaning of the novel.

Another favorite literary work, 'The Three Musketeers', was brought to the screen by Richard Lester. The film, starring Michael York, Oliver Reed, and Raquel Welch, was generally described as witty and entertaining.

Jon Voight starred in still another film adapted from a book, 'The Odessa File'. Ronald Neame directed the thriller about a journalist purusing Nazi war criminals in West Germany in the 1960's.

'The Apprenticeship of Duddy Kravitz', the work of Canadian director Ted Kotcheff, was generally well received by critics. The film starred Richard Dreyfuss, who had achieved recognition for his role in 'American Graffiti'.

'Lacombe, Lucien', directed by Louis Malle of France, explored the issue of collaboration with the Nazis during World War II. In a lighter and warmer vein, the renowned director Federico Fellini of Italy offered his 'Amarcord', an impressionistic reminiscence of his youth.

Rainer Werner Fassbinder, perhaps West Germany's most promising director, made a film called 'Fear Eats the Soul'—detailing an offbeat courtship and marriage. 'La Prima Angélica', by director Carlos Saura of Spain, chronicled the turmoil of that country in the 1930's.

Ingmar Bergman's 'Scenes from a Marriage', originally made for television in Sweden, was generally acclaimed as one of the director's best films ever. Liv Ullmann and Erland Josephson starred in the portrait of a union that survived separation and divorce. (*See also* Television and Radio; Theater.)

## MUSEUMS.

**MUSEUMS.** The financial problems of the U.S. museum in 1974 were highlighted at the debt-ridden Pasadena Museum of Modern Art in California where the board of directors accepted a complex offer by Norton Simon, a West Coast financier and art collector. Simon offered to give the museum almost $1 million and continue to underwrite its debts in exchange for 75% of its area for the display of his own vast collection. "Modern" was dropped from the museum's title, and several shows of recent art were canceled. Critics pointed to Simon's antipathy to contemporary art and lamented the loss of the showcase for its display.

The museum world reflected society's general concern during the year with acts of political terrorism—an anxiety perhaps not felt as strongly since the late 1960's. Although U.S. museums were hit with only one major example, when Pablo Picasso's 'Guernica' was spray-painted at the Museum of Modern Art (MOMA) in New York City, the major thefts of significant art works for ransom elsewhere haunted the security staffs of U.S. museums. (*See* Great Britain; Ireland; Sweden.) Conservation continued to be a prime concern of museums. Late in 1973 the National Conservation Advisory was founded, and regional laboratories were planned in 1974 that would be able to handle the problems of the many museums too small to afford their own conservation staffs. The National Endowment for the Arts continued to distribute federal grants for conservation projects, and a National Institute for Conservation was spoken of as a strong probability for the future.

The two newest states of the Union announced museum building activity in 1974. In Hilo, Hawaii, the Lyman House Memorial Museum was to be built, and the city of Anchorage, Alaska, raised a $1.2-million bond issue to fund a new wing for its Historical and Fine Arts Museum. In Minneapolis, Minn., the Institute of Arts completed a $26-million addition to its school, theater, and museum complex—the first U.S. buildings by the renowned Japanese architect Kenzo Tange. In Baltimore, Md., the new $4-million wing at the Walters Art Gallery substantially doubled its exhibition area. The Pennsylvania Academy of Fine Art in Philadelphia, one of the country's major collections of early American art, announced a $6-million renovation, and at the other end of the state Pittsburgh's Carnegie Institute expanded its exhibition area with the installation of the Sarah Scaife Gallery. The Houston, Tex., Museum of Fine Arts dedicated its new addition, the Brown Pavilion, in January. The Tucson, Ariz., Museum of Art announced a ten-year expansion program; the Norfolk, Va., Museum announced a new wing; and Asheville, N.C., announced that an art museum was being planned for its civic center. The University of Chicago opened its first major museum facility, the Smart Gallery, in 1974; and, with the opening of the Neuberger Museum at New York State University at Purchase, that university had the largest museum facility of any state university system in the country.

California art patron B. Gerald Cantor donated the world's largest private collection of Auguste Rodin sculpture to several museums; 10 to MOMA, 29 to the Los Angeles County Museum of Art, and 88 to the Stanford University museum. The U.S. General Services Administration presented 200 pieces of art produced by the W.P.A. and the U.S. Treasury during the depression years to the National Collection of Fine Arts of the Smithsonian Institution in Washington, D.C. In New York City the Morgan Library, which cele-

*The Hirshhorn Museum and Sculpture Garden in Washington, D.C., opened in October. It is the world's largest free museum built and maintained in a capital city by the government and houses Joseph H. Hirshhorn's vast personal collection of 19th- and 20th-century art.*

brated its 50th anniversary as a public institution, announced the bequest of the Janos Scholz collection of Italian drawings, and John D. Rockefeller III presented 300 prime Oriental art objects to the Asia Society. The Minneapolis, Minn., Institute of Art received the Gale Collection of Japanese Ukiyo-e works that consisted of 100 paintings and 200 prints. The well-known photographer Eliot Elisofon bequeathed 600 African sculptures and a 50,000-photo archive on African art to the Museum of African Art in Washington, D.C. In Mexico, in January, painter Rufino Tamayo and his wife, Olga, gave their native city, Oaxaca, a museum and their vast collection of pre-Hispanic sculpture. (*See also* Architecture; Landmarks and Monuments; Painting and Sculpture; Photography.)

**MUSIC.** Scholars deciphered and performed in 1974 the earliest notated music yet found. The tablet containing the notation was discovered in the 1950's on the coast of Syria and was believed to date from about 1800 B.C. Previously, the oldest known notation of music was on a 400 B.C. Greek papyrus. The most startling discovery was that the music used a diatonic, or Western, scale, forcing musicologists to question their assumption that Western music came from the Greeks. The discovery also meant that Western music might be at least 1,400 years older than formerly thought.

The centennials of the births of composers Arnold Schönberg and Charles Ives were celebrated in 1974. The Schönberg Society in Vienna, Austria, held an international congress and bought the composer's home to be used as a museum. Among performances of Schönberg's music throughout the world in 1974 was the Hamburg State Opera's new production of his unfinished opera 'Moses und Aron'. New York City held a festival, "Around Charles Ives," that included performances by Pierre Boulez and the New York Philharmonic and performances of Ives's chamber music. The Charles Ives Festival Conference was held in New York City and in New Haven, Conn.; Ives's hometown, Danbury, Conn., also held a short festival of his music. At an Ives festival in Miami, Fla., which was to extend into 1975, it was planned to present nearly all of Ives's major works.

The Chicago Symphony Orchestra visited 12 European cities in 1974 and continued, under its music director, Sir Georg Solti, to receive rave reviews for its performances and recordings. The Los Angeles Philharmonic Orchestra, conducted by Zubin Mehta, also toured Europe in 1974. The Cleveland Orchestra, under Lorin Maazel, toured Japan and signed a recording contract with London Records, bringing to four the number of "big six" orchestras in the U.S. that recorded exclusively or in part for European companies. The London Sym-

**309**

KEN REGAN—CAMERA 5

*In early January Bob Dylan began a 40-concert tour in Chicago playing with the Band. It was Dylan's first tour in eight years.*

phony Orchestra with Andre Previn toured the U.S. in 1974, as did the Berlin Philharmonic Orchestra with Herbert von Karajan.

The future of the Dallas Symphony Orchestra remained unclear after financial and managerial problems caused the resignation of the conductor and some players and the cancellation of concerts. The San Francisco Symphony Orchestra temporarily settled a dispute over the members' decision not to grant tenure to two highly regarded players. The New York Pro Musica Antiqua, founded in 1952 and renowned for its performances of early music, disbanded in 1974.

Eugene Fodor of Denver, Colo., won a tie with two Soviet violinists for second place at the Tchaikovsky competition in Moscow and began what seemed a promising concert career. Myung Whun Chung of New York City won second place in piano at the competition; first place went to Andrei Gavrilov of the Soviet Union.

Henri-Louis de la Grange published the first volume of his biography of Gustav Mahler in 1974, acclaimed by critics as a definitive work. Composer Darius Milhaud, conductor Josef Krips, and violinist David Oistrakh died in 1974. Impresario Sol Hurok, who had brought many Soviet artists such as the Bolshoi Ballet to the U.S., also died during the year.

## Opera

The Metropolitan Opera completed its 'Ring' cycle with 'Götterdämmerung' in March 1974, conducted by Rafael Kubelik, who soon after resigned as music director. James Levine conducted a highly successful first Metropolitan production of Giuseppe Verdi's 'I Vespri Siciliana' with Montserrat Cabellé. The final new production of the 1973–74

season was a double bill consisting of Béla Bartók's 'Bluebeard's Castle' and Giacomo Puccini's 'Gianni Schicchi'. Benjamin Britten's 'Death in Venice' was the first new production of the 1974–75 season.

Beverly Sills's performance in Vincenzo Bellini's 'I Puritani' at the New York City Opera, its 30th anniversary production in February 1974, was highly praised. At the San Francisco Opera, Joan Sutherland sang a revival of Jules Massenet's rarely heard 'Esclarmonde'. At Chicago a Verdi Congress was held during September. The Chicago Lyric Opera, celebrating its 20th year, produced his 'Simon Boccanegra' to run concurrently with the congress and produced his 'Falstaff' later in the season. Chicago produced Britten's 'Peter Grimes' for the first time and completed its 'Ring' cycle, a four-year project. Sarah Caldwell's Opera Company of Boston staged a very successful production of Massenet's 'Don Quichotte' and gave the U.S. premiere stage production of Sergei Prokofiev's 'War and Peace'. Opera/South in Jackson, Miss., gave the world premiere of William Grant Still's 'A Bayou Legend'. Lawrence Kelly, founder and director of the Dallas Civic Opera, died in 1974.

Maria Callas and Giuseppe di Stefano toured in 1974 and appeared at the Verdi Congress in Chicago. In spite of the reservations of some critics, audiences were enthusiastic.

## Popular

The high standards of rock musicianship began to result in works of symphonic proportion in 1974 such as the popular 'Tubular Bells' by the young British musician Mike Oldfield and 'Quadrophenia' by the group Who. There was also in 1974 a revival of rock 'n' roll of the 1950's.

The Beatles' much publicized possible reunion failed to materialize, but a Broadway musical based on their music, 'Sgt. Pepper's Lonely Hearts Club Band on the Road', opened late in the year in New York City. The year seemed to be one for performers to reappear and for groups to reunite. David Bowie came out of an early and short retirement with a new show, two albums, and a television spectacular. One of the best rock guitarists, Eric Clapton, who had been inactive in the early 1970's, played several concerts in 1974. Soul singer Marvin Gaye, who had not performed publicly for some time in spite of his enormous success on records, made a number of appearances during the year. Frank Sinatra ended his retirement to perform in the U.S. and in other countries. Bob Dylan and the Band toured the U.S., performing the music that had made them famous and receiving wide acclaim. One of the most popular groups of recent years, Crosby, Stills, Nash & Young, reunited for a tour.

Stevie Wonder performed again in 1974 after recuperating from a serious automobile accident in 1973. Wonder received five Grammy awards in March 1974, and later released a new album, 'Fulfilling Ness's First Finale'. Critics praised Wonder

*The Minnesota Orchestra rehearses in Minneapolis' new Orchestra Hall, the 71-year-old orchestra's first permanent home. The acoustically sound, $10-million building opened to a capacity crowd of 2,573 on October 21.*

for his originality and growth and saw in his fusion of rock, blues, and jazz an eclectic musical form that might revitalize American popular music.

Waylon Jennings and other country and western singers had success in 1974 with their blend of country and rock. The Grand Ole Opry moved from the Ryman Auditorium in Nashville, Tenn., the home of the most famous country and western musicians for years, to a modern auditorium in Opryland, a combined music facility and amusement park outside the city.

The popular movie 'The Sting', which used the ragtime music of Scott Joplin on its soundtrack, brought Joplin's music to the attention of the general public in 1974. Several new recordings of Joplin's music were issued during the year. Jelly Roll Morton, one of the links between ragtime and early jazz, also began to receive recognition in 1974 when recordings of his music were rereleased.

The Newport Jazz Festival in New York City had its most successful year financially in 1974. Among the artistic highlights of the festival were tributes to Duke Ellington, who had died earlier in the year, and to Charlie Parker. The Modern Jazz Quartet, considered by many jazz critics to be one of the most important groups in the history of jazz, announced its decision to disband in 1974. The newest jazz was perhaps best represented by Herbie Hancock, who was playing an electronic fusion of jazz, blues, and rock—what some called "improvised funk"—that appealed to both jazz and rock fans. Hancock's album 'Headhunters' had sold more than one million copies by 1974 and was reported to be the biggest selling jazz album of all time.

"Mama" Cass Elliot died in 1974 after appearing at the Palladium in London. Bill Chase and three members of his group were killed in a plane crash. Two great jazz saxophonists, Eugene (Jug) Ammons and Harry Carney, also died, as did well-known jazz trombonists Tyree Glenn and Georg Brunis, exuberant jazz pianist of the Preservation Hall Jazz Band Billie Goodson Pierce, and popular country and western singer Tex Ritter. (*See also* Obituaries.)

# Music

## Special Report:
## An Art Form in Search of Itself

by Cooper Speaks

Opera is not an art form indigenous to the Western Hemisphere. It had its origins in attempts by the Florentine *Camerata* to revive Greek drama, and it flourished in the court life of 17th- and 18th-century Europe. Nevertheless, as an art encompassing all the others, its appeal has been universal, and there are few areas of the world today where an art combining drama and music does not flourish.

Though the Americas cannot be said to have contributed any operas to the permanent international repertoire, the performance of opera has long been popular here. Indeed the history of operatic performances in the New World and the list of great American opera singers are long and brilliant. In addition to such singers as Lillian Nordica, Sybil Sanderson, Minnie Hauk, Louise Homer, Geraldine Farrar, and Rosa Ponselle, to mention only a few native prima donnas, a major part of the singing careers of Europeans Jenny Lind, Enrico Caruso, Kirsten Flagstad, Lauritz Melchior, and Mary Garden made performance history in the United States an exciting one. By contrast, the failure of American composers to write operas of international permanent appeal seems all the more remarkable.

What this failure may indicate is that opera in America exists principally as a glittering showcase for society and its trappings rather than as an art form that has drawn from our cultural roots, reflecting our heritage in a meaningful way. Moreover, in a country that gives little financial recognition to the importance of the arts, those in the business side of opera have had little opportunity and often little desire to make of their art one appealing to democratic society.

### Artistic Wealth, Financial Failure

Nevertheless, in addition to its many fine performers, America has produced native operas deserving of comment. Though it has had no composers of the rank of Wolfgang Amadeus Mozart, Giacomo Puccini, Giuseppe Verdi, or Richard Wagner, it has had during the last half-century some composers of operas who rank on an equal footing with modern opera composers of other countries: George Gershwin, Virgil Thomson, Gian-Carlo Menotti, and Samuel Barber, for example. All attempts to make opera into a popular art, however, failed, despite such valiant attempts as those of the Ford Foundation in 1958 to sponsor performances of American works and to subsidize the composition of American operas.

Small wonder, therefore, that impresarios of American opera houses are reluctant to present works by American composers: they are nearly always financial failures. Those impresarios who have made brave attempts to encourage American composers have often found their efforts thwarted by a public that shuns the new and the native while flocking to performances of minor works by European composers. Those brave impresarios who perform American operas, therefore, are often left with only deficits as thanks. Surprisingly, the record of operatic performances of American works goes back before the American Revolution. Mainly these musical stage works—hardly deserving the name of "operas" or "musical dramas"—were in the style of John Gay's 'The Beggar's Opera' and were ballad operas of simple tunes strung together with spoken dialogue. Though the libretti of several of these interesting works have survived, most of the music has been lost.

One such work, much in the style of an oratorio, was 'The Temple of Minerva', composed in 1781 and performed in that year in Philadelphia, Pa., before a distinguished audience including George and Martha Washington and the French minister. Written by Francis Hopkinson, who signed the Declaration of Independence and helped to design the new country's flag, the work is a collection of solos, choruses, ensembles, and an overture; but the music has been lost, as is true of so many of these early operatic attempts. Other early American ballad operas include 'Tammany' (the name of a Cherokee chieftain; 1794), with music by James Hewitt and a libretto by Anne Julia Hatton, a sister of the actress Sarah Siddons, and 'Edwin and Angelina' (1796), with music by Victor Pelissier, a French musician who was residing in New York City at the time the work was composed.

### Culture Crosses the Sea

In the second quarter of the 19th century, foreign opera troupes began to visit America. The earliest of these (1825) was the Garcías, one of the century's most remarkable musical families, which included the great tenor Manuel García and his daughters, Maria Malibran and Pauline Viardot, as well as his son, Manuel, who was the teacher of Lind and Mathilde Marchesi. Other companies visiting these shores were the Montresors, who came in 1832, and the Seguins, who arrived in 1838. Meanwhile, Mozart's librettist, Lorenzo da Ponte, was encouraging the performance of Italian works in New York City and Philadelphia. Under all these stimuli American opera composers began to stir, and finally the first real opera composed by an American was performed in Philadelphia on June 4, 1845, by the Seguin company. It was 'Leonora' by William Henry Fry, with a libretto by the composer's brother, Joseph. This opera, modeled on the works of Gaetano Donizetti and Giacomo Meyerbeer, was later heard in New York City in 1858, translated into Italian (!), and was performed again in a concert revival there in 1929. However, 'Leonora', like Fry's other opera, 'Notre Dame de Paris' (1864), is based on European subject matter.

During the second half of the 19th century there were many operas composed by native musicians, including two by the brilliant, eccentric Louis Moreau Gottschalk; John Philip Sousa's 'El Capitan', first performed in Boston, Mass., in 1896 and slated for several bicentennial productions; 'The Scarlet Letter' (1896), based on Nathaniel Hawthorne's novel, by America's great musical friend Walter Damrosch; and Reginald de Koven's 'Robin Hood' (1890).

Most American opera houses, however, ignored these 19th-century efforts; and it was not until March 18, 1910, when Frederick Shepherd Converse's one-act 'The Pipe of Desire' was performed on a double bill with Ruggiero Leoncavallo's 'I Pagliacci', that a major American opera house (in this case the Metropolitan) produced a work by a native composer. Despite an all-American cast that included Louise Homer, the work was hampered by what one critic called "a hopeless text" and imitative Wagnerian music.

One of the early American efforts of the 20th century was 'Natoma', based on an Indian story with a California setting, libretto by Joseph Redding and music by Victor Herbert, who was later to become a popular writer of operettas. Herbert had begun his career as a cellist in the orchestra at the Metropolitan, and 'Natoma', produced in Philadelphia and New York City in 1911, revealed a knowledge of operatic structure along with unforgettable tunes, Herbert's trademark. It starred Mary Garden and John McCormack and was conducted by Cleofonte Campanini. Sadly, the opera has been lost. A second Herbert opera, the one-act 'Madeleine', was premiered at the Metropolitan in 1914. It had an 18th-century setting and starred Frances Alda.

The German influence was strong in American music during the early years of the century, as can be seen in both Henry Hadley's 'Azora', produced in Chicago in 1917, and Horatio Parker's 'Mona', which won the $10,000 prize offered by the Metropolitan for the best American opera. When premiered there in 1912, 'Mona' reminded many critics musically of Wagner's 'Tristan und Isolde'. Still this

Douglas Moore's 'The Ballad of Baby Doe' was based on actual figures in late-19th-century American history and premiered at the Central City Opera House in Colorado in 1956.

opera, which featured contralto Homer in the title role, has passages of great beauty and an astringent tone that is remarkably modern. It was undeservedly withdrawn from the Metropolitan after four performances, and it is certainly due a revival at a time when far less consequential minor works by foreign composers are being produced.

## The Renaissance of the Thirties

The great decade for the composition and production of American operas was the 1930's, beginning with a new work produced in the new Chicago Civic Opera on Dec. 10, 1930. The opera, called 'Camille', starred Mary Garden, who had suggested its composition to composer Hamilton Forrest. Far more significant, however, were the works of Deems Taylor, whose 'The King's Henchman' (1927), with a libretto by the U.S. poet Edna St. Vincent Millay, was first performed at the Metropolitan and established a record for longevity of an American opera until broken by the same composer's 'Peter Ibbetson', which was produced in 1931 and starred Edward Johnson, Lawrence Tibbett, and Lucrezia Bori. In 1933 'Peter Ibbetson' became the first American opera ever to open a Metropolitan season. Also starring Tibbett, a performer who did much for American opera, was Louis Gruenberg's 'The Emperor Jones' (1933), which was based on a play by U.S. dramatist Eugene O'Neill. This work has some nice choral passages and fine declamatory monologues. It received its world premiere over a Metropolitan radio broadcast on Jan. 7, 1933; another radio premiere opera was Howard Hanson's 'Merry Mount' (1934), based on a story by Hawthorne and starring Tibbett as a Puritan preacher. Thus, between 1927 and 1934 four American operas received their world premieres at the Metropolitan, all of them starring Tibbett and all conducted by Tullio Serafin.

Meanwhile, Gershwin—in some respects America's most original serious composer—was writing 'Porgy and Bess', which was premiered in Boston in 1935 and is perhaps the best claimant for a place in the international repertoire. Though it has little musical continuity, 'Porgy and Bess' shows the use of the jazz idiom as a basis for a work of real emotional depth. It was the first American opera to be a genuine success throughout the world. In 1952 a traveling production with an all-black cast including Leontyne Price, William Warfield, and Cab Calloway was enthusiastically received in the capital cities of Europe.

Within narrow limitations America's most original operatic talent has been Thomson, whose two finest works are based on libretti by the U.S. expatriate writer Gertrude Stein: 'Four Saints in Three Acts' (1934) and 'The Mother of Us All' (1947). Both of these works have been revived often and are always greeted with enthusiasm.

One of the most controversial modern American opera composers has been Menotti, one of the few serious composers who has written on truly American subjects. His music is strongly Italianate, nevertheless, and he is sometimes called "the American Puccini." The composer of both serious and comic works, his 'Amelia Goes to the Ball', a comic one-act work, was produced by the Metropolitan in 1938, and his serious 'The Island God' by the same company in 1942. Later works include 'The Medium' (1946), 'The Telephone' (1947), 'The Consul' (1950), 'The Saint of Bleecker Street' (1954), 'Maria Golovin' (1958), and more recently 'Tamu Tamu' (1973), as well as such popular television works as 'The Old Maid and the Thief' and 'Amahl and the Night Visitors'. Still Menotti has yet to compose a genuine American opera and appears more Italian than American in his musical idiom and his outlook.

Menotti also wrote the libretto to Barber's 'Vanessa' (1958), which, with its vaguely Scandinavian or Slavic setting, reminds one of Henrik Ibsen or Anton Chekhov; there is little in it that is American. It has enjoyed popularity in Italy and Austria and is frequently revived in America.

Another Barber opera, 'Antony and Cleopatra', was chosen to open the new Metropolitan Opera House in 1966. It starred Leontyne Price and was conducted by Thomas Schippers, but it was a disaster, principally because of its lavish production by Franco Zeffirelli, who also staged it. It is now being revised by its composer, and in a cleaner, less fussy setting it may enjoy new success.

Among those operas produced as a result of the Ford Foundation grant of 1958 were Norman Dello Joio's 'Blood Moon', produced in San Francisco, Calif.; Douglas Moore's 'The Wings of the Dove' and Robert Ward's 'The Crucible', produced in New York City by the City Opera; and Vittorio Giannini's 'The Harvest', produced by the Chicago Lyric Opera. All of these were mounted in 1961, and none is performed today. Money does not necessarily produce successful operas.

Moore's 'The Wings of the Dove' was perhaps the most successful of this group, but Moore was already an accomplished composer. In addition to 'The Devil and Daniel Webster' (1938), he had written 'The Ballad of Baby Doe' (1956), a real American "grand" opera in an American setting.

Another serious American composer is Carlisle Floyd, whose 'Susannah' (1955), the biblical story of Susannah and the Elders placed in a Tennessee setting, is one of the most widely performed American operas today. Still another is Thomas Pasatieri, who has composed operatic works for both television and the stage. Other works to be considered are those of Marc Blitzstein ('The Cradle Will Rock', 'Regina'), Lee Hoiby ('The Scarf', 'Summer and Smoke'), Kurt Weill ('Down in the Valley', 'Street Scene'), and many others. Still the question remains: Why has America not yet produced an opera capable of taking its place in the international repertoire?

*'Vanessa', Samuel Barber's first opera and ranked among America's best, explores the quest for and reality of love; it premiered at New York City's Metropolitan Opera House in 1958.*

## "Democratization" of Opera

The fault lies with its composers who think of romantic foreign subjects as being properly "operatic," with its audiences who wish to hear the 19th-century repertoire over and over again, and with its producers who see American opera only in terms of huge deficits. Though at the time of the bicentennial there are plans to produce American operas in many places around the country, there are too few commissions for new works, and not all of these are for American composers. While the New York City Opera will perform Leon Kirchner's 'Henderson, the Rain King', based on the novel by U.S. novelist Saul Bellow, it will also perform 'Barrabas' by the Argentinian composer Alberto Ginastera as a part of its bicentennial celebration. Seattle, Wash., has announced Leonard Kastel's 'The Pariahs' about America's early whaling era, but the Baltimore, Md., bicentennial entry will be Pasatieri's 'Ines de Castro', a 14th-century Portuguese subject. Chicago —perhaps in a bow to its Polish population—commissioned Krzysztof Penderecki to compose a bicentennial offering, announced as being based on John Milton's 'Paradise Lost'. General Manager Carol Fox stated flatly that "At the moment there's no American who could give us the kind of lasting work we wanted." There are surely reasons why she thinks this, though there were 43 world premieres of new American works in the U.S. in 1972. American operatic composers just do not succeed in opera houses in this country where all modern works are relatively suspect. Chicago, therefore, is by no means assured of a musical or financial success from its Polish composer either.

The trouble may be, as the *Atlanta Constitution* put it when the local company folded in 1973, that opera is "a particular form of cultural expression not too well suited to our country." Still, considering the thousands of people flocking to operatic performances in this country and the thousands of others studying to be opera singers, this hardly seems convincing. The trouble is more likely that opera is the last of the arts to become democratized. Growing out of an aristocratic tradition, it has yet to reflect the American experience profoundly and truthfully. Until it does, no American opera will really last.

The flurry of operatic activity accompanying the U.S. Bicentennial, however, offers some hope for the beginning of a truly American tradition in opera. Menotti has accepted a commission for a full-length work for the Philadelphia Lyric Opera. Carlisle Floyd will present 'Bilby's Doll', based on a novel about colonial times, for the Houston Grand Opera. Floyd is also said to be negotiating for the rights to Robert Penn Warren's political novel 'All the King's Men'.

A number of other works of American literature are in the process of becoming libretti for U.S. composers. They include Nathaniel Hawthorne's 'The Scarlet Letter' (Donald Lybert) and 'Dr. Heidegger's Experiment' (Stephen Burton), Edgar Allan Poe's 'The Masque of the Red Death' (Robert Haskins), Washington Irving's 'The Legend of Sleepy Hollow' (Robert Haskins), Stephen Crane's 'Maggie' (Stephen Burton), and Truman Capote's 'Other Voices, Other Rooms' (Alec Wilder). Perhaps the next hundred years will witness the long delayed democratization of opera and a native form.

*In accord with the National Park Service's new policy, a summer forest fire in Wyoming's Grand Teton National Park is allowed to burn, clearing land for new generations of trees and eliminating accumulated deadwood and underbrush, the fuel for more dangerous fires.*

**NATIONAL PARK SERVICE.** In 1974 the National Park Service (NPS) opened Gateway National Urban Recreation Area to provide the 30 million people of the New York Harbor region with waterfront recreation along the New York and New Jersey shores. A similar waterfront, Golden Gate National Recreation Area, near San Francisco, Calif., was opened to greater public use. The NPS, consolidating the recent addition of 25 new areas, had funded and staffed Gateway, Golden Gate, and 19 other new areas for the first time. The 19 were Fossil Butte (Wyo.), Hohokam Pima (Ariz.), and John Day Fossil Beds (Ore.) national monuments; Grant-Kohrs Ranch (Deer Lodge, Mont.), Longfellow (Cambridge, Mass.), Puukohola Heiau (Hawaii), Clara Barton (Glen Echo, Md.), Sewall-Belmont House (Washington, D.C.), Knife River Indian Villages (N.D.), Springfield Armory (Mass.), Tuskegee Institute (Ala.), and Martin Van Buren (Kinderhook, N.Y.) national historic sites; Big Cyprus (Fla.) and Big Thicket (Tex.) national preserves; the Buffalo National River (Ark.); the Cumberland Island National Seashore (Ga.); the John D. Rockefeller, Jr., Memorial Parkway (Wyo.); Boston National Historic Park (Mass.); and the Thaddeus Kosciuszko Home National Memorial (Philadelphia, Pa.). The Carl Sandburg Home National Historic Site (Connemora Farm, near Flat Rock, N.C.) was opened to the public for the first time in 1974.

Public use of the NPS increased sharply after an initial decline of 8.9% during the energy crisis period of the first six months of 1974. By September the decline from the record year of 1973 was less than 3%, and visits were approaching the 159.7 million recorded in the first eight months of 1973.

Tent camping from January 1 to August 1 increased 7% to 10% over 1973 figures for Acadia (Me.), Yellowstone (Wyo.), and Yosemite (Calif.) national parks, dropped 1.3% in Blue Ridge Parkway (Va., N.C., Ga.) and more than 23% in Everglades National Park (Fla.), where backcountry camping increased 187%. Recreational vehicle camping for the seven-month period dropped in all 5 parks from 3% on the Parkway to 29% in Everglades. Backcountry camping was up 72% in Yosemite and 18% in Yellowstone for the period. The NPS also extended its backcountry permit program to 5 more parks, bringing the number to 23.

Ronald H. Walker, NPS director since Jan. 8, 1973, announced on September 9 that he was resigning as of Jan. 1, 1975. A new NPS National Science Center began operations at the Mississippi Test Facility complex of the George C. Marshall Space Flight Center in Bay St. Louis, Miss. The center enabled NPS to use advanced aerospace technology to solve management problems and 25 NPS scientists to coordinate research programs for the park system.

On July 1, NPS began the final program to prepare its American Revolution-related areas for the 1976 Bicentennial. The program included restoration of historic structures and battlefields and the construction of visitor centers, roads, trails, parking areas, and other facilities. All active areas in the National Park System will observe the Bicentennial with special programs in keeping with their individual dominant natural, historical, or recreational significance.

Under the Wilderness Act of 1964, NPS had until Sept. 3, 1974, to complete studies in 57 areas and to recommend to Congress the addition of NPS acreage to the National Wilderness Preservation System. NPS had completed its studies and recommendations on 56 areas by the deadline, withholding action on 1 only because of pending legislation. NPS recommended against wilderness in 5 areas and that 15.5 million acres in 51 areas be added to the National Wilderness Preservation System. (*See also* Camping.)

**NETHERLANDS.**    As a consequence of the oil boycott of the Netherlands by the Arab countries, the Dutch government at the beginning of 1974 rationed gasoline. The measure was ineffective, however, and was revoked on February 4. On March 3, a British Airways VC10 plane was seized by two Palestinian terrorists. When it landed at Schiphol Airport, the 92 passengers and the crew were allowed to disembark. The hijackers set fire to the plane, in reprisal for Britain's having permitted its airports to be used to transport weapons and recruits to Israel during the Arab–Israeli October war, and then surrendered. The hijackers were sentenced to five years' imprisonment.

On May 29, elections for the provincial and municipal councils took place. As compared with the corresponding elections of 1970, they showed gains by left and right at the expense of the three confessional parties: the Roman Catholic People's party, the Protestant Antirevolutionary party, and the Christian Historical Union. Early in July the minister of defense, Henk Vredeling, presented a defense plan. Salient proposals were that the defense budget need not rise proportionately with the rise in national income and that there should be a shift from quantity to quality in weapons and a decrease in numbers of military personnel.

The 1975 budget presented to parliament in September provided for a 23% increase in government expenditures. Thanks to higher revenue from natural gas, however, an increase in taxation was not necessary. In the autumn, the minister of economic affairs, Ruud F. M. Lubbers, presented an energy policy directive to parliament. Its chief proposals were the planned reduction of power; increased government participation in the production, allocation, and use of energy; formation of a strategic reserve of natural gas; and the bringing into operation of three new nuclear power stations by 1985. (*See also* Europe.)

**NEWSPAPERS.**    Rising costs of newsprint, labor, postal rates, and distribution during 1974 drove the price of many 10¢ daily papers to 15¢ and even 20¢. Newsprint held to $200 a ton until August 1, but by the end of the year it had gone up to almost $260. The paper mills operated at near capacity during the year, producing 16.6 million tons, but forecasts predicted tight supplies until the early 1980's. (*See* Forest Products.)

The three major New York City dailies battled their printers, the 2,500-member Typographical Union No. 6, over automation. Most of the members were resigned to the inevitability of the new technology but wanted job guarantees and could not understand the lack of support from other newspaper unions. Mediation brought a final settlement in late August. The New York Newspaper Guild struck Reuters News Service in May over the refusal of management to include a cost-of-living increase clause in its new three-year contract. Other strikes affected newspapers in Akron, Ohio; Dallas,

*Pressmen examine the last issue of the afternoon tabloid* Chicago Today, *which ceased publication on September 13. Of the paper's 425 employees, about one fourth were offered jobs on the parent company's newspaper, the* Chicago Tribune, *which then expanded from its single morning edition to 24-hour production and three daily editions.*
WIDE WORLD

Tex.; Kansas City, Mo.; Pittsburgh, Pa.; and Washington, D.C., in 1974.

Democrat Joe L. Allbritton negotiated a controlling interest in the Republican *Washington Star-News*; the Washington Post Co. purchased *The Trenton Times* and its *Sunday Times-Advertiser*; and the New York Times Co. acquired *The Hendersonville Times-News* during the year. The Frank E. Gannett Newspaper Foundation awarded the Massachusetts Institute of Technology a $125,000 grant to promote the development of newspaper technology, and the American Press Institute, formerly centered at Columbia University, dedicated its own new building at Reston, Va. in 1974. (*See also* Awards and Prizes; Magazines.)

**NEW ZEALAND.** The Labour prime minister of New Zealand, Norman E. Kirk, died at the age of 51 on Aug. 31, 1974. (*See* Obituaries.) He was replaced by Wallace E. Rowling.

New Zealand had economic problems in 1974 common to many countries, paying more for imported oil and getting less for its exports of meat and wool in overseas markets. The government battled inflation, which ran at about 14% for the year. In April a general pay raise of 9% was granted, along with profit and cost controls that proved to be ineffective. The budget limited the size of new homes to conserve the short supply of building materials, increased pensions, increased loans for farmers, and extended special depreciation allowances for business. Later in the year the dollar was devalued 9%, and Prime Minister Rowling announced additional measures to combat inflation, including a compulsory savings plan for earnings of $78 and more per week to be credited against taxes.

Abortion became an issue in New Zealand again when police conducted a controversial raid on a clinic that liberally interpreted the country's abortion law. There was also controversy over the relationship of trade unions and the courts as well as over alleged irregularities in union management.

Immigration policies began in 1974 to put more emphasis on age and skills, and included British and Irish among those requiring entry permits. There was much objection to receiving South African whites-only sports teams. On the other hand, violence increased between police and nonwhites in New Zealand during the year. Like other countries in the area, New Zealand opposed the enlargement of the British-U.S. base at Diego Garcia in the Indian Ocean and also opposed French and Chinese nuclear testing in the Pacific.

**NICARAGUA.** As expected, the year 1974 marked the official return of Gen. Anastasio Somoza Debayle as head of state. Votes cast during the national election on September 1 were not yet tallied when the sole opponent, Conservative Edmundo Paguaga Irias, conceded defeat. The 1950 constitution prohibited the reelection of a president or any of his relatives up to the fourth degree of consanguinity or affinity, but in March a new constitution was approved (the country's 12th in 140 years) that provided legitimacy for Somoza's return. Since his previous term, the president's most notable position had been that of minister of reconstruction, following the December 1972 earthquake, and despite retiring from the armed forces' "active list" he retained his post as supreme chief, a job that could be held by a civilian under Nicaraguan law.

Guerrilla opposition to Somoza was dramatically displayed at year's end when members of the Sandinista Liberation Front seized Nicaragua's foreign minister and several other prominent persons, holding them hostage for 60 hours. Upon government ransom of $500,000, release of 14 jailed sympathizers, and safe passage to Cuba, the hostages were freed unharmed.

Censorship was imposed on the news media during April and May, ostensibly to curb inaccurate reports of a strike by hospital workers. They had asked for a 45% wage increase but settled for 25%. A Central America summit meeting, held in June on a Somoza tobacco farm in Jalapa, unsuccessfully discussed reconstruction of the Central American Common Market. More successful was a meeting between Costa Rican and Nicaraguan associates that agreed to the development of an electric power grid between the two countries and to a hydro scheme in the San Juan River basin. A preferential trade agreement was also signed with Honduras.

Though the annual gross national product growth rate dropped after the earthquake, foreign trade grew at a healthy rate. Imports grew faster than exports, however, leading to inflation. Increased energy costs made serious inroads in overall economic growth, but it was hoped that a domestic pilot project for generating electricity would prove successful in the future. (*See also* Latin America.)

**NIGERIA.** Provisional figures for the 1973 population census became the focus of Nigeria's greatest political controversy in 1974. Issued in May, they indicated that with a total population of 79.8 million, Nigeria was the eighth most populous country in the world—after China, India, the Soviet Union, the United States, Indonesia, Japan, and Brazil. But leaders of Nigeria's southern states disputed the count, which showed the population of the six northern states increasing from 29.8 million in 1963 to 51.4 million in 1973 and that of the six southern states from 25.9 million to only 28.4 million. It was feared by the South that the predominantly Muslim North, with an indicated 64% of the country's population, therefore would dominate the country's politics. It also was feared that the lopsided census figures would affect the sharing of more than $7 billion in oil revenues and the regional allocation of funds for education and economic development. The dispute broke into the open in July when Chief Obafemi Awolowo, leader of the

Yoruba people of the South, said in a public speech that the census figures were false.

With Southern leaders balking at the possible return of Nigeria to civilian rule in 1976 if political representation were based on the 1973 census, Gen. Yakubu Gowon, head of the country's military regime, announced in October that the 1976 date was unrealistic and would be postponed.

General Gowon visited the Soviet Union and China during the year. Increased Soviet technical aid was received by Nigeria, particularly in establishing an iron and steel industry and in further development of the booming oil industry. In September it was announced that the government was moving to acquire majority control of petroleum companies operating in Nigeria. Under the country's indigenization laws, government control also was extended over several small foreign-owned business enterprises earlier in the year.

Despite huge petroleum-export revenues, Nigeria's economic performance was disappointing in 1974. The vital peanut harvest in the drought-stricken North was expected to be less than half that of 1973. As a result, exports were drastically cut as farmers reserved the crop for possible use as food. (*See also* Africa.)

## NIXON, RICHARD M.

**NIXON, RICHARD M.** Undone by his own recorded words, Richard M. Nixon became in 1974 the first U.S. president to resign from office. With impeachment a certainty, he tendered his resignation on August 9. His vice-president, Gerald R. Ford, took office the same day in an orderly transition. (*See* Ford.) The electronic taping system that Nixon had installed to record his presidency provided the documentation that ended it.

In a unanimous vote on July 24, the U.S. Supreme Court ordered Nixon to surrender tape recordings and other documentation of 64 White House conversations sought by the special Watergate prosecutor as evidence for criminal proceedings. Among the last to be released were three that documented Nixon's personal order to stop investigation by the Federal Bureau of Investigation (FBI) of the break-in at Democratic party offices in the Watergate complex. The new information proved that only six days after the break-in on June 17, 1972, Nixon had authorized an effort to use the Central Intelligence Agency to sidetrack the FBI. Along with the transcripts, Nixon released a statement in which he admitted that the evidence was "at variance" with certain of his previous statements and that he had withheld it from investigators, staff, and his own attorney.

The House Judiciary Committee had already voted, on July 27–30, to recommend Nixon's impeachment on charges of obstructing justice, abuse of power, and refusal to honor the committee's subpoenas for evidence. With disclosure of the tapes of June 23, 1972, the committee members who had voted against impeachment changed their votes. A delegation of Republican Congressional leaders met with Nixon on August 7 to apprise him of the scant support he could expect in the House and the Senate. The next evening, Nixon told the country on television that he would resign because he had lost most of his "political base in the Congress." "I regret deeply," he said, "any injuries that may have been done in the course of the events that led to this decision." Citing his peace initiatives, Nixon said that he hoped they would be his legacy.

Shortly before noon on August 9, his formal let-

*The Nixon family poses for its last White House family picture on August 7, the day Nixon decided to resign.*
PICTORIAL PARADE

ter of resignation was delivered to the office of the secretary of state. After an emotional farewell to his Cabinet and the White House staff, Nixon was en route to his home in California, aboard Air Force One, when Ford took the oath of office.

The official opinion on the impeachment of Nixon was made public on August 22 in a 528-page report by the House Judiciary Committee. By a vote of 412 to 3, the full House accepted the report. In it, the ten Republican committee members who originally voted against impeachment emphasized that Nixon had not been " 'hounded from office' by his political opponents and media critics."

On September 8 Ford granted a full, free, and absolute pardon to Nixon for any offenses against the U.S. that he might have committed during his presidency. As a result, Nixon no longer faced the threat of indictment, prosecution, or imprisonment. In reply to the pardon, Nixon said, "No words can describe the depths of my regret and pain at the anguish my mistakes over Watergate have caused the nation."

The pardon was designed to direct the country's attention from Watergate, but it offended many citizens who felt that it put Nixon above the law and left the Watergate story unfinished. Special Watergate Prosecutor Leon Jaworski said, however, that evidence to be presented at the trial of former Nixon aides and campaign officials would reveal Nixon's guilt. Nixon had been named an unindicted coconspirator by the Watergate grand jury. Jaworski added that guilt was implicit in Nixon's acceptance of the pardon and, further, that Nixon could have invoked his Fifth Amendment guarantees against self-incrimination, pleaded quilty, and remained silent had he gone to trial.

When the House Judiciary Committee began on May 9, 1974, to formally consider impeachment, the country was outraged by the transcripts of private conversations about Watergate released by Nixon on April 30. Instead of complying with a House Judiciary Committee subpoena for more than 40 taped conversations between Nixon and his aides, Nixon decided to protest his innocence directly to the people. In a televised address, he said he was making public 1,254 pages of transcribed tape recordings to show once and for all "that the President has nothing to hide in this matter." Nixon admitted that the transcripts were ambiguous in places and that the talks would "become the subject of speculation and ridicule." (The transcripts were riddled with the phrase "expletive deleted.") The manipulative tone of the conversations lost Nixon many staunch and influential supporters.

Unedited tape recordings that were played in court during the Watergate cover-up trial (the trial of Nixon associates on charges involving perjury and conspiracy to obstruct justice) revealed that many incriminating passages had been deleted from the transcripts published in April. A recording never before made public disclosed that Nixon knew 16

months before he resigned that he had incriminated himself in discussing hush money for the Watergate burglars with former White House counsel John W. Dean III on March 21, 1973.

Nixon's voice on tape was at the center of courtroom proceedings that began early in October in Washington, D.C. Nixon had been subpoenaed by the defense and the prosecution both, but ill health precluded his appearance. The day after he resigned, a small blood clot that apparently had originated in his leg was discovered in his right lung. Nixon was hospitalized on September 23, released 11 days later, then readmitted on October 24. Five days later surgeons operated to block off blood clots in his leg. Nixon went into shock after surgery; his condition was described as critical, but on November 14 he was discharged.

U.S. District Court Judge John J. Sirica, who was conducting the Watergate cover-up trial, appointed three physicians to establish officially that Nixon was unable to testify. The doctors examined the former president on November 25, reporting that he was too ill even to give a legal deposition in his home before Jan. 6, 1975. Sirica then ruled that the trial could proceed without the Nixon testimony. Final arguments were completed in December, after three months of testimony, and on New Year's Day the jury pronounced a guilty verdict against former Attorney General John Mitchell, presidential assistants John Ehrlichman and H. R. Haldeman, and former Assistant Attorney General Robert Mardian. Kenneth Parkinson, an attorney for the Nixon reelection committee, was acquitted. Nixon stated he was "deeply anguished" by the verdict but refrained from further comment on the events.

Nixon remained involved in extensive litigation. At the request of the Watergate special prosecutor's office, a September agreement with the government giving Nixon ownership and control of White House tapes and presidential documents had not gone into effect. Nixon appealed to a federal court to force the government to honor the accord, but on December 19 Ford signed legislation giving custody of all the tapes and documents to the General Services Administration. Nixon in turn filed suit, contending the new law violated his "constitutionally protected privilege of confidentiality."

Late in August, Ford had asked Congress to provide Nixon $850,000 as the initial payment on his pension and for transition expenses through June 1975. In November Congress cut the amount to $200,000, and Ford signed the bill on December 27.

In April 1974, Nixon announced that he would pay $432,787.13 in back income taxes plus interest. Congressional investigators and the Internal Revenue Service had concluded that Nixon had underpaid his taxes by more than $400,000 during his first four years as president. After Nixon's resignation, the rights to his as yet unwritten autobiography were sold for a reported $2.5 million. (*See also* Congress; Law; Supreme Court; United States.)

**NORWAY.** Norwegians continued to enjoy a high level of prosperity during 1974. Demand remained strong for most of Norway's traditional export products, such as metals and paper, and the offshore oil boom created many new jobs along the western coast. Norway was expected to become Europe's first net exporter of oil, with the result that oil became a major consideration of foreign policy in 1974. Norway and the Soviet Union disputed their boundary in the oil-rich Barents Sea, and Norway—as an exporter—declined to join the U.S. and other oil-importing countries in the newly formed International Energy Agency.

Increased attention was devoted to environmental issues. In the autumn, the youth organizations of all the country's political parties united behind an appeal urging local authorities and organizations to fight against the introduction of nuclear power. Bowing to the trend, the Ministry of Industry ordered that planning on nuclear power projects should be taken no further than strictly necessary in order to allow parliament to reach a decision on the possible construction of such a plant.

The minority Labor government continued to govern without much difficulty, in spite of having only 62 of the 155 seats in parliament. It sought support for its policies from different groups within the opposition, which was split up among seven parties of varying size. At the same time, however, the Labor party's popularity with the voters fell. The budget for 1975 gave substantial tax concessions, and many Labor opponents saw it as a bid to regain popularity before the next major political contest. Prime Minister Trygve Bratteli, the party's 64-year-old chairman, announced in June that he would not continue in office beyond Labor's 1975 national congress. (*See also* Europe.)

**NURSING.** During 1974, the trend continued for more educated and competent registered nurses to function independently and interdependently in primary care as well as in long-term and acute-care centers. The American Nurses' Association (ANA) vigorously supported the concept of the nurse as a primary health care provider and called for unrestricted access in nursing services by the public. The ANA stated that this could be realized only through third-party payment of nursing fees, not covered in most health insurance policies.

More registered nurses in the U.S. opened private offices during 1974. These nurses took health histories, conducted screening tests, gave nursing care in their offices and in homes, helped clients assess their own conditions, and taught preventive health measures. Some offered public classes in such subjects as antepartum care, diabetes management, nutrition, and prevention of heart, respiratory, and other diseases. The acceptance of nurses in private practice varied from community to community, but for the most part they were received enthusiastically.

More than 10,000 registered nurses attended the

WIDE WORLD

*Three nurses picket outside a San Francisco hospital as part of the California Nursing Association strike against 43 hospitals in June.*

49th biennial convention of the ANA in San Francisco, Calif., in June. In an effort to strengthen nursing's position in politics on the state and national level, the Nurses Coalition for Action in Politics was formed. As nursing's political action arm, this group intended to stimulate nurses to take a more active role to help improve the country's health care.

The National League for Nursing (NLN) won a precedent-setting suit against impoundment of federal funds for nursing schools by the Department of Health, Education, and Welfare (HEW). A January decision forced the release of $21.7 million in capitation funds budgeted by Congress for the 1973–74 academic year, which meant that 948 nursing schools received grants as originally committed.

The ANA and the NLN joined in supporting extension of capitation and other provisions for funding of nurse training programs. They supported specific standards for nursing care under national health insurance and endorsed a national health insurance plan that would guarantee coverage of all people "for the full range of comprehensive health services." The ANA was awarded a contract by HEW providing $252,411 to develop criteria for measuring the quality of nursing care and to recommend ways in which nursing could participate in Professional Standards Review Organizations.

For the first time, consumers of health care services were considered for membership on state boards of nursing, the regulatory bodies pertaining to the practice of nursing in each state. The ANA formally called for the inclusion of one consumer on each state board of nursing, citing that "consumers are increasingly concerned with matters related to the quality and quantity, cost and accessibility of health care services." (*See also* Dentistry; Hospitals; Medicine; Race Relations.)

WIDE WORLD

JACK BENNY

# OBITUARIES. Among the notable people who died in 1974 were:

**William (Bud) Abbott,** straight man of the comedy team of Abbott and Costello; with partner Lou Costello, he made more than 40 movies and amassed a small fortune, which he later lost to the Internal Revenue Service; April 24, Woodland Hills, Calif., age 78.

**Gen. Creighton W. Abrams,** Army chief of staff (1972–74) and former U.S. commander in Vietnam; Sept. 4, Washington, D.C., age 59.

**Forrest C. (Phog) Allen,** master basketball coach for the University of Kansas for nearly 40 years; because of his efforts, basketball became an Olympic sport in 1936; Sept. 16, Lawrence, Kan., age 88.

**Stewart Alsop,** journalist who covered the Washington, D.C., scene in regular columns for the *Saturday Evening Post* and, later, *Newsweek*; he was respected by politicians and other newsmen for his direct, literate style and gentlemanly mien; May 26, Bethesda, Md., age 60.

**Gene (Jug) Ammons,** jazz saxophonist who played with such greats as Billy Eckstine, Woody Herman, Miles Davis, and Charlie Parker; Aug. 6, Chicago, age 49.

**Cliff(ord), Arquette,** comic actor known to TV audiences as Charley Weaver, the whimsical bumpkin from mythical Mount Idy, Ohio; Sept. 23, Burbank, Calif., age 68.

**Miguel Angel Asturias,** Guatemalan poet, novelist, and diplomat who won the Lenin peace prize, 1966, and the Nobel prize for literature, 1967; June 9, Madrid, Spain, age 74.

**Mohammed Ayub Khan,** Pakistani politician and field marshal, who in 1958 seized control of Pakistan in a bloodless military coup; confirmed as president in 1960, he was reelected in 1965 but resigned in 1969 following riots and growing civil strife; April 19, Islamabad, Pakistan, age 66.

**Jack Benny,** comedian who was a master of the pregnant pause and whose carefully created comic image of a vain, finicky tightwad earned him a large, devoted following; actually an accomplished violinist, he traded on the comic appeal of squeaky, off-key renditions and insisted for decades that he had just turned 39; Dec. 26, Beverly Hills, Calif., age 80.

**Helen Hemingway Benton,** owner and publisher of the *Encyclopaedia Britannica*; she assumed the title of publisher in April 1973 following the death of her husband, William Benton; May 3, Phoenix, Ariz., age 72.

**Alexander M. Bickel,** constitutional law expert and Yale professor who participated in the successful defense of *The New York Times* in the controversial 1971 Pentagon Papers case; Nov. 7, New Haven, Conn., age 49.

**Baron Patrick Blackett,** British experimental physicist who discovered the positive electron in 1933 and was awarded the Nobel prize for physics in 1948; July 13, London, age 76.

**Charles Eustis (Chip) Bohlen,** diplomat and expert on Soviet affairs; he served as interpreter—and adviser—to Presidents Roosevelt and Truman in the conferences at Teheran, Yalta, and Potsdam; his ambassadorial assignments included Moscow, Manila, and Paris; Jan. 1, Washington, D.C., age 69.

**Hal Boyle,** widely published human-interest columnist for the Associated Press since 1943, who was awarded a Pulitzer prize in 1945 for his distinguished coverage of the European front in World War II; April 1, New York City, age 63.

**Walter Brennan,** veteran actor especially known for his parts in Westerns and for his television portrayal of Grandpa on The Real McCoys; he won three Academy Awards for best supporting actor; Sept. 21, Oxnard, Calif., age 80.

**Jacob Bronowski,** Polish-born scientist, philosopher, and author who in 1964 left his career as a mathematician and adviser to the British government to join the staff of the Salk Institute at La Jolla, Calif.; author of 'Science and Human Values', 'William Blake and the Age of Revolution', and a 13-part television series entitled The Ascent of Man; Aug. 22, East Hampton, N.Y., age 66.

**Clive Brook,** suave, unflappable British actor of stage and screen famed for his character roles as the stiff-upper-lip hero; Nov. 17, London, age 87.

**Georg Brunis,** Dixieland jazz trombonist who was known for his antics onstage as well as his popular musical style; Nov. 19, Chicago, age 74.

**Vannevar Bush,** gifted and versatile engineer who planned and coordinated the urgent updating of American technology for World War II and who was instrumental in the development of the atomic bomb; his postwar report to President Truman on the peaceful uses of wartime lessons provided the basis for the eventual establishment of the National Science Foundation; June 28, Belmont, Mass., age 84.

**Henry Joel Cadbury,** biblical scholar and humanitarian who shared the 1947 Nobel peace prize for his creation in 1917 of the American Friends Service Committee, U.S.; Oct. 7, Bryn Mawr, Pa., age 90.

**Harry Carney,** jazz saxophonist who played during his career with such jazz notables as Benny Goodman and Duke Ellington; Oct. 8, New York City, age 64.

**Sir James Chadwick,** British physicist who won the 1935 Nobel prize for physics for his discovery of the neutron; July 24, Cambridge, England, age 82.

**Bill Chase,** trumpet player and leader of the jazz-rock band Chase whose recording 'Get It On' was nominated for a Grammy award in 1972; Aug. 9, Jackson, Minn., age 39.

**Erskine Childers,** English-born second Protestant president of the Irish Republic (1973–74) and a fierce patriot who pledged his efforts to the peaceful union of the Irish people; Nov. 17, Dublin, Ireland, age 68.

**Murray M. Chotiner,** lawyer, political tactician, and behind-the-scenes political adviser who greatly influenced the career of Richard M. Nixon; Jan. 30, Washington, D.C., age 64.

**Jack Cole,** choreographer trained at the Denishawn School, who had a worldwide influence on the development of stage dancing; his last Broadway hit was 'Man of La Mancha' (1965); Feb. 17, Los Angeles, age 59.

**Edward U. Condon,** expert physicist who was instrumental in the development of the atomic bomb and who directed a well-known U.S. Air Force report on unidentified flying objects; March 26, Boulder, Colo., age 72.

**Cyril Connolly,** witty and learned British literary critic and author who founded and edited *Horizon* magazine (1939–50), publishing among others the works of W. H. Auden, T. S. Eliot, and André Gide; in 1950 he joined the London *Sunday Times* as a regular contributor; Nov. 26, London, age 71.

**Katharine Cornell,** leading lady of the American stage for more than 30 years; national fame came from her 1925 portrayal of sultry Iris March in Michael Arlen's 'The Green Hat'; seeking richer dramatic roles for her talents, she founded in 1931 with her director-husband Guthrie McClintic the Katharine Cornell Presents company and in one of her greatest triumphs starred as Elizabeth in 'The Barretts of Wimpole Street', the company's first production; success continued with a variety of leading roles—Juliet, St. Joan, Candida, Antigone—until 1961; after her husband's death, she retired; June 9, Vineyard Haven, Mass., age 81.

**Donald Crisp,** veteran character actor who appeared in numerous films; his performance in 'How Green Was My Valley' won an Academy Award for best supporting actor in 1941; May 25, Van Nuys, Calif., age 93.

**Jean Cardinal Daniélou,** eminent French Jesuit theologian; known in the 1930's as a liberal Catholic intellectual, in later years he became more moderate, ultimately serving as a conservative spokesman in the cause of papal authority and priestly obedience; May 20, Paris, age 69.

**Lili Darvas,** Hungarian-American actress, discovered in 1925 by the celebrated director Max Reinhardt, whose 50-year career took her to the leading theaters of Europe and the U.S.; July 22, New York City, age 68.

**Rodger Davies,** U.S. ambassador to Cyprus; an expert on Middle Eastern affairs, he had previously worked in Washington, D.C., as a deputy assistant secretary of state; Aug. 19, Nicosia, Cyprus, age 53. (*See* Cyprus.)

**Adelle Davis,** pioneer in the health foods movement and author of four bestselling books on health and nutrition; May 31, Palos Verdes Estates, Calif., age 70.

**Jay Hanna (Dizzy) Dean,** star pitcher in the 1930's for the St. Louis Cardinals who was elected in 1953 to baseball's Hall of Fame; when injuries forced his early retirement in 1941, he became a sportscaster whose grammatically fractured reports and on-the-air antics earned him a large, devoted following; July 17, Reno, Nev., age 63.

**Maj. Alexander de Seversky,** Russian-born U.S. aircraft designer and aviator, whose efforts contributed to Allied air success in World War II; Aug. 24, New York City, age 80.

**Vittorio de Sica,** Italian film director whose films, such as 'Shoeshine' and 'The Bicycle Thief', ushered in the postwar era of cinematographic realism; four of his works received Oscars as best foreign films; Nov. 13, Paris, age 73.

**Billy De Wolfe,** dapper comedian of stage, screen, and television, whose film credits included 'Lullaby of Broadway' and 'Call Me Madam'; March 5, Los Angeles, age 67.

**Enrico Gaspar Dutra,** president of Brazil (1945–51); June 11, Rio de Janeiro, Brazil, age 89.

**Edward Kennedy (Duke) Ellington,** master jazz pianist and prolific composer whose more than 6,000 works ranged from popular tunes ('Sophisticated Lady', 'Mood Indigo') to lengthy orchestral pieces ('Black, Brown and Beige') and sacred compositions, all of which greatly influenced the course of contemporary American music; he gained national attention in the late 1920's leading his band, the Washingtonians, in a nightly radio broadcast from Harlem's Cotton Club; in later years he toured the world with his music, receiving numerous honors along the way; his creative drive never diminished, and later works included the scores for several movies, a ballet for Alvin Ailey, a theatrical pageant of black history, and in 1973 his autobiography, 'Music Is My Mistress'; May 24, New York City, age 75.

**(Mama) Cass Elliot** (Ellen Naomi Cohen), pop singer who rose to stardom in the 1960's as a member of the Mamas and the Papas and later went on to a successful nightclub and recording career on her own; July 29, London, age 33.

**Jacques Estérel,** engineer-turned-couturier who specialized in avant-garde design; April 14, Paris, age 56.

**Yekaterina Furtseva,** Soviet minister of culture and the only woman to enter the inner ruling circle of the Communist party; Oct. 25, Moscow, age 63.

**Tyree Glenn,** jazz trombonist who played with the big names of jazz—Louis Armstrong, Lionel Hampton, and Duke Ellington; May 18, Englewood, N.J., age 61.

**Prince Henry, Duke of Gloucester,** uncle of Queen Elizabeth II and the last surviving son of King George V; June 10, Barnwell, England, age 74.

**Samuel Goldwyn,** movie producer whose credits included about 70 films, which won 27 Academy Awards in various categories; a colorful personality, he coined such phrases as "Include me out" and "An oral agreement isn't worth the paper it's written on!"; Jan. 31, Los Angeles, age 91.

**Adolph Gottlieb,** noted painter and an early proponent of abstract expressionism; March 4, New York City, age 70.

**Georgios Grivas,** Greek army officer who led the National Organization for the Cyprus Struggle (EOKA B), the faction that sought by terrorist means to end British rule and bring about reunion of Cyprus and Greece; Jan. 27, Limassol, Cyprus, age 75.

**Ernest Gruening,** Alaska's governor (1939–53) and U.S. senator (1956–69); one of two senators to vote against the 1964 Gulf of Tonkin resolution, he remained an outspoken critic of U.S. military involvement in Vietnam; June 26, Washington, D.C., age 87.

**Alan Guttmacher,** obstetrician who pioneered the birth-control movement and was its most vocal spokesman; March 18, New York City, age 75.

**Seymour E. Harris,** influential political economist and advocate of Keynesian economics who was economic adviser to Presidents Kennedy and Johnson; Oct. 27, San Diego, Calif., age 77.

**Dame Sibyl Mary Hathaway,** 21st ruler to exercise feudal dominion over the tiny English Channel Island of Sark; July 14, Sark, age 90.

**Georgette Heyer,** British novelist known for historical romances of early 19th-century England; July 5, London, age 71.

**Luther H. Hodges,** governor of North Carolina (1954–60) and secretary of commerce under Presidents Kennedy and Johnson from 1961 to 1964; Oct. 6, Chapel Hill, N.C., age 76.

**Paul G. Hoffman,** businessman, philanthropist, and statesman who was the first administrator of the Marshall Plan, which reconstructed the postwar economies of Western Europe; Oct. 8, New York City, age 83.

**Tim Horton,** defenseman for the Buffalo Sabres and oldest regular in the National Hockey League; Feb. 21, St. Catharines, Ont., age 44.

**H(aroldson) L(afayette) Hunt,** eccentric billionaire Texas oil titan and entrepreneur known for his frugality; in the 1950's he championed right-wing causes and became an ardent supporter of Sen. Joseph McCarthy's anti-communist investigations; Nov. 29, Dallas, Tex., age 85.

**Chet Huntley,** television newscaster who co-anchored with David Brinkley from 1956 to 1970 the popular evening news program the Huntley-Brinkley Report; March 20, Bozeman, Mont., age 62.

**Sol Hurok,** Russian-born U.S. impresario who introduced American audiences to an international array of distinguished per-

ADELLE DAVIS

THE NEW YORK TIMES
ADOLPH GOTTLIEB

forming artists including Fyodor Chaliapin, Isadora Duncan, Anna Pavlova, Andrés Segovia, Marian Anderson, and Maria Callas; March 5, New York City, age 85.

**A(lexander) Y(oung) Jackson,** Canadian landscape painter and one of the founders in 1920 of the Group of Seven, whose work provided Canada with its first uniquely Canadian artistic expression; April 5, Pine Grove, Ont., age 91.

**Franz Jonas,** Austrian statesman and president of Austria (1965–74); he had previously served 14 years as mayor of Vienna and had held seats in both the upper and lower chambers of the federal parliament; April 23, Vienna, age 74. (*See* Austria.)

**B. Everett Jordan,** U.S. senator (D, N.C.) from 1958 to 1972 who led the 1964 Senate investigation of Bobby Baker; March 15, Saxapahaw, N.C., age 77.

**Louis I. Kahn,** Russian-born U.S. architect whose innovative buildings exploited the textures of raw, unfinished materials and exposed mechanical features such as pipes and ductwork as integral parts of the design; his best-known works include the Yale University Art Gallery, government buildings in Dacca, Bangladesh, the Salk Institute in La Jolla, Calif., and the Kimbell Art Museum in Fort Worth, Tex.; March 17, New York City, age 73.

**Alberta Williams King,** mother of slain civil rights leader Martin Luther King, Jr.; she was killed by a young black gunman during Sunday morning worship services at the Ebenezer Baptist Church where her husband, the Rev. Martin Luther King, Sr., was pastor; June 30, Atlanta, Ga., age 70. (*See* Crime.)

**Norman Eric Kirk,** prime minister of New Zealand (1972–74); chief of the country's Labour party since 1963, he ended the party's 12-year absence from power with his 1972 election; Aug. 31, Wellington, New Zealand, age 51.

**Anne Klein** (Rubinstein), fashion designer whose clothes were known for their casual sophistication; she was named to the Coty American Fashion Awards Hall of Fame in 1971; March 19, New York City, age 51.

**William Fife Knowland,** politician and newspaper executive; as Republican floor leader in the U.S. Senate (1953–58) he became known as an ardent opponent of Chinese Communism; Feb. 23, near Guerneville, Calif., age 65.

**Josef Krips,** Austrian-born conductor who directed many of the world's leading opera companies and orchestras; Oct. 12, Geneva, Switzerland, age 72.

**Otto Kruger,** veteran character actor of stage and screen whose more than 100 films included 'High Noon' and 'The Last Command'; Sept. 6, Woodland Hills, Calif., age 89.

**Pär Lagerkvist,** Swedish author and winner of the 1951 Nobel prize for literature; his best-known works include the novels 'The Dwarf', 'The Sibyl', and the prizewinning 'Barabbas'; July 11, Stockholm, Sweden, age 83.

**Rosemary Lane,** one of the four singing Lane sisters who broke into show business in the 1930's with Fred Waring's Pennsylvanians; Nov. 25, Hollywood, Calif., age 61.

**Lois Lenski,** prolific author-illustrator of children's books ('Strawberry Girl'); Sept. 11, Tarpon Springs, Fla., age 80.

**Elie Lescot,** president of Haiti (1941–46), whose virtual dictatorship was ended by a military coup; Oct. 22, Port-au-Prince, Haiti, age 90.

**Charles Lindbergh,** aviator who stunned the world in 1927 with his nonstop 33½-hour solo flight across the Atlantic in a single-engine plane called the *Spirit of St. Louis*; an instant hero, he returned home to ticker tape parades and the Congressional Medal of Honor and the Distinguished Flying Cross; shy by nature, he coveted privacy and after the widely publicized kidnap-murder of his infant son in 1932, sought seclusion with his family in Europe; in 1939 he returned home to oppose U.S. entry into World War II, advocating a negotiated peace for which he was widely criticized and regarded by many as anti-Semitic; with the bombing of Pearl Harbor, he abandoned his nonintervention campaign and tried to enlist for active duty but was rebuffed; instead he served in the Pacific theater as a consultant for United Aircraft Corp. and flew about 50 combat missions as a civilian; after the war, he withdrew from public view, devoting himself to rocketry and the development of the U.S. missile program and in later years became involved with ecology; Aug. 26, Maui, Hawaii, age 72.

**Walter Lippmann,** giant of American journalism, columnist, and author of 25 books; his syndicated column "Today and Tomorrow," begun in 1931, traced the political events in Washington, D.C., and the world; Dec. 14, New York City, age 85.

**Anatole Litvak,** Russian-born U.S. film director who maintained his residence in Paris and whose many films included such classics as 'Anastasia' with Ingrid Bergman and 'Mayerling' with Charles Boyer; Dec. 15, Paris, age 72.

**Harold A. Loeb,** member of the "Lost Generation" expatriate writers in Paris and publisher of the avant-garde literary magazine *Broom*, which printed the early works of such writers as Hart Crane, Gertrude Stein, Conrad Aiken, and E. E. Cummings; Jan. 20, Marakesh, Morocco, age 82.

**Frank McGee,** newsman and host since 1971 of NBC's Today program; known for his cool, competent reportorial style, he provided coverage of the nation's racial strife, political scene, and space program; April 17, New York City, age 52.

**Wayne Maki,** forward with the National Hockey League; May 12, Vancouver, B.C., age 29.

**Ilona Massey,** Hungarian-born film star and singer who appeared on Broadway in the Ziegfeld Follies (1943–44); Aug. 20, Bethesda, Md., age 62.

**V. K. Krishna Menon,** anti-Western Indian defense minister and leader in the fight for Indian independence; as defense minister, he failed to prepare India for the 1962 Chinese border assault and resigned in disgrace; Oct. 6, New Delhi, India, age 77.

**Darius Milhaud,** French composer who became known as the father of polytonality; in the 1920's he presided over a group of avant-garde composers known as Les Six; among his most famous works are 'La Création du monde' and 'Le Boeuf sur le toit'; June 22, Geneva, Switzerland, age 81.

**Agnes Moorehead,** versatile character actress of stage, screen, and television; she was best known to the American public for her portrayal of Endora in the TV series Bewitched, but her stage credits included 'Scarlet Pages', 'All the King's Men', 'Courage', and 'Don Juan in Hell'; she also made about 100 motion pictures and received five Academy Award nominations; April 30, Rochester, Minn., age 67.

**Wayne Morse,** U.S. senator from Oregon (1945–69) and one of two senators to oppose the Gulf of Tonkin resolution; July 22, Portland, Ore., age 73.

**Karl E. Mundt,** U.S. senator from South Dakota (1948–73), best known for presiding over the 1954 Army-McCarthy hearings; Aug. 16, Washington, D.C., age 74.

**Manuel Arturo Odria,** Peruvian army general and president (1948–56); Feb. 18, Lima, Peru, age 77.

**David Oistrakh,** renowned Soviet violinist who was among the first Soviet artists to perform in the U.S. after the cold war thaw; he continued to expand his vast repertoire throughout his lifetime and in 1958 took up conducting with considerable success; Oct. 24, Amsterdam, Netherlands, age 65.

**Marcel Paul Pagnol,** French filmmaker and author who was best known in the U.S. through 'Fanny', a musical adaptation of a film from his trilogy ('Marius', 'Fanny', and 'César') about life in Marseilles; April 18, Paris, age 79.

**Park, Yook Young Soo,** charming and extremely popular wife of South Korean President Park Chung Hee; she was shot by the would-be assassin of her husband; Aug. 15 (South Korea's Liberation Day), Seoul, South Korea, age 48. (*See* Korea.)

**Juan Domingo Perón,** president of Argentina and for more than 25 years the dominant—and most controversial—figure of that country's political scene; rising to power in 1943 in a bloodless military coup, he captured the presidency in 1946 and gained tremendous popularity among the working class with his progressive social reforms; after his second presidential victory in 1951, however, his political base was greatly diminished by the country's faltering economy and Roman Catholic opposition to certain of his policies; driven into exile in 1955, he returned 18 years later and was reelected to the presidency with 65% of the vote, but at his death left a badly divided nation to his successor and third wife, Isabel; July 1, Buenos Aires, Argentina, age 78.

**Billie Goodson Pierce,** exuberant jazz pianist and co-leader in the 1960's with her husband, DeDe Pierce, of the Preservation Hall Jazz Band; Oct. 1, New Orleans, La., age 67.

**Lucius Pitts,** civil rights leader and educator; Feb. 25, Augusta, Ga., age 59.

**Georges Pompidou,** French statesman and president of the Fifth Republic (1969–74); abandoning his teaching career in 1944, he became an aide to Gen. Charles de Gaulle and served in various government posts until joining the bank of Rothschild Frères in 1954; he returned to political service four years later as chief of the cabinet and helped to draft the constitution of the Fifth Republic; appointed premier in 1962, he consistently stayed in De Gaulle's shadow until an impressive handling of the 1968 student riots and strikes won him considerable prestige but subsequent ouster from his post by De Gaulle; when the latter resigned in 1969, Pompidou entered and won the presidential race; as president he provided France with a stable government, strengthened the economy, supported Great Britain's entry into the Common Market, and generally made France's political presence felt throughout the world; April 2, Paris, age 62.

**James Pope-Hennessy,** British biographer and writer who won wide acclaim for his official biography of Queen Mary, consort of George V; Jan. 25, London, age 57.

**John Crowe Ransom,** poet, critic, teacher, and founder of the Fugitives, a group of Southern poets that included Robert Penn Warren and Allen Tate; July 3, Gambier, Ohio, age 86.

**Peter Revson,** jet-set auto racer and nephew of cosmetics magnate Charles Revson; he established himself as a gifted driver in 1971 as winner of the Can-Am championship; March 22, Johannesburg, South Africa, age 35.

**Edgar (Sam) Rice,** baseball Hall of Famer of the Washington Senators (1915–33): Oct. 13, Rossmor, Md., age 84.

**Woodward Maurice (Tex) Ritter,** actor and country-and-western singer best known for throaty renditions of 'You Are My Sunshine', 'Jingle, Jangle, Jingle', and the theme song of the movie 'High Noon'; Jan. 2, Nashville, Tenn., age 67.

**Françoise Rosay,** leading lady of the French cinema for 60 years; March 28, Paris, age 82.

**Harry Ruby** (Rubinstein), songwriter who composed numerous popular tunes, including 'Three Little Words', 'Who's Sorry Now?', and 'I Wanna Be Loved by You'; Feb. 23, Woodland Hills, Calif., age 79.

**Louis B. Russell, Jr.** (*See* Medicine.)

**Cornelius Ryan,** Irish-born U.S. author who as a World War II correspondent began extensive research on the war that he later chronicled in the best-sellers 'The Longest Day', 'The Last Battle' and 'A Bridge Too Far'; Nov. 23, New York City, age 54.

**Eduardo Santos,** Colombian politician, journalist, and president (1938–42); March 27, Bogotá, Colombia, age 85.

**Sholom Secunda,** prolific composer and songwriter best known for 'Bei Mir Bist Du Schoen'; June 13, New York City, age 79.

**André Dunoyer de Segonzac,** widely respected French naturalist painter and printmaker who stubbornly rejected the turn-of-the-century experimental theories and movements in the Parisian artistic coterie, preferring instead to create Cézannesque still lifes and landscapes of southern France; Sept. 17, Paris, age 90.

UPI COMPIX

### AGNES MOOREHEAD

**Anne Sexton,** Pulitzer-prizewinning poet ('To Bedlam and Part Way Back', 'All My Pretty Ones', 'Live or Die') whose anguished verse recorded her relentless self-examination and fascination with death; Oct. 4, Weston, Mass., age 45.

**Clay L. Shaw,** New Orleans businessman, who was accused in 1967 by District Attorney Jim Garrison of being a coconspirator in the assassination of President Kennedy; in a 1969 trial, the jury took less than one hour to declare Shaw innocent; Aug. 15, New Orleans, La., age 60.

**Schneor Zalman Shazar,** Russian-born Israeli poet, biblical scholar, and president of Israel (1963–73), who helped to write Israel's declaration of independence in 1948; Oct. 5, Jerusalem, Israel, age 84.

**David Alfaro Siqueiros,** Mexican artist whose political activity and social protest gained as much notoriety as his bold, flamboyant artistic style; he was jailed several times, most notably in 1960 for inciting student riots; pardoned after four years, he retired from politics to resume painting with unabated vigor; his best-known works, murals depicting historical and revolutionary scenes, are at the National Preparatory School; Chapultepec Palace; the universities of Guadalajara, Mexico City, and Morelia; the Palace of Fine Arts; the National History Museum; and on the interior and exterior walls and in the gardens of the Polyforum Cultural Siqueiros—his largest and most ambitious work—in Mexico City; Jan. 6, Cuernavaca, Mexico, age 77.

**Josef Smrkovsky.** (*See* Czechoslovakia.)

**Lydia Sokolova** (Hilda Munnings), English ballerina who, in 1913, became the first English dancer to enter Sergei Diaghilev's Ballets Russes; Feb. 5, Sevenoaks, England, age 77.

**Moses Soyer,** Russian-born U.S. painter and brother of artists Raphael and Isaac Soyer; Sept. 2, New York City, age 74.

**Gen. Carl A. Spaatz,** first chief of staff of the U.S. Air Force and commander of U.S. strategic bombing forces in Europe and the Pacific in World War II; July 14, Washington, D.C., age 83.

**Bishop Stephen G. Spottswood,** chairman since 1961 of the board of the National Association for the Advancement of Colored People; Dec. 1, Washington, D.C., age 77.

**Lewis L. Strauss,** head of the U.S. Atomic Energy Commission (1953–58) who was instrumental in shaping the U.S. thermonuclear policy; Jan. 21, Brandy Station, Va., age 77.

**FRANK McGEE**

**DIZZY DEAN**

**WALTER BRENNAN**

**GEORGES POMPIDOU**

**DUKE ELLINGTON**

**ED SULLIVAN**

GERALD ISRAEL—PICTORIAL PARADE

SOL HUROK

UPI COMPIX

CHARLES LINDBERGH

WIDE WORLD

KATHARINE CORNELL

UPI COMPIX

U THANT

JUAN PERÓN
WIDE WORLD

EARL WARREN
WIDE WORLD

Ed(ward Vincent) Sullivan, television host of the "really big shew" that entertained the nation for 23 years with endless variety acts and introduced such stars as Jack Benny, Jerry Lewis, Dean Martin, Jackie Gleason, and Elvis Presley; Oct. 13, New York City, age 73.

Jacqueline Susann, actress-turned-author who became the first novelist to have three consecutive books, 'Valley of the Dolls' (1966), 'The Love Machine' (1969), and 'Once Is Not Enough' (1973), top the best-seller lists; her lusty, intricately plotted tales of show business and jet-set worlds brought little praise from critics, but the unprecedented sale of her first book (17 million copies) earned her a listing in the 'Guinness Book of World Records'; Sept. 21, New York City, age 53.

Earl W. Sutherland, Jr., physiologist who won a 1971 Nobel prize for hormonal research; March 9, Miami, Fla., age 58.

U Thant, Burmese statesman who became the third secretary-general of the United Nations (UN) in 1961 after Dag Hammarskjöld's death and was reelected to two full terms in his own right, serving a record ten years in that post; he assumed leadership when the UN was greatly weakened, and prevented its collapse by means of skillful mediation with the superpowers; perhaps his greatest peacekeeping accomplishment was his successful appeal to the U.S. and the U.S.S.R. for restraint during the 1962 Cuban missile crisis; a critic of the U.S. role in Vietnam and Hanoi's bombing of the south, he was himself criticized for acceding in 1967 to United Arab Republic (U.A.R.) President Nasser's demand for removal of the UN peacekeeping forces from the Sinai, a move many viewed as a prelude to the U.A.R.-Israeli six-day war; political foes in the Burmese government prevented his return home after retiring in 1971, and upon his death he was given the unprecedented honor of lying in state at UN headquarters; when his body was moved to Rangoon, Burma, for burial in a government-assigned cemetery, students and monks seized the casket for entombment in a site they felt more fitting for a world statesman; later recovered, the body was buried at the planned site; Nov. 25, New York City, age 65.

Stepan Cardinal Trochta. (See Czechoslovakia.)

Amy Vanderbilt, author and syndicated columnist who served as guardian of the nation's standards of etiquette; a staunch traditionalist on rules of etiquette, she recently admitted that she had modified her views in light of the changing times; Dec. 27, New York City, age 66.

Cornelius Vanderbilt, Jr., author, newspaperman, and lecturer; great-great-grandson of "Commodore" Vanderbilt, founder of the family fortune, he lost millions in ill-fated publishing ventures; July 7, Miami Beach, Fla., age 76.

Baldur von Schirach, Nazi leader who was the first head of Hitler Youth (1933–40) and later gauleiter of Austria responsible for the deportation of 50,000 Austrian Jews; Aug. 8, Munich, West Germany, age 67.

Yevgeny V. Vuchetich, Soviet sculptor whose works include the Soviet war memorial in East Berlin and the statue 'Let Us Beat Swords into Ploughshares' in front of the United Nations headquarters in New York City; April 12, Moscow, age 65.

Earl Warren, attorney general (1939–43) and governor of California (1943–53), Republican vice-presidential candidate (1948), and chief justice of the U.S. Supreme Court (1953–69); under his leadership the controversial "Warren court" became a force for libertarian reform with landmark decisions banning racial segregation in public schools, protecting the rights of accused criminals, and forcing reapportionment of legislative and Congressional districts in all 50 states; in 1963 a committee chaired by Warren investigated President Kennedy's assassination and in 1964 issued the Warren Report, concluding there was no evidence of group conspiracy; July 9, Washington, D.C., age 83.

Delbert Eugene Webb, real estate tycoon and former co-owner of the New York Yankees, who built a $100-million construction empire from a small building company founded in 1929; July 4, Rochester, Minn., age 75.

Sol Wilson, Polish-born U.S. expressionist painter known for his Cape Cod seascapes and New York cityscapes; Nov. 23, New York City, age 81.

Georgi K. Zhukov, Soviet military leader and war hero; chief of staff under Stalin, he commanded forces at key battles during World War II and later served as defense minister of the U.S.S.R.; June 18, Moscow, age 77.

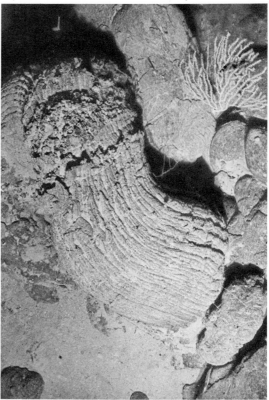

COURTESY, WOODS HOLE OCEANOGRAPHIC INSTITUTION

*In the rift valley of the Mid-Atlantic Ridge this "toothpaste" lava was photographed by a camera lowered from U.S. vessel* Atlantis II.

# OCEANOGRAPHY.

Potential and actual worldwide shortages of food, raw materials, and energy during 1974 highlighted interest in the oceans, not only as possible direct sources of these essentials but also as a perhaps major influence in establishing global climatic regimes upon which agricultural and marine biological sources of food and raw materials are dependent. Reconciliation of these international needs with claims of national sovereignty was the general subject of the third United Nations Conference on the Law of the Sea, an international meeting of more than 5,000 delegates from 148 countries lasting over two months during the summer in Caracas, Venezuela. The discussion articulated the many conflicting points of view that must be reconciled in the writing of an international treaty regulating exploitation of the sea. Elements of any final agreement on the basis of discussion to date included a relatively narrow (perhaps 12-mile-wide) territorial sea, with a considerably wider adjoining zone of economic priority (to 200-mile width or shelf width). Details of any such agreement remained to be specified, however, and it was clear that further work was necessary before the ultimate aim, an international treaty, could become reality.

Against this challenging background of resource

shortage and political uncertainty, studies of ocean circulation aimed at understanding not only how the oceans store and distribute dissolved and suspended substances but also how they absorb, transmit, and release heat, thus potentially exerting a profound influence on the global climate. Studies of the ocean bottom continued global study of its structure with added emphasis on detailed knowledge of conditions at one spreading center. The second phase of the Geochemical Ocean Sections (GEOSECS) study of ocean circulation ended on June 10, when the research ship *Melville*, operated by the Scripps Institution of Oceanography, put into port after a ten-month expedition. The cruise was the Pacific sequel of the nine-month Atlantic cruise a year earlier. Both had been planned to follow presumed trajectories of deep western ocean currents, hypothesized to supply the deep and bottom waters of the two major ocean basins. In addition to the traditional oceanographic measurements of temperature, salinity, and oxygen, GEOSECS concentrated upon measurements of dissolved constituents such as radioisotopes and suspended particulate matter.

The North Pacific experiment (NORPAX) was an attempt to understand the observed apparent correlation between shifts in the pattern of sea surface temperature in the Pacific and Northern Hemisphere climatic fluctuations. Early in 1974, NORPAX experimenters carried out the first of a series of projected studies aiming ultimately at understanding how ocean surface temperature anomalies form. Coherence between climate and ocean temperature was documented in equatorial as well as middle latitudes, and it was suggested that the oceans exert their causative effect upon climate primarily in the tropics. During the summer the Global Atmospheric Research Program, Atlantic Tropical Experiment, held a multinational three-month program of field work in an effort to understand the tropical interaction of the ocean and the atmosphere.

Coastal upwelling is a process occurring most conspicuously along the western coasts of continents. Equatorialward surface winds, plus the rotation of the earth, work together to force surface water seaward and to bring up in its place (upwell) cold and nutrient-rich water from the ocean depths. About 50% of the world's fish catch is taken from such areas. Coastal Upwelling Ecosystem Analysis studied both the physical and biological aspects of upwelling, attempting to develop predictive skill at forecasting the onset and duration of upwelling. Study of the ocean floor was continued by the Deep Sea Drilling Program (DSDP) aboard the drilling ship *Glomar Challenger*. Deep ocean drilling by DSDP generally confirmed the idea of sea floor spreading, according to which the oceanic crust spreads laterally from mid-ocean ridges at speeds of several centimeters per year toward trenches and zones of convergence.

A portion of the Mid-Atlantic Ridge, about 200 miles southwest of the Azores, was studied in unprecedented detail during repeated dives by the U.S. submersible *Alvin* and the French undersea vehicles *Archimède* and *Cyana* to depths of 9,000 feet. The dives were part of the French-American Mid-Ocean Undersea Study (FAMOUS). The Mid-Atlantic Ridge was believed, for indirect reasons, to mark the source of the sea floor underlying the Atlantic Ocean. During Project FAMOUS, numerous formations indicating frequent extrusion of lava were observed. There was evidence that modern volcanic eruptions were confined to a narrow zone of about 500 feet on either side of the ridge's rift valley centerline. (*See also* Earth Sciences; Fish and Fisheries.)

**PACIFIC ISLANDS.** Nationalism among the people of the Pacific islands continued to grow in 1974. The South Pacific Forum, a political group of independent and self-governing countries, and other alliances continued to play important roles in the area. Many leaders became increasingly critical of the U.S., which directly controlled the islands of Guam, American Samoa, and Micronesia. Some said that the U.S.-controlled states were being left behind in the nationalistic movement that had brought independence to many former colonies.

A U.S. offer to Samoa, similar to a system in effect in Guam, that the appointed governor be replaced with an elected official was defeated in 1974, however, in the third referendum to be held on the issue. Proponents of the change argued that the vote reflected Samoan fear that an elected governor would be less successful in getting U.S. aid than an appointed one. Some said that Samoans had been taught that they could not govern themselves. Proponents of an elected governor also charged that they were not given access to government-controlled radio and television to present their views. But it appeared that older and more conservative Samoans, who favored close ties to the U.S., still had great political and social influence.

The governor of American Samoa, John M. Haydon, was found innocent in 1974 of violating the Hatch Act, prohibiting federal employees from campaigning in elections, on grounds that the law did not apply to American Samoa. Critics had charged that Haydon had used his position to prevent them from using radio and television during the second referendum on the issue of electing a governor and were displeased with the acquittal.

Negotiations between Micronesia and the U.S. did not make progress in 1974. Micronesia, a United Nations trust territory, had asked for a subsidy for U.S. military rights and control of foreign affairs, as well as self-government in association with the U.S. There was growing Micronesian sentiment for total independence because of U.S. unwillingness to meet Micronesia's demands.

Papua New Guinea, which became autonomous

in domestic affairs from Australia in 1973, faced the problem of establishing a national identity. There were many rival factions in the country; more than 1,000 tribes spoke about 600 mutually unintelligible languages. The government tried to placate separatist movements on Bougainville and on New Britain by offering the areas autonomy. Another separatist movement began in Papua. Large profits from Bougainville Copper Ltd., controlled by a British firm, brought demands from many politicians that Papua New Guinea receive a larger share of the income.

During the year a number of Portuguese territories were promised the right of self-determination. Included among those territories was Portuguese Timor, on an island off northern Australia.

Fiji celebrated its fourth year of independence from Great Britain in 1974 but had mixed economic success. Record prices were received for crops, but rising import costs forced the government to seek loans and to link the Fijian dollar to the U.S. dollar to reduce currency fluctuations. The new Fijian National party, advocating indigenous interests and opposing multiracial policies, gained popularity.

Fiji and the republic of Nauru remained leaders in regional political and economic affairs, particularly in developing regional communication and transport. When France exploded a nuclear device on the Mururoa Atoll in June 1974, many Pacific and other nations protested the action. (*See also* Indonesia; New Zealand; Philippines.)

## PAINTING AND SCULPTURE.

The increasing interest in native American arts and crafts was marked by several exhibitions during 1974, the most important being "The Flowering of American Folk Art 1776–1876," organized by the Whitney Museum, New York City. The show illustrated the full range of American life and was certainly the most definitive exhibition of its kind ever held. In Chicago, the Art Institute held an exhibition of its entire collection of nearly 160 woven American coverlets, dating from about 1800 to the beginning of the 20th century.

A major exhibition devoted to "American Self-Portraits" was organized by the International Exhibitions Foundation of Washington, D.C., and

*'Universe', Alexander Calder's "wallmobile" in the lobby of the Sears Tower in Chicago, was unveiled and set in motion by the artist on October 25.*
WIDE WORLD

opened at the National Portrait Gallery there. The show, the first of its kind, consisted of 109 works lent by major museums and private collections and covered three centuries of changing tastes. "Art of the Pacific Northwest" was a major show held at the National Collection of Fine Arts at the Smithsonian Institution, also in Washington; 46 artists were represented by 117 paintings, drawings, and watercolors and 16 sculptures.

"Objects USA," featuring American decorative art, was presented at the Kunstgewerbemuseum, Cologne, West Germany, in 1974. Other exhibitions of works by American artists included one devoted to Everett Shinn; it was organized by the New Jersey State Museum in cooperation with the Delaware Art Museum and the Munson-Williams-Proctor Institute, Utica, N.Y. The show included 77 items lent by 33 public institutions and private collectors. The long-forgotten but recently rediscovered history painter and illustrator Edward Austin Abbey was the subject of an exhibition held at the Albany Institute of History and Art and at the Pennsylvania Academy. The show was assembled by the Yale University Art Gallery, which owned a large Abbey collection. A special exhibition of the works of the painter-sculptor Frederic Remington was held at the Whitney Gallery of Western Art, Cody, Wyo.

Following the huge international success of the previous year's "Treasures of Chinese Art" exhibition in Europe, several U.S. shows were devoted to objects from the Orient and the Middle East. The Boston Museum of Fine Arts held the first exhibition in the U.S. to explore recent archaeological discoveries in China; "Unearthing China's Past" included more than 100 works of Chinese art from Western collections, together with photographs of works unearthed since 1949. "Chinese Figure Painting" was one of a series of exhibits held to celebrate the 50th anniversary of the Freer Gallery, Washington, D.C., and showed the status achieved by figure painting in China long before landscape was accepted as an independent subject. The Hans Popper Collection of Oriental Art was first seen at the Asian Art Museum of San Francisco, Calif., and then traveled to Baltimore, Md., Cleveland, Ohio, and Seattle, Wash. The Los Angeles County Museum of Art in 1973 acquired the Palevsky-Heeramaneck Collection of Islamic art, one of the finest in the world; it was on display in the spring of 1974. It covered the period from A.D. 700 to 1900 and included paintings, bronzes, glass, textiles, calligraphy, and ceramics from the Middle East.

A good many exhibitions during the year were devoted to 20th-century artists. Works by the color-field abstractionist Jules Olitski were shown at the Pasadena Museum of Modern Art, Calif., and at the Boston Museum of Fine Arts. Olitski, who was born in the U.S.S.R. in 1922 and had had a strong influence on younger painters, was best known for his technique of spraying fine layers of acrylic paint on raw canvases to create soft expanses of color. A

*'Woman V', by Willem de Kooning, originally bought for under $3,000, was sold for a record $850,000 to the Australian National Gallery.*

"Tribute to Mark Tobey," consisting of 70 paintings, opened at the National Collection of Fine Arts in Washington, D.C., in early summer. Though the first American since Whistler to win Italy's Venice Biennale and the first living American to rate a retrospective at the Louvre in France, the 84-year-old Tobey remained the least known at home of all the American "old masters." A tribute to Joan Miró, the Spanish surrealist, was held at the Museum of Modern Art, New York City, to honor the artist's 80th birthday. The paintings, sculptures, and collages on display came from the museum's own extensive holdings, the best Miró collection in the world. An exhibition of 120 works by Belgian symbolists and surrealists organized by the Belgian Ministry of National Education and Culture was shown at the New York Cultural Center and later at the new Museum of Fine Arts, Houston, Tex. The two great Belgian 20th-century artists René Magritte and Paul Delvaux were well represented.

Some of the finest art collections in the U.S. were in the possession of universities. "Paintings from Midwestern University Collections," sponsored in 1974 by a group of 11 universities, included 42 paintings that encompassed a wide range of subjects and styles.

In Chicago three major sculptural works were unveiled in public areas within a four-week period. On September 27 Marc Chagall's free-form, five-paneled ceramic mosaic wall the size of a boxcar was unveiled. It was entitled 'The Four Seasons' and stood on one side of the First National Bank building's sunken plaza. Then on October 25 two monumental Alexander Calder sculptures were dedicated—'Flamingo', a bright red stabile on the Federal Center Plaza, and 'Universe', a moving "wallmobile" mural in the Sears Tower lobby. (*See* Cities.) Calder was also on display at the Perls Gallery in New York City in late autumn in an exhibition called "Crags and Critters of 1974."

Three American museums acquired rare old master works during the year. The Cleveland Museum of Art obtained 'Saint Catherine of Alexandria' by the mysterious 16th-century German artist Matthias Grünewald. The work, from a private German collection, was one of only two Grünewald works in the U.S. Its coming to light especially excited scholars because the painting was part of a larger altarpiece thought to have been lost at sea in the 17th century. The National Gallery of Art, Washington, D.C., after many years of negotiations with a private source in France, acquired a painting by the 17th-century French artist Georges de la Tour, 'Magdalene of the Mirror'. The fact that fewer than 40 of his paintings had been authenticated undoubtedly accounted for the purchase price, reputed to have been about $1.5 million. The Los Angeles County Museum of Art acquired 'The Holy Family' by Fra Bartolommeo, an important work transitional to the early-16th-century Italian High Renaissance.

The art world was dismayed in September when art historian Rosalind Knauss revealed that seven painted, welded steel sculptures by the late David Smith had been altered by being ground back to the bare metal. Clement Greenberg, an art critic and an executor of Smith's estate, had authorized the removal of the paint. Other of the sculptor's polychrome works had been left outdoors to rust, and their painted surfaces were beyond repair.

In Canada, the English sculptor Henry Moore presented more than 300 of his works to the Art Gallery of Ontario, in Toronto. The gift—including 18 bronzes, 41 plaster casts, and numerous graphic works—coincided with the opening of a new building facility by the museum. After four years of negotiation, the National Museum of Man, at Ottawa, Ont., acquired the Arthur Speyer, Jr., collection of Canadian Indian artifacts predating 1850. Canada's Emergency Purchase Fund, part of the National Museum policy, made possible quick responses in order to preserve works of art representing that country's cultural heritage.

### Art Abroad and Deaths

Australia again made art news headlines in 1974 by purchasing U.S. painter Willem de Kooning's 'Woman V' for about $850,000—the highest price ever paid for a work by a living American artist. The acquisition by the National Gallery in Canberra, during a period of economic ills, aroused heated criticism against the government.

One of the most pleasant exhibitions in London was "Landscape in Britain, 1750–1850" at the Tate Gallery, bringing together large quantities of diverse material. The collection illustrated the complexity of ideas behind the rendition of landscape and included work by unknown as well as by famous artists. The Tate also mounted a retrospective exhibition of "The Late Richard Dadd." A little-known English artist, Dadd painted pictures of remarkable intensity and originality in a style related to that of the Pre-Raphaelites. After murdering his father in 1843, he was confined to a hospital and prison for more than 40 years where he painted some of his finest works, the best-known painting being the Tate's own 'Fairy Feller's Master-Stroke'.

The Royal Academy in London held an exhibition entitled "Impressionism—Its Masters, Precursors, and Influence in Britain" to celebrate the centenary of the first impressionist show, held in Paris on April 15, 1874. There were 137 pieces from public and private collections in Great Britain, including works by the French founders of the movement and by their English followers. The academy also mounted a large exhibition of works by J. M. W. Turner to celebrate the centenary of his death.

At the Victoria and Albert Museum an exhibition of musical instruments entitled "Music in the 18th Century" included examples of work by the celebrated British and French instrument makers. Another exhibition that attracted crowds to the Victoria and Albert commemorated the 150th anniversary of the poet Lord Byron's death; it included paintings, manuscripts, and letters as well as relics such as the pillow from the traveling bed on which Byron died. An exhibition at Somerset House to mark the centenary of Sir Winston Churchill's birth was the first show held in the reopened 18th-century rooms designed by Sir William Chambers. London's Hayward Gallery held a number of worthwhile shows—including "Vorticism and its Allies," "Edvard Munch," and "Lucian Freud."

Major exhibitions in Paris in 1974 included one devoted to Georges Braque, a pioneer of cubism, and one honoring cubist Juan Gris, both at the Orangerie des Tuileries; "Pastels et miniatures du XVIIIème siècle," at the Louvre's Pavillon de Flore; and "Treasures of the Equator," featuring pre-Columbian art of equatorial South America, at the Museum of the Petit Palais. Other French shows included "Matisse Drawings," "Thracian Gold," "Miró," and "Cézanne."

Among those who died during the year were U.S. painter Adolph Gottlieb, Canadian artist A. Y. Jackson, French painter André Dunoyer de Segonzac, Mexican muralist David Alfaro Siqueiros, Russian-born U.S. painter Moses Soyer, and Soviet sculptor Yevgeny Vuchetich. (*See also* Great Britain; Ireland; Museums; Obituaries; Spain; Sweden; U.S.S.R.)

## Painting and Sculpture

## Special Report:
# Two Centuries of U.S. Painting

by Robert H. Glauber

The history of American art is, in great part, a long and continuing search for an image: one that in both its outward forms and inner drives would deal with the particular and peculiar reality in America at any given moment. The search has shifted as our realities have shifted.

Two European artists had visited America before the permanent settlers came. Jacques Le Moyne went to Florida with a French expedition in 1564 and did some paintings of the Indians. John White went to Sir Walter Raleigh's ill-fated colony at Roanoke in 1587 and made small studies of Indians and local plants, animals, and fish. Both artists intended their work as reports for their European sponsors.

The first paintings done in America for Americans were also done by European artists—largely English and Dutch. They were almost all portraits. The growing prosperity of the towns in New York and New England provided incentives for itinerant artists to settle and paint the local merchants. About 400 such portraits done in the 17th century have survived.

*'Paul Revere' by John Singleton Copley, c. 1768.*
COURTESY, MUSEUM OF FINE ARTS, BOSTON. GIFT OF
JOSEPH W., WILLIAM B., AND EDWARD H. R. REVERE

By the 18th century, interest in painting had begun to spread. The talented Scotsman John Smibert (1688–1751) arrived in 1728 and executed some splendid portraits, including 'The Bermuda Group', done in 1729. It set Colonial standards for years. John Wollaston and Joseph Blackburn were both English. They were active in America in the 1750's and 1760's. Both brought new technical glitter to their portraits, but they missed the souls of their sitters. Nevertheless, both were popular and influential.

Native-born talents began to flourish. Robert Feke was born, probably in New York, in about 1705. Little is known of his life, but he was most likely a sailor as well as a painter. That would explain the decidedly English touch to many of his cool, elegant canvases.

### Copley and West

In 1738 were born the two finest painters of 18th-century America. John Singleton Copley (1738–1815) came from Boston and grew up in an artistic atmosphere. His stepfather was a painter, engraver, and teacher of penmanship. Copley was a successful portraitist by the time he was 17. By 20, he had surpassed all previous American artists in painting techniques, use of color, and subtlety of composition. In the decade before the Revolution, he painted a remarkable group of portraits of some of the coming leaders in that struggle. His 'Paul Revere' is a penetrating, personal characterization of one artist by another. Done about 1768, it may well be the greatest work of its period.

Benjamin West (1738–1820) was born in rural Pennsylvania and was largely self-taught. His early works show traces of these beginnings, but his strong dramatic talent soon surfaced. West painted good enough portraits, but he was more interested in historical painting. So, in 1760 he sailed for Europe—never to return. In 1774 Copley joined him. He never came back either. The growing unrest of the coming Revolution had virtually eliminated Copley's market for fine portraits. Such work never really interested West, and what he wanted to paint the Colonials were not ready to buy. They worked, taught, and flourished in London, each producing some of the finest dramatic and historical canvases of the period. Copley's 'Watson and the Shark' and West's 'Saul and the Witch of Endor' are both extremely impressive works.

Many of the best American painters went to

*'The Oxbow' by Thomas Cole, 1846.*

COURTESY, THE METROPOLITAN
MUSEUM OF ART. GIFT OF
MRS. RUSSELL SAGE, 1908

study with West in London. To name a few: Charles Willson Peale (1741–1827), the first American painter-scientist; Gilbert Stuart (1755–1828), best known for his portraits of George Washington; John Trumbull (1756–1843), who painted important works for the Capitol rotunda in Washington, D.C.; and Samuel F. B. Morse (1791–1872), another painter-scientist and inventor of the telegraph.

Before the first 20 years of the 19th century had passed, it was clear that America had developed a flourishing group of highly competent artists. They still painted, however, in the styles and traditions of Europe, where most had been trained—the majority in London, but a few like John Vanderlyn (1775–1852) and John James Audubon (1785–1851) in Paris. Slowly, indigenous American influences started to arise.

### Americans Discover America

The so-called Hudson River School painters were the first to interest themselves seriously in the natural American landscape. This was not so much a school as a loose group of painters who shared a common attitude. The founder of the group was Thomas Cole (1801–48).

In the 1820's literary Romanticism burst upon the country from England. Cole adapted the picturesque and poetic ideas of the Romantics to produce great sentimental vistas of rivers, mountains, and farmlands. Other artists soon followed Cole's lead. Asher Durand (1796–1886) and John F. Kensett (1818–72) painted Hudson River School canvases that heavily romanticized the out-of-doors.

Working at about the same time was another group of artists who preferred the more human and homely aspects of American life. The genre painters were interested in the rural life of the common man. Their inspirations were the 17th-century Dutch and Flemish genre masters.

They worked in both the East and West in a variety of styles and with varying skills. Among the most interesting and satisfying of them were William Sidney Mount (1807–68), who detailed small-town life in New England in gentle, witty canvases; George Caleb Bingham (1811–79), who reported the movement westward in superbly composed, naturalistic paintings that have the look of absolute authenticity and honesty; Eastman Johnson (1824–1906), who was a compassionate observer and often put a stinging edge to his scenes of life among the poor; and Winslow Homer (1836–1910), who brought greatness to his accounts of the dramatic dangers of the sea and the isolation of the woods.

The frontier movement of explorers and settlers aroused the interest of artists. They, too, pushed west to report or romanticize what they saw. George Catlin (1796–1872), Seth Eastman (1808–75), and Alfred Jacob Miller (1810–74) lived with and painted the Indians, "their looks and their modes," with accuracy and sympathy. Their work is probably the finest source of information about Plains Indian life of the 1830's to 1850's. They were, in a sense, as much anthropologists as artists.

Albert Bierstadt (1830–1902) and Thomas Moran (1837–1926) created landscape fantasies that sought to capture the grandeur, the immensity, and the spectacular colors of the unspoiled Rockies in the 1860's and 1870's. They worked, however, firmly within the traditions of European, mostly German, monumental landscape painting.

Finally came the folklorists who dramatized the myths, heroes, and outlaws of the Old West as they imagined them. Frederic Remington (1861–1909), Charles Schreyvogel (1861–1912), Charles Russell (1865–1926), and William Leigh (1866–1955) gave vivid life to the solitary hunters and trappers, the battles between soldiers and Indians, the uproar of frontier towns. In the most melodramatic terms, they immortalized the cult of the horse and saddle.

As American artists mastered the techniques of painting, a small but talented group of them turned back to one of the oldest forms of art known—the still life. As early as 1815 Raphaelle Peale (1774–1825) had painted baskets of fruits and vegetables that clearly reflected Dutch origins. By the last quarter of the 19th century, the greatest of American still-life *trompe l'oeil* (literally, deceive the eye) painters were flourishing: William Harnett (1848–92), John Peto (1854–1907), and John Haberle (1856–1933). All three were masters of an illusionistic realism.

## The Arrival of Impressionism

In 1874 a group of young French artists organized the first impressionist exhibition in Paris. Its repercussions were enormous. Within a few years much of the art world was reacting to impressionism—one way or the other. In 1886 the first important impressionist paintings were shown in America. Many American artists were influenced—to widely varying degrees—by the impressionists' color use, loose composition, subject matter, and paint application, but they tended to utilize only the visual techniques rather than the scientific theories of vision and light that so fascinated the French.

The range of style and approach among the numerous American impressionists was great. Any list of the most significant among them must include Mary Cassatt (1844–1926), Theodore Robinson (1852–96), Julian Alden Weir (1852–1919), John Twachtman (1853–1902), Childe Hassam (1859–1935), and Ernest Lawson (1873–1939). Two of these artists had especially close ties to the French impressionists. Mary Cassatt studied and worked in France and, as early as 1877, was invited by Edgar Degas to join the impressionists' inner circle. Robinson was one of Claude Monet's very few pupils. All of its American followers adapted impressionism to American tastes and talents.

## Eakins and Ryder

Despite the pressures of schools and groups, there were a few great artists who went their own ways. Two of the most interesting were Thomas Eakins (1844–1916) and Albert Pinkham Ryder (1847–1917). Eakins admired scientific detachment and painted coolly precise outdoors scenes, ingeniously characterized portraits (his masterpiece is a group portrait, 'The Gross Clinic'), and curiously prosaic views of sporting events. There is a directness and solidity in the handling of light and form that Eakins made his own.

Ryder was a mystic visionary. The sources of his inspiration are still unknown. He was interested in expressing "his thought and not the surface of it." Shape, rhythm, and elemental harmony were what he sought without reference to any specifics in nature. Neither Eakins nor Ryder influenced the art that followed. They were powerful but private artists with little fame in their own time.

As American artists moved confidently into the 20th century, they were still searching for a positive and specifically American identity. They had been successful in many fields, with many techniques and approaches. As the country shifted, expanded, and reorganized, so did its art, but almost all of the changes had grown from basically European traditions. Great numbers of artists still studied abroad.

## A Wholly American Art

At just about that time, the search was rewarded. Life had shifted from rural to urban, from farms to

*'Raftsmen Playing Cards' by George Caleb Bingham, 1847.*

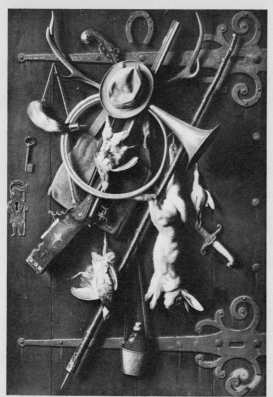

*'After the Hunt' by William Harnett, 1885.*

cities. Within the first decade of the 20th century, American painters recognized the artistic potential of life in the new big cities.

The so-called Ash Can School held its first show in 1908. A thoughtful group of eight illustrator-artists found their inspiration in the city streets around them. "Art cannot be separated from life" was their credo—the first time such an idea had been advanced in America.

Soon others joined the original eight—and a powerful, imaginative, extremely varied group of compassionate artists lifted painting from mere narrative to poetry. They exchanged impersonal chronicles for social commentaries and made their art out of the clamor and confusion of the city.

Each saw the city and its inhabitants in his own way and according to his own social lights. Robert Henri (1865–1929), George Luks (1867–1933), William Glackens (1870–1938), John Sloan (1871–1951), and George Bellows (1882–1925) brought alive the tragedies, trivialities, amusements, and labors of what, more and more, was becoming the pulse of America—the Big City.

In 1913 the Armory Show opened in New York City. Later it went to Chicago and Boston, Mass. More than 300 of the most progressive artists of Europe and America exhibited their works. Fau-

vism, cubism, and expressionism burst on the local art scenes to shock, complicate, and inspire. The door was opened to a rush of new ideas with which American artists were anxious and able to experiment. But they had their own subject matter now, their own basis for inspiration.

John Marin (1870–1953) started with images of the city and grafted cubist techniques upon them to produce works that were wholly his own and wholly American. Later he produced many versions of the Maine islands that were equally distinctive: not realism, not cubism, not impressionism—but all pure Marin.

For the next half-century—up to the present moment—American artists were off and running through the numerous and often perplexing mazes of what is loosely termed Modern American Art. The speed may have varied, the directions may have changed, the emphases may have shifted—but they are still running.

Step by step, with amazing productivity and inventiveness, school has replaced school, movement has followed movement, innovation has spawned reaction and then fresh innovation. The history of the past 50 years of American art has been richer and more complex than all the years that went before. We now have a highly diversified art—image and idea—that is rooted in American perceptions. Its influences are everywhere. The creative center of the world painting scene has shifted from Europe to America. It is likely to stay here quite a while.

*'Chez Mouquin' by William Glackens, 1905.*

**PAKISTAN.** The government of Prime Minister Zulfikar Ali Bhutto consolidated its ties to other Islamic nations in 1974 by strongly supporting the Arab cause in the Middle East, identifying itself with the Turkish cause in Cyprus, and taking an active part in an Islamic summit conference. Relations with the Soviet Union became more cordial, partly because of Soviet help in construction of the country's first steel mill, near Karachi.

On February 22, President Bhutto recognized Bangladesh and thus removed the last major obstacle to repatriation of Pakistani prisoners of war in India, of Bengalis in Pakistan, and of considerable numbers of Biharis in Bangladesh who chose to live in Pakistan. Bangladesh announced that it would not try Pakistani war prisoners for atrocities.

Hopes for restoring normal relations with India were at least temporarily set back when India exploded a nuclear device in May, an act that Pakistan considered threatening. Later in the year, Pakistan secured pledges of support from numerous countries to declare South Asia a nuclear-free zone. At a September meeting, India and Pakistan restored travel and mail. Perhaps the most serious obstacle to good relations with India, however, was Pakistan's fear that India was supporting forces within Pakistan that were trying to set up independent states in underdeveloped provinces. The Pakistani government continued its program of subsidizing the less developed provinces to bring them up to the level of the prosperous areas.

An earthquake that struck northern Pakistan on December 28 killed about 5,200 and injured an estimated 16,000, according to early reports. The final casualty toll was expected to be much higher.

Pakistan enjoyed a remarkable economic revival in 1974. The end of the program of nationalization—which included banking, shipping, and oil distribution—helped restore business confidence. In April former President Mohammed Ayub Khan died. (*See also* Asia; Bangladesh; India; Obituaries.)

**PANAMA.** In February 1974 Panama and the U.S. agreed on guidelines to be used in drafting a new treaty governing the Panama Canal Zone. The agreement provided for abrogation of the 1903 treaty and for negotiation of a treaty to be in force not in perpetuity but for a fixed number of years. The U.S. would continue to have rights to land, water, and air spaces necessary to operate and defend the canal but would surrender the rest of the Canal Zone to Panamanian sovereignty. Panama would be assured a share in administering and defending the canal and in plans for enlarging the present canal or building a new one. Panama's share of revenue from canal operations also would increase.

The U.S. Congress was hostile to the agreement. The chief opposition was to U.S. surrender of sovereignty over the Canal Zone. Without that control, critics contended, defense of the canal would be impossible. A resolution in the Senate calling for a continuation of U.S. sovereignty drew enough support to defeat a treaty if one were presented.

The achievements of Brig. Gen. Omar Torrijos' rule were evident in apartment house construction, new schools, and higher living standards for the poor. His success brought him the loyalty of the urban masses but at the cost of dissent from business and investment leaders who continued to protest General Torrijos' 1973 order that landlords freeze rents and banks set aside as much as half of their domestic savings to finance low-cost housing.

Panama proposed levying an export tax on bananas in 1974. United Brands Co., the major exporter, stopped production for more than a month in protest. In September the company apparently agreed to Panama's demands and resumed production and exports. (*See also* Latin America.)

**PARAGUAY.** President Alfredo Stroessner's fifth five-year term of office entered its second year in 1974 in an atmosphere of political stability in which effective opposition was virtually absent and the president remained firmly in control with the support of the Colorado party and the armed forces. Rumors of plans to manipulate the constitution so as to make Stroessner president for life had yet to be confirmed, although it seemed that potential problems of succession were being kept in mind as Stroessner's eldest son, Gustavo, also an army officer, came increasingly into the limelight.

The joint project embarked upon with Brazil in 1973 for the huge Itaipu hydroelectric plant had led many people to assume that plans for cooperation with Paraguay's other large neighbor, Argentina, would be shelved. A similar agreement, however, was reached with Argentina for the construction of a large plant at Yacyretá-Apipé, also on the Paraná River. Both Brazil and Argentina later agreed to provide funds and assistance for a number of development projects, so it seemed that Paraguay was successfully playing one against the other.

On the domestic front, soaring oil and wheat prices led to a massive increase in the cost of living, provoking the country's only legal labor union for the first time in many years to request a wage increase. The main source of protest, however, was the traditional alliance of students and clergy on behalf of the peasants. Protests centering on demands for economic reform to reduce hardship in the countryside and for the release of political prisoners flared briefly at the University of Asunción, but calm was quickly restored when about 100 demonstrating students and peasants were rounded up and handed over to the military tribunals.

In the economic sphere, Paraguay continued to benefit from worldwide high prices for its principal exports, notably beef. Moreover, while the world energy crisis was a source of short-term detriment to the external economic position, in the long run the country's prospects as an energy producer were considerably enhanced. (*See also* Latin America.)

WIDE WORLD
*Philippe Petit*

*Evel Knievel*
ALLEN GREEN—GAMMA

WILLIAM E. SAURO—THE NEW YORK TIMES
*Frank Sinatra*

UPI COMPIX
*Rep. Wilbur Mills
and wife, Polly*

SYNDICATION INTERNATIONAL/PHOTO
TRENDS

*Richard Burton, Princess
Elizabeth of Yugoslavia,
and her daughter.*

WIDE WORLD
*Fanne Foxe*

UPI COMPIX
*David Kunst*

UPI COMPIX

*Lieut. Hiroo Onoda (left)*

MARK SENNET

*Rachel Fitler*

WIDE WORLD

*Michael Wilson*

**PEOPLE OF THE YEAR.** The following persons were among the newsmakers of 1974. For other noted names check the index.

**Elizabeth Taylor** and **Richard Burton** ended their stormy, ten-year marriage in a June divorce. Shortly thereafter, Burton announced plans to marry another Elizabeth—**Princess Elizabeth of Yugoslavia.** Within days the plans were rumored off and later on again with the outcome pending as the New Year arrived. Wedding plans for lesser-known figures usually draw little attention from the press. In this case, however, the media seized on the scoop with such fury that by year's end **Rachel Fitler,** 77-year-old Philadelphia heiress and aunt to "Happy" Rockefeller, seemed inclined to bow out of the planned union with **Michael Wilson,** her 29-year-old ex-chauffeur. The press also found time to turn up another alleged fiancé and earlier Fitler chauffeur, 38-year-old **Hans von Aczel.**

**Frank Sinatra,** who became a grandfather in March, made headlines during a July tour of Australia but not for the old crooner's tunes. Beset by the press upon his arrival, Sinatra interrupted one concert to vent his fury, calling the men reporters "bums" and women in the press "buck and a half . . . hookers." The Australian Journalists Association demanded an apology. Sinatra countered with his own demand for an apology and a cancellation of the tour, only to find his private jet grounded when airport refuelers in support of their compatriots refused him service. Hasty negotiations produced mutual apologies and a resumption of the tour, but no diplomatic laurels for "Ol' Blue Eyes." The Australian fiasco proved of little import to home fans, however, who flocked to Sinatra's New Year's Eve performance at a Hollywood, Fla., hotel where $200-apiece tickets quickly sold out.

For **Rep. Wilbur Mills** of Arkansas the year proved an exceptionally difficult one. The early October Tidal Basin incident that thrust him into headlines with former stripper **Annabella Battistella** —alias Fanne Foxe and the "Argentine Firecracker"—seriously threatened Mills's reelection fight against his tough Republican opponent, Judy Petty. While Mills struggled to victory in the election, Fanne was reviving her act in Boston, Mass.,

this time as the "Tidal Basin Bombshell." Mills unwisely sought to dispel rumors by making an onstage appearance with the ecdysiast. Congressional colleagues, worried about his health, urged Mills's hospitalization and accepted with relief his resignation as chairman of the powerful House Ways and Means Committee. At year's end Mills acknowledged a problem of alcoholism, vowing to lick it and return to his seat in the 94th Congress, while Fanne announced her retirement.

Life was looking up for several figures in the news. **Clifford Irving,** bogus biographer of Howard Hughes, was paroled after serving nearly 18 months of his 2½-year term, and his wife, **Edith Irving,** was freed after 16 months in U.S. and Swiss jails for her part in the fraud. They returned to the island of Ibiza, Spain, to spend Christmas with their children.

In 1970, while officers of a Soviet ship and a U.S. Coast Guard vessel anchored off the New England coast were discussing fishing rights, Lithuanian sailor **Simas Kudirka** attempted to defect aboard the U.S. vessel. Kudirka was returned to his ship and later imprisoned for treason. With the May 1974 revelation that Kudirka's mother had been born in New York, the State Department granted both U.S. citizenship. Kudirka was released by the Soviets and returned with his family to the U.S.

"Without orders, I couldn't surrender," explained Japanese **Lieut. Hiroo Onoda** as he emerged from the Philippine jungles, ending 29 years of guerrilla warfare and intelligence gathering ordered by his commanding officer, Maj. Yoshimi Taniguchi, in 1944. Though search parties over the years had several times spotted Onoda, he agreed to come out of hiding only after Taniguchi posted formal cease-fire and surrender orders issued by the emperor. On Christmas Eve another World War II Japanese soldier gave up the fight. **Teruo Nakamur,** a native of Taiwan, exited the jungles on the Indonesian island of Morotai, where he had held out for 31 years. Still another military man made news in 1974, albeit 56 years late. The U.S. Army presented **Ernest A. Sheen** of Rock Island, Ill., a Silver Star, the nation's third highest military decoration, for "extraordinary heroism" in World War I.

After months of publicity, daredevil **Evel Knievel**

was embarrassed when his life-or-death attempt to rocket 1,600 feet across the Snake River Canyon in Idaho fizzled into anticlimax for fans. Even before his Sky-Cycle reached the end of the launch ramp, the drogue parachute had appeared prematurely, slowing the craft down, and when the major chute deployed shortly thereafter, the cycle bobbed about in midair and finally drifted down to the canyon bed. Knievel's take for the abortive stunt, which he once boasted would bring in $20 million, was closer to $3 million when a final count of ticket sales proved disappointing and backer Robert Arum stated the much-touted $6-million guarantee was in fact a publicity gimmick.

Brazilian soccer superstar **Pelé** hung up his professional T-shirt, ending a brilliant 18-year career during which he had become the first player to score more than 1,000 goals. Pelé, whose real name was Edson Arantes do Nascimento, led Brazil to three World Cup championships during his career.

French aerialist **Philippe Petit** stunned New Yorkers on their way to work one morning as he gracefully cavorted on a cable, strung with the help of friends, 1,350 feet in the air between the two towers of the World Trade Center. Arrested for disorderly conduct after his unauthorized 45-minute performance, Petit eagerly agreed to a supervised high-wire act in Central Park for the city's children in exchange for a dismissal of charges.

There's nothing unusual about returning to one's hometown, but when **David Kunst** strolled into Waseca, Minn., in October, people took note. He had completed a 4½-year, 15,000-mile trek around the world (aided by planes to cross the oceans) that took him through 13 countries and 21 pairs of shoes.

Among the charges that caused **Doris Judd** to be ousted from her job in the University of California at Davis cafeteria were her curious inability to spread mayonnaise to the edge of sandwich bread, her penchant for making ten too many sloppy joes and too much egg salad, and her slow track record in putting sauerkraut on franks. While the egg salad and mayonnaise charges were dropped in a campus hearing, the firing was upheld until Judd took her case to the county court. The judge ordered her reinstated with $7,500 back pay; the university appealed. Meanwhile, at California State University in Los Angeles, **Hurlin Hall** was fired from his cafeteria job for making hashed brown potatoes too greasy. The California State Employees Association filed suit and won him reinstatement in the cafeteria but with a switch from hashbrowns to sandwiches.

While society hurled itself forward with ever increasing speed, **Lawrence Gilbert Broadmoore, 23,** of tiny Tivoli, N.Y., chose to move backward in time and custom and plant his spatted feet firmly in the Victorian era. Refusing telephone, television, indoor plumbing, electric lights, and all else introduced within the past 60 years, Broadmoore lived a true *fin de siècle* existence that he supported by re-

pairing player pianos, Victrolas, and other period artifacts. His allegiance to the era was verbalized in a controlled-Victorian vocabulary, though he acknowledged being "capable of discoursing in modern terms." Broadmoore stated a simple preference for the past, calling his lifestyle "an experiment," which incidentally appeared to work jolly well! (*See also* Awards and Prizes; Births; Ford; Marriages; Nixon; Obituaries; Rockefeller; Trudeau.)

**PERU.** The military government of Peru continued to follow a middle course between capitalism and socialism in 1974. President Juan Velasco Alvarado emphasized his government's intention ultimately to nationalize major industries. Early in the year several U.S. companies were nationalized, for which Peru agreed to pay $150 million. In April the government approved a law establishing "social ownership" enterprises, with the state supplying capital and workers participating in management and sharing profits. On July 27 government-appointed committees took over the daily newspapers, a move that provoked violent right-wing demonstrations in Lima.

In spite of the government's policy of nationalization, there was large foreign investment for copper mines and irrigation projects in 1974. Foreign oil companies signed contracts for exploration and development of oil in the Peruvian Amazon. Several wells proved successful, and the prospects were excellent. By 1974 Peru was producing about two thirds of its oil requirements but hoped to become a substantial exporter by the end of the decade. During the year the government also arranged foreign financing for construction of a 530-mile oil pipeline from the Amazon fields to the Pacific coast.

One of Peru's most successful industries in 1974 was shipbuilding: major contracts were won from foreign countries, and plans were made to expand capacity at the major shipyards. During the year carefully controlled anchovy fishing was resumed, with the catch limited to allow stocks to maintain themselves. Peru's exports increased substantially in value during 1974, but rapid inflation and severe food shortages adversely affected daily life at home. (*See also* Latin America.)

**PETS.** With the U.S. pet population rising more rapidly in 1974 than the human rate of increase, some veterinarians and government officials recommended birth control measures. Although several breakthrough had been made in a search for drugs to control animal births, none had been totally effective, and an estimated 60,000 unwanted pets had to be destroyed each day by humane institutions. A veterinarian at Michigan State University found that many people who became pet owners were unaware of obligations that accompany such ownership, or that vaccinations, disease preventatives, and food costs have made pet ownership much more expensive than before.

SYNDICATION INTERNATIONAL/PHOTO TRENDS

*Pet snail Katy-Jane is patched up after a dog mistook her for a biscuit and took a bite out of her shell, requiring emergency bandaging.*

Viewing the situation from an economic standpoint, U.S. Secretary of Agriculture Earl Butz declared that a reduction by half of the country's dogs, cats, and horses would release a vast amount of grain for hungry peoples abroad. Sales of pet food in the U.S. during 1974 exceeded $2 billion, four times that of baby food.

That there had been no diminution in the American public's high regard for its pets was indicated by the storm of protest that arose over proposed military experiments that would have caused several hundred beagle puppies to breathe poisonous aviation fumes. Typical of the thousands of letters that flooded the offices of congressmen and Pentagon officials was that of a 15-year-old Chicago boy: "What would they do if there wasn't no dogs, would they kill humans?" As a result of the protests, an amendment was attached to Department of Defense appropriations bills prohibiting use of dogs for certain chemical and biological military research experimentation.

Public health officials reported that laws requiring vaccination of dogs against rabies have virtually eliminated that animal as a source of the disease in human beings. The few victims reported yearly are now infected primarily by wild animals such as the bat, skunk, fox, and raccoon.

In Sweden, regular fares were required for dogs riding on buses and trains unless they were small enough for their owners to carry them in a bag. In Idaho, friends of female dogs forced the state legislature to pass an equal rights bill, making it illegal for license fees of females to be higher than those of male dogs. In Philadelphia, Pa., a German shepherd named Tim led police to the house of a mugger who had robbed his blind owner of $237; in Louisville, Ky., a German shepherd named Duchess tore out the seat of a burglar's pants, the back pocket of which held a wallet with the name and address of the intruder; in Mountain Brook, Ala., a Labrador retriever named Clyde began making daily trips to a building and loan office when he discovered the organization was giving free dog biscuits to depositors. (*See also* Animals and Wildlife; Zoos.)

**PHILIPPINES.** The economic outlook for the Philippines in 1974 was one of optimism, with a gross national product that had expanded by 5%. A balance of payments surplus of $64 million was reported for the first nine months of the year, and government revenues for the same period had grown by 46%. As a result of a determined campaign by the government, foreign investments entering the country during the first half of the year totaled $85 million and accounted for almost 65% of all new investments. Sugar, a major export commodity, continued to command high prices throughout the year.

On the other hand, inflation raised the Manila consumer index by 26%. Of the labor force of 14 million, 7% were unemployed and about 20% were underemployed. A growth rate of 3% in the population of 42 million people added half a million new job seekers to the labor market in 1974. During the year, alternating floods and drought plagued the farmers. On November 7, President Ferdinand E. Marcos suspended trading and export of sugar

*A woman returns to her ruined home in Jolo after a Muslim rebellion in February destroyed most of the town. Muslim insurgents cited abuse by the ruling Christian majority in the Philippines and demanded establishment of a separate Muslim state.*

SYDNEY H. SCHANBERG—THE NEW YORK TIMES

while assessing damage to the crop caused by six typhoons within a five-month period. The annual national average per capita income for the Philippines was less than $330.

In September, in an effort to diversify the country's oil suppliers, the Philippines negotiated a deal with the People's Republic of China for 750,000 tons of crude oil for 1975, representing 9% of the country's annual requirements. At the same time, China promised to purchase raw materials from the Philippines. In November President Marcos took another step toward implementation of land reform by issuing a proclamation limiting all land devoted to the raising of rice and corn to 17.3-acre units that ultimately would belong to the tenant farmer. The proclamation would permit all of the one million tenant farmers who worked corn and rice fields to take steps toward eventual ownership of land they tilled. Marcos said, "Land reform will continue unabated until we attain our goal of emancipating every farmer."

Violent opposition to governmental policy was being exerted by the New People's Army, described by Marcos as waging "an armed insurrection and rebellion . . . based on the Marxist-Leninist-Maoist teachings and beliefs." The group, whose activity covered the central and northern provinces of the country, was estimated to be composed of 1,800 armed guerrillas, backed by 4,200 propagandists charged with organizing support for the rural population. In December Marcos, in the spirit of "reconcilation," ordered released 622 political foes who had been imprisoned since his 1972 proclamation of martial law.

Marcos' biggest problem in the south was from continued clashes between the army and the Moro National Liberation Front, whose avowed aim was complete independence for Muslim-inhabited areas, which included most of the southern portion of the Philippines. A peace plan that was being considered by the central government had been initiated by Islamic groups abroad, including Malaysia and Indonesia. This consisted of creating an autonomous Muslim state within Philippine jurisdiction. A border agreement between the Philippine government and Indonesia had led to both countries' patrolling their waters to check the flow of weapons and other contraband into the Philippines. The insurgency in the south had been sustained by a flow of arms and funds believed to have come from Malaysian Sabah across the Sulu straits in the southern part of the Philippines.

# PHOTOGRAPHY.

Worldwide expenditure on photography climbed in 1974 to about $15 billion, some 20% more than in the previous year. Rising costs of raw materials and labor, however, indicated that the rate of expansion seen in the photographic trade in recent years would probably not be sustained. Increasingly manufacturers sought to deal with rising production costs via international

WIDE WORLD

*Free-lance photographer Anthony Roberts won a Pulitzer prize for his first news photos—a series of pictures showing the death of a man holding a hostage in a parking lot.*

mergers. Following the 1972 West German-Japanese lead in the merger of the Leitz and Minolta companies, a partnership was formed between Zeiss of West Germany and Yashica of Japan. In search of cheaper labor, the Japanese firms of Canon, Asahi Optical, and Yashica took steps to begin production in Hong Kong and Taiwan, with an additional Asahi factory planned for São Paulo, Brazil. With the devaluation of the dollar and the simultaneous floating of the yen, the Japanese government's 1972–73 measures to restrict exports were essentially canceled out.

A great many firms produced cameras to take the new subminiature 110 cartridge films, but no designs were marketed with reflex focusing or interchangeable lenses. Among the best compact designs was that introduced by Rollei at the 1974 Photokina exhibition. The unit, measuring only 32 x 44 x 84 mm., featured a 23-mm. $f/2.8$ lens and a 4 to 1/400-second silicon photocell exposure control. Vivitar's new 110 design included an integral electronic flash unit. Plagued by manufacturing problems and decreased sales of the much touted SX-70, Polaroid introduced to the U.S. market an inexpensive black-and-white camera, called ZIP, which produces 2¼-inch square photos in 30 seconds.

New rangefinder 35-mm. cameras included the compact Rollei 35 S with a $f/2.8$ five-element lens and the Konica C35 EF. The latter had a small built-in retractable electronic flash for use in fill-in flash work as well as dim-light photography.

The most interesting new camera of the year was the 2¼-inch square format Rolleiflex SLX, whose design replaced the largest possible number of mechanical functions by electronic control. It featured a built-in, through-the-lens light meter, and newly designed differential electromagnets (described as linear motors) replaced the conventional spring-loaded shutter mechanism. Exposure signals were given by light-emitting diodes.

Lenses introduced in 1974 were for the most part only slightly improved versions of previously known types. Significant, however, was Canon's announcement that they had solved the problems of machine-produced aspheric lens surfaces, cutting in half the cost of the previously hand-produced lens.

The new improved Kodachrome color transparency films became available in the U.S., though not elsewhere, in 1974. New films introduced included Agfa-Gevaert's Agfachrome 64, an improved reversal film, and CT21, twice as fast as the existing Agfa CT18. Notable in the black-and-white field was the new, concentrated liquid developer Aculux.

Accompanying the growing photographic mania, the value of collectible photographs continued to increase. Early in the year $35,000 was paid for an 1848 daguerreotype of Edgar Allan Poe. At London's Sotheby auction an album of portraits by Victorian photographer Julia Margaret Cameron sold for an unheard-of $100,000. Among the year's notable U.S. exhibitions were individual shows of the works of Man Ray and Edward Weston. In London a retrospective of the work of U.S. photog-

rapher Diane Arbus was mounted, consisting of 136 photographs taken between 1962 and her suicide in 1971. She had concentrated on freaks of all descriptions, emphasizing the physical and psychological flaws in humanity. An international exhibit, 'One World for All', was prepared in conjunction with the United Nations' World Population Year, and in November New York City's Whitney Museum mounted its first major photographic show. Two major galleries were established in 1974. The International Center of Photography, at Audubon House, New York City, contained a book and print shop, library, workshops, several galleries, and an archive. In Chicago the Center for Photographic Arts was opened to display contemporary works. (*See also* Awards and Prizes; Museums.)

**PHYSICS.** Physicists continued to look for a unifying theory that could explain gravitation, electromagnetic force, the "strong" force holding together the nucleus of an atom, and the "weak" force underlying the behavior of subatomic particles as aspects of one grand force. Steven Weinberg of Harvard University, a strong advocate of such a central force theory, explained at an April gathering of the Optical Society of America that nature tends to work as simply as possible. Weinberg felt that nature supported only one force rather than four separate forces.

On May 11, the Fermi National Accelerator Laboratory was dedicated at Batavia, Ill. Formerly the National Accelerator Laboratory but renamed in honor of pioneer nuclear physicist Enrico Fermi, the site contains the world's most powerful atom

Antony Hewish (center, with tie) of the Cavendish Laboratory in England and Sir Martin Ryle (far right), astronomer royal of Britain, shared the 1974 Nobel prize for physics.
JOHN DEVERILL— CAMERA PRESS/PICTORIAL PARADE

smasher, an accelerator able to generate a record 400-billion-electron-volt beam of protons. As of 1974 it could send 10 trillion protons per pulse.

Lawrence Berkeley Laboratory in California planned to build the world's first particle accelerator entailing superconducting magnets, provided that funds became available in 1975. Because superconducting magnets require less power than conventional ones, the Experimental Superconducting Accelerator Ring would be less costly to operate.

What moves faster than the speed of light? Nothing, most people would say. Some particle physicists, however, suggest that something called a tachyon moves in excess of 186,200 miles per second, the approximate speed of light. The tachyon is believed to be a particle that is always in motion, never at rest. The existence of such an entity is admittedly based on scanty findings, but two Australian scientists, Roger Clay and Philip Crouch, reported statistical evidence of the tachyon.

Nuclear laser research was under way after a long hiatus, at least in the United States. Soviet physicists, however, after more than a decade of their own theoretical work in the field, were eager to work jointly with U.S. scientists toward the development of "grasers," or gamma-ray lasers. The Soviet scientists were hopeful that U.S. technology could provide the sophisticated materials needed in "graser" construction.

In November West Coast physicists reported the discovery of a new subatomic particle they called psi. At the same time, physicists on the East Coast announced finding a new particle that they dubbed J. In the end psi and J were found to be the same new particle, the heaviest atomic fragment ever found. Hailed as a top event "in years" in high energy physics, discovery of psi amazed scientists because psi lives 1,000 times longer than other such entities. Within days of the first discovery, a second new particle, called psi(3700), was found. The similarly weighty and long-lived psi(3700) further fueled speculation that these particles, which defy classification in existing theories, are held together by an entirely "new kind of structure."

**POLAND.** On July 22, 1974, the Polish People's Republic celebrated its 30th anniversary. The new regime had sought to repair the country's enormous war ravages in the shortest possible time and to transform Poland from a mainly agricultural country into a modern industrial power. In 1974 this ambitious and difficult task was almost complete. Speaking in the Sejm (parliament), Polish United Workers' (Communist) Party First Secretary Edward Gierek attributed the achievement to hard work, correct policy, and cooperation with the Soviet Union and other socialist countries.

On February 16 Stanislaw Wronski was dismissed as minister of culture and art and replaced by Jozef Tejchma, who retained his position of deputy premier. Kazimierz Barcikowski left the

party secretariat to succeed Jozef Okuniewski as minister of agriculture. Three new secretaries of the Central Committee were elected: Wincenty Krasko, member of the Council of State; Andrzej Werblan, deputy speaker of parliament; and Jozef Pinkowski, former Planning Commission deputy chairman.

Gierek paid an official visit to the U.S. in early October. After talks with President Gerald R. Ford and Secretary of State Henry Kissinger, six technical agreements and two political declarations were signed. An official communiqué noted the rapid increase of Polish-U.S. trade. As a result of the freeing of credits by the U.S. Export-Import Bank, Poland's trade turnover with the U.S. had grown between 1971 and 1973 from $180 million to $543 million. (*See also* Europe.)

**POLICE.** Major detective forces might not be necessary except in the largest U.S. cities, according to conclusions reached in 1974 after a three-year study on robbery prevention and control. The study, conducted by the Center on Administration of Criminal Justice at the University of California at Davis, revealed that detectives were not a major factor in robbery arrests. Another noteworthy finding was that the controversial U.S. Supreme Court decisions restricting police activity in search and sei-

*Atlanta, Ga., policewoman Marilyn Stone is among the growing number of mounted officers reappearing in cities after these patrol units were assessed as effective for crime control.*
MIKE KEZA—THE NEW YORK TIMES

zure and in interrogations of suspects had had little effect on conviction robbery cases.

Law enforcement administrators continued in 1974 to use civilian employees in greater numbers to relieve more sworn personnel for active duty. In city agencies, males represented 98% of all sworn personnel.

In November 1973 two women were sworn in as deputy U.S. marshals. They were the first in the 184-year history of the service to be given the same responsibilities as their male counterparts. New York City's experiment in teaming policemen and policewomen in patrol cars was attacked on the ground that a woman could not provide adequate backup in a dangerous situation, but superior officers considered women to be as effective as men on patrol.

Suffolk County, N.Y., initiated a drive to recruit minority members to reflect more accurately the county's ethnic composition. In a "reverse discrimination" suit, a New York State Supreme Court justice ruled against hiring three Hispanic men who scored lower than others on a civil service exam.

On the other hand, a court decision in Albany, N.Y., rejected a suit by male state patrol officers who objected to the selective certification of women. The court held that women officers were needed to process women offenders.

The Philadelphia, Pa., police department initiated a program in August under which persons arrested for petty crimes would no longer be subjected to fingerprinting and mug shots. Instead, they would receive a citation similar to a traffic ticket. If acquitted at a court hearing within five days after arrest, they would have no police record.

In Baltimore, Md., a five-day strike by police officers ended July 16, 1974. By August 1, the police commissioner had dismissed 91 and suspended 75 for taking part. Local 1195 of the American Federation of State, County, and Municipal Employees lost its exclusive bargaining right and its dues checkoff, and all its officials were suspended.

As a result of felonious criminal action, 127 law enforcement officers were killed in the U.S. during 1973. All but 7 of the murders were committed with the use of firearms—86 with handguns. Firearms had been used by felons to commit 95% of the 858 police killings since 1964, and 71% of the weapons had been handguns. Some police departments were planning in 1974 to use bullet-proof vests. The New York and Connecticut state police were replacing the .38 calibre police special with the more powerful .357 magnum. The Baltimore police began in August to pay a $50 bounty to persons turning in firearms and $100 for information leading to the seizure of an illegal gun.

Police corruption remained a major problem in 1974. In New York City and Indianapolis, Ind., policemen were accused of narcotics trafficking, extortion, perjury, and bootlegging. Several Chicago captains were indicted on charges of taking bribes

UPI COMPIX

*Part of the new equipment acquired by police in Bogota, Colombia, at a cost of $2.5 million, this new attire to protect against bombs and mob attacks was unveiled in April.*

from tavern owners. The Pennsylvania Crime Commission reported corruption in every Philadelphia district or precinct. (*See also* Cities and Urban Affairs; Crime; Law; Prisons.)

**POLITICAL PARTIES.** The two major political parties in the United States ended 1974 amid efforts at far-reaching restructuring of their party machinery in preparation for the 1976 presidential election campaign. The Republicans had the advantage of an incumbent president who would probably be a candidate. They suffered, however, from severe erosion of their base of support in the 1974 elections. As a result, there were fewer Republican governors than at any time since the 1930's. Moreover, the Democrats had made important inroads into the state legislatures, and there were fewer Republican members of Congress than at any time since the administration of Lyndon B. Johnson. This meant that in 1976 there would be fewer officeholders campaigning to bring out the Republican vote.

Despite their 1974 election triumph, the Democrats also had problems in planning for 1976. There was no clear-cut leader in the contest for the presidency. There also was a problem of holding together the liberal, labor, and minority elements that had been the source of Democratic political strength since the 1930's—the coalition that shattered when Richard M. Nixon won the presidency in 1972 by an unprecedented Republican margin.

Further, the sheer size of the Democratic election victory in 1974 conferred responsibility unusual for a party not in control of the White House. Party leaders agreed that voters expected them to find legislative solutions to the country's twin economic problems, inflation and unemployment. By year's end, the party and its Congressional leaders had begun outlining approaches to these solutions.

In the November election—the first since President Nixon resigned and Gerald R. Ford replaced him—the voter turnout was estimated at only 38% of those eligible. The low level of participation was viewed as either a reaction to the political corruption exposed in the Watergate scandals or a failure of the major parties to present meaningful alternatives on important issues—or both.

The problem was particularly acute for the Republicans. A sharp distinction was drawn, during both the 1972 campaign and the subsequent Watergate scandals, between the Republican party and the Committee to Re-Elect the President, the organization directly involved in the scandals. Nevertheless, as the controversy leading to the resignation of President Nixon neared its climax, a Gallup Poll found that only 23% of Americans identified themselves as Republicans, the lowest figure in more than 30 years of polling. In 1972, the figure was 28%.

This trend did not mark a simple shift in party preference. Those identifying themselves as Democrats increased only from 43% to 44%. The number of persons who regarded themselves as independents, however, increased from 29% in 1972 to 33%

in 1974. Thus an increasing number of Americans were concluding that neither party offered a consistently attractive answer to questions of public policy.

### The Republicans

The Republicans had a particular problem in 1974 of finding attractive candidates to campaign under their party label, which was given much of the blame for the party's election losses. Another difficulty was the cutoff of many usual sources of campaign funds. A key factor in the Watergate scandals had been misuse of campaign contributions, some of them illegal. As the scandals unfolded, indictments were brought against those involved in such misuse. A new campaign-financing law providing for public contributions to national campaigns was expected to alter significantly the financial structure of both parties by 1976.

President Ford took the first step toward restructuring the Republican party in September, when he chose Mary Louise Smith of Iowa to head the Republican National Committee, replacing George Bush of Texas. Smith was a moderate conservative with no rigid ties to any faction of the party. She announced that she would appoint Richard D. Obeshain, chairman of the Virginia Republican party, as her cochairperson, thus offering conservative southern Republicans a significant voice in the party. There was speculation that she might be an interim appointee, and that before the end of 1975 the president would replace her with the person he expected to manage his likely 1976 election campaign.

In December, a Republican policy committee drafted party reform rules for approval by the Republican National Committee. One proposal, designed to broaden participation in party affairs, called for state Republican organizations to "take positive action and endeavor to assure greater and more equitable participation of women, young people, minority and heritage groups and senior citizens in the political process and to increase their representation at the 1976 national convention." Quotas would be forbidden, but the National Committee would have the right to report to the 1976 convention on positive action programs in each state. States failing to comply presumably would be subject to delegate challenges; state organizations with a reasonable degree of compliance would be assumed to be acting in good faith.

Other recommendations by the Republican policy committee were: National Committee meetings and meetings of its committees should be open to the public unless closed by majority vote. Committeemen and committeewomen, presently nominated by state groups but elected by the National Committee, would be elected by state organizations. The chairperson of the National Committee would be elected by the committee for a two-year term beginning in June and could be removed only

STEVE MILLER—NEWS & OBSERVER, RALEIGH, N.C./ROTHCO

WIDE WORLD

*José Angel Gutierrez, the driving force behind La Raza Unida, a Chicano alternative to the Republican and Democratic parties, works at party headquarters in Crystal City, Tex., where Mexican Americans had won control of city government over a period of four years.*

by a two-thirds vote of the committee. (This would eliminate the practice of a presidential nominee naming the committee chairperson.) The National Committee would be given the right to keep a close check on the finances of the presidential campaign committee and would possibly be opened to participation by Republican auxiliary groups. Regional caucuses would be held to elect regional Republican vice-chairpersons.

The call for a positive action program before the 1976 Republican convention was an interpretation of a rule adopted in 1972. It and all of the other actions were to be subject to approval by both the National Committee and the 1976 convention. The Republican National Committee decided to increase its spending in an effort to recoup party strength. The first phase of its new program was to be a study of voter attitudes toward the Republican party. This would be followed by a large-scale advertising campaign, based on results of the survey.

### The Democrats

Two major events shaped Democratic actions in preparation for the 1976 election campaign: the disastrous presidential campaign of 1972 and the triumph in the 1974 elections. To win in 1976, the Democrats needed a strong candidate, an organization with a vigorous campaign, and a program that would attract a broad spectrum of voters.

The strongest and one of the most controversial candidates took himself out of the race in September. Senator Edward M. Kennedy (Mass.), reportedly worried about the health of his wife and his son, announced: "I will not accept the nomination. I will not accept a draft." At year's end, a nationwide poll found that Senators Edmund Muskie (Me.) and Henry M. Jackson (Wash.), two of the best-known presidential possibilities, were slightly below President Ford in voter preference, with a large bloc of voters undecided. Ford had a somewhat larger edge over Gov. George Wallace (Ala.), with a smaller percentage undecided.

The Democrats came through a December crisis in party affairs comparatively united. The 1972 convention had ordered a 1974 national convention to adopt a charter for the Democratic party. The delegates met in Kansas City, Mo., for the first midterm convention of a major party in history. It resulted in the first constitution ever adopted by a major party in the United States, but it was not to become fully effective until 1980. Its rules for delegate selection, however, were adopted for the 1976 nominating convention. They provided that state parties must take "affirmative action" to secure participation of youth, blacks, and women in party affairs, including the selection of delegates, but banned quotas.

The charter envisaged far-reaching changes in primary elections. It declared that only Democrats

*Dressed as rabbits to draw attention to the world population crisis, members of the Population Action Group deliver a demand in October to No. 10 Downing Street in London for better public education on birth control and increased aid to Third World countries.*

should select the Democratic presidential nominee. This referred to the so-called open-primary laws in some states, which permitted persons to vote in the primary elections of either party without declaring party preference. The charter ordered state parties to make reasonable efforts to bring their states' laws into compliance. The charter also provided that presidential candidates were to be awarded delegates in proportion to the preferences of those participating in the selection process. In states where slates of delegates were chosen on a winner-take-all basis, the party would have to seek changes in the primary election law.

Also, a judicial council was set up to judge the affirmative action program, the Democratic National Committee was expanded in an effort to make it reflect more accurately the makeup of the party, and a national educational and training council was set up to publicize party activities and encourage greater participation.

The delegates adopted an economic program to cope with a recession that appeared to be deepening as they met. The program called for across-the-board economic controls on wages, prices, rents, and profits; lower taxes for lower- and middle-income groups; easier credit; and a compulsory system of energy conservation that could, as a last resort, include rationing of gasoline and fuel oil. It also called for more public service jobs for the unemployed. (*See also* Cities and Urban Affairs; Elections; State Governments; Women.)

**POPULATION.** The U.S. Bureau of the Census estimated the total population of the United States at 211,210,000 as of Jan. 1, 1974. This represented a gain of only 1,505,000—or less than 1%—over the figure for the preceding year.

This was the lowest rate of increase in the U.S. population for any year since 1937 and less than half the annual growth rate registered in the 1950's.

The birthrate of 14.9 for 1973 was 41% below the 1957 rate of 25.2 per 1,000 persons. In 1970 the crude birthrate was 18.2 per 1,000.

The Census Bureau reported that in 1973 the general fertility rate—the number of births per 1,000 women of childbearing age (15 to 44)—was 69.3. By contrast, the general fertility rate had been 122.9 per 1,000 women in 1957.

A survey by the Census Bureau revealed that the small family of two or three children appeared to be the wave of the future. More than half the white wives aged 18 to 24 expected to give birth to only two children. Another 20% anticipated having three children. The proportion of young black women expecting to have two to three children was somewhat less than that of white women. Only one in ten of young wives of all racial groups expected to have four children or more.

### Social Indicators

Early in 1974 the president's Office of Management and Budget released a study of various social statistics entitled "Social Indicators 1973." The study listed 71.1 years as the life expectancy for the average American. Nonwhites, however, had a life expectancy of about ten years less than that of whites.

Aside from health and welfare, the study also

dealt with population growth, education, economic status, and leisure time. By 1972, the study reported, the average American family spent 6.2 hours per day watching television—up from 4.8 hours in 1954.

"Social Indicators 1973" confirmed information brought out in other studies. The report, for example, verified the fact that low-income blacks were more likely to be the victims of violent crime than were high-income whites.

### Income Distribution Stagnant

In February the president's Council of Economic Advisers disclosed that the distribution of wealth among the rich and the poor had changed very little since World War II. The poor had stayed poor, and the rich had suffered little.

The 20% of the population with the lowest income shared only 5.4% of the total national wealth in 1972. Those percentages were nearly the same in 1947. On the other hand, the top 20% in affluence shared 41.4% of the total "pie" in 1972—a slight drop from their 43.3% share in 1947.

### World Population Conference

In August the United Nations convened the World Population Conference in Bucharest, Romania. The conference opened at a time when famine was spreading in the less developed countries, and the threat of mass starvation was a real one.

The U.S. proposed that all the world's countries adopt an official policy of promoting the two-child family. Other delegates countered with resolutions condemning "vulgar affluence" in the consumption of world resources. The general resolution finally adopted called for economic and social development policies as a means to reducing population, leaving decisions on birth control up to individual governments. It also stressed women's equality and a more equitable utilization of the world's natural resources. (*See also* Families.)

**PORTUGAL.** The military coup that took place on April 25, 1974, radically changed Portugal internally and in its relationship to the world. The coup derived from the work of a group known as the Captains' Movement (Armed Forces Movement), which had been formed to press for better pay and conditions for junior officers in the armed forces. In early 1974 it became more political, especially after the February publication of Gen. António Sebastião Ribeiro de Spínola's revelatory book 'Portugal and the Future', which stated that the wars in Africa could not be settled by military means but only by a political solution. In early March, after the clandestine circulation by the movement of a document voicing aspirations sprung from similar conclusions, the government decided to act, seized the movement's leaders, and placed about 200 officers under virtual house arrest. On March 14 Gen. Francisco da Costa Gomes and Spínola were dismissed after they failed to attend a ceremony to pledge loyalty to Prime Minister Marcello José das Neves Alves Caetano's government.

On the night of March 15–16, part of an infantry regiment at Caldas da Rainha mutinied. They held

*Troops of the "Armed Forces Movement" block off city streets in Lisbon, Portugal, on April 25, the first morning of the military coup headed by Gen. António de Spínola that ousted the government of Prime Minister Marcello Caetano.*

SYGMA

*Members of the military junta that took over the Portuguese government on April 25 (left to right), Gen. Costa Gomes, Gen. Spínola, Gen. Silverio Marques, and Col. Galvao de Melo, meet with the press on April 29.*
KEYSTONE

their senior officers captive and left for Lisbon, the capital, but were turned back by police and troops. The ensuing calm was deceptive, however, and early on April 25 a force of about 5,000 men converged on Lisbon. The army insurgents, calling themselves the Armed Forces Movement (A.F.M.), overthrew the government, detained President Américo Tomás, Caetano, and members of his cabinet, and installed a "Junta of National Salvation" headed by Spínola. On the following day Spínola promised a provisional civil government within three weeks, immediate dismissal of Tomás and Caetano, free elections by universal suffrage, freedom of political association and free trade unions, abolition of censorship, disbandment of the secret police, immediate amnesty for political prisoners, and dismissal of all overseas civil governors and governors-general. On May 15 Spínola assumed the presidency; and on the following day a new cabinet was sworn in.

The junta offered self-determination to Portugal's African territories, and the Portuguese Socialist leader Mario Soares, as foreign minister, negotiated throughout the summer with African revolutionary leaders. Complete independence was demanded, and on September 10 it was granted to Portuguese Guinea. (*See* Guinea-Bissau.) An agreement was signed with Mozambique that it would become independent on June 25, 1975. (*See* Africa; United Nations; Zambia.)

In July Prime Minister Adélino da Palma Carolos and three other ministers resigned. Brig. Gen. Vasco dos Santos Gonçalves, a "moderate" member of

the A.F.M., became prime minister, and a new cabinet was announced. Then, on September 30 in a power struggle with left-wing officers, Spínola resigned and was replaced by Gomes, chief of staff of the armed forces, but the leadership was shared by Gonçalves. Both went out of their way to assure Portugal's Western allies that the government would honor its treaties and international commitments, would not withdraw from the North Atlantic Treaty Organization, and, though steering a leftward course, would not turn Communist. At year's end, elaborate rules had been drawn up in preparation for the country's first free elections since the fall of the republic in 1926. Incidents in December, however, resulted in a serious split in the coalition government, initiating speculation that the elections planned for March 1975 might be canceled. (*See also* Europe.)

**POSTAL SERVICE.** The third fiscal year of the U.S. Postal Service as a semi-independent government agency ended with a record $385-million deficit. Because of inflation, a two-month delay in rate increases, and the rising cost of wages and benefits, the deficit for fiscal 1975 was projected at around $500 million. The rate increases were postponed as a result of a Cost of Living Council ruling that restricted increased postal revenues. On March 2, instead of January 5, first-class postage rose from 8¢ to 10¢ an ounce, and airmail went from 11¢ to 13¢. Increases for second-class and fourth-class mail were to be phased in over a period of years.

A 1.2% rise in the cost of living in September 1974 triggered a $458 annual pay raise for postal workers, effective November 9. That raise brought the amount of salary increases won under the current contract to $2,098 over a period of 15 months. Another raise was expected before expiration of the contract in July 1975.

On Nov. 17, 1974, the postal service stopped delivering mail that carried no postage. It was returned to the sender if a return address was given. Utility companies and others that mail quantities of bills had protested that an increasing volume of payments were coming to them minus postage.

In September the postal service decided not to allow private companies to deliver some intra-company mail for certain businesses. The service had considered the plan a year earlier but decided against any proposal that might cut revenues.

The most publicized slow mail delivery of 1974 involved a subpoena ordering U.S. President Richard M. Nixon's appearance at a Los Angeles court. Sent by certified mail on February 4, it reached its destination at the District of Columbia Superior Court eight days later. (*See also* Stamps; U.S. Special Report.)

*A Huntsville, Tex., State Prison guard stands watch on the night of August 1 during the second week that three inmates held 15 hostages in an attempt to gain their freedom.*

**PRISONS.** As prisoners and guards alike demanded more bearable conditions, alternatives to the prison system increased in the U.S. in 1974. More states experimented with furloughs for prisoners nearing the end of their terms. Opportunities grew for work or study outside the prison walls. Still another coed facility was opened, with the goal of creating a more normal environment for inmates before their return to the outside world.

Some authorities held that crime would be reduced and billions of tax dollars saved if only the most dangerous criminals were imprisoned and the rest put on probation. In light of the high percentage of repeaters, the prison had failed as an instrument for rehabilitation, and it was estimated that imprisonment cost about 15 times as much as community supervision of an offender.

The longest siege in U.S. prison history took place in Texas in late July and early August 1974. Three armed inmates at Huntsville State Prison seized 15 hostages in an escape attempt. After 252 hours, the siege ended with a 20-minute shoot-out in which 2 convicts and 2 of the 12 hostages still held were killed. The leader of the escape attempt was Fred Gomez Carrasco, a convicted murderer and narcotics dealer.

A federal district judge ordered the state of Oklahoma in 1974 to stop mistreating inmates at the state prison at McAlester and to end racial segregation there. In the summer of 1973, convicts had burned the prison during a week of riots.

Unarmed prisoners overpowered four guards at Menard State Penitentiary in Illinois in May in order to discuss grievances with the warden. He agreed to meet with representatives of the inmates, and the incident ended peacefully. Also in May prisoners at the Jackson County Jail in Kansas City, Mo., seized three guards and took control of a section of the jail for three hours. They wanted to complain about practices regarding visitors.

The Bureau of Prisons established a new grievance procedure during the year in order to relieve the federal courts, which were overburdened with prisoners' lawsuits. Wardens were to answer all written protests within 15 days, and if the prisoner was dissatisfied with the response, an appeal could be made to the bureau director.

In July a federal judge ordered New York City to close the Manhattan House of Detention for Men, known as the Tombs. He said that he would reconsider his order if the city submitted a detailed plan for eliminating conditions that he declared unconstitutional in January 1974. The renovation plan fell short of the court's specifications, and the Tombs was closed on December 20.

The National Prison Project of the American Civil Liberties Union estimated in 1974 that at least 20 state prisons and 3 federal institutions were using some form of behavior modification. Federal involvement in the modification of an individual's personal behavior patterns raised many legal and ethical questions, however, and in February two federal agencies, the Federal Bureau of Prisons and the Law Enforcement Assistance Administration, announced the at least temporary halt of the federally sponsored penal behavior-modification programs. (*See also* Crime; Law; Mental Health; Police; Psychology.)

**PSYCHOLOGY.** The effectiveness and ethics of behavior-modification (human conditioning) programs proved the major issue in 1974 for the behavioral sciences. Although a number of researchers reported impressive results using simple behavior-modification techniques to treat autistic or severely retarded children and a variety of nervous habits, more traditional therapists voiced concern at the treatment of symptoms rather than the causes of problems. While the debate little affected behavior-modification work in most sectors, the future for similar programs instituted in prisons in the early 1970's looked none too bright. Prompted by the pressures of Congressional inquiries, the media, and protesting civil rights groups, the Federal Bureau of Prisons announced in February the demise of its controversial Project START (Special Treatment and Rehabilitative Training), a behavior-modification program for "unusually aggressive" inmates in Springfield, Mo. Shortly thereafter, the government's Law Enforcement Assistance Administration announced the cutoff of funds for all programs involving behavior modification. (*See* Prisons.) In response to these events Albert Bandura, president of the American Psychological Association, stated that all such programs should be subject to careful public scrutiny and called for the development of ethical guidelines for those working in the field.

The subject of ethics also dominated the 1974 meeting of the American Psychiatric Association. The meeting focused on the violation of rights of involuntarily confined mental patients and the problems resulting from the growing wholesale release of "nondangerous" patients from many state hospitals.

Parapsychology, the study of alleged psychic phenomena, was recently gaining ground as an "acceptable" science. In August, however, parapsychologists were dealt a severe blow when Walter Levy, Jr., director of the Institute for Parapsychology in Durham, N.C., admitted falsifying data in an extrasensory perception experiment.

The behavioral sciences did not escape the effects of inflation. Many researchers expressed difficulty in completing surveys at a reasonable cost, and the American Statistical Association cited increasing costs among the determining factors in whether some research could be done at all. In considering inflation's psychological effects, psychologists generally agreed that the stress it caused would exaggerate already existing personality problems.

Among the results of the year's research was a Tufts University study indicating that sex stereotyping begins within 24 hours after a child's birth. Though hospital records showed little difference between male and female children in the study, the parents saw their daughters as softer, finer-featured, smaller, and more inattentive than did the parents of boys. On the other hand, child psychiatrist Arthur Kornhaber reported increasing sexual identity problems in adolescents whose parents tended to wholly reject traditional sexual roles.

Initial research conducted by John Ott of the Environmental Health and Light Research Institute indicated that conventional fluorescent lighting in schools may contribute to hyperactivity in children. To counter the problem, he proposed a lighting design that blocked X rays and radio waves and included ultraviolet wavelengths present in sunlight.

New York City psychiatrists Jan Frank and Harold Levinson published a new theory pinpointing a faulty connection between the brain and inner ear as the cause of primary dyslexia, a common learning disorder affecting a child's ability to read. (*See also* Families; Mental Health.)

*Edward Eismann (top right, gesturing) conducts a psychotherapy session for youngsters in a closed-off Bronx, N.Y., street. The sessions that Eismann termed part of a therapeutic community were an extension of the nearby Lincoln Community Mental Health Center.*

DON HOGAN CHARLES—THE NEW YORK TIMES

*After a peaceful march from the predominantly black Roxbury section of Boston, Mass., demonstrators rally on Boston Common in mid-October in support of a court-ordered busing program aimed at integrating the city's schools. The orderliness on the Common was in sharp contrast with the scene at several white-neighborhood schools, where violent incidents had already become commonplace.*
UPI COMPIX

**RACE RELATIONS.** Blacks and other minorities made further political gains in the November 1974 elections. Blacks won an additional House seat and the lieutenant governorships of California and Colorado. In Hawaii, George Ariyoshi became the first Japanese American to be elected governor of a state. Two Spanish-surnamed candidates, Raul Castro in Arizona and Jerry Apodaca in New Mexico, also won their races for governor. The Democratic party, traditionally the party of blacks and other minorities, announced in March, however, new rules for selecting delegates to their national convention that could reduce minority participation. (*See* Elections.)

Many court decisions and federal initiatives promoted the interests of American Indians in 1974. The Supreme Court granted the Oneida Indians the right to sue upstate New York counties for fair rental value of 5 million acres the Oneida claimed were illegally ceded to the state before 1800. A federal court ruled that most state fishing regulations did not apply to 14 Indian tribes in Washington because Indian fishing rights were guaranteed by existing treaties.

The Supreme Court unanimously upheld the right of Indians living off reservations to receive welfare benefits from the Bureau of Indian Affairs. The Supreme Court declined to review a decision upholding the election of a Navajo as a county supervisor in Arizona whose eligibility had been challenged on the grounds that as a reservation resi-

dent he was immune from taxes and normal legal processes.

The Department of the Interior agreed that coal contracts on the Northern Cheyenne reservation in Montana would have to be renegotiated on terms more favorable to the Indians. The Federal Trade Commission announced an agreement under which operators of 19 trading posts on Navajo and Hopi reservations would cease employing unfair practices. (*See* Indians, American.)

In January, Joseph Remiro and Russell Little of the Symbionese Liberation Army (SLA) were charged with the slaying of Marcus Foster, the black superintendent of schools in Oakland, Calif. Clark Squire, a reputed member of the Black Liberation Army, was found guilty in March of the 1973 fatal shooting of a state policeman in New Jersey and was sentenced to life in prison. In May four Black Muslims from Philadelphia, Pa., were convicted of the 1973 murders of seven Hanafi Muslims in their Washington, D.C., home. Donald DeFreeze, an escaped convict and reputed leader of the SLA, was killed in Los Angeles in May. The American Civil Liberties Union got a temporary injunction against San Francisco, Calif., police, who tried to stop, search, and question all black males who resembled a man who had allegedly shot and killed whites at random in the city. (*See* Crime.)

The U.S. Supreme Court declined to rule on a case involving a white applicant who had sued the University of Washington on the grounds that he

JACK MANNING—THE NEW YORK TIMES

*At Confucius Plaza, a major cooperative housing project being built in New York City's Chinatown, protesters charge discrimination by the builder against Asian-American workers.*

had been denied admission although 36 minority applicants with lower grade averages had been admitted. Courts did rule in several cases involving busing and desegregation of schools in 1974. (*See* Education.)

Efforts to increase minorities in nursing received federal aid during the year. The National Student Nurses' Association received a $286,000 federal grant to expand its Breakthrough to Nursing project in which minority high school students were recruited through assistance, counseling, and tutoring. The American Nurses' Association received a $1-million federal grant to provide 35 fellowships for minority nurses seeking graduate education leading to doctoral degrees.

The Department of Justice and the Equal Employment Opportunity Commission secured court orders and consent decrees with industries, including trucking and utilities firms, in 1974. In April a major agreement was reached with steel companies and the United Steelworkers of America, who consented to $30.9 million in back pay, one half of openings in trade and craft positions to be filled by minorities and women, and easier access for jobs previously reserved for white males. The NAACP, however, sued to have the agreement set aside as inadequate. In May, the American Telephone and Telegraph Co. signed a similar agreement. The U.S. Department of Labor imposed mandatory minority hiring goals on building contractors and construction unions doing some federally funded work.

The Los Angeles Fire Department, the Chicago Police Department, and state police in Maryland, Mississippi, and Alabama were among other municipal and state agencies that had judgments against them in 1974 for failure to hire and to promote minorities. A report of the Police Foundation said that minority officers constituted only 6% of the nation's police, a figure highly inflated by Washington, D.C. (37% black officers), and Hawaii (more than 95% minority officers).

Although the alliance between blacks and Jews in

the U.S. had broken apart in recent years, leaders of both groups held talks in 1974 to begin to rebuild the coalition. Air Force Gen. George S. Brown, chairman of the Joint Chiefs of Staff, was rebuked by U.S. President Gerald R. Ford for public comments that Jews controlled U.S. newspapers and banks and exerted undue influence on U.S. foreign policy toward Israel. (*See also* Employment; Literature; State Governments; Youth Organizations.)

**RELIGION.** The release of the Watergate tapes in the U.S. in 1974 raised shocked questions in religious circles about U.S. President Richard M. Nixon's earthy language. Religious leaders called his comments "insensitive," "reprehensible," and "cynical." New U.S. President Gerald R. Ford's pardon of Nixon created a sentiment among religious spokesmen that "the great absolutes of the Judeo-Christian tradition have been diluted or discarded." Many said that the time had come for churches to speak out on ethics to help create a better moral climate.

Two popular religious figures, thought by many to be heretical or even fraudulent, continued to exert an influence on young people in the U.S. and other countries. The Rev. Sun Myung Moon, through his Unification Church, preached a Christianity mixed with conservative politics and morality. His critics questioned the sources of his financial support and speculated about the enormous sums involved. Guru Maharaj Ji, leader of the Divine Light Mission, claimed 8 million followers, 50,000 of them in the U.S. Believers said that the guru was a perfect spiritual master who had completely transformed their lives through his teachings. Doubters, including most of the people of his native India, saw the guru as an opportunist.

In more established religions, familiar themes ap-

*The Gyalwa Karmapa, head of the Kagyu order of Tibetan Buddhism, blesses one of the more than 1,000 persons who attended the first Western celebration of the solemn Black Crown ceremony in New York City on September 21.*

MEYER LIEBOWITZ—THE NEW YORK TIMES

The 16th temple of the Church of Jesus Christ of Latter-day Saints was opened to the public in September, prior to its dedication in November. Rising 288 feet over Kensington, Md., and faced in white marble, the temple cost $15 million, striking testimony to the prosperity of the rapidly growing Mormon church.
COURTESY, THE CHURCH OF JESUS CHRIST OF LATTER-DAY SAINTS PUBLIC COMMUNICATIONS DEPT.

peared again in 1974. There was concern about the apparent decline of the influence of religion in the world, particularly among young people. Various Christian groups worked to achieve ecumenical agreements, although there were many disagreements between sects of various religions. Theologically conservative, as well as evangelistic, Christian movements continued to grow.

## Judaism

The foreign policy of Israel affected Jews throughout the world in 1974. Nearly all Jews continued to support Israel following the Yom Kippur war late in 1973. Most Orthodox Jews persisted in viewing Israel in the messianic tradition and supported the Israeli position against surrendering any land to Arab sovereignty. Some more modern Orthodox and some non-Orthodox Jews, however, rejected this position in favor of compromise and conciliation. Some Jewish leaders expressed fear that a new kind of anti-Semitism would arise, related to Israeli politics in the Middle East. Whereas earlier anti-Semitism had originated with rightist political groups, some Jews saw evidence of anti-Semitism among leftist groups that favored the Arabs politically.

The number of Jews immigrating to the U.S. from the U.S.S.R. reached nearly 4,000 in 1974. Most came directly to the U.S. from the U.S.S.R., but increasing numbers came after first trying and rejecting Israel, often because of the difficulty non-religious Jews and mixed couples found in living in Israel. Some Soviet Jews, who noted that Jewish culture had effectively died in the U.S.S.R. 50 years earlier, said that Soviet Jews sometimes found adjustment to the sectarian state of Israel impossible.

Orthodox Jewish rabbis admitted in 1974 that they had failed to influence large numbers of Jews in the U.S. Studies disclosed that as many as 60% of young Jews were unaffiliated with any Jewish religious institution. Nearly 90% of the young had attended college, the rabbis said, and had adopted secular intellectual positions opposed to the traditional values of Judaism. The rabbis attributed rising rates of intermarriage between Jews and Gentiles to the increasing alienation of young Jews from their heritage.

## Protestantism

More than 2,000 participants at the International Congress on World Evangelization at Lausanne, Switzerland, signed a covenant that proclaimed, among other things, that the Old and New Testaments were divinely inspired and without error and composed the only infallible guide. The meeting also called for "the liberation of (humankind) from every kind of oppression" and expressed "penitence both for our neglect and for having sometimes regarded evangelism and social concern as mutually exclusive." The statement on social action seemed to move evangelical Christianity closer to the position of the World Council of Churches (WCC). The meeting, however, was evidence of the growing strength of the evangelical movement, and some people speculated that evangelical leaders might eventually set up a rival organization to the WCC.

Two major Protestant denominations found themselves embroiled in bitter controversy in 1974. The question of ordaining women to the Episcopalian priesthood created a furor when four bishops ordained 11 women in July. The new presiding bishop, John M. Allin, called a special session of the House of Bishops, which, by a vote of 128 to 9, declared the ordinations invalid and ordered the women not to exercise their functions. The 1976 General Convention was to vote on the question. (*See* Women.)

The 2.8-million-member Lutheran Church-Missouri Synod remained seriously divided on interpretation of Scripture and administrative policies. Conservative officers took disciplinary action against the faculty of Concordia Seminary who had refused to sign a new creed in 1973. In February 1974 the faculty formed a new Seminary in Exile, taking most of the students with them, resulting in the near collapse of Concordia. Efforts at conciliation were under way at year's end.

### Roman Catholicism

The Roman Catholic church reached some limited ecumenical agreements in 1974. Roman Catholic and Lutheran scholars agreed that both groups could modify their positions on papal authority and that the issue should not be a barrier to reconciliation between their two groups. The Roman Catholic church in Scotland and the Anglican church came to agreements about the meaning of the Eucharist. In Great Britain, the Roman Catholic church joined the other four major churches, including the Anglican church, to form a national commission to discuss reunion.

The Roman Catholic church, however, appeared to have less success dealing with its own members. In Italy, Pope Paul VI strongly opposed the referendum legalizing divorce, but voters approved it.

In the U.S. the disagreement between pro- and anti-abortion Roman Catholics continued in 1974. The most publicized incident involved a Roman Catholic woman in Massachusetts who had supported the opening of an abortion clinic in her heavily Catholic hometown. When the woman took her three-month-old baby to be baptized, the parish priest refused because of her stand on abortion. Another priest, affiliated with Catholics for a Free Choice in New York City, later baptized the infant.

At year's end Pope Paul decreed the sainthood of Elizabeth Ann Bayley Seton, founder of the Sisters of Charity and the first American-born saint. On Christmas Eve, Pope Paul opened the 25th Holy Year of the Roman Catholic Church.

**RHODESIA.** Intensified terrorist activity by black guerrillas forced the white minority government of Rhodesia to adopt broadened security measures in 1974. Because the guerrillas began directing their terrorist activities more at Rhodesia's African population than its white farmers, the government stepped up its program of building protected villages to house threatened blacks.

In June the executive committee of the African National Council (ANC) flatly rejected a government proposal that promised to increase the number of black seats in the Rhodesian parliament from 16 to 22. The ANC, under its leader Bishop Abel Muzorewa, argued that under the government plan it would take 40 to 60 years for blacks to achieve

The first female Episcopal priests, ordained in July, serve communion with Bishop Daniel Corrigan (center); the church's House of Bishops declared the ordinations invalid.
WIDE WORLD

*Former New York Gov. Nelson A. Rockefeller testifies before the Senate Rules Committee in September during the lengthy hearings on confirming his nomination as U.S. vice-president.*

PICTORIAL PARADE

equal parliamentary representation with whites. Responding angrily, Prime Minister Ian D. Smith dissolved parliament. In the new general elections held July 30, Smith's Rhodesian Front party won all 50 of the non-African seats in parliament.

In December, however, amidst diminishing hope of suppressing Rhodesia's black militants, increasing numbers of hostile black neighbors, and pressure from South African Prime Minister B. J. Vorster, Smith relented in a dramatic political about-face. He announced that a conference would be held shortly to work out increased political rights and representation for Rhodesian blacks.

In September Rhodesia completed a new 90-mile railway to South Africa. The only direct rail link with that country, it was designed to stave off economic strangulation in the event that Rhodesia's outlet to the Indian Ocean through Mozambique were to be closed by a hostile government.

Earnings of Rhodesian farmers reached a record level in 1974, mainly as a result of the heavy world demand for agricultural products. Rhodesia's 1974 mineral production also brought in a record return. (*See also* Africa; Uganda.)

**ROCKEFELLER, NELSON A.** The U.S. had its third vice-president in little more than a year when Nelson Aldrich Rockefeller took the oath of office on Dec. 19, 1974. He became the 41st vice-president at televised ceremonies in the Senate Chamber. With his installation, the U.S. had for the first time a president and a vice-president chosen outside the normal election process. (*See* Ford.) U.S. President Gerald R. Ford nominated Rockefeller on August 20. He was confirmed by the U.S. Senate, 90–7, and by the House, 287–128, under provisions of the 25th Amendment to the Constitution.

Rockefeller, who governed New York from 1959

to the end of 1973, sought the presidential nomination in 1960, 1964, and 1968. He was widely quoted as calling the vice-presidency "standby equipment" and saying that he was not a "number two type." At 66 years of age, however, the dynamic Rockefeller accepted the nomination with enthusiasm. After he left the governorship of New York, he devoted his time to the Commission on Critical Choices for Americans, which he had founded. With that organization as a base, he had planned to speak throughout the country, and many observers thought he might hope to emerge as his party's presidential candidate in 1976. Before entering politics, Rockefeller had served in appointive posts relating to both foreign and domestic affairs under U.S. Presidents Franklin D. Roosevelt, Harry S. Truman, and Dwight D. Eisenhower.

Rockefeller's nomination was generally popular in Congress, but because of his enormous wealth, exhaustive hearings concerning his financial affairs faced the grandson of the country's first billionaire, John D. Rockefeller. The nominee estimated that during his lifetime he had given away $33 million, had promised to donate another $20.5 million in art and real estate to public use, and had paid $69 million in taxes. He put his total holdings at $218 million, mostly in trusts, and his net worth at $62.5 million. Wary of great economic power combining with political power, members of the House Judiciary Committee sought figures on the Rockefeller family's holdings. The family's senior financial adviser testified that the 84 living members had assets of more than $1 billion—not including real estate, Nelson's $33-million art collection, or the Rockefeller Foundation and charitable institutions, with assets of more than $1 billion.

Rockefeller defended gifts and loans totaling approximately $2 million that he had made to friends and associates, including public officials. The mo-

KEYSTONE

*Romanian athletes participate in the celebrations marking the 30th anniversary of their nation's liberation from Nazi rule.*

nies were not intended to corrupt, he said, but were made for "friendship and hardship." Another stumbling block to the confirmation was the disclosure that Rockefeller's brother Laurance underwrote the publication of an unflattering book about former Supreme Court Justice Arthur J. Goldberg when he ran for governor against Rockefeller in 1970.

Witnesses testifying for and against Rockefeller raised the controversial issues of abortion and Attica. Rockefeller had signed the country's first open abortion law in 1970. In 1971, he had ordered a state police attack on rebellious prisoners at the Attica Correctional Facility in New York, where 43 persons died.

Rockefeller was born on July 8, 1908, to John D. Rockefeller, Jr., and Abby Greene Aldrich Rockefeller in Bar Harbor, Me. He was graduated from Dartmouth College in 1930. In 1962, after 32 years of marriage and the births of five children, he and his first wife, Mary Todhunter Clark, were divorced. He had two sons by his second wife, Margaretta (Happy) Fitler Murphy.

## ROMANIA.
The premier of Romania for 13 years, Ion Gheorghe Maurer, retired on March 26, 1974, citing his age and ill health. He was replaced by a deputy premier, Manea Manescu. At the same time, Nicolae Ceausescu, head of the Communist party and titular head of state, was named president. Ceausescu's new position gave him almost unlimited power in the country.

In August 1974 Romania celebrated the 30th anniversary of its freedom from Nazi Germany. At the celebrations, President Ceausescu said that Romanian industry was producing nearly 30 times more than at the time of World War II. Steel production rose from 280,000 tons to 9 million tons in 1974. Electric power generation rose from 1.5 billion kilowatt-hours to 55 billion kilowatt-hours. Agricultural production also increased greatly. Between 1950 and 1974, the value of Romanian foreign trade rose 18 times. But visitors to Romania reported that that consumer goods were scarce and that currency black markets thrived.

The foreign policy of Romania continued on a course somewhat independent of the Soviet Union in 1974. Romania reportedly refused to allow the Soviet Union to build a rail corridor through the country to facilitate movements of troops. Romania continued only limited participation in the Warsaw Pact and pursued an economic policy largely independent of the Soviet bloc. The 11th congress of the Romanian Communist party approved the country's first political charter in November, rejecting Soviet satellite status and seeking a "new type of unity in the international Communist movement, based on the equality of each (state's) party." Romania remained on friendly terms with the People's Republic of China in 1974. In August U.S. President Gerald R. Ford accepted an invitation to visit Romania, but no date was set for the visit. (*See also* Europe.)

**RWANDA.** President Juvénal Habyalimana continued his military rule in 1974, and he and his government sought to raise the standard of agriculture. However, although Rwanda was one of the poorest, least productive African states, yet with an annual population increase of 3%, the government both increased expenditure on entertainment and forbade government employees to hold trade licenses. Intertribal relations were improved, and one Tutsi was included in the government. Dependence on foreign aid, mainly Belgian and Swiss, was crucial; the International Development Association provided $6.3 million for road projects, and the European Development Fund gave further aid for tea planting, though coffee was the chief export.

During the year the Home de la Vierge de Pauvres, commonly known as the Father Fraipont Mission (supported by the Rwandan and Belgian governments and other organizations), became the largest private employer in the country. It produced the cheapest transistor on the African market; its semi-industrial shirt factory captured almost all the local market, using local handicapped labor; and its orthopedic workshop produced needed invalid aids. The mission itself also had a wholly self-supporting farm. (*See also* Africa; Burundi.)

**SAFETY.** Total traffic deaths during the first eight months of 1974 declined 21%, as compared with the same period in 1973—due chiefly to the mandatory 55-mph speed limit. This and other gasoline-saving measures brought about many changes in the driving habits of the public. During the first eight months alone, an estimated 7,000 lives had been saved as a result of the reduced speed, and shifts in time, place, and circumstance of motor vehicle travel, as well as reduced travel generally, according to Vincent L. Tofany, president of the National Safety Council (NSC).

During the same period about 1.1 million persons suffered disabling injuries in traffic accidents, with a resultant estimated cost to the national economy of more than $10.6 billion. As total annual costs for all accidents climbed to $41.5 billion in 1973, the NSC pointed out that fatalities and disabling injuries created a national loss contributing to inflation. Approximately one million man-years were thought to be lost annually because of work accidents alone.

Public deaths accounted for 17,500 fatalities for the first eight months of 1974, a decrease of 2% from the same period the previous year. Both home and work deaths were down 3%. Fire deaths were down 4%, but drownings were up 14% in 1973. Falls continued to be the second highest cause of accidental deaths, after motor vehicles, with some 16,900 fatalities in 1973. Persons in the 65-and-over age group accounted for 12,000 of these deaths.

In October the U.S. House of Representatives completed Congressional approval of a bill to eliminate the Transportation Department's ruling that made a seat-belt interlock system mandatory on all U.S.-built cars, beginning January 1974. The bill also restricted the department's authority to require the controversial air-bag system it had planned for 1977 model cars. During 1974, also, growing worker concern over job hazards prompted labor

*Stuntman Dar Robinson, halfway through a seven-story leap, is about to demonstrate a new fast-inflating air cushion rescue device to fire and police officials in New York City.*

*Due to sharp edges, excessively leaded paint, and breakable and hence swallowable clips, the U.S. Consumer Product Safety Commission recalled in November its own "Think Toy Safety" buttons.*

unions to give increased attention to job safety and accident prevention in negotiations with employers. (*See also* Consumer Affairs; Crime.)

**SAUDI ARABIA.** The largest Arab oil producer and world petroleum exporter, Saudi Arabia, exerted major influence on world affairs in 1974 as de facto leader of the Organization of Petroleum Exporting Countries (OPEC). The OPEC oil price hikes from $3.44 per barrel in late 1973 to more than $10 a year later proved a devastating blow to the oil-consuming nations while raking in a $112-billion profit in 1974 for the 13 OPEC countries.

Of that sum Saudi Arabia's oil revenues for the year totaled $28.9 billion, despite petroleum production cutbacks late in the year due to surpluses. The government pumped its vast earnings into both domestic and foreign projects. At home, subsidies were allocated for consumer goods and services in order to reduce the cost of living, school and hospital construction was begun in a massive development program, $2 billion in modern weapons were added to the growing Saudi defense force, and by year's end arrangements were under way for the government's purchase of the Arabian American Oil Co., previously owned by U.S. companies. Abroad Saudi Arabia contributed $50 million to the World Food Program, $750 million to the World Bank, and pledged millions more to Arab neighbors and to less developed non-Arab nations.

Saudi Arabia entered into agreements with U.S. industries and announced plans to purchase several billion dollars of U.S. Treasury bonds. In October, following a visit to King Faisal by U.S. Secretary of State Henry A. Kissinger, sources claimed that the U.S. had agreed to double, or possibly even triple, sales of arms to Saudi Arabia, perhaps as an inducement to lower oil prices.

King Faisal, however, continued to emphasize in 1974 the importance to the West, particularly the U.S., of achieving a stable peace in the Middle East. The king insisted that Israeli withdrawal from occupied lands was a necessary condition for peace and for stable agreements, including agreements concerning oil supply, between Saudi Arabia and the U.S. King Faisal said that Saudi Arabia might again use its "oil weapon." (*See also* Middle East.)

**SHIPS AND SHIPPING.** For several of the world's great luxury liners, 1974 was an unusually eventful year. In January, salvage workers began cutting apart the superstructure of the *Queen Elizabeth*, which had been resting on the bottom of Hong Kong Harbor for two years. Formerly the world's largest passenger liner, the 83,673-ton ship had burned, capsized, and sunk in 43 feet of water on Jan. 9, 1972.

In February, the United States passenger liners *Constitution* and *Independence* were sold by American Export Lines to the C. Y. Tung shipping group, based in Hong Kong and Taiwan. The 30,293-ton sister ships, built in 1950 and 1951, had not been in

*Prince Fahd bin Abdul Aziz of Saudi Arabia and U.S. Secretary of State Henry Kissinger sign an agreement in Washington, D.C., on June 8, pledging the two countries to greater economic cooperation, including a review of U.S. military aid.*
WIDE WORLD

*Firing a salute, the* Golden Hind *passes under Tower Bridge in London. The ship, a replica of the one on which Sir Francis Drake became the first English captain to sail around the world, was preparing to set sail for San Francisco, Calif., on a 13,000-mile voyage retracing the first leg of Drake's historic circumnavigation of 1577–80.*

UPI COMPIX

service for five years. The purchase price was slightly more than $5 million, as compared with the original construction cost of $50 million.

On April 1, the British liner *Queen Elizabeth 2* developed boiler trouble and stalled about 270 miles southwest of Bermuda while en route to the Caribbean from New York City. About 1,640 passengers were then transferred to the Norwegian cruise ship *Sea Venture*, which took them to Bermuda. The disabled vessel was towed back to the U.S. On April 17, the *Queen Elizabeth 2* resumed service, sailing with passengers to Great Britain.

The 66,000-ton *France*, the world's longest passenger ship, was withdrawn from service on September 18, following prolonged operating losses. The French vessel had sailed for 14 years, as compared with a normal operating period of 20 years.

On September 12, the 480-foot *Ambassador*, of Britain's Cunard line, caught fire about 40 miles

southwest of Key West, Fla., while en route from Miami, Fla., to New Orleans, La. The ship's 309 crew members were evacuated. The $27-million liner was carrying no passengers.

On March 7, oceanographer John G. Newton of Duke University, Durham, N.C., reported that the sunken wreck of the U.S.S. *Monitor* had been identified in 220 feet of water about 15 miles southeast of Cape Hatteras, N.C. The vessel had taken part in a historic Civil War battle with the Confederate warship *Virginia* (popularly called the *Merrimack*) at Hampton Roads, Va., on March 9, 1862. The naval engagement had been the first encounter between ironclad vessels. The *Monitor* had sunk during a storm the following December 31.

Newton reported that the 172-foot vessel had been discovered several months earlier, but murky water and treacherous currents had hindered attempts to examine and identify it. The hull was in-

*Gustavo Thoeni of Italy skis to victory in the giant slalom event of the World Cup competition at Adelboden, Switzerland, in January. The three-time Cup winner lost narrowly in the final standings to Italian teammate Piero Gros.*
WIDE WORLD

spected by means of suspended television cameras, sonar, and magnetometer, and pieces of wood were taken from the hull by mechanical scoops and analyzed. The wreck had not yet been examined by divers. According to Newton, the hull probably would not be raised from the bottom.

Gordon P. Watts, underwater archaeologist for the state of North Carolina, observed that "the wreck has to be the *Monitor* because the outline of the stern, the screw, the keel, the turret, even the plating and riveting . . . matched the historical description we have of the ship." Cost of the search, partly funded by the National Geographic Society and the National Science Foundation, was more than $75,000.

In August, the U.S. Merchant Marine Academy, at Kings Point, N.Y., accepted women cadets for the first time since the school was opened in 1943. Fifteen women were admitted along with 1,024 men for the new term—the largest enrollment in the school's history.

**SKIING.** In 1974, the golden jubilee year of the International Ski Federation (FIS), the installation of more plastic practice slopes for preseason training accelerated early progress and aided the growth of recreational skiing. An ever increasing choice of skis, boots, safety-release gadgets, and specialized clothing improved the efficiency and appearance of skiers.

Thirty-five nations were represented by 271 skiers (181 men and 90 women) in the 23d world Alpine championships held at St. Moritz, Switzerland, on February 2–10. The fact that Austrian skiers won three of the eight gold medals and French and Italian two each was a fair reflection of international strength, but a first-ever gold for the tiny principal-ity of Liechtenstein (Hanny Wenzel in the women's slalom) was as sensational as the relative failure of U.S. racers.

Gustavo Thoeni of Italy, with convincing slalom and giant slalom victories, stressed his comparative downhill weakness by not even contesting that event and thus forfeiting a combined rating. Only a great second descent by Hans Hinterseer, the Austrian runner-up, prevented a grand slam in the giant slalom by the Italians, for whom Piero Gros won the bronze. Some 30,000 spectators lined the downhill course when David Zwilling and Franz Klammer, both Austrians, took the first two places after Roland Collombin, the Swiss favorite, crashed halfway down. Klammer's consistency in all three events secured him the combined title. Annemarie Moser-Proell of Austria took the women's downhill.

In the eighth World Cup series, Gros became the second Italian to win the men's cup, narrowly preventing Thoeni, the runner-up, from scoring a fourth consecutive success. Moser-Proell won the women's cup, outstripping her rivals for a record fourth successive win. The Nations' Cup, decided concurrently by combining men's and women's aggregate points, went to Austria.

In the fourth Can-Am Ski Trophy series, the victors were Gary Aiken of Canada and Leith Lende of the U.S. The third European Cup series winners were Christian Witt-Döring of Austria and Elena Matous from San Marino. Hugo Nindl of Austria was the season's outstanding professional.

Thirty nations were represented by 324 skiers, including 58 women, in the 30th world Nordic championships at Falun, Sweden, held February 16–24. Overcoming sparse snow conditions, East Germany won five of the seven men's events, and Soviet skiers came first in all three women's races.

**SOCIAL SERVICES.** In September 1974, U.S. President Gerald R. Ford signed into law new provisions regulating private pension plans that cover nearly 30 million American workers. The new law set up the Pension Benefit Guaranty Corp. to underwrite private pension systems against financial collapse and thus to guarantee retirement benefits to members of such plans. The new law also established standards for "vesting," guaranteeing a contributor to a private pension fund the right to at least a percentage of his pension after a number of years of service. The new pension law also allowed increased tax deferment for savings used to establish personal pension funds by people not covered by other plans. The law imposed more stringent regulations on the handling of pension funds, and it required other changes designed to assure that private pension programs in the U.S. would operate with greater financial responsibility and with more equitable benefits to workers.

Changes in Social Security took effect in 1974, increasing benefits by as much as 11% for some people. The new regulations also guaranteed a new minimum monthly benefit of $146 ($219 for married couples) by July 1974 and tied minimum benefits to future cost-of-living increases. The federal government increased benefits to disabled veterans by $566.9 million in 1974. Other legislation extended educational benefits, which otherwise would have expired at midyear, to 285,000 veterans in school.

The Office of Economic Opportunity (OEO), threatened in 1973, got at least another temporary extension in 1974. The agency continued to supervise the highly regarded legal services program, the Economic Development Corp., and many community action programs disliked by many local politicians. In some areas of the country, OEO workers helped poor people develop ways to minimize the effects of inflation and the energy shortage. Many programs of the OEO, particularly legal aid, seemed likely to be transferred to other departments of government, and it appeared that the agency itself might eventually disappear.

Two major social programs, welfare reform and national health insurance, continued to be topics of political debate in 1974, but there was no action on either. The Department of Health, Education, and Welfare (HEW) issued a study discussing alternatives to the present welfare system. They included a negative income tax, refundable tax credits, and major overhaul of the present system—all of which had been proposed before. The continuing debate over a system of national health insurance centered around funding and administration. Republican proposals generally favored using and building on existing private insurance. Democratic proposals, however, advocated health insurance modeled on Social Security, administered by the federal government and paid for through a tax.

Charges of poor administration and corruption continued to plague federal and state social programs. HEW acknowledged that a five-year-old program to screen and treat underprivileged children for physical disorders had reached only 2 million of the 13 million eligible children. Hearings in New York City exposed malpractice among physicians who treated Medicaid patients. An audit in the state of New York uncovered more than $4.5 million in unwarranted claims to Medicaid by nursing homes.

**SOUTH AFRICA.** In April 1974, more than a year earlier than required by law, South African Prime Minister B. J. Vorster called for general elections. As expected, Vorster's ruling National party was victorious; the opposition United party—suffering from internal division—lost five seats in the House of Assembly but was returned to power in Natal. The anti-apartheid Progressives made the most gains in the House, going from one representative to six.

The Legislative Assembly of the partially self-governing Transkei—homeland for the 4-million-member Xhosa tribe—voted in March to ask for full independence within five years. A major condition was that land promised to the Transkei under the original 1936 legislation should be transferred within five years and that such transfer should not prejudice rights of the Transkei to specific districts originally claimed but not falling within the 1936 terms. Vorster announced in September his government's approval of the request. No agreement was reached on defense or on the Transkei claim to the city of Port St. Johns, hitherto regarded as a white enclave.

In September the General Assembly of the United Nations (UN) rejected the credentials of the South African delegates and referred South Africa's UN membership to the Security Council, where a triple veto (by the U.S., Great Britain, and France) prevented eviction. In November, however, South Africa was barred from participation in the General Assembly debate.

Perhaps in response to the pressure of international opinion as well as to Portugal's withdrawal from southern Africa, South Africa softened its stand on the issue of independence for Namibia (South West Africa) and announced policies of economic cooperation and political nonintervention toward black governments in Mozambique and Angola. Vorster, faced also with a growing liberal element in his own party, began to express interest in removing some external manifestations of apartheid and in opening dialog with the black nations of Africa. But at the same time, the year was marked by repressive legislation affecting right of assembly and freedom of speech and potentially limiting the activities of organizations considered to be engaged in politics. Harsh action was taken against attempts to unionize black workers. (*See also* Africa; Rhodesia; United Nations.)

# SPACE EXPLORATION.

The U.S. Skylab 4 mission, although plagued by the failure of gyroscopes and by other problems, was completed successfully in February 1974. The mission, which began in 1973, lasted 84 days as scheduled. The crew's work included studying solar flares, experimenting with processes such as welding and melting under weightless conditions, producing new data about the earth's surface, and providing information on humans' ability to live for extended time in space.

Before leaving Skylab 4, the astronauts—Lieut. Col. Gerald P. Carr, Lieut. Col. William R. Pogue, and Edward G. Gibson—raised the altitude of the laboratory so that it would remain in orbit for about eight years, increasing the possibility of its use in the future, although no projects were definitely planned. The astronauts returned to earth safely, and doctors reported that they were in good health, having adjusted well to the return to gravity.

## Other Manned Spaceflights

During 1974 there were three Soviet manned spaceflights. Soyuz 14 lifted off on July 3 with two cosmonauts aboard. They docked with the Salyut 3 space station and entered it for a 15-day stay. The cosmonauts performed medical tests, biological ex-

Technicians inspect the Apollo command module (background) and the docking module (foreground) in preparation for the joint U.S.-Soviet orbital rendezvous mission planned for 1975.
WIDE WORLD

periments, earth observations, and military reconnaissance and returned to earth on July 19.

On August 26, Soyuz 15 was launched with two other cosmonauts aboard who failed, however, to achieve an expected docking with Salyut 3, apparently because of equipment failure. The possible malfunction worried some U.S. officials because of its implications for the Apollo-Soyuz Test Project (ASTP), the joint Soviet-U.S. manned mission planned for 1975. U.S. officials were reassured, however, with the successful testing of a new docking mechanism on the two-man, six-day Soyuz 16 flight, launched December 2. Soyuz 16 was identical to the Soviet spacecraft to be used for ASTP.

U.S. and Soviet scientists and astronauts exchanged visits in 1974 to work on the ASTP project. Joint crew training took place in both countries. Late in 1974 the equipment for the mission was tested and the U.S. and Soviet equipment mated. The agreement on U.S. press coverage of the program, a difficult issue with the Soviet Union, stipulated that no U.S. news people would be permitted at the U.S.S.R. launch site or control center.

## U.S. Unmanned Satellites

The future of U.S. manned spaceflights remained unclear, but the U.S. continued to lead the world in 1974 in the use of unmanned satellites for communications and scientific research. There were a number of satellites launched or becoming operational during the year. In April, Western Union launched the first domestic communications satellite in the U.S. In May, Applications Technology Satellite-6 was launched for educational programs and for use in communications.

Explorer 51, launched late in 1973, began in 1974 to measure the earth's thermosphere, particularly energy transfer affecting the earth's weather. The first Synchronous Meteorological Satellite (SMS-A), a new type of weather satellite, began to provide as much as 72 hours of continuous coverage of North and South America and Western Africa. The satellite was designed to provide weather data at night and specifically to seek out hurricanes and conditions that might cause tornadoes.

## Interplanetary Probes

Mariner 10, launched in November 1973, reached the vicinity of Venus early in 1974. The craft's two television cameras photographed the planet's atmosphere, while instruments on board made extensive measurements, revealing greatly detailed information on the makeup and behavior of Venus' atmosphere.

Mariner 10 flew near Mercury in March and returned photographs of the planet. Scientists were particularly interested in the photographs of the large scarp that ran for hundreds of miles southward across the planet from its northern hemisphere and of a huge circular basin 800 miles in diameter. Although Mariner 10's tape recorders had jammed, the craft did transmit additional photographs when it flew by Mercury again in September.

Pioneer 10, launched in March 1972, reached Jupiter in December 1973. Information from Pioneer 10's probe of Jupiter was released in 1974. Scientists learned more about the planet's strong magnetic field, its high radiation, its atmosphere, its high temperature, and the varying densities of its moons. Pioneer 11, launched in April 1973, reached Jupiter in December 1974, successfully passing through the intense Jovian radiation belts at one third the distance of Pioneer 10, swinging back out into space for its planned probe of Saturn in 1979.

The U.S.S.R. also made space news in 1974. The Mars 4, 5, 6, and 7 probes, launched in July and August 1973, reached Mars in February and March 1974. Malfunctions, however, prevented three of the probes from carrying out their missions. In May the Soviet Union launched Luna 22 to the moon, and it entered lunar orbit in June to make television photographs of the moon's surface and to study the moon's gravitational field. (*See also* Astronomy; Communications; Earth Sciences.)

**SPAIN.** Rumblings of political reform and the possible loosening of Generalissimo Francisco Franco's rule of Spain were heard during 1974. The year began with the taking office on January 2 of Carlos Arias Navarro, former interior minister and mayor of Madrid, as the nation's new premier. He succeeded Adm. Luis Carrero Blanco, who had been assassinated just two weeks earlier.

In Arias Navarro's first major speech, delivered on February 12 to the Cortés, or parliament, he proposed electing all mayors and provincial assembly presidents and a larger proportion of the Cortés, giving workers more bargaining power, and allowing limited rights of political organization. This new "spirit of February 12" seemed to herald a reform in Spain's political life, but action was slow.

Skepticism toward Arias Navarro was fed by the execution on March 2 of left extremist Salvador Puig Antich, who had been convicted of killing a policeman when resisting arrest on a bank robbery charge, and by the house arrest and attempted exile of Monsignor Antonio Añoveros Ataún, bishop of Bilbao in the Basque country, after he had publicly called for greater freedom for the Basques.

The overthrow of Marcello Caetano's authoritarian regime in neighboring Portugal at the end of April heightened the Spanish government's uneasiness. Apparent fear that a similar move might occur in Spain led to the dismissal in June of Gen. Manuel Díez Alegría, the liberal chief of the joint chiefs of staff. Hopes for political reform revived when ill health obliged the 81-year-old Franco to temporarily relinquish his post as head of state to Prince Juan Carlos de Borbon from July 19 to September 1. In December the upper legislative chamber approved a bill allowing for limited political activity.

CIFRA GRAFICA/PHOTO TRENDS

*More than 200 entries in the competition for sculptural works to be placed along the Mediterranean Highway were exhibited in San Pedro de Galligans Church in Gerona, Spain.*

For much of the year the government concentrated on sustaining a high economic growth rate at the expense of controlling inflation. Growth of the nation's gross national product was estimated at 6.2% between the first halves of 1973 and 1974. Despite a freeze on wages, prices, and dividends imposed at the end of 1973, the cost-of-living index showed a 14% rise during 1974. Wage controls were removed in August, largely in response to mounting worker unrest.

The higher cost of petroleum imports and declining income from tourists and from Spanish workers abroad prompted Finance Minister Antonio Barrera de Irimo to introduce an economic austerity program on October 26. Just three days later, however, Franco dismissed Information Minister Pio Cabanillas Gallas, who had been a champion of a freer press. And on the same day Barrera de Irimo also resigned, ostensibly as a gesture of sympathy. Subsequent resignations among other liberals in the government were interpreted either as a retightening of the rightist grip or as a move by liberals to disassociate themselves from a regime that they believed was doomed. (*See also* Europe.)

**SRI LANKA.** The price of tea, Sri Lanka's main export, rose slightly in 1974, but increased prices for fertilizer and food imports further eroded the country's balance of payments. The economy, shaky in 1973, did not improve; in January 1974 nearly 800,000 persons were unemployed. Foreign loans came from the International Monetary Fund, Great Britain, West Germany, and Sweden.

The leader of the opposition United National party organized a series of rallies to protest the government's food and prices policies. When, on April 21, as many as 150 rallies were organized for the same day, Prime Minister Sirimavo Bandaranaike used the government's emergency powers to forbid them. Publication of newspapers supporting the opposition was halted and a curfew was imposed, despite angry protests in the National State Assembly.

In June an important measure—the Companies (Special Provisions) Act—was passed. Effective as of June 1975, the act stated that any companies working in Sri Lanka must be incorporated there. The law was primarily aimed at ending the longstanding ownership of tea plantations by British "sterling companies."

The Tamils of northern Sri Lanka at last obtained their own branch of the Sri Lanka University. But this community was still dissatisfied, and talk of federalism, even of separation, did not cease in 1974.

Prime Minister Bandaranaike was active in foreign affairs during the year. She took exception to the development of a joint U.S.-British naval base at Diego Garcia in the Indian Ocean. In conjunction with Indira Gandhi, prime minister of India, Bandaranaike arranged during a visit to New Delhi to settle the long-standing problem of the South Indian laborers on ceylon tea estates, of whom some 150,-000 were stateless. Half were to be granted Sri Lanka citizenship and the remainder repatriated to India. (*See also* Asia.)

**STAMPS.** Aided by the flight from currency, the international stamp market continued extremely buoyant when the 1973–74 season opened in September 1973 and stayed that way until the philatelic year ended in July 1974, with considerably increased turnovers from major philatelic auctioneers in Europe and the U.S. The controversy on the practical value of self-adhesive stamps created interest by the issue of a booklet of such stamps by Gibraltar and the experimental issue of a 10¢ self-stick precanceled Christmas stamp by the U.S. The

*The 1974 set of "Bicentennial Era" stamps was issued on July 4 in Philadelphia, Pa.*

COURTESY, U.S. POSTAL SERVICE

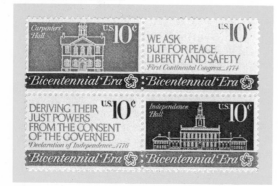

U.S. Postal Service held three seminars designed to bring philatelists and the postal service together to consider the extension of philatelic facilities through marketing by the postal service. In Great Britain, the experimental issue, in January 1975, of its first charity-cum-postage stamps was announced: the post office would sell the stamp at 1½ pence above postal value, and an independent committee would give advice on the distribution of the money raised among recognized charitable organizations. Two "omnibus" issues were launched, one with worldwide support for the centenary of the Universal Postal Union and the other (largely confined to the British Commonwealth territories) for the centenary of Sir Winston Churchill's birth at Blenheim Palace, Oxfordshire, in 1874. Unlike the previous omnibus issues, each of these included a wide variety of designs by different artists.

The American Philatelic Society (APS) published *The Yucatan Affair: The Work of Raoul Ch. de Thuin, Philatelic Counterfeiter*, a record of the forged overprints and postmarks made by De Thuin before the APS bought his business and closed it down after negotiations in Mérida, Yucatán, Mexico, in 1967. (*See also* Postal Service; U.S. Special Report.)

**STATE GOVERNMENTS, UNITED STATES.** During 1974 ethics and energy were important priorities for the 50 state governments. As federal programs dealing with the energy crisis of the 1973–74 winter seemed ineffective, state governors and legislators stepped forward to take up the challenge. To prevent Watergate-type scandals at the state level, an unprecedented number of disclosure and reform laws were approved—all enhancing citizen ability to learn about public officials and public affairs. Budget balancing was also a preoccupation of state governments, along with efforts toward land use regulation and environmental protection.

Forty-three states held regular legislative sessions during 1974, and eight held special sessions. Also, state legislative elections were completed in 44 states, and referenda balloting on a variety of questions was held in 38 states.

The Democratic party—aided by fallout from Watergate, a troubled economy, and some dissatisfaction with incumbents in general—scored marked gains in the November 5 elections. Democrats gained control of nine governorships held by Republicans; one independent and four Republicans won seats held by Democrats. The Democrats went into the elections controlling 32 governorships and came out with 36. One Democratic victor was Ella T. Grasso of Connecticut, the first woman to be elected governor in her own right. (*See* Political Parties; Women.)

During 1974 Democrats controlled both houses of 28 state legislatures; Republicans, 16. After the elections, Republicans remained in two-house con-

*Democrats Richard Lamm (left) and George Brown won the offices of governor and lieutenant governor in Colorado. Brown and new California Lieut. Gov. Mervyn Dymally were the first blacks elected to that post since Reconstruction.*

trol of only 4 state legislatures. Democrats had captured two-house control of 37 legislatures.

State budgets continued to grow, as business expansion and inflation caused a 15% boost in general revenue from state income, sales, and other taxes. Most states were successful in holding the line on tax rates, or reducing them. The pressure on state treasuries was relieved by the infusion of federal revenue-sharing funds. The U.S. Treasury reported that about 65% of the states' revenue-sharing money was being used for improving education.

As in 1973, legislators enacted a variety of tax reform measures to assist those persons hardest hit by inflation. Property tax reductions for the elderly were approved in nine states; for farmers in two. Three states reduced their income tax rates, and one reduced its sales tax rate. For the second consecutive year, no state imposed new personal income, corporate, or sales taxes.

State tax collections in the 1974 fiscal year totaled $68.1 billion, up 13.7% from the 1973 figure. Figures accumulated in 1974 showed that state revenue totaled $129.8 billion in fiscal 1973, an increase of 15.6% from 1972. Of that 1973 total, the federal government provided $31.4 billion.

A trend toward reorganization of state executive branches—usually involving a consolidation of agencies along with increased centralized power in the governor's office—continued in 1974. Twelve states enacted consolidation and reorganization plans. In Colorado, on the other hand, state govern-

ment was partially decentralized, with effective control of many agencies moving from the capital to eight regional offices. A new constitution approved by the voters in Louisiana provided increased powers for the legislature, rather than the executive.

Alaska's voters decided to move their state capital from Juneau, accessible only by water and air, to a site to be determined later. The capital would probably be constructed between the state's two largest cities, Anchorage and Fairbanks.

State legislatures passed an unprecedented number of ethics, disclosure, open meeting, and campaign financing statutes in 1974. Various campaign finance reforms were passed during the year in 21 states.

By the end of 1974, eight states had provided for partial public financing of elections. Laws requiring candidates or officeholders to disclose personal finances and potential conflicts of interest were passed in 14 states. Judicial ethics laws were adopted in New Jersey and Kansas.

California's Lieut. Gov. Edward Reinecke was convicted of perjury in connection with the 1972 Senate Judiciary Committee, which was investigating his role in a federal antitrust case involving the International Telephone and Telegraph Corp. (ITT). Despite his indictment in April, Reinecke remained on the ballot for the Republican primary race for governor in June; he was defeated. He was convicted on one count of perjury in July but resigned his office in October—only minutes before receiving an 18-month suspended sentence.

Attempts to revive capital punishment, outlawed as "arbitrary and capricious" by the U.S. Supreme Court in 1972, continued during 1974. Nine more

*Hawaii's Governor-elect George Ariyoshi, here celebrating his October Democratic primary victory, became in November the first Japanese American to reach a governor's mansion.*

WIDE WORLD

*Raul Castro, the Democratic candidate who became Arizona's first Mexican American governor, arrives at his Tucson campaign headquarters to await the final results in the close race.*

states approved new death penalty statutes supposedly tailored to the court's stipulation for any future laws; this brought to 27 the total number of states adopting such statutes; none of the new state laws had yet been reviewed by the court.

Illinois, Ohio, Delaware, Maine, and Rhode Island established new state-run lotteries during the year, bringing to 13 the total of states operating lotteries. In September U.S. Attorney General William Saxbe warned that lotteries must not violate federal gambling laws; he threatened that all of the lotteries would have to be closed down unless Congress exempted states from existing laws. The director of Pennsylvania's lottery pointed out that the state could derive far more revenue if lottery advertisments were permitted on radio or television. In December Congress passed a bill that would exempt from federal prosecution the transporting, mailing, and broadcasting of information on legal state-run lotteries.

Strong bills to protect environmentally choice areas and provide for state parklands were approved by California and North Carolina. A number of states legislated new strip-mining curbs.

Water pollution control measures were inaugurated or tightened in Florida, Georgia, New Jersey, New York, Virginia, West Virginia, and Wisconsin. Laws encouraging use of solar energy through tax exemptions were passed in Arizona and Indiana.

During the gasoline shortage in early 1974, the governor of Oregon introduced a voluntary odd-even plan for motorists, allowing them to purchase fuel on alternate days by license plate number. Shortly thereafter, Hawaii became the first state to make such a plan mandatory by law. (*See also* Education; Environment; Fuel and Power; United States.)

## GOVERNORS OF THE STATES
(With Party Affiliations and Current Terms)

| | | |
|---|---|---|
| Ala. | George C. Wallace (D), | 1975–79 |
| Alaska | Jay S. Hammond (R), | 1974–78 |
| Ariz. | Raul H. Castro (D), | 1975–79 |
| Ark. | David Pryor (D), | 1975–77 |
| Calif. | Edmund G. Brown, Jr. (D), | 1975–79 |
| Colo. | Richard D. Lamm (D), | 1975–79 |
| Conn. | Ella T. Grasso (D), | 1975–79 |
| Del. | Sherman W. Tribbitt (D), | 1973–77 |
| Fla. | Reubin O'D. Askew (D), | 1975–79 |
| Ga. | George Busbee (D), | 1975–79 |
| Hawaii | George Ariyoshi (D), | 1974–78 |
| Idaho | Cecil D. Andrus (D), | 1975–79 |
| Ill. | Dan Walker (D), | 1973–77 |
| Ind. | Otis R. Bowen (R), | 1973–77 |
| Iowa | Robert D. Ray (R), | 1975–79 |
| Kan. | Robert F. Bennett (R), | 1975–79 |
| Ky. | Julian Carroll * (D), | 1971–75 |
| La. | Edwin W. Edwards (D), | 1972–76 |
| Me. | James B. Longley (I), | 1975–79 |
| Md. | Marvin Mandel (D), | 1975–79 |
| Mass. | Michael S. Dukakis (D), | 1975–79 |
| Mich. | William G. Milliken (R), | 1975–79 |
| Minn. | Wendell R. Anderson (D), | 1975–79 |
| Miss. | William L. Waller (D), | 1972–76 |
| Mo. | Christopher S. Bond (R), | 1973–77 |
| Mont. | Thomas L. Judge (D), | 1973–77 |
| Neb. | J. James Exon (D), | 1975–79 |
| Nev. | Mike O'Callaghan (D), | 1975–79 |
| N.H. | Meldrim Thomson, Jr. (R), | 1975–77 |
| N.J. | Brendan T. Byrne (D), | 1974–78 |
| N.M. | Jerry Apodaca (D), | 1975–79 |
| N.Y. | Hugh L. Carey (D), | 1975–79 |
| N.C. | James E. Holshouser, Jr. (R), | 1973–77 |
| N.D. | Arthur A. Link (D), | 1973–77 |
| Ohio | James A. Rhodes (R), | 1975–79 |
| Okla. | David L. Boren (D), | 1975–79 |
| Ore. | Robert Straub (D), | 1975–79 |
| Pa. | Milton J. Shapp (D), | 1975–79 |
| R.I. | Philip W. Noel (D), | 1975–77 |
| S.C. | James B. Edwards (R), | 1975–79 |
| S.D. | Richard F. Kneip (D), | 1975–79 |
| Tenn. | Ray Blanton (D), | 1975–79 |
| Tex. | Dolph Briscoe (D), | 1975–79 |
| Utah | Calvin L. Rampton (D), | 1973–77 |
| Vt. | Thomas P. Salmon (D), | 1975–77 |
| Va. | Mills E. Godwin, Jr. (R), | 1974–78 |
| Wash. | Daniel J. Evans (R), | 1973–77 |
| W.Va. | Arch A. Moore, Jr. (R), | 1973–77 |
| Wis. | Patrick J. Lucey (D), | 1975–79 |
| Wyo. | Ed Herschler (D), | 1975–79 |

* Succeeded **Wendell H. Ford** (resigned after election to U.S. Senate) in January 1975.

**STOCKS AND BONDS.** As the worst year for the stock market since the depression-ridden 1930's, 1974 would long be remembered. The most reliable of the stock market indicators, the Dow-Jones industrial average (DJI), opened at 850.86 on January 2, the year's first day of trading, and closed on December 31 at 616.24—a 27.6% decline for the year. The year's low was 577.60 on December 6, the DJI's lowest point in 12 years. A customary year-end rally brought the DJI up from the 580's and 590's where it had remained through most of December.

On January 2 the minimum down payment, or margin rate, for most stocks bought on credit was reduced by the Federal Reserve Board from 65% to 50%. The move was prompted by the sharp reduction in stock market credit that had occurred since the last margin-rate increase in November 1972.

DuPont Walston, Inc., which operated the second largest network of stock brokerage offices in the United States, announced in January that it was going out of business. The company, which had about 300,000 clients and 143 branch offices, had suffered a financial loss in every month since its formation in July 1973 by merger of duPont Glore Forgan, Inc., and Walston & Co.

On August 2 the U.S. Treasury Department approved a 9% interest rate on $4 billion in Treasury securities—the highest rate ever offered on Treasury notes with maturities greater than one year. The new rate applied to notes in denominations of $1,000 and higher. They were sold to help refinance $10.2 billion in notes with a 5⅝% interest rate maturing on August 15.

Beginning October 1, the New York Stock Exchange (NYSE) attempted to boost trading volume by extending daily trading hours from a closing time of 3:30 P.M. to 4 P.M. Exchange officials believed that the extension would be reflected particularly in increased trading volume on the Pacific Coast, where it had been 12:30 P.M. at closing.

The sagging economy increased moonlighting by stockbrokers. The NYSE, which had generally prohibited moonlighting by salesmen of firms with membership on the exchange, was receiving—and granting—more applications for outside employment. (*See also* Banks; Business and Industry; Money and International Finance; United States.)

**SUDAN.** President Maj. Gen. Gaafar al-Nimeiry, in a speech in April 1974, foresaw a future in which Sudan's role would be that of granary and sugar supplier to the Arab world and even beyond. Emphasis in economic development was set toward this objective. Work was in progress on a trunk road system, as well as an oil products pipeline, to link Port Sudan with Khartoum, the capital, and the central agricultural region; work on the Rahad River irrigation project, which would bring an extra 300,000 acres under cultivation, was under way; and contracts were awarded for construction of two new sugar refineries to supplement the two already operational. However, declining cotton exports and severe inflation, running at more than 30%, made it difficult for the government to sustain bright hopes for the future among a population increasingly disturbed by food shortages, the rising cost of sugar, and the inefficiency of the transportation system.

*Built under the auspices of the United Nations emergency relief program, the $2.4-million bridge across the White Nile at Juba, Sudan, opened March 15, replacing antiquated ferry service.*

COURTESY, SUDANESE MINISTRY OF INFORMATION & CULTURE, PHOTOGRAPHY SECTION

President Nimeiry's visit to President Anwar el-Sadat of Egypt in Cairo in February ended a period of tension and resulted in agreement on gradual economic integration with Egypt, followed later by the appointment in each country of a minister specially charged with forging closer ties with the other, but the practical results of this new policy were few by the year's end. Plans were laid for future joint projects, however, including irrigation and conservation of the waters of the White Nile for cultivation. (*See also* Africa; Zaire.)

## SUPREME COURT OF THE UNITED STATES.

Except for two important decisions at the end of the 1973–74 term, the year was a relatively undistinguished one for the Supreme Court. Generally the court reaffirmed the position it had held since World War II as a civil liberties court, with one important difference—persons alleging deprivation of civil liberties were losing appeals with greater frequency.

A record number of 3,876 cases were disposed of. As was customary, most of these were cleared from the docket by the court's refusing to hear them because of what the justices viewed as adequate treatment in the lower courts.

The court remained in session later than any other term in modern history, in order to hear evidence and hand down the decision in the "Watergate tapes" case, United States *vs.* Nixon. This was undoubtedly the most momentous case of the year, inasmuch as the decision was a key link in the chain of events that led to the resignation of U.S. President Richard M. Nixon.

United States *vs.* Nixon concerned the validity of a subpoena issued by U.S. District Court Judge John J. Sirica. The subpoena ordered President Nixon to surrender tape recordings and other materials in connection with the Watergate criminal cover-up trial (*See* Law; Nixon; United States.)

The court held that Judge Sirica's subpoena was valid and that President Nixon must relinquish the disputed materials. The decision was unanimous, 8–0; Justice William H. Rehnquist disqualified himself from the case because he had worked for former Attorney General John N. Mitchell, one of the Watergate cover-up defendants.

Chief Justice Warren Burger wrote the unanimous opinion in United States *vs.* Nixon. The court rejected the argument that executive privilege and separation of powers were applicable to the case. The basic issue was deemed to be withholding of evidence in a criminal proceeding. The court noted that the conversations recorded on the Watergate tapes did not involve sensitive military or diplomatic matters.

The other important case heard at the end of the term was the Detroit, Mich., school busing case, Milliken *vs.* Bradley. In order to desegregate the Detroit public schools, the lower federal courts had ordered the busing of pupils across city boundaries into the suburbs. The high court overruled the lower courts, 5–4, stating that there had been no violation of 14th Amendment rights by the various school boards involved. The court also noted that the principle of local control of schools was deeply rooted in the history of U.S. public education. The constitutional right of blacks in Detroit, the court held, was to attend a unitary school system in that district—not in outlying districts. (*See* Education.)

The decision in DeFunis *vs.* Odegaard shed no light on the issue of alleged discrimination against whites in favor of members of minority groups. Marco DeFunis sued a law school that refused to admit him; applicants with lower grade averages and test scores had been admitted to the school. By the time the case reached the high court, DeFunis had been admitted to the school on a lower court order. The court thus ruled the case moot and did not consider the substantive constitutional issues.

Watergate Special Prosecutor Leon Jaworski leaves the Supreme Court July 24 after the court ruled unanimously that President Nixon had to surrender the subpoenaed Watergate tapes as evidence in the Watergate cover-up trial. Surrender of the tapes was followed by Nixon's resignation on August 9 and later conviction of four key Nixon associates in the cover-up trial.

UPI COMPIX

SUPREME COURT 8
WHITE HOUSE 0

"Stonewalled"

Under Florida's "right of reply" statute, a political candidate could demand from a newspaper the right to equal space to answer criticism by the newspaper. This statute was invalidated in Miami Herald Publishing Co. *vs.* Tornillo, as a violation of 1st Amendment guarantees of a free press.

A local political candidate sued the city of Shaker Heights, Ohio, because of the city's policy of not permitting political advertisements on public transit vehicles. In Lehman *vs.* City of Shaker Heights the court held that the city's policy was valid and did not constitute a violation of the guarantees invoked —free speech and equal protection.

The case O'Shea *vs.* Littleton involved allegations of discrimination in the administration of the criminal justice system in Illinois, especially in matters of bail and sentencing. The court did not deal with the issues of the case but ruled instead that the plaintiffs had no "standing"—they themselves had sustained no injury and therefore had no power to sue.

The court struck down a residency requirement for free, public medical treatment in nonemergency cases. In Memorial Hospital *vs.* Maricopa County, the court held that interstate travel was a basic constitutional freedom and that the state of Arizona had created an "invidious" classification of persons, violating the equal protection clause of the 14th Amendment.

The village of Belle Terre on Long Island, N.Y., had adopted a zoning ordinance to prevent groups of more than two unrelated persons from living together in "a one-family dwelling." The court upheld the ordinance in Village of Belle Terre *vs.* Boraas, noting that the exercise of police power of the state may include defining family needs and community standards.

Under Florida tax law, provision is made for a special exemption for widows. A widower who was denied the same exemption sued on the grounds of discrimination. In Kahn *vs.* Shevin the court held that there was no invalid discrimination because a reasonable distinction was involved. The opinion stated that the financial difficulties confronting the lone woman exceed those facing the lone man.

Pittsburgh, Pa., operated public parking facilities and at the same time imposed a 20% tax on private commercial parking lots. In City of Pittsburgh *vs.* Alco Parking Corp. the court upheld the tax against the charge that it was unreasonably high and burdensome to private business, and thus violative of due process. The court specifically declined to set terms under which governments may compete with private businesses.

California law required a filing fee for candidates in primary elections, with no waiver provision for indigent persons. In Lubin *vs.* Allison the court struck down the fee requirement, noting that qualifications for a place on the ballot may not be measured solely in terms of dollars.

The court ruled in Wolff *vs.* McDonnell that prisoners subject to disciplinary hearings were not entitled to all of the rights of due process normally accruing in a criminal proceeding. In another criminal case, United States *vs.* Edwards, the court broadened the power of police to seize the clothing of a suspect without a warrant.

A number of criminal cases, involving more than 600 persons, were dismissed in May when the court ruled that the Nixon Administration had engaged in illegal wiretapping to gather evidence. The Omnibus Crime Control Act of 1968 clearly states that requests for wiretaps must be approved by the U.S. attorney general or a specially appointed assistant attorney general. An executive assistant in the Department of Justice had been approving taps in organized-crime cases and others.

Early in the 1974–75 term the court upheld as constitutional the 1973 Regional Rail Reorganization Act that provided for revamping six bankrupt Northeastern railroads into one financially profitable system. A lower court had ruled the act unconstitutional because of the possible loss of assets by Penn Central's creditors, but the high court cited existing recourse for the recovery of losses.

**SWAZILAND.** Though the most prosperous of the three countries, Swaziland shared with its southern African neighbors Botswana and Lesotho many of the problems of being landlocked. In addition Swaziland shared a border with Mozambique, where 1974 was a year of political upheaval. (*See* Africa.) The "political holiday" continued through 1974 as the royal commission had not completed its study on the country's constitutional future; yet opposition leader Ambrose Zwane was detained in March for criticizing the government and was threatened with rearrest if he continued his political activities. In March and April, meetings were held by the three states to coordinate matters of common interest, in particular problems arising from the oil crisis, monetary policy, and migration (Swaziland had 4,500, or 1.2%, of its labor force in South Africa, as against Botswana's 4.7%, and Lesotho's 20%). Although remaining in the rand currency zone, Swaziland in September issued its own currency of emalangeni (singular, lilangeni) and cents, equal to and convertible into rand and backed by the South African Reserve Bank.

In his March budget, the finance minister indicated the linkage between the Swazi economy and world inflation. Current high prices indicated good prospects, particularly in the important sugar industry. Wood pulp exports increased by 5.5% and asbestos by 46%. The value of the cotton crop increased dramatically for the 1974 season, and a textile factory for processing was established in the Nhlangano area after talks with Hong Kong experts. The tourist industry expanded to a record 92,000 visitors. Shell had been given a concession for the extensive coal deposits known to exist in eastern Swaziland. The capital budget for 1974 was increased by 30%. The spectacular increase in government spending was met by world prices for Swaziland commodities, but the finance minister pointed out that Swaziland's capacity to absorb loans was limited by a lack of personnel to carry out projects rather than by repayment difficulties.

**SWEDEN.** Prime Minister Olof Palme's Social Democratic government was put to an early test in 1974 by the oil crisis. Energy shortages created immediate concern about Sweden's ability to maintain its standard of living, since it was heavily dependent on imported oil. The situation was aggravated by Sweden's small refining capacity. In spite of the oil crisis, however, the economy enjoyed an excellent year. In June, the number of job vacancies exceeded the number of unemployed for the first time in three years.

In January the government introduced an economic package designed to maintain employment, dampen price increases, and strengthen purchasing power. It affected child allowances, old-age pensions, housing construction, energy-saving investments, and the subsidy of basic foods. In February the government increased the package in a compromise with the Center and Liberal parties, the main element of which was a decision to lower the general value-added tax between April 1 and September 15. The bank rate was raised twice in 1974 to counteract a further drain on currency exchange reserves.

On February 27 a new constitution, effective Jan. 1, 1975, was adopted for the second time by the new Riksdag (parliament), following its primary adoption by the preceding Riksdag, as required by law. The constitution reduced the role of king to that of a figurehead, whose formal assent to legislation was no longer required. It reduced the number of seats in the Riksdag from 350 to 349, to avoid ties in votes between parliamentary blocs and the consequent drawing of lots. In May a new and more liberal abortion law, also effective January 1975, was approved. At midyear a state commission proposed the establishment of national casinos to be run by the state. Sweden was allowed to become a member of the Energy Coordinating Group on condition that it could withdraw if its neutral status were threatened. Diplomatic relations between the U.S. and Sweden, severed in December 1972 over Vietnam, improved with respective appointments of ambassadors in March. (*See also* Europe.)

*Members of the Stockholm police display in November some of about 50 recovered Russian icons, smuggled from the U.S.S.R. by two employees of the Swedish embassy in Moscow.*
UPI COMPIX

Swimming in Concord, Calif., on August 25, Tim Shaw heads for the finish and a new world record—his third in four days—for the 1,500-meter freestyle event with a time of 15:31.75.

## SWIMMING.

**SWIMMING.** Five international regional championships plus the U.S.-East Germany dual meet provided the spark for a record-shattering 1974 in amateur competitive swimming. The year began with the tenth British Commonwealth Games at Christchurch, New Zealand, January 25–February 1, when Wendy Cook of Canada and Stephen Holland of Australia each lowered world records. The Canadian high school student set her record in the 100-meter backstroke with a time of 1:04.78, and the Australian teenager stroked to a record of 8:15.88 for the 800-meter freestyle, on his way to a victory in the 1,500-meter freestyle, clocking 15:-34.73, less than three seconds off his own world mark of 15:31.85 set in 1973.

In the 12th Central American and Caribbean Games in Santo Domingo, February 28–March 6, Mexico led the medal parade, winning 14 gold, 10 silver, and 8 bronze. Twenty-two Central American records were broken in the meet.

The 22d South American Swimming Championships were held at Medellín, Colombia, May 1–5. Jorge Delgado of Ecuador was the outstanding swimmer, winning six individual gold medals. Brazil produced two outstanding women swimmers—Maria Elisa Guimaraes and Flavia Nadalutti—both of whom won three events. Brazil dominated the meet, winning 38 medals, 21 of them gold.

The 13th European Championships were held in Vienna, Austria, on August 18–25. In this meet 17 world records and 23 European records were set. East Germany continued its ascent to a world ranking just below the U.S. Their women won every event but the 100-meter breaststroke, and it took a world record time of 1:12.55 by West Germany's Christel Justen to halt the awesome East German team. In the men's competition, the 15 titles were divided by five countries. In the medal count East Germany outdistanced its rivals, capturing 17 gold and a total of 35. West Germany with 6 gold and a total of 12 was a distant runner-up.

Only a suspension of the Fédération internationale de natation amateur (FINA) rules permitted the People's Republic of China to compete in the seventh Asian Games in Teheran, Iran, September 2–16. By world standards, the performances were not outstanding. Japan held onto its overwhelming superiority, winning the medal count with 21 gold and a 42 total in the swimming events.

The Amateur Athletic Union (AAU) Senior Short Course Championships were held at Dallas, Tex., on April 10–14. The women set American records in every one of their 15 events, and the men set 7 new standards. The Santa Clara Swim Club won the women's team crown, their 40th AAU championship, dating back to 1957. The University of Southern California won the men's title.

In the National Collegiate Athletic Association (NCAA) championships Indiana University's swimming streak was halted at six when the University of Southern California (U.S.C.) pulled out a one-point victory at Belmont Plaza Olympic Pool in Long Beach, Calif. The score was 339 to 338. While Indiana was being defeated by U.S.C., the Arizona State University women were winning their fourth Association for Intercollegiate Athletics for Women (AIAW) championship at Penn State University on March 14–16.

Rosemarie Kother of East Germany races through the 100-meter butterfly event on September 1 in Concord, Calif., finishing with a time of 1:01.88 to set a new world record.

## WORLD SWIMMING RECORDS SET IN 1974 (through September)

| | Event | Name | Country | Time | |
|---|---|---|---|---|---|
| **MEN** | 200-meter freestyle | Tim Shaw | U.S. | 1 minute | 51.66 seconds |
| | 400-meter freestyle | Tim Shaw | U.S. | 3 minutes | 56.96 seconds |
| | 400-meter freestyle | Tim Shaw | U.S. | 3 minutes | 54.69 seconds |
| | 800-meter freestyle | Stephen Holland | Australia | 8 minutes | 15.88 seconds |
| | 1,500-meter freestyle | Tim Shaw | U.S. | 15 minutes | 31.75 seconds |
| | 100-meter breaststroke | John Hencken | U.S. | 1 minute | 3.88 seconds |
| | 200-meter breaststroke | John Hencken | U.S. | 2 minutes | 18.93 seconds |
| | 200-meter breaststroke | John Hencken | U.S. | 2 minutes | 18.21 seconds |
| | 200-meter individual medley | David Wilkie | Great Britain | 2 minutes | 6.32 seconds |
| | 200-meter individual medley | Steve Furniss | U.S. | 2 minutes | 6.32 seconds |
| | 400-meter individual medley | Andras Hargitay | Hungary | 4 minutes | 28.89 seconds |
| | 400-meter freestyle relay | U.S. National Team | U.S. | 3 minutes | 25.17 seconds |
| **WOMEN** | 100-meter freestyle | Kornelia Ender | East Germany | | 57.51 seconds |
| | 100-meter freestyle | Kornelia Ender | East Germany | | 56.96 seconds |
| | 200-meter freestyle | Kornelia Ender | East Germany | 2 minutes | 3.22 seconds |
| | 200-meter freestyle | Shirley Babashoff | U.S. | 2 minutes | 2.94 seconds |
| | 400-meter freestyle | Heather Greenwood | U.S. | 4 minutes | 17.33 seconds |
| | 400-meter freestyle | Shirley Babashoff | U.S. | 4 minutes | 15.77 seconds |
| | 800-meter freestyle | Jenny Turrall | Australia | 8 minutes | 50.1* seconds |
| | 800-meter freestyle | Jo Harshbarger | U.S. | 8 minutes | 47.5* seconds |
| | 1,500-meter freestyle | Jenny Turrall | Australia | 16 minutes | 48.2* seconds |
| | 1,500-meter freestyle | Jenny Turrall | Australia | 16 minutes | 43.4* seconds |
| | 1,500-meter freestyle | Jenny Turrall | Australia | 16 minutes | 39.28 seconds |
| | 1,500-meter freestyle | Jenny Turrall | Australia | 16 minutes | 33.94 seconds |
| | 100-meter backstroke | Wendy Cook | Canada | 1 minute | 4.78 seconds |
| | 100-meter backstroke | Ulrike Richter | East Germany | 1 minute | 4.43 seconds |
| | 100-meter backstroke | Ulrike Richter | East Germany | 1 minute | 4.09 seconds |
| | 100-meter backstroke | Ulrike Richter | East Germany | 1 minute | 3.30 seconds |
| | 100-meter backstroke | Ulrike Richter | East Germany | 1 minute | 3.08 seconds |
| | 100-meter backstroke | Ulrike Richter | East Germany | 1 minute | 2.98 seconds |
| | 200-meter backstroke | Ulrike Richter | East Germany | 2 minutes | 18.41 seconds |
| | 200-meter backstroke | Ulrike Richter | East Germany | 2 minutes | 17.35 seconds |
| | 100-meter breaststroke | Renate Vogel | East Germany | 1 minute | 12.91 seconds |
| | 100-meter breaststroke | Christel Justen | West Germany | 1 minute | 12.55 seconds |
| | 100-meter breaststroke | Renate Vogel | East Germany | 1 minute | 12.28 seconds |
| | 200-meter breaststroke | Ann Katrin Schott | East Germany | 2 minutes | 37.89 seconds |
| | 200-meter breaststroke | Karla Linke | East Germany | 2 minutes | 34.99 seconds |
| | 100-meter butterfly | Rosemarie Kother | East Germany | 1 minute | 2.09 seconds |
| | 100-meter butterfly | Rosemarie Kother | East Germany | 1 minute | 1.99 seconds |
| | 100-meter butterfly | Rosemarie Kother | East Germany | 1 minute | 1.88 seconds |
| | 200-meter individual medley | Ulrike Tauber | East Germany | 2 minutes | 18.93 seconds |
| | 400-meter individual medley | Ulrike Tauber | East Germany | 4 minutes | 52.42 seconds |
| | 400-meter freestyle relay | U.S. National Team | U.S. | 3 minutes | 51.99 seconds |
| | 400-meter medley relay | East Germany National Team | East Germany | 4 minutes | 13.78 seconds |

*Watch time, recorded in 1/10 increments

The AAU National Senior championships were held at Concord, Calif., on August 21–25. Eleven world records, 18 American records, 1 American citizen's, 2 Australian and Commonwealth marks, plus 1 civilian and 3 Brazilian records were set.

At the AAU Senior National Indoor championships in Dallas on April 4–6, the winners were Christine Loock, one-meter springboard; Jennie Chandler, three-meter springboard; and Janet Ely, ten-meter platform. In the men's events, Tim Moore won the one-meter, Phil Boggs took the three-meter, and Steve McFarland captured the platform competition.

In the AAU Senior National Outdoors Diving championships at Decatur, Ala., August 13–17, the winners were Tim Moore in the ten-meter springboard and Keith Russell in the three-meter springboard and platform. Cynthia Potter won the women's one-meter, Christine Loock the three-meter, and Canada's Teri York won the platform.

KEYSTONE

*The Swiss army comes to the rescue when early winter snows in October threaten to trap herds of sheep in the Swiss Alps.*

**SWITZERLAND.** The state of the 1974 federal budget was grave, with the annual deficit—due to a large increase of federal expenditure, especially for social security and welfare, highway construction, nuclear power plants, and education—constantly increasing. The government sought to obtain additional revenue from the national defense tax, the sales tax, and import levies on oil products.

The federal government's report on defense policy was approved by parliament in June. After considerable discussion, the U.S. Tiger IIF-5E fighter plane was preferred for purchase to the French Mirage 30 and the British Hunter. In November the government limited the influx of foreign capital to prevent the Swiss franc from rising excessively. After more than a year's discussion in parliament, the draft constitutional article authorizing the federal government to institute economic systematic controls gained more definitive shape. It was to be submitted to popular vote in 1975.

After an exceptionally heated campaign, the people on October 20 rejected the "third antiforeign influence initiative" calling for the departure from the country by January 1978 of about 500,000 foreign workers and their families. Meanwhile, the government pursued its policy of stabilizing and gradually diminishing the volume of resident foreign workers. In December Foreign Minister Pierre Graber was elected president of Switzerland for 1975 in accord with the annual rotation of the presidency among cabinet members. (*See also* Europe.)

**SYRIA.** Full-scale renewal of the October 1973 war seemed imminent through early 1974 as artillery and tank duels broke out between Syria and Israel on the Golan Heights. No progress was made toward a military disengagement despite visits to Damascus, the Syrian capital, by U.S. Secretary of State Henry Kissinger in January and February. The main dispute was over prisoner exchange and the return home of 170,000 Syrian refugees.

Kissinger tried again, and after shuttling between Damascus and Jerusalem 14 times he brought about a disengagement agreement on May 29. Israel agreed to withdraw to the pre-1973 lines and to yield a band of territory, including the Golan Heights capital. In June U.S. President Richard M. Nixon visited Syria, and an accord was reached restoring U.S.-Syrian relations, broken off in 1967. On November 29, with Syrian agreement, the United Nations approved a six-month extension for its peacekeeping force on the Golan Heights.

The Soviet Union and other Communist countries continued to play a vital role in Syrian affairs. In April President Hafez al-Assad led a Syrian delegation to Moscow, where he signed several economic and military agreements. In September he visited Romania and Bulgaria. It was announced in August that the U.S.S.R. would build, in addition to the almost completed Tabka Dam on the Euphrates River, a large dam on the Nahr el-Kebir.

Economic losses from the October war were estimated by the government at $2.3 billion, with the full cost of repairing power stations, bridges, and other installations still to be assessed. The Syrian cereal crop was well above average in 1974, although early spring floods cut it somewhat. The new cotton crop was expected to be down, but exports for 1974 were up. Early in the year the government relaxed controls on currency and on capital flow in order to encourage private trade. A new cabinet was formed on August 31 by Premier Mahmoud Ayoubi, with the Baathist Socialist party still in control. (*See also* Middle East.)

*In a last ceremonial lowering of the flag, Israeli soldiers prepare to withdraw on June 24 from El Quneitra, Syria, captured in the October 1973 war.*
CAMERA PRESS/PHOTO TRENDS

# TAIWAN.

There was renewed optimism in Taiwan in 1974 as the Chinese Nationalist regime there remained determined to resist Chinese Communist attempts to isolate and eventually absorb the island republic. Premier Chiang Ching-kuo, acting as chief executive under the nominal presidency of his father, Chiang Kai-shek, broadened the base of his administration and lifted public morale by adding more Taiwan-born Chinese, thus reducing antagonisms toward the minority mainland Chinese refugees.

The Taiwan government also was encouraged by continued diplomatic recognition by the United States. U.S. Ambassador Leonard Unger pledged on May 25 that his government would continue to safeguard the island's security. In fact, despite a 1972 agreement with China on withdrawal of troops from Taiwan, U.S. forces still numbered about 4,000 men in July. Relations with Japan, however, deteriorated. In April the Taiwan government retaliated against Japan's signing an air agreement with China by shutting off its own air service with Japan and banning Japanese planes from Taiwan's airspace.

Taiwan's export-oriented industries were threatened during the year by steep price increases in imported oil and raw materials. They also were losing their competitive advantage as wages also rose. The island's economy nevertheless continued to grow during 1974—at an estimated annual rate of 8.5%, down just a little from an average of 11% for the preceding few years. In the belief that a strong economic base was its best guarantee for political survival, the government increasingly emphasized capital-intensive, technologically advanced industry. Plans were pushed for a major development program that would include railway electrification, highway building, new ports, a new steel mill, a shipyard, an international airport, and a petrochemical complex.

It was reported that Taiwan's trade had reached an all-time high of $8.2 billion in 1973 and then of $8.5 billion for the first eight months of 1974. The U.S. remained in first place among Taiwan's trading partners. (*See also* Asia; China.)

# TANZANIA.

On July 7, 1974, the Tanganyika African National Union, Tanzania's ruling party, celebrated the 20th anniversary of its founding with trade shows, football matches, and other festivities. Seven months earlier, in January, the Zanzibar government had celebrated the 10th anniversary of its revolution by releasing 545 prisoners. In May the year-long trial for treason of 81 people charged with complicity in the assassination of Sheikh Abeid Karume came to an end. In all, 54 were found guilty, of whom 43 were sentenced to death.

In March President Julius K. Nyerere paid a visit to China, as the result of which the Chinese government offered an interest-free loan of about $75 million during the following five years to develop coal and iron ore deposits in southern Tanzania and to link them with the railway system. This offer was followed shortly afterward by a further loan of

*In July Presidents Nyerere of Tanzania (with white hat) and Kaunda of Zambia (to Nyerere's left) tour a workshop built to serve the Great Uhuru Railway that would soon link the two countries.*
CAMERAPIX/KEYSTONE

about $400,000 by West Germany to help counter the difficulties arising from increased oil prices and the probability of crop shortages because of poor rainfall. In June Great Britain resumed economic aid that had been stopped in 1965 when Tanzania left the Commonwealth. The British minister of overseas development agreed to make money available to assist rural development. The agreement also envisaged the payment of compensation to British farmers whose land might subsequently be nationalized. One of the first results of this clause was a government proposal to take over British land that was producing coffee and tea in the region of Mount Kilimanjaro, causing discontent among uncompensated farmers whose land had been nationalized the previous October.

In April new price controls were introduced, any breach of which rendered traders liable to fines and imprisonment. In September Nyerere toured the Caribbean. (*See also* Africa; Burundi; Uganda.)

## TELEVISION AND RADIO.

In 1974 the number of television and radio sets in use throughout the world passed the one-billion mark, reaching an estimated 1,007,500,000. There were approximately 702.5 million radio sets in use throughout the world, with 356.5 million of those—slightly more than half—in the United States. Television sets throughout the world totaled approximately 305 million, of which about 112 million were in the United States.

Estimates published in the 1974 *Broadcasting Yearbook* ranked the Soviet Union, with about 30 million TV sets, second behind the U.S. Japan was close behind the U.S.S.R., with 25 million sets; Great Britain had 20 million.

U.S. homes equipped with color TV sets numbered 48,635,000, or 71% of all television homes, as of Oct. 1, 1974—according to estimates compiled by *Broadcasting* magazine. This represented a one-year gain of 5,235,000, or 12%.

There were about 6,435 television stations on the air throughout the world. That total broke down as follows: 2,100 in the Far East, 2,000 in Western Europe, 947 in the U.S., 910 in Eastern Europe, 175 in South America, more than 80 in Canada, and 35 in Africa.

About 13,850 radio stations were operating worldwide; most of those were of the amplitude modulation (AM) variety, but the number of frequency modulation (FM) stations continued to increase. The U.S. had 7,715 of the world's radio stations, or about 55%.

### Cable TV in the U.S.

In 1974 the progress of cable television remained slow as some of its principal problems intensified. High interest rates continued to hold down borrowing for construction of new systems, particularly in larger cities. This led operators to put more emphasis on developing old franchises, seeking rate in-

COURTESY, CBS TELEVISION NETWORK

*Rhoda*

COURTESY, NBC, INC.

*The Little House on the Prairie*

COURTESY, CBS TELEVISION NETWORK

*'The Autobiography of Miss Jane Pittman'*

LONDON WEEKEND TELEVISION

*Upstairs, Downstairs*

creases for their services, and adding subscribers to existing systems.

Cable TV operators received a favorable Supreme Court decision on their liability under existing copyright law. Efforts by lobbyists to obtain favorable treatment in pending copyright legislation bogged down, however—along with the legislation itself, which seemed destined to wait still another year for final Congressional action.

## Programming

The House Judiciary Committee's public impeachment proceedings, the subsequent resignation of U.S. President Richard M. Nixon, and the swearing-in of President Gerald R. Ford were carried in full by TV and radio. *Broadcasting* estimated that about 70 million viewers, almost double the entire U.S. population when President Andrew Johnson was impeached in 1868, saw some or all of the impeachment proceedings. The total cost to the three commercial TV networks, which covered the deliberations on a rotation basis, was estimated at about $3.4 million for the six days of hearings.

The regular network season that opened in September 1974 was dominated by situation comedies and action-adventure series, with 12 new entries in each category spread among the three networks. From the standpoint of audience ratings, reaction to the new lineup as a whole was the most negative in recent years. Within a month after the opening of the season, the first cancellation notices had gone out; among the series canceled were Kodiak, Sierra, Sons and Daughters, and The Texas Wheelers.

Some new series did win viewer support, however. Rhoda, a spin-off from The Mary Tyler Moore Show, was especially popular; Valerie Harper starred. Other new shows with good ratings included Chico and the Man, Little House on the Prairie, Rockford Files, and Police Woman.

The networks continued to present contemporary problems and themes—including rape, homosexuality, and prostitution—in regular programming and in specials. Viewer complaints, when they occurred, tended to focus on the language used, rather than the fact of covering such issues.

The National Academy of Television Arts and Sciences presented its 26th annual Emmy Awards for excellence in the 1973–74 season. Upstairs, Downstairs, a British series carried on public TV in the U.S., was chosen best drama series; M*A*S*H, best comedy series. Mary Tyler Moore was voted best actress in a series; Alan Alda of M*A*S*H, best actor.

'The Autobiography of Miss Jane Pittman', the story of a black woman from her childhood in slavery to her old age during the civil rights movement of the 1960's, was voted best special. Cicely Tyson, who played Miss Jane, was voted best actress in a special. Hal Holbrook was named best actor for his starring role in the special 'Pueblo'.

Zoom, produced by the Public Broadcasting Service (PBS), was voted best children's series. In the news and documentaries awards, PBS took Emmies in five major categories—beating out two of the three commercial networks. (*See also* Magazines; Newspapers.)

**TENNIS.** Effective control of tennis by the traditional governing body, the International Lawn Tennis Federation (ILTF), continued to be a problem in 1974. Accord was reached with the Association of Tennis Professionals (ATP), to which most leading male players belonged and with which there was serious dispute in 1973, but the formation in the U.S. of World Team Tennis (WTT) complicated the administration of the game. Harmony between the ILTF and ATP was reached in September 1974, with the formation of a Men's International Professional Tennis Council with joint representation. The council was authorized to regulate all men's tournaments offering prize money in excess of $17,500.

The WTT, a purely commercial organization, began active operations in May. It was composed of 16 teams on an intercity league basis, with its administration based on the pattern of other professional sports in the U.S., such as baseball and football. The various franchise holders in WTT gave lucrative contracts to leading players of both sexes.

## Men's Competition

In the tennis circuit promoted by World Championship Tennis (WCT), there were three groups of

*Jimmy Connors displays superb form in early play at Wimbledon in July, later winning the title with an easy defeat of Ken Rosewall.*

LONDON DAILY MAIL/PICTORIAL PARADE

SYNDICATION INTERNATIONAL/PHOTO TRENDS

*In a preliminary round at Wimbledon, Chris Evert follows through with the determined skill that eventually secured her the title.*

28 players who competed in eight tournaments (24 in all) at various sites throughout the world. The eight most successful players qualified for a final tournament in Dallas, Tex., in May. They were John Newcombe and Rod Laver of Australia, Stan Smith and Arthur Ashe of the U.S., Tom Okker of the Netherlands, Jan Kodes of Czechoslovakia, Ilie Nastase of Romania, and Björn Borg of Sweden. In the final contest, Newcombe beat Borg 4–6, 6–3, 6–3, 6–2. But Borg had a good year, winning the Italian, French, and Swedish Open championships.

Jimmy Connors of the U.S. won the Australian championship, and, more importantly, captured the Wimbledon title. In the final he easily beat Ken Rosewall of Australia 6–1, 6–1, 6–4. The success of 39-year-old Rosewall as runner-up was the most surprising aspect of the event. He beat the number one seed, Newcombe, in the quarterfinal and the 1972 champion, Smith, in the semifinal, after being within a point of losing. Rosewall's first Wimbledon singles final was in 1954. In the year he first competed there, 1952, his final opponent of 1974 had not been born. Connors maintained compelling form to take the U.S. Open title at Forest Hills, N.Y., in September. At that tournament Rosewall again surprised by reaching the final, again beating Newcombe in the course of doing so. In the last match Connors overwhelmed Rosewall 6–1, 6–0, 6–1, the most one-sided final match on record.

The finals of the Davis Cup competition between South Africa and India resulted in a walkover for South Africa when India announced their inability, for political reasons, to compete against them. The U.S. team lost to Colombia in an early round.

### Women's Competition

In the absence of Margaret Court of Australia, who gave birth to her second baby during the year,

the outstanding player was Chris Evert of the U.S., who won the Italian, French, and Wimbledon titles, events in which she was runner-up in 1973. Evonne Goolagong of Australia won her own Australian title for the first time after three previous years as a finalist. She beat Evert in the final 7–6, 4–6, 6–0. Evert defeated Martina Navratilova of Czechoslovakia 6–3, 6–3 in the final to win in Rome. In Paris she won the final against Olga Morozova of the Soviet Union 6–1, 6–2, and then met the same opponent in the final at Wimbledon, where she triumphed 6–0, 6–4.

Billie Jean King, an outstanding performer at Wimbledon for many years, defended all three titles, but achieved success only in the mixed doubles with Australian Owen Davidson. It brought her total of Wimbledon championships to 18, one short of the record established by another Californian, Elizabeth Ryan, 1914 to 1934. King compensated for her Wimbledon losses by taking the U.S. Open at Forest Hills. Goolagong beat Evert in the semifinal 6–0, 6–7, 6–3 to reach the final for the second year. King beat Goolagong 3–6, 6–3, 7–5.

**TEXTILES.** In 1974 inflation and recession, prevalent in the major industrial countries, created problems for the textile industry worldwide. Producers of synthetic fibers, for example, faced higher prices for raw materials—especially petroleum—along with decreasing demand. In recent years synthetics had been in great demand for clothing and for home furnishing items such as rugs. Experts predicted that polyester and nylon would emerge as the most expensive synthetics, based on their complicated manufacturing processes; acrylics and polypropylene, simpler to produce, would become the general-purpose, moderately priced synthetics.

Wool prices dropped more than 40% from the high levels of 1973. By spring of 1974 the fine grade of Australian wool brought about $2.35 a pound at auction, down from about $4.15 a pound a year previously. Japan, a major wool customer at the high prices of 1972 and 1973, was unable to sustain high demand for wool because of severe economic problems within the textile industry.

Cotton consumption, increasing steadily for a decade, rose in 1973–74 by more than 1.5 million bales worldwide from the figure for the preceding year. U.S. cotton growers found a brisk market for their crop; prices rose about 225% from 1970 to 1974. A severe shortage was expected in the U.S. for 1974, but the shortage was less serious than expected—because of reduced demand from Japan. Rising prices and a still lively demand encouraged U.S. cotton farmers to increase their crops by more than 15% for the 1974–75 growing season.

Japan, again, was the key to the falloff in silk trade. The People's Republic of China was forced to reduce silk prices from the record-high levels of early 1973, after buying decreased. (*See also* Agriculture; World Trade.)

**THAILAND.** Political unrest and instability characterized 1974, Thailand's first full year as a civilian democracy. Prime Minister Sanya Dharmasakti had to contend with severe impatience from the students who had helped to oust the military dictatorship in October 1973. At first the students backed Sanya vigorously, but they soon felt that democratic reforms were too slow in coming. Groups of students demonstrated, rioted, and occupied government buildings early in the year.

Prime Minister Sanya also encountered strong resistance to his legislative proposals in the National Assembly. He was further disturbed by the resignation from his cabinet of the deputy education minister. Faced with a variety of pressures, the prime minister resigned on May 21. A national military alert was declared, and Thailand's experiment with democracy was feared already dead. Various civilian factions united to urge Sanya to withdraw his resignation; he did so on May 24.

A draft of the new constitution was completed in January. The constitution was duly approved by the legislature in October and promulgated by the king, with certain reservations, shortly thereafter, with elections scheduled to be held Feb. 1, 1975.

Rioting erupted in the Chinese section of Bangkok, the capital, in July; after three days of street fighting, the official death toll was placed at 25 persons. A minor incident triggered the riot—thought to have roots in serious economic and social problems among Thailand's Chinese.

The secret return home on December 27 of exiled former Premier Thanom Kittikachorn threatened to renew violence and endanger the scheduled 1975 elections. Foregoing legal action, the government had him quickly removed from the country.

United States troops and B-52 bombers were being gradually withdrawn from Thailand, under an agreement with the new government. In January a 14-year-old ban on trading with the People's Republic of China was rescinded. (*See also* Asia.)

**THEATER.** In the American theater, the great symbolic event of 1974 was the First American Congress of Theater, a four-day meeting of theater people from all over the country, held in June at Princeton, N.J., and organized under the leadership of the Broadway producer Alexander H. Cohen.

The great dramatic success of the 1973–74 Broadway season was 'A Moon for the Misbegotten' by Eugene O'Neill. It had been professionally produced in New York City twice previously; this time—in a production that originated at the Academy Playhouse outside Chicago—it connected fully with both press and public. José Quintero directed a cast that included Jason Robards, Colleen Dewhurst, and Ed Flanders; Quintero, Dewhurst, and Flanders all won Tony awards.

The musical success of the season was 'Candide', a revival of a Broadway failure of 1956, based on Voltaire, with a score by Leonard Bernstein. It opened at the Chelsea Theater Center in the Brooklyn Academy of Music, with a new book by Hugh Wheeler and an inventive staging by Harold Prince that had the actors dashing among several small stages through the midst of the audience. The production then moved to the Broadway Theater and later won the New York Drama Critics Circle Award as best musical of the season.

Another success from Brooklyn was 'Scapino', adapted and directed by Frank Dunlop. This free version of Molière's 'Les Fourberies de Scapin' was first produced by the Young Vic in London and taken to the Brooklyn Academy of Music. From there it transferred to a noncommercial theater in Manhattan, then to a regular Broadway theater. It featured a virtuoso low-comedy performance by Jim Dale as the athletic and irrepressible Scapino.

A number of other Broadway offerings came from Great Britain by various routes. Late in 1973 'Good Evening', a revue by Peter Cook and Dudley Moore, opened; it was received as a sterling example of British hilarity. 'Find Your Way Home', by the British playwright John Hopkins, was not in general well received, but young American actor Michael Moriarty became a star as a result of his performance. 'Noël Coward in Two Keys', a bill of two one-act plays by the late British playwright, starred Hume Cronyn, Jessica Tandy, and Anne Baxter. 'Jumpers' by Tom Stoppard, a meditation on modern life in the form of a farcical comedy, arrived on Broadway in a production mounted by the Kennedy Center in Washington, D.C., directed by Peter Wood, with Brian Bedford in the lead.

The most prominent dramatic success of the fall season was 'Equus' by Peter Shaffer, a play about a boy who is passionately and dangerously drawn to horses, first presented at the British National Theatre and given on Broadway with two British actors heading the cast: Peter Firth and Anthony Hopkins. The Circle in the Square-Joseph E. Levine Theatre opened its 1974–75 season with 'The National Health' by Peter Nichols, a comedy about mortality set in a hospital ward, also first presented by the British National Theatre but shown in New York City in a production from the Long Wharf Theatre in New Haven, Conn. The comedy success of the new season was a West End farce with serious overtones, 'Absurd Person Singular' by Alan Ayckbourn. Yet another British import was 'Flowers', a mime adaptation of Jean Genet's novel 'Our Lady of the Flowers', created by Lindsay Kemp, who also played the leading role. The Royal Shakespeare Company sent its productions of two 19th-century plays: 'London Assurance' by Dion Boucicault and 'Sherlock Holmes' by Arthur Conan Doyle and William Gillette.

'The Freedom of the City', by the Irish playwright Brian Friel, which dealt with the troubles in Northern Ireland, arrived in New York City in a production mounted by Chicago's Goodman Theatre Center. 'Bad Habits', a pair of sourly witty

Winner of the New York Drama Critics Circle Award for the best musical of the season, Candide' revived the ill-fated 1956 Broadway show based on Voltaire's work with an exciting score by Leonard Bernstein.

MARTHA SWOPE

one-act comedies by Terrence McNally, transferred to Broadway from off-Broadway. A revival of 'Cat on a Hot Tin Roof' by Tennessee Williams, with Elizabeth Ashley in the leading role, transferred to Broadway from the American Shakespeare Theater in Stratford, Conn. 'Hosanna', by the French-Canadian playwright Michel Tremblay, was originally presented in Montreal, Que., and then went to Broadway in an English-language production mounted by the Tarragon Theater in Toronto, Ont.

'The Good Doctor', adapted by Neil Simon from the work of Anton Chekhov, was less successful than most of Simon's work. 'Ulysses in Nighttown', an adaptation from James Joyce's novel 'Ulysses', starring Zero Mostel as Leopold Bloom, was less successful on Broadway than it had been off-Broadway 16 years before. There was a comedy about the stresses of New York life, 'Thieves', by Herb Gardner. 'The Magic Show', starring a young Canadian magician named Doug Henning, was a super suc-

cess, and there were a number of nostalgia-laden musicals: 'Lorelei', a reworked version of 'Gentlemen Prefer Blondes', once again starring Carol Channing; 'Over Here!', set in the "happy days" of World War II and starring the Andrews Sisters; a revival of 'Gypsy' starring Angela Lansbury; 'Mack and Mabel', about the early days of Hollywood, with Robert Preston and Bernadette Peters; and a revival of 'Good News' with Alice Faye and Gene Nelson (John Payne did the role pre-Broadway).

## Off-Broadway and Noncommercial Theater

A successful production of 'Moonchildren'—Michael Weller's sensitive play about a group of brilliant, unhappy young Americans—opened in November 1973 and ran until the following fall. Two old-fashioned realistic plays transferred to off-Broadway from one off-off-Broadway theater, the Circle Repertory. One was a melodrama, 'When You Comin' Back, Red Ryder?' by Mark Medoff,

Ed Flanders (left), Colleen Dewhurst, and Jason Robards starred in a new production of Eugene O'Neill's play 'A Moon for the Misbegotten', which proved one of the highlights of the theatrical season.

R. BRAATEN—AUTHENTICATED NEWS INTERNATIONAL

the other a romantic two-character play called 'The Sea Horse' by "James Irwin," which turned out to be a pseudonym for Edward J. Moore, who played the leading role in his own play. Medoff eventually replaced Kevin Conway in the leading role of *his* play. Another play by Medoff, 'The Wager', was produced off-Broadway after an off-off-Broadway tryout at the Manhattan Theater Club.

The Dallas Theater Center in Texas continued to produce new plays about its own region, including 'Jack Ruby: All-American Boy' by John Logan and the 'Bradleyville Triology', three plays about West Texas, by Preston Jones. In addition to its regular season of classical plays, the Tyrone Guthrie Theater in Minneapolis, Minn., commissioned an original musical presentation, 'The Portable Pioneer and Prairie Show' by David Chambers and Mel Marvin, based on Midwestern history, and sent it out for a ten-week tour.

The Trinity Square Repertory Company moved into new headquarters in downtown Providence, R.I., late in 1973 and celebrated with a season that included new plays by Stuart Vaughan ('Ghost Dance'), Israel Horovitz ('Alfred the Great'), and Oliver Hailey ('For the Use of the Hall') as well as a musical, 'Aimee', about Aimee Semple McPherson, with book and lyrics by William Goyen and music by Worth Gardner. The Yale Repertory Theater in New Haven, Conn., did a successful production of the Kurt Weill-Bertolt Brecht opera 'Mahagonny' and presented new plays by Sam Shepard ('Geography of a Horse Dreamer'), Adrienne Kennedy ('An Evening with Dead Essex'), and Isaac Bashevis Singer ('Shlemiel the First') as well as Albert Camus's adaptation of Fedor Dostoevski's 'The Possessed' staged by the Polish film director Andrzej Wajda. The Arena Stage in Washington, D.C., presented 'The Madness of God', a new play about Russian Jewry by Elie Wiesel. Several more British plays made their first U.S. appearances at regional theaters. Two plays by David Storey had their U.S. premieres in Washington: 'In Celebration' by the Arena Stage and 'The Farm' by the Folger Theater Group. 'The Sea' by Edward Bond was produced at the Goodman in Chicago.

For Joseph Papp, the producer of the New York Shakespeare Festival and the most prominent figure in the American noncommercial theater, it was a relatively poor season. His first production at the Vivian Beaumont Theater in Lincoln Center, 'Boom Boom Room' by David Rabe, provoked furious controversy. 'What the Wine-Sellers Buy' by Ron Milner, a play about a young man's maturation set in a black ghetto, was presented both at the Beaumont and in the touring Mobile Theater. Papp's only unqualified success, however, was 'Short Eyes', a prison drama written by an ex-convict, Miguel Piñero, and performed under the direction of Marvin Felix Camillo by "The Family," a group consisting mostly of ex-convicts. The play was chosen best American play of the season by the New York Drama Critics Circle.

## Canadian Theater

In Niagara-on-the-Lake, Ont., the Shaw Festival mounted a successful production of 'Charley's Aunt', starring Paxton Whitehead; and the Stratford Festival, in Jean Gascon's last season as artistic director, produced 'The Imaginary Invalid' as a vehicle for William Hutt. The most important theatrical news in Canada, however, was made by Canadian playwrights. The most prominent among them was Michel Tremblay, whose play 'Hosanna' was described by the author as a political allegory about the nationhood of Quebec. A new play by David Freeman, 'Battering Ram', was produced both in Toronto and in Vancouver. The Toronto Free Theater presented 'Red Emma', a play by Carol Bolt about anarchist Emma Goldman. James Reaney was working on a trilogy entitled 'The Donnellys'. 'Sticks and Stones', the first part, was produced in 1973, and the second, 'The St. Nicholas Hotel', was scheduled for 1974. (*See also* Motion Pictures; Television and Radio.)

Jim Dale called upon his athletic as well as dramatic skills in the starring role of the successful Young Vic production 'Scapino', a freely adapted version of Molière's 'Les Fourberies de Scapin'.

MARTHA SWOPE

*At a new toy library for the mentally retarded in Bloomfield, Conn., a child tries out a toy before deciding whether to take it home.*

## TOYS AND GAMES.

A decline in the number of children in the U.S. under 15 years of age began to affect the toy industry in 1974. The estimated number of them at the beginning of the year was 55.3 million, a full million less than in 1973. The annual retail toy sales figure was expected to exceed $80 per child in 1974, up from $76 in 1973. Substantial price increases followed as costs climbed for petroleum-derivative plastics.

A return to simple unmechanized dolls was a trend in 1974. Some sellers believed that the walking, talking, wetting, crying dolls discourage a child's imagination. Kewpie dolls, dressed in new fashions, were still popular in their 60th year. The Shirley Temple doll, long a best-seller, was enhanced in 1974 by costumes from Shirley's films.

Electronic games gained in popularity. Among them were Finders Beepers, an electronic hide-and-seek game, and a table tennis game in which an electronic screen showed a ball moving from side to side, complete with sound effects. Players used serving control buttons and a speed control.

The fuel shortage in 1974 kept more families at home. Many enjoyed playing games such as Got A Minute, a word game; the Old Shell Game, a game of chance reminiscent of riverboat days; Air Traffic Controller; and Pro Draft, for football fans.

A new Sesame Street pushbutton toy for preschool children and a U-Drive-It game simulating actual driving conditions were among the educational toys offered in 1974. Pour 'N Play kits containing molds, pouring compound, wheels, axles, paint, and decals gave miniature-car racers the thrill of building their own entries.

Evel Knievel and his exploits inspired a Stunt and Crash Car, a Canyon Sky Cycle, and a Stunt Stadium. The 48-inch × 12-inch grandstand provided a realistic environment. (*See also* Hobbies; People of the Year; Safety.)

## TRACK AND FIELD.

Rick Wohlhuter of the University of Chicago Track Club dominated U.S. track and field in 1974 by setting two world records and one U.S. record, all outdoors. At Eugene, Ore., on June 8, Wohlhuter ran 880 yards in 1 minute 44.1 seconds, bettering his own world record by 0.5 second. His time became the new U.S. record for 800 meters. Later in June, in Los Angeles, Wohlhuter lowered the 800-meter time to 1 minute 43.9 seconds, a time he repeated at Stockholm, Sweden, on July 18. Wohlhuter captured his second world record in the 1,000 meter with a time of 2 minutes 13.9 seconds at Oslo, Norway, on July 30, becoming the first U.S. runner in 21 years to hold the 1,000-meter record.

Three other U.S. runners set world outdoor records. Ivory Crockett of the Philadelphia Pioneer Club ran 100 yards in 9 seconds at Knoxville, Tenn., on May 11. In the Amateur Athletic Union (AAU) national championships, Steve Williams of San Diego State ran the 100 meter in 9.9 seconds to equal the world mark. Jim Bolding ran the 440-yard intermediate hurdles in 48.7 seconds, a world record, at Turin, Italy, on July 24. Bolding also claimed a U.S. record in the 400-meter hurdles with 48.1 seconds at Milan, Italy, on July 2.

Steve Prefontaine of the Oregon Track Club set no world marks in 1974, but he did claim an unparalleled total of nine U.S. records in eight events. Indoors, Prefontaine won the two mile in 8 minutes 22.2 seconds at Portland, Ore., on January 26; and

*At the San Diego Indoor Games in February, North Carolina's Tony Waldrop sets a new world record of 3:55.0 for the indoor mile.*

*Mike Whitehead jumps 6 feet 8 inches to a state high school championship in the high jump on May 24 in Columbus, Ohio.*
UPI COMPIX

he lowered the time to 8 minutes 20.4 seconds at San Diego, Calif., on February 17. In the latter race he ran 3,000 meters in 7 minutes 50 seconds, another U.S. record. Outdoors, on April 27 at Eugene, Ore., Prefontaine earned two records in one race, 26 minutes 51.8 seconds for six miles and 27 minutes 43.6 seconds for 10,000 meters. At Eugene, on June 6, he ran three miles in 12 minutes 51.4 seconds. Prefontaine ran 5,000 meters in 13 minutes 22.2 seconds at Helsinki, Finland, on June 26; 3,000 meters in 7 minutes 42.6 seconds at Milan, Italy, on July 2; and two miles in 8 minutes 18.4 seconds at Stockholm on July 18.

Two additional U.S. running records fell in 1974. Doug Brown of the University of Tennessee reduced the 3,000-meter steeplechase record to 8 minutes 23.2 seconds. Manhattan College ran the four-mile relay in 16 minutes 14.4 seconds.

Indoors, George Woods of the Pacific Coast Club raised the amateur shot-put mark to 72 feet 2¾ inches at Inglewood, Calif., on February 8. Tony Waldrop of North Carolina lowered the world indoor mile record to 3 minutes 55 seconds at San Diego, Calif., on February 17; in the same race he received credit for a U.S. record of 3 minutes 39.8 seconds for 1,500 meters. The indoor 60-yard high hurdle record of 6.8 seconds was matched three times by Rod Milburn of the Baton Rouge Track Club. Dwight Stones of the Pacific Coast Club high jumped 7 feet 4¼ inches, a U.S. indoor record for amateurs. Neil Cusack of East Tennessee State won the Boston Marathon on April 15 in 2 hours 13 minutes 39 seconds, the third-best ever.

### Team and Professional Competition

The U.S. won the annual men's competition over the U.S.S.R. at Durham, N.C., on July 5–6, 117 to 102, but lost the women's meet 90 to 67 and was defeated in the combined scoring, 192 to 184. In junior competition, for those under 20, the U.S. won 197 to 181 at Austin, Tex., on June 29. The U.S. and the U.S.S.R. met indoors at Moscow on March 2, with the U.S.S.R. winning 158 to 124.

The Beverly Hills Striders won the indoor AAU championship at New York City on February 22 and the outdoor championship at Los Angeles on June 21–22. The University of Texas at El Paso won the indoor National Collegiate Athletic Association (NCAA) title meet at Detroit, Mich., on March 8–9. Tennessee won the outdoor NCAA championship at Austin, Tex., on June 6–8. Eastern Illinois and Norfolk State shared the NCAA Division II championship; Ashland won the Division III meet.

Joining the professional International Track Association midway through the season, Rod Milburn established a world indoor record of 6.7 seconds for the 60-yard hurdles. Steve Smith twice vaulted to an indoor record of 18 feet 1 inch and 18 feet 1¾ inches. In other indoor professional competition, Paul Gibson set a record for the 70-meter hurdles with a time of 8.7 seconds; John Carlos set a record of 7.3 seconds for the 70 meters.

### Women's Competition

Among women, runners also broke many records. Francie Larrieu set three U.S. records outdoors: 4 minutes 10.3 seconds for 1,500 meters; 4 minutes 33.1 seconds for one mile; and 9 minutes 3.2 seconds for 3,000 meters. Indoors, she set four world records: 4 minutes 12.2 seconds for 1,500 meters; 4 minutes 34.6 seconds for one mile; 9 minutes 2.4 seconds for 3,000 meters; and 9 minutes 39.4 seconds for two miles.

Mary Decker broke three indoor records: 880 yards in 2 minutes 2.3 seconds, 800 meters in 2 minutes 1.8 seconds, and 1,000 yards in 2 minutes 26.7 seconds. Wyomia Tyus set an indoor world record for the 70 meters with 8.3 seconds.

**TRANSPORTATION.** In 1974 the cost of fuel and the general inflationary conditions had a serious effect on transportation in the U.S. Demand was high for improved commuter facilities to offset fuel shortages and traffic congestion, but there was little agreement on who should pay. Most cities were counting on the federal government for most of their transit-building funds. Mass-transit systems already in operation in urban centers also looked to Washington, D.C., for subsidies to help cover huge operating losses. A sharply revised six-year bill for mass-transit aid won the approval of U.S. President Gerald R. Ford in October. After threatening a veto, Ford succeeded in having the bill cut from $20 billion to $11.8 billion. The legislation, enacted in November, met his requirements that it include $1.4 billion already appropriated for the Urban Mass Transportation Administration (UMTA) and that state governors would be the sole allocators of money for areas of less than 200,000 population.

In June, the U.S. Department of Transportation released $500 million in highway money from funds impounded by several administrations in order to hold down spending and limit road building. Several states had sued for release of their impounded highway money, and Missouri had already won its suit. The Transportation Department, through UMTA, made six grants totaling $160 million for mass-transit projects in the New York City; Philadelphia, Pa.; and San Francisco, Calif., areas.

In San Francisco, the Bay Area Rapid Transit (BART) district planned in October to sue the companies that designed and built certain equipment for the 75-mile line. Four years behind schedule, BART opened its final and key link—the underwater tunnel between San Francisco and Oakland, Calif.—in September 1974. Much of the delay was caused by the line's unique all-automatic control system.

### Airlines

The major inflationary pressure on the country's airline industry, its 200 million annual passengers, and its shippers in 1974 was the price of fuel. The cost practically doubled for domestic carriers and nearly tripled for international lines. Fuel costs increased by more than $1 billion in 1974, totaling more than $2 billion for the year. The number of flights was reduced as a fuel-saving measure, and fares were raised repeatedly during the year.

A relatively slow rate of traffic growth in 1974 reflected the depressed economic state. For the first eight months of 1974, domestic passenger traffic in-

*Though final construction was not expected to be completed until at least 1985, service was begun in March at France's 75,000-acre Aéroport de Charles de Gaulle, northeast of Paris.*
FREDERIC PROUST–SYGMA

*Coffered concrete ceilings were used to eliminate noise in the new $4-billion Metro in Washington, D.C. The first 4.6-mile section of the rail system was scheduled to open in 1975.*

creased 4.8% over the same period in 1973, but international passenger traffic was down by 9.6% for the same period. Revenue ton miles of freight flown through August 1974 registered only a 3.1% increase domestically. International operations, however, rose 12.4% as shortages of many products brought increased reliance on air freight to move them quickly and as high interest rates required many businesses to keep inventories low.

In September Pan American World Airways (Pan Am) and Trans World Airways, Inc. (TWA), both in financial trouble, reached an agreement with British Airways and British Caledonia to reduce winter passenger service by 20%. Both Pan Am and TWA appealed to the federal government for direct subsidy to remedy their financial ills; the Ford Administration refused the request but recommended such economy measures as fare increases and route swapping to eliminate costly competition between lines. Subsequently, TWA and Pan Am agreed to divide the major European and Asian travel routes; United, American, and TWA took similar action to reduce domestic competition.

The Civil Aeronautics Board (CAB) also acted to relieve the airlines' financial troubles. It approved an agreement calling for a 6%–11% fare increase on all scheduled transatlantic flights and proposed higher minimum fares for transatlantic charters. It also approved a 4% fare hike on domestic flights and made permanent an earlier, temporary 6% increase. CAB actions were widely criticized. A group of congressmen demanded price roll-backs, and the Justice Department's antitrust division began action against the proposed charter-flight minimum. In December, however, Congress attempted to aid the

faltering airlines with legislation aimed at eliminating discriminatory landing fees and other practices that put U.S. international carriers at a competitive disadvantage with foreign airlines.

In 1974 the airlines spent $2.7 billion for new aircraft. These included Boeing 727's, Boeing 737's, Boeing 747's, Douglas DC-9's, Douglas DC-10's, and Lockheed L-1011's. (*See also* Aerospace.)

### Railroads

While economic conditions in the U.S. threatened to slow the rate of growth later in the year, railroad traffic volume during the first nine months of 1974 ran 4.4% ahead of 1973's all-time record level. Operating revenues also increased, but operating expenses, taxes, and rents increased even more.

In October the Ford Administration asked for a supplemental appropriation of $84.9 million in federal funds for the National Railroad Passenger Corp. (Amtrak). The money was requested to help cover a $72-million deficit in the 1974 fiscal year and in order to keep Amtrak trains running after February 1975. The Supreme Court's decision upholding a 1973 railroad reorganization plan provided for continuation of the merger of six bankrupt railroads, including the Penn Central, into one federally subsidized system. How the merger would be effected was in dispute. (*See* Supreme Court.)

The energy crisis brought good business to the piggyback trains, which haul truck trailers and large containers on railroad flatcars. It was estimated that trucks burned four times as much diesel fuel as trains hauling the same amount of freight between cities. In June the Interstate Commerce Commission gave the country's railroads permission to boost freight rates 10% provided they promised to use the added revenue for improving service.

The demand for new freight cars continued at high levels, with more than 82,000 units ordered in the first nine months of 1974—an increase of 10,700 over the same period in 1973. The American Rail Box Car Co. was founded in 1974 to acquire and operate a nationwide pool of modern boxcars. (*See also* Tanzania.)

### Trucks and Trucking

In 1974 the truck fleet in the U.S. increased by nearly 1.8 million, reaching 23.8 million. The industry transferred approximately the same number of ton miles—505 billion—as it did in 1973. Operating revenues of for-hire trucks engaged in interstate commerce were expected to reach $23 billion—up $2 billion from 1973. Nevertheless, net profit declined for a second year because of the higher costs of fuel, labor, and equipment.

In a protest against high fuel prices and low trucking rates, thousands of independent truckers went on strike on Jan. 31, 1974. The strike was brought to an end by an agreement with the federal government on concessions that included a surcharge on freight rates.

Faced by a lawsuit filed by the U.S. Department of Justice, major trucking companies agreed in 1974 to fill from $33^1/_3$% to 50% of vacancies and new jobs with blacks and applicants with Spanish surnames. (*See also* Fuel and Power; Ships and Shipping; Travel.)

**TRAVEL.** Higher oil prices, worldwide inflation, and expectations of lower economic growth in North America and Europe combined to moderate the growth of international tourism in 1974. While some destinations reported a falloff in visitors of 2%–7%, in many others tourism continued unimpeded. The main beneficiaries of the new situation were domestic travel and international movements to neighboring countries. The main casualties were organized travel and, latterly, air charter vacations.

In 1974, international tourism faced, for the first time in its postwar history, a zero-growth situation. The travel year began slowly, but, as the impact of fuel costs on prices became clearer, confidence returned, and operators who had made drastic cutbacks in hotel bookings in response to pessimistic predictions frequently found themselves unable to satisfy last-minute demand. The international tourist responded to higher, oil-price inflated prices in a number of ways: first, there was an attempt to keep within the confines of the previous year's travel budget by substituting lower-cost air charter travel for scheduled air carriers. Then, as the effects of higher air transport costs filtered through to charter lines in the form of "fuel surcharges," there was a drop in bookings of "inclusive tour" arrangements involving high air-travel content. Finally, fears of economic recession and short-time working in European industry led to the postponement of travel plans from January–February, the traditional booking season, to the late spring and the approach of the holiday season. This last effect, although it did

The Otis Electrobus, a fume-free, fuel-saving vehicle that is battery powered, began regular runs in New York City at year's end. The bus, which accommodates about 45 passengers, runs at a top speed of 35 mph and requires a battery charge every 50 miles.
COURTESY, ELECTROBUS DIVISION, OTIS ELEVATOR CO.

*Among the major hotels completed in 1974 were several abroad, including the imposing Paris-Sheraton that adds to the changing Parisian skyline.*

COURTESY, AMERICAN HOTEL & MOTEL ASSOCIATION

not affect the ultimate numbers of travelers, had serious repercussions on the activities of tour operators, whose slender profit margins could ill withstand the dual impact of booking uncertainty and a serious shortage of liquidity, occasioned by delay in receiving deposits.

News came from Geneva, Switzerland, in July that—almost four years after the Extraordinary General Assembly of the International Union of Official Travel Organizations held in Mexico City, Mexico, in September 1970—tourism was to have its own intergovernmental body, the World Tourism Organization (WTO). The new organization was to raise tourism, a rapidly rising item in world trade, to the decisive level of full governmental responsibility. The first General Assembly of WTO was to be held in November 1975.

Income of U.S. hotels and motels climbed to a record $8.6 billion in 1974, a gain of 6% over the 1973 total. Inflation, however, fueled much of this increase, as the average room rate rose nearly 10% during the same period, while the average room occupancy rate slipped about 1.5%.

To increase income as one means of offsetting higher costs, a number of chains turned to or increased diversification. Knott Hotels expanded its contract catering business, Resorts International operated a sea-animal-theme park, and Sonesta Hotels' food-processing subsidiary grossed $48 million. To improve cash flow, a number of systems sold their properties in 1974 and operated them under management contract. The Sheraton Corp., for example, sold several Hawaiian hotels to Japanese investors. Higher interest rates, uncertainty over fuel availability, and the threat of overbuilding in a number of areas led to a sharp decline in hotel and motel construction; 30% fewer U.S. hotel and motel guest rooms were built, reversing a six-year upward trend.

The largest new hotel completed in the U.S. in 1974 was the $21-million 1,000-room Hyatt Regency Chicago. Other major hotels completed in 1974 included the 1,000-room Paris-Sheraton; 922-room Sheraton-Hong Kong; 850-room Plaza, Hong Kong; 866-room Borobudur Inter-Continental, Jakarta, Indonesia; and the 752-room Forum, Warsaw, Poland. The new Otani Hotel, Tokyo, Japan, added a 1,005-room tower, doubling its number of rooms. New interest in South America as a tourist destination was shown among at least two major U.S.-based lodging companies. Holiday Inns opened its first South America inn at Caracas, Venezuela, and other inns at Campinas and São Bernardo, Brazil. The Sheraton Corp. also completed a 617-room hotel in Rio de Janeiro, Brazil. (*See also* Camping; Environment Special Report; Landmarks and Monuments; National Park Service; Ships and Shipping; Transportation; U.S. Special Report; articles on individual countries.)

**TRUDEAU, PIERRE ELLIOTT.** With a skill rarely shown in his six years as prime minister of Canada, Pierre Elliott Trudeau engineered a stunning election victory in 1974 and reestablished himself solidly as the central figure in Canadian

*Rejection of Prime Minister Trudeau's fiscal policy in May forced a national election in July in which he won a solid victory.*

CANADIAN PRESS

political life. Trudeau burst on Canada's national scene when he won the leadership of the ruling Liberal party early in 1968 and swept to a large parliamentary majority in a national election later that year. A penchant for inflammatory statements and what critics called his arrogance, however, helped contribute to a loss of popularity that all but cost him power when he went to the polls again in 1972. Operating at the head of a minority government throughout 1973 and early 1974, Trudeau managed to stay in office by adroit policy compromises, most of them designed to win support of the socialist New Democratic party (NDP), which held the balance of power in the House of Commons.

The NDP turned on the Liberals in May when they sensed a waning of national support for their unofficial marriage with the government. The NDP joined the main opposition party, the Progressive Conservatives, in rejecting Liberal fiscal policy by voting against the federal budget. Forced by this parliamentary defeat to call an election, Trudeau set aside his customary academic discussion of policy and campaigned primarily on a single issue recognized by all parties: the Conservative proposal for a national system of wage and price controls as a means of combating inflation. Trudeau won a convincing victory in the voting July 8, returning to power with 141 of the 264 seats in the Commons, a gain of 32 from his position in 1972. All other parties were weakened, with NDP leader David Lewis beaten in his own constituency and Conservative leader Robert Stanfield forced into a caretaker role pending a leadership convention in his own party. Trudeau was only the second prime minister in history to regain a majority after being in a minority.

His parliamentary position secure, Trudeau undertook a long-delayed trip to Europe in October to mend fences with France and other members of the Common Market. In terms of domestic policy, the highlight of Trudeau's year was his personal negotiation of a settlement of oil prices with provincial governments. The deal served to keep the domestic costs of oil far below the international price and to help contain inflation in Canada.

In December Trudeau went to Washington, D.C., where he met with President Gerald R. Ford and also spoke to a Congressional group. The talks centered around Trudeau's earlier announcement of a plan to phase out oil exports to the U.S. (*See also* Canada.)

**TUNISIA.** Although President Habib Bourguiba of Tunisia and Col. Muammar el-Qaddafi of Libya, after two days of talks on the Tunisian island of Djerba, announced on Jan. 12, 1974, that their countries would be united in a single state, the referendum on the merger was postponed. During the year Tunisia and Libya cooperated, however, in the fields of agriculture and transport coordination.

The Tunisian government moved toward the right in 1974. Unrest among students at the Univer-

WIDE WORLD

*Acceding in November to the demands of hijackers of a British plane, authorities allow two Palestinians freed from a Dutch prison to join the hijackers. All were to be granted asylum in Tunisia.*

sity of Tunis led to trials and prison sentences for left-wing activists. Forty students sentenced in April were pardoned by the president in July to mark the 16th anniversary of the republic, but at an August trial of alleged left-wing plotters 175 men and women were sentenced and 27 were acquitted. Another 31 persons accused of belonging to illegal organizations endangering state security were tried in late December. In general elections that took place in November, Bourguiba was reelected unopposed for a fourth term of office, and the ruling Destour Socialist party (PSD) won all 112 seats unopposed in the new enlarged National Assembly. Earlier, at the ninth congress of the PSD at Monastir, Bourguiba had been acclaimed chairman of the party for life.

A $7.8-million trade agreement was reached with Egypt in March. France and Belgium made loans for light engineering equipment, telecommunications, rural development, health, and agriculture. A phosphate extraction and treatment complex was inaugurated in the Gafsa Basin in October, in cooperation with Romania. And an electrical power and gas station with 42,000-kw. capacity in southern Tunisia was contracted to a French firm. (*See also* Middle East.)

**TURKEY.** The political crisis that had dragged on since the inconclusive general elections of October 1973 was temporarily resolved on Jan. 25, 1974, when Bülent Ecevit was named to replace caretaker Premier Naim Talu. Ecevit, leader of the left-of-center Republican People's party (RPP), largest party in the Turkish National Assembly, formed a coalition with the right-wing traditionalist National Salvation party (NSP), whose leader, Necmettin Erbakan, became deputy premier.

Ecevit promised a general amnesty to include political prisoners and guarantees for free speech and a free press. On May 15, however, the National Assembly passed an amnesty bill that excluded those jailed by the country's former military regime for advocating "Communist" and "anarchist" ideas. Ecevit threatened to resign, but on July 3 Turkey's Constitutional Court reversed the Assembly's amnesty exclusion. Included in the amnesty bill were greatly reduced sentences for several Americans convicted of drug crimes.

On July 1 the government lifted its 1971 ban on cultivation of the opium poppy. Protests from the U.S. government, which feared that Turkey would once again become a major source of illegal narcotics, failed to reverse the decision. The Turks pointed to the economic hardships suffered by poppy farmers and insisted that there was a worldwide shortage of legitimate medicinal opium. In October, United Nations officials reported that a new processing method would effectively curb the diversion of Turkish opium into illegal channels. (*See* Drugs.)

*After signing a disengagement agreement July 30 in Geneva, Switzerland, Turkish Premier Ecevit answers reporters' questions regarding Cyprus.*
WIDE WORLD

The new Ecevit government continued a dispute with Greece over oil-exploration rights in the Aegean Sea. Despite several high-level Turkish-Greek meetings during the year, the issue was not resolved. On July 20, a few days after the Greek nationalist military coup in Cyprus, Turkey landed troops on the island's northern coast, ostensibly to protect the large Turkish population there. As guarantors of Cyprus' constitution, Turkey, Greece, and Great Britain began cease-fire talks on July 24 and reached an agreement on July 30. With the Turks insisting on a federal structure for Cyprus, however, subsequent negotiations broke down. Turkish forces resumed hostilities, occupying more than one third of Cyprus before a further cease-fire on August 16. In reaction to the invasion of Cyprus, the U.S. Congress threatened to terminate military aid at year's end. The foreign assistance bill passed by Congress in December extended to Feb. 5, 1975, the cut-off date for all U.S. military aid to Turkey.

Having won considerable popularity at home as a result of the successful Cyprus operation, Premier Ecevit resigned his office on September 18 in an attempt to shake loose the distasteful partnership with the NSP. The immediate issue was NSP opposition to a planned Scandinavian visit by Ecevit after he had refused to name Vice Premier Erbakan as acting premier while he was to be gone, but Ecevit was unable to form a new coalition with other possible partners in the National Assembly. On November 17, independent Senator Sadi Irmak became interim premier, but 12 days later the National Assembly rejected Irmak in a vote of no confidence. This was seen as a victory for Ecevit, who was pushing for new elections in an effort to gain a majority.

Despite the expense of the Cyprus operation and rising prices, the Turkish economy remained healthy, growing at a rate of about 8% during the year. In August the giant $400-million Keban hydroelectric station on the Euphrates River was commissioned. (*See also* Cyprus; Europe; Greece.)

## UGANDA.
In March the body of Lieut. Col. Michael Ondoga, dismissed from the post of foreign minister on Feb. 19, 1974, was found in the Nile River. The news triggered an attempted coup led by Brig. Charles Arube, former army chief of staff, and supported by soldiers from the Lugbara tribe among whom there had been unrest as the result of the dismissal of a number of officers from that tribe. President Idi Amin acted promptly, and the rising was crushed. Many of the dissidents were killed, Arube among them. In December Amin fired Ondoga's successor as foreign minister, Princess Elizabeth of Toro, for alleged personal misconduct.

In June the International Commission of Jurists, in a report submitted to the United Nations secretary-general with the request that it be put before a Commission on Human Rights, accused Amin's government of maintaining a reign of terror in Uganda. Amin responded by threatening to close

CAMERA PRESS / PICTORIAL PARADE

*President Amin maintained a high profile in 1974, despite unrest inside and outside Uganda.*

down the office of the British High Commission in Uganda and to expel all Britons working in the country. Then in November he ordered a reduction of the British High Commission staff from 50 to 5, to which the British government reacted by ordering a corresponding reduction of Uganda High Commission staff in London.

In June Amin urged committed African countries to attack Rhodesia. This followed an earlier call to abandon guerrilla tactics in southern Africa and instead to launch a military attack under African leadership. He had offered seven battalions of troops as Uganda's contribution to any such force that might be raised. Amin repeatedly accused Tanzania and Zambia of plotting to invade Uganda and threatened in December to launch preemptive action against Tanzania. In this fluctuating political situation the country's economy remained unsteady. High prices for cotton and coffee exports brought in a welcome flow of foreign currency, and a continuing fall in imports improved the country's balance of payments. Nevertheless, the availability of foreign exchange was severely limited, and shortages of many commodities such as salt and sugar remained acute. (*See also* Africa.)

## UNION OF SOVIET SOCIALIST REPUBLICS (U.S.S.R.).
Rumors about impending changes in the Soviet Union's top leadership proved unfounded when the entire Politburo was confirmed in office by the Communist party's Central Committee in July 1974. Leonid I. Brezhnev, whose dominating position as general secretary of the party remained unchallenged, celebrated his 68th birthday during the year. Both President Nikolai V. Podgorny and Premier Aleksei N. Kosygin were continued in office by the nation's parliament, the Supreme Soviet, which met in July. Nationwide elections to the Supreme Soviet had been held on June 16, with the Communist list of candidates getting more than 99% of the votes.

Despite this evidence of political stability, under-

V. YEGOROV—TASS/SOVFOTO

*Restoration of Moscow's Red Square, begun in May, was completed in time for the November 7 celebration of the 57th anniversary of the Bolshevik Revolution. Paving stones laid 44 years earlier were reset, and new granite grandstands (foreground) were installed.*

currents of discontent continued to cause official concern. The most famous dissenter, novelist Aleksandr I. Solzhenitsyn, was expelled from the country and deprived of citizenship in February. He ultimately settled with his family in Switzerland, and in December he visited Stockholm, Sweden, to accept the Nobel prize for literature that he had won in 1970. (*See* Literature.) Dissident writer Vladimir Maksimov was allowed to leave in March. Shortly afterward, Pavel Litvinov, a grandson of former Commissar for Foreign Affairs Maxim Litvinov and a critic of the Soviet invasion of Czechoslovakia in 1968, was also permitted to leave. Cellist Mstislav Rostropovich and his wife, soprano Galina Vishenevskaya, also went to live and work abroad. In June, Jewish ballet dancer Valery Panov and his wife, ballerina Galina Ragozina, were given permission to leave for Israel, and a few days later the main male dancer of Leningrad's Kirov Ballet defected while on tour in Canada. (*See* Dance.) Later in the year Kirov ballerina Kaleriya I. Fedicheva sought to emigrate, having married U.S. dancer

Martin Friedman in January, but was ignored by the authorities.

The resurgence of underground literature known as *samizdat* also troubled the authorities. In particular was the appearance early in the year, for the first time since October 1972, of the illegal *Chronicle of Current Events*.

Following the death of longtime Minister of Culture Yekaterina Furtseva in October and her replacement by party leader Pyotr Demichev, it was thought that Soviet cultural policy might undergo some changes. Renewed Western proposals for a free exchange of ideas between East and West, however, were rejected by Soviet authorities as "a convenient cloak for subtle anti-Soviet propaganda." They dismissed the attention given to a few "dissenting" writers in the Soviet Union as "raving anti-Sovietism." (*See* Obituaries.)

Meanwhile, the strict laws controlling the movement of Soviet citizens inside their own country were relaxed a little in August. Internal passports were to have unlimited validity.

## The Economy

The Soviet Union suffered relatively little from the world energy crisis during 1974. Soviet oil production was expected to reach more than 450 million metric tons in 1974, an increase of almost 30 million over that of 1973. In October it was reported that the U.S.S.R. had overtaken the United States as the world's leading oil producer. Natural gas production was expected to total almost 260 billion cubic meters, 21 billion more than in 1973. Although the country was virtually self-sufficient in energy production, a discreet campaign was launched during the year to encourage the conservation of energy resources, apparently because of their use as a major bargaining counter in the country's commercial dealings with Western countries.

The opening of a huge new gas field near Orenburg, east of the Volga River, was announced in February. Because of a shortage of high-quality basic equipment to exploit new oil fields, special grants were obtained from West Germany for the purchase of nearly one million tons of large-diameter steel pipe. In return, Soviet natural gas would be supplied to West Germany.

The newly established U.S.-U.S.S.R. Trade and Economic Council began meeting during the year. In October Brezhnev estimated that the volume of U.S.-Soviet trade would reach $1 billion in 1974 as compared with only $200 million three years before. Earlier it had been announced that total Soviet trade with the capitalist world had jumped by more than 40% between 1972 and 1973.

In September an agreement was concluded with Japan to finance the production of coking coal, the extraction of natural gas, and the processing of timber in Siberia. In January a big dry-cargo container terminal had been opened at the Pacific port of Nakhodka. It was expected to expedite high-speed freight movements across the Soviet Union between Japan and Europe.

Trade talks in May produced a ten-year agreement with Great Britain on economic, scientific, technical, and industrial cooperation—with computers and scientific instruments as items of special interest. As the result of a meeting between Brezhnev and President Valéry Giscard d'Estaing of France in December, the French agreed to help construct an aluminum plant in Siberia in exchange for Soviet natural gas.

To further the development and military security of Siberia the decision was made in 1974 to resume construction of the long-delayed 2,000-mile Baikal–Amur railway. To be completed in 1983, it would parallel the Trans-Siberian line and open up virgin territory rich in copper and iron ore, asbestos, and coking coal.

Soviet economic growth in 1974 was impressive. Industrial output increased by 8% over that of 1973, exceeding the planned 6.8%. Generally, labor productivity was up and production costs down, although Soviet industry continued to be troubled by inefficient management, underuse of capacity, and failure to complete construction projects on time. Serious shortfalls in the production of chemicals, oil industry equipment, and farm machinery were reported, and production of almost all consumer goods once again lagged behind the ambitious long-range plans.

Nevertheless, the 195-million-ton grain harvest in 1974 was second only to the record 225 million tons of the previous year. Although sugar beet and sunflower oil production fell short, the cotton harvest reached a record 8.4 million tons. Early in the year the Soviet Union claimed to have passed the U.S. in the production of chemical fertilizer for its farms. At the same time, a multibillion-dollar agricultural development project was announced for the non-black-soil steppes of northern Russia. A new $2.4-billion-per-year program for financial support to large low-income families was announced in September.

*A child peers at a painting entitled 'Love and Peace' at an officially sanctioned September exhibit of avant-garde art in a Moscow park that drew thousands of viewers. Two weeks earlier, Soviet authorities had used bulldozers and sprayed water to disrupt a similar show, but Western pressure, following foreign reporters' denunciation of the incident, apparently caused the turnabout in Soviet policy.*
WIDE WORLD

### Foreign Affairs

The major preoccupation of Soviet diplomacy during the year continued to be the maintenance of international stability in order to foster the growth of economic relations with the West. In the Soviet view this was based largely on the development of a détente with the U.S. and the avoidance of any direct military confrontations. During U.S. President Richard M. Nixon's visit to the Soviet Union in June, Brezhnev described the achievement of "stable peace" as "the chief task in the development of Soviet-American relations." Throughout the Watergate affair Soviet comment was reserved and cautious, and with Nixon's resignation from office in August the Soviets emphasized that U.S. foreign policy could not be identified with any single politician.

At the end of November Brezhnev met with U.S. President Gerald R. Ford and reached a tentative understanding on limiting the numbers of offensive strategic nuclear weapons and delivery systems. Obviously not wanting to engage in a runaway nuclear arms race, the Soviet Union also was making efforts to reduce total military spending. Although some military items undoubtedly were concealed under other budget headings, official defense spending for 1974 was budgeted at 9.1% of total government expenditures, down from 9.9% in 1973. The economic motives behind Soviet readiness to limit nuclear spending were believed genuine, but the Soviets may also have been seeking to gain time for technological developments. (*See* Arms Control.)

The same overriding policy of international détente was pursued in Soviet relations with other major capitalist powers where there were changes in top leadership during the year—such as France, West Germany, and Japan. Brezhnev's December meeting with Giscard ended with a call for a 35-nation European summit meeting and reflected a new alignment of Soviet and French positions on many international issues.

The crisis in the Middle East was treated cautiously, although the Soviet Union continued its diplomatic support of the Arab cause. Exchanges at high level took place during the year, including visits by the Syrian president to the Soviet Union and of Soviet officials to Iraq, Syria, and Egypt. Yasir Arafat, leader of the Palestine Liberation Organization, was officially welcomed to Moscow in July. Soviet-Egyptian relations, earlier on an upswing, appeared to have soured, however, when on December 30 Brezhnev suddenly postponed a scheduled January 1975 visit to Egypt, ostensibly for poor health. (*See* Middle East.)

Relations with China remained in a state of plaintive hostility, expressed principally by frequent commentaries in the Soviet press and at the United Nations. Early in the year charges were traded on the Chinese detention of a Soviet helicopter and its crew that had strayed across the border. Each country also expelled nationals of the other on charges of spying. In January, however, nonstop air service was begun between Moscow and Peking. In October and November the two Communist giants made counterproposals for a nonaggression pact.

*As if questioning what the talks would bring, U.S. President Nixon and Soviet leader Brezhnev gesture at the outset of their Moscow summit meeting in June at the Kremlin.*
WIDE WORLD

The Soviet Union's desire for closer economic ties with the U.S. ran head on into the issue of Jewish emigration from the Soviet Union during the year. An informal agreement giving the Soviets trade benefits in return for a liberalized emigration policy was reportedly reached in midyear. But as the U.S. was enacting legislation in December giving the Soviet Union "most favored nation" trading status, the Soviet Union "flatly rejected as unacceptable" any such attempts to "interfere" in its "internal affairs." As the year ended, Soviet authorities warned that economic relations with the U.S. were in danger. Meanwhile, the total number of Jews leaving the Soviet Union had declined from 35,000 in 1973 to 21,000 in 1974. (*See also* Engineering Projects; Europe; Space Exploration; World Trade.)

**UNITED NATIONS (UN).** Much of the attention of the United Nations in 1974 was taken up with unresolved problems in the Middle East. Early in the year the UN Emergency Force supervised the disengagement of Egyptian and Israeli troops. In June the UN Disengagement Observer Force (UN-DOF) took up positions between Syria and Israel. UN Secretary-General Kurt Waldheim visited the Middle East in late November and secured the agreement of the Syrians to renew the UNDOF until April 24, 1975.

Palestinian guerrillas allegedly based in Lebanon attacked Israeli villages several times in 1974, provoking Israeli attacks on Lebanese villages and ports. On April 24 the Security Council voted to condemn Israel for violating Lebanon's territorial integrity and for committing acts of violence and asked Israel to refrain from further military actions against Lebanon. U.S. efforts to amend the resolution so that it would allude to Palestinian guerrilla attacks on Israel were defeated.

In October the General Assembly voted to invite representatives of the Palestine Liberation Organization (PLO) to participate in a debate on the Palestinian question. The PLO thus became the first nongovernmental organization in UN history to address a plenary session of the General Assembly. On November 13 the head of the PLO, Yasir Arafat, called for the establishment in Palestine of "one democratic state where Christian, Jew, and Muslim can live in justice, equality and fraternity." Such a state would presumably require dismantling Israel, whose spokesmen replied by saying that they would never deal with the PLO. On November 22 the General Assembly acknowledged the right of Palestinian refugees "to return to their homes and properties," affirmed their rights to self-determination, national independence, and sovereignty "inside Palestine," and, in a second resolution, granted observer status in the UN to the PLO. The U.S. and Israel opposed both resolutions.

In November the UN Educational, Scientific, and Cultural Organization (UNESCO) voted to suspend a $12,000 Israeli cultural grant for 1975 and denied

T. CHEN—UNITED NATIONS/KEYSTONE

*PLO leader Yasir Arafat addresses the UN in November after the UN's controversial October vote to seat the PLO in discussions of the Palestinian question.*

expansion of Israel's observer status to full membership in the European regional UNESCO group. Incensed Western nations took action to cut their UNESCO contributions. (*See also* Israel; Jordan; Lebanon; Middle East.)

In July a coup led by Greek officers deposed the Cypriot president, Archbishop Makarios, and Turkey intervened militarily on July 20. The Security Council immediately asked all nations to respect Cypriot sovereignty and to withdraw all military personnel not sanctioned by international agreement. Great Britain, as a guarantor of the 1960 treaty on the independence of Cyprus, requested Greece and Turkey to open peace negotiations.

On July 30 the three nations issued a declaration in Geneva, Switzerland, demanding an immediate end to the fighting on Cyprus and asking for further talks. The Geneva talks later broke down, however, and Turkey launched heavy air and sea attacks on Cyprus. Turkey's military action prompted the Security Council in August to issue repeated ceasefire demands, to urge new political negotiations, and to call on all parties to alleviate human suffering and to ensure respect for human rights.

Secretary-General Waldheim flew to Cyprus, Greece, and Turkey in August and afterward told the Security Council that all parties wanted a negotiated settlement and that the UN Force in Cyprus needed a new mandate. The 250,000 persons left destitute by the fighting received attention from the UN High Commissioner for Refugees, who estimated that the UN needed $9 million to provide emergency medicine, food, blankets, and shelter. By year's end about 35,000 refugees were still living under canvas. (*See also* Cyprus; Greece; Turkey.)

### Mixed Success with African Policies

Secretary-General Waldheim visited Lisbon, Portugal, in August and received from the new government pledges that it would cooperate fully with UN efforts to decolonize Africa. Portugal announced that it was ready to recognize Guinea-Bissau as an independent state and that it would support the nation's application to join the UN. When Portuguese President Gen. Francisco da Costa Gomes addressed the General Assembly in October, he confirmed Portugal's intentions to speed decolonization in the Cape Verde Islands, in Mozambique, and in Angola and to consider sanctions against Rhodesia.

In October the General Assembly rejected the credentials of South Africa's delegation and asked the Security Council to review South Africa's relations to the UN because of its "constant violation" of the principles of the UN charter. France, Great Britain, and the U.S. vetoed on October 30 an African resolution recommending that the General Assembly expel South Africa for maintaining apartheid, for refusing to surrender authority over Namibia, and for violating the UN boycott of Rhodesia. The General Assembly voted on November 12 to suspend South Africa for the rest of the session. (*See also* Portugal; South Africa.)

### Food and Economics

The drought in Sahelian Africa was in its seventh year by 1974. In May the UN Economic and Social Council (ECOSOC) asked nations to double their aid to the people of Chad, Gambia, Mali, Mauritania, Niger, Senegal, and Upper Volta. Secretary-General Waldheim visited the Sahelian countries and other West African nations in early 1974. UN Undersecretary-General Bradford Morse toured Western European nations to ask for additional aid. One private group estimated that by 1974 as many as 100,000 drought victims had died.

Delegates to the World Food Conference met in Rome in November to consider worsening worldwide food shortages. It was estimated that, if current trends continued, there would be a deficit of 80 million tons by 1985. The conference reached no conclusive short-term solutions but did create a World Food Council to work through ECOSOC to coordinate a long-term global war against hunger.

Representatives of more than 130 nations met in Bucharest, Romania, at the first UN World Population Conference. Members adopted plans to improve the quality of life for all people and to coordinate population and development trends.

The General Assembly met in a special spring session to consider problems of raw materials and development, particularly the disparities between affluent and destitute nations. It adopted a declaration for a new world economic order emphasizing sovereignty of nations over their natural resources and increased development of poor nations.

Former UN Secretary-General U Thant of Burma died on November 25. The UN honored Thant with an unprecedented lying-in-state at UN headquarters in New York City prior to removal of his body to Burma for burial. (*See* Obituaries.)

*Archbishop Makarios (bottom left), ousted Cypriot president, appealed to the UN Security Council in July for restoration of constitutional order on the embattled island.*
WIDE WORLD

*Artpark, the country's first park dedicated to the arts, opened in 1974 on 172 acres of reclaimed wasteland along the Niagara River at Lewiston, N.Y. Artpark's $7-million, 2,500-seat theater could accommodate a variety of artistic performances and would in the future be enhanced by an outdoor amphitheater, a restaurant, artists' studios, and a Town Square building for special events.*

DRISCH—ARTPARK

# UNITED STATES.

Vice-President Gerald R. Ford took the oath of office as 38th president of the United States on Aug. 9, 1974. Referring to the two-year-long ordeal of Watergate—the series of political scandals that crippled and finally destroyed the administration of President Richard M. Nixon—he said, "My fellow Americans, our long national nightmare is over."

But the new Republican president's honeymoon with the Democratic Congress and the public ended on September 8, when he granted Nixon a full pardon. Public confidence in Ford was further eroded by his seeming inability to combat rising inflation and unemployment. At year's end the country seemed to be facing a long economic recession.

## Nixon's Downfall

As 1974 began, President Richard M. Nixon was firmly resolved to remain in office until his second term expired in January 1977. In his state of the union message to Congress on January 30 he vowed that he would not quit—but wished the Watergate investigators would. "One year of Watergate is enough," the president said. But Special Prosecutor Leon Jaworski refused to back off, charging that the White House had not turned over the tapes and documents he had requested. And on February 6 the U.S. House of Representatives directed its Judiciary Committee to investigate the president's conduct to determine if grounds existed for his impeachment.

On March 1, several former top Nixon aides, including John N. Mitchell, H. R. Haldeman, John D. Ehrlichman, and Robert C. Mardian, were indicted by a federal grand jury for conspiring to hinder the Watergate investigation. In a further cloudy development, a Congressional committee reported on April 3 that Nixon owed almost $500,000 in federal income taxes for 1969 through 1972.

The White House was temporarily heartened by the acquittal on April 28 of Mitchell and Maurice H. Stans, officials in Nixon's 1972 reelection campaign. They had been tried for conspiracy, perjury, and obstruction of justice in connection with their handling of a secret $200,000 contribution from fugitive financier Robert L. Vesco. Their acquittal weakened the credibility of former White House adviser John W. Dean III, a key prosecution witness in the trial as well as Nixon's principal accuser before the Senate Watergate Committee.

The next day Nixon told a nationwide TV audience that in response to a subpoena of April 11 he was turning over to the House Judiciary Committee the edited transcripts of more than 40 tapes of private discussions he had with his advisers concerning Watergate. The transcripts were widely reprinted, and public reaction was highly unfavorable. There was dismay at the occasionally vindictive tone of the conversations and at gaps in them marked "unintelligible" or "expletive deleted."

Meanwhile, the White House refused to turn over tapes and documents of other presidential conversations to Special Prosecutor Jaworski. The U.S. Supreme Court, responding to a petition by Jaworski, agreed to hear the case. In an 8–0 decision on July 24, the high court ruled against Nixon, ordering him to provide "forthwith" the materials sought by Jaworski. It held that Nixon's claim of executive privilege "must yield to the demonstrated, specific need for evidence in a pending criminal trial," namely that of the former Nixon aides indicted on March 1 for the Watergate cover-up. (*See* Supreme Court of the U.S.)

On the same day the House Judiciary Committee began nationally televised hearings on the possible impeachment of the president. By the end of July the committee approved, by large bipartisan majorities, three articles of impeachment—charging Nixon with obstruction of justice, abuse of presidential powers, and impeding the impeachment process. Rejected were two other articles of impeachment, one charging that Nixon had usurped the powers of Congress by ordering the secret bombing of Cambodia in 1969, the other concerning possible income tax fraud and use of government funds on his homes in California and Florida.

The White House expressed confidence that the president would survive an impeachment vote in the full House. Then came the final development that sealed Nixon's fate. On August 5 he released transcripts of conversations he had on June 23, 1972, six days after the Watergate break-in, with Haldeman, then White House chief of staff. They clearly implicated the president in the overall Watergate cover-up.

Virtually all remaining support for Nixon then collapsed. His supporters in the House Judiciary Committee announced that they would vote for impeachment on the House floor. Congressional leaders called on the president to resign and thus spare the country the ordeal of his impeachment by the House and sure conviction and removal from office by the Senate. Nixon wavered. But on August 8 he went on nationwide television to announce that he would resign as president the next day. He said "I no longer have a strong enough political base in the Congress to justify continuing" the struggle to remain in office. (*See* Nixon.)

---

### THE 11 EXECUTIVE DEPARTMENTS

#### (January 1975)

Secretary of State . . . . . . . . . Henry A. Kissinger
Secretary of the Treasury . . . William E. Simon
Secretary of Defense . . . . . James R. Schlesinger
Attorney General . . . . . . . . . William B. Saxbe
Secretary of the Interior . . Rogers C. B. Morton
Secretary of Agriculture . . . . . . . . Earl L. Butz
Secretary of Commerce . . . . . Frederick B. Dent
Secretary of Labor . . . . . . . . . Peter J. Brennan
Secretary of Health, Education,
    and Welfare . . . . . . . . Caspar W. Weinberger
Secretary of Housing and
    Urban Development . . . . . . . James T. Lynn
Secretary of Transportation . . Claude S. Brinegar

PICTORIAL PARADE

*Becoming the second U.S. president in history to appear before a Congressional committee, Ford explains his pardon of Nixon in October.*

### Transition to Ford

Gerald Ford's accession to the presidency was greeted with a mixture of relief and euphoria. He was glowingly portrayed as a forthright, plain-spoken man ideally suited to the task of binding up the nation's Watergate wounds. Ford's surprise announcement in September, however, that he was pardoning Nixon for all crimes he "committed or may have committed" while president and agreeing to give him his presidential papers and tape recordings abruptly ended the period of good feeling. There were widespread reactions of shock and outrage, especially after Nixon, in accepting the pardon, admitted no guilt. Many persons felt it was a miscarriage of justice to let him escape possible criminal prosecution. There even was speculation that the pardon was part of a "deal" made with Ford before Nixon resigned.

Ford's standing with the public appeared to have suffered lasting damage. His relations with Congress also deteriorated as he vetoed 20 bills during his first five months in office. Included among the vetoes were a cutoff of military aid to Turkey, later extended in a compromise bill, and freer public access to government-held information, later overridden by Congress. Ford also was criticized for campaigning around the country for Republican Congressional candidates in the fall elections instead of concentrating on economic problems.

The president's economic policies came in for particular criticism, partly because the anti-inflation program he presented to Congress on October 8 contained few mandatory features, relying instead on appeals for "self-discipline" and "voluntary restraint." Senate Majority Leader Mike Mansfield, of Montana, rejected Ford's program as too similar to the "policies of the previous administration—policies which have long since proved to be inadequate."

Meanwhile, Ford's nomination of former New York Gov. Nelson A. Rockefeller to be vice-president, submitted to Congress on August 20, ran into unexpected difficulty. During his appearances before the Senate and House committees, Rockefeller, a multimillionaire, was criticized for substantial gifts of money he had made to various associates while governor. He also was criticized for sanctioning a hostile biography of Arthur J. Goldberg, his Democratic opponent for governor in 1970, and for his involvement in the Attica, New York, prison-riot deaths in 1971. Nevertheless, Rockefeller was confirmed as vice-president and sworn in on December 19. (*See* Ford; Rockefeller.)

### Watergate Trial

Ford's pardon of Nixon did not lay Watergate to rest. Although not physically present, the former president soon emerged as the central figure in the Watergate cover-up trial, which got under way in U.S. District Court in Washington, D.C., on October 1. Several tape-recorded conversations between Nixon and his aides were played in the courtroom. The tapes, some never before made public even in transcript form, tended to confirm Nixon's deep involvement in the Watergate cover-up.

One defendant, John Ehrlichman, insisted that Nixon's testimony was vital to his defense. Nixon, however, had been hospitalized in California for phlebitis of his left leg. Undergoing surgery on October 29, he was in critical condition for a while. A team of three court-appointed physicians examined Nixon and concluded that his appearance as a witness at the trial would endanger his recovery. Judge John J. Sirica thereupon ordered the Watergate trial to proceed without Nixon's testimony. On New Year's Day, after 15 hours of deliberation, the jury of nine women and three men found Mitchell, Haldeman, Ehrlichman, and Mardian guilty of conspiracy to obstruct justice in trying to cover up the Watergate scandal. Kenneth W. Parkinson, a lawyer for Nixon's reelection committee, was acquitted.

### Election Results and Congressional Action

As expected, Watergate and the twin specters of inflation and recession were decisive in the November elections. The Democrats gained more than 40 seats in the House of Representatives, three seats in the Senate, and four state governorships. The new Congress was expected to be considerably more liberal. (*See* Elections.)

Although Congress failed to complete action on several key bills, including tax reform, national health insurance, and a consumer protection agency, it approved several important laws during the year. In response to campaign irregularities disclosed by the Watergate scandal, Congress passed a law that set limits on campaign contributions and expenditures and provided for public financing for Congressional and presidential races. Congress also authorized $11.8 billion for a six-year mass transit program and set minimum standards guaranteeing payment of private pension benefits in, for example, the event of a company bankruptcy. (*See* Congress.)

### Foreign Affairs

Presidents Nixon and Ford both engaged in an unusual amount of high-level diplomacy during the year. In June and July Nixon visited the Middle East and the Soviet Union. The trip to the Middle East came just two weeks after U.S. Secretary of State Henry A. Kissinger had persuaded Israel and Syria to sign a cease-fire agreement and to exchange prisoners captured in the October 1973 war. As a result, Nixon got a hero's welcome in the Middle East. A week later Nixon was in the Soviet Union for inconclusive talks with Leonid I. Brezhnev.

Ford went on his first overseas trip as president when he visited Japan in November. Then, after a brief stopover in South Korea, he flew to Vladivostok, U.S.S.R., to confer with Brezhnev. A major agreement was reached on limiting the number of strategic nuclear weapons through 1985. Also as part of a general détente with the Soviet Union,

*U.S. deserters of the Vietnam war arrive at Camp Atterbury, Ind., in September as President Ford's conditional amnesty program begins.*
WIDE WORLD

Congressional legislation giving the president broad authority to reduce trade barriers with Communist countries was passed and signed in December. (*See* Arms Control; World Trade.)

### The Economy

*Stagflation* was the word used by most analysts to characterize the country's economy during 1974. It meant that business was foundering amid acute material shortages while prices of just about everything shot relentlessly upward at an annual inflation rate of 12%, the sharpest rise since 1946. The U.S. economy seemed troubled in a new way; the well of capital, minerals, and energy that once seemed bottomless was running dry. President Ford's proposed remedies, outlined before Congress in October, were, many observers felt, more placebo than panacea. His suggested 5% surtax on corporations and middle-to-upper-income taxpayers drew tepid response from legislators and public alike and was dropped at year's end. Other portions of his program fared better. On December 31 Ford signed legislation creating 100,000 new public-service jobs, extending unemployment benefits from a maximum 39 weeks to 52 weeks, and making eligible for benefits 12 million workers previously uncovered.

The country's gross national product (GNP), or total output of goods and services, in "real" dollars —that is, adjusted for price increases—plummeted 7% during the first quarter. It then continued to slide downward, although more slowly, throughout the rest of the year. This was the first time since the recession of 1960–61 that the GNP had declined for more than two consecutive quarters. Industrial production stopped rising early in the year and by October had fallen below the level of 1973. Auto production in particular was cut back, and mass layoffs began as sales dwindled. By the end of the

year President Ford was referring to the economic slump as a recession. Earlier, Secretary of Commerce Frederick B. Dent had called it an "energy-related spasm," resulting apparently from dislocations caused by the quadrupling of the price of imported oil during the year. Soaring oil costs had in fact sent the country's trade balance into the red in 1974, after a surplus, or excess of exports over imports, was posted for 1973. (*See* Money and International Finance.)

The slowdown in such industries as autos, appliances, building materials, and plumbing products began to take some of the pressure off materials shortages in other industries toward the end of the year. Nevertheless, in October the wholesale industrial price index was about 28% ahead of that of a year earlier. Shortages persisted in many key commodities, which in earlier years would have prompted immediate planning for expansion of production capacity.

Profits held up during the third quarter, but much of them were from inventories acquired before recent price increases. They disappeared as many companies changed their accounting systems and revalued inventories at their replacement costs, which in inflationary times are much higher.

The utilities and railroads, heavy users of coal, oil, and natural gas, were hit hard by soaring fuel prices. As rate increases were approved by government regulatory bodies, millions of dollars were added to the electric bills of households and businesses across the country. Mounting fuel costs, flak from environmentalists, and operating problems of nuclear power stations combined with steep costs of capital borrowing to discourage electric utilities from building much-needed new generating capacity. (*See* Fuel and Power.)

The oil crisis and farming disasters added enormously to the already raging inflation. In October, in fact, the government yanked its approval from a $500-million grain-export deal with the Soviet Union and imposed controls to restrict grain sales to other foreign buyers as well, mostly in the hope that this would reduce the upward pressure on food prices at home. Personal income did not keep up with soaring prices, even with the help of cost-of-living escalator clauses in many labor contracts. By year's end unemployment had climbed to 7% of the country's labor force, or more than 6 million persons, the highest figure since 1940. Equally alarming, total employment had begun dropping by the end of the year. (*See* Employment.) Such trends were even more ominous against a background of staggering business, government, and consumer debt—$2.5 trillion in 1974. There was doubt whether these debts could be paid off or be refinanced when due and whether enough new debt could be added to keep the U.S. economy growing at a rate comparable to that during nearly three decades following World War II. (*See also* Business and Industry; Intelligence Operations.)

U.S. Mint officials prepare for the Fort Knox, Ky., facilities' inspection by ten congressmen whose September visit quelled rumors that some of the gold was missing.

GEORGE TAMES – THE NEW YORK TIMES

# United States

## Special Report:
# A New Spirit for 1976

by John W. Warner

The Bicentennial—the 200th anniversary of the founding of the United States—is to be a many-splendored, many-sided event. It will be a community-by-community celebration. It will be a time to appreciate America's origins and what's happened in the past 200 years. It will be a time to look ahead to the problems and likely achievements of the next hundred years. And it will be a time of festival, of fireworks, and of the reenactment of famous historic events.

Every American should, if he or she wishes, have a hand in the celebration. Each community should contribute, develop, and celebrate. An infinite variety of projects are under way. A slum is to be eradicated here. A children's theater is to be inaugurated there. An encyclopedia of Indian history is to be published. A Revolutionary skirmish is to be restaged. A statement of goals for America's 3d century is to be published. An array of tall sailing ships is to reach New York Harbor on July 4, 1976.

A giant folk festival highlighting many foreign countries will be running during the summer of '76 on the mall in Washington, D.C. A series of ethnic paintings and sculpture will be unveiled. A bicycle trail from the Pacific to the Atlantic oceans will be opened. Trees—of the types that played roles in early American history—are to be planted.

Whatever celebrates the United States of America, recalls its past, projects its future, or improves its environment is grist for the Bicentennial. Plus some fun and enjoyment in the celebrating of all this. From Alaska to Maine and from Guam to the Virgin Islands, the Bicentennial is growing.

Every city, town, village, county, or Indian tribe whose program is approved by the American Revolution Bicentennial Administration (ARBA) will have won designation as a "Bicentennial Community." A community is expected to include in its plans at least one project to improve life there—in such fields as art, recreation, education, and housing—not just for 1976 but for the years ahead.

There is a further aspect to the Bicentennial. Americans are also memorializing and examining something that began to happen in 1776, the translation into national policy of the outlook and aspirations contained in three tremendous documents: the Declaration of Independence, the Constitution, and the Bill of Rights. Americans, when they stop to think about it, realize that it is the wisdom and the direction embedded in these that has made the U.S. the oldest, continuously existing republic oper-

ating under its original constitution. Celebrated, too, will be the idealistic yet pragmatic genius of the men who, on the shores of a wilderness, drafted these powerful fundamental documents: George Washington, Thomas Jefferson, Benjamin Franklin, Alexander Hamilton, John Adams, John Jay, James Madison—the men of Virginia, Massachusetts, South Carolina, and the other colonies.

On July 4, 1966, the U.S. Congress established ARBA, which was updated by further legislation on Christmas Eve 1973, establishing an administration with a policy board of 11 and providing for a direct administrator nominated by the president and confirmed by Congress. The basic mission of the Bicentennial Administration was "to coordinate, to facilitate, and to aid in the scheduling of events, activities, and projects of local, state, national, and international significance of the American Revolution Bicentennial." The overall goals of the Bicentennial are to gain the greatest individual participation and to forge a new national commitment—a new Spirit for 1976—a spirit to revitalize the ideals for which the Revolution was fought. Nearly all Bicentennial programs—be they national, state, or local—will fall within three thematic areas:

—*Heritage '76.* A survey of America's past achievements and history that shows how the country grew as a nation, in stature and in responsibility.

—*Festival USA.* A celebration of present-day America and its culture and traditions, both for citizens and for travelers from all over the world.

—*Horizons '76.* A program by which Americans can look ahead and examine the conditions, problems, and goals of their country in its next century.

State Bicentennial Commissions are operative in 50 states, the District of Columbia, the Commonwealth of Puerto Rico, and the Territories of Guam, American Samoa, and the Virgin Islands. An ARBA-matching-grants program to assist state and local Bicentennial projects was approved by Congress, with funds derived from such activities as the sale of commemorative medals struck by the U.S. Mint.

The Bicentennial Communities Program offers all qualifying communities an opportunity to obtain national Bicentennial recognition by implementing projects on any of the three themes. The program makes it possible for any one of the 41,000 governmental structures across the country to be officially recognized as a Bicentennial Community through a simple procedure. The community organizes a special Bicentennial planning and coordinating committee that is representative of all its segments. It plans a Bicentennial program that will have at least one lasting reminder—one permanent program—to show the special effort the community undertook for the '76 commemoration. It must obtain the approval of the chief executive officer or the governing body of the community. It must submit the application to ARBA through the appropriate State Bicentennial Commission. It must notify the local members of Congress that it is undertaking this activity. These are easy requirements, and thousands of communities have already chosen projects.

## Heritage '76

Under the theme of Heritage '76, for instance, there is a project entitled "Above-Ground Archaeology" that has attracted much attention. In essence, the program seeks to recover, restore, and make available important historical artifacts now gathering dust in trunks, attics, and storage areas across the country. The program has special appeal to youth, particularly students who can have fun while learning about the history of their community.

Another Heritage project—"Herstory 1776," the brainchild of Linda Grant DePauw, a professor of history at George Washington University and consulting historian to the Women's Coalition for the Third Century—is aimed at furthering the study of women in America's Revolutionary era. Its thesis was summarized in the proposing manuscript: "Americans of today who wish to commemorate the Bicentennial of our nation by studying the history of its early days do not find much mention of the founding mothers. This guidebook . . . is designed to help such readers uncover the missing half of Revolutionary history—the herstory of 1776."

There is also a Heritage project to develop the South Street Seaport—an urban, historical, and cultural area in lower Manhattan, New York City. It will "make the multiple meanings of our maritime history accessible to the public." The city will end up with a park and a restored port area. Another project in Manhattan is an "American Museum" sponsored by the Metropolitan Museum of Art. It is coming to fruition as a new wing of the Metropolitan Museum devoted entirely to Americana.

A project entitled the "Meeting House" program proposes that 55 historic U.S. sites be saved, restored, and used thereafter as meeting places for citizens concerned with preserving the nation's cultural heritage and the quality of the physical environment. It is being sponsored by the National Trust for Historic Preservation.

## Festival USA

A vast array of projects are planned under the theme of Festival USA. They encompass travel, hospitality, fairs, athletics, exhibits, educational and special events, and the arts. Current projections estimating how many travelers will be arriving, leaving, and crossing the U.S. during the Bicentennial are staggering. It is clear that there will be an increased number of visitors from abroad, and more Americans will be traveling within the country than ever before. Federal agencies are participating with city officials to help cope with the "tourist influx."

One Festival project is the "Bikecentennial"—a proposal to set up a bike trail or trails, using secondary and nonsuperhighway roads, from coast to coast. Two couples, riding across the continent on bicycles, traversed the west–east route and pronounced it feasible. Hostels, waystations, and attractions along the route must be added, however, if it is to be used extensively. Meanwhile, low-cost accommodations for travelers are being readied, and underutilized facilities such as church buildings, schools, college dormitories, and other public buildings are being designated as temporary accommodations for travelers during peak travel periods.

The Bicentennial presents a compelling challenge to widen the opportunity for the people of the U.S. and the people of the world to enjoy the multiple expressions of American culture. Thus, a major Festival project is in the area of folk and ethnic expression, with special emphasis on the Smithsonian Institution's Annual Festival of American Folklife. In 1973, ARBA gave a $200,000 grant to the Smithsonian Institution to permit it to conduct several pilot projects in preparation for an expanded nationwide festival in 1976. The theme "Old Ways in a New World" was introduced, which in effect says that America is a nation of immigrants. The music, dance, crafts, and customs of ethnic groups in the U.S. will be brought together with their Old World antecedents in a series of celebrations presented in cooperation with participating countries. The annual focus of the Smithsonian Festival, which has previously centered upon one of the 50 states, will be expanded in 1976 to encompass many of the states and territories, which are being encouraged to identify and inventory their characteristic folk traditions, skills, and customs.

As one Festival project, the World Theatre Festival—composed of top-ranking productions, companies, and artists from the U.S. and more than 25 other countries—will tour the country in 1975–76. Theatrical producer Alexander H. Cohen, the moving force behind the program, described it as "a 15-month-long pageant of the best in theater art in the world today, performed by the world's greatest theatrical troupes and artists, in commemoration of the 200th anniversary of our nation's birth."

In another Festival project an experimental pilot program has been put into action to stimulate communities across the country to "rediscover" their own individual cultural heritage. Under the direction of state arts councils, in three cities—Galveston, Tex., Quincy, Ill., and Tacoma, Wash.—task forces of professional artists are working to identify evidences of local artistic expression and cultural heritage. These will then be dramatized by using the facilities and resources available in each community. In this home-front project, community participation of all sorts is encouraged—such as displays of native artistic handiwork and industry products, tours of homes, development of children's museums, exhibits by local artists, and the publishing of cookbooks compiled by residents.

Other Festival projects include a plan to add to the facilities at Mt. Rushmore in South Dakota; an international people-to-people invitational program sponsored by the "Ninety-Nines," a women's flying group, which has also proposed extensive tree planting at airports to build an "International Forest of Friendship"; and a highly mobile Children's Theater, sponsored by the Eugene O'Neill Memorial Theater Center, for New York City that will provide a home for more than 120 community and ethnic theater groups.

### Horizons '76

The third thematic component of the Bicentennial, Horizons '76, is that area through which Americans can commemorate their past by looking to the future. It provides not only the challenge but also the opportunity for citizens to dedicate themselves to worthy activities that, begun during the Bicentennial, will constitute a national commitment toward the improvement of the quality of life during the next century.

To help individuals and groups in the development of significant Horizons projects, a National Action Guide was prepared. It delineates ten areas of program emphasis, all of which can have a profound impact on the future while providing a means of focusing on contemporary concerns: Citizenship, Community Development, Communications, Transportation, Health, Human Values and Understanding, Learning, Leisure, Environment, and Economy.

A large number of projects have already been recognized officially and are being developed. Among them is the "Johnny Horizon '76 Program," sponsored by the U.S. Department of the Interior, eight other federal agencies, and about 2,000 organizations. The program's slogan, "Let's Clean Up America for Our 200th Birthday," calls for environmental and ecological improvement across the land, cleaning up pollution in any and every form.

Another Horizon project, sponsored by the National Medical Association, aims at directing major effort toward abolishing sickle-cell anemia. It includes an information campaign, a research clearinghouse, and new counseling procedures.

Still another project, sponsored by the American Forest Institute, calls for the collection of seeds from trees that have contributed prominently to the nation's development and their distribution throughout the country for planting. These are only a few of the activities that have sprung to life from the basic concept—a befitting celebration of "Bicentennial."

### Something for Everybody

Many more happenings—which do not fit directly under the themes of Heritage, Festival, or Horizons—are under way. Commemorative medals, stamps, and coins, for example, have been designed. It was agreed that at least one Bicentennial commemorative stamp issue would be planned for each July 4 from 1972 through 1976. Preferably the postal issue would be a block of four thematically related first-class stamps. The 1972 issuance depicted 18th-century American crafts; the slogan "Bicentennial Era" appeared on each stamp, and the Bicentennial symbol was printed on the border of each sheet of 50 stamps. In 1973, four stamps depicting the Boston Tea Party were released. In 1974 the four stamps issued depicted Independence Hall and Carpenters' Hall in Philadelphia, Pa., and contained quotations from the Declaration of Independence and the First Continental Congress. (*See* Stamps.)

On Feb. 16, 1972, legislation was signed authorizing the U.S. Mint to strike a series of special Bicentennial commemorative medals. The 1972 medal

*Delegates from the original 13 colonies meet at Carpenters Hall in Philadelphia, Pa., on September 5 to celebrate the bicentennial of the first Continental Congress.*

WILLIAM E. SAURO—THE NEW YORK TIMES

*In one series of Bicentennial medals, the U.S. Mint is reproducing some of the first medals voted by the Continental Congress to celebrate noted leaders and victories in the Revolution.*

carried on its obverse the renowned Jean Antoine Houdon bust of George Washington; the reverse dramatized the Liberty Tree, the Stamp Act, and the "Join or Die" slogan of the American Revolution. The 1973 medal—designed by Robert Weinman, president of the National Sculptors' Society—presented Samuel Adams and Patrick Henry on the obverse and the Committees of Correspondence, which relayed revolutionary sentiments among the various colonies, on the reverse. The 1974 medal depicted John Adams and the First Continental Congress. The 1975 medal carries Paul Revere's likeness; and the 1976 medal, Thomas Jefferson's.

A Congressional act of Oct. 18, 1973, provided that there be new Bicentennial designs of the reverse side of the dollar, the half-dollar, and the quarter-dollar that are minted between July 4, 1975, and Jan. 1, 1977. They will each bear the dates 1776–1976 in lieu of the actual year of coinage. (*See* Coins and Medals.)

Congress called on ARBA to develop and maintain a Bicentennial register of programs and projects, and in other ways to provide a central clearinghouse for information and coordination regarding dates, events, places, documents, artifacts, and personalities of commemorative significance. This was accomplished by means of the "Bicentennial Information Network" (BINET)—a computer into which is fed a description of each project, sponsor, dates, locations, associated events, subject matter, and methods of presentation. Questions to BINET produce answers on any of these subjects. In addition, BINET can supply listings of books, parks, medals, surveys, and almost any other data that pertain to the Bicentennial. Since BINET presents a comprehensive picture of Bicentennial plans across the country, the system can be used to identify funding problems, crowd patterns, traffic flow, gaps in programs, and so forth.

The Bicentennial began slowly and haltingly. It suffered, in its early days, from haphazard direction and a multiplicity of counsels. At first it was thought that the Bicentennial should be celebrated as some sort of "Expo" world fair centered in Philadelphia. When that idea was abandoned, a plan was put forward for the creation of a new "Bicentennial

Park" in each of the 50 states, which could have cost $1.2 billion in federal money. A study showed that the use of excess federal lands for parks was not really feasible and that only nine states had population concentrations large enough to make their parks self-sufficient. So the parks plan died. A third idea, however—that the local communities across the country should make their own Bicentennial, out of their own efforts—gathered strength and support. And that is what the Bicentennial has largely become—a series of thousands of local celebrations, attached to a few big concepts that are always valid, about freedom and the Founding Fathers and the wisdom of the Constitution. The Bicentennial is developing realistically. Its funding is a bit reduced from early expectations, but its governing board is of high caliber, and it is at work on new initiatives.

Much interest, for example, is being generated by what is called the "American Issues Forum," which was announced at a May 1974 press conference by ARBA in conjunction with Ronald Berman, chairman of the National Endowment for the Humanities. This forum, first proposed by Walter Cronkite of CBS-TV News, involves the selection of fundamental American issues drawn from the Founding Documents. Through the work of the media and various organizations, one issue per month will be considered—focused upon and widely discussed—during the main Bicentennial period of 1975–76. A "national planning group" of distinguished citizens has been set up to select the issues for discussion. If all works as planned, the whole country will be considering some very fundamental issues—in world affairs and in mankind's quest for freedom. It will be like the early pre-1776 discussions that went into the Declaration of Independence and the Constitution, but keyed to today.

The Bicentennial is also planned as an occasion for other countries to help celebrate our 200th birthday. On June 21, 1973, invitations were dispatched through diplomatic channels to heads of state around the world, expressing the hope that government leaders, tourists, and visiting groups including artists and performers would travel to the U.S. and participate in commemorative events. Many of the countries now have official Bicentennial organizations and plans. The first foreign government to present the U.S. with a gift for its 200th anniversary was France. The French government announced in July 1974 that it would present a *son et lumière* (sound and light) show at historic Mt. Vernon in 1976. This concrete international interest is most encouraging, because it is certain to strengthen the mechanisms of international mutual understanding in ways that will continue to be beneficial long after the commemoration is over.

One of the prominent Bicentennial exhibitions that will be sent abroad is an ARBA exhibit created by Charles Eames, distinguished American designer, entitled the "Age of Franklin and Jefferson."

The exhibit was planned to open at the Grand Palais in Paris in January 1975. Later showings will be seen in Warsaw (Poland) and London. Then in 1976 the exhibit will return to the U.S. and tour New York City, Chicago, and San Francisco, Calif.

Another exhibit with international influence will be the "Nation of Nations," a presentation by the Smithsonian Institution that seeks to show the U.S. as a country composed of "many nations"—people who have come together from Europe, Latin America, Asia, and Africa to form one nation on the North American continent. Of special interest to Latin America is the "Interama" International Trade Fair to be held in Miami, Fla. It is to be a permanent inter-American Cultural and Trade Center at the new Florida International University.

"Pacific 21," a regional trade fair and cultural festival project sponsored by private business, will involve the participation of countries in the Pacific Ocean area. Its overall theme is "Third Century and Its Opportunities," and it was planned to open in Los Angeles in July 1975. Iowa State University has planned a Bicentennial World Food Conference of recognized international experts in the fields of food production, distribution, and nutrition. Most of the countries of the United Nations, as well as each state of the U.S., are expected to participate.

A number of performing arts groups from other countries are planning U.S. tours during the Bicentennial. Notable among these will be the Vienna Symphony, the Vienna Philharmonic, and the Lipizzaner horses of Austria; the new Opera Company of West Germany; the National Ballet of Canada; the Royal Danish Ballet; the Israeli Philharmonic Orchestra; and the London Symphony and the Royal Ballet of Great Britain.

Many federal departments are participating in the Bicentennial. The National Archives, for example, through its Center for the Documentary Study of the American Revolution, will bring together the most comprehensive collection of documentary source material on the American Revolution ever assembled. Its value to scholars will be considerable, because it will help overcome the problems of time, travel, and expense usually associated with such research. The Archives will also publish the complete papers of the Continental and Confederation congresses. The Department of Defense will be busy with worldwide ceremonies in recognition of the 200th anniversaries of the Army (June 14, 1975), the Navy (Oct. 13, 1975), and the Marine Corps (Nov. 10, 1975). Other military projects include a major renovation of Arlington National Cemetery, an overhaul of the warship *Constitution*, and a 1974 Air Force Academy Symposium on "The Military History of the American Revolution."

So the Bicentennial moves ahead, with more projects being added daily. As ARBA spokesmen have said, "the Bicentennial will not be confined at all to one area, but will have something for everybody." (*See also* the ten other special reports.)

**URUGUAY.** The progressive militarization of the government that had begun in 1973 when President Juan María Bordaberry dissolved Congress and began to rule by decree with the support of the armed forces proceeded apace in 1974, putting an end to Uruguay's long tradition of democracy. The process resembled a military coup in slow motion, the president remaining in office while other civilian members of the government were gradually ousted. Bordaberry remained partly by skillful political maneuvers and partly, perhaps, because the military was content with its already substantial stake in the leadership and saw in the president a potential scapegoat should its policies fail.

During the year the military gradually extended its control from a mere handful of functions, such as transport, communications, and police, to most of the country's major institutions. As part of a series of changes in the governmental structure, Bordaberry reinforced the Central Planning and Budget Office with the participation of military advisers and created an Economic and Social Council, comprised of the joint chiefs of staff, among others, that would advise the government. At the end of July military officers were put in charge of the major state-owned enterprises, including the power and fuel monopolies and the Central Bank. The process seemed to be nearly complete when in September Bordaberry announced that a return to parliamentary government was no longer possible and that a new constitution was in preparation.

Inflation, though reduced somewhat in 1973, remained a sizable problem during 1974. Moreover, the restrictive stance adopted by traditional importers of Uruguayan beef, plus the rocketing price of oil supplies, for which Uruguay was totally dependent upon imports, was expected to bring about a severe setback in the country's external economic position. (*See also* Latin America.)

**VENEZUELA.** Foremost among the advantages of the new administration of President Carlos Andrés Pérez was the huge sums received as oil income in 1974. Averaging $833 million a month, it supplied the government the funds to finance its many plans. The underlying concern in drafting new policies, however, was that social problems might reach a point where an ineffective democratic government would simply be overwhelmed and fall victim to a populist regime. The government, therefore, undertook to expand the economic and social content of the political framework to include "the large part of Venezuelans who live under conditions of extreme poverty."

In late March Pérez launched his attack on inflation, decreeing a 90-day price freeze at mid-January levels for basic consumer goods and services, while expanding jobs and raising health standards. On May 1 Pérez asked Congress for extraordinary powers to issue economic and financial measures, programs, and policies.

Venezuelan President Pérez (fourth from left) watches an inaugural parade in Caracas on March 13, the day after he was sworn into office.
WIDE WORLD

The government was ambitious to adjust the distribution both of income and to some extent of economic power, transforming the structure of the economy—substituting "a society of producers in place of a society of consumers," to quote the new president's phrase. To help achieve these aims, the Central Bank and two major mining enterprises, subsidiaries of U.S. Steel Corp. and Bethlehem Steel Corp., were to be nationalized. In addition, the Andean Pact's Decision 24 was adopted—a measure that reserved 80% of the electric power generation, radio and television broadcasting, Spanish-language publication, local transport, advertising, and department stores to ownership by Venezuelan nationals. In December Venezuela joined the growing number of Latin American countries that were reestablishing diplomatic relations with Cuba. (*See also* Latin America.)

**VIETNAM.** President Nguyen Van Thieu of South Vietnam seemed firmly entrenched in power at the beginning of 1974. Opposition to him was scattered and uncoordinated, and in January the National Assembly approved a constitutional amendment that permitted Thieu to run for a third term in 1975 and extended the term of office from four to five years.

The cabinet was reshuffled in February, and five ministers were removed. This was directed more to dealing with the country's rapidly mounting economic problems, however, than with the growing agitation against dictatorial rule, maladministration, and corruption that became the main anti-Thieu rallying points in subsequent months.

Corruption charges were leveled against Thieu himself by the Catholic-directed Anti-Corruption Movement, led by Father Tran Huu Tranh and by the Buddhist organization known as the National Reconciliation Force. Misuse of power, it was charged, had resulted in great financial gains for Thieu and members of his immediate family. Thieu responded by denying the charges and accused those agitating for his removal as "Communists and people working for the Communists."

Nonetheless, Thieu seemed unusually conciliatory, offering to root out corruption and to curb the powers of the Democracy party, the country's sole legal political organization. But Thieu's opponents rejected his promises of reform. Repressive police measures against antigovernment demonstrations in the country's major cities of Saigon, Da Nang, and Hue tended to unite the opposition. The violent church-led demonstrations and suicides by fire reminded many of the events preceding the overthrow of President Ngo Dinh Diem in 1963.

During October Thieu removed four members of Premier Tran Thien Khiem's cabinet, including his cousin, Information Minister Hoang Duc Nha, who was widely detested for his arrogant treatment of dissidents. Thieu also ousted three of South Vietnam's four military corps commanders and dismissed several hundred army officers on charges of corruption.

To a great extent Thieu was hurt by his inability to forestall reductions in U.S. military and economic aid. This allegedly blunted his ability to meet inflationary problems and to respond fully to military moves by the Communist Provisional Revolutionary Government (PRG). Renewed Communist attacks forced a series of pullbacks by government troops all across the country. By August tank-led Communist forces had penetrated to within 15 miles of Saigon. Government casualty figures were raised to near-record levels. Hue and Da Nang were exposed to artillery and assault groups. In the Central Highlands the government was almost completely shut out, with some local forces actually joining the PRG. In the densely populated Mekong Delta, North Vietnamese tanks took part in fighting for the first time, and as many as 100 government outposts were lost.

The South Vietnamese economy was severely af-

Three years after the end of the massive U.S. defoliation program in South Vietnam, leafy trees once again shade a country lane near Can Gio village. According to a study done by the National Academy of Sciences for the Defense Department, however, some varieties of trees might take many more years to recover from the herbicides, and there was concern about other side effects of defoliation, including toxic residue in the food chain.

WIDE WORLD

fected by inflationary pressures during the year. For the average South Vietnamese, who suffered from a 65% price rise in 1973, the prospect was for at least a 100% rise in 1974. Unemployment soared to more than one million. Imports—including critically needed petroleum, machinery, rice, sugar, and fertilizers—were down by one third from the peak year of 1969. Stricter tax collection increased revenue income by 40%, however, and helped offset inflation losses to some extent.

In North Vietnam the government declared economic reconstruction to be its primary goal for 1974 and 1975. Le Duan, first secretary of the ruling Communist (Workers) party, said, "The war has rolled back our originally underdeveloped economy, which had just made one step forward, to where it was more than ten years ago."

Of immediate concern was agricultural output, critically reduced by winter drought and then by typhoon damage and floods. Rice crops on about 400,000 acres were totally lost, and yields were greatly reduced on another 700,000 acres. Nevertheless, an increase of 21% in gross industrial output and of 16% in agricultural output was expected from 1973 to 1974. Even with $1.2 billion in aid from Communist countries (mainly the Soviet Union and China), capital was a limiting factor in the country's reconstruction program. North Viet-

nam had anticipated fulfillment of a U.S. pledge of $2.5 billion in economic aid. In the face of what it considered continuing North Vietnamese violations of the peace accord, however, the U.S. government refused any funds to North Vietnam.

North Vietnam's other pressing domestic problems centered on rising consumer demands from a war-weary population and acknowledged corruption in what was described as a "reversion" to the "old social (capitalist) system." Moving to consolidate the country's socialization, the government pushed for the mergers of farm cooperatives and increasingly discouraged private retailing.

Crucial to North Vietnam's long-term economic rehabilitation was the attitude the government would adopt toward its continued goal of reunification with the South. In a major speech on September 1, Premier Pham Van Dong emphasized reconstruction of the North but did not discount "liberation" of South Vietnam. North Vietnam's standing army was estimated at 370,000 men, with all but a home defense force of 50,000 believed to be stationed outside its borders—about 150,000 in South Vietnam, 90,000 in Laos, and 80,000 in Cambodia. Massive stockpiles of weapons and supplies were believed to have been set up in strategic locations in the event of future major military action. (*See also* Asia.)

**WEATHER.** From mid-June through mid-September 1974, the field phases of man's most ambitious environmental study were conducted on and over the tropical Atlantic Ocean. The project, Global Atmospheric Research Program Atlantic Tropical Experiment (GATE), based in Dakar, Senegal, brought together 38 research ships, an international squadron of research aircraft, instrumented buoys and balloons, earth-orbiting satellites, and some 4,000 scientists, technicians, and other personnel.

The mass of data collected was to provide scientists with their first systematic look at the processes linking the tropical atmosphere and ocean, where much of the world's weather begins. GATE was sponsored by the United Nations' World Meteorological Organization and the International Council of Scientific Unions, and involved participants from about 70 countries.

Other regional Global Atmospheric Research Program experiments being planned included an Air Mass Transformation Experiment for the westernmost Pacific Ocean, a Monsoon Experiment for the Arabian Sea monsoon, and a Polar Experiment, concerned with energy transfer processes in the polar regions. The target date for the First Global Atmospheric Research Program Global Experiment (FGGE) was set for 1978.

In the United States, the National Hail Research Experiment was continued over northeastern Colorado in 1974 by the National Center for Atmospheric Research, supported by the National Science Foundation. The National Oceanic and Atmospheric Administration (NOAA) of the U.S. Department of Commerce continued its research into lightning suppression through the introduction of metallized chaff "hairs." During the 1974 season, investigators used two seeding aircraft to determine whether seeding *within* the cloud system mitigates the eventual lightning output of a thunderstorm.

Although no hurricane modification was attempted in 1974, NOAA continued its preparations for renewal of Project Stormfury in 1976. In August, the agency announced the purchase of two Lockheed WP-3D "Orion" aircraft for its Research Flight Facility. Scheduled for delivery in mid-1975 and early 1976, the new aircraft, when equipped with instrumentation and data systems, would be among the world's most advanced environmental airborne research platforms.

NOAA's annual summary of weather modification projects in the U.S. showed that 67 projects took place in 19 states between Nov. 1, 1972, and the start of 1974. Oklahoma and California had 12 and 11 projects, respectively. North and South Dakota had 6 each; Idaho, 5; Washington, 4; Michigan, Texas, and Utah, 3 each; Iowa, Montana, Oregon, and Wyoming, 2 each; and Arkansas, Colorado, Illinois, Nebraska, Nevada, and New

After heavy rains caused widespread flooding across southwestern Ontario, Canada, in mid-May, a policeman with no traffic to direct stands idle in a Cambridge street.
UPI COMPIX

York, 1 each. The report was required by 1971 legislation that became effective in November 1972, asking for the reporting of all nonfederally sponsored weather modification activities in the U.S. and its territories.

### Weather Forecasting and the Year's Results

A major technological step for weather forecasters came with the May 1974 launch of the first Synchronous Meteorological Satellite, SMS-1, by the National Aeronautics and Space Administration. Positioned in geostationary orbit about 22,000 miles over the equator at 45° west longitude, SMS-1 provided day-and-night pictures of cloud cover over the Atlantic Ocean every half hour, greatly improving GATE scientists' ability to plan aircraft missions. SMS-2 was scheduled for a year-end launch.

Meteor 16, a new Soviet weather satellite, was launched on March 5. And in the polar-orbiting satellite series, NOAA-3 became the prime operational spacecraft in March.

NOAA's National Weather Service moved closer to implementing its Automatic Forecasting and Observation System (AFOS). The new computer-centered system was to automatically assemble and analyze weather data, display weather information, and predict trends on television consoles. What was believed to be the world's largest operating computer was put into use at NOAA's Geophysical Fluid Dynamics Laboratory in Princeton, N.J., permitting the testing of the laboratory's complicated mathematical models of the atmosphere and ocean systems.

The 1974 tornado season in the U.S. was one of the most devastating in history. Although the number of tornadoes did not match the record of more than 1,100 set in 1973, the twisters of 1974 ran to the large, destructive variety weathermen called "maxi tornadoes." The worst outbreak of the year came from April 2 to 5. More than 100 tornadoes struck 14 midwestern states during a single 12-hour period, killing more than 300 people. This was the worst one-day death toll since the tristate tornado of March 18, 1925, killed 689 people in four hours.

Atlantic hurricanes stayed away from the U.S. coastline in 1974 except for Carmen, which struck across the Louisiana coastline west of New Orleans on September 8, spoiling much of the Louisiana sugarcane crop.

Atlantic hurricane Fifi, however, brought one of history's worst natural disasters to the Western Hemisphere. The storm struck Honduras on September 18 and 19 with 110-mile-per-hour winds and inundating rains and storm tides. Fifi left an estimated 5,000 persons dead, and damage estimated at $450 million. (See Honduras.) It also hit Nicaragua, El Salvador, Guatemala, and Belize, killing several thousand more persons.

In the eastern Pacific area there was above-average activity. During August, four tropical storms— Joyce, Kirsten, Lorraine, and Ione—were tracked simultaneously. Early Christmas day a cyclone destroyed or damaged about 90% of Darwin, northern Australia's major city.

### Will We Weather the Storm?

The meteorological preoccupation of 1974, however, was the growing concern over the effects of weather and climate upon the world's ability to feed its inhabitants. A persistent drought still stretched around the globe at the lower latitudes, afflicting the sub-Saharan nations of Africa and a broad strip through the Indian subcontinent. In the U.S., hard spring freezes, heavy spring rains, summer drought, and early fall freezes caused failures of some important crops, draining reserves and boosting food prices. The crops of other countries were similarly hurt by ill-timed heavy rains and dry periods.

Accordingly, there was increasing concern among scientists and governments that more effort be applied to comprehending the crucial relationships between weather, climate, and global food production, and toward solving the difficult problems they posed. (See also Disasters of 1974; Environment; Food; Oceanography.)

*Equipped with sensors to record meteorological data that are radioed to a shore station for processing, this 35-ton buoy is designed to be an automatic weather watcher that may enable more accurate and longer-range forecasts.*
UPI COMPIX

**WEST INDIES.** Because of offshore oil and natural gas, the economy of Trinidad and Tobago was generally strong in 1974. The government took over Shell Trinidad, Inc., and helped finance an aluminum smelter in its own country and one in Guyana. Trinidad worked to establish a fund to assist the eight less developed members of the Caribbean Community and Common Market. There were serious domestic problems, however, in education, unemployment, violent crime, and labor unrest under the virtual one-party government of Prime Minister Eric Williams.

Barbados was hurt by rising import costs, inflation, economic slowdown, and increased unemployment in 1974. In March the government proposed a development plan to create new jobs in manufacturing, construction, and tourism. The sugar crop was slightly smaller than it had been in 1973, but high world prices increased revenue. Constitutional changes, vesting more power in the executive, aroused some protest but were adopted.

Guyana perhaps suffered most from the energy crisis. Its foreign currency reserves were drastically reduced during the year. Guyana's economic problems were also compounded by the effects of droughts and floods in 1973 that had ruined its sugar and rice crops. There was a serious increase in crime in 1974, partly attributable to extremely high unemployment.

As a solution to a depressed economy, citizens of the Turks and Caicos Islands, colonies of Great Britain, advocated union with Canada as a territory or as a tourist haven. There was some support in Canada for the proposal, but such a union seemed unlikely. In the U.S. Virgin Islands, there were 14 murders during 1974, many of the victims being white Americans apparently murdered by native blacks because of racial hostility. (*See also* Bahamas; Cuba; Dominican Republic; Grenada; Haiti; Jamaica.)

**WOMEN.** In the 1974 U.S. elections, women candidates scored some impressive victories. Democrat Ella T. Grasso was elected governor of Connecticut; she thus became the first woman to be elected governor of any state in her own right (not as a wife or widow of a male officeholder). Grasso was one of three women to run for gubernatorial office in 1974; the other two were defeated.

Three women ran for the U.S. Senate, in Maryland, Oregon, and South Carolina. All three lost, and the Senate remained 100% male. In the House of Representatives, 4 of the 16 women incumbents chose not to run for reelection; however, with six new victorious female candidates, the total of women in the House rose from 16 to 18.

Janet G. Hayes was elected mayor of San Jose, Calif.; she became the first woman elected to a mayoral post in any U.S. city with a population exceeding 500,000. North Carolina became the first state to elect a woman to the office of chief justice of the state supreme court; she was Associate Justice Susie Sharp.

Supporters of the equal rights amendment (ERA) to the U.S. Constitution conceded that they had little hope of seeing the amendment ratified in 1975. Resistance to the ERA was a major issue at the conference of the National Women's Political Caucus in June. Thirty-three states had approved the ERA by the end of 1974, but two of those— Nebraska and Tennessee—voted to rescind their approval. Court tests of the rescinding votes were expected. Thirty-eight of the 50 state legislatures were required to approve the ERA before it could become law.

The Supreme Court of the U.S. handed down two major decisions in 1974 relating to the rights of women who are pregnant; one was considered a victory for the women's movement, the other a setback. In January the court ruled that public school boards cannot force pregnant teachers to take long

*Dancer Martha Graham (left) accepts the first MacDowell Colony medal ever awarded in the field of dance from choreographer Agnes DeMille and William Schuman, MacDowell Colony chairman, on November 7 during the colony's annual benefit dinner in New York City.*
WIDE WORLD

*Rep. Bella Abzug (D, N.Y.) speaks at Federal Hall Memorial in New York City during an Equal Rights Amendment rally held by feminists in celebration of Women's Equality Day on August 26.*

leaves of absence before their babies are born. In June the court ruled, however, that states do not have to pay disability benefits to women unable to work because of normal pregnancy symptoms.

In the fall the Congress passed the Equal Credit Opportunity Act, barring discrimination because of sex in the granting of credit. The law was to become effective one year after enactment. Observers noted that the enforcement procedures provided for in the act were neither quick nor simple.

The nation's economic problems were largely responsible for a long delay in the opening of the First Women's Bank, to be located in New York City. The bank was scheduled to open in September, but the organizers were unable to raise the authorized capital. Many of the persons who had pledged financial support were involved in the stock market or in construction—two areas of the economy hardest hit by inflation and recession. Opening of the bank was rescheduled for sometime in 1975.

A study of male and female police patrol officers revealed that both sexes were equally effective on the job. The private Police Foundation studied the records of 86 male and 86 female police recruits in Washington, D.C. The study pointedly noted that women performed patrol duty as well as men; one woman had subdued a "belligerent, 250-pound intoxicated man" in the course of her patrol. The yearlong study, prepared by the Urban Institute, was designed to show whether there were barriers to the equal hiring practices required by law.

Women were also making inroads in the male-dominated field of medicine. For the 1973–74 school year, women comprised 19.7% of the entering class in U.S. medical schools—up from 7.8% ten years before. Women composed 15.4% of the total enrollment in medical schools for the 1973–74 year, up from 9.6% only three years before.

Eleven women were ordained Episcopal priests in July, and their ordination touched off a major controversy. In 1972 the denomination's House of Bishops had approved priesthood for women "in principle," but in the following year the House of Deputies had voted not to accept women as priests. The 11 women, deacons of the Episcopal church, were ordained by four bishops in a church in Philadelphia, Pa. Shortly after the ordination, the Rt. Rev. John M. Allin, presiding bishop of the church, stated that the women could not perform priestly offices. In August the House of Bishops in emergency session declared the ordinations invalid. This action was based on a complex interpretation of canon law; the four bishops who performed the ordinations did not have the permission or approval of the bishops in charge of the candidates' dioceses. In November the Rev. Alison Cheek, one of the 11 new priests, celebrated the eucharist in an Episcopal church in Washington, D.C., becoming the first woman to do so in the U.S. In October, however, the Rev. Cheek and two of her colleagues had celebrated holy communion in a non-Episcopal Christian church in New York City.

Young girls and their parents were victorious in their campaign to be accepted on Little League baseball fields. League headquarters announced in June that the formerly all-boy teams could admit girls; 22 class-action suits had been filed across the country, and the league petitioned Congress to amend its charter. On Christmas Day President Gerald R. Ford signed the bill making the change legal. (*See also* Colleges and Universities; Elections; Families; Political Parties.)

Steel rods from Belgium and France are unloaded in New York City. The shortage of American steel production capacity forced increased U.S. purchases abroad at prices 20% to 30% higher than domestic costs.
THE NEW YORK TIMES

**WORLD TRADE.** In 1974 the trade expansion that had characterized the preceding year came to an abrupt end, giving way to accelerated inflation and the possibility of a serious and protracted recession. Uncertainties about the future development of prices and about the availability of energy resources and foodstuffs further aggravated an already ominous economic outlook for 1975.

The principal unanswered question at the end of 1974 was whether the industrial countries would get together and coordinate their individual policies in order to cope jointly with the oil-induced balance of payments deficits—or whether each would resort to stringent deflationary moves, increased exports, and controls on imports to cope with such deficits. Experts predicted that the latter course would lead to the further deterioration of an already precarious world economy.

Amid this growing crisis, the industrial countries and less developed countries alike felt the need to take stock in the economic situation and to explore the possibility of joint international programs. The Organization for Economic Cooperation and Development (OECD), at a ministerial level meeting in Paris in May, warned of the dire consequences of a nationalistic approach to growing deficits. The ministers agreed to a standstill, for a period of one year, on the application of new restrictions on trade and current invisible transactions, and on any new artificial stimulation of exports. The OECD ministers, representing industrial countries in the main, directed one of the group's committees to disperse relief assistance to less developed countries with low per capita incomes. This assistance would take the form of providing essentials such as food, fertilizers, and debt relief.

A new textiles agreement, concluded in late 1973 under the auspices of the General Agreement on Tariffs and Trade (GATT), went into effect on Jan. 1, 1974. The agreement was intended to aid in the expansion and liberalization of world trade in tex-

tiles, without disruption in individual markets, in both importing and exporting countries. The GATT participants hoped that such a policy would secure a substantial increase in the foreign exchange earnings derived by the less developed countries from the textile market. (*See also* Textiles.)

Specifically, the textile agreement forbids further restraints on textile imports and provides for a gradual phasing out of existing bilateral restraints on imports. A Textiles Surveillance Body was established to implement the agreement.

Long-standing negotiations between the United States and the European Economic Community (EEC) resulted in a new trade agreement in May 1974. The U.S. sought compensation for economic losses caused by the enlargement of the EEC. The agreement provided for tariff concessions by the Europeans on a number of products that constitute major exports for the U.S. These products included excavating machinery, tobacco, and citrus fruits. No agreement was made concerning U.S. grain exports, but the U.S. reserved the right—under the provisions of GATT—to enter into negotiations on grain in the future. Canada was still negotiating with the EEC along the same lines.

The multilateral trade negotiations begun in Tokyo in September 1973, under GATT auspices and direction, marked time awaiting final passage of the trade reform bill by the U.S. Congress. The bill, finally passed and signed in December, gave U.S. President Gerald R. Ford the authority to enter into trade agreements.

One version of the trade reform bill had been passed by the House of Representatives in late 1973. The bill was extensively debated and amended in the Senate Finance Committee. In mid-December the Senate voted to link trade concessions for Communist countries with those countries' emigration policies; this move, in effect, provided economic pressure on the U.S.S.R. and its allies to allow emigration of Jews and other minorities.

The Senate version of the trade bill required Congressional approval of the president's negotiations to eliminate nontariff barriers. The Senate Finance Committee tried to ensure, also, that the United States would be able to gain concessions in obtaining vital resources from the less developed countries by offering them other types of concessions in return.

Forty-four less developed countries were involved in negotiations with the EEC on future trade relations. Ministers from the countries—located in Africa, the Caribbean, and the Pacific—met in Jamaica in July 1974 to clarify their common objectives; they agreed to pursue the goal of free and unlimited access to EEC markets for all their exports, along with the elimination of tariff reciprocity. (*See also* Fuel and Power; Money and International Finance.)

## YOUTH ORGANIZATIONS.

In 1974 the youth organizations of America continued to grow. One of the most important developments was the attempt to broaden membership and programs to serve youth of different backgrounds.

### Boys' Clubs of America

During 1974, the Boys' Clubs of America had more than one million members and grew at the rate of one new club each week. During National Boys' Club Week, March 31–April 6, George R. Clark was selected 1974 Boy of the Year. Clark attended a special White House conference later in the year with U.S. President Gerald R. Ford to discuss youth problems.

Under a program called Design for the Seventies, Boys' Clubs of America concentrated on urban problems, health services, job training, and preparation for adulthood and parenthood. The clubs began an Urban Fellows Training Program. In three test cities, with the cooperation of the U.S. Department of Labor, the clubs placed more than 400 persons in permanent jobs.

### Boy Scouts of America

Two incidents marred the image of the Boy Scouts of America in 1974. Investigations showed that membership rolls in several cities had been padded by professional staff members of the Boy Scouts. The staff members claimed that they had created the phony members out of fear of being fired for not meeting increased membership goals, in some cases necessary to justify federal aid under Model Cities programs. Scout officials announced new procedures to prevent such abuses in the future.

In Utah, the National Association for the Advancement of Colored People and two black youths brought suit against the Boy Scouts on the grounds that one of the boys had been unfairly denied promotion to the position of senior patrol leader. The youths, members of Mormon-sponsored troops, could not qualify for the position because of Mormon practices restricting the participation of blacks. The suit was later dropped after the court was assured that discriminatory policies in church-sponsored troops had ceased.

Two of the important programs of the Boy Scouts of America during 1974 were its environmental and bicentennial programs. In Project SOAR (Save Our American Resources) Scouts worked with the environment, energy conservation, and recycling. In GIFT (Get Involved for Them) Scouts studied America's past and its revolutionary ideals.

### Camp Fire Girls

In November 1974 the 64-year-old organization of Camp Fire Girls received the report of a planning

*George R. Clark, 18, named national Boy of the Year by the Boys' Clubs of America, speaks with President Ford in Washington, D.C., in a September meeting that Ford called to elicit the opinions and concerns of today's youth.*
U.S. NEWS SERVICE

committee, established in 1972, with recommendations and conclusions about the future purpose and programs of the organization. By 1974 nearly 60% of all members of Camp Fire Girls lived in metropolitan or urban areas.

The organization sponsored a national art competition, among other activities, during the year. The winning painting, 'Wingding Dilly', by eight-year-old Barbara Bovee of Salem, Ore., a pastel blue and green bug, was to be used on the cover of the 1975 calendar. A group of 39 of the winning paintings was used in a traveling art show.

## 4-H

There were more than 5 million members of 4-H groups throughout the U.S. in 1974. Members worked in a variety of projects. Some groups developed antilitter and environmental projects. Others developed practical health programs—testing for diseases, eradicating rats, and teaching dental hygiene. Some 4-H members not only raised food but also taught poor people how to have nutritious meals at low cost.

## Future Farmers of America

Renewed interest in food production attracted students to the Future Farmers of America (FFA) in 1974. Membership rose to over 465,000 in 7,726 chapters. Nearly half of all members participated in contests and award programs to recognize achievement, including new programs such as a national horticultural contest and proficiency awards in beef, sheep, and swine production, and for achievement in the horse industry.

President Gerald R. Ford was the keynote speaker at the FFA's 47th national convention and was presented the Honorary American Farmer degree. In his televised address, President Ford urged FFA members and the nation to fight inflation.

## Future Homemakers of America

In 1974 there were more than 400,000 members, young men and women, in Future Homemakers of America (FHA). At their 1974 national convention in Chicago, delegates and advisers developed projects to help youth assume their roles in personal growth, family life, vocational preparation, and community involvement.

## Girls Clubs of America

There were about 164,000 members of Girls Clubs of America in 1974. Approximately 68% of Girls Clubs were in low income areas, and about 30% of the members were from minority groups. Girls Clubs continued to emphasize career education, but other activities included working with senior citizens, high school tutoring, and ballet. Most Girls Clubs, however, concentrated on the dilemmas of poor urban youth.

## Girl Scouts of the United States of America

In 1974 the Girl Scouts of the United States of America continued projects to increase membership in Appalachia, remote rural areas, migrant camps, inner cities, and on Indian reservations. The Girl Scouts also developed plans to increase membership among Mexican Americans.

The programs of the Girl Scouts continued to broaden to include special projects in education for parenthood, child development, family relationships and management, work with handicapped children, and physiological and emotional development. The Girl Scouts' bicentennial project, America's Hidden Heroines, worked to discover unknown women in American history. As in the past, under the "wider opportunities" program, Girl Scouts traveled outside the U.S. and were hosts to Girl Scouts from other countries.

*Some of the more than 17,000 boy and girl scouts from 12 countries meeting in a July scout camp in Jutland, Denmark, take to the water in a variety of boats, including oil-barrel rafts.*

TAGE JENSEN—NORDISK PRESSEFOTO/PICTORIAL PARADE

### Young Men's Christian Association

The wide range of services of the Young Men's Christian Association (YMCA) continued in 1974. Nearly one fourth of all associations offered alternatives to institutionalization for youth in trouble. The YMCA spent more than $3 million on juvenile justice programs in 1974. The YMCA expanded its aquatic program, with funding by the United States Bureau of Education, to teach the handicapped to swim.

The YMCA established a commission on women, who made up nearly one third of its membership in 1974. It continued its programs in family life and worked with its international organization to help drought areas in Africa and to train young Africans for jobs.

### Young Women's Christian Association

In 1974 the Young Women's Christian Association (YWCA) further developed its formal programs to create a society free of racism and of bias against women and youth. The YWCA attempted to become pluralistic in its own organization and to contribute toward pluralism in all institutions.

The YWCA sought advice from various groups, including teenage women, on their needs. The YWCA operated juvenile "intervention" centers in YWCA residences and a consumer education program for women. (*See also* Baseball; Women.)

# YUGOSLAVIA.
The country's fourth constitution since World War II was promulgated on Feb. 21, 1974. While maintaining single-party Communist government, it considerably modified the legislative system, including the replacement of the 620-member, five-chambered Federal Assembly with two houses, a Federal Chamber of 220 delegates and a Chamber of Republics and Provinces of 88. The State Presidency, the supreme body, was reduced from 23 members to 9. A slight shift away from the policy of close collaboration with the Soviet Union and a sharp deterioration of the country's economic position were the main features of the year. The internal political situation continued to be uncertain, reflecting the ambiguities of Soviet intentions toward Yugoslavia. In April, Yugoslav security services discovered and arrested a group of pro-Soviet Communists who had held a secret party "congress" at Bar in Montenegro. The news of their arrest was delayed until September 12, and on September 20 it was announced that 32 members of the group had been tried at two separate trials at Pec and Titograd and had been given sentences ranging from 1 to 14 years. Warsaw Pact forces maneuvers in Hungary at the end of September were followed by Yugoslav military exercises close to the borders of Hungary and Bulgaria.

The dinar was devalued by 7% at the end of October. Yugoslavia's trade gap was expected to reach $3.5 billion by the end of the year, and its balance of payments deficit was estimated at $720 million. Yugoslavia had a record wheat harvest of 6.3 million tons, but heavy floods in northern Croatia and Serbia in October destroyed much of the corn and sugar-beet crops and damaged property. Inflation reached a level of about 30%.

The most important political event of 1974 was the tenth Congress of the League of Communists in Belgrade in late May. The congress reelected President Tito party leader "with an unlimited mandate." The congress also adopted new party statutes that emphasized party discipline and gave greater powers to the central party bodies. (*See also* Europe.)

# ZAIRE.
A search for offshore oil in 1974 proved extremely expensive, but it was hoped that some return would begin to be seen by the middle of 1975. At a conference of the leading copper-producing countries held in Zambia in June, however, representatives of Zaire joined with other delegates in severely criticizing the system under which copper prices were fixed by the London Metal Exchange. Encouraged by the actions of oil-producing countries, the conference set out to make plans to enable copper-producing countries to fix prices themselves.

Relations with Belgium became strained early in the year over the publication of a critical biography of Zaire's President Mobutu Sese Seko by a Belgian lawyer. Later the situation improved with the arrival of a new Belgian envoy in Kinshasa, the capital. Potentially more serious were Portuguese fears that Zairian forces might unite with the Angolan guerrilla movement, with an eye, perhaps, on the oil resources of the Cabinda enclave. Portuguese border defenses were strengthened, but the Zairian government took no action although it was thought that Mobutu was anxious to abandon the moderate role he had played for years and emerge as a leader of the militant African nationalists. The president joined with Sudan's President Maj. Gen. Gaafar al-Nimeiry in criticizing the Organization of African Unity for failing to unite the various guerrilla movements in Angola. On December 30 it was announced that as of Jan. 1, 1975, Zaire's industry, building trades, and distribution services were to be nationalized.

With Mobutu's encouragement, the promoters of a boxing match between George Foreman and Muhammad Ali for the heavyweight championship of the world successfully staged it in Kinshasa, the first African city to be chosen to hold such a title fight. (*See also* Africa; Boxing.)

# ZAMBIA.
The economic situation in Zambia in 1974 seemed promising, though there remained obstacles to be overcome. Negotiations took place early in the year with a view to increasing the export of copper to China that had first begun when the government took control of the copper mines in 1970, and in February President Kenneth D.

Kaunda paid a goodwill visit to China. As a result of technical developments by the Nchanga copper mines group, the output of copper in the future was expected to be greatly increased and the cost of production to remain relatively low. A conference of the leading copper-producing countries was held in Lusaka, the capital, in June. (*See* Zaire.) There were hopes, too, that by the end of the year Zambia would no longer need, because of its own rising production of sugarcane, to import sugar.

Inadequate transport facilities resulted in the pileup of imported goods intended for Zambia at the docks in Dar es Salaam, Tanzania, early in the year. Metal goods rusted in the heavy rains, while perishable goods, including food, deteriorated in the heat. One section of the Tanzam Railway was brought into operation in April ahead of schedule to try to reduce the backlog. Also in April President Kaunda ordered the death sentence for convicted armed robbers.

Probably the most important development in foreign affairs was the change of government in Mozambique. In May Kaunda called upon the new military government in Portugal to grant independence to Mozambique and Angola, and in September, due to the president's initiative, Lusaka was the meeting place of Frelimo leaders and the Portuguese foreign minister when final details were arranged for Frelimo's participation in an interim government in Mozambique. In November President Kaunda visited the U.S.S.R. (*See also* Africa.)

**ZOOS.**   During 1974 most zoos continued to emphasize the breeding of animals. Many zoos throughout the world operated loan plans in which animals were exchanged with other zoos to form breeding pairs. The National Zoological Park announced plans to set up a farm at Front Royal, Va., to provide facilities that most small zoos could not offer for breeding in large groups. Although zoos in the past had contributed to conservation by successfully breeding large numbers of a few endangered species, some critics charged that zoos were a drain on, rather than a contributor to, animal life. Park zoos in New York City reported abuse and even severe injuries to animals by visitors and were charged themselves with keeping animals in unclean and overcrowded conditions.

For years zoos had been trying to achieve second-generation breeding in captivity. The Washington, D.C., Zoo was successful in 1974 with golden marmosets, a species in danger of extinction, as was Chicago's Lincoln Park Zoo with a pair of snow leopards. The Washington, D.C., Zoo also hatched a bald eagle; only three others of this uncommon species, the official bird of the U.S., had ever been born in captivity. And the Chicago zoo recorded a litter of Asian lions, the first born in captivity in the Western Hemisphere. The Point Defiance Aquarium in Tacoma, Wash., recorded the first births from captive sea otters, and the Toledo Zoo in Ohio had the first chimpanzee birth from artificial insemination.

Red-fronted macaws, found in a restricted area of Bolivia and hunted by natives, were captured alive for the first time; ten were taken into captivity to form a breeding nucleus. The West Berlin Zoo in Germany received from New Guinea two vulturine parrots, birds that could be seen at only two other zoos in the world. London Zoo received a pair of giant pandas as a gift from the People's Republic of China. (*See also* Animals and Wildlife; Pets.)

*Female panda Ching-ching (Crystal Bright) rests against the fence of her cage in the London Zoo with her younger male companion Chia-chia (Most Excellent) looking on. The pandas, a gift of the Chinese government to the people of Great Britain, were transferred to their new home in September. The London Zoo had been without a panda since its female, Chi-chi, died in 1972.*

LONDON DAILY EXPRESS/PICTORIAL PARADE

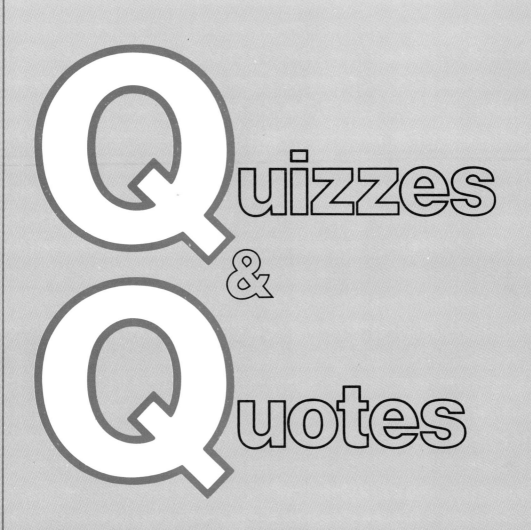

# Quizzes & Quotes

with a foreword
by
clifton fadiman

## Clifton Fadiman

Although perhaps best known to the American public as an author and lecturer, Clifton Fadiman has also had a long career as an educator and educational consultant. His literary credits include essays, anthologies, and criticism. Among his many current interests is *Cricket,* a new children's magazine of which he is senior editor.

A long time ago I held down a job as master of ceremonies on a radio show called Information Please. Those readers who have reached what is known (for no sound reason) as the age of discretion may remember it. Fact questions on all sorts of subjects were mailed in by the listening audience. A panel of four experts (they really did know a lot—sometimes) tried to answer them. The program ran for more than ten years. It reached an enormous audience—young and old, for this was a family program. It actually brought people together, whereas today's average television show can tend to isolate the viewer in his own private cocoon of glassy-eyed impassivity.

Though Dr. I.Q. preceded it in time, Information Please was the real ancestor of the quiz show craze that has even now not entirely subsided, though it has taken forms of show business vulgarity that are not to everyone's liking. What was the secret of the appeal of the original Information Please?

Partly, it was the light, amusing, *genuine* conversation generated among the experts. But, just as important, the secret lay in our national passion for isolated facts, which Information Please satisfied divertingly. There is a curious pleasure, akin to treasure hunting, in uncovering hitherto unsuspected areas of memory in that odd storehouse, the mind. All of us know more than we think we know. It's just that the requirements of daily living rarely make it necessary for us to ransack our memories. All of us once learned in school when Abraham Lincoln was born, but it is quite possible to live a long life without ever being challenged to recall the date. (I blush to tell you that I just looked it up in my encyclopedia—it's 1809, of course.)

It seems that the owners of all encyclopedias love the challenge of questions and the search for answers. The editors of *Compton's Encyclopedia,* for example, discovered that one of its most popular features was the "Exploring" question pages at the beginning of each volume. Readers, experiencing the self-discovery pleasures I've been discussing, have frequently written the *Compton* editors, asking for more such questions. Apparently those readers make a kind of family game out of challenging each other's memories. So we have prepared a whole volume of questions in this *Compton's Book of Quizzes & Quotes*.

As you see, there are 72 quizzes of 25 questions each, alphabetically arranged by subject matter, from Aerospace to Youth Organizations, including several of a general nature. They cover a lot of factual territory: geography, technology, history, literature, animals and plants, the arts, military matters, communications, games, holidays, biography, legends, religion, sports, and (it's about time) women's rights. And a lot of other stuff besides, including a notable quote at the beginning of each quiz.

With this book you can test yourself in the fields you think you know best; or learn hundreds of facts in fields you're unfamiliar with; or match your own knowledge against that of a friend or member of your family; or astound your teacher by coming up with information that may be new to him or her; or enrich your school assignments with relevant factual data; or win (or lose) a bet; or just browse around, learning odd bits and pieces of information that may come in handy sometime—you never can tell.

Facts aren't, of course, wisdom; they're not even truth, though they are, in the narrow sense, true. But they do help to furnish the mind with the nitty-gritty materials that may help us a step or two toward wisdom and truth. Best of all, they satisfy human curiosity and then excite it further. You may be looking up something about Holidays and Festivals, and then, idly turning the page, suddenly find yourself fascinated by the next section, which deals with Insects and Spiders. Unsystematic education, of course—but education of a kind nonetheless, with the added attraction of a game, a challenging indoor sport that any number can play.

We hope that these quizzes will give the whole family both instruction and many hours of innocent diversion. Authors of the 72 quotes and the answers to the 1,800 questions are given after the quizzes.

*The old engravings illustrating the alphabetical quizzes are used by permission and courtesy of the G. & C. Merriam Company of Springfield, Massachusetts, publishers of* Webster's Third New International Dictionary, Webster's New Collegiate Dictionary, *and other dictionaries in the Merriam-Webster series.*

# aerospace

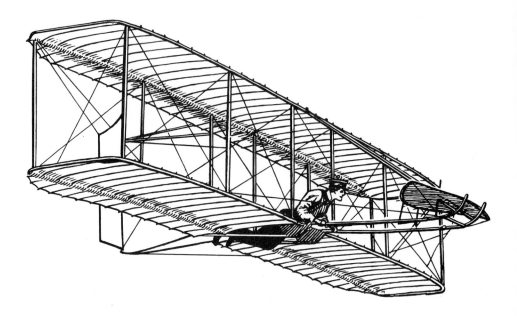

*"No national sovereignty rules in outer space. Those who venture there go as envoys of the entire human race."*

1 What were the first bombs used in World War I aerial fighting?

2 What mythological Greek met his death when he flew too near the sun?

3 What early flying vehicle was powered by smoke from a straw fire?

4 Charles Lindbergh was the first man to fly alone nonstop across the Atlantic Ocean. Who made the first transcontinental flight across the U.S.?

5 Who was piloting the plane in which the first modern airplane fatality occurred?

6 Who built the first power-driven, heavier-than-air machine that flew for more than a few seconds?

7 The air crash in which American humorist Will Rogers died occurred in 1935. What famous aviation pioneer also died in that crash?

8 Who was the American physicist known as the "father of modern rocketry"?

9 When did air navigators use the stars for determining their position?

10 What are probably the earliest written records of the use of rockets in warfare?

11 What aircraft, controlled by a propellerlike rotor on its topside, was invented in 1923?

12 The Wright brothers, Orville and Wilbur, are famous for achieving the first "true" airplane flight. What did they do for a living?

13 What did many World War I fliers use their skills for after the war was over?

14 What was the first plane to fly faster than the speed of sound?

15 Wiley Post made the first round-the-world solo flight in 1933. Who was the first woman to make such a flight?

16 When did the first regular airmail postal delivery service begin?

17 What was the first heavier-than-air flying machine called?

18 What is an oleo strut?

19 What are the small hinged flaps near the tips of airplane wings called?

20 What, technically, is a sonic boom?

21 Who was the medieval monk who predicted that men would fly in winged machines?

22 In 1855 Capt. Jean Marie le Bris used an unusual model for a glider. What did he pattern it after?

23 Who made the first jet-propelled device?

24 When was the first instance of aerial jet combat?

25 Who followed Lindbergh by making the first nonstop flight from New York to Germany?

# africa

*"Always something new out of Africa."*

1. Most people have heard of the famous explorer of Africa, David Livingstone, but two Scottish explorers traveled in the African interior many years before Livingstone did. Who were they?

2. What is the oldest nation in Africa?

3. In what part of Africa do tigers live?

4. Which West African country bears the name of a great empire of the Middle Ages?

5. Several African countries lead the world in production of certain materials. Name three of these countries and their main products.

6. What is the longest river in Africa?

7. Who was the first Egyptian leader to believe in one god?

8. Which of the foreign explorers built the great stone city of Zimbabwe, whose ruins still stand in Rhodesia?

9   The Sahara is the most famous desert in Africa, but the continent has two other large desert regions. What are they?

10  The people of North Africa were traditionally divided into two groups: Hamitic and Semitic. Where did these names originate?

11  In the 15th century, European slave traders began to carry off Africans as slaves. Where were these slaves first used?

12  Approximately how many slaves were brought to the West Indies and North America between 1680 and 1786?

13  The people of what African country are not racially related to other African peoples, but to Polynesians?

14  Which African country is totally surrounded by another?

15  Mount Kilimanjaro is the highest mountain in Africa. What is the second highest?

16  Where do the famous Watusi, or Tutsi, people live?

17  What famous Italian sculptor and painter was so impressed by African art works that he incorporated many of their ideas into his own creations?

18  The Great Sphinx in Egypt is one of the world's best-known statues, but whom does it represent?

19  Which African country was founded by Americans? When?

20  The Cape of Good Hope, a landmark for sea travelers for centuries, was known by a much less complimentary name during the days of exploration. What was this name and who coined it?

21  South Africa is noted for its fine gem diamonds. What was the largest diamond ever taken from a South African mine?

22  The nomadic peoples of the Arabian Desert are known as Bedouins. What does this name mean?

23  What was Africa's "year of independence," when 17 former colonies became self-governing?

24  Two of the most ancient peoples in Africa are nearing extinction. Who are they?

25  Which African country bears an ancient Greek name?

# american history

*"There were human beings aboard the Mayflower,*
*Not merely ancestors."*

1    What was the first permanent English settlement to be established in North America?

2    Who were the famous American explorers who traveled the vast area west of the Mississippi around 1800?

3    What event marked the beginning of fighting in the Civil War?

4    Who was the only man to be elected to four terms as president of the U.S.?

5    In 1824, none of the four candidates for president received a majority of the electoral votes cast. Who was elected president in the subsequent balloting in the House of Representatives?

6    Who was the British general who surrendered to General George Washington at Yorktown in 1781?

7   What Spanish territories did the U.S. acquire as a result of the Spanish-American War?

8   The U.S. went to war with Mexico in 1846 over their common boundary. What was the outcome?

9   Which war was fought "to make the world safe for democracy"?

10   A historic Supreme Court decision established the right of the judiciary to review legislation—thus strengthening the concept of "checks and balances" in government. What was the name of the court case?

11   In 1775 Paul Revere made his famous ride to warn of the redcoats' coming. What were the redcoats coming to get?

12   Who led the last major military victory for the Indians in the late 19th century?

13   What event precipitated U.S. entry into World War II?

14   Who was the black man killed in the Boston Massacre in 1770?

15   When did the gold rush take place in California?

16   Which president established the "war on poverty" program?

17   Which European explorer was the first to venture inland substantially on the North American continent?

18   What was the major unforeseen consequence of Prohibition?

19   Which U.S. president created the Peace Corps?

20   How and when did the U.S. first acquire the territory of Alaska?

21   What was the largest city in the U.S. in 1790?

22   The cost of food and clothing increased about 100% in a seven-year period in the 20th century. What was that period?

23   Who wrote the following: "If I could save the Union without freeing *any* slave, I would do it; and if I could save it by freeing *all* the slaves I would do it"?

24   Which was the 50th state to be admitted to the Union?

25   When was cross-country air-mail service inaugurated?

# american literature

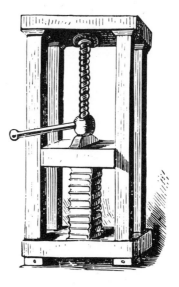

*"All modern American literature comes from one book by Mark Twain called* Huckleberry Finn.*"*

1 What early 19th-century American writer created the forerunner of many fictional detectives?

2 What little magazine founded in Chicago in 1912 published the first or early work of nearly every distinguished American poet?

3 Name the writer and editor who was instrumental in developing the school of realism in American fiction.

4 What 19th-century American poet who wrote hundreds of poems had only six published in a lifetime?

5 Who wrote the novel 'Main Street'?

6 What author changed Oxford in Lafayette County, Miss., to Jefferson in Yoknapatawpha County, Miss.?

7 Whom did the English appreciate as the first important American writer?

8  John Steinbeck wrote a novel about farmers who fled to California from the Oklahoma dust bowl. What was its name?

9  Who was the first person to write about the English settlements in the New World?

10  What post-Puritan writer examined the darker side of life, which his contemporaries were generally ignoring?

11  Who wrote about Americans in the process of experiencing Europe in the late 19th and early 20th centuries?

12  What underlay Ralph Waldo Emerson's inspirational writings?

13  The manuscript for Thomas Wolfe's first novel filled a large packing crate before it was edited. What best-selling novel did it become?

14  Who wrote 'Moby-Dick'?

15  Who was the best-known poet who wrote lovingly of rural New England?

16  Name the novelist who depicted the disillusioned rich of what he called the Jazz Age.

17  U.S. President Theodore Roosevelt helped a New England poet obtain a position in the New York customs house. Who was he?

18  What effect did Noah Webster have on spelling?

19  A post-World War II black novelist won high critical acclaim with his novel 'Invisible Man'. Who is he?

20  Name three famous midwestern poets who were born late in the 19th century and lived well into the 20th.

21  In what river town did Mark Twain gather material for his best-known stories?

22  The poem 'The Waste Land' made many poets disciples of its author. Who was he?

23  Who wrote the novel 'The Fixer'?

24  Nebraska Pioneer days were the subject of 'My Antonia' and 'O Pioneers'. Who wrote them?

25  What was the paramount virtue of Ernest Hemingway's heroes?

# american minorities

*"In the American design—as we perceive it—each group in our nation has special problems. None has special rights. Each has peculiar needs. None has peculiar privileges."*

1 A black slave leader headed a revolt in Southampton, Va., in 1831 that resulted in the death of about 60 whites. Who was that leader?

2 Which is the largest Indian tribe in the U.S. today?

3 Which people comprise the largest single foreign-born group in the Los Angeles area?

4 Name the famous black nationalist leader assassinated in early 1965.

5 When was the civil rights march on Washington, D.C.?

6 Who was the Shawnee chief whose tribe was defeated in a battle over Indian lands at Tippecanoe?

7 New York City's Harlem has long been known as a black community. What other group is represented in considerable numbers?

8 What was Marcus Garvey's major contribution to the "new Negro" of the 1920's?

9   What was the specific issue in the battle between Custer and Sitting Bull at the Little Bighorn?

10  Which city contains the largest group of Chinese people outside of Asia?

11  Who were the two black leaders from the U.S. to win the Nobel peace prize?

12  Several hundred Indians—men, women, and children—were murdered by the U.S. Army in 1890 in a now-famous massacre. Where did this massacre occur?

13  Japanese-Americans from Hawaii compiled an exemplary battle record during World War II. Where were they sent to fight?

14  Who founded the abolitionist journal *North Star* in 1847?

15  How many lynchings of blacks were recorded between 1900 and 1914?

16  Which U.S. president refused to enforce a Supreme Court ruling entitling the Cherokees to retain their Georgia lands?

17  About one third of the people in which state regard Spanish as their mother tongue?

18  Approximately how many black soldiers served in the Union army during the U.S. Civil War?

19  What event, in 1886, marked the end of Indian resistance in the Southwest?

20  An immigration law enacted in 1882 excluded natives of which country from becoming naturalized citizens?

21  Which four cities had black populations of more than 50% in 1970?

22  Which amendment to the Constitution granted citizenship to black people?

23  The National Association for the Advancement of Colored People (NAACP) was organized in 1910; who was the editor of the NAACP journal, *Crisis*, in those early days?

24  Which federal office was placed in charge of the Indian treaties in 1789?

25  Who was the only Indian leader in the West to win a major victory against the U.S. government?

# animals of the wild

*"Tiger! Tiger! burning bright
In the forests of the night."*

1 Which is the largest living animal?

2 The most familiar animals are vertebrates, those with backbones. If they are divided down the middle the two halves match each other but in reverse. What is the proper name for this matching?

3 All animals must take in oxygen in order to change food into a form the body can use. How do fish and tadpoles do this?

4 When sea squirts, sponges, corals, and similar creatures reproduce themselves, lumps appear along a branchlike organ and develop into young. What is this form of reproduction called?

5 Marsupials are animals that carry their young in pouches. There is only one native to the Americas. What is it?

6 There are two types of elephants, African and Asian. How do they differ?

7 An ostrich can run faster than a horse, but how fast can it fly?

8 The kangaroo is one of the best-known jumping animals and is able to leap five times its length. What tiny animal is a far better jumper, able to leap 200 times its own length?

9   Some birds swim well under water, but can you name a fish that can walk on land?

10  What animal cuts palm fronds so that they droop to form a shelter from the sun or rain?

11  How do squids defend themselves when threatened?

12  Where do you find the organs for the sense of sound on a cricket?

13  Most insects die when cold weather comes; which one hibernates instead?

14  What do we mean when we say ants, bees, and wasps are social insects?

15  Which are the most intelligent of the animals?

16  Which animal can expect to live the longest?

17  The land areas of the earth can be divided into regions where the animals differ from those in any other region. How many such regions are there?

18  Australia's koala is threatened with becoming extinct because it refuses to eat anything but one kind of food. What does it eat?

19  Sponges are among the simplest many-celled animals. They have no mouth or digestive cavity. How do they acquire food?

20  Which is the most primitive animal to have a definite head with sense organs and a differentiated body?

21  The largest group of animals is the arthropods, which includes the insects. Instead of a skeleton they have a framework on the outside of the body. What is the substance that makes up this framework?

22  Which of the apes customarily walks erect, standing on its hind legs?

23  There are four kinds of apes. Gorillas and chimpanzees are natives of equatorial Africa, but where do orangutans and gibbons live?

24  True anteaters, with long snouts and tongues, but no teeth, are found only in what part of the world?

25  Antelopes come in many sizes and are found in many parts of the world. Which is the smallest one of all?

# architecture

*"A house is a machine for living in."*

1 Which modern architect coined the phrase "Form follows function"?

2 Which of the world's greatest artists was one of the architects for St. Peter's basilica in Rome?

3 What material was used throughout the building of the Parthenon in Greece?

4 Which famous church in New York City is an imitation of the great Gothic cathedrals of the Middle Ages?

5 Who was the architect for the Johnson Wax Building in Racine, Wis.?

6 Which architect initiated the concept of the "split-level" house?

7 What is the name of the famous office building in St. Louis, Mo., designed by Louis Sullivan and completed in 1891?

8   What were the three styles, or "orders," of ancient Greek architecture?

9   Who designed the geodesic dome?

10  The ancient Egyptian structures that have survived to the present day are made of what material?

11  The London Fire of 1666 destroyed most of the heart of the city. Who was the architect most influential in rebuilding the city?

12  Which style of architecture incorporates minarets and bulbous domes?

13  Name the five great Gothic cathedrals in the Ile de France.

14  What is the oldest dwelling in Boston, Mass., and when was it built?

15  Who is the architect generally credited with inventing the skyscraper?

16  Which technological invention paved the way for skyscrapers and made them practical?

17  What is an "eclectic" design in architecture?

18  Which renowned architect designed the Barcelona chair to harmonize with his buildings?

19  When was the Church of Holy Wisdom (Santa Sofia) in Istanbul, Turkey, completed?

20  What advantages did Gothic architects gain through the use of the flying buttress?

21  Few of the structures built in ancient Mesopotamia have survived, though many Egyptian structures of the same period did survive. Why?

22  Shah Jehan was a Mogul emperor who ordered a magnificent tomb built for his favorite wife in the 17th century. What is the name of the resulting structure?

23  Which 19th-century U.S. architect was highly influential in reviving the Romanesque style?

24  How many stories are there in the Empire State Building?

25  Which 17th-century British architect brought Italian influence to major structures in England?

# armed forces & military history

*"An army marches on its stomach."*

1  In what 19th-century war were the commanders of the opposing armies both graduates of the U.S. Military Academy?

2  What warriors used coconut-fiber suits for armor?

3  In what ancient battle does legend credit the mythical twins Castor and Pollux with aiding the victors?

4  What is "Fabian policy"?

5  The city of Candia, in Crete, once underwent what was probably the longest military siege in history. When was this siege and how long did it last?

6  In what battle of what war did the 'Charge of the Light Brigade' immortalized by the poet Tennyson occur?

7  What modern country first revived the ancient Roman and Greek system of universal conscription into the military?

8 Why do the people of Moscow owe so much to "General Winter"?

9 In what U.S. war did nearly eight soldiers die of disease for every one who died in combat?

10 What famous modern painting protests the use of aerial bombing on a small town in the 1930's?

11 What U.S. general was once court-martialed after demanding that the U.S. have a strong and independent air force?

12 George Armstrong Custer gained lasting fame at the Battle of the Little Bighorn, but he was renowned long before that for other military exploits. What were they?

13 Who developed the modern battle tank, and what was used as a prototype?

14 One of the great Allied heroes of World War I refused all honors and decorations, changed his name twice to avoid publicity, and died as an obscure enlisted man. Who was he?

15 Aside from observation, what were the German Zeppelin balloons used for in World War I?

16 The armistice ending World War I was signed in an unlikely place. Where?

17 Where did the term "Fifth Columnist" originate?

18 When did blacks and whites first serve in integrated combat units for the U.S. Army?

19 What military leader first supplied his troops from fixed bases, thus eliminating the practice of pillaging and foraging for supplies?

20 What was the longest war in recorded history?

21 Who first said "Don't give up the ship"?

22 What war was fought over a drug?

23 What country was once known as the "cockpit of Europe" because of the many battles that took place on its soil?

24 What American Revolutionary War general was also a successful playwright and librettist?

25 Where did the term "Parthian shot" originate?

# asia

*" Oh, East is East, and West is West, and never the twain shall meet."*

1   The Srivijava empire was a major power from the 7th century to the 13th century. Where was it located?

2   Which Asian country was the first United Nations member ever to withdraw from the organization?

3   What was the name of the first kingdom established in Vietnam?

4   What ancient Asian kingdom was one of the world's first totalitarian states?

5   Why do the Chinese people often refer to themselves as Hans?

6   When did the famous warrior Genghis Khan live?

7   In the 18th century Laos was divided into two kingdoms, whose names are still known today. What were they?

8   What were the Three Kingdoms?

9   Yi Sunsun, a Korean military hero, invented a modern naval weapon in 1592. What was it?

10   According to legend, who was the first emperor of Japan?

11   What did Marco Polo call Japan?

12   What great Japanese city was, by the 18th century, larger than any European city?

13   When did Japan first establish formal relations with China by sending emissaries there?

14   In what Asian country was built the largest religious building in the world?

15   The East Indies were originally populated by Malay people. Who were the first foreigners to gain influence there?

16   From what country did the original inhabitants of Burma come?

17   What Mongol leader ruled over more people than had any Roman emperor?

18   The poet Rudyard Kipling wrote of being "on the road to Mandalay." Where is this famous city?

19   How old was Marco Polo when he first entered the court of the Chinese emperor?

20   Although the Japanese and the Mongols both conquered much of Asia, another group controlled almost all of Indochina from the 9th century to the 15th century. Who were they?

21   English playwright Christopher Marlowe based his play 'Tamburlaine the Great' on an Asian warrior named Timur Leng. What people did he lead?

22   When did the Vietnamese, then known as the Annamese, gain freedom from China?

23   What Asian ruler was the subject of the musical comedy 'The King and I'?

24   Who was "Chinese Gordon"?

25   How were the Philippines named?

# astronomy

*"There is no light in earth or heaven
But the cold light of stars."*

1  The planet Mars sometimes looks like a red star in the sky.
   How does it make its light?

2  How far from Earth is the nearest star?

3  How old is the universe?

4  Who made the first telescope?

5  When does a meteoroid become a meteorite?

6  Many centuries ago people thought that the stars and the sun
   and its planets revolved around Earth. What famous
   astronomer thought otherwise and provided the modern theory
   of solar system movement?

7  How long does it take for a ray of sunlight to reach Earth?

8  What ordinary substances are thought to make up the unique
   system of rings that encircle the planet Saturn?

9  In time the sun will grow brighter and larger and then will cool off. When will this change begin?

10  The Milky Way, the galaxy in which we live, contains how many stars?

11  In the skies relatively close to the North and South poles, solar wind causes spectacular displays called the aurora borealis and the aurora australis. What is solar wind?

12  What is the unit of astronomical measurement?

13  White-dwarf stars are composed of densely compact matter about the size of the planet Earth. If the superdense white-dwarf material could be put into a teaspoon, how much would a teaspoonful weigh?

14  Some places in the universe are so dense that they act like sponges and suck in nearby radiation and matter. What are these sites called?

15  What ancient people believed that the sun was a god who sailed across the sky in a kingly ship?

16  How far away from Earth is the most distant galaxy?

17  Though this Danish astronomer disbelieved Copernican views of planetary movements, his careful calculations were actually used to support the Copernican theory. Who was he?

18  What famous British tourist attraction is believed to have once been a sophisticated observatory for predicting eclipses, phases of the sun and moon, and other astronomical phenomena?

19  Which great astrophysical mathematician also dabbled in alchemy?

20  What would happen if a wayward star passed through our solar system?

21  What is possibly the most plentiful element in the universe?

22  Does the universe have a shape?

23  What is an inferior planet?

24  Which is the largest planet in the solar system, and which is the smallest?

25  Just as the planets orbit the sun, the sun moves in an orbit around the center of the Milky Way. How long does it take for the sun to complete an orbit?

# australia

*" Once a jolly swagman camped by a billabong,*
*Under the shade of a coolibah tree,*
*And he sang as he sat and waited till his billy boiled,*
*'You'll come a-waltzing, Matilda, with me'."*

1 The name *Australia* gradually replaced what name given to the continent by early Dutch explorers?

2 What is the highest point on the Australian continent?

3 Zoogeographers divide the world into regions each of which has plants and animals more or less distinct from those of the other regions. What areas are included in the Australian region?

4 Who was the first explorer to sight Australia's coast?

5  What substance constitutes the Great Barrier Reef off the northeast coast of Australia?

6  Why is Australia known as "the land down under"?

7  How does Australia rank in geological age with the other continents?

8  What is Australia's chief waterway?

9  The aborigines of Australia are believed to have come from what area of the world?

10  Who was "Flynn of the Inland"?

11  How fast can the great gray kangaroo hop along the ground?

12  The eucalyptus is the best known of all Australian trees. What does its name mean?

13  More than 50% of the population live in Australia's five largest cities. Name them.

14  Who is Australia's closest neighbor?

15  What is Australia's single largest export?

16  Who established England's claim to eastern Australia and when?

17  An immigration drive after World War II brought nearly one million people to Australia in nine years. Of the continental Europeans, what nationality predominated?

18  What are the two beasts of prey found only in Tasmania?

19  Was Australia ever attacked during World War II?

20  Which of the performing arts benefited most from the wealth of Australia's gold rush?

21  How do children separated by hundreds of miles take part in lessons with a teacher and each other?

22  Name two outstanding modern-day Australian novelists.

23  Who is Australia's head of state?

24  Who was Albert Namatjira?

25  Which of Australia's six states is the most populous?

# birds

*" Birds of a feather flock together."*

1 Which birds once flew in flocks of up to 2 billion and yet today are extinct?

2 Peacocks are native to what area of the world?

3 What bird figures prominently in Samuel Taylor Coleridge's poem 'The Rime of the Ancient Mariner'?

4 What was the earliest-known "true" bird?

5 How many known varieties of birds are there?

6 What one feature makes birds different from all other animals?

7 The eagle has been chosen as the symbol of many governments. What was probably the first state to use it?

8 What members of the heron family were almost exterminated because of demand for their magnificent feathers?

9 What country's soldiers are nicknamed for the bird that is also the country's emblem animal?

10 Hawks are, for the most part, solitary birds. When do they flock together?

11 What birds are credited with saving ancient Rome from the Gauls?

12 What animals serve as food for vultures?

13 To what continents is the turkey native?

14 What bird is known as the "whisky jack" or "camp robber"?

15 What early-spring songbird is the state bird of six different states?

16 What is the largest living bird?

17 John James Audubon was the greatest of all American ornithologists (students of birds). What was the name of his most famous work?

18 What birds make the longest known nonstop flight?

19 What bird has a kinked vertebra in its neck so that it cannot raise its face?

20 What bird's cry is thought to be a sign of death by superstitious people?

21 The dodo, extinct since 1681, was a clumsy and unattractive bird. What did early Portuguese explorers call it?

22 What is the rarest woodpecker?

23 After enjoying great popularity during the Middle Ages, the sport of falconry declined. When was it next revived?

24 What bird lays its eggs in other birds' nests and lets them hatch and raise its young?

25 What unusual bird has become a major pest to Australian wheat farmers?

# canada

*"This is the Law of the Yukon, that only*
*the Strong shall thrive;*
*That surely the Weak shall perish, and*
*only the Fit survive."*

1 What is the most densely populated province in Canada?

2 Uranium for the first atomic bomb came from Canada. Where was the uranium mine?

3 What three Canadian provinces lead in the manufacture of pulp and paper?

4 What percentage of Canada's people are of French origin?

5 In what century did European fishing fleets begin to visit Canada's eastern waters?

6 What is Canada's most valuable mineral?

7 About how many Eskimos live in Canada?

8 Which plant and animal region of Canada has nearly 300 botanical species that occur nowhere else in the country?

9 The Canadian government provided transportation and found employment for more than 35,000 immigrants from one country in 1956–57. Who were they?

10 In what year did Canada adopt an act similar to the U.S. Bill of Rights?

11 The best-known descendants of the Acadians who were deported from Nova Scotia in 1755 live in Louisiana. What are they called?

12 What has been an outstanding development in Canada's English-language theater?

13 Which Canadian province ranks first in waterpower resources?

14 What was the chief export of New France?

15 What are Canada's two major political parties?

16 About half of Canada's area consists of some of the oldest rock in the world. What is this mass called?

17 What are the two largest metropolitan areas of Canada?

18 What is Canada's unique role in the United Nations?

19 In which natural region is Mount Logan, the highest point in Canada (19,580 feet)?

20 Who were the United Empire Loyalists?

21 In what year was the last spike driven in the Canadian Pacific Railway?

22 Who chose Ottawa as the capital of Canada?

23 What are the rich fishing grounds off the north Atlantic coast of Canada called?

24 In what year was the Hudson's Bay Company granted a charter by King Charles II of England?

25 What is the most important statute in Canadian constitutional history?

# careers

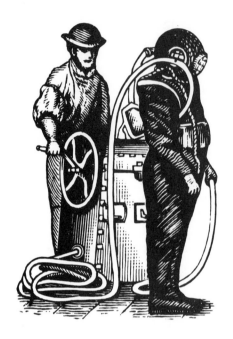

*"There is no substitute for hard work."*

1   According to 1960 figures, in what general area of work is the largest percentage of Americans employed?

2   What percentage of U.S. workers earned their living on farms in 1960?

3   What are the three largest professional fields?

4   What fraction of the U.S. work force is represented by semiskilled and unskilled workers?

5   What type of education is generally required for professional work?

6   What does a county agricultural agent do?

7   What is the technical title used by weathermen to describe their profession?

8   When most people think of rigging, they think of ships and sailing, but a high rigger is employed in an entirely different kind of work. What is it?

9   What does a milk receiver do?

10   "Mule skinners" were the men who worked with mules in the 18th and 19th centuries. What do present-day mule spinners do?

11   What is a stope?

12   How long have men been mining the earth?

13   How many people in the U.S. work in iron and steel manufacturing?

14   Where did the earliest ironworkers get their iron ore?

15   What was the average workday for a seaman in the days of sailing?

16   How often does the first mate of a modern ship stand watch?

17   Many states license two types of nurses. What are they?

18   What were probably the first organized nursing groups?

19   What kind of work does a civil engineer do?

20   What, generally, are the three areas in which a college teacher is expected to work?

21   In many states, after a medical student completes his studies in medical school, he must take a different type of training. What is this phase called?

22   What three factors are considered by the admissions committee of a medical school when they are weighing a student's application?

23   What proportion of the average newspaper staff are women?

24   What is truck farming?

25   How many commercial fishermen are there in the U.S.?

# children's literature

*"I cannot think of any work that could be more agreeable and fun than making books for children."*

1 When did the first collection of Mother Goose rhymes as we know them today appear in English?

2 What was the title of the first book in the rags-to-riches series of novels by Horatio Alger?

3 Books to please children rather than teach them were late in coming. When did they begin to proliferate?

4 What country was the setting for the international best-seller 'Anne of Green Gables'?

5 The Caldecott Medal has been awarded annually since 1938 for the most distinguished American picture book for children. Why is it named Caldecott?

6 Who composed the musical fairy tale 'Peter and the Wolf'?

7 'Millions of Cats' was one of the first fine picture books in the U.S. for young children. Who created it?

8  Why were the Grimm brothers' collected folktales called House Stories?

9  What beloved Scottish writer was known by Samoans as "Tusitala" (teller of tales)?

10  Of what national background was the collection of folktales called 'East o' the Sun and West o' the Moon'?

11  Orchard House in Concord, Mass., where 'Little Women' was written, was made a memorial in 1911. Who was the author so honored?

12  Whose illustrations helped to make Lewis Carroll's 'Alice in Wonderland' so popular when it was published in 1865?

13  Who was the Danish author who wrote more than 150 fairy tales, among them 'The Snow Queen'?

14  Who wrote 'Tale of Peter Rabbit' (1901) and in what country?

15  In what country were the Moomins created?

16  Sir James Barrie's story of a little boy who lived in a world of Indians, pirates, and fairies was a play before it was published in book form. What is the title of the play?

17  More children's literature of Asia has become available in English recently. What is the Japanese Tom Thumb story in excellent translation?

18  When were children's libraries first opened in many European countries?

19  What was the Cuban liberator José Martí's contribution to children's literature?

20  Who wrote 'Bronzeville Boys and Girls'?

21  Who was the title character of Mark Twain's most famous juvenile book?

22  Who wrote 'Visit from St. Nicholas' or 'The Night Before Christmas'?

23  What African country has been outstanding in its attention to books for children?

24  What was the first library in the U.S. to have a story hour for children?

25  What is the setting for the book 'Heidi'?

# cities of the world

*"The reason American cities are prosperous is that there is no place to sit down."*

1 Tokyo, with 9 million inhabitants, is regarded as the most populous city in the world, but what major city is regarded as among the largest in land area?

2 In which city was the world's first cinema theater established?

3 More retail clothing, dry goods, and department store business is transacted in six blocks of what famous street in what city than in any other similar area in the world?

4 The city of Washington, D.C., was laid out according to a grid plan devised by Maj. Pierre Charles L'Enfant, a French engineer who had fought in the American Revolution. What other major U.S. city also adopted this plan?

5 What modern city is shaped like a huge swept-wing airplane?

6 Name three major cities of the world that were seriously ravaged by fire.

7 In at least three modern capitals walls of the original ancient cities are still easily visible. Which are they?

8 What capital city is sacred to three major world religions?

9 Many cities have nicknames. Which city is called the "Eternal City," which the "City of Light," and which the "City of Brotherly Love"?

10 What city has a postal system that delivers brief messages anywhere in about an hour?

11 The Latin Quarter is one of the oldest parts of Paris. Why is it called the Latin Quarter?

12 Paris is famous for its boulevards, wide thoroughfares, many of which were built under Napoleon III. What was the emperor's main purpose in building wide streets.

13 What was the first city park to be established in the U.S.?

14 In what city will you find the Golden Triangle?

15 What was the original name of Mexico City and of what ancient civilization was it the capital?

16 What European capital is called the "Venice of the North" because, like Venice, Italy, it is built on islands?

17 What capital city is actually two cities with long separate histories united under a single administration only just more than 100 years ago?

18 The modern civic center is a grouping of public buildings built for what specific purposes?

19 A city is usually defined as a large, organized community with a considerable population. In what country will you find that an area will always be called a town, no matter how large or crowded it is, unless it was given the special title of city many centuries ago?

20 The largest city in one European country is completely surrounded by another country. What city is it?

21 What city was the birthplace of Christopher Columbus?

22 What city has established a special role for itself in the crusade for world peace and cooperation?

23 Which African city serves as headquarters for pan-African organizations and meetings?

24 In what city will you find the Hockey Hall of Fame?

25 What city serves as headquarters for the Royal Canadian Mounted Police?

# climate & weather

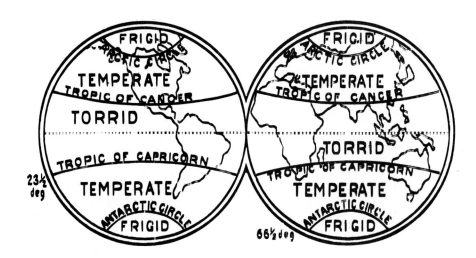

*"Four seasons fill the measure of the year."*

1 What are the two factors determining length of daylight?

2 When did temperatures on the earth as a whole reach their lowest point?

3 What is the only area in the world to receive the vertical rays of the sun?

4 What is the average annual precipitation in Death Valley in California?

5 What is an anemometer?

6   Name the science of observing and predicting the weather.

7   What is the wind speed in a hurricane or typhoon?

8   What was Nimbus III?

9   What are the principal tropical deserts in Africa?

10   In which climate type is there the difference of more than 100° between the January and June mean temperatures?

11   What is the largest highland climate zone in South America?

12   Which of the U.S. armed forces provides weather information for transoceanic ships and planes and also operates an ice patrol in the North Atlantic?

13   What was the record height achieved by kites carrying weather instruments?

14   More than one million people died in a flood in 1887. Where was it?

15   What does a barometer measure?

16   Where is the National Meteorological Center located?

17   What was the greatest rainfall recorded in a 12-month period—where and when?

18   What kind of weather should you expect if a farmer says, "When ropes twist, forget your haying"?

19   How many districts are covered by the flood-forecasting system of the National Weather Service?

20   How many inches of snow equal one inch of rain?

21   When were commercial rainmakers first able to "seed" clouds successfully?

22   What is generally considered the maximum wind velocity in a tornado?

23   Dull red sunsets are a sign of what kind of storm?

24   What is the average number of people killed by lightning in any year?

25   What is the highest temperature ever recorded in an inhabited area of the world—where and when?

# clothing

*"Every generation laughs at the old fashions, but follows religiously the new."*

1 How much filament is spun in an average silkworm cocoon?

2 When were left and right shoes first made?

3 What is the fabric jean?

4 Who were the first people to master the basic processes still used in clothing manufacture?

5 What was the first synthetic dye named?

6 In what period did dress in the Western world make a complete break with tradition?

7 Who founded the trade association that works to preserve the dominance of France in dress design?

8   What was the earliest hoop skirt?

9   Of what materials were the Greek *chitons* made?

10  Which of the coal-tar products are transformed into dyes?

11  When did dress design become a profession?

12  What feature distinguished fine Byzantine garments?

13  What was the first man-made fiber?

14  Who was Beau Brummell?

15  More than half the world's textiles are still provided by what
    fiber?

16  What is the distinction between yarn and thread?

17  What factor has been the most influential in determining the
    kind and quantity of clothing worn in different parts of the
    world?

18  Two plants, cotton and flax, are grown mainly for use in cloth.
    What are the two most important animal fibers used to make
    cloth?

19  What are tenterhooks?

20  Using the raw materials of their locality, early civilizations
    learned to make cloth. What cloth was made in Egypt, in
    Mesopotamia, in India, and in China?

21  During what period did Englishmen first wear clothing similar
    to men's clothing today?

22  Dry-cleaning establishments generally use one of two kinds of
    solvents. What are they?

23  The U.S. leads in textile manufacture, but which country is
    second?

24  What is the highest-paid trade in the garment industry?

25  What unique method of ornamentation marked the German
    Renaissance?

# communications

*"Where the press is free, and every man able to read, all is safe."*

1 In what year was the launching of the first satellite for worldwide communications?

2 Who was the U.S. photographer who patented flexible roll film?

3 What people invented torch-signaling?

4 What is the difference between telegraph and radio transmission?

5 What is the literal meaning of the word *propaganda*?

6 What are the two methods of transmitting television programs for long distances?

7   Why would space exploration probably be impossible without the help of computers?

8   In what century and where was movable type invented?

9   Upon what principle is stereophonic sound based?

10  What is a creole language?

11  What organization binds the postal systems of member countries into a vast communication network?

12  Because the earth is practically spherical, a globe represents it better than a map. What advantage, then, does the map have for viewing?

13  Who spanned the Atlantic Ocean by wireless telegraphy in 1901?

14  How did the railroad term "highball" originate?

15  What was the first weather surveillance satellite called?

16  What is cinematography?

17  Name the regulatory agency that supervises the operations of telephone systems.

18  Who invented the first telegraph system?

19  Before hieroglyphic writing evolved, how did people record events?

20  Why do airplane pilots in distress use the word *Mayday*?

21  What is a teleprinter?

22  A great seafaring and trading people of ancient times spread the alphabet to other nations. Who were those mariners?

23  When was the first wirephoto transmitted?

24  How were messages sent to Rome from the front lines during the Gallic Wars?

25  Which Amendment to the U.S. Constitution guarantees freedom of speech?

# consumer affairs & protection

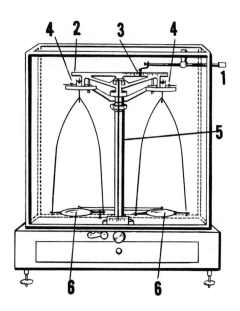

*"The buyer needs a hundred eyes, the seller not one."*

1 What are the typical carrying charges on a credit card from a department store?

2 How do newspapers deal with advertising that is fraudulent or potentially so?

3 When did bank cards come into popularity?

4 The U.S. government publishes a Consumer Price Index every month to show changes in the prices of common items such as food, clothing, and rent. What are the base years used for comparison?

5 What is the chief federal agency charged with administering pure food laws?

6 Ralph Nader is probably the best-known consumer advocate in the U.S. What was the name of his landmark book on auto safety?

7 How does the Federal Deposit Insurance Corp. protect bank deposits?

8   A bureau of weights and measures might be termed the first consumer protection agency in the U.S. When was the first such bureau established?

9   What are the disadvantages of installment buying?

10   Which country started the first mandatory program of unemployment insurance, and when?

11   Which U.S. agency has the power to forbid false advertising in some fields?

12   What is the chief means of financing the purchase of a home in the U.S.?

13   How do the 50 states ensure that insurance companies remain solvent?

14   What is a "collateral" loan?

15   When did consumers' cooperatives begin to flourish in the U.S.?

16   Where do extension home economists ply their trade of aiding consumers?

17   An important federal law passed in 1968 requires institutions to state the true interest rate on all credit transactions. What is that law called?

18   The U.S. Department of Agriculture puts its stamp of approval directly on any meat to be sold at retail in interstate commerce. What are the exact words used in the stamp?

19   What term is used to designate the highest quality grade of beef?

20   About what percentage of your food budget should be spent for produce?

21   What is the top U.S. grade for canned fruits and vegetables?

22   Supermarkets use colorful, eye-catching displays to attract the shopper's eye. What is an important aid in preventing "impulse buying" of products from such displays?

23   What percentage of "liveweight" good-grade cattle amounts to salable, edible meat?

24   What major meat product is generally sold precooked?

25   Name two ways the U.S. government regulates the quality of bread sold in retail trade.

# dance

*"On with the dance! let joy be unconfin'd:*
*No sleep till morn, when Youth and Pleasure meet*
*To chase the glowing Hours with flying feet."*

1   What kind of music made American social dancing distinctive?

2   What has research shown about the dance patterns of primitive people?

3   What kind of folk dance is 'Dive for the Oyster, Dig for the Clam'?

4   In oriental traditions, the footwork is not the most important part of the dancer's movement. What is?

5   What is the name of a celebrated Mexican courtship dance?

6   No and kabuki are Japanese dance dramas in which performers use pantomime and dance. How do the two forms differ?

7   What is ballet dancing?

8   What countries are represented by the following folk dances: polonaise, tarantella, schottische?

9   Dancing had a religious connotation in ancient times. Where are religious dances still performed in church?

10   All ballet movements start from a set number of positions. How many?

11   Why did ballerinas learn to dance on the tips of their toes?

12   What is the outstanding characteristic of modern dance?

13   Why is French the universal language of ballet?

14   Who is the leading exponent of modern dance in the U.S.?

15   Who are the best-known line dancers in the world?

16   What is choreography?

17   Many ballets from the period of 1909–29 are still popular. Who dominated ballet at that time?

18   What significant innovation did the British and American choreographers bring to ballet?

19   Who was Isadora Duncan?

20   In ballet, what is a variation?

21   Who started the use of dance as an important part of story development in musical comedy?

22   What tiny island has developed the best-known dances of any Indonesian land?

23   Why is 'Skip to Ma Lou' considered to be a play-party game and not a dance?

24   Who was the greatest dancer in Sergei Diaghilev's company?

25   What is an ethnic dance?

# discoverers & inventors

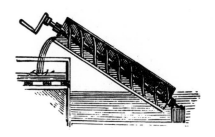

*"Invention breeds invention."*

1 Sir Alexander Fleming discovered penicillin while he was engaged in studying in a different area. What was he researching when he found the penicillin mold?

2 Who first discovered that arteries contained blood?

3 For what discovery did the German physicist Wilhelm Roentgen win the 1901 Nobel prize?

4 When did William Harvey first announce his discovery of blood circulation in the human body?

5 Who developed antiseptic surgery?

6 Robert Koch, a German physician, discovered tuberculin in 1890. It was believed at the time to be a cure for tuberculosis, but in reality it serves what other purpose?

7 Who developed the system of classification of animal and plant life that is used today?

8 Charles Darwin, who formulated the theory of evolution, was greatly inspired by a famous English book. What was it and who wrote it?

9 Who pioneered classical conditioning of animals and was one of the pioneers of the study of animal behavior?

10 In the 1930's, several important discoveries were made by physicists Ernest O. Lawrence, Sir John Cockcroft, E.T.S. Walton, Carl Anderson, and Sir James Chadwick. What area of investigation were these scientists studying?

11 While legend credits an apple with having inspired Isaac Newton to discover gravity, his theory actually developed from his questions about another spherical object. What was it?

12 What other element did Marie and Pierre Curie discover at about the same time they discovered radium?

13 Russian chemist Dmitri Mendeleev discovered that there were repeated patterns of characteristics among the physical elements. What valuable tool did he develop from this discovery?

14 An Italian astronomer made the accurate telling of time possible when he compared the swing of a pendulum with his own pulse. Who was he?

15 At what point in his life did Nicolaus Copernicus see the first copy of his revolutionary treatise on the rotation of the planets?

16 What did Clyde W. Tombaugh contribute to modern astronomy?

17 Samuel Slater is noted for having secretly brought the plans for an advanced spinning machine from England to the U.S. Who originally designed this machine?

18 Alexander Graham Bell's invention of the telephone was actually a digression from his life's work. What was his primary occupation?

19 When he died, Thomas Alva Edison had patented 1,093 inventions. For what did he take out his first patent?

20 When did German inventor Paul Nipkow first attempt to transmit images by wire and thus open the way for the development of modern television?

21 In 1785 William Withering first prescribed digitalis for treatment of heart disease. What was the source of this new drug?

22 Who discovered that smallpox could be prevented by vaccination?

23 The first man to describe the red corpuscles of the blood is better known for his pioneering work with microscopes. Who was he?

24 Louis Pasteur is renowned for having developed a treatment for rabies. What other deadly animal disease did he conquer?

25 Who was the "father of modern surgery"?

# domesticated animals

*"When I play with my cat, who knows whether she is not amusing herself with me more than I with her."*

1 After a successful period during which man domesticated many kinds of wild animals, domestication came to an abrupt end. When?

2 What was the first domesticated animal?

3 Do scientists find special meaning in the fact that most domesticated animals are meat-eaters?

4 What was the last important animal to be domesticated?

5 Why did cattle and the other domesticated animals yield so readily to man's mastery, while the majority of wild animals never did?

6 When cattle are used as work animals, what are they called?

7 How long does a cow carry a calf before it is born?

8   The llama's chief value is as a beast of burden, but the fur of two of its close relatives is highly prized. What two animals?

9   How long has the dog been a companion of man?

10  How many kinds of domesticated animals did the North American Indians have before the arrival of the Europeans?

11  What is the difference between taming and domesticating an animal?

12  In India the tail of a certain domestic animal is used as a flyswatter? What animal?

13  Which extinct ancestor of modern cattle was graphically described by Stone Age artists on the walls of France's Lascaux Cave?

14  Some of the wild forebears of domesticated animals still exist. Name one and its domesticated relative.

15  Some domesticated animals have reverted to a wild state. Name one.

16  When and where were the first horses domesticated?

17  One member of the horse family was first domesticated by the ancient Egyptians and still is used as a beast of burden. Which?

18  Of the domesticated animals one type is quite despised by the very people it serves. Which?

19  Some people are so fond of the tail fat of one kind of domesticated animal that they prefer it to butter. What is the animal, and where is it found?

20  How many head of cattle are raised in the U.S. each year?

21  A semifluid butter called ghee is made from the milk of which Asian domesticated animal?

22  Modern civilization is said to have its origins coincide with the domestication of which domestic animals?

23  One type of domestic animal also played a part in ancient rites of sin riddance. What animal?

24  The ancestors of domestic animals usually ran in herds. What North American game animal, the largest, ran in herds but was never domesticated?

25  What domestic animal is held sacred by certain people?

# earth

*"The earth, that is sufficient."*

1   The most common type of rock found in the crust of the earth was formed from molten rock under the crust. What is the crustal rock called?

2   Mt. Everest (29,028 ft.) is the highest point on earth. What is the deepest?

3   In 1902 a volcano in Martinique erupted and killed 40,000 people. What volcano?

4   Conglomerate and shale are two kinds of sedimentary rock. Name two others.

5   How old is the earth?

6   Rain is a great chemical weathering force because by the time it strikes the ground it contains two acids. What are they?

7   Granite, a common constituent of mountains, is used as a building material because of its great hardness. Which American state leads in the production of granite?

8   Diamond is the hardest mineral. Which is the softest?

9   The Appalachian Mountains are generally thought to be very old, but the range was actually uplifted twice; the first uplift was eroded to a level plain. When did the second uplift occur?

10 Is the earth composed of more land area or more ocean area?

11 The hardness of the diamond makes it extremely valuable as a gem stone. Where is the location of the sole diamond mine in the U.S.

12 Where are the world's oldest gem mines located, and what is mined there?

13 The focus of an earthquake is the part below the earth's surface where rock movements begin. At what depth was the deepest known focus of an earthquake?

14 Earth scientists think that many years ago the seven continents were united in one land mass surrounded by water. What was the name of the original continent, and how long ago did it exist?

15 Who first accurately calculated the circumference of the earth (about 25,000 miles)?

16 The earth's core is made up of what substance?

17 Why are the "horse lattitudes"—between 30° and 40° north and south latitudes—so called?

18 On Nov. 14, 1963, an underwater volcano erupted and formed a new island in the ocean. What is its name, and where is it located?

19 Minerals make up the earth's rocks. How many kinds of minerals have been discovered?

20 The surface features of the earth are constantly changing. What are the natural processes that are responsible for these changes?

21 What is the most abundant substance in the earth's atmosphere?

22 What earth locale has more rainfall than any other each year?

23 Carbon, one of the earth's most common elements, is found in two native (uncombined) forms, of which diamond is one. What is the other?

24 In the Northern Hemisphere the winds move from west to east; in the Southern Hemisphere from east to west. What is the name of the process responsible for this action?

25 Two kinds of rocks were highly valued by ancient man as tool-making materials. Which?

# europe

*"The lamps are going out all over Europe; we shall not see them lit again in our Lifetime."*

1 What is Benelux and when was it started?

2 When was Napoleon defeated at Waterloo?

3 What was the Dawes Plan?

4 Which city is nicknamed "the Venice of the North"?

5 The Magyars became the principal people of Hungary in the 10th century. What group of people were they supplanting?

6 Which European leader continued to champion nationalism, and to oppose European unity, in the 1960's?

7 Which country lost the most land in World War II?

8   In the late 19th century, three countries formed the Triple Entente to deal with Germany's growing naval strength. What were the three countries?

9   Name the two Russian rulers who built up their country's status as an international power in the 18th century.

10  How long was Mohammedanism established in Spain?

11  When did Hitler gain power in Germany?

12  In 1928 the major powers signed the Kellogg-Briand Pact. What was the aim of this pact?

13  Where did the earliest civilization begin in Europe, and when?

14  Who was Romulus?

15  Who was the leader of the Puritans in the Civil War in England?

16  What was the incident that precipitated World War I?

17  When was the Trojan War?

18  What were the three names that devolved, in succession, for the city that was the capital of the Byzantine Empire?

19  What was Metternich's crowning achievement?

20  When was the Permanent Court of International Justice established at The Hague?

21  What event in 1963 allayed European fears of Soviet nuclear power and the general possibility of a nuclear confrontation?

22  What is "Sinn Fein"?

23  Norway, Sweden, and Denmark were unified in 1397—the beginning of a long string of arrangements between and among the three. When did Norway finally become independent and free?

24  What country was known as "the mother of Parliaments" for its leadership in representative government?

25  When and why was the Thirty Years' War fought?

# explorers & settlers

*"Dr. Livingstone, I presume?"*

1 From what country did the first known explorer set out?

2 About how much of the world's land area was practically unknown at the beginning of the 19th century?

3 Whose writings about his 13th-century travels in the Far East inspired future explorers to search for a sea route to the Orient?

4 What mountain is named for an American who explored the Arkansas River in 1806?

5 In 32 observations, Robert E. Peary, the first man to reach the North Pole, met the test that proves one *is* at the pole. What is the test?

6   What U.S. physicist launched the world's first successful liquid-propellant rocket in 1926?

7   On what date did man land on the moon?

8   Who was the first explorer to reach the South Pole?

9   Identify the first space traveler.

10  What theory was Thor Heyerdahl trying to prove by his ocean journey on a balsa raft from Peru to the Tuamotu Archipelago?

11  Who was the first white man to cross Canada to the Pacific Ocean?

12  Whom do most historians believe to be the discoverer of the North American mainland?

13  Who discovered the Grand Canyon?

14  In about 800 B.C., the Phoenician seafarers and traders settled an area of North Africa and made it a powerful city. What was its name?

15  A Canadian explorer of the Arctic helped to convince the world that transarctic airlines were possible. Who was he?

16  From what country did Eric the Red take settlers to Greenland?

17  Name the French undersea explorer who pioneered in underwater color photography.

18  Utah's settlement began with the arrival of a wagon train of religious exiles. Who were they?

19  Who was the first man to orbit the earth?

20  Who were two of the great sailors who explored the New World in the service of Queen Elizabeth I of England?

21  Where was France's first permanent Canadian colony?

22  In what year was Mount Everest, "the roof of the world," finally scaled?

23  Where did the London Company establish the first permanent English settlement in North America?

24  What U.S. president sent Lewis and Clark on their expedition?

25  Whose expedition was the first to go around the world?

# food &
# nutrition

*" Other men live to eat, whereas I eat to live."*

1 What is the best source of calcium in the human diet?

2 Which is "the sunshine vitamin"?

3 Iodine is important to which part of the body?

4 Approximately how many calories are there in a tablespoon of mayonnaise?

5 Which nut is native to Australia and is now grown extensively in Hawaii?

6    Which spice provides one of the more concentrated sources of vitamin C?

7    Which countries produce the most lemons and limes?

8    What are frijoles?

9    In the Middle Ages, "trenchermen" were hearty eaters who consumed vast quantities of food at their lord's table. What did they use for trenchers, or plates?

10   Which American state leads in cheese production?

11   Which protein is found in wheat?

12   Food experts recommend minimum quantities of milk (and/or other dairy products) for people of different ages. What is the recommended minimum for teenagers?

13   What does the term "braise" mean in cooking?

14   What is the leading source of food (and of export funds, also) in Iceland?

15   Which vitamin prevents the disease pellagra?

16   What is the minimum weight set by the U.S. government for large Grade A eggs?

17   What is the recommended quantity, for one week, of citrus fruits and tomatoes for nursing mothers?

18   What is the most popular drink in the world?

19   Name the famous gourmet cook who popularized instructional television shows on cooking.

20   When did the first known advertisement for ice cream appear in the U.S.?

21   What percentage of a potato consists of carbohydrates?

22   What percentage of the U.S. fisheries catch is smoked or salted before sale?

23   Which type of lettuce is easiest to grow in a home garden?

24   What is generally considered a safe rate for losing weight?

25   Which fruit should never be refrigerated?

# games & hobbies

*"If you watch a game, it's fun. If you play it, it's recreation. If you work at it, it's golf."*

1 How many points win a game of table tennis?

2 Approximately when did the game of croquet originate?

3 Why is tennis sometimes called "lawn tennis"?

4 The British National Tournament is an important annual event in the world of tennis. Where is this tournament held?

5 Proof coins are made especially for collectors at which mint?

6  How many people can play in a game of handball?

7  One 20th-century U.S. president played the piano as a hobby—sometimes to accompany his daughter's singing. Who was he?

8  The game known as *Damenspiel* in Germany is called what in the U.S.?

9  What do the initials "O.G." mean to stamp collectors?

10  What is the slang bowling term used to describe three strikes in a row?

11  Which is the key marble in a player's collection?

12  How many balls are used in "pool," or pocket billiards?

13  Who was the first golfer to earn more than $200,000 in one season?

14  Why was the game "ninepins" changed to "tenpins"?

15  How many dominoes are there in the customary set?

16  The most popular comic strip since World War II has fostered many games, toys, and hobby materials. What is that strip?

17  What popular sport played in the Middle Ages involved birds?

18  What is Origami?

19  What does the term "still fishing" mean?

20  What two games have computers been programmed to play?

21  What is the minimum age recommended for a child's first electric train set?

22  Which of the martial arts was introduced into Japan in the 17th century and became popular in the U.S. in the 20th century?

23  The development of which type of film was a boon to amateur photographers?

24  When did the children's game Blind Man's Buff originate?

25  The chain stitch and featherstitch are used in what type of needlework?

# holidays & festivals

*"Thanksgiving Day . . . the one day that is purely American."*

1  When is Flag Day in the U.S.?

2  What important holiday is celebrated in France on July 14?

3  Guy Fawkes Day is celebrated in England on November 5. Who was Guy Fawkes?

4  What is Kuhio Day?

5  What is the English name of the Jewish holiday Yom Kippur?

6    How is Children's Day observed in Japan?

7    Who was the first U.S. president to issue a proclamation on the observance of Mother's Day?

8    Who was St. Valentine?

9    How is the date for Easter determined each year?

10   Jefferson Davis's birthday is a holiday celebrated in many Southern states. When is it?

11   Mardi Gras is a famous festival held before Lent, as in New Orleans, La. What do the French words *mardi gras* mean in English?

12   When is Thanksgiving Day observed in Canada?

13   What was the original name for Memorial Day?

14   When was December 25 established as the date for celebrating the birth of Christ?

15   When is Independence Day celebrated in Mexico?

16   When is the birthday of the late Rev. Martin Luther King, Jr.?

17   Central and northern European countries celebrate an important religious holiday on December 6. What is that day?

18   Which U.S. city is famous for its Tulip Festival?

19   When is Dominion Day in Canada?

20   May 1 has been celebrated as International Labor Day since what year?

21   When and what is Boxing Day?

22   When is the Jewish holiday Hanuka observed?

23   Will Rogers Day, November 4, is a legal holiday in which state?

24   Which famous music festival is held each year at Lenox, Mass.?

25   When was New Year's Day celebrated during the Middle Ages in Europe?

# insects & spiders

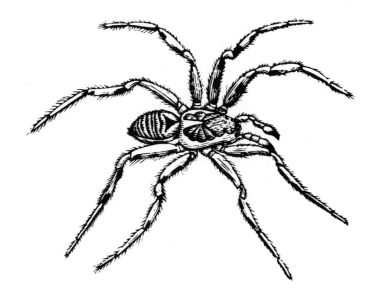

*" 'Will you walk into my parlour?' said a spider to a fly;*
*' 'Tis the prettiest little parlour that ever you did spy'."*

1  How old are the most ancient insect fossils believed to be?

2  What insect is probably the worst hazard to human health?

3  The common housefly is a pest and a disease carrier, but it does provide at least one service to man. What is this?

4  By what name, other than "insect," are these animals sometimes called?

5   How do insects breathe?

6   What insect is known as the mosquito hawk?

7   How many eyes do flies have?

8   When were cockroaches probably the most numerous insects on earth?

9   What insect is considered by the Chinese to be a creature of good omen?

10  How did a flea kill Pericles, the great leader of ancient Greece?

11  Why are the eggs of the wheel bug so unusual?

12  What insects were the first papermakers?

13  What are the policemen of the insect world?

14  What, technically, were the insects referred to in the Bible as locusts?

15  The "San José scale" insect is one of the worst pests in the U.S. Where is it believed to have come from?

16  Where did caterpillars get their name?

17  What insects were symbols of immortality in the ancient world?

18  What are the only insects to carry on organized warfare?

19  The tsetse fly is known to be a carrier of African sleeping sickness. What lesser-known disease is also carried by some species of this fly?

20  What is the largest known spider?

21  How many U.S. spiders are poisonous to human beings?

22  What European dance is named for a spider?

23  According to Greek mythology, where did spiders come from?

24  What king of Scotland was inspired to win his country's independence by a spider?

25  The "red spider," which preys on household plants, is not a true spider. What is it?

# languages & writing

| 1 | 2 | 3 | 4 | 5 | 6 | 7 | 1 | 2 | 3 | 4 | 5 | 6 | 7 |
|---|---|---|---|---|---|---|---|---|---|---|---|---|---|
| A | A A | A A A | ⚡ | | | aˡ | N | N | N | | | | n |
| B | B B | B B | | | | b | O | O | O | O | | | P |
| C | C < | C ⌐ Γ | ⌐ 7 ∧ | | | k² | P | P Γ | Γ | ⌐ | | | qᴷ |
| D | D | D Δ | ◁ ◁ | | | t³ | Q | Q | ℗ | Φ | | | r |
| E | E | E F | ⴺ | | h | R | R ℟ | R ℟ P | ◁ | | | sh |
| F | F | F | | | f | S | S | ⑀ ⑀ | W | | | t |
| G | G C | | | | | T | T | T | + X | | | |
| H | H | H ⊟ | ⊟ ⊟ | | | 4 | U | | | | | | |
| I | I | I | | | iy | V | V | V Y | | | | |
| J | I | I | | | | W | | | | | | | |
| K | K | K | | | k | X | X | X + | | | | |
| L | L ⌐ | ⌐ V | | | lr | Y | (Y) | Y | | | | |
| M | M | M M | | | m | Z | (Z) | Z I | I | | | |

*"Good heavens! I have been talking prose for over forty years without realizing it."*

1 Who introduced the interlanguage Esperanto?

2 What is a dialect?

3 The phrase "kick the bucket" is an example of which language term?

4 What is the name of the reading alphabet for the blind?

5 Which are the first two letters of the Greek alphabet?

6    What are uncials?

7    Which is the oldest living Indo-European language?

8    What are the four principal Romance languages?

9    The oldest known system of writing is Sumerian. How far back in time has Sumerian been traced?

10   Which form of the German language has prevailed officially and in literary circles?

11   Where is Pashto spoken?

12   What is connotative meaning?

13   Which ancient city is famous for its export of the writing material papyrus?

14   Approximately how many languages are spoken in Ghana?

15   The renowned rabbi Maimonides wrote mainly in which language?

16   What is the minimum number of words needed to make a sentence?

17   The Malay and Tagalog languages belong to which language family?

18   Which language was shared by the writers Cicero, Lucretius, and Juvenal?

19   What is usually the key word in a predicate?

20   Which were the last two letters to be added to the Latin alphabet?

21   When were French and English declared the official languages of Canada?

22   How did cuneiform writing get its name?

23   What language was spoken by the Aztecs?

24   How many other languages belong to the family that includes Japanese?

25   What are homophones?

# latin america

*"In that island also, which I have before said we named Española, there are mountains of very great size and beauty, vast plains, groves, and very fruitful fields, admirably adapted for tillage, pasture, and habitation."*

1  What are the two landlocked countries of Latin America?

2  More than two thirds of the Argentine people live in the fertile plain that covers about one fourth of the country? What is it called?

3  Six countries of Latin America revere a statesman and general as their liberator. Who is he?

4  What are trogons, motmots, and hoatzins?

5  Where is the Mayan temple Chichen Itzá?

6  What industry dominates Venezuela's economy?

7  Where is the geographical point that marks the joining of North and South America?

8   In nearly half the continent of South America, the people do not speak Spanish. What is their country and language?

9   Modern Mexican artists are famous for a particular kind of painting. What is it?

10   What is the world's longest continuous mountain system?

11   Who is the Chilean poet who won the Nobel prize for literature in 1945?

12   The staple food of the Mexican people is the tortilla. From what crop is it made?

13   By what designation is the racial mixture of white European and Indian known?

14   Bullfighting, Spain's favorite sport, is the main spectator sport in many Latin American countries. Name another popular sport introduced from Spain.

15   What is the difference between Hispanic America and Indo-America?

16   In 1961 two organizations were formed to further mutual economic development among Latin American countries. What do their initials—CACM and LAFTA—stand for?

17   Who is Oscar Niemeyer?

18   What kind of reform is a major rallying point for political reformers in Latin America?

19   For whom was Mexico named?

20   In which Central American countries are there ruins of Mayan civilization?

21   What is Central America's only extensive industry?

22   What is the beast of burden commonly seen along roadsides in Mexico?

23   Who was the leading champion of free public schools in Latin America?

24   In what year did Panama declare its independence from Colombia?

25   The rate of population growth in Latin America is the highest of any major region in the world. What population figure is projected for Latin America by 1990?

# leaders of the world

*"Some are born great, some achieve greatness, and some have greatness thrust upon 'em."*

1   What South American dictator was reelected to the presidency of his country after 17 years in exile?

2   What Roman leader defeated Hannibal in 202 B.C. and ended the Carthaginian threat?

3   What great Roman warrior was the author of the phrase "I came, I saw, I conquered"?

4   Who led Athens during its most brilliant and productive period?

5   Tutankhamen and Amenhotep were probably the best-known Egyptian pharaohs, but under whose leadership did the ancient empire reach its peak?

6   When Cleopatra first inherited the throne of Egypt, she was forced to share it with someone. Who?

7   Alexander the Great was a renowned conqueror, but in ancient times his father was equally famous. What was his name?

8   Who was Alexander the Great's tutor?

9   The code of Hammurabi remains a highly respected legal system. When did he rule, and where?

10  Was the famous King Solomon of Israel a real king or a legendary one?

11  How many nonreligious historians writing in the time of Jesus Christ chronicled his life and work?

12  "Count Roland," a medieval hero, died at the battle of Roncesvalles in A.D. 778. What even more famous medieval leader was his ruler?

13  What was the name of the great census that William the Conqueror ordered taken of all the lands and people in England?

14  Who was the last Stuart ruler of England?

15  Elizabeth I of England was once said to have owed her throne to another ruler, whose navy was later destroyed by hers. Who was he?

16  A single family ruled Austria from 1278 to the end of World War I. What was its name?

17  The great champion of the Protestant cause in the Thirty Years' War came to his throne when he was 17 years old. Who was he and where did he rule?

18  The man who controlled most European foreign policy and decision making in the last half of the 19th century was neither a king nor an emperor. Who was he and what was his title?

19  Which Russian ruler is credited with bringing his country from a backward and feudal kingdom to a modern state?

20  The founder of one of the most influential social movements of modern times spent most of his life in grinding poverty in London. Who was he?

21  Who ruled England for the longest period in history?

22  What was Martin Luther studying to be when he decided to renounce the world and join a religious order?

23  Who wrote a book entitled 'The Army of the Future', in which he suggested the idea of mechanized infantry, and later led resistance against a huge mechanized army?

24  Who was the prime minister of England during World War II?

25  Who, in his first term as U.S. president, called a special session of Congress and pushed through more legislation in a 99-day period than had ever been passed before?

# libraries

*"No place affords a more striking conviction of the vanity of human hopes, than a public library."*

1    How were valuable books protected in medieval libraries?

2    How does an almanac differ from a handbook?

3    How many main subjects are included in the Dewey Decimal System?

4    Name two of the famous cathedral libraries and tell what country they were in.

5    Who was Lao Tse?

6    On what part of the cards in library card catalogs is the call number listed?

7  The University of Paris, France, founded its library on the gift of a collection of books in 1250. Who was the donor?

8  What is the best-known periodical that indexes articles in other periodicals?

9  What is a library page?

10  How do academic libraries and research libraries differ?

11  What was a scriptorium?

12  In what year was the Library of Congress founded?

13  What is necessary in order to read microforms?

14  Besides bookmobiles, what are some library services for people who live in areas remote from cities?

15  Papyrus rolls shelved in ancient Roman libraries were called by a name from which came a name now given to books. What was that name?

16  What kind of librarian is classified as a media specialist?

17  In what century did today's great academic libraries start to develop?

18  How many countries are represented in the International Federation of Library Associations?

19  What is the function of a glossary?

20  How many clay tablets were there in the renowned palace library of Ashurbanipal in Assyria?

21  What is a bibliography?

22  What famous ancient libraries survived?

23  In what do libraries keep clippings from newspapers and magazines?

24  Where was the most famous library built by the ancient Greeks?

25  In 1947, the manuscripts from an ancient Hebrew library were found stored in pottery jars in a cave. What are these manuscripts called?

# mathematics

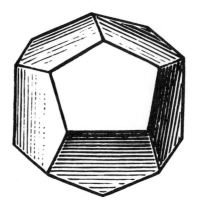

*"Euclid alone has looked on beauty bare."*

1   Who wrote the first organized work on geometry?

2   What is a *great circle*?

3   What were the three classical problems of geometry?

4   What does the word *geometry* mean?

5   The great Greek mathematician Pythagoras is known for his theorem concerning triangles. What progressive theory did he hold concerning the earth?

6   What great astronomer was first able to mathematically calculate the paths of the planets?

7   Sir Isaac Newton is one of two mathematicians credited with having discovered the calculus. Who was the other?

8   What noted mathematician wrote one of the most famous children's books of all time?

9   The winner of the 1950 Nobel prize for literature was a mathematician. Who was he?

10   Who first recognized and used the power of the lever?

11   What symbol did the ancient Egyptians use for the number 1,000?

12   Current numeration uses the decimal system, based on the number 10. What number was the Mesopotamian system based on?

13   Who developed the system of numbers that eventually replaced Roman numerals?

14   "Pi" ($\pi$) stands for the number representing the circumference of a circle whose diameter is 1. How many decimal places has pi been calculated to?

15   Why are the numbers used today called Arabic numbers?

16   There are many famous mathematical formulas that describe physical reactions. What does the formula $F=ma$ describe?

17   What is the formula that can be used to calculate the momentum of a moving object?

18   The scientific definition of work is stated in terms of a force acting on an object. What is the formula that describes this process?

19   Albert Einstein's formula $E=mc^2$ is probably the best known of all mathematical descriptions of physical processes. What does this formula represent?

20   What formula can be used to determine the area of a circle?

21   What was the *comptometer*?

22   The slide rule is based on logarithms, a kind of mathematical notation. Who invented logarithms, and when?

23   Computers are an important part of modern industry; yet their many capabilities are based on one simple mathematical process. What is the one act on which all computer calculations are based?

24   Punched cards, an essential part of most computer systems, were invented for use in a different manner. What were they intended for by their inventor?

25   In 1949 Albert Einstein completed one of the most ambitious mathematical projects in history. What was it?

# medicine & first aid

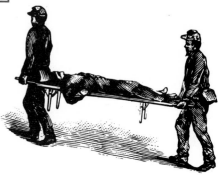

*"There are some remedies worse than the disease."*

1 The Royal Flying Doctor Service provides medical treatment to tens of thousands of persons each year in remote parts of what country?

2 After completing medical school and internship, a physician must be licensed by a state before he can practice medicine. Which state was the first to establish licensing procedures?

3 A sign is evidence detected by the physician of something wrong with the patient. What is a symptom?

4 Most of the people who work in the medical field are not doctors or nurses. Name three other careers for persons interested in medicine.

5 Although there are about 323,000 physicians practicing in the U.S., there is a severe doctor shortage. How many persons would one doctor have to serve for everyone in the country to have equal medical care?

6 Today surgery is a medical speciality requiring special postgraduate training. Who were the first surgeons?

7 The treatment of disease has two major divisions. What are they?

8 In what branch of medicine does tissue typing play an important role?

9 Louis Pasteur, the famous French scientist, did considerable research on ways to make milk germfree. When did he develop the homogenization process?

10     In what country did Walter Reed, U.S. Army surgeon and bacteriologist, do the research that led to control of yellow fever?

11     The English surgeon Joseph Lister was the first person to use various surgical instruments and to try a number of different operations. What technique did he pioneer that added considerably to the chances of the success of any operation?

12     A chemist who has received two Nobel prizes has written a book suggesting a way to prevent and cure colds. Who is this man and what does he suggest?

13     When and where was the first human heart transplant performed?

14     What group of persons in the U.S. has special hospitals to provide it with free hospital care?

15     How many years of training are required to become a doctor? To become a nurse?

16     Opportunities for careers in medicine have increased in recent years for women and members of minority groups. What percentage of recent medical school students are women and minority groups?

17     What is the Red Crescent Society?

18     What woman was instrumental in the founding of the American Red Cross?

19     In addition to providing aid to disaster victims at home, what activities does the American National Red Cross carry out in wartime?

20     How does the League of Red Cross Societies differ from the American Red Cross?

21     Knowing what to do to help someone who is hurt or suddenly ill can be very important. What else can be just as important to know to save someone's life?

22     Why is it a good idea to try to keep an injured person warm?

23     When a person collapses from heat, he may have either sunstroke or heat exhaustion. Why is it important to know which one he has?

24     What are the two best methods of artificial respiration?

25     Burns and scalds are common accidents. What is the difference between them?

# middle eastern affairs

*"A land flowing with milk and honey."*

1 Who was the first prime minister of Israel?

2 What was Israel's chief gain from the Suez crisis of 1956?

3 The Arab states relied heavily on Communist support in the 1967 war. Which Arab state departed from that policy to seek Western aid?

4 When did the Kurds begin their revolt in Iraq?

5 Jordan was once part of which country (20th century)?

6   When did the People's Republic of Southern Yemen come into being?

7   What is the capital of the United Arab Emirates?

8   The Moslem holy cities of Mecca and Medina are located in what country?

9   When did Egypt gain its independence from Great Britain?

10  After World War I, Syria was placed under the mandate of a European country. Which country was that?

11  What was the ancient Greek name for all northern Africa?

12  When did the Yemeni civil war begin?

13  Approximately how many Arabic-speaking people are there in the Middle East?

14  Which country sponsored the first Aswan Dam project?

15  Who was the original leader of the Arab League?

16  When did Israel gain control of the Golan Heights?

17  What small country on the Persian Gulf became extraordinarily wealthy after the discovery of oil there in 1937?

18  Which country controlled Libya at the start of World War II?

19  What is the average annual rainfall in Arabian countries?

20  What is probably the oldest continuously inhabited city in the world?

21  When did Hebrew tribes first settle in Palestine?

22  Which Arab country waged a bitter struggle with France for its independence from 1954 to 1962?

23  What is the largest city in Morocco?

24  Which two Arab countries merged in 1958, only to separate again in 1961?

25  What important area of Palestine was occupied by the Israelis in 1956 and then given over to the United Nations Emergency Force in 1957?

# motion pictures

*"Tell me, how did you love the picture?"*

1 Which film won the Academy Award for best picture in 1943?

2 Who was the famous Russian filmmaker who produced 'Potemkin'?

3 What is the function of a grip on a film crew?

4 Where was the world's first motion picture studio, "Black Maria"?

5 Japanese films first won wide acclaim in 1951, when 'Rashomon' won the grand prize at the Venice International Film Festival. Who directed that movie?

6 When did copyright laws first apply to motion pictures in the U.S.?

7 What was Walt Disney's first full-length animated film?

**8** Censorship of films for adults was banned in what country in 1969?

**9** Who is the only man to have won the Academy Award for best actor two years in a row?

**10** D.W. Griffith made a number of major films such as 'Birth of a Nation' and 'Intolerance'. When was 'Intolerance' released?

**11** What post-World War II artistic trend was established by the films of Roberto Rossellini and Vittorio De Sica?

**12** German director Robert Wiene in 1919 released a horror film that has become a major classic. What is that film?

**13** Which film is considered the first important documentary?

**14** Marion Michael Morrison was the given name of which famous U.S. film star?

**15** 'The Seventh Seal' is generally considered one of the greatest films ever made. Who directed it?

**16** When did the Los Angeles area first gain preeminence as a locale for filmmaking?

**17** Which film was voted best picture in the 1950 Academy Awards?

**18** Who was the leading producer of slapstick comedies, starring such notables as Charlie Chaplin and Ben Turpin, in the early 1900's?

**19** Federico Fellini of Italy has won the Oscar for best foreign film several times. Which of his films won that award in 1958?

**20** When was *Cinema-Scope* first introduced?

**21** Who played the female lead in 'The Maltese Falcon'?

**22** For which picture did Marlon Brando win his first Oscar for best acting?

**23** In making his classic, 'Citizen Kane', Orson Welles drew heavily on his theater experience and his theater colleagues. What was the drama company he founded?

**24** Who directed the character study 'The 400 Blows'?

**25** For which film did Greta Garbo win an Oscar?

# music

*" Music, the greatest good that mortals know,*
*And all of heaven we have below."*

1   What are some musical instruments mentioned in the Bible?

2   During what age did keyboard instruments—including clavier, harpsichord, and organ—come into use?

3   One of Johann Sebastian Bach's most famous works is 'The Well-Tempered Clavier'. What was Bach's purpose in writing this collection of preludes and fugues?

4   Which of the great composers of the Romantic period were concert pianists as well?

5   One of the 20th-century Russian composers, Sergei Prokofiev, created a work to introduce children to the instruments in an orchestra by using individual instruments and descriptive themes for each character in a story. What work is this?

6   What are the three main groups of musical instruments?

7   The piano, or pianoforte, is a descendant of what ancient instrument?

8   Stringed instruments are placed in three groups, according to how they are played. What are the three groups?

9   In symphony orchestras the wind instruments are usually grouped as woodwinds and brasses. How are they grouped in dance and marching bands?

10     There are single-reed instruments, such as the clarinet, and double-reed instruments, such as the oboe. What instrument uses both single and double reeds?

11     What is composer Arnold Schoenberg's contribution to modern music?

12     Some of the more novel instruments are the free-reed instruments. What are two of these instruments?

13     What wind instrument produces more tones than any other?

14     The orchestra instrument that has the lowest working range is in the same section as the instrument with the highest working range. What are these two instruments?

15     The works of composers Dvořák, Glinka, Musorgski, Grieg, and Sibelius represent a musical trend of the late 19th century. What is that trend?

16     The newest musical instruments are the electronic ones. How do most of them produce sounds?

17     The mandolin is a popular instrument for accompanying the voice in Spain and Italy. What similar instrument is popular in Latin America and Spain?

18     Today the bagpipe is the national instrument of the Scottish Highlanders. Who were among the first people to use this instrument?

19     The banjo, a popular instrument for accompanying Western and hillbilly songs, originated in what part of the world?

20     Which bugle call is blown for the ceremonial lowering of the U.S. flag?

21     What instrument does the Old Testament say was played by the seven priests who marched around Jericho "till the walls came tumbling down"?

22     According to Greek legend, one of the gods is credited with making the first lyre from a tortoise shell a few hours after his birth. Which god was it?

23     Who was responsible for improvements in the piano and for perfecting the harp into an instrument for orchestral use?

24     The two great violin makers, Andrea Amati and Antonio Stradivari, came from the same town. What is its name?

25     Jazz is a musical form that uses elements from many other kinds of music. What are some of these borrowed elements?

# myths & legends

*"Was this the face that launch'd a thousand ships
And burnt the topless towers of Ilium?"*

1   For Aeolus, legendary keeper of the four winds, a musical
    instrument was named. What is it?

2   The name of which Greek god stands as a symbol of speed and
    movement?

3   According to Irish legend, what is the origin of mermaids?

4   In Norse mythology, what were man and woman made from?

5   A legendary serpent was so horrible that it died of fright from seeing its own reflection. What was that serpent called?

6   Who was Gilgamesh?

7   What did the ancient Greeks call their king of the underworld?

8   Who had the idea for the hollow wooden horse in which Greek troops entered Troy?

9   According to Polynesian legend, who fished up the islands of the South Pacific?

10   Who was Cupid's mother?

11   What was the first written record of the Greek mythology?

12   What was the Greek goddess Artemis called by the Romans?

13   Of the American Indians, which civilization had a hummingbird-god?

14   The Greek gods lived on Mount Olympus. Where did the Norse gods live?

15   What are trolls?

16   Why was Athens, Greece, named for the goddess Athena?

17   What are the Eddas?

18   Who was the legendary black railroad construction worker—the "steel-driving man"?

19   Aeneas, legendary Trojan war hero, was celebrated in the 'Aeneid'. What ancient Roman poet composed it?

20   In Scandinavian myth, who was the father of the gods?

21   Who best captured the essence of the mass of legends about King Arthur?

22   Who was the most popular god in Egyptian mythology?

23   In ancient Rome each family had its own god who was the spirit of an ancestor. What was it known as?

24   Name a legendary lumberjack of American folklore.

25   From whose gods came the names of the days of the week (in the English language)?

# national parks

*"The Nation behaves well if it treats the natural resources as assets which it must turn over to the next generation increased, and not impaired, in value."*

1   What was the first U.S. national park to be officially established?

2   Approximately how many national parks are there in the world?

3   Africa's national parks preserve large tracts of land in a natural state; what other important purpose do they serve?

4   By what process are U.S. national parks officially created?

5   What are the three types of national park areas in Canada?

6   What Canadian national historic park honors a world-famous inventor?

7   What was the first national seashore established in the U.S.?

8   A unique breed of wild ponies live in a U.S. national park area. What is the name used for these horses and where do they live?

9    What U.S. national monument shows the longest record of human cultural progress in the southwestern U.S.?

10    A U.S. national historic park stands on a site where social outcasts were once sent. Where is it?

11    What area, now a U.S. national monument, served as a rugged natural fortress for American Indians who were engaged in a bitter struggle with the U.S. Army?

12    Which U.S. national park is still largely unexplored?

13    What is unique about Olympic National Park in the state of Washington?

14    One of Colorado's national park areas is named Mesa Verde, or "Green Table" in Spanish. To what does this name refer?

15    Both the Canadian and the U.S. national park systems include a theater among their domains. Why are these two structures famous?

16    Which African national park shelters many wildebeest, zebra, and gazelle herds?

17    In which English national park can some of the oldest mountains in Europe be found?

18    Which European national park is named for a semiprecious stone that is found in its vicinity?

19    Which U.S. national park contains two active volcanoes?

20    Where was the first international park in Europe established?

21    What is Italy's largest national park, and in what part of the country is it located?

22    Daniel Defoe's novel 'Robinson Crusoe' is based on a true story of a man's survival. In what area, now a South American national park, did this struggle for life occur?

23    What South American national park, which rests on an international boundary, includes one of the world's most famous waterfalls?

24    Longfellow's poem 'Evangeline' tells the tragic story of the expulsion of the French-speaking Acadians from Canada. What national historic park also marks this event?

25    What U.S. national park's name honors both a unique species of tree and a Cherokee Indian leader?

# oceans & islands

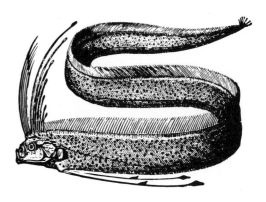

*"The sea never changes and its works, for all the talk of men, are wrapped in mystery."*

1  What part of the earth's total area is occupied by the Pacific Ocean?

2  Which is the largest island among the group included in the state of Hawaii?

3  Where is the deepest known spot in the Atlantic Ocean?

4  How high does the tide rise in the Bay of Fundy (Canada)?

5  On which island is the grave of Algernon Swinburne located?

6  How long is the Great Barrier Reef of Australia?

7  Greenland is the largest island in the world. What is the second largest?

8  Agana is the capital of which island?

9  What do the Bermudas and New Caledonia have in common physically?

10  What is the Gulf Stream?

11  How many islands are there in the Galápagos chain?

12  The Shackleton Ice Shelf of Antarctica borders on which ocean?

13  The mutiny on the ship HMS *Bounty* centered on what island?

14  What is the general name for any coral island not attached to visible land?

15  Why does the Pacific Ocean appear to be "bluer" in color than the Atlantic?

16  Which is the largest island in the West Indies?

17  How many islands are there in the Pacific Ocean?

18  How did the Canary Islands come to be so named?

19  Which are the two most abundant chemical elements in the ocean?

20  The Virgin Islands of the U.S. consist of 3 major isles and about 50 islets. What are the 3 major isles?

21  What was the name of the famous British research ship that cruised the oceans from 1872 to 1876, gathering information that formed the basis for the science of oceanography?

22  What is the greatest depth to which a free-swimming diver can descend in an ocean—without special breathing equipment?

23  What is the island nation in the Mediterranean that has been suffering from civil strife for at least ten continuous years (much longer intermittently)?

24  On which group of islands did Charles Darwin find unusual animal and plant species that helped him form his theory of evolution?

25  Where are the Pescadores Islands?

# painting & the graphic arts

*"Artists don't see the world the way it wants to be seen and the world reciprocates."*

1    Which Mexican artist painted 'Echo of a Scream'?

2    What is the name of the most famous painting by the *pointillist* artist Georges Seurat?

3    Where was Pablo Picasso born?

4    What is the name of Michelangelo's only easel painting?

5    When did Rembrandt live?

6    Most Japanese prints are made by what process?

7    Name two brothers who were renowned painters in Flanders in the early 15th century.

8 Who did the surrealist oil painting 'The Persistence of Memory'?

9 Which process was used extensively by the French artist Honoré Daumier in creating his graphics?

10 Approximately how many paintings were done by Vincent Van Gogh in his lifetime?

11 Which pop artist has used a comic-strip image in much of his work?

12 When did Da Vinci paint the 'Mona Lisa'?

13 A prehistoric drawing, given the name 'The Stag Frieze', was found on a wall in the Lascaux caves in France. What is the earliest date generally assigned to this work?

14 Which early American painter is especially known for his portraits of George Washington?

15 Who painted the impressionist master work 'Two Little Circus Girls'?

16 An American-born painter sued English critic John Ruskin for libel, after Ruskin savagely attacked his work. Who was that painter?

17 Who is the contemporary black artist known particularly for his collages?

18 Where was artist Marc Chagall born?

19 A French impressionist painter often called the "father of modern painting" was a failure in his own time and had to turn to writer Émile Zola for money to survive. Who was he?

20 What is a burin?

21 The work of Jackson Pollock belongs to which school of painting?

22 Who was Domenikos Theotokopoulos?

23 Which famous woman painter was born in Pittsburgh, Pa., but lived and worked in Paris?

24 Victor Vasarely is known for which style of art?

25 A great artist of 16th-century Venice was known especially for his portraits. Who was he?

# physiology & health

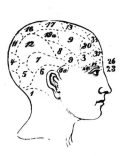

*"Good health is a prerequisite to the enjoyment of the 'pursuit of happiness'."*

1  All of the blood cells are formed in the bone marrow, but one type must complete its development in another part of the body. Which one and where?

2  How long does it take for antibodies to begin fighting against an infection?

3  Penicillin, the first antibiotic, was first mass-produced in the 1940's, but even earlier another powerful infection-fighting drug was available. What was it?

4  Measles, mumps, chicken pox, and polio were once common childhood diseases. Vaccination can now prevent most of them. Which of these virus-caused diseases is not currently preventable by vaccine?

5  Cancer is the second most common cause of death in the U.S. and Canada. What disease ranks first?

6  A person's physical characteristics are determined by his genetic code, the varying sequence of only four chemicals that form paired bases in the DNA of a cell's nucleus. What are the four chemical bases?

7  All cells in the body have the ability to become any other type of cell. Does this mean that all cells have the same chromosomes?

8  The central nervous system carries nerve signals to and from the brain and various parts of the body. What vital functions are not regulated by the CNS?

9  For nine months a baby develops in the well-protected environment within the mother's body. How do nourishment and oxygen get to the baby?

10 Kwashiorkor is a strangely named disease that is common in what highly industrialized country?

11 The average person will have 200 bones in the body or may have as many as 212. Where might these extra bones be found?

12 Muscles can be either striped or smooth. Which are striped and which are smooth?

13 How does the chest cavity get bigger when a person breathes in?

14 Hormones, which govern many bodily activities, are produced in the endocrine glands. What is the chief endocrine gland?

15 Which of the glands provides the hormones that stimulate the heart or other bodily functions in times of stress?

16 Sweat can pour out onto the surface of the skin and keep it cool by evaporation, and nerves in the skin can make a person aware of things outside the body. What can be absorbed into the body through the skin?

17 In what part of the body do you find the medulla oblongata, the mandible, and the pons?

18 In what part of the body do you find the intercostal muscle, the scapula, and the aorta?

19 In what part of the body do you find the saphenous vein, the quadriceps femoris, and the femur?

20 What function does the spleen have?

21 What disease does a person have when the body cannot make proper use of the sugars and starches in food?

22 What disease does a person have when the air passages in the lungs contain too much mucus?

23 What condition may result from the lack of use of a part of the body?

24 Some people believe that certain parts of the DNA that control rapid cell division before birth become locked up by chemical repressors after their use is past, but in some people something happens to free this genetic message so that cells will again behave as they did in the embryo. What disease are they talking about?

25 What disease was once thought to be caused by a blood clot in an artery but is now known to result from a lack of oxygen in a muscle?

# plants

*"Rose is a rose is a rose is a rose."*

1   Where is the only place on earth one cannot find a growing plant?

2   What are the principal characteristics that plants have that animals do not have?

3   The oldest living thing on earth is a tree that has been growing in California for more than 4,600 years. What kind of tree is it?

4   Why do leaves usually turn their upper surfaces toward the sun?

5   What would happen if the stomata, the tiny openings that permit gases to enter a leaf and water and gases to leave, were on the side of the leaf exposed to the sun?

6   Some plants, such as mistletoe and mushrooms, lack chlorophyll and are colorless. How do they live?

7   If you plant a seed sideways, which direction will the sprouting root go?

8   Most of the water that enters a plant through its roots passes out through the leaves by a process called transpiration. How much water does a single oak tree give off in one day?

9   Plants fall into three general groups—trees, shrubs, and herbs. In which category would you place the banana plant?

10  Two sets of tubes in plant stems carry water and minerals upward from the roots and sugars downward from the leaves. What are these tubes called?

11  What purpose does the pith, the center of a tree stem, have?

12  Cambium is the growing layer of stems and accounts for their growth in diameter. What happens to those plants that do not have cambium?

13  What are the brown or black dots that can be found on the undersides of fern leaves?

14 The process of making new plants by means of seeds took millions of years to evolve. What were the first plants to develop this ability?

15 A potato plant can be grown from a seed. Why, then, is it better to use vegetative reproduction instead and grow the plant from the tuber?

16 Although plants cannot move freely, they can twist, bend, and grow in response to stimuli. What is this kind of movement called?

17 To what family of plants does Spanish moss, which hangs on trees in the Southern states, belong?

18 Air plants, such as orchids and mosses, lie on branches of trees in tropical areas. They live entirely on what they get out of the air and do not feed off the trees as parasite plants do. Why, then, do they cling to the trees?

19 In many cases very different plants will form natural partnerships. For example, bacteria supply alfalfa and other legumes with nitrates and get carbon-made foods in return. What is this type of partnership called?

20 Why do tree leaves change color in the autumn?

21 Why are the plants in eastern Asia and North America closely related?

22 Many common vegetables are cultivated only by man and are unknown in the wild state. Cabbage, cauliflower, kohlrabi, broccoli, and Brussels sprouts, however, can all be traced back to a single plant. What is this plant?

23 Modern plant breeding to increase usefulness, disease or weather resistance, or other desirable traits is based on the laws of heredity first worked out by an Austrian monk, Gregor Mendel. What plant did Mendel use for his experiments?

24 In 1930 the U.S. government passed a law giving breeders of new plants the protection of patents for their products. What was the first plant protected in this way?

25 Long-day plants will flower only when the day is 12 or more hours in length, while short-day plants begin to flower when the day is less than 12 hours long. What is one common plant that is not bothered by these photoperiod conditions and will flower under a wide range of daylight conditions?

# polar regions

*"I felt the keenest exhilaration, and even exultation, as I climbed over the pressure ridge and breasted the keen air sweeping over the mighty ice, pure and straight from the Pole itself."*

1  What did the Russian inhabitants of the Alaskan settlement at Sitka in the early 1800's call their home?

2  The Bering Sea separates Alaska and the Aleutians from the Soviet Union. Who explored these waters before Vitus Bering did?

3  What peculiar celebration takes place in Nenana, Alaska, each year?

4  When was the first undersea crossing of the North Pole?

5  What geological formation on Ross Island, Antarctica, seems to be an oddity for the region?

6  There is an oasislike area of Antarctica that is free of ice. What kinds of wildlife live there?

7    Who are the native peoples of Antarctica?

8    There are indications that Antarctica was not always a glacial region. What kind of climate once prevailed there?

9    Admiral Richard Byrd was one of the pioneers of polar exploration. What did he call the large section of Antarctica that he claimed for the U.S.?

10   At which pole do polar bears live?

11   What bear is named after the Arctic island on which it lives?

12   How tall were prehistoric penguins?

13   Penguins are found in large numbers in Antarctica. Where else do they live?

14   What is "white out" and why is it dangerous to polar air explorers?

15   Who was probably the first polar explorer?

16   The bitterly cold weather of the polar regions caused the deaths of many explorers, but what killed 16 members of A.W. Greely's Arctic party in 1881?

17   What is pelagic hunting?

18   Where in the U.S. are the skins of fur seals that are taken in sanctioned hunts processed?

19   What is Siberia named for?

20   How large is Siberia as compared to the U.S.?

21   The last lines written by a dying polar explorer were, "It seems a pity but I cannot write any more." Who was he and when did he die?

22   The Vikings were probably the first people to extensively explore the Arctic. What does the name Viking come from?

23   Who were the first explorers to reach the North and South poles?

24   Of what nationality are the Lapps of Arctic Europe?

25   How many months of the year is Hudson Bay frozen over?

# religions of the world

*"Every religion is good that teaches man to be good."*

1 Which was the first great monotheistic religion?

2 What is the chief religion of India?

3 In what country did Buddhism originate?

4 What is the name of Mohammed's sacred book?

5 Which religion claims the greatest number of followers worldwide?

6 In 1867 Japan adopted a state religion that was repudiated by the emperor after World War II. What was that religion?

7   In what country did the custom of using a Christmas tree begin?

8   Who was the Chinese philosopher whose system of ethics is commonly considered a religion?

9   Who was the Roman ruler who began a major persecution of Christians in the year 64?

10   Who was the leader of the Reformation in Switzerland?

11   What is the holy city of Islam?

12   Two religious leaders were killed by a mob in Carthage, Ill., in 1844. Which religion did they represent?

13   What is the name of the service that marks the coming of age for Jewish boys?

14   What is the Quaker group organized in the U.S. to provide relief and service projects around the world?

15   For which religious denomination did Johann Sebastian Bach write his music?

16   In ancient Greece, which god was thought to rule the waters of the earth?

17   Where is the most famous shrine to the Madonna?

18   The 'Epic of Gilgamesh', possibly 5,000 years old, tells the story of a semidivine ruler. In what ancient city was the story found?

19   What group was attacked in the Massacre of St. Bartholomew in the 16th century?

20   How many martyrs are included in the records of the Roman Catholic Church?

21   Which Indian tribe makes sand paintings for religious purposes?

22   When was the ecumenical World Council of Churches formed?

23   Who was the famous Protestant missionary who worked in Africa?

24   In what city was the Church of Christ, Scientist, founded?

25   The Eastern Orthodox, or Greek, church and the Roman church split apart in a great schism. When did that occur?

# reptiles &
# prehistoric
# animals

*"It is the wisdom of the crocodiles, that shed tears when they would devour."*

1   Most people think of dinosaurs as being giant beasts, but the first dinosaurs were about the size of which modern animal?

2   Most of the major groups of animals are believed to have evolved during the Paleozoic era. How long ago was it?

3   Which was the largest dinosaur of all?

4   The savage Tyrannosaurus and other formidable reptiles prospered for more than 50 million years and then disappeared. Why?

5   What dinosaur looked and acted like an ostrich?

6   The elephantlike mammoths and mastodons are well known because whole frozen carcasses have been recovered. Have the bodies of any other prehistoric animals been uncovered intact?

7   The first horses had four front toes and three hind toes. How long ago did they live?

8   Which dinosaur had the smallest brain?

9   Which of the prehistoric reptiles could fly?

10  Where are the world's largest known dinosaur bone deposits located?

11  In what desert did the famous explorer Roy Chapman Andrews discover dinosaur eggs that were several million years old?

12  The largest land mammals lived in prehistoric times. What were they?

13  Trachodon was a plant eater with a ducklike bill containing numerous teeth. How many?

14  What kind of animals were the first to inhabit the land?

15  When and where did "giant pigs" that grew six feet high live?

16  Many prehistoric animals were much larger than their modern counterparts. What was the wingspan of dragonflies that lived during the Coal Age?

17  What insect has changed little since prehistoric times?

18  Which reptile of the Chalk Age greatly resembled its modern descendant?

19  How did the long-necked sea-living dinosaurs of the Jurassic period snare their prey?

20  Although the woolly mammoth seemed well adapted to the cold glacial areas of the Northern Hemisphere some 10,000 years ago, it died out. Why?

21  From what predecessor group and when did mammals evolve?

22  How do scientists know the age of prehistoric fossils?

23  When did the first prehistoric men emerge?

24  What land-living dinosaur looked like a sailfish?

25  A prehistoric fish thought extinct for millions of years was found in 1938 to still exist. What is it called?

# rivers & dams

*"It is with rivers as it is with people: the greatest are not always the most agreeable nor the best to live with."*

1 In what American state does the Rio Grande rise?

2 What is a sluice?

3 In what country is the first dam that furnishes hydroelectric power from ocean tides?

4 Between what rivers did the earliest known civilization flourish?

5 How did Boulder City, Nev., originate?

6   On the average, how much soil does the Mississippi River dump into the ocean each year?

7   The Amazon is the world's longest river. How does the Nile rank?

8   What river and its tributaries make up Europe's busiest waterway?

9   In which two ways do rivers shape land surfaces?

10   What is a cofferdam?

11   What river is sacred to millions of Hindus, and why?

12   What causes a flash flood?

13   What organizations generally build federal dams in the U.S.?

14   What is Europe's longest river?

15   What are oxbow lakes?

16   Where does the Ohio River begin?

17   For what purpose is the Soviet Union building Nurek, the world's highest dam?

18   Lake Mead stores more than a two-year normal flow of the Colorado River. How was this vast lake created?

19   What is England's most important river?

20   Besides irrigation, for what purposes are dams built?

21   When was Egypt's Aswan Dam finished?

22   What is the storage volume of Tennessee Valley Authority dams?

23   What river is the largest source of hydroelectric power in North America?

24   Which dam design holds back the water by its own weight and requires the least maintenance?

25   On what river is Paris, France?

# sculpture

*"The more the marble wastes, the more the statue grows."*

1   In ancient and medieval times, what was the source of style, subject matter, and inspiration for sculptors?

2   What majestic statue is considered to be Michelangelo's masterpiece?

3   What terms are used to identify Alexander Calder's abstract sculptures?

4   What is the most versatile metal for casting?

5   As early as 1909 an influential artist was doing work in sculpture akin to his cubist paintings. Who was he?

6   What external element is necessary for the appreciation of sculpture?

7   The Greek sculptor Phidias created the giant statue of Athena for the Parthenon. Of what was it carved?

8   Name the Romanian-born sculptor who pioneered in the use of abstract forms.

9   Who was Jean Goujon?

10  François Rodin popularized a rugged, expressive style. With what group of bronze figures did he probably reach his peak?

11  What Florentine sculptor is known as the father of Renaissance art?

12  In the work of what modern English sculptor is space, as an element to be molded and shaped, as important as mass?

13  What Italian Renaissance sculptor brought relief sculpture to its highest level?

14  What modern Swedish sculptor carried on the tradition of 17th- and 18th-century fountain sculpture?

15  Who created the figure of Abraham Lincoln in the Washington, D.C., Lincoln Memorial?

16  What modern sculptor carved massive and sometimes grotesque figures expressing what he called the "problems of man?"

17  What American sculptor created the 'Prometheus' fountain in Rockefeller Center, New York City?

18  What was the purpose of the chimeras on Notre Dame Cathedral?

19  What method of casting did Benvenuto Cellini make famous?

20  Who was the sculptor that specialized in cowboys and Indians and their horses?

21  What is the function of *distortion* in sculpture?

22  What school of sculpture did Alberto Giacometti represent?

23  From about 1100 B.C. to 250 B.C., master craftsmen were producing bronze sculpture of a quality still unsurpassed. Where did they live?

24  What is terra cotta?

25  'Kneeling Woman' is a graceful example of the work done by an expressive German sculptor who studied with Rodin. Who was he?

# team sports

*"Pro football is like nuclear warfare. There are no winners, only survivors."*

1  How many regular-season games are scheduled for each major league baseball team?

2  In what year was the first All-Star baseball game between the National and American leagues played?

3  What is the maximum number of players a major league baseball team can carry?

4  What major league baseball player holds the record for the highest batting average for one season, and what was the average?

5  Where is the Baseball Hall of Fame located?

6   Who was the first baseball commissioner?

7   What Canadian city is represented in major league baseball?

8   What major league baseball team has won the most World Series?

9   How high above the floor are the goals in basketball?

10  Who invented the game of basketball?

11  How many free throws does a basketball player receive when he is fouled while not in the act of shooting?

12  How long are the quarters in high school basketball?

13  How long is a football field?

14  A safety in football is worth how many points?

15  A football team that is charged with "clipping" is penalized how many yards?

16  In what city is college football's Rose Bowl game played?

17  What two colleges played in the first American intercollegiate football game?

18  What professional football team won the first Super Bowl game?

19  How many players constitute a football "backfield"?

20  How long do field hockey games last?

21  How many players are there on a soccer team?

22  How many chukkers (periods) are in a polo match?

23  How many players are there on a volleyball team?

24  When was volleyball invented?

25  How many points does a volleyball team have to score to win a game?

# theater & drama

*"Drama—what literature does at night."*

1 Did William Shakespeare ever act in his own plays?

2 With what subject matter did miracle plays deal?

3 Where did the drama of the Western world originate?

4 In acting, what is "the method"?

5 The most popular actors in the 1800's included Ellen Terry, Sarah Bernhardt, and Edwin Booth. In what country was each born?

6 The first great modern playwright was Norwegian. What was his name?

7 What poet, sometimes known as the father of English tragedy, wrote 'The Tragical History of Dr. Faustus'?

8 Who wrote 'William Tell'?

9 The works of two French tragic dramatists of the 17th century still live. Who are they?

10 Oscar Wilde was probably the wittiest man of the Victorian Era. Which one of his plays is still popular?

11 What is the most effective tool for establishing mood and atmosphere in the theater?

12 Who was Pedro Calderón de la Barca?

13 The popular musical play and movie 'Carousel' was adapted from 'Liliom', by Hungary's leading playwright. Who was he?

14 Which great playwright of the Irish Renaissance in literature wrote 'The Playboy of the Western World'?

15 Lorraine Hansberry wrote a fine play about a black family in a multiracial society. What is its name?

16 Which modern French dramatist wrote 'Waltz of the Toreadors'?

17 What is the home country of the Abbey Players?

18 Who wrote 'The Cherry Orchard' and 'Three Sisters'?

19 Who wrote 'Pygmalion', the play from which the musical comedy 'My Fair Lady' was adapted?

20 In the theater, what is a flat?

21 Name the two dramatists who dominated the American theater in the 1940's and 1950's.

22 What is the difference between a farce and a comedy of manners?

23 The first performances of many of Shakespeare's tragedies were staged in a theater that opened in London in 1599. What was its name?

24 About when did drama in the U.S. become a major literary form, and who was largely responsible?

25 Who are two stock comic characters in commedia dell'arte?

# tools

*" Man is a tool-making animal."*

1 What is the machine tool used to perform turning operations?

2 When did blade tools apparently make their first appearance in history?

3 Which is the most versatile kind of drill press?

4 Who is generally credited with the invention of the first practical sewing machine?

5 What is the large machine used to dig soil from the bottom of bodies of water?

6   The punch press is widely used in which industry?

7   Which kind of hand saw is used to cut metal?

8   Tools from the Paleolithic era have been discovered in the Far East. What were they made of?

9   What complex device is at the heart of the "new industrial revolution" developing since World War II?

10  Who is credited with the discovery of the compound microscope?

11  What is a ball-peen hammer used for?

12  When was the first power loom for weaving cloth installed in the U.S.?

13  What is "tolerance" in manufacturing?

14  A vernier scale is found on what tool?

15  What is the chief use for photoelectric cells in automated machinery?

16  About how many kinds of machine tools are in use in modern U.S. industry?

17  What name do anthropologists give to any chunk of raw material suitable for fashioning tools?

18  What are the two main styles of type found on U.S. typewriters?

19  Name the most effective man-made abrasives used in grinding machines.

20  Which is the most common industrial method for making plastic tools?

21  What is an important safety device to be utilized while operating a grinding or chipping machine?

22  What tool is used by campers for splitting firewood?

23  Who developed the first successful milling machine?

24  When did the "projectile-point" industry begin in the Americas?

25  What was the average work week in 1850—before machine tools came into widespread use?

# transportation & travel

*"All travelling becomes dull in exact proportion to its rapidity."*

1 Transportation usually means the movement of people and goods. When can transportation be an end in itself?

2 What is the most expensive and least efficient carrier of goods?

3 Is the flow of traffic greater between two places that are far apart or close together?

4 Transportation facilities are often built before there is an economic need for them. What two projects were completed by 1825 to open up to settlement vast sections of the U.S.?

5 Before the use of sails to harness the wind, what were the earliest watercraft made of?

6 The leading commodity in international trade is carried in a vessel that accounts for about half of the tonnage capacity of all oceangoing merchant ships. What is the product and ship?

7 When were the earliest long-distance overland trade routes established?

8 Which form of transportation handles the largest volume of freight in the U.S., and which receives the most revenues?

9 Coastal tankers and railroad tankcars used to carry crude oil and petroleum products. What has largely replaced them?

10 Steam power to drive vehicles was a most successful and enduring means of water transportation. To what use was it first applied?

11 Robert Fulton is credited with having established the first successful steamboat service, on the Hudson River in 1807, but who was the first person to try this and when?

12 Who established the first regularly scheduled steamship line between England and North America?

13 A large container ship first built in large numbers in the 1960's requires less loading and unloading time than a regular freighter. How many conventional vessels can it replace?

14 Terminals often must be huge to accommodate the goods being transferred in them. How much adjoining land is required for assembling and distributing cargo carried on a container ship?

15 On the first railroads men and animals pushed wagons along wooden tracks. When and where was this first done?

16 When was the first transcontinental railroad route to the U.S. Pacific coast completed?

17 In the early 1970's there were about 200 daily intercity passenger trains in the U.S. How many had there been 30 years before?

18 Before it was closed to traffic in 1967, the Suez Canal was a major sea-traffic link between the European and Indian Ocean trade routes. What route became a substitute?

19 How many miles of surfaced highways are there in the U.S.?

20 Limited-access highways were not an American invention. Who were the first people to build them?

21 When and where were the first subways built?

22 All-water transportation routes via southern Africa, the Panama Canal, or the Suez Canal used to be the principal link between such distant markets as Japan and Europe or the western U. S. and Europe. What made land–sea combination routes between such distant places increasingly competitive?

23 The automobile was responsible for the paving of many roads. What was the reason for paving them as early as the 1890's, when automobiles were not yet a serious form of transportation?

24 Orville and Wilbur Wright accomplished the first successful manned, engine-powered flight in a heavier-than-air craft. What was their principal occupation?

25 What are the most heavily used air routes in the U.S.?

# united states

*"America is a state of the mind—a point of view—a love of moving on—beyond the next hill—the next filling station—the next frontier. Expanding—growing—living beyond the horizon."*

1 How many countries in the world exceed the U.S. in land area?

2 What is the average growing season in the Alaska Panhandle?

3 New York state contains what part of the total U.S. population?

4 The name Massachusetts comes from two Indian words. What do they mean?

5 What was the increase in life expectancy in the U.S. from 1900 to 1967?

6  Which is the Cornhusker State?

7  What is the official U.S. bird?

8  In what state is the geographic center of the U.S.?

9  Where is the most extensive dinosaur collection in the U.S.?

10  Hugo Black and George Washington Carver are primarily associated with which state?

11  What is the state bird of New Mexico?

12  What is the lowest point in the U.S.?

13  Where is Haleakala National Park?

14  The reverse side of the Great Seal of the U.S. bears the words "Annuit Coeptis." What does that phrase mean?

15  Which state has adopted the black-eyed Susan as its official flower?

16  Who designed the Statue of Liberty?

17  Where is the U.S. Merchant Marine Academy located?

18  Which amendment to the U.S. Constitution limits the president to two terms?

19  On a per capita basis, which state boasts the highest number of patents granted to its inventors?

20  Which state adopted Stephen Foster's "Swanee River" as its official song?

21  What type of product is the leading export of the U.S.?

22  What percentage of the U.S. population was counted as rural in the 1970 census?

23  What is the address of the White House?

24  Which state customarily raises the largest cotton crop in modern times?

25  According to the U.S. census for 1970, what was the average number of persons per square mile of the country?

# water life

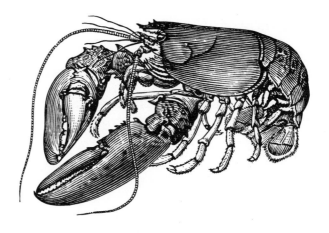

" 'Will you walk a little faster?' said a whiting to a
    snail.
'There's a porpoise close behind us, and he's treading on my
    tail'."

1 What is the organ that most fish use for breathing?

2 Caviar is an important product of the sturgeon. What is another?

3 What fish's life cycle was a major factor in determining the living patterns of the Chinook Indians?

4 What was the armor plate of the gar once used for?

5   What is the largest member of the pike family?

6   Why should sticklebacks not be included in aquariums?

7   What fish is honored by a carving in the Massachusetts State House?

8   What fish is known as the "silver king"?

9   How does the torpedo fish defend itself?

10  What sea animals are probably the subjects of most sea monster legends?

11  The octopus and the squid are related to each other; what lesser known, nonshelled animal is closely related to both of them?

12  Do all starfish have five arms?

13  The shell of the sand dollar, when found on the beach, is gray and lifeless. What color are these animals when living?

14  What sea animal has the largest shell?

15  What is the most ferocious of all sharks?

16  What are "mermaids' purses"?

17  What kind of animal is the sea horse?

18  What water animal was responsible for the almost total destruction of the Lake Michigan and Lake Huron trout fisheries?

19  Where are the world's greatest lobster waters?

20  To what other kind of animal is the horseshoe crab closely related?

21  What animals built the Great Barrier Reef of Australia?

22  The most primitive of the multicelled animals lives in water. What is it?

23  What looks like a cross between a snail and a squid and has a unique vision system?

24  Who thought that young eels grew spontaneously from mud?

25  The most abundant form of sea life is also the most important; what is it?

# winter & water sports

*"There is nothing—absolutely nothing—half so much worth doing as simply messing about in boats."*

1 What is the name of the first practical method for teaching skiing?

2 Which team won the Stanley Cup for five consecutive hockey seasons beginning with 1955–56?

3 What is Scotland's national winter sport?

4 A standard springboard for sport diving is made from what kind of wood?

5   What is the minimum vertical drop for a giant slalom in Olympic competition?

6   Where did surfing originate?

7   What is the regulation weight for an ice hockey puck?

8   How many sails does a catboat have?

9   What is the most famous international yachting competition, and when did it begin?

10   What is a common nickname for snowshoes?

11   Iceboats on the Hudson River conduct informal races with what type of vehicle?

12   When were the Winter Olympics first staged?

13   The catamaran design has been widely adopted by modern boatbuilders. Where did catamarans originate?

14   What is the swimming stroke adapted from the breast stroke and used mainly for racing?

15   The American Water Ski Association holds national tournaments that focus on three major events. What are the events?

16   How did the Head ski differ from earlier skis?

17   How many players are there on a water polo team?

18   Who popularized the outboard motor in the U.S.?

19   In competitive rowing, how many oars are used by each man?

20   Where is the Hockey Hall of Fame located?

21   Which national U.S. organization offers a widely respected program of water safety instruction?

22   Who developed the aqualung?

23   Bobby Hull joined the Winnipeg Jets hockey team in 1972, in a widely publicized deal. On what team did he develop his reputation?

24   Which boat rig is considered best for racing?

25   How does the blade on a figure skate differ from that on other types of skates?

# women & women's rights

*"The capacity of the female mind for studies of the highest order cannot be doubted, having been sufficiently illustrated by its works of genius, of erudition, and of science."*

1 Who was the first woman to be elected to the U.S. House of Representatives?

2 Approximately how many women served in the U.S. Army and Navy during World War II?

3 Where and when did the first women's rights convention take place?

4 What was the name of Betty Friedan's landmark book on women published in 1963?

5 Which was the first U.S. political party to recognize the right of women's suffrage in its official platform?

6 Who was the leader of the women's suffrage movement in Great Britain?

7 What is "purdah"?

8 Which sex is longer-lived?

9 What percentage of U.S. doctoral degrees were earned by women in the late 1960's?

10 Who was the first woman Cabinet member?

11 One U.S. woman stood out, from the early 20th century, as a crusader for the right to disseminate birth control information. Who was she?

12 What were the median incomes for U.S. men and women in sales jobs in 1969?

13 Who was the male abolitionist leader who actively supported feminist causes in the mid-19th century?

14 Who was the first black woman to be elected to the House of Representatives?

15 Thomas Aquinas, the 13th-century Christian theologian, stated that women have one, and only one, major role in life. What was that role?

16 When did the American Medical Association begin to admit women members?

17 Which country drafts women into its armed forces for combat duty?

18 Who was a prominent leader in the settlement house movement in the 19th century and an ardent feminist as well?

19 In 1953—between the larger "waves" of feminism—Simone de Beauvoir of France wrote a now-famous book on women. What is its name?

20 What is a major consumer problem for divorced women?

21 What is a "passion shooting," and how is the concept discriminatory?

22 Susan B. Anthony, renowned U.S. feminist, worked for women's suffrage for 50 years and more. Who was the first U.S. president to whom she pleaded her cause?

23 To test the law, Susan B. Anthony voted unlawfully in an election in 1872. What happened then?

24 When did women finally receive the right to vote in the U.S.?

25 When was the Female Medical College of Pennsylvania established?

# world literature

*" 'Classic'. A book which people praise and don't read."*

1 Where did Rudyard Kipling write the tales that were to make up his 'Jungle Books'?

2 Italy's first great poet wrote 'The Divine Comedy'. What is his name?

3 Who is considered to be the founder of modern Russian literature?

4 'The Tales of the Marshes', by Chinese novelist Sze Nai-an, was translated into English under the title 'All Men Are Brothers'. Who was the American translator?

5 What modern novelist of Nigeria wrote 'Arrow of God'?

**6** When and where was the first book published in the New World?

**7** Who was the greatest poet of ancient Greece?

**8** What is the native land of Selma Lagerlof?

**9** Whose place in German literature is comparable to Shakespeare's in English literature?

**10** What novel marked the high point of Spain's "golden age" of literature?

**11** India was the country of the Nobel laureate in literature for 1913. Who was he?

**12** The fortunes of the Whiteoak family were followed by Canadian novelist Mazo de la Roche in a popular series that began in 1927. What was the series called?

**13** Who was the pivotal figure of the Irish literary revival, which began in the late 1800's?

**14** What Cuban poet-journalist of the late 19th century was influential in that country's independence movement?

**15** Which two post-World War II French novelists examined man's existence in a "meaningless universe"?

**16** What modern Italian novelist wrote 'Bread and Wine'?

**17** Who were the three poetic geniuses of England's Elizabethan period?

**18** Who was François Villon?

**19** What contemporary German writer is the author of 'The Tin Drum'?

**20** What American writer captured the mood of the "Roaring Twenties" in his novels and short stories?

**21** In 'Endymion', one of England's greatest Romantic poets wrote "A thing of beauty is a joy forever." Who was he?

**22** What are haiku and tanka?

**23** What novelist introduced the "stream of consciousness" technique into modern fiction?

**24** Who was known as Chile's Balzac?

**25** What Russian novelist was awarded the Nobel prize for literature for 1958?

# youth organizations

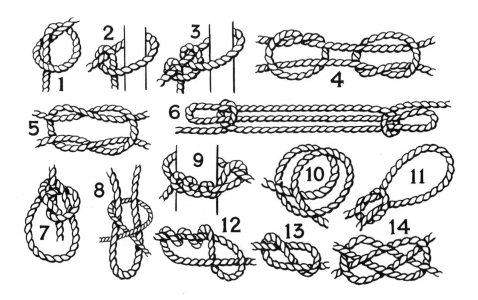

*"We have got to bring these young people into the active life of the community and make them feel that they are necessary."*

1   Where and when is the National 4-H Club Congress held?

2   What are Tri-Hi-Y Clubs?

3   Which group initiates a new member as a "green hand" in high school?

4   Who founded the Camp Fire girls?

5   What is the Cub Scout motto?

6   Which organization is devoted to helping young people acquire practical business experience?

7 When was the first Girl Scout troop founded in the U.S.?

8 Housing for women is provided at low cost by one national group. What is that group?

9 What are the 5-V's?

10 What is the age range served by the Camp Fire Girls of America?

11 How many merit badges are necessary to become an Eagle Scout?

12 Which organization is devoted to promoting the study of birds among young people?

13 What is the Order of De Molay?

14 At what age do Brownies become Girl Scouts?

15 What is the national organization formed to honor high school students for scholarship and leadership?

16 Which youth organization has a flag bearing crossed logs and a flame?

17 What is the national organization for high school students interested in teaching as a career?

18 The Komsomol is a youth organization in which country?

19 Which U.S. president successfully urged American youth to form their own Red Cross group?

20 When did the Future Homemakers of America become a national group?

21 Where was the Little League founded?

22 Which adult group sponsors Girls States to provide citizenship training?

23 What is the "umbrella" group for the major youth organizations in the U.S.?

24 The Catholic Youth Organization has long been nationally known for its activities—particularly in sports. Who founded it?

25 George Junior Republic is a large community founded to promote self-government among teenaged males and females. Where is it located?

# general quiz one

*"No race can prosper till it learns that there is as much dignity in tilling a field as in writing a poem."*

1   What is the difference between an artesian spring and an artesian well?

2   Why will frost not damage crops on hillsides but destroy them in the adjacent valley?

3   Who led the most formidable slave uprising in the history of Rome?

4 What emperor was the last monarch in the Americas, and what country did he rule?

5 What two countries occupy the Iberian peninsula?

6 What plant lives on insects?

7 What is implied by the adjective "Spartan"?

8 What are some effects of weightlessness on the human body?

9 What war began as a result of the sinking of the American battleship *Maine*?

10 Who was known as the "George Washington of South America"?

11 What speed is required for a spacecraft to escape from the earth's gravitational force?

12 What does a philatelist collect?

13 Which one of the 50 states has a one-house (unicameral) legislature?

14 What is the largest body of fresh water in the world?

15 What are "full-fashioned" hose?

16 What is the world's rarest postage stamp? How much is it worth?

17 Which is the brightest of all the stars?

18 Does all issued stock have par value?

19 Who are the "star boys"?

20 What is the meaning of the term "star chamber"?

21 What event stirred a khedive of Egypt to entertain more than 6,000 persons?

22 How can you estimate the age of a tree?

23 What fish electrocutes its prey?

24 Why do some tigers become man-eaters?

25 Private automobiles account for how much of all cross-country passenger transportation in the United States?

# general quiz two

*" Music is essentially useless, as life is."*

1    Where is the center of worldwide time?

2    Why should young fruit trees be pruned at planting?

3    What American patriotic society developed into a powerful political machine?

4    What was the writer Thoreau trying to prove in his Walden experiment?

5    What birds sometimes line their nests with hair they snatch from squirrels' tails?

6   How did the thistle save the Scots from the Norse invaders?

7   Does handling toads cause warts?

8   What general of the Civil War won a battle while the order for his removal was on the way?

9   What is the nation's oldest state police force?

10   Where did iced tea originate?

11   What is the only country in Southeast Asia that has never been under European rule?

12   Who was named the greatest football player and the greatest male athlete of the first half of the 20th century?

13   What is the "American twist"?

14   How does the standard relay race differ from a medley relay race?

15   What Italian poet wrote some of his best works in a madhouse?

16   How can termites be distinguished visually from ants?

17   Is the bite of the American tarantula fatal to human beings?

18   What is considered the most complex and difficult of all track and field events?

19   How much water may a medium-sized apple tree soak up on one summer day?

20   What are "fixed" expenses?

21   Who was the old woman whom no Norse god could conquer?

22   How are magnetic mines fired?

23   How many years were required to build the Taj Mahal?

24   What tree must be at least 100 years old before it can be cut for timber?

25   How do the permanent teeth drive out the primary teeth?

# general quiz three

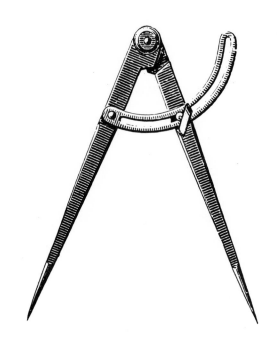

*"There is no royal road to geometry."*

1    Who was the only man ever to win both the pentathlon and the decathlon in Olympic competition?

2    What president of the United States later became chief justice of the United States?

3    What inventor refused to share the Nobel prize for physics with Edison?

4    Which continent is the home of the tiger?

5   Harry Truman was given the middle initial "S." For what did it stand?

6   What are free ports?

7   What is the most populous city, and one of the most congested in the world?

8   What famous composer was helped for many years by a wealthy woman he never met?

9   In what century did William Tell first appear in Swiss literature?

10   What metal brought the Phoenicians all the way to the British Isles?

11   What country lies on the "roof of the world"?

12   What is the world's longest paved national road?

13   How has the TVA improved the health and economy of the people of the Tennessee Valley?

14   What is registered by a tachometer?

15   What city manufactures more handmade cigars than any other city in the world?

16   In what country is Africa's highest peak?

17   What delicious pudding is derived from the roots of the cassava plant?

18   Who were the first white men to observe tobacco being smoked?

19   Two beasts of prey that attack sheep are found only in Tasmania. Name them.

20   Where was the earliest known civilization?

21   Do both frogs and toads have teeth?

22   In the United States when does the fiscal year begin and end?

23   What tree is sacred to Buddhists?

24   What is the law of primogeniture (first born)?

25   Can treaties be made by other than sovereign nations?

# general quiz four

*"Water, water, every where,*
*And all the boards did shrink;*
*Water, water, every where,*
*Nor any drop to drink."*

1   Who were the "forty-niners"?

2   Tierra del Fuego, the island group making up the southern tip
of South America, is divided between what two countries?

3   What mollusk does millions of dollars of damage every year to
wooden ships and wharf pilings?

4 Which president signed the first national Thanksgiving proclamation?

5 What bird is an expert tailor?

6 Are the Morse code and the International code similar?

7 What are the Buddhist monasteries of Thailand called?

8 Why are lenses more than 40 inches in diameter not suitable for use in refracting telescopes?

9 Who were the Teutonic Knights?

10 What was the first city in North America to adopt a government for a whole metropolitan area?

11 What queen ruled Great Britain and Ireland for 64 years?

12 What painted smile has puzzled the world for more than four centuries?

13 Who has been called the "painter's painter"?

14 Why is Leonardo da Vinci justly called a versatile genius?

15 How long may a United States president hold office?

16 Does a ventriloquist really "throw" his voice?

17 What kind of mountains build themselves?

18 What state is called the Mother of Presidents?

19 How many pieces of wood are there in a violin?

20 What is the Dead Man's Chest, popularized in the 'Treasure Island' pirates' song?

21 In what way are ants, ladybugs, and dragonflies helpful to man?

22 What plant's leaves have hair-trigger traps?

23 Why are Geiger counters used to prospect for uranium ores?

24 When was the violin invented?

25 Are vitamins food?

# general quiz five

*"We are the Romans of the modern world—the great assimilating people."*

1 What is the meaning of the word *vinegar*?

2 In what decade of the 20th century was Vitamin D first isolated?

3 Who are the Baganda of Buganda?

4 Do vultures kill living prey?

5   Who were the "abolitionists"?

6   What was the name of the first permanent English settlement in North America?

7   Can a person who contracts a venereal disease acquire immunity?

8   What war was ended by the Treaty of Ghent?

9   What is the meaning of "manifest destiny"?

10  What are animals with backbones called?

11  What war was ended by the Treaty of Guadalupe-Hidalgo?

12  Where is the world's longest railroad?

13  What two Americans were the first to cross the vast region of the United States west of the Mississippi River?

14  What city has 170 canals that serve as its streets and avenues?

15  From where do all vitamins originally come?

16  What is the Bill of Rights?

17  Why do today's armies wear dull-colored uniforms in combat?

18  What is the name of the highest known falls on earth?

19  The Central Pacific and the Union Pacific railroads were connected to form the first transcontinental railway. Where were they joined?

20  What is the "Holy See"?

21  How much did the colonists of Virginia pay for their future brides' passage?

22  Against what dread disease was the first vaccine used?

23  What was the name of the first steamer to cross the Atlantic Ocean?

24  What vitamin, found in fresh fruits and vegetables, prevents the disease called scurvy?

25  What newspaper first carried the text of the United States Constitution?

# general quiz six

*" I like rivers*
*Better than oceans, for we see both sides."*

1 What constitutional amendment gave 18-year-olds the right to vote?

2 Where is the largest Christian church in the world?

3 How many permanent member nations are there in the United Nations Security Council?

4 What is the national bird of the United States, and when was it adopted?

5   What is the largest nation in the world in area?

6   Which vitamin is produced in the body by ultraviolet rays?

7   What site within the borders of the United States is international territory?

8   Which United States presidents have taken office by majority vote of the electoral college although another candidate had a larger popular vote?

9   In what building are the Declaration of Independence, the Constitution, and the Bill of Rights on display?

10  How many active volcanoes are there?

11  Why does a teenage boy's voice "crack"?

12  To punish the American colonies, the British passed the Five Intolerable Acts. What were the provisions of these acts?

13  Who were the Vandals?

14  What modern French painter produced his finest paintings when he was drunk?

15  What great service do vultures perform for mankind?

16  Where was the first permanent white settlement north of the Ohio River?

17  What is the oldest institution of higher learning in the United States? When was it founded?

18  In what year was Vatican City established?

19  Where was the first steel-skeleton skyscraper erected? What was its name?

20  How many states were carved out of the Northwest Territory?

21  What is South America's smallest nation?

22  Does the British Crown (the king or queen) have the right to veto an act of Parliament?

23  What canal linked the Great Lakes with the Atlantic Ocean?

24  What was the chief duty of the Vestal Virgins of ancient Rome?

25  What is Africa's largest lake?

# general quiz seven

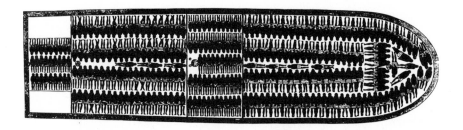

*"Whenever I hear anyone arguing for slavery, I feel a strong impulse to see it tried on him personally."*

1 Where did Leonardo da Vinci paint his masterpiece 'The Last Supper'?

2 What animal makes a ten-ton elephant look small?

3 What plant depends upon the moth for its survival?

4 Why do many water plants have long slender leaves?

5 What birds build community nests?

6 Are whales fish?

7 What beast of burden makes its home highest in the mountains?

8 What are the two great classes of trees?

9 What is "Big Ben" and where is it located?

10 Why does the woodpecker peck?

11 What insects are the original papermakers?

12 How do wolves hunt when food is scarce?

13 What sea animals furnish ivory?

14 How does the wasp paralyze its prey?

15 What bearlike animal is the largest member of the weasel family?

16 Why are weeds so successful in the battle for life?

17 What did the invention of the telegraph have to do with weather forecasting?

18 Who was the mystic poet whose greatest work was done after he was 50 years old?

19 Who originated mass production in industry?

20 Why is Wisconsin called the Badger State?

21 What bird uses its tongue to spear food?

22 Where is the land of King Arthur?

23 What wife of a United States president was also his secretary?

24 What place on earth has the greatest average rainfall? The least?

25 What is the oldest written material yet discovered?

# general quiz eight

*"Sensible and responsible women do not want to vote."*

1   What French writer emphasized the effects of heredity and environment in his novels?

2   What is the source of the term "wasp waist"?

3   What man had to found a city and a state before he could worship in his own way?

4   Where are Canada's highest mountains?

5   What is the 'Anabasis'?

6 Why do whales "blow"?

7 Where is the Poets' Corner in which England honors its great writers?

8 What famous orator was too shy as a lad to speak a piece in school?

9 How many bushels of wheat are required to make a barrel of flour?

10 What is the best wood for making gunstocks?

11 What was the first universal religion?

12 Why are sapphires and rubies used in watch movements?

13 In which room in the White House does the woman guest of honor sleep? The man honor guest?

14 Who was the Apostle of the Indies?

15 Why is the home of the president of the United States called the White House?

16 What is the Smithsonian Institution?

17 What did Englishmen of the 12th century use for runners on their ice skates?

18 What is a waterspout?

19 In what war was the most important land battle fought after peace was declared?

20 What first lady was married in the White House?

21 In what state was the Northwest's first full-scale oil refinery built?

22 Which brothers came to America as missionaries and founded a religious denomination?

23 Who was the wife of one president of the United States and the mother of another?

24 What great conqueror was born in the same year as the man who finally defeated him?

25 Who were the first men to fly in an airplane?

# general quiz nine

*"Seeing is deceiving. It's eating that's believing."*

1　How many islands are in the West Indies?

2　What is a cap rock fall, in geology?

3　What president first lived in the White House?

4　What ruler had a crippled arm from birth?

5   What king and queen jointly ruled England?

6   What water plant has leaves large enough and firm enough to support a child?

7   What is the meaning of "Rainbow in the morning, travelers take warning; rainbow at night, travelers' delight"?

8   Who founded the first zoo in history?

9   How many years did Noah Webster work on his dictionary?

10   Did the invention of the cotton gin make Eli Whitney rich?

11   What four children are said to have slept crosswise on the long bed built for Abraham Lincoln?

12   How did people tell time in the Middle Ages?

13   What are planetary winds?

14   What people were the first to use the toboggan?

15   What is meant by dying intestate?

16   Who was the hero of the Dutch struggle against Spanish rule?

17   How are bacteria both a nuisance and a help to the food industry?

18   What is a clearinghouse?

19   What two famous Missourians, one a United States senator and the other an artist, bore the same name?

20   What state capital is named after a chancellor of Germany?

21   Who broke the monotony of his bookkeeping job by working on a story or poem at the noon hour?

22   What country has the oldest of existing parliaments?

23   What are some of the reasons the Industrial Revolution began in England?

24   How may the atoms of a single element differ?

25   To what U.S. state does Israel's area correspond?

# general quiz ten

*" It is the privilege of genius that to it life never grows commonplace as to the rest of us."*

1   Who made the first voyage by ship on the Great Lakes?

2   Whom do the citizens of the Soviet Union regard as their greatest national hero?

3   What saint lived in the cell of an unused jail when she was a child?

4   What caused Martin Luther to take up a religious life?

5   Why is the Canadian city of Montreal often called the Paris of the New World?

6   What are the four basic elements of music?

7   How many songs did Robert Schumann write in the year 1840?

8   Name some of the patriotic songs that were inspired by the Civil War?

9   Where are the world's greatest cod fishing grounds?

10   What is one of the oldest intercollegiate athletic contests in the United States?

11   What kind of belt encircles the world?

12   How do orchids grow?

13   Why is it illegal to hunt the Alpine ibex?

14   How far south in America did the ice sheet extend during the fourth glaciation period of the Ice Age?

15   Iceland's warmest temperature averages 48°, so what furnishes the heat for its hot springs and geysers?

16   What country established the first colony in Iceland?

17   In most years, the state of Idaho produces more of what mineral than any other state?

18   In what year was Idaho, the 43d state, admitted to the Union?

19   Who made the first idols?

20   What is the chief trade center of northwestern Illinois?

21   The Galena, Ill., home of what president of the United States has become a memorial to him?

22   Does imagination help solve a practical problem?

23   Who are the only native Americans?

24   Did more or fewer Germans than Italians immigrate to the United States?

25   When was the federal constitutional amendment permitting a tax on incomes adopted in the United States?

# general quiz eleven

*"The newspapers must not be taken too seriously."*

1 If you were to vacation in Indiana, what interesting recreation areas might you find?

2 Why have the Navajo Indians been called nomads?

3 In a room that has north light, what kind of colors should be used in a decorative scheme?

4 Do colors always look the same?

5   What was the first great invention to come out of the new United States?

6   About how many patents for newly invented products does the United States Patent Office issue each year?

7   What is smog?

8   Where can the famous Peacock Throne of Persia be seen today?

9   Why is Ireland called the Emerald Isle?

10   What was a night watchman in 17th-century England called?

11   How did the Ivory Coast get its name?

12   Do jackals hunt during the day?

13   What is Andrew Jackson's home near Nashville, Tenn., called?

14   Why was Andrew Jackson sometimes called King Andrew?

15   Who was appointed the first governor of Florida by President James Monroe?

16   What two Jacobins helped inaugurate the Reign of Terror in France?

17   How does a jaguar hunt?

18   What trees, important in the making of furniture, grow on the island of Jamaica?

19   What is the "King James Version"?

20   Which king of England was defeated at the battle of the Boyne?

21   For what Roman god was January named?

22   Who were the earliest inhabitants of Japan?

23   Why is Thomas Jefferson one of the two heroes (with George Washington) of the American Revolution whose fame has spread around the world?

24   What is a petty jury?

25   Why is the name of the mountains in southwest Idaho so appropriate?

# general quiz twelve

*"Jazz will endure as long as people hear it through their feet instead of their brains."*

1   How does a dam use waterpower to generate electricity?

2   Which state in the Union has the nickname Mountain State?

3   Why is Phidias important in the history of art?

4   Which bird has the greatest wingspread?

5 On what code of ancient Rome is modern European law based?

6 What contours do landforms tend to have in humid areas?

7 What engineering feat of the Romans forecast construction of a public utility?

8 When was the first U.S. census taken?

9 Which state in the United States has the smallest forest area?

10 What velocity rates in air conditioning are agreeable to most people?

11 From which fable has come the saying "Practice what you preach"?

12 How are plants helped by the color and scent of their flowers?

13 What is the largest island of the Malay Archipelago?

14 How did Alexander Hamilton and Thomas Jefferson chiefly differ in their theories of government?

15 What president is regarded as having established the "spoils system"?

16 In what year did the Bill of Rights go into effect?

17 What did the 13th Amendment to the U.S. Constitution do?

18 What was the first written agreement providing for a people's government?

19 What country in Central America does not touch the Caribbean Sea?

20 What legend led to the discovery of Florida?

21 What animal washes its food before eating it?

22 What is probably the most widely used clock of the 20th century?

23 How far apart are the pins placed in bowling?

24 What is a lehr in glassmaking?

25 What are Tanagra figurines?

# answers

## aerospace

*Quotation: Lyndon B. Johnson*

1 Grenades dropped from open airplane cockpits.
2 Icarus.
3 The Montgolfier brothers' balloon.
4 Calbraith Perry Rodgers, 1911.
5 Orville Wright.
6 Samuel Pierpont Langley, 1896.
7 Wiley Post.
8 Robert Hutchings Goddard.
9 They still do.
10 Chinese chronicles of the Mongol wars, A.D. 1232.
11 The Autogiro.
12 They owned a bicycle shop.
13 They became daredevil barnstorming pilots.
14 The rocket plane Bell X-1, 1947.
15 Jerrie Mock, 1964.
16 1918, U.S.
17 A biplane.
18 A shock absorber to cushion the impact of landing.
19 Ailerons.
20 A shock wave caused by an airplane colliding with air particles.
21 Roger Bacon.
22 An albatross.
23 Hero of Alexandria, 1st century A.D.
24 The Korean War, 1950.
25 Clarence Chamberlain and Charles Levine.

## africa

*Quotation: Pliny the Elder*

1 James Bruce and Mungo Park.
2 Egypt.
3 They don't; tigers are native to Asia.
4 Ghana.
5 Zaire—industrial diamonds; Ghana—cacao; South Africa—gold; and Tanzania (Zanzibar)—cloves.
6 The Nile, then the Congo, then the Niger.
7 Amenhotep IV, or Ikhnaton, more than 1,000 years B.C.
8 Nobody knows who built Zimbabwe, but it was built long before the days of foreign explorers.
9 The Kalahari Desert, Botswana, and the Namib Desert, Namibia.
10 By tradition, it is believed they were named for two of Noah's sons, Ham and Shem.
11 Europe, especially Spain.
12 More than 2 million.
13 Malagasy Republic.
14 Lesotho is totally surrounded by South Africa.
15 Mount Kenya, 17,058 feet.
16 Rwanda and Burundi.
17 Amedeo Modigliani.
18 The pharaoh Khafre, about 2600 B.C.
19 Liberia, founded in 1822.
20 Portuguese explorer Bartholomew Diaz called it "Cabo Tormentoso"—the Stormy Cape.
21 The Cullinan—3,106 carats (1⅓ pounds).
22 Desert people.
23 1960.
24 The Hottentots and the Bushmen.
25 Libya.

## american history

*Quotation: Stephen Vincent Benét*

1 Jamestown.
2 Lewis and Clark.
3 Confederate attack on Ft. Sumter.
4 Franklin D. Roosevelt.
5 John Quincy Adams.
6 Lord Cornwallis.
7 Puerto Rico, Guam, and the Philippines.
8 Mexico ceded California and Texas to the U.S. and agreed on the Rio Grande as a boundary.
9 World War I—according to President Woodrow Wilson.
10 Marbury vs. Madison.
11 Military supplies in Concord.
12 Sitting Bull and Crazy Horse.
13 Japanese attack on Pearl Harbor, 1941.
14 Crispus Attucks.
15 1849.
16 Lyndon B. Johnson.
17 Hernando de Soto, 1539.
18 Widespread bribery of public officials to circumvent Prohibition.
19 John F. Kennedy.
20 The U.S. purchased Alaska from Russia in 1867.
21 New York (pop. 33,131).
22 1939-46.
23 Abraham Lincoln.
24 Hawaii.
25 1924.

## american literature

*Quotation: Ernest Hemingway*

1 Edgar Allan Poe.
2 *Poetry: A Magazine of Verse.*
3 William Dean Howells.
4 Emily Dickinson.
5 Sinclair Lewis.
6 William Faulkner.
7 Washington Irving.
8 'The Grapes of Wrath'.
9 Capt. John Smith.
10 Nathaniel Hawthorne.
11 Henry James.
12 The faith that man has in him a spark of divinity, an inner light.
13 'Look Homeward, Angel'.
14 Herman Melville.
15 Robert Frost.
16 F. Scott Fitzgerald.
17 Edward Arlington Robinson.
18 He Americanized English spellings such as colour and centre.
19 Ralph Ellison.
20 Edgar Lee Masters, Vachel Lindsay, and Carl Sandburg.
21 Hannibal, Mo.
22 T. S. Eliot.
23 Bernard Malamud.
24 Willa Cather.
25 Bravery, or courage.

## american minorities

*Quotation: Dwight D. Eisenhower*

1 Nat Turner.
2 The Navajo.
3 Mexicans.
4 Malcolm X.
5 1963.
6 Tecumseh.
7 Puerto Ricans.
8 Rediscovery of the African heritage.

9 Gold was discovered on Sioux land in the Black Hills, and the government insisted the Indians give up the land.
10 San Francisco, Calif.
11 Ralph Bunche (1950) and the Rev. Martin Luther King, Jr. (1964).
12 Wounded Knee Creek, South Dakota.
13 Italy.
14 Frederick Douglass.
15 More than 1,000.
16 Andrew Jackson.
17 New Mexico.
18 More than 186,000.
19 Geronimo's surrender.
20 China.
21 Washington, D.C., Atlanta, Ga., Newark, N.J., and Gary, Ind.
22 14th Amendment, ratified in 1868.
23 W. E. B. Du Bois.
24 The secretary of war.
25 Red Cloud of the Oglala Sioux.

## animals of the wild

*Quotation: William Blake*

1 The blue whale.
2 Bilateral symmetry.
3 By means of gills.
4 Budding.
5 The opossum.
6 Asiatic elephants have smaller ears and can be trained to serve man.
7 Ostriches cannot fly.
8 The flea.
9 The mudskipper, or skippiup goby, pulls itself along mud on its front fins.
10 Certain tropical bats.
11 Squid squirt a cloud of inky material and escape behind it.
12 The "ears" of a field cricket are on its forelegs.
13 The ant.
14 They live together in highly organized societies.
15 Apes and monkeys.
16 The giant tortoise.
17 Six.
18 Eucalyptus leaves.
19 Water flows through their tiny holes or pores, which filter out organisms for their food.
20 The flatworm.
21 Chitin.
22 The gibbon.
23 In Southeast Asia.
24 Tropical America.
25 The African dik-dik.

## architecture

*Quotation: Le Corbusier*

1 Louis Sullivan.
2 Michelangelo.
3 Marble.
4 St. Patrick's Cathedral.
5 Frank Lloyd Wright.
6 Le Corbusier.
7 The Wainwright Building.
8 Doric, Ionic, and Corinthian.
9 Buckminister Fuller.
10 Stone.
11 Sir Christopher Wren.
12 Moorish, or Mohammedan.
13 Paris, Bourges, Chartres, Reims, and Amiens.
14 Paul Revere's house, 1676.
15 William LeBaron Jenney.

16 The elevator.
17 One that combines elements from different styles.
18 Mies van der Rohe.
19 A.D. 537.
20 They were able to build higher and to open up the walls to large stained-glass windows.
21 The Mesopotamians used clay, rather than stone, and it crumbled.
22 The Taj Mahal.
23 H.H. Richardson.
24 102.
25 Inigo Jones.

## armed forces and military history

*Quotation: Napoleon Bonaparte*

1 The U.S. Civil War.
2 The Gilbert Islanders.
3 The Battle of Lake Regillus, won by the Romans.
4 Use of caution and delay in combat; taken from the name of Quintus Fabius Maximus, a Roman general.
5 The Turks besieged Candia from 1648 to 1669.
6 The Battle of Balaklava, in the Crimean War.
7 France, in 1793.
8 The fierce Russian winters, known to the people of Moscow as "General Winter," have helped defeat many invaders—notably Napoleon I and Hitler.
9 The Spanish-American War.
10 Pablo Picasso's 'Guernica'.
11 Gen. William L. Mitchell.
12 He was a U.S. Civil War hero.
13 The British based the modern tank on American farm tractors.
14 T. E. Lawrence ("Lawrence of Arabia").
15 They were used for bombing.
16 A railroad car.
17 The Spanish Civil War.
18 During the Korean War.
19 Gustavus Adolphus of Sweden.
20 The Hundred Years' War.
21 U.S. Navy Capt. James Lawrence.
22 The Opium War (China *vs.* Great Britain).
23 Belgium.
24 British Lieut. Gen. John Burgoyne.
25 The Parthian horsemen fired arrows back at their foes as they rode away from them.

## asia

*Quotation: Rudyard Kipling*

1 In what is now Malaysia.
2 Indonesia (March 1, 1965).
3 Nam-viet.
4 The Ch'in Dynasty in China (221–206 B.C.).
5 In honor of the great Han Dynasty (206 B.C.–A.D. 220).
6 1162–1227.
7 Vientiane and Luang Prabang.
8 Koguryo, Paekche, and Silla (in Korea).
9 An ironclad ship.
10 Jimmu, 660 B.C.
11 Xipangu.
12 Edo (now Tokyo).
13 A.D. 607.

14 Cambodia (Angkor Wat).
15 People from India.
16 China.
17 Kublai Khan.
18 Burma.
19 21 years old.
20 The Khmer.
21 The Mongols.
22 The 10th century.
23 King Mongkut of Thailand (1851–68).
24 A British officer who put down the Taiping Rebellion.
25 By Ruy López de Villa-Lobos, who in 1542–43 explored the islands and named them for King Philip II of Spain.

## astronomy

*Quotation: Henry Wadsworth Longfellow*

1 It doesn't; all planets reflect sunlight.
2 The sun, the nearest star, is about 93 million miles away.
3 No one knows for sure, but many astronomers think it is about 10 billion years old.
4 Probably Hans Lippershey, a Dutch optician, in 1608.
5 When it survives passage through Earth's atmosphere and falls to the ground.
6 Nicolaus Copernicus, whose theory was published in 1543.
7 8 minutes and 19 seconds.
8 Ice and ice-coated dust.
9 About 4 billion or 5 billion years from now.
10 About 100 billion.
11 Streams of electrically charged particles from the sun.
12 The light-year, the distance through space that light travels in one year— about 5 trillion, 900 billion miles.
13 Ten tons.
14 Black holes.
15 The Egyptians.
16 More than likely 5 billion light-years.
17 Tycho Brahe.
18 Stonehenge.
19 Sir Isaac Newton.
20 It would destroy the solar system, but the event is unlikely.
21 Hydrogen.
22 Curved, some astronomers think.
23 One whose orbit lies between Earth's orbit and the sun; Mercury and Venus.
24 Jupiter; Mercury.
25 200 million years.

## australia

*Quotation: Andrew Paterson*

1 New Holland.
2 Mt. Kosciusko (7,316 feet).
3 Australia, Tasmania, New Guinea, New Zealand, and nearby Pacific Islands.
4 Nobody knows; early explorers who sailed nearby didn't know they were skirting the shores of a continent.
5 Coral.
6 It lies almost halfway around the world from England, "the mother country."
7 It is the oldest.
8 The Murray River.
9 Somewhere in southeast Asia.
10 The Reverend John Flynn, who supervised the first medical service to people in the remote areas of Australia.

11 At 30 miles an hour.
12 "Well-covered," referring to the cap that covers each bud.
13 Sydney, Melbourne, Brisbane, Adelaide, and Perth.
14 New Guinea.
15 Wool.
16 Capt. James Cook on April 29, 1770.
17 Italian.
18 The Tasmanian zebra wolf and the Tasmanian devil.
19 Yes; the Japanese bombed Darwin in 1942.
20 The theater expanded nationwide.
21 By two-way radio.
22 Patrick White and Morris West.
23 The British sovereign.
24 Aboriginal artist who achieved international renown.
25 New South Wales.

## birds

*Quotation: Miguel de Cervantes*

1 Passenger pigeons.
2 The Indian subcontinent and Ceylon (Sri Lanka).
3 The albatross.
4 The archaeopteryx.
5 About 30,000.
6 No other kind of animal has feathers.
7 Sumeria.
8 The egrets.
9 New Zealand; the bird is the kiwi.
10 During migration.
11 The sacred geese of the Temple of Juno (390 B.C.).
12 All kinds of dead or dying animals.
13 North and Central America.
14 The Canada jay.
15 The meadowlark.
16 Ostrich.
17 'Birds of America', 1827.
18 The blue goose and the snow goose.
19 The pelican.
20 The owl.
21 "Simpleton."
22 Ivory-billed woodpecker.
23 The 18th century.
24 The European cuckoo.
25 The emu.

## canada

*Quotation: Robert William Service*

1 Prince Edward Island.
2 At Great Bear Lake in the Northwest Territories.
3 Quebec, Ontario, and British Columbia.
4 About 29%.
5 In the 15th, after 1497.
6 Crude petroleum.
7 About 18,000.
8 The Great Lakes Region.
9 Hungarians who fled after the unsuccessful uprising against the Soviet Union.
10 In 1960.
11 Cajuns.
12 The Stratford (Ont.) Festival, founded in 1953.
13 Quebec.
14 Furs.
15 The Progressive Conservative (Tory) and the Liberal.
16 The Laurentian Plateau or Canadian Shield.

17 Montreal, Que., and Toronto, Ont.
18 It is the only country that has regular troops designated for future UN peacekeeping and observation duties.
19 The Cordilleran Region.
20 Thousands of settlers from the newly created United States who chose to remain under British rule.
21 In 1885.
22 Queen Victoria in 1857.
23 The Grand Banks.
24 In 1670.
25 The British North America Act of 1867.

## careers

*Quotation: Thomas A. Edison*

1 Clerical and sales work.
2 About 4%.
3 Teaching, nursing, and engineering.
4 Less than one fifth.
5 College education is usually required.
6 Distributes information and instructions on improved agricultural methods.
7 Meteorologist.
8 Forestry.
9 Tests milk for sweetness.
10 Work with spinning machines.
11 The excavated area in which a miner works.
12 Since prehistoric times.
13 About 250,000.
14 From meteorites.
15 Twelve hours a day.
16 As a rule, he does not stand watch.
17 Registered nurses and practical nurses.
18 Religious orders.
19 Plans, designs, and supervises construction of roads, bridges, harbors, railroads, tunnels, dams, and other such projects.
20 Instruction, research, and publication.
21 Internship.
22 The student's premedical scholarship record, his letters of recommendation, and his score on the Medical College Admissions Test.
23 One in five.
24 Growing of vegetables, fruits, and specialty crops.
25 About 132,000.

## children's literature

*Quotation: Arnold Lobel*

1 The English publisher John Newbery's collection 'Mother Goose's Melody' was published in 1760.
2 'Ragged Dick' (1867).
3 After 1850.
4 Canada.
5 It honors Randolph Caldecott, a 19th-century English illustrator famous for his drawings for children's books.
6 Sergei Prokofiev.
7 Wanda Gág.
8 Because in the preface the brothers said that the tales would "remain an inheritance in the house."
9 Robert Louis Stevenson, who settled in Samoa for his health.
10 Norwegian.
11 Louisa May Alcott.
12 English cartoonist and artist Sir John Tenniel.
13 Hans Christian Andersen.
14 Beatrix Potter, in England.
15 In Finland.
16 'Peter Pan'.
17 'Issun Boshi, the Inchling'.
18 In the early 1900's.
19 He founded an early children's magazine.

20 Gwendolyn Brooks.
21 Tom Sawyer.
22 Clement Moore.
23 Nigeria.
24 Carnegie Library in Pittsburgh, Pa., in 1899.
25 Switzerland.

## cities of the world

*Quotation: Alfred J. Talley*

1 Los Angeles, Calif., with 454 square miles.
2 Paris, in 1896.
3 State Street, Chicago, Ill.
4 Detroit, Mich., after a fire in 1805.
5 Brasília, Brazil.
6 San Francisco, Calif., after the earthquake of 1906; Chicago, in 1871; London, in the Great Fire of 1666; and Moscow, in 1812, to prevent Napoleon's army from living there.
7 Moscow, Rome, and Jerusalem.
8 Jerusalem is regarded as a holy city by Jews, Christians, and Moslems.
9 Rome (the Eternal City); Paris (City of Light); and Philadelphia, Penn. (City of Brotherly Love).
10 Paris, where letters are sent through a network of pneumatic tubes.
11 For centuries only Latin was spoken in and around its educational institutions.
12 In case of riots or revolution they could be raked by artillery fire.
13 Boston Common, Boston, Mass., in 1634.
14 Pittsburgh, Penn.
15 Tenochtitlán; Aztec.
16 Stockholm, Sweden.
17 Buda and Pest became the single city of Budapest, Hungary, in 1872.
18 Three possible uses are for government affairs, cultural affairs, or community and business affairs.
19 England.
20 West Berlin.
21 Genoa, Italy.
22 Geneva, Switzerland, which is the headquarters for many international organizations.
23 Addis Ababa, Ethiopia.
24 Toronto, Ont., Canada.
25 Ottawa, Ont., Canada.

## climate and weather

*Quotation: John Keats*

1 Latitude and time of year.
2 Ice ages of the Pleistocene Epoch.
3 The equator and its surroundings.
4 Less than five inches.
5 A device for measuring surface wind speeds.
6 Meteorology.
7 75 mph or more.
8 A weather satellite launched in 1969.
9 The Sahara and the Kalahari.
10 Subarctic.
11 Andes Mountains.
12 Coast Guard.
13 23,835 feet (1910).
14 Honan Province, China.
15 Atmospheric pressure.
16 Suitland, Md.
17 1042 inches, Cherrapunji, India, 1860–61.
18 Rain.
19 90.
20 10 to 12.
21 1946.

22 300 mph.
23 Hurricane.
24 500.
25 136° F., El Azizia, Libya, on Sept. 13, 1922.

## clothing

*Quotation: Henry David Thoreau*

1 About 600 yards.
2 Around the time of the U.S. Civil War.
3 A heavy twilled cotton woven in white, plain colors, or stripes.
4 The Shang people of the Far East in about 1550 B.C.
5 Purple in color, it was called *mauve*, a French word for a purple color yielded in nature by the mallow plant.
6 In the late Middle Ages, known as the Gothic period.
7 Charles Frederick Worth, an English tailor who in 1858 opened a fashion house in Paris.
8 The Spanish farthingale, beginning in mid-16th century.
9 Wool, cotton, linen, or silk.
10 Xylene and naphthalene.
11 As early as the 1600's.
12 Ornamentation with jewels and precious metals.
13 Rayon.
14 George Bryan Brummell, who influenced men's fashion in England during the early 19th century.
15 Cotton.
16 The product of spinning is usually known as yarn if it is to be made into cloth and thread if it is to be used for sewing.
17 Climate.
18 Wool and silk.
19 Clamps on a machine that grip out-of-shape fabric and jerk the cloth back into shape.
20 Linen in Egypt, wool in Mesopotamia, cotton in India, and silk in China.
21 During the late 18th century.
22 Petroleum and synthetic solvents.
23 The U.S.S.R.
24 Cutting.
25 Slashing—an outer layer of cloth was slashed to reveal a contrasting inner layer in gowns, shoes, and caps.

## communications

*Quotation: Thomas Jefferson*

1 In 1965.
2 George Eastman, in 1884.
3 The Greeks.
4 Telegraphy uses wires; radio does not.
5 The spreading of a doctrine.
6 By coaxial cables or by relay towers.
7 Their speedy handling of complex equations permits the calculation of trajectories and orbits needed to control the flight of space vehicles.
8 In the 15th century in Germany.
9 The principle that sounds from two directions are heard differently because the ears are on opposite sides of the head.
10 When a pidgin language becomes the first, or primary, language of a group, it is known as a creole language.
11 The Universal Postal Union.
12 Maps are cheaper; they can be stored flat, folded, or rolled; and on maps the viewer can see the entire surface of the earth at one time.
13 Guglielmo Marconi.

14 In an early signal system, a colored ball hoisted to the top of a pole beside the track meant "go ahead."

15 Tiros (Television and Infra Red Observation Satellite).

16 Knowing how to compose the images to be filmed and how to use the motion-picture camera to capture the images in the desired way.

17 The Federal Communications Commission.

18 Samuel F. B. Morse.

19 By drawing pictures of it.

20 It comes from and sounds like the French *m'aider*, "help me."

21 A primitive telegraph machine that transmits signals direct over a telegraph line to another teleprinter.

22 The Phoenicians.

23 In 1904.

24 By carrier pigeon.

25 The First Amendment.

## consumer affairs and protection

*Quotation: George Herbert*

1 1½% a month, or 18% a year.

2 Refuse to print a suspect ad; or, if the ad is already in print, file suit against the advertiser.

3 Late 1960's.

4 1957–59.

5 Food and Drug Administration (FDA).

6 'Unsafe at Any Speed'.

7 By insuring each account up to $20,000.

8 In 1830.

9 Allotting too much income to payments; risking inability to pay in case of illness or unemployment.

10 Great Britain, 1911.

11 Federal Trade Commission (FTC).

12 A loan from a savings and loan association.

13 By regulating the investment of insurance companies' funds.

14 One for which the borrower signs over secured property to the bank.

15 1850's.

16 Rural and urban areas both.

17 Popular name: "truth in lending"; official name: Consumer Credit Protection Act.

18 "U.S. Inspected and Passed."

19 U.S. Prime.

20 25%.

21 Grade A, or Fancy.

22 A shopping list.

23 44%.

24 Ham.

25 Prohibiting deceptive trade names; prohibiting the use of chemical softeners; and regulating the amount of moisture in each loaf.

## dance

*Quotation: Lord Byron*

1 Ragtime.

2 They usually imitate or reflect the animal life of the region the people live in.

3 A square dance.

4 Movement of the head, hands, and arms.

5 The Mexican hat dance.

6 Kabuki is a more lively version of the slow and majestic no.

7 A theatrical performance in which dancing and pantomime accompanied by music tell a story or express an idea.

8 Poland, Italy, and Scotland.

9 In the cathedral of Seville, Spain.

10 Five.

11 To better express the supernatural quality of the characters they portrayed.

12 Experimentation and changing forms for the sake of expressiveness.

13 Because the first great ballet company and school were established in France.

14 Martha Graham.

15 The Rockettes, of Radio City Music Hall in New York City.

16 The arrangement of the steps and patterns of a dance.

17 The Russian impresario Sergei Diaghilev.

18 Reality and psychological impact.

19 The first great performer to follow the principles of the modern dance.

20 A solo dance.

21 The choreographer Agnes de Mille in 'Oklahoma!'

22 Bali.

23 Because of the absence of musical instruments.

24 Vaslav Nijinsky.

25 An art expression of a racial group.

## discoverers and inventors

*Quotation: Ralph Waldo Emerson*

1 Staphylococcus microorganisms.

2 Claudius Galen, an ancient Greek physician.

3 X rays.

4 1616.

5 Baron Joseph Lister.

6 It is used to detect the presence of tuberculosis.

7 Carl von Linné.

8 'An Essay on the Principle of Population', by Thomas Malthus.

9 Ivan Pavlov.

10 The structure and nature of the atomic nucleus.

11 The moon.

12 Polonium.

13 The periodic table.

14 Galileo.

15 On his deathbed.

16 He discovered Pluto.

17 Sir Richard Arkwright.

18 Helping the deaf.

19 An electric vote counter.

20 1884.

21 The foxglove.

22 Edward Jenner.

23 Anthony van Leeuwenhoek.

24 Anthrax.

25 Ambroise Paré.

## domesticated animals

*Quotation: Michel de Montaigne*

1 About 4,000 years ago.

2 The dog.

3 No, because most domestic animals are plant-eaters.

4 The horse.

5 No one knows why.

6 Oxen.

7 About 282 days.

8 Alpaca and vicuña.

9 Some 15,000 years.

10 Only one, the dog.

11 Single animals are tamed; whole groups are domesticated.

12 The yak of Tibet.

13 The aurochs.

14 The boar and the pig.

15 The dhole, a feral (wild) dog of India, is one; the dingo of Australia is another.

16 About 4,000 years ago in what is present-day Turkestan.

17 The ass, the first of the domesticated horse family.

18 The camel, considered by its Arab owners to be stupid and spiteful.

19 The Tunis sheep found in parts of Africa and Asia.

20 More than 100 million head.

21 The Indian buffalo, similar to the Philippine carabao.

22 Cattle.

23 The goat ("scapegoat").

24 The bison.

25 The zebu by Hindus.

## earth

*Quotation: Walt Whitman*

1 Igneous rock.

2 The Mariana Trench (about 36,000 feet deep), in the Pacific Ocean.

3 Mont Pelée.

4 Limestone and sandstone.

5 Scientists think it is about 4.5 billion years old.

6 Carbonic acid and sulfuric acid.

7 Vermont.

8 Talc.

9 25 million years old.

10 Ocean area; ocean water covers 71% of the earth's surface.

11 Near Murfreesboro, Ark.

12 Afghanistan, where lapis lazuli has been mined for 6,000 years.

13 447 miles beneath the surface.

14 Pangaea; 200 million years ago.

15 The 3rd-century B.C. Greek scientist Eratosthenes.

16 Molten iron perhaps; scientists are unsure.

17 Perhaps because the light winds there becalmed sailing ships, and horses aboard often died.

18 Surtsey Island, off Iceland in the North Atlantic.

19 About 1,500 kinds.

20 Weathering, erosion, earthquakes, and volcanoes.

21 Nitrogen, making up 78% of the atmosphere near the earth's surface.

22 Waialeale, a peak on the Hawaiian island of Kauai, with 472 inches of rain a year.

23 Graphite.

24 The coriolis effect.

25 Flint and obsidian, a volcanic glass.

## europe

*Quotation: Lord Grey of Fallodon*

1 A customs union formed by Belgium, the Netherlands, and Luxemburg in 1947.

2 1815.

3 A reparations plan agreed to by Germany after World War I—shortly after that country had defaulted on a more severe reparations plan.

4 Bruges, Belgium.

5 The Asian Avars.

6 France's President Charles de Gaulle.

7 Italy.

8 Great Britain, France, and Russia.

9 Peter the Great and Catherine II.

10 More than 700 years.

11 1933.

12 To renounce war "as an instrument of national policy."

13 In the Aegean Sea area (present-day Greece), in about 2000 B.C.

14 A mythical person credited, in legend, with the founding of Rome.

15 Oliver Cromwell.

16 Assassination of the Austrian crown prince, Francis Ferdinand, in Sarajevo on June 28, 1914.
17 In about 1200 B.C.
18 Byzantium, Constantinople, Istanbul.
19 Maintaining the status quo among the major European powers for 30 years after the Congress of Vienna.
20 1920.
21 The signing of the nuclear test ban treaty.
22 Sinn Fein ("We Ourselves") is an Irish nationalist movement founded in 1900.
23 1905.
24 Great Britain.
25 1618–48; a dispute between Catholics and Protestants within the Holy Roman Empire.

## explorers and settlers

*Quotation: Henry Morton Stanley*

1 From Egypt.
2 About four fifths.
3 The writings of Marco Polo.
4 Pikes Peak.
5 Seeing the sun and stars going around the sky in horizontal circles.
6 Robert Hutchings Goddard.
7 July 20, 1969.
8 Roald Amundsen.
9 It was Laika, a dog carried in Russia's Sputnik 2 in 1957.
10 The theory that the Polynesians originally came from South America.
11 Sir Alexander Mackenzie.
12 Leif Ericson.
13 Francisco Coronado.
14 Carthage.
15 Vilhjalmur Stefansson.
16 Iceland.
17 Jacques-Yves Cousteau.
18 The Mormons, or members of the Church of Jesus Christ of Latter-day Saints.
19 Yuri Gagarin.
20 Sir Francis Drake and Sir Walter Raleigh.
21 At Quebec.
22 In 1953.
23 At Jamestown, Virginia.
24 President Thomas Jefferson.
25 Ferdinand Magellan's.

## food and nutrition

*Quotation: Socrates*

1 Milk.
2 Vitamin D.
3 Thyroid gland.
4 90.
5 Macadamia nut.
6 Paprika.
7 U.S., Italy, and India.
8 Beans, a staple of the Mexican diet.
9 Large slabs of bread.
10 Wisconsin (more than 40% of the U.S. total).
11 Gluten.
12 4 or more glasses (8 ounces each) per day.
13 To cook slowly in moist heat, usually in a covered utensil.
14 Fish.
15 Vitamin $B_5$ (Niacin).
16 24 ounces a dozen.
17 7 pounds.
18 Tea.
19 Julia Child.
20 1777.

21 Less than 20%.
22 About 2%.
23 Leaf lettuce.
24 Two pounds per week.
25 Bananas.

## games and hobbies

*Quotation: Bob Hope*

1 21 (or, if the game becomes tied at 20, any number thereafter that represents a two-point lead).
2 The 1600's.
3 Because it was originally played on a grass court.
4 Wimbledon.
5 Philadelphia.
6 Two, three, or four.
7 Harry Truman.
8 Checkers.
9 "Original gum."
10 "Turkey."
11 The shooter.
12 16—15 and a cue ball.
13 Billy Casper.
14 To evade a law banning the game "ninepins."
15 28.
16 "Peanuts," by Charles Schulz.
17 Falconry.
18 Japanese craft of making figures from folded paper.
19 The technique of catching fish without moving from one spot.
20 Chess and checkers.
21 Six years.
22 Karate.
23 Fast film.
24 By the time of the Roman Empire.
25 Embroidery.

## holidays and festivals

*Quotation: O. Henry*

1 June 14.
2 Bastille Day.
3 A soldier caught and executed in the Gunpowder Plot (1605) to blow up King James I and Parliament.
4 An official holiday in Hawaii commemorating Prince Kuhio, Hawaii's first delegate to the U.S. Congress.
5 Day of Atonement.
6 Every house in which there is a son flies a paper carp.
7 Woodrow Wilson.
8 Several saints had this name; one was a Roman priest, another was the bishop of Terni.
9 Easter is the first Sunday after the first full moon on or after the Vernal Equinox.
10 June 3.
11 Fat Tuesday (before Ash Wednesday).
12 The second Monday in October.
13 Decoration Day.
14 Middle of the 4th century.
15 September 16.
16 January 15.
17 Feast of St. Nicholas.
18 Holland, Mich.
19 July 1.
20 1889.
21 A holiday celebrated on December 26 in England—deriving its name from the custom of giving boxes of money to servants and tradesmen.
22 About winter solstice (December 21).
23 Oklahoma.
24 The Berkshire Music Festival at the Tanglewood estate.
25 March 25.

## insects and spiders

*Quotation: Mary Howitt*

1 About 350 million years old.
2 The mosquito.
3 Its larvae feed on decaying refuse.
4 *Hexapod.*
5 Through breathing pores (*spiracles*).
6 A common dragonfly.
7 Five.
8 The Coal Age.
9 The cricket.
10 He died of bubonic plague, which is carried by fleas.
11 They resemble milk bottles.
12 Social wasps.
13 Ladybugs.
14 Short-horned grasshoppers.
15 China.
16 From the Latin *catta pilosa*, which means "hairy cat."
17 Scarabs.
18 Ants.
19 *Nagana*, a disease of cattle and other animals.
20 The bird spider.
21 Three.
22 The tarantella (after the tarantula).
23 A mortal girl named Arachne, who was turned into a spider by the goddess Athena.
24 Robert Bruce.
25 A mite.

## languages and writing

*Quotation: Molière*

1 Dr. L.L. Zamenhof of Poland.
2 A variety of a language.
3 An idiom.
4 Braille.
5 Alpha and beta.
6 Decorative capital letters drawn by hand in books during the Middle Ages.
7 Sanskrit.
8 French, Italian, Spanish, and Portuguese.
9 To about 3100 B.C.
10 High German.
11 Afghanistan and Pakistan.
12 Personal associations called up by a word or words.
13 Byblos.
14 50.
15 Arabic.
16 One.
17 Austronesian.
18 Latin.
19 The verb.
20 The letters j and w.
21 1969.
22 From the Latin *cuneus* ("wedge"); wedge-shaped marks were made by pressing a reed into clay.
23 Nahuan, or Nahuatl.
24 None.
25 Words that sound alike but are spelled differently and have different meanings —*e.g.*, meet and meat.

## latin america

*Quotation: Christopher Columbus*

1 Bolivia and Paraguay.
2 The Pampa.
3 Simón Bolívar.
4 Birds of the tropical rain forests.
5 In Yucatán.
6 The petroleum industry.
7 At the Isthmus of Panama.
8 Brazil; Portuguese.

9 Mural painting.
10 The Andes.
11 Gabriela Mistral.
12 Corn.
13 Mestizo.
14 Jai alai.
15 None. Each is another term for Latin America.
16 Central American Common Market and Latin American Free Trade Association.
17 Brazilian architect who designed all public buildings in Brasília.
18 Land reform, or redistribution of huge estates that orginated as grants from kings of Spain or Portugal.
19 The Aztec god of war, Mexitli.
20 Guatemala and Honduras.
21 Agriculture.
22 The burro.
23 Domingo Sarmiento of Argentina.
24 In 1903.
25 400 million.

## leaders of the world

*Quotation: William Shakespeare*

1 Juan Perón of Argentina.
2 Scipio Africanus.
3 Julius Caesar.
4 Pericles (460–430 B.C.).
5 Thutmose III.
6 Ptolemy XIII, her brother.
7 Philip II of Macedon.
8 Aristotle.
9 About 1800 B.C., in Babylon.
10 A real king, who ruled around 960 B.C.
11 None.
12 Charlemagne.
13 The Domesday Book.
14 Queen Anne (1665–1714).
15 Philip II of Spain.
16 Hapsburg.
17 Gustavus Adolphus of Sweden.
18 Otto von Bismarck, chancellor of Prussia.
19 Peter the Great.
20 Karl Marx.
21 Queen Victoria.
22 A lawyer.
23 Charles de Gaulle.
24 Winston Churchill.
25 Franklin Delano Roosevelt.

## libraries

*Quotation: Samuel Johnson*

1 They were chained to the shelves.
2 An almanac gives up-to-date facts on many subjects, and a handbook is a guide to a particular subject.
3 Ten.
4 Canterbury and York in England; Notre Dame and Rouen in France; Bamberg and Hildesheim in Germany; and Toledo and Barcelona in Spain.
5 This philosopher was the first known Chinese librarian, about 550 B.C.
6 The upper left-hand corner.
7 Robert de Sorbon.
8 'Readers' Guide to Periodical Literature'.
9 A library employee who sorts returned materials and puts them back in the right place.
10 A research library is not always attached to a college or university; and, also, it frequently concentrates on a special subject.
11 A room in a monastery where books were copied by hand.

12 In 1800.
13 A machine that enlarges the print.
14 Books by mail, book sleds, book boats, book trains, and book planes.
15 Volumen.
16 An expert on the use of all library materials, both print and nonprint.
17 In the 13th century.
18 More than 50.
19 It explains foreign or uncommon words.
20 More than 30,000.
21 A list of books and other materials on the subject that is being explored.
22 None survived.
23 In cabinets known as vertical files.
24 In Alexandria, Egypt.
25 The Dead Sea Scrolls.

## mathematics

*Quotation: Edna St. Vincent Millay*

1 Euclid.
2 The largest circle that can be drawn on a sphere.
3 Trisecting an angle, squaring a circle, and doubling a cube.
4 "Earth measurement."
5 He believed the earth was round.
6 Johannes Kepler.
7 Gottfried W. Leibnitz.
8 Lewis Carroll, 'Alice in Wonderland'.
9 Bertrand Russell.
10 Archimedes.
11 A lotus flower.
12 Sixty.
13 The Hindus.
14 More than 2,000 decimal places.
15 The Hindu system was translated into Arabic and then was introduced in Europe around the 13th century.
16 Newton's second law of motion.
17 $M = mv$.
18 $W = Fs$.
19 The relationship between mass and energy.
20 $A = \pi r^2$
21 The first commercially successful key-driven calculator.
22 John Napier, 1614.
23 A computer can tell the difference between "1" and "0."
24 To govern the operation of weaving looms.
25 He linked the phenomena of light, motion, gravity, and electromagnetism in one set of equations.

## medicine and first aid

*Quotation: Publilius Syrus*

1 Australia.
2 New Jersey.
3 Evidence of abnormality detected by the patient.
4 Therapists, physician's assistants, social workers, medical technologists, and laboratory technicians and assistants.
5 There is one doctor for every 650 persons in the U.S.
6 Barbers.
7 Surgery, treatment by manual or operative procedures, and medicine, treatment with drugs, diet, and others.
8 Transplant surgery, where a recipient will reject a graft unless its chemical patterns match his own.
9 Pasteur developed pasteurization in 1857; homogenization is a development of the modern dairy industry.
10 Cuba.
11 Antiseptic surgery.

12 Linus Pauling recommends heavy use of Vitamin C.
13 Cape Town, South Africa, on Dec. 3, 1967, by a team headed by Christiaan Barnard.
14 All veterans of the U.S. Armed Forces, at Veterans Administration facilities.
15 A doctor must study seven years or longer after high school graduation; and a registered nurse must have at least two years of special training.
16 In 1972–73, 13% of all U.S. medical school enrollments consisted of women and 8% of members of minority groups.
17 The name of the Red Cross organization in some Mohammedan countries.
18 Clara Barton.
19 Provides relief to air raid victims, distributes medical supplies, handles correspondence with people in enemy territory, gathers information on the missing, sick, or dead, and sends supplies to prisoners.
20 Acts as a clearinghouse for information from 75 national societies.
21 What not to do.
22 It helps to prevent severe shock.
23 The right treatment for one could be fatal for a person with the other.
24 Mouth-to-mouth, for both children and adults; and back pressure-arm lift, for adults.
25 Burns are injuries from dry heat; scalds, from moist heat.

## middle eastern affairs

*Quotation: Exodus 3:8*

1 David Ben-Gurion.
2 Access to the Gulf of Aqaba.
3 Jordan.
4 1961.
5 Turkey.
6 1967.
7 Abu Dhabi.
8 Saudi Arabia.
9 1922.
10 France.
11 Libya.
12 1962.
13 98 million.
14 Great Britain.
15 Gamal Abdel Nasser, president of Egypt.
16 June 1967.
17 Kuwait.
18 Italy.
19 Less than five inches.
20 Damascus, Syria.
21 About 2000 B.C.
22 Algeria.
23 Casablanca.
24 Egypt and Syria.
25 Gaza Strip.

## motion pictures

*Quotation: Samuel Goldwyn*

1 'Casablanca'.
2 Sergei Eisenstein.
3 Moving cameras, equipment, and scenery.
4 West Orange, N.J.
5 Akira Kurosawa.
6 1912.
7 'Snow White and the Seven Dwarfs'.
8 Denmark.
9 Spencer Tracy.
10 1916.

11 Realism.
12 'The Cabinet of Dr. Caligari'.
13 'Nanook of the North'.
14 John Wayne.
15 Ingmar Bergman.
16 1908.
17 'All About Eve'.
18 Mack Sennett.
19 'Nights of Cabiria'.
20 1953.
21 Mary Astor.
22 'On the Waterfront'.
23 Mercury Theater.
24 François Truffaut.
25 None (she did receive an Oscar on a special basis, for her work overall, in 1955).

## music

*Quotation: Joseph Addison*

1 Harp, lyre, trumpet, and cymbal.
2 The baroque age (1600–1750).
3 To show the advantages of a method of tuning keyboard instruments.
4 Felix Mendelssohn, Frédéric Chopin, and Franz Liszt.
5 'Peter and the Wolf'.
6 Stringed, wind, and percussion.
7 The Greek lyre, which was a primitive harp.
8 Bowed, plucked, and struck.
9 As reeds and brasses.
10 The bagpipe.
11 He abandoned traditional scales and substituted 12-tone series.
12 The group includes the harmonica, accordion, piano accordion, concertina, and reed organ.
13 The organ.
14 The double bass has the lowest range and the violin the highest.
15 Nationalism.
16 By varying the oscillations of radio tubes.
17 The bandola, as it is called in Latin America, which is also called the bandurria in Spain.
18 Egyptians, Greeks, and Romans.
19 Africa; it was brought to colonial America by the first blacks.
20 Retreat.
21 "Trumpets of ram's horns."
22 Hermes, or Mercury.
23 Sébastien Erard (1752–1831), a French musical-instrument maker.
24 Cremona, Italy, near Venice.
25 Spirituals, work songs, blues, minstrel music, ragtime folk songs, African rhythms, and others.

## myths and legends

*Quotation: Christopher Marlowe*

1 The Aeolian harp.
2 Hermes, or Mercury, messenger of the gods.
3 Irish legend says that mermaids were pagan women banished from earth by St. Patrick.
4 The gods made man from an ash tree and woman from an elm.
5 A basilisk, or cockatrice.
6 Legendary king of Babylonia and hero of an epic poem written on clay tablets and found in the ruins of Nineveh.

7 Hades.
8 Odysseus.
9 Maui, their most famous folktale character.
10 Aphrodite, or Venus (Roman).
11 The 'Iliad', an epic poem attributed to Homer.
12 Diana.
13 The Aztec.
14 In the city Asgard on a plain named Ida.
15 In Norwegian myth, they are sometimes giants and sometimes dwarfs who live in forests and caves and own the earth's minerals.
16 Her father, Zeus, offered the city to the god who gave it the most useful gift; she gave it the olive tree.
17 Two collections of Icelandic literature that relate myths and legends of the early Scandinavians.
18 John Henry.
19 Virgil.
20 Odin.
21 Sir Thomas Malory in 'Morte d'Arthur'.
22 Osiris, a good king who became god of the sun.
23 A lar.
24 Paul Bunyan.
25 From the Norse gods.

## national parks

*Quotation: Theodore Roosevelt*

1 Yellowstone National Park, Wyo.
2 More than 1,200.
3 Preservation of threatened wildlife.
4 Acts of Congress.
5 National parks, national historic parks, and national historic sites.
6 Alexander Graham Bell National Historic Park, N.S.
7 Cape Hatteras National Seashore, N.C.
8 Chincoteague ponies, Assateague National Seashore, Md. and Va.
9 Canyon de Chelly National Monument, N.M.
10 City of Refuge National Historic Park, Hawaii.
11 Lava Beds National Monument, Calif.
12 Mount McKinley National Park, Alaska.
13 It is the site of the finest primeval rain forest in the U.S. and the home of the rare Roosevelt elk.
14 A plateau area covered with cedar and piñon trees.
15 The Palace Grand Theatre National Historic Site in Dawson, Yukon Territory, was a famous Gold Rush site; Ford's Theatre and Lincoln Museum in Washington, D.C., was the site of U.S. President Abraham Lincoln's assassination.
16 Serengeti National Park, Tanzania.
17 Lake District National Park, England.
18 Cairngorms National Nature Reserve, Scotland. The cairngorm is a quartz.
19 Hawaii Volcanoes National Park.
20 On the Luxemburg-West German border.
21 Gran Paradiso, a former royal hunting reserve in the Alps.
22 Juan Fernandez Islands, a Chilean national park.
23 Iguassú, on the Argentine-Brazilian border.
24 Grand Pré National Historic Park, N.S.
25 Sequoia National Park, Calif.

## oceans and islands

*Quotation: Joseph Conrad*

1 Almost one third.
2 Hawaii ("Big Island"), *not* Oahu.
3 Puerto Rico Trench (27,498 feet).
4 More than 50 feet.
5 Isle of Wight.
6 About 1,250 miles.
7 New Guinea.
8 Guam.
9 They're volcanic islands.
10 A major current in the North Atlantic.
11 Nine major islands, plus about 50 islets and reefs.
12 Indian Ocean.
13 Pitcairn Island.
14 Atoll.
15 The Atlantic contains more plankton—which dulls the surface color—than the Pacific does.
16 Cuba.
17 No one knows (too many to count).
18 Early explorers found many dogs there, chose Canary after the Latin word for dog, *canis*.
19 Hydrogen and oxygen.
20 St. Croix, St. Thomas, and St. John.
21 HMS *Challenger*.
22 About 100 feet.
23 Cyprus.
24 The Galápagos Islands.
25 In the China Sea, between mainland China and Formosa.

## painting and the graphic arts

*Quotation: Archibald MacLeish*

1 David Alfaro Siqueiros.
2 'Sunday Afternoon on the Island of the Grand Jatte'.
3 Malaga, Spain.
4 'The Holy Family'.
5 17th century (1606–69).
6 Woodcut.
7 Jan and Hubert van Eyck.
8 Salvador Dali.
9 Lithography.
10 800.
11 Roy Lichtenstein.
12 About 1505.
13 30,000 B.C.
14 Gilbert Stuart.
15 Auguste Renoir.
16 James Abbott McNeill Whistler.
17 Romare Bearden.
18 Russia.
19 Paul Cézanne.
20 A cutting tool used in the engraving process.
21 Abstract expressionism.
22 El Greco—a Greek-born painter who lived and worked in Spain.
23 Mary Cassatt.
24 "Op."
25 Titian.

## physiology and health

*Quotation: John F. Kennedy*

1 The white cells called lymphocytes mature in the lymph tissues.
2 About two days after infection.
3 Sulfanilamide, predecessor of the sulfa drugs, was in clinical use in the 1930's.
4 Chicken pox. (Scarlet fever, for which there is no practical vaccine, is caused by a bacterium, not a virus.)
5 Cardiovascular disease, or disease of the heart and blood vessels.

6 Adenine, thymine, cytosine, and guanine.

7 No. Prior to fertilization sperm and egg cells have half the number of chromosomes characteristic of the species.

8 None. The CNS can make occasional adjustments to the autonomic nervous system (outside the spinal column).

9 Through the umbilical cord, which is linked with the placenta, where the exchange of chemicals between mother and baby takes place.

10 None. It is a protein deficiency that occurs as a result of conditions common in underdeveloped countries.

11 Around certain joints, where they are small accessory bones.

12 Voluntary muscles are striped; involuntary ones are smooth, except for heart muscle, which is branched and striped.

13 The diaphragm, the sheet of muscle dividing the chest from the abdomen, is drawn downward.

14 The pituitary gland.

15 The adrenal gland, which produces epinephrine, also called adrenalin.

16 Almost nothing; oil glands keep the skin waterproofed.

17 The head. The medulla and pons are parts of the lower brain; the mandible is the lower jawbone.

18 The chest. The intercostal is a rib muscle, the scapula is the breastbone, and the aorta is the artery of the heart.

19 The leg. The saphenous is the large skin vein in the leg, the femur is the long thighbone, and the quadriceps femoris is one of the thigh muscles.

20 It destroys used red blood cells.

21 Diabetes mellitus, caused by the lack of insulin hormone.

22 Asthma, which may follow a lung infection or result from an allergic reaction.

23 Atrophy, the lessening in size of cells or tissues.

24 Cancer, which is characterized by rampant, abnormal cell growth.

25 Myocardial infarction, or heart attack. The clot is now thought to form after the infarction.

## plants

*Quotation: Gertrude Stein*

1 The black depths of the sea.

2 Plants contain cellulose and chlorophyll, and they manufacture their own food (photosynthesis).

3 Bristlecone pine.

4 Most of the chlorophyll needed for photosynthesis is in the upper surfaces.

5 The leaf would lose too much water and die.

6 They live on other plants and decaying material.

7 Roots always turn downward no matter what way the seed is planted.

8 90–100 gallons.

9 The banana plant is an herb; its trunk is not woody.

10 Vascular bundles.

11 It stores reserve food.

12 They will grow in height but not diameter.

13 Spore cases, used for reproduction.

14 The gymnosperms—pines, cedars, and various other evergreens.

15 Vegetative reproduction produces larger plants more rapidly.

16 Tropism.

17 The pineapple family.

18 To get sunlight.

19 Symbiosis.

20 Chlorophyll breaks down chemically and becomes colorless, allowing the other colors that were always in the leaf to show.

21 Plants, as well an animals, migrated over the Bering Sea in ancient times.

22 A wild cabbage native to the eastern Mediterranean.

23 The garden pea.

24 New Dawn, an everblooming rose.

25 The tomato.

## polar regions

*Quotation: Robert Peary*

1 New Archangel.

2 Simon Dezhnev.

3 The Nenana Ice Classic, during which people guess when the ice on the Tanana River will break up.

4 1958, by the submarine *Nautilus*.

5 Mount Erebus, an active volcano.

6 Only birds.

7 There are none.

8 Tropical.

9 Marie Byrd Land, for his wife.

10 North Polar (Arctic) area.

11 Kodiak bear.

12 As tall as six feet.

13 Pacific islands, New Zealand, Australia, and South America.

14 The blending together of sky and snowy ground to make the horizon and other points of reference virtually invisible.

15 Pytheas, an ancient Greek.

16 Starvation.

17 Hunting of seals on the open sea.

18 Greenville, S.C.

19 The Tatar khanate of Sibir.

20 Siberia is nearly one and a half times as large as the U.S.

21 Robert Falcon Scott, 1912.

22 From the Norse word *vik*, meaning harbor or bay.

23 Robert E. Peary, North; and Roald Amundsen, South.

24 They are citizens of whatever town— Swedish, Danish, Norwegian, or Soviet —they live in.

25 The bay does not freeze over; there is only drifting ice.

## religions of the world

*Quotation: Thomas Paine*

1 Judaism.

2 Hinduism.

3 India.

4 The Koran.

5 Christianity.

6 Shinto.

7 Germany.

8 Confucius.

9 Nero.

10 Ulrich Zwingli.

11 Mecca.

12 The Church of Jesus Christ of Latter-day Saints (Mormons).

13 Bar Mitzvah.

14 American Friends Service Committee.

15 Lutheran church.

16 Poseidon.

17 Lourdes, France.

18 Ancient Nineveh.

19 The Huguenots.

20 About 14,000.

21 The Navajo.

22 1948.

23 David Livingstone.

24 Boston, Mass.

25 A.D. 1054.

## reptiles and prehistoric animals

*Quotation: Francis Bacon*

1 The turkey.

2 About 570 million years ago.

3 Brachiosaurus, weighing some 50 tons.

4 Inability to adapt to major geological and climatic changes, maybe.

5 Struthiomimus ("ostrich mimic").

6 Oligocene spiders and insects have been preserved in amber.

7 About 60 million years ago.

8 Stegosaurus, an armored dinosaur with a walnut-size brain.

9 The pterosaurs.

10 Dinosaur National Monument, on the Colorado-Utah border.

11 The Gobi of Mongolia during the 1920's.

12 Titanotheres, similar to rhinoceroses and horses.

13 About 2,000 teeth.

14 Scorpionlike animals about 430 million years ago.

15 About 30 million years ago in North America.

16 Two and a half feet wide.

17 The cockroach.

18 The sea turtle.

19 By darting their heads into the water and snagging fish as herons do today.

20 No one knows.

21 The reptiles, about 225 million years ago (the Triassic period).

22 By measuring the radioactive decay of some of their components.

23 When man emerged is uncertain; humanlike teeth 20 million years old have been found.

24 The pelycosaurs.

25 The coelacanth.

## rivers and dams

*Quotation: Henry Van Dyke*

1 In Colorado.

2 A passage through a dam for lowering the water level of the reservoir.

3 In France.

4 The Tigris and the Euphrates.

5 It was built to house more than 5,000 persons engaged in building Hoover Dam.

6 About 400 million tons.

7 It is the third longest.

8 The Rhine.

9 They drain off surplus water to the sea and carry soil and rocks with the water.

10 A temporary dam that is built to hold back water so that work can be done on the permanent dam.

11 The Ganges, because the crops depend upon its waters.

12 An unusually torrential rain or the collapse of a dam and reservoir when weakened by heavy rains.

13 The U.S. Army engineers if navigation is involved and the Bureau of Reclamation for irrigation projects.

14 The Volga, 2,325 miles in length.

15 The abandoned meanders, or windings, of a river.

16 At the juncture of the Monongahela and Allegheny rivers at Pittsburgh, Pa.

17 For electric power and irrigation.

18 By Hoover Dam.

19 The Thames.

20 Water supply, flood control, electric power, and improved navigation.

21 In 1902.

22 More than 23 million acre-feet of water.

23 The Columbia River.

24 The solid gravity dam.

25 The Seine.

## sculpture

### Quotation: Michelangelo

1 Religion.
2 'Moses'.
3 "Stabiles" and "mobiles."
4 Bronze.
5 Pablo Picasso.
6 Proper lighting.
7 Ivory and gold.
8 Constantin Brancusi.
9 The greatest sculptor of the French Renaissance.
10 'The Burghers of Calais'.
11 Donatello.
12 In the statues by Henry Moore.
13 Lorenzo Ghiberti.
14 Carl Milles.
15 Daniel Chester French.
16 Sir Jacob Epstein.
17 Paul Manship.
18 They were intended to frighten people into mending their ways.
19 The lost-wax process.
20 Frederic Remington.
21 Alteration of literal truth to achieve a desired effect.
22 The surrealist.
23 In China.
24 Baked clay.
25 Wilhelm Lehmbruck.

## team sports

### Quotation: Frank Gifford

1 162.
2 1933.
3 25.
4 Rogers Hornsby; .424.
5 Cooperstown, N.Y.
6 Kenesaw M. Landis.
7 Montreal, Que.
8 New York (American League).
9 Ten feet.
10 Dr. James A. Naismith.
11 One.
12 Eight minutes.
13 100 yards.
14 Two.
15 15.
16 Pasadena, Calif.
17 Princeton and Rutgers.
18 Green Bay Packers.
19 Four.
20 70 minutes.
21 11.
22 Eight.
23 Six.
24 1895.
25 15.

## theater and drama

### Quotation: George Jean Nathan

1 By 1592 he was already recognized as an actor and playwright. He probably acted in some of his plays.
2 Lives of the saints.
3 In Greece.
4 The Stanislavsky approach, in which the actor identifies himself with the emotional life of the character he is portraying.
5 England, France, and the U.S.
6 Henrik Ibsen.
7 Christopher Marlowe.
8 Johann Christoph Friedrich von Schiller.
9 Pierre Corneille and Jean Baptiste Racine.
10 'The Importance of Being Earnest'.
11 Lighting.
12 The last great playwright of the Golden Age of Spanish drama.
13 Ferenc Molnár.
14 John Millington Synge.
15 'A Raisin in the Sun'.
16 Jean Anouilh.
17 Ireland.
18 Anton Chekhov.
19 George Bernard Shaw.
20 The basic unit for scene construction.
21 Arthur Miller and Tennessee Williams.
22 A farce is broad comedy, full of horseplay; a comedy of manners is subtle, witty, and often mocking.
23 The Globe.
24 About 1920; Eugene O'Neill.
25 Harlequin and Pierrot.

## tools

### Quotation: Benjamin Franklin

1 Lathe.
2 30,000 years ago.
3 Radial type.
4 Elias Howe (1846).
5 Dredge.
6 Metalworking.
7 Hack saw.
8 Quartz or quartzite.
9 Computer.
10 Zacharias Janssen, about 1590.
11 Bending and shaping metal.
12 1814.
13 The amount of deviation permitted in the size of a part.
14 Micrometer.
15 Operating relays for control purposes.
16 400.
17 A "core."
18 Pica and elite.
19 Aluminum oxide and silicon carbide.
20 Casting.
21 Goggles.
22 Hatchet.
23 Eli Whitney.
24 About 11,000 B.C.
25 70 hours.

## transportation and travel

### Quotation: John Ruskin

1 In recreational activities, such as pleasure driving.
2 Human porter.
3 Close together.
4 The Cumberland Road and the Erie Canal.
5 Reeds or branches for rafts; skins for boats; or logs for dugout canoes.
6 Crude oil, in tankers.
7 About 2000 B.C.
8 Railroads carry 40% of the total volume, while trucks account for more than half of the revenues.
9 Oil pipelines.
10 A Frenchman, Nicolas Cugnot, demonstrated a steam carrier intended for use on common roads in 1769.
11 John Fitch, on the Delaware River in 1790.
12 Samuel Cunard, in 1840.
13 Four to six.
14 As much as 25 acres.
15 In European mines as early as the mid-1500's.
16 In 1869.
17 More than 20,000 a day in the early 1940's.
18 A branch of the route between Western Europe and South America curves around southern Africa to fill the gap.
19 About 3 million, including 35,000 miles of expressways.
20 The Italians built the autostrada and the Germans the Autobahn in the 1920's and 1930's.
21 In London, beginning in 1863.
22 Speedier transfer of cargo between ships and overland carriers.
23 The popularity of the bicycle.
24 They ran a bicycle shop.
25 Between Boston, Mass., New York City, and Washington, D.C.; New York City and Chicago; and Los Angeles and San Francisco, Calif.

## united states

### Quotation: Thomas Wolfe

1 Only three.
2 120 to 180 days.
3 About 10%.
4 "Near the great mountain."
5 About 23 years, to age 70.5.
6 Nebraska.
7 Bald eagle.
8 South Dakota.
9 Dinosaur Quarry, near Kenton, Okla.
10 Alabama.
11 Roadrunner.
12 Death Valley, Calif. (282 feet below sea level).
13 Maui, Hawaii.
14 "He Has Favored Our Undertakings."
15 Maryland.
16 F.A. Bartholdi.
17 Kings Point, N.Y.
18 22d Amendment.
19 Connecticut.
20 Florida.
21 Motor vehicles.
22 26.5%.
23 1600 Pennsylvania Avenue, N.W., Washington, D.C.
24 Texas.
25 57.5.

## water life

### Quotation: Lewis Carroll

1 Gills.
2 Isinglass.
3 The salmon.
4 Covering ploughshares.
5 The muskellunge.
6 They will fight incessantly.
7 The cod.
8 The tarpon.
9 By generating a powerful electric current.
10 Giant squids.
11 The cuttlefish.
12 No.
13 Purple.
14 The giant clam of the Indian and Pacific oceans.
15 The man-eater or great white shark.
16 The egg cases of skates and rays.
17 A fish.
18 The lamprey.
19 Canada.
20 Spiders and scorpions.
21 Corals.
22 The sponge.
23 The nautilus.
24 Aristotle.
25 Plankton.

## winter and water sports

*Quotation: Kenneth Grahame*

1 Arlberg system.
2 Montreal Canadiens.
3 Curling.
4 Oregon pine or fir.
5 1,000 feet.
6 Hawaii.
7 About 6 ounces.
8 One.
9 The America's Cup Race (1851).
10 "Rackets."
11 Railroad trains on land.
12 1924.
13 In the South Pacific and off the coast of India.
14 Butterfly stroke.
15 Trick riding, slalom, and jumping.
16 It was made of metal rather than of wood.
17 Seven.
18 Ole Evinrude.
19 Two in single sculling; only one in all other types.
20 Toronto, Ont.
21 Red Cross.
22 Jacques-Yves Cousteau and Émile Gagnan.
23 Chicago Black Hawks.
24 Marconi.
25 The blade is convex and has teeth at the front.

## women and women's rights

*Quotation: James Madison*

1 Jeanette Rankin.
2 Almost 300,000.
3 Seneca Falls, N.Y., 1848.
4 'The Feminine Mystique'.
5 Prohibition party, in 1872.
6 Emmeline Pankhurst.
7 The Moslem custom requiring women to cover their faces in public.
8 Female.
9 About 13%.
10 Frances Perkins, secretary of labor, appointed by U.S. President Franklin D. Roosevelt.
11 Margaret Sanger.
12 Men: $9,454; women: $3,818.
13 William Lloyd Garrison.
14 Shirley Chisholm.
15 Conception.
16 1915.
17 Israel.
18 Jane Addams.
19 'The Second Sex'.
20 Obtaining credit.
21 Killing of a wife by her husband in crimes of "passion"—adequate defense against murder in many states but does not apply if wife attacks husband.
22 Abraham Lincoln.
23 She was tried, found guilty, and fined $50.
24 1920.
25 1850.

## world literature

*Quotation: Mark Twain*

1 Near Brattleboro, Vt.
2 Dante Alighieri.
3 Aleksander Sergeevich Pushkin.
4 Pearl S. Buck.
5 Chinua Achebe.
6 In Mexico City, Mexico, in about 1539.
7 Pindar.
8 Sweden.
9 Johann Wolfgang von Goethe's.
10 'Don Quixote'.
11 Rabindranath Tagore.
12 The Jalna series.
13 William Butler Yeats.
14 José Martí.
15 Albert Camus and Jean Paul Sartre.
16 Ignazio Silone.
17 William Shakespeare, Christopher Marlowe, and Edmund Spenser.
18 The first great lyric poet of France.
19 Günter Grass.
20 F. Scott Fitzgerald.
21 John Keats.
22 Two kinds of short Japanese poems that suggest a mood or picture.
23 James Joyce.
24 The Realist Alberto Blest Gana.
25 Boris Pasternak.

## youth organizations

*Quotation: Eleanor Roosevelt*

1 In Chicago, concurrently with the International Livestock Exposition.
2 Teenage girls' groups sponsored by the YMCA.
3 Future Farmers of America.
4 Dr. and Mrs. Luther Halsey Gulick.
5 "Do your best."
6 Junior Achievement.
7 1912.
8 Young Women's Christian Association (YWCA).
9 Venezuela's equivalent of 4-H Clubs.
10 Six to 16.
11 24.
12 Audubon Junior Clubs.
13 A Masonic group for young men aged 14 to 21.
14 Nine.
15 National Honor Society.
16 Camp Fire Girls.
17 Future Teachers of America (FTA).
18 U.S.S.R.
19 Woodrow Wilson.
20 1945.
21 Williamsport, Pa.
22 American Legion Auxiliary.
23 The Young Adult Council.
24 Bishop Bernard J. Sheil.
25 Near Freeville, N.Y.

## general quiz one

*Quotation: Booker T. Washington*

1 An artesian spring is pressurized underground water spurting out a natural opening. If the opening is man-made, the water is known as an artesian well.
2 After nightfall, as the air on the hillside cools, it falls a little, and the warmer air from above settles in its place.
3 Spartacus.
4 Emperor Dom Pedro II of Brazil.
5 Spain and Portugal.
6 The sundew.
7 A vigorous, disciplined, and laconic person.
8 Loss of weight, some disorientation, orthostatic collapse, or "lazy heart," and softening of bones.
9 The Spanish-American War.
10 Simón Bolívar.
11 About 420 miles per minute, or 25,000 miles per hour.
12 Stamps.
13 Nebraska.
14 Lake Superior.

15 Stockings that fit tightly to the leg.
16 The British Guiana one-penny black stamp is worth $60,000.
17 Sirius.
18 No.
19 Dressed in white and carrying a glowing star on a staff, these boys in Sweden perform brief biblical scenes or sing during the Christmas season.
20 It means any secret, arbitrary court.
21 The opening of the Suez Canal.
22 Every year the cambium adds a layer of new cells to the older wood, and each layer forms a ring. Counting the rings reveals the age of the tree.
23 Torpedo fish.
24 They lose the ability to kill their natural prey because of broken teeth or claws or failing strength of an old tiger.
25 More than 86%.

## general quiz two

*Quotation: George Santayana*

1 Greenwich, England.
2 The newly transplanted roots can nourish only a limited amount of foliage.
3 The Society of St. Tammany.
4 That the best life is a simple life.
5 Titmice.
6 In a night attack on the Scottish camp, a barefoot Norseman trod on a thistle. Crying out in pain, he alerted the Scots, and the attack failed.
7 No, that is a superstition.
8 General George Thomas.
9 The Texas Rangers.
10 At the Louisiana Purchase Exposition of 1904, in St. Louis, Mo., where the weather was very hot.
11 Thailand.
12 Jim Thorpe.
13 It is a tennis term. When the racket is swung from left to right, the ball clears the net, drops sharply to the receiver's right, and "breaks" high to his left.
14 In a standard relay race, each member of a team runs one fourth of the total distance. In a medley relay, the team members run varying distances.
15 Torquato Tasso.
16 By their lack of a waistline such as the ant has where its thorax joins its abdomen.
17 No, only to insects.
18 Pole vault.
19 About 800 pounds, or 94 gallons.
20 Expenses for constant necessities such as food, shelter, and transportation.
21 Old Age.
22 By electromagnetic force when a metal ship approaches.
23 About 20 years.
24 Teak.
25 When a permanent tooth is ready to replace a primary tooth, the root of the primary tooth has been absorbed by the tissue of the jaw.

## general quiz three

*Quotation: Euclid*

1 Jim Thorpe.
2 William Howard Taft.
3 Nikola Tesla.
4 Asia.
5 His grandfathers, Anderson Shippe Truman and Solomon Young.
6 Ports where goods intended to be sent to another country may be landed and reshipped tax-free.

7 Tokyo, Japan.
8 Peter Tchaikovsky.
9 In the second half of the 15th century.
10 Tin.
11 Tibet.
12 The Trans-Canada Highway.
13 By eliminating malaria and raising individual income.
14 The revolutions per minute of a revolving shaft.
15 Tampa, Fla.
16 In Tanzania.
17 Tapioca.
18 Two of the men who sailed with Christopher Columbus.
19 Tasmanian zebra wolf and Tasmanian devil.
20 In Mesopotamia.
21 The frog has, but the toad has not.
22 It begins on July 1 of one year and ends on June 30 of the next.
23 The bo tree.
24 Titles and property are inherited by the eldest son.
25 No.

## general quiz four

*Quotation: Samuel Taylor Coleridge*

1 The people who settled in California during the gold rush of 1849.
2 Chile and Argentina.
3 The teredo.
4 Abraham Lincoln.
5 The tailorbird.
6 Yes, they are both in dots and dashes.
7 Wats.
8 Because lenses bigger than 40 inches are too distorted by their own weight.
9 A military and religious order that arose during the Crusades.
10 Toronto, Ont.
11 Queen Victoria.
12 The Mona Lisa's.
13 Diego Velasquez.
14 Because he was a painter, sculptor, scientist, engineer, and inventor.
15 For two terms.
16 No, he only produces the illusion that the voice originates elsewhere.
17 Volcanoes.
18 Virginia.
19 About 70 pieces.
20 A rocky key in the Virgin Islands.
21 They eat other insects that prey on plant and human life.
22 Those of the Venus's-flytrap.
23 Because the ores are radioactive.
24 In the 1550's.
25 No.

## general quiz five

*Quotation: Oliver Wendell Holmes*

1 "Sour wine" (in Latin).
2 In the 1920's.
3 The dominant tribe of Buganda.
4 No.
5 People in the North who were talking of abolishing slavery in the name of humanity.
6 Jamestown, Va.
7 No.
8 The War of 1812.
9 The national feeling in mid-19th century that the United States should expand across the continent.
10 Vertebrates.
11 The Mexican War of 1848.

12 Leningrad-Vladivostok, U.S.S.R.
13 Meriwether Lewis and William Clark.
14 Venice, Italy.
15 From plants.
16 The first ten amendments to the United States Constitution.
17 Because conspicuous shades are hazardous in combat.
18 Angel Falls in Venezuela.
19 At Promontory, Utah.
20 Vatican City.
21 They paid 120 pounds of tobacco.
22 Smallpox.
23 Sirius, from London.
24 Vitamin C.
25 The *Pennsylvania Packet, and Daily Advertiser*, of Philadelphia.

## general quiz six

*Quotation: Edwin Arlington Robinson*

1 The 26th Amendment.
2 At Vatican City.
3 Five.
4 The bald eagle, adopted June 20, 1782.
5 The Union of Soviet Socialist Republics.
6 Vitamin D.
7 The United Nations.
8 John Quincy Adams, Rutherford B. Hayes, and Benjamin Harrison.
9 In the National Archives Building in Washington, D.C.
10 More than 400.
11 Because the larynx has not attained its full growth and development and because the vocal cords have not yet adjusted to the larger voice box holding them.
12 To close the port of Boston; limit self-government in Massachusetts; allow British officials accused of crimes in America to stand trial in Great Britain; order the colonies to furnish additional quarters for British troops; and extend the southern boundary of Quebec to the Ohio River.
13 Teutonic barbarians who wrecked buildings and looted churches.
14 Maurice Utrillo.
15 They dispose of carrion.
16 In Marietta, Ohio.
17 Harvard University, founded in 1636.
18 In 1929.
19 In Chicago; the Home Insurance Building.
20 Five.
21 Uruguay.
22 Yes.
23 The Erie Canal.
24 To keep the sacred fire burning in the Temple of Vesta.
25 Lake Victoria.

## general quiz seven

*Quotation: Abraham Lincoln*

1 On the plaster wall of the convent church of Santa Maria delle Grazie in Milan, Italy.
2 The whale.
3 The yucca.
4 To present a greater surface to the water, from which they draw their nourishment.
5 Weaverbirds.
6 No, they are warm-blooded mammals.
7 The yak.
8 Softwoods and hardwoods.

9 The Westminster clock on the Victoria Tower of the Houses of Parliament in London.
10 It is searching for food.
11 Social wasps.
12 They hunt in packs, working together to bring down game.
13 Walruses.
14 By thrusting a stinger into the body of a victim.
15 Wolverine.
16 They are able to stand extremes of heat and cold, drought, high winds, and even fire.
17 It made possible the rapid collection and dissemination of weather observations.
18 William Yeats.
19 Eli Whitney.
20 Because the Wisconsin lead miners were called "badgers."
21 The woodpecker.
22 In Wales.
23 Sarah Childress Polk.
24 Mount Waialeale, Kauai, Hawaii, has the greatest; Arica, Chile, the least.
25 A cuneiform tablet from the Sumerian city of Uruk, dating from about 3100 B.C.

## general quiz eight

*Quotation: Grover Cleveland*

1 Émile Zola.
2 Many wasps have a slender joint between the thorax and the abdomen.
3 Roger Williams.
4 In the Yukon Territory.
5 A famous book about the march and retreat of the Greek auxiliary army in the service of the Persian prince, Cyrus, who was trying to overthrow his brother, the Persian king.
6 When the whale surfaces, the pent-up air is expelled from its lungs through the nostril, or blowhole, on top of its head.
7 In Westminster Abbey.
8 Daniel Webster.
9 Five bushels.
10 Black walnut.
11 Zoroastrianism.
12 Because they can be ground with great precision, are extremely hard, and do not corrode.
13 The woman guests occupy the Rose Room; the men, the Lincoln Room.
14 Saint Francis Xavier.
15 Because the gray sandstone walls of the Executive Mansion were painted white.
16 A center of scientific knowledge in the United States.
17 They were made from the brisket bone of an ox and fastened by thongs to the sole of the skater's boot.
18 The twisting column of water seen between clouds and the surface of the sea.
19 The War of 1812.
20 Frances Folsom Cleveland.
21 In Washington.
22 John and Charles Wesley.
23 Abigail Smith Adams.
24 The Duke of Wellington.
25 Wilbur and Orville Wright.

## general quiz nine

*Quotation: James Thurber*

1 About 100 islands.
2 A hard formation of rock over soft layers.
3 John Adams.
4 William II, emperor of Germany.
5 William III and his queen, Mary.
6 The water lily.
7 A morning rainbow indicates humid air and the coming of stormy weather; an evening rainbow indicates the passing of stormy weather.
8 Chinese Emperor Wu Wang.
9 For 17 years.
10 No, because his machine was stolen and copied.
11 Four of Theodore Roosevelt's children.
12 By using hourglasses with sand.
13 Vast movements that occur on a worldwide scale in response to worldwide temperature variations.
14 American Indians.
15 Dying without having made a will.
16 William the Silent, prince of Orange.
17 The bacteria that bring about decay are the chief cause of food spoilage. Other bacteria produce fermented foods such as sour cream, buttermilk, and other dairy products.
18 An association established by banks to collect and distribute checks.
19 Thomas Hart Benton.
20 Bismarck, N.D.
21 Walter de la Mare.
22 Iceland.
23 Expansion of commerce and growing interest in scientific investigation and invention.
24 In size and weight.
25 New Jersey.

## general quiz ten

*Quotation: James Russell Lowell*

1 Sieur de La Salle.
2 Lenin.
3 St. Bernadette of Lourdes.
4 During a storm he was struck by lightning. He was filled with a fear of death and a consciousness of sin. He renounced the world and entered a monastery.
5 Because about two thirds of its inhabitants speak French, and evidences of French culture can be seen everywhere.

6 Rhythm, melody, harmony, and form.
7 More than 100.
8 'Dixie', 'Maryland, My Maryland', and 'Battle Hymn of the Republic'.
9 Off Newfoundland, the Grand Banks.
10 The Harvard-Yale regatta.
11 A submarine mountain ridge that continues 40,000 miles.
12 Some grow on the ground, others grow in marshy places, and the most valuable grow on tree trunks and branches.
13 Because it was threatened with extinction by overhunting.
14 Well into Illinois.
15 The volcanic rocks.
16 Ireland.
17 Silver.
18 In 1890.
19 Primitive man.
20 Rockford.
21 Ulysses S. Grant.
22 Yes. The fancies that enable an Edison to give electric light to the world represent imagination made to work to a useful end.
23 The Indians.
24 Fewer.
25 In 1913.

## general quiz eleven

*Quotation: Benjamin Harrison*

1 The sand dunes along Lake Michigan in the north; mineral springs and Wyandotte Cave in the south; and Brown County, in south-central Indiana.
2 Because they followed their herds from place to place seeking pasture.
3 Warm colors, containing red or yellow.
4 No, they change under different lighting conditions.
5 The cotton gin.
6 About 40,000 to 50,000.
7 A mixture of smoke and fog.
8 In Tehran's Central Bank of Iran.
9 Because wherever there is drainage enough to prevent marshes, the abundant moisture produces lush green grass.
10 Jack-o'-lantern.
11 It grew out of 15th-century European trade in ivory along the Gulf of Guinea.
12 No, at night.
13 The Hermitage.
14 Because he assumed so much power as president.
15 Andrew Jackson.

16 Robespierre and Danton.
17 Both by pursuit and by pouncing on its victims from trees.
18 Mahogany, rosewood, and ebony.
19 A translation of the Bible published in 1611.
20 James II.
21 Janus.
22 Hunters, gatherers, and farmers.
23 He played the major part in planning the principles of U.S. democracy.
24 A trial jury.
25 The name Sawtooth is well suited to the jagged peaks of the mountain.

## general quiz twelve

*Quotation: John Philip Sousa*

1 Water from a lake rushes down the penstock and spins the turbine. The turbine shaft whirls the armature of the generator, and the electricity produced flows along transmission lines to the user.
2 West Virginia.
3 He supervised the building of the Parthenon, carved the giant statue of Athena in ivory and gold, and sculpted a statue of Zeus that was one of the wonders of the ancient world.
4 The albatross.
5 The Code of Justinian.
6 Rounded contours.
7 Aqueducts.
8 In 1790.
9 Delaware.
10 From 15 to 35 feet per minute.
11 'The Wolf and the Ass'.
12 They attract pollen-carrying insects and birds.
13 New Guinea.
14 Hamilton believed in a strong central government, but Jefferson believed in states' rights.
15 Andrew Jackson.
16 In 1791.
17 It abolished slavery.
18 The Mayflower Compact.
19 El Salvador.
20 The legend of the Fountain of Youth.
21 The raccoon.
22 The alarm clock.
23 Their centers are placed 12 inches apart.
24 An annealing oven.
25 Small terra-cotta figures made by the ancient Greeks.

# calendar for 1975

## JAN

| | | |
|---|---|---|
| Wed. | 1 | New Year's Day. Major football bowl games. Tournament of Roses and Mummers Day parades. International Women's Year begins. |
| Sun. | 5 | Twelfth Night. |
| Mon. | 6 | Epiphany, or Twelfth Day. |
| Tues. | 7 | Millard Fillmore's birthday. |
| Thurs. | 9 | Richard M. Nixon's birthday. |
| Mon. | 13 | Stephen Foster Memorial Day. Muslim Era New Year begins. |
| Wed. | 15 | Martin Luther King, Jr.'s birthday. Eagles return to Dunderbergh, N.Y. |
| Fri. | 17 | Benjamin Franklin's birthday. |
| Sun. | 19 | World Religion Day. |
| Mon. | 20 | Robert E. Lee's birthday. |
| Sun. | 26 | Septuagesima Sunday. |
| Mon. | 27 | National MIA (Missing in Action) Awareness Day. |
| Wed. | 29 | William McKinley's birthday. |
| Thurs. | 30 | Franklin D. Roosevelt's birthday. |

## FEB

| | | |
|---|---|---|
| Sat. | 1 | National Freedom Day. American Heart, History, and Music months begin. |
| Sun. | 2 | Candlemas. Groundhog Day. International Clergy Week begins. |
| Sat. | 8 | Boy Scouts of America 65th birthday. |
| Sun. | 9 | William H. Harrison's birthday. |
| Mon. | 10 | National Nurse Week begins. |
| Tues. | 11 | Mardi Gras (Fat Tuesday). Shrove Tuesday. National Inventors' Day. Pancake Day. |
| Wed. | 12 | Ash Wednesday. Lent begins. Abraham Lincoln's birthday. |
| Fri. | 14 | St. Valentine's Day. |
| Sat. | 15 | Susan B. Anthony Day. |
| Sun. | 16 | First Sunday in Lent. Brotherhood and National Engineers' weeks begin. |
| Mon. | 17 | George Washington's birthday observed. National Parent-Teacher Associations Founders Day. |
| Tues. | 25 | Purim, or Feast of Lots. |

## MAR

| | | |
|---|---|---|
| Sat. | 1 | Red Cross Month begins. |
| Sun. | 2 | Save Your Vision Week begins. |
| Sun. | 9 | Girl Scout Week begins. |
| Sat. | 15 | Andrew Jackson's birthday. Ides of March. Buzzards return to Hinckley, Ohio. |
| Sun. | 16 | James Madison's birthday. Camp Fire Girls Birthday, National Poison Prevention, and National Wildlife weeks begin. |
| Mon. | 17 | St. Patrick's Day. |
| Tues. | 18 | Grover Cleveland's birthday. |
| Wed. | 19 | Swallows return to San Juan Capistrano, Calif. |
| Fri. | 21 | Spring begins. World Forestry Day. |
| Sun. | 23 | Palm Sunday. Holy Week begins. |
| Thurs. | 27 | Passover begins. Maundy Thursday. |
| Fri. | 28 | Good Friday. |
| Sat. | 29 | John Tyler's birthday. Holy Saturday. Vietnam Veterans Day. |
| Sun. | 30 | Easter Sunday. |

## APR

| | | |
|---|---|---|
| Tues. | 1 | April Fool's Day. National Laugh and Publicity Stunt weeks begin. Cancer Control, Freedom Shrine, and American Lawn and Garden months begin. |
| Wed. | 2 | International Children's Book Day. |
| Sun. | 6 | Low Sunday. |
| Wed. | 9 | Sir Winston Churchill Day. |
| Sun. | 13 | Thomas Jefferson's birthday. Pan American Week begins. |
| Mon. | 14 | Pan American Day. |
| Sun. | 20 | National Coin, National YWCA, and Secretaries weeks begin. |
| Mon. | 21 | Earth and National Volunteer weeks begin. |
| Wed. | 23 | James Buchanan's and William Shakespeare's birthdays. |
| Fri. | 25 | National Arbor Day. |
| Sun. | 27 | Ulysses S. Grant's birthday. |
| Mon. | 28 | Confederate Memorial Day. James Monroe's birthday. |

# MAY

| Thurs. | 1 | May Day. Law Day. Older Americans and Steelmark months begin. |
| Sat. | 3 | Kentucky Derby. |
| Sun. | 4 | Humane Sunday. National Be Kind to Animals Week begins. |
| Thurs. | 8 | Harry S. Truman's birthday. |
| Sun. | 11 | Mother's Day. Police and National Transportation weeks begin. |
| Mon. | 12 | Legal Rights for Retarded Citizens Week begins. |
| Fri. | 16 | National Defense Transportation Day. Shavout, or Feast of Weeks, begins. |
| Sat. | 17 | Armed Forces Day. |
| Sun. | 18 | Pentecost, or Whitsunday. Small Business and World Trade weeks begin. |
| Mon. | 19 | Empire Day, Canada. Whitmonday. |
| Thurs. | 22 | National Maritime Day. |
| Sat. | 24 | Total eclipse of the moon. |
| Sun. | 25 | Indianapolis 500-mile race. |
| Thurs. | 29 | John F. Kennedy's birthday. |

# JUNE

| Sun. | 1 | America the Beautiful Week begins. Fight the Filthy Fly, National Ragweed Control, and National Rose months begin. Carnivals Against Dystrophy begins. |
| Tues. | 3 | Jefferson Davis' birthday. |
| Thurs. | 5 | World Environment Day. |
| Sun. | 8 | Children's Day. Race Unity Day. National Flag and National Fraternal weeks begin. |
| Mon. | 9 | National Little League Baseball Week begins. |
| Sat. | 14 | Flag Day. Queen Elizabeth II's birthday observed. |
| Sun. | 15 | Father's Day. |
| Sat. | 21 | Summer begins. |
| Thurs. | 26 | United Nations Charter signed by 50 countries 30 years ago. Freedom Week begins. |
| Sun. | 29 | National Safe Boating Week begins. |

# JULY

| Tues. | 1 | Dominion Day, Canada. |
| Fri. | 4 | Independence Day, or Fourth of July. Calvin Coolidge's birthday. |
| Sat. | 5 | Dog Days begin. |
| Tues. | 8 | Nelson A. Rockefeller's birthday. |
| Fri. | 11 | John Quincy Adams' birthday. |
| Sun. | 13 | Captive Nations Week begins. |
| Mon. | 14 | Bastille Day, or Fête National, France. Gerald R. Ford's birthday. |
| Tues. | 15 | St. Swithin's Day. |
| Wed. | 16 | U.S. Space Week begins. |
| Fri. | 18 | International Railway Day. |
| Sat. | 19 | First Women's Rights Convention Anniversary. |
| Sun. | 20 | Moon Day. America's Dependence on God Day. Expo '75 (International Ocean Exposition), Okinawa, Japan, begins. |
| Thurs. | 24 | Simon Bolivar's birthday. |
| Fri. | 25 | National Farm Safety Week begins. |

# AUG

| Fri. | 1 | U.S.A. Sports Day. Beauty Queen and National Clown weeks begin. Good Nutrition and August Is Sandwich months begin. |
| Sun. | 3 | Friendship Day. National Smile Week begins. |
| Mon. | 4 | Coast Guard Day. Civic Holiday, Canada. |
| Wed. | 6 | Hiroshima Day. Peace Festival, Japan. |
| Fri. | 8 | International Character Day. National Hobo Convention begins. |
| Sun. | 10 | Herbert C. Hoover's birthday. Family Reunion Day. |
| Mon. | 11 | Dog Days end. |
| Thurs. | 14 | Atlantic Charter Day. Victory, or VJ, Day. |
| Tues. | 19 | National Aviation Day. |
| Wed. | 20 | Benjamin Harrison's birthday. |
| Tues. | 26 | Women's Equality Day. |
| Wed. | 27 | Lyndon B. Johnson's birthday. |

# SEPT

| | | |
|---|---|---|
| Mon. | 1 | Labor Day. Mackinac Bridge Walk. American Youth Month begins. |
| Sat. | 6 | Rosh Hashanah, or Jewish New Year (Tishri 1, 5736). |
| Sun. | 14 | National Hispanic Heritage Week begins. |
| Mon. | 15 | Yom Kippur, or Day of Atonement. William H. Taft's birthday. |
| Wed. | 17 | Citizenship Day. Constitution Week begins. |
| Sat. | 20 | Succoth, or Feast of Tabernacles, or Ingathering, begins. Harvest Moon. |
| Sun. | 21 | American Newspaper Anniversary Week begins. |
| Mon. | 22 | National Hunting and Fishing Day. |
| Tues. | 23 | Autumn begins. National Highway Week begins. |
| Fri. | 26 | American Indian Day. |
| Sun. | 28 | Gold Star Mother's Day. National Port Week begins. |

# OCT

| | | |
|---|---|---|
| Wed. | 1 | Country Music Month begins. |
| Sat. | 4 | Rutherford B. Hayes's birthday. |
| Sun. | 5 | Chester A. Arthur's birthday. National Employ the Physically Handicapped and Fire Prevention weeks begin. |
| Mon. | 6 | Child Health Day. |
| Thurs. | 9 | Leif Erickson Day. |
| Sat. | 11 | General Pulaski's Memorial Day. |
| Mon. | 13 | Columbus Day. |
| Tues. | 14 | Dwight D. Eisenhower's birthday. |
| Wed. | 15 | White Cane Safety Day. |
| Sat. | 18 | Sweetest Day. Pierre Elliott Trudeau's birthday. |
| Sun. | 19 | National Forest Products Week begins.. |
| Fri. | 24 | United Nations Day. |
| Sun. | 26 | American Education Week begins. |
| Mon. | 27 | Veterans, or Armistice, Day. Theodore Roosevelt's birthday. |
| Thurs. | 30 | John Adams' birthday. |
| Fri. | 31 | Halloween. National UNICEF Day. |

# NOV

| | | |
|---|---|---|
| Sat. | 1 | All Saints', or All Hallows', Day. National Model Railroad Month begins. |
| Sun. | 2 | All Souls' Day. Warren G. Harding's and James K. Polk's birthdays. |
| Tues. | 4 | General Election Day. |
| Wed. | 5 | Guy Fawkes Day. |
| Mon. | 10 | Marine Corps birthday. Youth Appreciation Week begins. |
| Tues. | 11 | Remembrance Day, Canada. Martinmas. |
| Sat. | 15 | Sadie Hawkins Day. |
| Sun. | 16 | National Farm-City Week begins. |
| Tues. | 18 | Total eclipse of the moon. |
| Wed. | 19 | James A. Garfield's birthday. |
| Fri. | 21 | Aviation Month—International begins. |
| Sun. | 23 | Franklin Pierce's birthday. |
| Mon. | 24 | Zachary Taylor's birthday. |
| Thurs. | 27 | Thanksgiving Day. |
| Sat. | 29 | Hanuka, or Feast of Lights, or Dedication, begins. |
| Sun. | 30 | First Sunday of Advent. |

# DEC

| | | |
|---|---|---|
| Tues. | 2 | Pan American Health Day. World Community Day. |
| Fri. | 5 | Martin Van Buren's birthday. |
| Sun. | 7 | Pearl Harbor Day. |
| Wed. | 10 | Human Rights Day. Human Rights Week begins. |
| Sat. | 13 | Army and Navy Union Day. |
| Mon. | 15 | Bill of Rights Day. Halcyon Days begin. |
| Wed. | 17 | Wright Brothers Day. Pan American Aviation Day. |
| Mon. | 22 | International Arbor Day. Winter begins. |
| Wed. | 24 | Christmas Eve. |
| Thurs. | 25 | Christmas Day, or Feast of the Nativity. |
| Fri. | 26 | Boxing Day, Commonwealth countries. |
| Sun. | 28 | Woodrow Wilson's birthday. |
| Mon. | 29 | Andrew Johnson's birthday. Halcyon Days end. |
| Wed. | 31 | New Year's Eve. |

# New Words

Language constantly changes. New words and word meanings are forever coming into the vocabulary; old ones die out. The new words are often only passing fads. One group uses a word, but the novelty may never gain wide acceptance. The word dies when the group gives it up or changes if it is given fresh meaning.

Sometimes, however, a new word does become a part of the living language. How do dictionary makers know when that has happened? And how do lexicographers go about giving a new word recognition in a reference work as part of the English language?

Dictionary and reference-set staffs and individual professionals employ continuous word-watching systems. Readers and editors record and analyze the language as it is actually spoken and written. Almost everything printed in English—books, magazines, newspapers, catalogs, and even business forms—is sampled. Each marked item is recorded and filed along with the content of its usage. These citations are tangible proof that each word was used in a particular way to convey a particular meaning at a particular time.

The following list of new words and meanings contains a sampling of the continuing change and growth of our language. Some of the entries may be forgotten next year; some may last as long as man himself.

## a

**acronymology** *n* : study of words formed from the initial letter or letters of the parts of compound terms

**ALADDIN** *n* : acronym used by the U.S. National Aeronautics and Space Administration (NASA) for Atmospheric Layering and Density Distribution of Ions and Neutrals

**Anik** *n* : Canadian domestic communications satellite placed in geostationary orbit above the Equator; after an Eskimo word meaning "little brother"

**anthropozoology** *n* : study of man as "naked ape"

**antitechnology** *n* : attitude of opposition to technological developments, based on concern for environmental consequences

**arteriograft** *n* : platinum or tantalum plastic graft to replace a defective or worn-out artery

**aspartame** *n* : aspartylphenylalanine methyl ester used as an artificial sweetener

## b

**bacat** *n* : special type of containerization for transporting freightboats; barge aboard catamaran

**bigskirt** *n* : voluminous flared skirt, knee-length or longer

**bioceramics** *n* : technique of inducing bone regrowth through porcelain implants that provide a natural matrix for renewed ossification

**biocybernetics** *n* : science of techniques for manipulating and transforming human personality

**biofeedback** *n* : use of techniques for the precise measurement of bodily functions previously regarded as automatic and unconscious

**bourgeoisification** *or* **embourgeoisement** *n* : blurring of distinction between the working and middle classes

**bug juice** *n* : medicine, prison slang

## c

**Caad** *abbr* : computer-aided architectural design

**cardiotocograph** *n* : saving technique in difficult childbirth by recording the heartbeat of the unborn baby by means of a mini-electrode attached to its scalp

**community home** *n* : establishment for delinquent children, replacing penal institutions and approved schools

**consensocracy** *n* : form of government or administration based on consensus of opinion

**cryosphere** *n* : permanently frozen land

# d

**dead-on-arrival** *adj* : in electronics, used of circuits that don't work when first plugged in

**diamond mine** *n* : good location to earn diamonds—see DIAMONDS

**diamonds** *n pl* : highest international soaring awards, earned for altitude gain of at least 16,404 feet, distance beyond 310.7 miles, and flight of at least 186.4 miles to predetermined goal

**disintermediation** *n* : the outflow of funds from banks and savings-and-loan institutions when interest rates on investment vehicles such as Treasury bills rise relative to interest rates on savings

**divirace** *n* : form of reverse discrimination in which members of racial minorities are singled out, or resegregated, solely on the basis of race

**doomwatch syndrome** *n* : pessimistic signs and symptoms of those prophesying resource depletion by the end of the century

**drivotrainer** *n* : simulator aid to help train a beginner at home to learn to drive an automobile

# e

**earth resources satellite** *n* : man-made vehicle placed in orbit around the earth for the purpose of gathering and transmitting information regarding meteorology, geology, agriculture and forestry, mapping

**earthwatch** *n* : plan of action directed against anything that might lead to the destruction of a whole countryside

**ecodoom** *n* : inevitable resource depletion on the earth as predicted by the pessimistic ecological doomsters

**electrothanator** *n* : apparatus for electrocuting stray animals; a speedier and less expensive means of killing than by intravenous injection of barbiturates

**embourgeoisement** *n* : BOURGEOISIFICATION

**English disease** *n* : in economics, certain profit-reducing labor practices, such as working to rule, absenteeism, wildcat strikes

**ethnoscience** *n* : area of study within field of comparative anthropology

**Eurobank** *n* : bank of the European Economic Community (EEC), or Common Market

**Exclusive Economic Zone (EEZ)** *n* : 200-mile offshore area, or patrimonial sea, wherein a nation would hold fishing and mineral rights; proposed for coastal countries by the United Nations Conference on the Law of the Sea at Caracas, Venezuela

# f

**floater** *n* : light sailplane well suited to weak lift conditions

**freshpersons** *n pl* : first-year high school or college students, including both females and males

# g

**genetic bank** *n* : nature reserve in which rare and dying species of animals and birds are preserved under permanent surveillance

**gigamillion** *n* : French and U.S. billion, which is one thousand million —compare TERAMILLION

**glass ship** *n* : sailplane made of fiberglass

**godfather** *n* : prison superintendent, prison slang

**graser** *n* : gamma-ray laser

**guestworker** *n* : foreign laborer working on temporary basis

**gurudom** *n* : office of preceptor or spiritual guide in the realm of transcendental meditation

# h

**HIO** *n* : acronym for highly important occasion

**hit** *n* : rejection of a prisoner for parole, prison slang

**hyphens** *n pl* : show business trade term for writer-producers

# i

**identikit** *n* : highly specialized police identification kit that forms a composite portrait from interchangeable facial parts

**inquorate** *adj* : having too few members present to constitute a quorum

**Iris** *abbr* : infrared intruder system

**island of silence** *n* : area of quietness within a complex of pedestrian malls and stores within a shopping center

**Ivy-League tower** *n* : dwelling place of the academic loner

# j

**jacket** *v* : to label someone, prison slang

**jitterbug** *n* : young gang fighter, prison slang

# k

**katikia** *n* : rented or purchased house, on or near the southern coast of France, for vacation or retirement

# l

**lacertid** *n* : new object in the cosmos, thought to be a quasar embedded in a galaxy

**laughter curtain** *n* : fear of ridicule that prevents people from treating controversial subjects—such as UFO's—seriously

**launder** *vt* : to obliterate the origin of money being used for illegal or unethical purposes

**lexicometrics** *n* : controlled vocabulary

# m

**mag-lev** *n* : magnetically levitated high-speed train; a kind of land hovercraft equipped with superconducting magnets that repel the image magnets on the aluminum plates beneath and so raise the train above the track

**mainstream speech** *n* : prevailing manner of speaking among given group of people, as opposed to standard language

**maxi-taxi** *n* : a "people-moving" vehicle halfway between an automobile and a bus

**megabyte** *n* : computer measurement equal to $2^{20}$ (1,048,576) bytes, or eight times that number of bits or binary digits

**minibennies** *n pl* : illicitly made amphetamine tablets

**monetarist** *n* : specialist in the study of money and monetary systems

**multicausal** *adj* : attributable to many causes

**multispectral scanner** *n* : instrument that detects a wide range of electromagnetic radiation; chief information-gathering system of EARTH RESOURCES SATELLITE

# n

**never ever** *adv* : never at any time

**nonanswer** *n* : any answer that fails to give a straight reply

**nuke,** *or* **newk** *n* : slang, short for "nuclear test"

# o

**optacon** *n* : electronic minicamera that converts printed texts into tactile patterns that can be felt by a blind person's fingertips, enabling him to read print by touch

**ostrich syndrome** *n* : signs and symptoms of optimistic critics when they bury their heads in sand and refuse to face realities

# p

**patrimonial sea** *n* : EXCLUSIVE ECONOMIC ZONE (EEZ)

**petrodollars** *n pl* : huge sums of money flowing into Arab oil-exporting countries as result of increased petroleum prices

**physician's associate** *n* : one who is qualified by special medical training to perform limited physicians' duties without holding a doctor of medicine degree

**phytotron** *n* : electric plant breeder used by botanists

**pipe-in-pipe** *n* : system whereby fluid-bearing tubes are encased in other protecting pressure-tight tubes

**pillow** *n* : plastic bag of illegal amphetamines, or MINIBENNIES

**plate tectonics** *n* : conflicting stresses and strains between rock masses in the cooling-down period that resulted in the earth's present structural formation

**polyversity** *n* : large university having many component divisions with widely diverse functions

**postcode** *n* : United Kingdom equivalent of the U.S. Zip code

**prespeech** *n* : lip movements made by young children before they are able to enunciate meaningful words

# q

**QUANGO** *n* : acronym for quasi-non-government organization

**quasarology** *n* : study of quasi-stellar radio sources

# r

**rebunk** *v* : to reestablish a reputation previously damaged or destroyed by debunking

**recflation** *n* : economic condition in which recession and inflation exist simultaneously

**retrofit hushkit** *n* : device used on certain types of aircraft that greatly reduces noise

# s

**safari lodge** *n* : luxury hotel in African nature reserve from which guests can view wildlife from a sort of reverse zoo, with animals at large and humans enclosed

**salyut-skylab** *n* : proposed space station to be orbited and manned both by Soviet cosmonauts and U.S. astronauts

**shamateur** *n* : contestant at Olympic Games who is sham amateur, posing as nonprofessional

**socioecology** *n* : study of the influence of the environment upon social grouping

**sortie module** *n* : space vehicle, as Spacelab

**Spacelab** *n* : sortie module, planned in Europe, that would be taken into orbit by a reusable space shuttle

**stepped-back** *adj* : in architecture, designed so as to be approached by access galleries and to admit maximum light and air

**stereoscan** *n* : microscope capable of resolving details as small as one millionth of a centimeter, such as the branching processes of nerve cells

**streak** *v* : to run nude from one point to another in a public place to startle unexpecting observers

**subvocalization** *n* : practice of mouthing words silently when reading, a habit that demonstrably retards speed of intake

# t

**tachyon** *n* : a particle that moves faster than the speed of light

**tardyon** *n* : a particle that moves slower than the speed of light

**technoeconomics** *n* : assessment of wealth resulting from technological research and development

**teleradio** *n* : television and sound radio grouped together

**telethermics** *n* : system of transmitting heat to towns and cities from a central source

**teramillion** *n* : United Kingdom billion, which is one million million—compare GIGAMILLION

**transmodality** *n* : linked transportation by sea, road, rail, and inland motorway

**tweeter-woofer** *n* : coaxial two-in-one loudspeaker that combines the separate functions of both tweeter and woofer in reproducing high and low frequencies

# u

**ufology** *n* : study of unidentified flying objects (UFO's)

**ultrafiche** *n* : microfilm bearing a photographic record of printed matter reduced more than 50 times that can be enlarged for reading

**unimate** *n* : multipurpose robot used in European factories—compare VERSATRAN

# v

**verisign** *n* : electronic device for verifying signatures in order to safeguard checks and credit cards against fraud

**versatran** *n* : multipurpose robot used in U.S. factories—compare UNIMATE

# w

**wallmobile** *n* : moving wall mural; term first used to describe work of U.S. sculptor Alexander Calder, originator of "mobiles" and "stabiles"

**wasteplex** *n* : recycling machine that eliminates useless from reusable materials that can be put back into circulation

# z

**zex** *interj* : be careful, someone's coming, prison slang

**zoosemiotics** *n* : all systems of communication in the animal world, especially those employed by bees and dolphins

# Contributors and Consultants

These authorities either wrote the articles listed or supplied
information and data that were used in writing them:

**Stener Aarsdal,** Economic Editor, 'Børsen', Copenhagen, *Denmark*

**Joseph J. Accardo,** Washington, D.C., Columnist, *Fuel and Power* (in part)

**Jacob B. Agus,** Visiting Professor of Modern Jewish Philosophy, Dropsie University, Philadelphia, Pa., *Religion* (in part)

**J. A. Allan,** Lecturer in Geography, School of Oriental and African Studies, University of London, *Libya*

**Gustavo Arthur Antonini,** Associate Professor, Center for Latin American Studies, University of Florida, Gainesville, *Dominican Republic*

**Bruce Arnold,** Free-lance Journalist and Writer, Dublin, *Ireland*

**Eric A. Astrom,** Executive Assistant to the President, The Ontario Jockey Club, and Director, National Association of Canadian Race Tracks, Toronto, *Horse Racing*

**Vincent P. Barabba,** Director of the U.S. Bureau of the Census, Washington, D.C., *Population*

**Robert F. Barkley, D.D.S.,** Author, Lecturer in Preventive Dentistry and Behavior Modification in the Dental Office, and Practicing Dentist in Macomb, Illinois, *Dentistry SPECIAL REPORT: Preventistry—The Dentist as Teacher* (in part)

**Kenneth de la Barre,** Director, Montreal, Que., Office, Arctic Institute of North America, *Arctic*

**Paul Charles Bartholomew,** Professor of Government, University of Notre Dame, Ind., *Supreme Court of the United States*

**Howard Bass,** Journalist, Author, Editor, Broadcaster, and Winter Sports Correspondent, 'Ski Racing', 'Sportsworld', and 'Daily Telegraph', London, *Ice Skating; Skiing*

**John V. Beall,** Author and Business Development Engineer, New York City, *Mines and Mining*

**David Carmeron Beckwith,** Washington, D.C., Correspondent, 'Time', *State Governments*

**R. H. Beddoes,** Sports Columnist, 'Toronto Globe and Mail', Ont., *Ice Hockey*

**William Beltrán,** Senior Economic Research Officer, Lloyds Bank International Ltd., London, *Latin America*

**Sue Benedetti,** Program Leader, 4-H Information, Washington, D.C., *Youth Organizations* (in part)

**Anne O. Bennof,** Coordinator of College Services, Office of Information and Public Affairs, Association of American Railroads, Washington, D.C., *Transportation* (in part)

**Clyde Richard Bergwin,** retired U.S. Air Force Information Officer, and Author of 'Animal Astronauts', St. Petersburg, Fla., *Aerospace*

**Alan G. Blyth,** Music Critic, London, *Music* (in part)

**Erma Bombeck,** Syndicated Columnist, Publishers—Hall Syndicate, *Food SPECIAL REPORT: Good-Bye, Frozen Rhubarb*

**Dick Boonstra,** Assistant Professor, Department of Political Science, Free University, Amsterdam, *Netherlands*

**Kooman Boycheff,** Supervisor of Physical Education and Coordinator of Recreation, University of California at Berkeley, *Hobbies; Toys and Games*

**Arnold C. Brackman,** Author of 'Indonesian Communism: A History', Brookfield Center, Conn., *Indonesia*

**Robert J. Braidwood,** Professor of Old World Prehistory, Oriental Institute and Department of Anthropology, The University of Chicago, *Archaeology and Anthropology* (in part)

**William A. Bresnahan,** President, American Trucking Associations, Inc., Washington, D.C., *Transportation* (in part)

**Manell P. Brice,** Newswriter, Special Projects Office, Division of Information, Headquarters Marine Corps, Washington, D.C., *Armed Forces, United States* (in part)

**Jack Brickhouse,** Vice-President and Manager of Sports, WGN Continental Broadcasting Co., Chicago, *Baseball* (in part)

**D. A. Brown,** Agriculture Librarian Emeritus, University of Illinois, Urbana, *Animals and Wildlife; Environment; Pets*

**Ardath W. Burks,** Professor and Associate Vice-President for Academic Affairs, Rutgers University, New Brunswick, N.J., *Japan*

**Allen D. Bushong,** Associate Professor of Geography, University of South Carolina, Columbia, *El Salvador; Honduras*

**Frank Butler,** Author, and Sports Editor, 'News of the World', London, *Boxing*

**Alva Lawrence Campbell,** Staff Consultant, Corporate Communications Dept., Metropolitan Life Insurance Co., New York City, *Insurance*

**James B. Cardwell,** Commissioner of Social Security, U.S. Department of Health, Education, and Welfare, Social Security Administration, Baltimore, Md., *Social Services*

**Kenneth F. Chapman,** Author, Editor, 'Stamp Collecting', and Philatelic Correspondent, 'The Times', London, *Stamps*

**Robin Chapman,** Senior Economic Research Officer, Lloyds Bank International Ltd., London, *Cuba; Mexico*

**Robert Chaussin,** Government Civil Engineer, SETRA (Service d'Études Techniques des Routes et Autoroutes), Bagneux, France, *Engineering Projects* (in part)

**Hung-Ti Chu,** Expert in Far Eastern Affairs, United Nations Area Specialist, and formerly Chief, Asia-Africa Section and Trusteeship Council Section, and Professor of Government, Texas Tech University, Lubbock, *China, People's Republic of; Taiwan*

**583**

**Donald F. Clifton,** Professor of Metallurgy, University of Idaho, Moscow, *Metals*

**Fletcher Coates,** Executive Director for Information of the National Council of Churches, New York City, *Religion* (in part)

**Leslie Collins,** Lecturer in Bulgarian History, University of London, *Cyprus*

**Stanley H. Costin,** London, British Correspondent, 'Australian Tailor and Menswear', 'Herrenjournal' (Germany), and Past President, Men's Fashion Writers International, *Fashion and Cosmetics* (in part)

**Rufus W. Crater,** Chief Correspondent, New York City, 'Broadcasting', *Television and Radio* (in part)

**Norman Crossland,** Bonn Correspondent, 'The Guardian' and the British Broadcasting Corp. (BBC), London, *Germany*

**K. F. Cviić,** Leader Writer and East European Specialist, 'The Economist', London, *Czechoslovakia; Yugoslavia*

**Hiroshi Daifuku,** Chief, Sites and Monuments Division, United Nations Educational, Scientific, and Cultural Organization (UNESCO), Paris, *Landmarks and Monuments*

**Geoffrey Dempsey,** Fellow of Institute of Practitioners in Advertising, J. Walter Thompson Co. Ltd., London, *Advertising*

**John Dennis,** Editorial Consultant, Quality of Life Center, Model Cities/CCUO, and Associate Creative Director, Nahser Agency, Chicago, *Dentistry SPECIAL REPORT: Preventistry —The Dentist as Teacher* (in part)

**Mary Ellen Dienes,** Assistant State's Attorney of Cook County, Chicago, *Law*

**Elfriede Dirnbacher,** Civil Servant, Vienna, *Austria*

**Patricia Dragisic,** Free-lance Writer and Editor, Chicago, *Awards and Prizes; Cities and Urban Affairs SPECIAL REPORT: Safety in the Streets; Indians, American; Women*

**Jim Dunne,** Detroit Editor, 'Popular Science Monthly', *Automobiles*

**Raul d'Eca,** Author, and formerly Fulbright Visiting Lecturer on American History, University of Minas Gerais, Belo Horizonte, *Brazil*

**Jan R. Engels,** Editor, 'Vooruitgang' (Quarterly of the Belgian Party for Freedom and Progress), Brussels, *Belgium*

**Robert J. Fendell,** New York Editor, 'Automotive News', Automobile Columnist, 'Gentlemen's Quarterly', and President Emeritus, International Motor Press Association, *Auto Racing*

**Monica J. Fenrich,** Articles Editor, 'Friday Review of Defense Literature' Office, Secretary of the Air Force, Washington, D.C., *Armed Forces, United States* (in part)

**R. W. Ferrier,** Group Historian, British Petroleum, London, *Fuel and Power* (in part)

**Judith Field,** Publicity Manager, Girls Clubs of America, New York City, *Youth Organizations* (in part)

**David A. Fredrickson,** Associate Professor of Anthropology, Sonoma State College, Rohnert Park, Calif., *Archaeology and Anthropology* (in part)

**Irving S. Friedman,** Senior International Policy Adviser, First National City Bank of New York, formerly Economic Adviser to the President of the World Bank and Department Director, International Monetary Fund, *Money and International Finance* (in part)

**Colonel James A. Fyock,** Information Officer, U.S. Army Forces Command, Fort McPherson, Ga., *Armed Forces, United States* (in part)

**Peter Gaddum,** Chairman, H. T. Gaddum and Co. Ltd., Silk Merchants, Macclesfield, England, and President, International Silk Association, Lyons, France, *Textiles* (in part)

**Fabio Galvano,** Special Correspondent, 'Gazzetta del Popolo', Turin, *Italy*

**Albert Ganado,** Lawyer, Valetta, *Malta*

**T. J. S. George,** World Population Year Secretariat, United Nations, New York City, *Cambodia; Korea; Laos; Thailand*

**Robert H. Glauber,** Curator, American Telephone and Telegraph Co., Art Critic and Editor, Chicago, *Painting and Sculpture SPECIAL REPORT: Two Centuries of U.S. Painting*

**Fay Gjester,** Oslo Correspondent, 'Financial Times', London, *Norway*

**Paul Glikson,** Secretary, Division of Jewish Demography and Statistics, Institute of Contemporary Jewry, Hebrew University of Jerusalem, Israel, *Religion* (in part)

**Harry Golombek,** British Chess Champion (1947, 1949, 1955), Author, and Chess Correspondent, 'The Times' and 'Observer', London, *Chess*

**R. M. Goodwin,** Free-lance Writer, London, *Guinea; Malagasy Republic; Tunisia*

**Robert Goralski,** Washington, D.C., Correspondent, NBC News, *Vietnam*

**A. R. G. Griffiths,** Senior Lecturer in History, Flinders University of South Australia, *Australia*

**Dorothy C. Grosvenor,** Writer-Editor, Specialized Publications, YWCA, New York City, *Youth Organizations* (in part)

**Michael Phillip Guerin,** Assistant Director, Division of Officer Services, Bureau of Public and Community Relations, American Hospital Association, Chicago, *Hospitals*

**Joseph H. S. Haggin,** Staff Writer, 'Chemical and Engineering News', Washington, D.C., *Chemistry*

**David A. Harries,** Director, Kinnear Moodie Ltd., Peterborough, England, *Engineering Projects* (in part)

**Gerard A. Harrison,** Associate Professor of Recreation, Springfield College, Mass., *Camping*

**William E. Hawkins,** Assistant Director, Public Information, National Safety Council, Chicago, *Safety*

**John Heap,** Sometime member of the British Antarctic Survey, London, *Antarctica*

**Peter Hebblethwaite,** Deputy Editor, 'Frontier', Cambridge, England, *Religion* (in part)

**Myrl C. Hendershott,** Associate Professor of Oceanography, Scripps Institution of Oceanography, La Jolla, Calif., *Oceanography*

**Patrice Daily Horn,** Editor, 'Behavior Today', and Senior Editor, 'Psychology Today', Del Mar, Calif., *Psychology*

**Louis Hotz,** Author, and formerly Editorial Writer, 'The Johannesburg Star', *South Africa*

**Kenneth Ingham,** Author, and Professor of History, University of Bristol, England, *Guinea-Bissau; Kenya; Rhodesia; Tanzania; Uganda; Zaire; Zambia*

**Stephen K. James,** Assistant Manager, Public Relations Department, American Bowling Congress, Greendale, Wis., *Bowling*

**Lou Joseph,** Author, and Manager of Media Relations, Bureau of Public Information, American Dental Association, Chicago, *Dentistry*

**William A. Katz,** Author, and Professor, School of Library Science, State University of New York at Albany, *Magazines*

**John A. Kelleher,** Editor, 'The Dominion', Wellington, *New Zealand*

**Peter Kilner,** Editor, 'Arab Report and Record', London, *Algeria; Morocco; Sudan*

**Jon Kimche,** Author, and Expert on Middle East Affairs, 'Evening Standard', London, *Israel*

**Joshua B. Kind,** Author, and Associate Professor of Art History, Northern Illinois University, De Kalb, *Museums*

**Resa W. King,** Correspondent, 'Business Week', New York City, *Business and Industry; Housing; United States* (in part)

**Frances M. Kirkham,** Information Officer, British Non-Ferrous Metals Federation, Birmingham, England, *Argentina; Peru*

**Alfred P. Klausler,** Author, Religion Editor, Westinghouse Broadcasting Co., and Editor at Large, 'Christian Century', Chicago, *Religion* (in part)

**Jean M. Knecht,** formerly Assistant Foreign Editor, 'Le Monde', Paris, Permanent Correspondent in Washington, D.C., and Vice-President of the Association de la Presse Diplomatique Française, *France*

**John Kneeshaw,** Economist, Bank for International Settlements, Basel, Switzerland, *Money and International Finance* (in part)

**Albert E. Kudrle,** Director of Public Relations, American Hotel and Motel Association, New York City, *Travel* (in part)

**G. C. Last,** Author, and Adviser, Ethiopian Ministry of Education and Fine Arts, Addis Ababa, *Ethiopia*

**Colin Legum,** Associate Editor and Commonwealth Correspondent, 'Observer', Editor, 'Africa Contemporary Record' and 'Travellers' Guide to Africa', and Author, London, *Africa*

**Michael Leifer,** Reader in International Relations, The London School of Economics and Political Science, *Malaysia*

**Chapin R. Leinbach,** Assistant to Vice-President, Public Relations, Air Transport Association of America, Washington, D.C., *Transportation* (in part)

**Peter Lennox-Kerr,** Editor and Publisher, 'Textile Manufacturer', and Author, Manchester, England, *Textiles* (in part)

**Richard M. M. McConnell,** Associate Editor, 'Banking', Washington, D.C., *Banks*

**Barrie Keith MacDonald,** Lecturer in History, Massey University, New Zealand, *Pacific Islands*

**Irene McManus,** Associate Editor, 'American Forests', Washington, D.C., *Forest Products*

**H. M. F. Mallett,** Editor, 'Weekly Woolchart', Bradford, England, *Textiles* (in part)

**Andrew J. A. Mango,** Orientalist and Broadcaster, London, *Turkey*

**Peter Mansfield,** Free-lance Writer, and formerly Middle East Correspondent, 'Sunday Times', London, *Egypt; Iraq; Jordan; Kuwait; Lebanon; Middle East; Saudi Arabia; Syria*

**Aldo Marcello,** Civil Engineer, Milan, Italy, *Engineering Projects* (in part)

**Björn Matthíasson,** Iceland Correspondent, 'Financial Times', London, *Iceland*

**N. F. Maude,** Consultant Editor, 'British Journal of Photography' and 'Photo Trader', Editor, 'Photographic Processor', and Author, London, *Photography*

**Jerome Mazzaro,** Author, and Professor of English and Comparative Literature, State University of New York at Buffalo, *Literature; Literature SPECIAL REPORT: America's Contribution to World Literature*

**R. S. Millard,** Deputy Director, Transport and Road Research Laboratory, Department of the Environment, Crowthorne, England, *Engineering Projects* (in part)

**William B. Miller,** Manager, Department of History, United Presbyterian Church, U.S.A., Philadelphia, Pa., *Religion* (in part)

**Sandra Millikin,** Architectural Historian, London, *Architecture; Painting and Sculpture*

**Mario Modiano,** Athens Correspondent, 'The Times', London, *Greece*

**Hazel Morgan,** Production Assistant (Sleevenotes and Covers) E.M.I. Records Ltd., London, *Music* (in part)

**Molly Mortimer,** Commonwealth Correspondent, 'The Spectator', London, *Burundi; Ghana; Nigeria; Rwanda; Swaziland*

**G. S. Mottershead,** Director-Secretary, Chester Zoo, England, *Zoos*

**Pauline G. Mower,** Director of Information, Future Homemakers of America, Washington, D.C., *Youth Organizations* (in part)

**Edward Harwood Nabb,** Vice-President, Union of International Motorboating, and formerly President of International Boating Writers Association, Cambridge, Md., *Boats and Boating*

**Colin Narborough,** Reuters Correspondent, Helsinki, *Finland*

**National Oceanic and Atmospheric Administration,** Office of Public Affairs, Boulder, Colo., *Weather*

**Raymond K. Neal,** Executive Editor, Editorial Service, North Brunswick, N.J., *Youth Organizations* (in part)

**Bert Nelson,** Editor and Publisher, 'Track and Field News', Los Altos, Calif., *Track and Field*

**Bruce C. Netschert,** Author, and Vice-President, National Economic Research Associates, Inc., Washington, D.C., *Fuel and Power* (in part)

**William A. Neubauer,** Chicago Sales and Public Relations Representative for Betterman's (Fortuny, Kent-Bragaline, Louis W. Bowen, Henry Cassen), and formerly for Scalamandré Silks, *Interior Design*

**H. S. Noel,** Managing Editor, 'World Fishing', London, *Fish and Fisheries*

**Julius Novick,** Author, Associate Professor of Literature, State University of New York at Purchase, and Dramatic Critic, 'Village Voice' and 'The Humanist', New York City, *Theater*

**Jeremiah A. O'Leary,** Author, and State Department Correspondent, 'Washington Evening Star-News', D.C., *Chile*

**Sidney A. Pakeman,** Historian, and Author of 'Ceylon', London, *Sri Lanka*

**Rafael Pargas,** Free-lance Writer, Washington, D.C., *Philippines*

**Anne Parsons,** Economic Research Officer, Lloyds Bank International Ltd., London, *Ecuador; Paraguay; Uruguay*

**George P. Patten,** Professor of Geography, Ohio State University, Columbus, *Nicaragua*

**Sheila Patterson,** Author, and Research Associate, Department of Anthropology, University College, London, *Bahamas; Grenada; Jamaica; West Indies*

**Joan Pearce,** Research Officer, Economics Department, Lloyds Bank International Ltd., London, *Colombia; Costa Rica; Guatemala; Spain*

**Virgil W. Peterson,** Author, and formerly Executive Director, Chicago Crime Commission, *Crime; Police*

**Thomas F. Pettigrew,** Author, and Professor of Social Psychology, Harvard University, Cambridge, Mass., *Race Relations*

**Otto Pick,** Professor of International Relations, University of Surrey, Guildford, England, and Director, Atlantic Information Centre for Teachers, London, *Union of Soviet Socialist Republics (U.S.S.R.)*

**Derek Prag,** Author, Business Consultant, Free-lance Journalist, and Director, London Information Office of the European Communities, *Europe*

**H. Y. Sharada Prasad,** Director of Information, Prime Minister's Secretariat, New Delhi, *India*

**Margaret H. Quinn,** Reporter, 'Sun-Gazette', Williamsport, Pa., *Baseball* (in part)

**Robert J. Ranger,** Assistant Professor, Department of Political Science, St. Francis Xavier University, Antigonish, Nova Scotia, *Defense*

**Francis W. Reichelderfer,** Aeronautical and Marine Meteorology Consultant, formerly Chief, Weather Bureau, U.S. Department of Commerce, Washington, D.C., *Earth Sciences* (in part)

**A. Daniel Reuwee,** Director of Information, Future Farmers of America, Alexandria, Va., *Youth Organizations* (in part)

**Richard Daniels Ritter,** Writer, Public Affairs Division, Office of Public and International Affairs, U.S. Coast Guard, Washington, D.C., *Armed Forces, United States* (in part)

**David Robinson,** Author, and Film Critic, 'The Times', London, *Motion Pictures*

**Lief J. Robinson,** Associate Editor, 'Sky and Telescope', Sky Publishing Corp., Cambridge, Mass., *Animals and Wildlife SPECIAL REPORT: Birding—A Living Heritage; Astronomy*

**Rocco A. Sacci,** Manager, Public Information, Boys' Clubs of America, New York City, *Youth Organizations* (in part)

**Alex Sareyan,** President, Mental Health Materials Center, Inc., New York City, *Mental Health*

**Albert Schoenfield,** Editor, 'Swimming World', North Hollywood, Calif., *Swimming*

**John Schulian,** Reporter, 'Baltimore Evening Sun', Md., *Basketball; Football*

**Stephen E. Scrupski,** Senior Editor, 'Electronics', New York City, *Electronics*

**Byron T. Scott,** Assistant Professor of Journalism, College of Communication, Ohio University, Athens, *Medicine*

**Peter Shackelford,** Research Adviser, International Union of Official Travel Organizations (IUOTO), Geneva, Switzerland, *Travel* (in part)

**Michell R. Sharpe,** Science Writer, and Author of 'Living in Space' and 'Satellites and Probes', Huntsville, Ala., *Space Exploration*

**Harvey R. Sherman,** Environmental Policy Division, Congressional Research Service, Library of Congress, Washington, D.C., *Agriculture; Food*

**C. Chung-Tse Shih,** Senior Adviser on Trade Negotiations, United Nations Conference on Trade and Development (UNCTAD), Geneva, Switzerland, *World Trade*

**Glenn B. Smedley,** Governor, American Numismatic Association, Colorado Springs, Colo., *Coins and Medals*

**K. M. Smogorzewski,** Founder and Editor, 'Free Europe', Author, and Writer on Contemporary History, London, *Albania; Hungary; Poland; Romania*

**Leonard M. Snyder,** Associate Director, Bureau of Communications, National Council YMCA's, New York City, *Youth Organizations* (in part)

**Cooper Speaks,** Correspondent-Critic, 'Opera Magazine' and 'Opera News', Bloomington, Ind., *Music SPECIAL REPORT: An Art Form in Search of Itself*

**Melanie F. Staerk,** Member, Swiss National Commission for UNESCO (Information), Zurich, *Switzerland*

**Tom Stevenson,** Author, and Garden Columnist, 'Baltimore News American', 'Washington Post', and Washington Post-Los Angeles News Service, *Flowers and Gardens*

James Glen Stovall, Journalist Second Class, News Staff, 'All Hands', U.S. Navy, Bureau of Naval Personnel, Washington, D.C., *Armed Forces, United States* (in part)

Carol Brooks Stroughter, Writer, Public Information, Girl Scouts of the U.S.A., New York City, *Youth Organizations* (in part)

Naomi S. Suloway, Editor, Institute of Gas Technology, Chicago, *Interior Design SPECIAL REPORT: Decorating with Green Plants*

Zena Sutherland, Editor, Children's Books, 'Chicago Tribune', Editor, 'Bulletin of the Center for Children's Books', and Lecturer, The University of Chicago, *Literature for Children*

James Strouder Sweet, Assistant Director for Science Information Services, Office of Public Information, The University of Chicago, *Biology*

Thelma Sweetinburgh, Paris Fashion Correspondent, 'International Textiles' (Amsterdam, Netherlands) and the British Wool Textile Industry, *Fashion and Cosmetics* (in part)

Richard N. Swift, Author, and Professor of Politics, New York University, New York City, *United Nations (UN)*

Sol Taishoff, Chairman and Editor, 'Broadcasting', Washington, D.C., *Television and Radio* (in part)

Arthur Tattersall, Textile Trade Expert and Statistician, Manchester, England, *Textiles* (in part)

Walter Terry, Author, and Dance Critic, 'Saturday Review/World', New York City, *Dance*

Harford Thomas, City Editor, 'The Guardian', London, *Great Britain and Northern Ireland, United Kingdom of*

Anthony Thompson, Author, European Linguist, College of Librarianship, Aberystwyth, Wales, and formerly General Secretary, International Federation of Library Associations, *Libraries*

Christine Timmons, Editor, 'The Britannica Discovery Library', Chicago, *Births; Disasters; Marriages; Obituaries; People of the Year*

Lance Tingay, Lawn Tennis Correspondent, 'Daily Telegraph', London, *Tennis*

Edward Townsend, Associate Editor, 'Business Week', New York City, *Labor Unions*

Govindan Unny, Agence France-Presse Special Correspondent for India, Nepal, and Ceylon, *Asia; Bangladesh; Burma*

Leslie Verter, Public Relations Coordinator, Camp Fire Girls, Inc., New York City, *Youth Organizations* (in part)

John Vosburgh, Public Information Specialist, Office of Public Affairs, National Park Service, U.S. Department of the Interior, Washington, D.C., *National Park Service*

David M. Walsten, Editor, Field Museum of Natural History 'Bulletin', Chicago, *Ships and Shipping; Stocks and Bonds*

P. A. Ward-Thomas, Golf Correspondent, 'The Guardian', London, *Golf*

Anne R. Warner, Program and Communications Director, National Health Council, New York City, *Nursing*

John W. Warner, Administrator, American Revolution Bicentennial Administration, Washington, D.C., *United States SPECIAL REPORT: A New Spirit for 1976*

Edith Wasserman, Staff Editor, 'Compton's Encyclopedia', Chicago, Free-lance Writer, and formerly Reporter, 'Pittsburgh Post-Gazette', *Environment SPECIAL REPORT: Expo '74; Ford, Gerald R.; Intelligence Operations; Nixon, Richard M.; Postal Services; Rockefeller, Nelson A.*

Jack Waugh, Free-lance Writer, and formerly Staff Correspondent, 'The Christian Science Monitor', Washington, D.C., *Families*

L. F. Rushbrook Williams, Author, and formerly Fellow of All Souls College, Oxford University, England, and Professor of Modern Indian History, Allahabad, India, *Iran; Pakistan*

Alan David Wilson, Associate Editor, 'Scanorama', Bromma, *Sweden*

J. Tuzo Wilson, Professor of Geophysics, University of Toronto, Ont., *Earth Sciences* (in part)

Michael Wooller, Economic Research Officer, Lloyds Bank International Ltd., London, *Bolivia; Haiti; Portugal; Venezuela*

Richard L. Worsnop, Writer, Editorial Research Reports, Washington, D.C., *United States*

Almon R. Wright, retired Senior Historian, U.S. Department of State, Washington, D.C., *Panama*

Paul Ziemer, Copy Editor, 'Detroit Free Press', Mich., *Congress, United States; Elections; Political Parties*

Joseph Zullo, Author, Free-lance Medical Writer, and member, American Medical Writers Association, Sacramento, Calif., *Medicine SPECIAL REPORT: The Progress of Medicine*

This index is arranged in alphabetical order. Words beginning with "Mc" are alphabetized as "Mac," and "St." is alphabetized as "Saint."

The figures shown in brackets [71, 72] indicate earlier editions of **The Compton Yearbook** in which the topic has appeared since 1971.

Entry headings in boldface type indicate articles in the text.

The first page reference is the main discussion.

Cross-references refer to index entries in this volume.

MAJOR SECTIONS OF THE YEARBOOK APPEAR ON THE FOLLOWING PAGES:

**Compton's Pictured Highlights and Chronology of 1974,** 4–29
**Feature articles**—*A New American Art—By the People, for the People,* 30–45; *Paul Dirac, Antimatter, and You,* 46–61; *The Women's Sports Revolution,* 62–79; *Canada Is Not the 51st State,* 80–95
**Special reports**—Animals and Wildlife: *Birding—A Living Heritage,* 107–108; Cities and Urban Affairs: *Safety in the Streets,* 158–160; Dentistry: *Preventistry—The Dentist as Teacher,* 184–186; Environment: *Expo '74,* 206–208; Food: *Good-bye, Frozen Rhubarb,* 218–219; Interior Design: *Decorating with Green Plants,* 253–256; Literature: *America's Contribution to World Literature,* 283–285; Medicine: *The Progress of Medicine,* 296–298; Music: *An Art Form in Search of Itself,* 312–315; Painting and Sculpture: *Two Centuries of U.S. Painting,* 333–336; United States: *A New Spirit for 1976,* 401–405
**Events of the Year 1974,** 96–416
**Compton's Encyclopedia Quiz Book,** 417–576
**Calendar for 1975,** 577–579
**New Words,** 580–582
**Contributors and Consultants,** 583–587

n

# q

# r

# X

# y

# z